PALESTINE BETRAYED

PALESTINE BETRAYED

EFRAIM KARSH

PUBLIC ENLIGHT-ENMENT IS THE FORE-RUNNER OF JUSTICE

Code of Ethics, Society of Professional Journalists

Committee for
Accuracy in
Middle East
Reporting in
America
CAMERA®
P.O. Box 35040
Boston MA 02135
www.camera.org

YALE UNIVERSITY PRESS
NEW HAVEN AND LONDON

Copyright © 2010 Efraim Karsh

For information about this and other Yale University Press publications, please contact:
U.S. Office: sales.press@yale.edu   www.yalebooks.com
Europe Office: sales @yaleup.co.uk   www.yaleup.co.uk

Set in Garamond by IDSUK (DataConnection) Ltd
Printed in Great Britain by TJ International Ltd, Padstow, Cornwall

Library of Congress Cataloging-in-Publication Data

Karsh, Efraim.
    Palestine betrayed/Efraim Karsh.
      p. cm.
    Includes bibliographical references and index.
    ISBN 978–0–300–12727–0 (cloth:alk. paper)
    1. Palestine—History—Partition, 1947. I. Title.
    DS126.4. K245 2010
    956.94′04—dc22   2009040202

A catalogue record for this book is available from the British Library.
10 9 8 7 6 5 4 3 2 1

IN MEMORY OF ELIAS KATZ (1901–47) AND SAMI TAHA (1916–47),
VICTIMS OF THEIR QUEST FOR ARAB-JEWISH COEXISTENCE

Contents

Illustrations and Maps

Unless otherwise acknowledged all pictures are courtesy of the State of Israel Government Press Office.

Acknowledgments

I would like to thank my departmental colleague, Professor Rory Miller, who not only read the entire manuscript but has also been my toughest critic, improving my ideas and saving me from not a few mistakes. I am grateful to my son, Matan, for indispensable research assistance at the Israeli archives, and to the two anonymous readers for their useful suggestions. Professor Moshe Brawer of Tel Aviv University graciously read the Appendix and suggested revisions and amendments. Heather McCallum at Yale University Press has provided her usual guidance and expertise. Needless to say, responsibility for any errors that may remain is mine and mine alone.

Last but not least, I would like to extend my gratitude to Roger and Susan Hertog, without whose generosity and support this book would never have been written.

Introduction

"There is no place in Palestine for two races. The Jews left Palestine 2,000 years ago, let them go to other parts of the world, where there are wide vacant places."

Hajj Amin Husseini, 1936

"We do not wish and do not need to expel Arabs and take their place. All our aspiration is built on the assumption – proven throughout all our activity in the Land of Israel – that there is enough room in the country for ourselves and the Arabs."

David Ben-Gurion, 1937

On November 29, 1947, the United Nations General Assembly passed a resolution calling for the partition of Palestine into two independent states – one Jewish, the other Arab – linked in an economic union. The city of Jerusalem was to be placed under an international regime, with its residents given the right to citizenship in either the Jewish or the Arab state. Thirty-three UN members supported the resolution, thirteen voted against, and ten abstained, including Great Britain, which had ruled Palestine since the early 1920s under a League of Nations mandate.

For Jews all over the world, this was the fulfillment of a millenarian yearning for national rebirth in their ancestral homeland. For Arab political and intellectual elites, it was a shameful surrender of (a however minute) part of the perceived pan-Arab patrimony to a foreign invader. In Jewish localities throughout Palestine crowds danced in the streets. In the Arab capitals there were violent demonstrations. "We are happy and ready for what lies ahead," the prominent Zionist official and future Israeli prime minister Golda Meyerson (Meir) told thousands of revelers in Jerusalem. "Our hands are extended in peace to our neighbors. Both States can live in peace with one another and cooperate for the welfare of their inhabitants."[1]

To this, however, the response of the Arab Higher Committee (AHC), the effective "government" of the Palestinian Arabs, headed by the militant ex-Mufti of Jerusalem, Hajj Amin Husseini, was an all-out war. In the five-and-a-half months between the passing of the UN resolution and the end of the British mandate, the former Mufti's forces, assisted by a sizeable pan-Arab irregular army, carried out thousands of attacks on their Jewish neighbors in an attempt to prevent them from establishing their state. This failed, and by the time the last British high commissioner for Palestine, General Sir Alan Cunningham, left the country and the state of Israel was proclaimed on May 14, 1948, Palestinian Arab society had all but disintegrated, with 300,000–340,000 of its members fleeing their homes to other parts of Palestine and to the neighboring Arab states.

A concerted attack by the regular Arab armies on the nascent Jewish state within hours of its proclamation proved equally counterproductive. Rather than drive the Jews into the sea, as promised by the Arab League's secretary-general, Abdel Rahman Azzam, the assault served to confirm Israel's independence within wider boundaries than those assigned by the partition resolution, albeit at the exorbitant human cost of 1 percent of its population,[2] and raised the number of refugees to about 600,000 – nearly half the country's Arab population.

Yet nowhere at the time was the collapse and dispersion of Palestinian Arab society – *al-Nakba*, "the catastrophe," as it would come to be known in Palestinian and Arab discourse – described as a systematic dispossession of Arabs by Jews. To the contrary: with the partition resolution widely viewed by Arab leaders throughout the region as "Zionist in inspiration, Zionist in principle, Zionist in substance, and Zionist in most details" (in the words of the Palestinian academic Walid Khalidi),[3] and with those leaders being brutally candid about their determination to subvert it by force of arms, there was no doubt whatsoever as to which side had instigated the bloodletting and the attendant defeat and exodus. As Sir John Troutbeck, head of the British Middle East Office in Cairo and no friend of Israel or the Jews, discovered to his surprise during a fact-finding mission to Gaza in June 1949:

> while [the refugees] express no bitterness against the Jews (or for that matter against the Americans or ourselves) they speak with the utmost bitterness of the Egyptians and other Arab states. "We know who our enemies are," they will say, and they are referring to their Arab brothers who, they declare, persuaded them unnecessarily to leave their homes. . . . I even heard it said that many of the refugees would give a welcome to the Israelis if they were to come in and take the district over.[4]

In his influential 1948 pamphlet *The Meaning of the Catastrophe* (*Ma'na al-Nakba*), which introduced the term into the Palestinian and Arab historical vocabulary, the Syrian historian Qustantin Zuraiq spoke of the flight – not the expulsion – of some 400,000 Arabs. So did the prominent Palestinian Arab leader Musa Alami. "If ultimately the Palestinians evacuated their country, it was not out of cowardice, but because they had lost all confidence in the existing system of defense," he wrote in October 1949. "They had perceived its weakness, and realized the disequilibrium between their resources and organization, and those of the Jews. They were told that the Arab armies were coming, that the matter would be settled and everything return to normal, and they placed their confidence and hopes in that."[5]

It was only from the early 1950s onward, as the Palestinians and their Western supporters gradually rewrote their national narrative, that Israel, rather than the Arab states, became the *Nakba*'s main, if not sole, culprit. The ex-Mufti led the way by casting his countrymen as the hapless victims of a Jewish grand design to dispossess them of their patrimony, as a steppingstone to regional domination,[6] and this fantastic claim was quickly picked up by many of his contemporaries. Some ascribed these supposed designs to *The Protocols of the Elders of Zion*, a virulent anti-Semitic tract fabricated by the Russian secret police at the turn of the twentieth century, from which the Jewish leadership allegedly drew inspiration and operational guidelines; others attributed them to religious and historical sentiments.[7] All viewed Zionism as omnipotent, with tentacles that reached the world's most powerful spots. In the words of the prominent Islamist leader in mandatory Palestine, Muhammad Nimr Khatib: "We are fighting an organized, educated, cunning, devious, and evil people that has concentrated the world's wealth and power in its hands. . . . We are fighting the forces that have prevailed over the entire world, we are fighting the power that buried Hitler and defeated Japan, we are fighting World Zionism that has Truman in its pay, enslaves Churchill and Attlee, and colonizes London, New York, and Washington."[8]

Echoing this obsession with the demonic power of "World Zionism" some four decades later, Walid Khalidi attributed the *Nakba* to "the vast chasm in the balance of power between, on the one hand, the resources of the World Zionist Organization and its sponsors in London and Washington, and, on the other hand, those of the pre-industrial Palestinian community"; while Edward Said put the supposed Jewish machinations in similarly stark terms, claiming that "from the beginning of serious Zionist planning for Palestine (that is, roughly, from the period during and after World War I), one can note the increasing prevalence of the idea that Israel was to be built on the ruins of . . . Arab Palestine."[9]

If it is understandable for leaders and politicians, culpable for their nation's greatest ever disaster, to revert to hyperbole and lies in their quest for personal and collective exoneration, it is inexcusable for future generations of scholars and intellectuals to substitute propaganda for incontrovertible facts. Yet such is the state of Palestinian and Arab historiography that the foremost, indeed the only comprehensive, study of the *Nakba* was written in the 1950s, without the necessary detachment and introspection, let alone access to the minefield of archival source material that has subsequently come to light, by the mandatory official, politician, journalist, and historian Arif Arif.

Younger generations of Palestinian scholars and intellectuals have avoided the *Nakba* like wild fire. They have, of course, evoked, lamented, and apportioned blame for this tragedy at every possible turn, yet none has attempted to explore what actually transpired: why and how it happened. Rashid Khalidi's *Palestinian Identity: The Construction of Modern National Conscience* (1997), for instance, devotes only a few pages to this most formative event in the development of Palestinian national identity. Yezid Sayigh's *Armed Struggle and the Search for Statehood* (1997) pointedly starts its narrative in the immediate wake of the 1948 war, though it was this conflict that witnessed the widest and most extensive use of armed struggle by the Palestinian Arabs until then and for decades to come, while Nur Masalha's *Expulsion of the Palestinians* (1992) focuses exclusively on the Zionist side to the total disregard of Palestinian Arab desires, goals, and activities. "[F]or all their flaws, the versions of history produced by . . . traditional Arab historiography are fundamentally different from the Israeli myths of origin that are currently being deconstructed by the Israeli 'new historians.' " Rashid Khalidi justified the absence of Palestinian rethinking of the foremost event in their history. "This is true notably because it is not a myth that a determined enemy bent on taking control of their homeland subjected the Palestinians to overwhelming force. It is not a myth, moreover, that as a result of this process the Palestinian people were victims, regardless of what they might have done differently in this situation of formidable difficulty, and of the sins of omission or commission of their leaders."[10]

It is indeed a historical irony that, since the late 1980s, much of the Palestinian historiography has been written by the Israeli "new historians" noted by Khalidi – younger, politically engaged academics and journalists who claim to have discovered archival evidence substantiating the anti-Israel case. These politicized historians have turned the saga of Israel's birth upside down, with aggressors transformed into hapless victims and vice versa. Rarely mentioned in these revisionist accounts are the Arabs' outspoken commitment to the destruction of the Jewish national cause; the sustained and repeated Arab efforts to achieve that end from the early 1920s onward;

and the no less sustained efforts of the Jews at peaceful coexistence. Zionism emerges, instead, as "a colonizing and expansionist ideology and movement" (in the representative words of one "new historian"),[11] an offshoot of European imperialism at its most rapacious.

Ignoring the total unfamiliarity of most "new historians" with the Arab world – its language, culture, history, and politics – and their condescending treatment of the Palestinians as passive objects, Arab propagandists and anti-Israel forces everywhere have embraced their seemingly authoritative shifting of the blame for the *Nakba*. Prominent Palestinian politicians such as President Mahmoud Abbas (Abu Mazen) and Hanan Ashrawi have cited their "findings" to support extreme Palestinian territorial and political claims. Academics have lauded them for using newly available documents to expose the allegedly immoral circumstances of Israel's creation.

Such plaudits, however, are undeserved. For one thing, rather than unearth new facts or offer novel interpretations, the "new historians" have recycled the standard Palestinian Arab narrative of the conflict.[12] For another, the recent declassification of millions of documents from the period of the British mandate and Israel's early days, documents untapped by earlier generations of writers and ignored or distorted by the "new historians," paint a much more definitive picture of the historical record, and one that is completely at odds with the anti-Israel caricature that is so often the order of the day. They reveal that there was nothing inevitable about the Palestinian-Jewish confrontation, let alone the Arab-Israeli conflict, corollaries, on the one hand, of the total rejection of the Jewish right to national self-determination, and, on the other, of the desire to annex Palestine, or parts of it, to the neighboring Arab states, or to a prospective regional empire; that the claim of premeditated dispossession is not only baseless but the inverse of the truth; and that far from being the hapless victims of a predatory Zionist assault, it was Palestinian Arab leaders who, from the early 1920s onward, and very much against the wishes of their own constituents, launched a relentless campaign to obliterate the Jewish national revival which culminated in the violent attempt to abort the UN partition resolution.

Had these leaders, and their counterparts in the neighboring Arab states, accepted the resolution, there would have been no war and no dislocation in the first place, for the simple reason that the Zionist movement was amenable both to the existence of a substantial non-Jewish minority in the prospective Jewish state on an equal footing, and to the two-state solution, raised for the first time in 1937 by a British commission of inquiry and reiterated by the partition resolution. That they chose to reject this solution and to wage a war of annihilation against Palestine's Jewish community amounted to nothing short of a betrayal of their constituents, who would

Map 1 Mandatory Palestine Administrative Division (1920–1948)

rather have coexisted with their Jewish neighbors yet instead had to pay the ultimate price of this folly: homelessness and statelessness.

These facts, as we have seen, were fully recognized at the time by the Gaza refugees, who claimed that "they have no quarrel with the Jews, that they have lived with the Jews all their lives and are perfectly ready to go back and live with them again."[13] They were likewise acknowledged by millions of contemporary Arabs, Jews, and foreign observers of the Middle East, only to be erased from public memory by decades of relentless pro-Arab propaganda. It is to reclaim the historical truth that this book has been written.

CHAPTER 1

Jews and Arabs in the Holy Land

"Though the Arabs have benefited by the development of the country owing to Jewish immigration, this has had no conciliatory effect. On the contrary . . . with almost mathematical precision the betterment of the economic situation in Palestine meant the deterioration of the political situation."

Peel Commission Report, 1937

More than any other conflict, the dispute between Arabs and Jews over the tiny piece of land on the eastern shore of the Mediterranean epitomizes the intricate linkage between past and present. The roots of this conflict date back to the Roman destruction of Jewish statehood, which had existed intermittently for over a millennium in the country that had subsequently come to be known as Palestine. Since then, exile and dispersion had become the hallmark of the Jewish people. Even in its ancestral homeland, it was progressively relegated to a small minority under a long succession of imperial occupiers – Byzantines, Sassanids, Arabs, Umayyads, Abbasids, Fatimids, Seljuks, Crusaders, Ayyubis, Mamluks, and Ottomans – who inflicted repression and dislocation upon Jewish life. At the time of the Muslim occupation of Palestine in the seventh century, the country's Jewish population ranged in the hundreds of thousands at the very least;[1] by the 1880s, Palestine's Jewish community had been reduced to about 24,000, or some 5 percent of the total population.

This forced marginalization notwithstanding, not only was there always a Jewish presence in Palestine, but the Jews' longing for their ancestral homeland, or Zion, occupied a focal place in their collective memory for millennia and became an integral part of Jewish religious ritual. Moreover, Jews began returning to Palestine from the earliest days of dispersion. When in 538 B.C.E. King Cyrus the Great of Persia, conqueror of Babylon, issued his famous proclamation allowing the Jews, exiled some fifty years earlier by the fallen empire, to return to their homeland and rebuild the Temple in Jerusalem with funds from the royal treasury, tens of thousands of exiles seized the historic opportunity for national restoration. Some 2,000 years later, the expulsion of the Jews from Spain (in 1492) brought in its wake waves of new immigrants; an appreciable influx of religious Jews from Eastern Europe occurred in the late eighteenth century, the same from Yemen a hundred years later.

In the 1880s, the latest type of returnees began arriving: young nationalists who rejected Diaspora life and sought to restore Jewish sovereignty in the historic homeland. Dozens of committees and societies for the settlement of the Land of Israel mushroomed in Russia and Eastern Europe, to be transformed before long into a full-fledged national liberation movement known as Zionism.

In August 1897, the First Zionist Congress was held in the Swiss town of Basle, under the chairmanship of Theodor Herzl, a young and dynamic Austro-Hungarian journalist. A milestone in modern Jewish and Middle Eastern history, the congress defined the aim of Zionism as "the creation of a home for the Jewish people in Palestine to be secured by public law." It also established institutions for the promotion of this goal. By the outbreak of World War I in 1914, the Jewish community in Palestine (or the Yishuv as it was commonly known) had grown to some 100,000 people (nearly 15 percent of the country's total population): twice its size at the turn of the century and four times its size in the early 1880s.[2]

This growth in numbers reflected the broader development of the Yishuv into a cohesive and organized national community, with its own economic, political, and social institutions. The "old" agricultural settlements of the late nineteenth century were flourishing, while a string of new villages were sprouting up across the country. An influx of capital from the Diaspora allowed the development of the urban sector and laid the foundations of an industrial infrastructure. While half of Palestinian Jewry still lived in Jerusalem, the Jewish population in the coastal cities of Jaffa and Haifa grew rapidly, and in 1909 Tel Aviv was established as the first modern Hebrew city. The Hebrew language had been revived and was rapidly establishing itself as the community's national language.

Palestine at the time did not exist as a unified geographical entity; rather, it was divided between the Ottoman province of Beirut in the north and the district of Jerusalem in the south. Its inhabitants, like the rest of the Arabic-speaking communities throughout the region, viewed themselves as subjects of the Ottoman Empire, which had ruled the Middle East and much of Eastern Europe and North Africa for hundreds of years, rather than as members of a wider Arab nation, and were totally impervious to the nationalist message of the tiny Arab secret societies operating throughout the empire prior to World War I. Their immediate loyalties were parochial – to one's clan, tribe, village, town, or religious sect – and coexisted alongside their overarching submission to the Ottoman sultan-caliph in his capacity as the religious and temporal head of the world Muslim community. Not even the repressive Ottoman measures in the Levant from the autumn of 1915 onward could turn the local population against their suzerain. As late as June 1918, less than three months before the end of hostilities in the Middle East, Brigadier General Gilbert Clayton, chief political officer of the Egyptian Expeditionary Force which expelled the Ottomans, who fought the war on the German-Austro-Hungarian side, from Palestine, noted the absence of "real patriotism amongst the population of Palestine." Two months later a British report stated that "the Muslim population of Judea took little or no interest in the Arab national movement. Even now the Effendi [i.e., upper] class, and particularly the educated Muslim-Levantine population of Jaffa, evince a feeling somewhat akin to hostility toward the Arab movement very similar to the feeling so prevalent in Cairo and Alexandria. This Muslim-Effendi class which has no real political cohesion, and above all no power of organization, is either pro-Turkish or pro-British."[3]

In these circumstances, the growing Jewish presence in Palestine encountered no nationwide opposition. There was, of course, the atavistic fear and xenophobic rejection of the "Other," with his alien habits, culture, and political ideals, but this was matched by the evolution of peaceful coexistence as a growing number of Arabs benefitted materially, or even earned their livelihood, from the budding Jewish presence in the country. There were also clashes over pasturing and farming lands, as well as marauding attacks on individuals and communities, but these did not fundamentally differ from the other acts of violence and lawlessness that plagued Palestine at the time.[4]

Even the Balfour Declaration of November 1917, made in a letter from British Foreign Secretary Arthur James Balfour to the Anglo-Jewish dignitary, Lord Lionel Walter Rothschild, in which the British government endorsed "the establishment in Palestine of a national home for the Jewish people" and pledged to "use its best endeavors to facilitate the achievement of this object, it being clearly understood that nothing shall be done which may prejudice the civil and religious rights of existing non-Jewish communities in Palestine," generated no immediate antagonism. It took one full year for the first manifestation of local opposition to emerge in the form of a petition by a group of Arab dignitaries and nationalists demanding Palestine's incorporation into Syria and proclaiming their loyalty to the short-lived Arab kingdom established in Damascus in the wake of World War I.[5]

But then the head of the very government to which they swore their allegiance, Emir Faisal ibn Hussein of Mecca, the celebrated hero of the "Great Arab Revolt" against the Ottoman Empire and the effective leader of

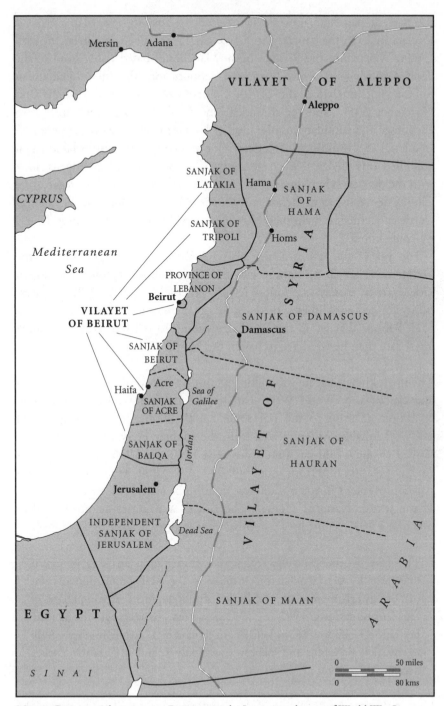

Map 2 Ottoman Administrative Divisions in the Levant on the eve of World War I

the nascent pan-Arab movement, evinced no hostility toward the Balfour Declaration. On the contrary, in January 1919 he signed an agreement with Chaim Weizmann, the Russian-born, Manchester-based rising head of the Zionist movement, which expressed support for "the fullest guarantees for carrying into effect the British Government's Declaration of the 2nd November 1917" and for the adoption of "all necessary measures . . . to encourage and stimulate immigration of Jews into Palestine on a large scale." In a letter to a prominent American Zionist a couple of months later, Faisal amplified this pledge: "We Arabs, especially the educated among us, look with the deepest sympathy on the Zionist movement . . . and we regard [the Zionist demands] as moderate and proper. We will do our best, in so far as we are concerned, to help them through: we will wish the Jews a most hearty welcome home."[6]

For years after its issuance many Arabs remained ignorant of the Declaration's actual substance, with the name Balfour instead denoting an idea – power, money to promote Jewish settlement, or better still an opportunity for self-enrichment. In the words of a sheik in the vicinity of Gaza: "Tell Balfour that we in the South are willing to sell him land at a much lower rate than he will have to pay in the North."[7]

The sheik knew what he was talking about. An inflow of Jewish immigrants and capital after World War I had revived Palestine's hitherto moribund condition. If prior to the war some 2,500–3,000 Arabs, or one out of 200–250 inhabitants, emigrated from the country every year, this rate was slashed to about 800 per annum between 1920 and 1936, while Palestine's Arab population rose from about 600,000 to 950,000 owing to the substantial improvement in socio-economic conditions attending the development of the Jewish National Home.[8] The British authorities acknowledged as much in a 1937 report by a commission of inquiry headed by Lord Peel:

> The general beneficent effect of Jewish immigration on Arab welfare is illustrated by the fact that the increase in the Arab population is most marked in urban areas affected by Jewish development. A comparison of the Census returns in 1922 and 1931 shows that, six years ago, the increase percent in Haifa was 86, in Jaffa 62, in Jerusalem 37, while in purely Arab towns such as Nablus and Hebron it was only 7, and at Gaza there was a decrease of 2 percent.[9]

Raising the standard of living of the Palestinian Arabs well above that in the neighboring Arab states, the general fructifying effect of the import of Jewish capital into the country was not limited to the upper classes, or the *effendis*, who "sold substantial pieces of land [to the Jews] at a figure far above the price it could have fetched before the War," but extended to the country's predominantly rural population, the *fellaheen*, who "are on the whole better off than they were in 1920." The expansion of Arab industry and agriculture, especially in the field of citrus-growing, Palestine's foremost export product, was largely financed by the capital thus obtained, and Jewish know-how did much to improve Arab cultivation. In the two decades between the world wars, Arab-owned citrus plantations grew sixfold, as did vegetable-growing lands, while the number of olive groves quadrupled and that of vineyards increased threefold.[10]

No less remarkable were the advances in Arab social welfare. Perhaps most significantly, mortality rates in the Muslim population dropped sharply and life expectancy rose from 37.5 years in 1926–27 to 50 in 1942–44 (compared with 33 in Egypt). Between 1927–29 and 1942–44, child mortality was reduced by 34 percent in the first year of age, by 31 percent in the second, by 57 percent in the third, by 64 percent in the fourth, and by 67 percent in the fifth. The rate of natural increase leapt upward by a third (from 23.3 per 1,000 people in 1922–25 to 30.7 in 1941–44) – well ahead of the natural increase (or the total increase) of other Arab/Muslim populations.[11]

That nothing remotely akin to this was taking place in the neighboring British-ruled Arab countries, not to mention India, can be explained only by the decisive Jewish contribution to mandatory Palestine's socio-economic wellbeing. While the neighboring Arab countries struggled to balance their budgets, the tens of millions of pounds brought to Palestine by Jewish immigration, much of which flowed into the coffers of the mandatory exchequer, placed the country's finances on exceptionally solid grounds. In the words of the Peel commission, "much the greater part of the customs duties are paid by [the Jews], and the rising amount of customs-revenue has formed from 1920 to the present day the biggest item in the rising total revenue." Though the commission was unable to calculate the precise share of customs revenue borne by the Jews, this was estimated at approximately 65 percent by a later official survey, while the Jewish contribution to revenue from income tax in 1944–45 amounted to 68 percent (compared with 15 percent paid by the Arabs).[12]

This massive contribution to state revenues was accompanied by the Yishuv's extensive public health provision which benefitted a substantial part of the country's Arab population. Jewish reclamation and anti-malarial work slashed the prevalence of this lethal disease (during the latter part of 1918, for example, 68 out of 1,000 people in the Beit Jibrin region died of malaria; in 1935, the number of malaria-related deaths in the whole of Palestine was 17), while health institutions, founded with Jewish funds primarily to serve the Jewish National Home, also served the Arab population. The Hadassah Medical Organization, in particular, treated many of the poorer classes among the Arabs, notably at the Tuberculosis Hospital in Safad and the Radiology Institute in Jerusalem, admitted Arab countryfolk to the clinics of its rural Sick Benefit Fund, and did much infant welfare work for Arab mothers. It is hardly surprising therefore that the greatest reductions in Arab mortality, as well as the most significant rise in the quality and standard of living, occurred in localities in or near those in which Jewish enterprise had been most pronounced.[13]

Had the vast majority of Palestinian Arabs been left to their own devices, they would most probably have been content to get on with their lives and take advantage of the opportunities afforded by the growing Jewish presence in the country. Throughout the mandate era (1920–48), periods of peaceful coexistence were far longer than those of violent eruptions, and the latter were the work of a small fraction of Palestinian Arabs.

In the 1920s and 1930s, Jewish representatives held hundreds of formal meetings with their Arab counterparts in Palestine and the neighboring Arab states, and were frequently welcomed at social gatherings and official events held by rural and urban leaders, as well as at the homes of prominent Arab families. There were also various joint Arab-Jewish projects and enterprises, ranging from the association for orange-growers in Jaffa, to mixed committees for the building of the Jaffa port and similar enterprises in Haifa; from active cooperation by Arab and Jewish villagers in anti-malarial drainage and in the improvement of water supplies, to a joint organization for the benefit of the poor and the aged, to Arab-Jewish professional unions. In 1923, about a hundred Arab children attended private Jewish schools while 307 Jewish children attended private Arab schools. Three years later, the number of Jews attending Arab schools grew by some 50 percent to 445 – including 315 Jewesses in Arab all-girl schools.[14]

In the course of a brief trip to the Galilee in April 1923, for example, Colonel Frederick Kisch, the most senior Zionist official in Palestine between 1923 and 1931, conferred with the local mufti and the "very friendly" mayor of Tiberias, a city of mixed Arab-Jewish population where "none of the Arabs are definitely opposed to us." He met Arab farmers visiting the Deganya kibbutz, was informed by the Rosh Pina villagers of the cordial relations with their Arab neighbors, and noted with satisfaction the treatment of Arab patients at the Hadassah hospital in Safad. The following month, having returned from a festive event at a Jewish village attended by at least 100 Arabs, Kisch recorded in his diary: "It was gratifying to see so many Arabs, most of them inhabitants of the neighboring villages, participating happily in such a ceremony under the shadow of the blue and white flag. No better answer could be given to the constantly repeated charge that all Arabs are opposed to Zionist work."

Even Gilbert Clayton, a prominent champion of the pan-Arab cause who in 1923 became Palestine's chief political secretary, acknowledged that "on non-political matters, such as taxation, agriculture, etc., the Jewish colonies and Arab villages speak with the same voice and sometimes from the same hall." He once recalled how he had arrived in a Jewish village to deliver a speech on the National Home, only to find a mixed gathering of Jews and Arabs engaged in an animated discussion, which necessitated a complete change in the nature of his own remarks.[15]

In a valedictory report summing up his term in office (1920–25), Sir Herbert Samuel, the first Jew to serve as a British cabinet minister, who subsequently became the first high commissioner for Palestine, painted an upbeat picture of the development of Arab-Jewish relations:

> In the first place, the people discovered that the disasters, which they had been told were about to fall upon them, did not in fact occur. The attacks upon their villages by well-armed Jewish colonists, which some of the agitators had announced, did not take place. The day when a hundred thousand Jews were to disembark in Palestine in order to occupy their lands, came and went, and there was no such invasion. Month followed month and year followed year, and no man had his land taken from him. So far from the mosques [being] closed and turned into synagogues, a new, purely Moslem, elected body was created to which the control of all Moslem religious buildings, and of their endowments, was transferred; it rebuilt those that were in ruins and began to restore those that needed restoration. It is difficult, under such conditions, to maintain indefinitely an attitude of alarm; people cannot be induced to remain constantly mobilized against a danger which never eventuates.[16]

Unfortunately for Arabs and Jews, the hopes and wishes of ordinary people were not taken into account – they rarely are in authoritarian communities hostile to the notions of civil society or liberal democracy. As Musa Alami, one of the foremost Palestinian Arab moderates during the mandate era, told David Ben-Gurion, "he would prefer the land to remain poor and desolate even for another hundred years" if the alternative was its rapid development in collaboration with the Zionists.

This bravado, however, did not prevent Alami from making a handsome profit by selling 225 acres (91 ha) to the Jews, as did thousands of Arabs from all classes and walks of life. In the three-year period from 1933 to 1936, for example, 2,809 of the 3,076 Arab-Jewish land transactions (or 91 percent) involved ordinary people selling smallish plots of less than 25 acres (10 ha), rather than absentee landlords selling large tracts of land. Even the radical leadership, which put the Palestinian Arabs on the tragic course that was to result in their collective undoing, unabashedly prospered from the Jewish national revival which it vowed to eradicate.

In Palestine, ordinary Arabs were persecuted and murdered by their alleged betters for the crime of "selling the country" to the Jews. Meanwhile, those same betters were enriching themselves with impunity. The staunch pan-Arabist Awni Abdel Hadi, scion of a distinguished Nablus-based family who accompanied Emir Faisal to the 1919 Paris peace conference, mediated the transfer of 7,500 acres (3,038 ha) to the Zionist movement, for which he was rewarded to the tune of £2,700 (about £1.2 million in today's terms),[17] and some of his relatives, all respected political and religious figures, went a step further by selling actual plots of land. So did the prominent leaders Muin Madi, Alfred Rock, As'ad Shuqeiri (father of Ahmad, later the founder of the PLO), and numerous members of the Husseini family, the foremost Palestinian Arab clan during the mandate period, including Musa Kazim (longtime Jerusalem mayor and father of Abdel Qader Husseini, the famous guerrilla leader) and Muhammad Tahir, father of Muhammad Amin Husseini, the militant leader of the Palestinian Arabs since the early 1920s.[18]

But then, socio-economic progress has never been a recipe for political moderation and intercommunal coexistence. In the modern world it has not been the poor and the oppressed who have led the great revolutions or carried out the worst deeds of violence, but rather militant vanguards from among the better-educated and more moneyed circles of society. So it was with the Palestinians. In the words of the Peel report: "We have found that, though the Arabs have benefited by the development of the country owing to Jewish immigration, this has had no conciliatory effect. On the contrary . . . with almost mathematical precision the betterment of the economic situation in Palestine meant the deterioration of the political situation."[19]

The driving force behind this deterioration was Muhammad Amin Husseini. Born in Jerusalem in 1895,[20] the minute and frail Amin, self-conscious to a fault owing to a lisp, had a rather unremarkable childhood that showed little of the ruthlessness that was to make him the most influential Palestinian Arab leader of the twentieth century. In 1912, at the age of seventeen, he was sent to Cairo for religious education, only to leave the city the following year on a pilgrimage to Mecca, which won him the honorific title of Hajj (Arabic for "pilgrim") that was to become his main moniker. From Mecca, Hajj Amin returned to Jerusalem, served in the Ottoman army during World War I, and in its wake became an ardent proponent of the ideal of a Greater Syrian empire, coediting the Jerusalem-based paper *Suria al-Janubiyya* (Southern Syria), as Palestine is named by pan-Arabists, and presiding over the Jerusalem-based Arab Club, which advocated Palestine's incorporation into Syria.

In April 1920, Hajj Amin played a major role in instigating an anti-Jewish pogrom in Jerusalem in which five people were murdered and 211 wounded. He was subsequently sentenced by a British military court to ten years in prison, but managed to flee the country and a few months later was pardoned by High Commissioner Samuel. "Like most agitators, having incited the man in the street to violence and probable punishment, he fled," the British governor of Jerusalem, Ronald Storrs, commented derisively.[21] Yet a year later Storrs supported Hajj Amin's elevation to Palestine's top religious post following the death of Kamil Husseini, the mufti of Jerusalem and Amin's half-brother. Initially Amin failed to make the final shortlist owing to his poor religious credentials, receiving only nine of the electors' sixty-four votes; but the Husseinis and their British champions forced one of the final three candidates to step down in his favor. Meanwhile Samuel, having been warned by Storrs and other advisors that the selection of another candidate would cause "great dissatisfaction among the people of the country," relented and in April 1921 appointed Hajj Amin to Palestine's highest Islamic post, though no official letter of appointment was issued, nor was it ever gazetted.[22]

Nine months later the Mufti consolidated his power still further by assuming the presidency of the newly established Supreme Muslim Council (SMC), which managed the religious affairs of the country's Muslim community and controlled its religious appointments and extremely well-funded endowments (*awqaf*). In subsequent years Hajj Amin used his joint appointments to become the foremost Palestinian Arab political figure, placing numerous members of his family in key posts, silencing the proponents of coexistence, and putting his constituents on a relentless collision course with the Zionist movement. "Palestine is a purely Arab land," argued his close associate, the staunch pan-Arabist Izzat Darwaza, "and there is no possibility that another people, with their own language, customs and traditions and a contradictory political goal, could live with them." Awni Abdel Hadi was no less forthright, telling a Jewish acquaintance that "we will not rest until Palestine is either placed under a free Arab government or becomes a graveyard for all the Jews in the country. We will finish them off one by one: if not in a month, then in a year, if not in a year – then in ten years. But our goal will be achieved, and there is nothing that can prevent us from achieving it, slowly but surely."[23]

The Mufti put the idea in similarly stark terms. "Just as it is impossible to put two swords into the same sheath," he claimed in a press interview, "it is impossible to squeeze two peoples into one small country." In private he was even blunter, telling the British high commissioner that "there was no place in Palestine for two races." "The Jews left Palestine 2,000 years ago," he averred. "Let them go to other parts of the world, where there are wide vacant places."[24]

By way of achieving this goal, the Mufti utilized the immense inflammatory potential of Islam, which had constituted the linchpin of the Middle Eastern social and political order for over a millennium, and its deep anti-Jewish sentiment. Reflecting the Prophet Muhammad's outrage over the rejection of his religious message by the Jewish community, both the Koran and later biographical traditions of the Prophet abound with negative depictions of Jews. In these works they are portrayed as a deceitful, evil, and treacherous people who in their insatiable urge for domination would readily betray an ally and swindle a non-Jew, and who tampered with the Holy Scriptures, spurned Allah's divine message, and persecuted His messenger Muhammad just as they had Jesus of Nazareth and other previous prophets. For this perfidy, they would incur a string of retributions, both in the afterlife, when they would burn in Hell, and here on earth, where they were justly condemned to an existence of wretchedness and humiliation. "I never saw the curse denounced against the children of Israel more fully brought to bear than in the East," wrote an early nineteenth-century Western traveler to the Ottoman Empire, "where they are considered rather as a link between animals and human beings, than as men possessed by the same attributes."[25]

Given the millennial disparagement of Jews in the House of Islam, it required an exceptional open-mindedness to view them with equanimity. The previous mufti, Kamil Husseini, was endowed with this rare virtue. A man of great religious learning and a peaceful disposition, largely free of bigotry and political machinations, he went out of his way to prevent the radicalization of his Muslim constituents and to promote coexistence with the Jewish community, so much so that in July 1918 he was given the honor of laying the foundation stone of the Hebrew University in Jerusalem. Hajj Amin had no such pacific intentions, despite the pledge to follow in his predecessor's footsteps that had won him the top spot.

Not that the Mufti, like other members of his family, had any qualms about seeking Jewish aid and support whenever this suited his needs. Prior to his appointment, he pleaded with Jewish leaders to lobby (the Jewish) Herbert Samuel on his behalf, and in 1927 he asked Gad Frumkin, the only Jewish Supreme Court judge during the mandate era, to influence Jerusalem's Jewish community to back the Husseini candidate in the mayoral elections. He likewise employed a Jewish architect to build a luxury hotel for the SMC, while ordering his constituents to boycott Jewish labor and products.[26]

"Arab nationalist feelings were never allowed to harm the interests of the Husseini family," wrote the prominent Jerusalem lawyer and Zionist activist Bernard (Dov) Joseph, a future minister of justice in the Israeli government. "One of [the Mufti's] kinsmen, Jamil Husseini, had once engaged my services in land litigation which went as high as the Privy Council in London. . . . For years one of the Mufti's close relations prospered mightily by forcing Arab small-holders to sell land, at niggardly prices, which he then resold to Jews at a handsome profit."[27] This instrumental approach notwithstanding, Hajj Amin was consumed with a burning hatred of Jews and Judaism. "How can the Jews be respected for their wealth at a time when they spread wickedness and misery throughout the world?" he recorded in his diary. "They tortured their innocent prophets, killed John [the Baptist] and rejected Jesus; they corrupt morality in every single country, destroy all religions and sympathize with [communist] Russia; they rob people's property, steal money by usury, and distort the prophets' preaching."[28]

Having discovered *The Protocols of the Elders of Zion* in the early 1920s, the Mufti spared no effort to disseminate them. Sprinkling his speeches, sermons, and writings with themes and ideas from this virulent anti-Semitic tract (his memoirs, for example, are rife with fulminations about world Jewry's designs on the Middle East),[29] the Mufti ensured that the SMC gave these canards the widest possible exposure through its daily newspaper *al-Jami'a al-Arabiyya*, the free distribution of newsletters and pamphlets, and the indoctrination of pupils in its school network with a regular diet of anti-Jewish propaganda. "O Arab! Remember that the Jew is your strongest enemy and the enemy of your ancestors since older times," read a typical SMC-printed proclamation. "Do not be misled by his tricks for it is he who tortured Christ, peace be upon him, and poisoned Muhammad, peace and worship be with him. It is he who now endeavors to slaughter you as he did yesterday."[30]

Temple Mount, or al-Haram al-Sharif as it is known to Muslims, became the centerpiece of the Mufti's hate-mongering. By way of rallying Palestine's Muslim community behind his ambitions and attracting the support of the Arab and Muslim nations, Hajj Amin spared no effort to place Jerusalem, which for most of Islam's history had been a sleepy backwater, at the forefront of Muslim attention. Time and again Muslims were reminded that it was Jerusalem toward which the Prophet Muhammad initially turned in prayer (before the direction was changed to Mecca), whence he made his famous journey to Heaven, and in which Islam's third most important mosque (al-Aqsa) was located. It was indeed in this mosque that the most virulent sermons were held and whence the bloodiest pogroms ensued, with a false rumor about a Jewish plot to destroy al-Aqsa (and the adjacent Dome of the Rock) and to rebuild a temple on their ruins becoming the standard battle cry. "No Muslim will accept that a foreigner should convert his house into a synagogue," lambasted Abdel Hadi. "How would he accept then that a *masjed* [mosque, i.e., al-Aqsa] be converted into a synagogue?"[31]

Matters came to a head in August 1929 when, after a year of systematic incitement and escalating efforts to restrict Jewish prayers at the Wailing Wall, a remnant of King Solomon's Temple, Judaism's holiest site, the Mufti exploited a youth rally nearby on the occasion of a Jewish religious event to unleash a tidal wave of violence throughout the country, in which 133 Jews were massacred and hundreds more were wounded. A particularly gruesome fate befell the ancient Jewish community of Hebron, which dated back to biblical times, where sixty-seven people were brutally slaughtered by their Arab neighbors, dozens more were wounded, property was ransacked, and synagogues were desecrated. A list compiled shortly after the massacre, and confirmed by the city's two rabbis, identified a mere nineteen Arabs, compared to the thousands of rioters, as having helped the persecuted Jews.

In his evidence given before a British commission of inquiry, the commander of police in Hebron, Raymond Cafferata, recalled how he "shot dead a man who was in the act of committing murder and saw another Arab raising his sword to strike a girl who was already bleeding at the neck. He was about to shoot when the man cried out, 'I am a policeman.' After a second's hesitation, Cafferata fired, wounding the man in the thigh."[32] Still, three of the commission's four members ruled against all the available evidence that the riots were "not premeditated."[33]

The repeated Arab resort to violence seemed to be working. It was particularly effective in influencing the British, who in April 1920 had been appointed the mandatory power in Palestine by the League of Nations, the newly established world organization and the United Nations' predecessor. Though the explicit purpose of the mandate was to facilitate the establishment of a Jewish National Home in Palestine as envisaged by the Balfour Declaration, the British government repeatedly gave in to Arab violence aimed at averting that purpose and to the demands that followed upon it. As early as March 1921, they sought to appease Emir Abdullah ibn Hussein of Mecca, Faisal's older brother, who resented his exclusion from the division of war spoils by severing the vast and sparsely populated territory east of the Jordan River, or Transjordan as it came to be widely known, from the prospective Jewish

National Home (though not from the Palestine mandate) and making the emir its effective ruler.[34] In two White Papers, issued in 1922 and 1930, respectively, Britain severely compromised the Jewish National Home by limiting immigration to the "economic capacity of the country at the time to absorb new arrivals" and imposing harsh restrictions on land sales to Jews.

No less important, the mounting violence placed a big question mark over an age-old Zionist hope: that the material progress resulting from Jewish settlement of Palestine would ease the path for the local Arab populace to become permanently reconciled, if not positively well disposed, to the project of Jewish national self-determination. As early as 1899, Herzl had reassured a leading Jerusalem notable that, rather than endanger them in any way, growing Jewish immigration into Palestine held great economic promise for its Arab inhabitants. Three years later, in his utopian Zionist novel *Alteneuland* (Old-New Land), Herzl painted an idyllic picture of Arab-Jewish coexistence in the Palestine of 1923, which by that time had become a modern, prosperous, liberal, and egalitarian Jewish state. "It was a great blessing for all of us," said Rashid Bey, the voice of the Palestinian Arab population in the novel, as he explained the impact of Zionism to an enquiring foreigner:

> The Jews have enriched us. . . . They dwell among us like brothers. . . . Naturally, the land-owners gained most because they were able to sell to the Jewish society at high prices, or to wait for still higher ones . . . [but] those who had nothing stood to lose nothing, and could only gain. And they did gain: Opportunities to work, means of livelihood, prosperity. . . . These people are better off than at any time in the past. They support themselves decently, their children are healthier and are being taught something. Their religion and ancient customs have in no wise been interfered with. They have become more prosperous – that is all.[35]

In his report to the Eleventh Zionist Congress (1913), Arthur Ruppin, head of the Zionist movement's Palestine office, advocated a greater effort to convince the Arabs of the material gains attending the Jewish national awakening. He noted the significant benefits already brought to the Arab population in the fields of employment, modern agricultural methods, and improved health services, yet insisted that still more was to be done. "In my report to last year's annual meeting I showed that the Jews could substantially improve Arab wellbeing by stamping out epidemics in Palestine, especially the frightfully common eye diseases," he argued. "Since then, this idea has been realized by [the American Jewish philanthropist] Nathan Strauss, assisted by a number of charitable societies, and one hopes that this work will win us the Arabs' sympathy."[36]

Two years later, the twenty-nine-year-old political activist David Ben-Gurion, who had arrived in Palestine in 1906, argued that "the Jewish settlement is not designed to undermine the position of the Arab community; on the contrary, it will salvage it from its economic misery, lift it from its social decline, and rescue it from physical and moral degeneration. Our renaissance in Palestine will come through the country's regeneration, that is: the renaissance of its Arab inhabitants." As late as December 1947, shortly after the Mufti had initiated a violent effort to subvert the UN partition resolution, Ben-Gurion, soon to become Israel's first prime minister, argued that, despite appearances of implacable enmity: "If the Arab citizen will feel at home in our state . . . if the state will help him in a truthful and dedicated way to reach the economic, social, and cultural level of the Jewish community, then Arab distrust will accordingly subside and a bridge will be built to a Semitic, Jewish-Arab alliance."[37]

Not all Zionists shared this prognosis. Fresh from an extended visit to Palestine, in 1891 the eminent thinker Asher Zvi Ginsberg (aka Ahad Ha'am) warned of the potential threat to the Jewish national project from the country's vast Arab population. "The Arabs, especially the city dwellers among them, are perfectly aware of our activities and goals in the country yet keep their own counsel and feign ignorance because they don't deem our present activities as endangering their future," he wrote.

> On the contrary, they exploit us to the best of their ability and try to extract the greatest possible profit from the newcomers, while laughing at us in their hearts. The peasants marvel at the establishment of Hebrew villages in their midst as they are handsomely remunerated for their labor and, as experience shows, prosper steadily by the year; while the great landowners are equally forthcoming toward us because we pay them exorbitant prices they have never imagined in their wildest dreams for stony lands and sand dunes. Yet should our national development in Palestine reach such a stage as to encroach upon them to a greater or lesser extent, they will not give in easily.[38]

Writing in the same vein shortly after Zionism had won its greatest political success until then – the Balfour Declaration – Max Nordau, Herzl's second-in-command, identified the Arab question as the foremost obstacle to the Zionist enterprise. "When we return to our ancestral homeland we will find there some 600,000 Arab inhabitants," he argued.

> This figure is of course an estimate, as Turkish statistics, the only source at our disposal, are highly questionable. But even in the event of large and

rapid Jewish immigration it is likely that initially, and for some time to come, we will remain a minority within, or beside, an Arab majority. This majority may or may not welcome us; it may be sympathetic, hostile or indifferent to our cause, and can facilitate our settlement in the Holy Land or make the lives of our pioneers difficult. We must therefore prepare ourselves without delay for the looming challenge of coexistence with our future neighbors.[39]

It was indeed Arab political hostility in the wake of World War I, as opposed to grassroots coexistence, that largely underlay the emphasis on Zionism's economic payoffs as an ameliorating factor. And even prominent champions of the "economic option," such as Kisch, acknowledged the latter tactic's limited value. "There is one point on which everyone who has studied the situation here seems to agree: namely, that it is futile now to try to create [an Arab] party that will formally accept the Balfour Declaration," he recorded in his diary on May 5, 1923. "Arabs can be won over for a specific action of limited duration, but it is impossible to persuade them definitely to attach themselves to an unpopular cause. We might get a strong Arab party to work with us to a certain extent on the basis of economic cooperation leaving the question of the political regime out of account. This seems to me the right policy to pursue for the time being."[40]

Ze'ev (Vladimir) Jabotinsky, the founding father of the branch of Zionism that was the forebear of today's Likud party, put the matter in stronger terms. In an address to the Zionist leadership in July 1921, two months after Arab violence claimed ninety Jewish lives, he dismissed the possibility of peaceful coexistence in the foreseeable future since the Arabs were not going to acquiesce in what they considered an alien encroachment on their patrimony. And while Arab hostility could be ameliorated through economic incentives, these measures were necessarily of limited value so long as the Arabs retained the hope of destroying the Jewish National Home by force of arms.[41]

Jabotinsky famously amplified this stark prognosis two years later in an article entitled "The Iron Wall," where he repeated the claim that Arab acquiescence in the Jewish national revival in Palestine would only follow upon the establishment of an unassailable Zionist power base – political, diplomatic, and military. "As long as the Arabs feel that there is the least hope of getting rid of us, they will refuse to give up this hope in return for either kind words or for bread and butter, because they are not a rabble, but a living people," he wrote in his characteristically direct manner:

And when a living people yields in matters of such a vital character it is only when there is no longer any hope of getting rid of us, because they can make no breach in the iron wall. Not till then will they drop their extremist leaders, whose watchword is "Never!" And the leadership will pass to the moderate groups, who will approach us with a proposal that we should both agree to mutual concessions. Then we may expect them to discuss honestly practical questions, such as a guarantee against Arab displacement, or equal rights for Arab citizens, or Arab national integrity.

And when that happens, I am convinced that we Jews will be found ready to give them satisfactory guarantees, so that both peoples can live together in peace, like good neighbors.

Keenly aware of his militant reputation, Jabotinsky went to great lengths to deny any connection between the "iron wall" concept and the possible expulsion of the Palestinian Arabs. "I am reputed to be an enemy of the Arabs, who wants to have them ejected from Palestine, and so forth," he wrote. "It is not true. Emotionally, my attitude to the Arabs is the same as to all other nations – polite indifference. . . . I consider it utterly impossible to eject the Arabs from Palestine. There will always be two nations in Palestine – which is good enough for me, provided the Jews become the majority."[42]

Jabotinsky reiterated this position on numerous occasions. In the autumn of 1936, he told a Jewish gathering in Warsaw that "Palestine can offer a solution to our immigration problem without expelling any Arabs or harming them in any way." A few months later, he testified before the Peel commission that "there is no question of ousting the Arabs. On the contrary, the idea is that Palestine on both sides of the Jordan should hold the Arabs, their progeny, *and* many millions of Jews."[43] At a meeting with British parliamentarians in July 1937, Jabotinsky criticized the Peel commission's recommendation of a population exchange between the prospective Arab and Jewish states as a means of reducing intercommunal tensions. "The commission's report describes me as an extremist," he said.

> But at least I never dreamt of demanding the Arab inhabitants of the Jewish state to emigrate. This might be a most dangerous precedent that will jeopardize the interests of the Jewish Diaspora. Nor will the prospective Arab state, once deprived of Jewish energy and capital [following the transfer of its Jewish inhabitants as suggested by the Peel report], be able to absorb these Arabs. Hence the notion of "uprooting" masses of people is nothing but idle talk.[44]

Jabotinsky upheld this view to his dying day. "The transformation of Palestine can be effected to the full without dislodging the Palestinian Arabs.

All current affirmations to the contrary are utterly incorrect," he wrote in 1940, the year of his death.

> A territory of over 100,000 square kilometers settled at the average density of France (87 inhabitants per square kilometer) would hold over 8 million inhabitants; at the density of Switzerland (104) over 10 million; at the density of Germany or Italy (140) about 14 million. It now holds, counting Arabs and Jews and Transjordanians and all, just over one million and a half inhabitants. There is margin enough for Palestine to absorb the better part of East-Central Europe's ghetto – the better part of 5 million souls – without approaching even the moderate density of France. Unless the Arabs choose to go away of their own accord, there is no need for them to emigrate.[45]

What about the Arabs' position in the prospective Jewish state? In Jabotinsky's view, they would be full-fledged citizens who would participate on an equal footing "throughout all sectors of the country's public life."[46] As early as 1905, he protested the mistreatment of Arabs by some Jewish villagers, insisting that "we must treat the Arabs correctly and affably, without any violence or injustice." He reiterated this position in "The Iron Wall": "I am prepared to take an oath binding ourselves and our descendants that we shall never do anything contrary to the principle of equal rights, and that we shall never try to eject anyone. This seems to me a fairly peaceful credo."[47]

Eleven years later, in 1934, Jabotinsky presided over the drafting of a constitution for Jewish Palestine. According to its provisions, Arabs and Jews were to share the prerogatives and the duties of statehood, including most notably military and civil service. Hebrew and Arabic were to enjoy the same legal standing, and "in every cabinet where the prime minister is a Jew, the vice-premiership shall be offered to an Arab and vice versa." Asked by the Peel commission whether he still subscribed to the position that "on a long view the Jewish village cannot prosper unless the Arab village prospers with it," Jabotinsky replied: "Yes. I think on the whole it is true and I think Palestine, such as I dream of it, should be a country of very happy Arabs. . . . When we shall become a majority and make the country rich and develop all its possibilities and utilize all its resources, then it will be a prosperity in which the Arabs will be happy."[48]

If this was the position of the more "militant" faction of the Jewish national movement, mainstream Zionism not only took for granted the full equality of the Arab minority in the future Jewish state but went out of its way to

foster Arab-Jewish coexistence. As early as 1918, Ben-Gurion argued that
"had Zionism desired to evict the inhabitants of Palestine it would have been
a dangerous utopia and a harmful, reactionary mirage." Eight years later,
as secretary-general of the federation of Jewish workers (Histadrut), the
foremost Jewish socio-economic organization in Palestine with responsibility
for the Yishuv's nascent clandestine military arm, the Hagana (meaning
"defense" in Hebrew), Ben-Gurion argued that "the Arab community is an
organic, inextricable part of Palestine; it is embedded in the country, where
it toils and where it will stay. It is not to disinherit this community or to
thrive on its destruction that Zionism came into being. . . . Only a madman
can attribute such a desire to the Jewish people in Palestine. Palestine will
belong to the Jewish people and its Arab inhabitants."[49]

In a letter to his son Amos on October 5, 1937, Ben-Gurion stressed:
"We do not wish and do not need to expel Arabs and take their place. All our
aspiration is built on the assumption – proven throughout all our activity
in the Land [of Israel] – that there is enough room in the country for
ourselves and the Arabs." At the Twentieth Zionist Congress in Zurich in
August 1937, he outlined his vision of the position of the Arab minority in
the prospective Jewish state:

> No Jewish state, big or small, in part of the country or in its entirety, will be
> [truly] established so long as the land of the prophets does not witness the
> realization of the great and eternal moral ideals nourished in our hearts for
> generations: one law for all residents, just rule, love of one's neighbor, true
> equality. The Jewish state will be a role model to the world in its treatment
> of minorities and members of other nations. Law and justice will prevail in
> our state, and a firm hand will eradicate all evil from within our ranks. This
> eradication of evil will not discriminate between Jews and non-Jews. Just as
> an Arab policeman helping Arab rioters will be severely punished, so a
> Jewish policeman failing to protect an Arab from Jewish hooligans will be
> severely punished.[50]

In its July 1938 submission to the Palestine partition commission, headed
by Sir John Woodhead and charged with re-evaluating the Peel recommendations, the Zionist movement undertook "not only to respect the civil and
religious rights of its non-Jewish citizens [as required by the Balfour
Declaration], but also to safeguard and, to the best of its ability, to improve
their positions." Insisting that "there can be no question of any citizen of the
Jewish State being at a disadvantage by reason of his race or religion," the
Jewish leaders pledged "to bring about a greater measure of real equality
in education and standards of life" between the state's Arab and Jewish

communities. Specifically, the Arabs were to participate in elections "for any representative Legislature which may be set up in the Jewish State" and to be represented in the national government, were promised full religious freedoms, and were assured that "no citizen of the Jewish State shall be at a disadvantage as a candidate for public employment by reason of his race or religion," that the state would do its utmost to narrow the gap between Jewish and Arab wage levels, and that while Hebrew would be the language of the Jewish state, "Arabic will have full recognition as the language of an important section of its citizens."[51]

Even the sporadic outbreaks of Arab violence did not destroy the Zionist movement's hope for peaceful coexistence. Writing in the immediate wake of the 1921 pogroms, a few months after arriving in Palestine, the twenty-two-year-old political activist Haim Arlosoroff, the Zionist movement's future "foreign minister," insisted that for all the pain and frustration, "we have only one way – the way of peace – and only one national policy: that of mutual understanding."[52] Echoing this prognosis, the Twelfth Zionist Congress, convened in the Czechoslovak town of Carlsbad in September 1921, pronounced "the determination of the Jewish people to live with the Arab people on terms of concords and mutual respect, and together with them to make the common home into a flourishing community." Two years later, the Thirteenth Zionist Congress (convened yet again in Carlsbad) reaffirmed that "the Jewish people who are beginning to rebuild their National Home are resolved with all their spiritual, moral and material powers to associate themselves with this new world now only coming into being [in the Middle East], but so rich in energies and possibilities, and to collaborate on a footing of equality with the peoples whose destinies they share, in close communion and fruitful harmony of interests."[53]

Arlosoroff also sought to downplay the nature and significance of the 1929 massacres, stressing that they involved only a small fraction of the country's rural classes and hardly any Christian Arabs. "How many of Palestine's 930 Arab villages actively responded to the venomous slogans from Jerusalem? No more than a few dozens," he reasoned. "How many of the country's 750,000-strong Arab population participated in these riots? No more than a few thousands." Even then, religious fanaticism (let alone nationalist militancy) played only a limited role in the crisis since "after the first frenzied days of rioting, when the masses responded to the calls for a jihad, which made the violence so horrific, pillage emerged as the main motivation."[54]

This view was largely shared by Ben-Gurion. Although ten years earlier he had expressed doubts over whether there was a viable solution to the Arab-Jewish dispute since "we, as a nation, want this country to be ours; the Arabs, as a nation, want this country to be theirs,"[55] he was loath to resign himself to this stark prognosis and was repeatedly tempted to look for fragments of hope even in the gloomiest situations. He thus acknowledged that the 1929 massacres were an "eruption of the most atavistic instincts of rampaging mobs – religious zealotry combined with a thirst for plunder, pillage, and blood – geared toward a clear and terrible goal: extermination of the entire Jewish community in Palestine and the destruction of its enterprise." Yet he took comfort in the fact that "many Arab neighborhoods, including most localities adjacent to our villages, refrained from participating in this attack. The large majority of Arab villages didn't support the murderers and marauders, despite the venomous propaganda, constant incitement and countless calls to attack their Jewish neighbors."

This, in Ben-Gurion's view, meant that the Jewish community "has no war with the Arab people" and that it had to do its utmost to avoid any actions that could exacerbate any strains between the two communities while at the same time consolidating its demographic base through mass immigration. Ideally, this should be done with Arab consent, which Ben-Gurion was prepared to reward with a generous quid pro quo; yet immigration had to continue even in the face of implacable Arab opposition, for, in the final analysis, as long as the Jewish community remained small and vulnerable, there was little incentive for the Arabs to reach an agreement.[56]

The Nazi rise to power in January 1933 heightened Ben-Gurion's sense of urgency and drove him to cast his sights much higher. Utterly convinced that Hitlerism endangered the entire Jewish people, rather than the German Jews alone, and that before long the Nazis would launch "a war of vengeance against France, Poland, Czechoslovakia and other countries where a German population is to be found, or against Soviet Russia with its vast expanses," he advocated the significant acceleration of immigration to Palestine – as a means of saving the largest possible number of Jews from persecution and consolidating the only place in the world where Jews constituted a major, if not yet the decisive, factor, and which would "prescribe our entire future as a nation." In December 1933, he spoke about bringing 250,000 Jews to Palestine in the next four to five years. Three years later, he was already talking about a million immigrants in five to ten years, or 100,000 to 200,000 per annum.[57]

By now Palestine's Labor faction (or Mapai) had become the largest party in the World Zionist Congress and Ben-Gurion, who in 1933 was elected to the Zionist Executive and two years later became chairman of the Jewish Agency Executive (JAE), the effective "government" of the Yishuv,[58] embarked on a sustained effort to explore the feasibility of an Arab-Jewish agreement that would allay fears of Jewish domination and lay the ground for future coexistence. In the spring and summer of 1934, he held a series of conversations with Musa Alami, the Mufti's close associate, as well as with Awni Abdel Hadi, Riad Sulh, Lebanon's future prime minister, and the prominent Syrian pan-Arabists Shakib Arslan and Ihsan Jabri. An overture to Jamal Husseini, the Mufti's distant cousin and right-hand man (as well as Alami's brother-in-law), was unceremoniously rebuffed.

A great believer in the direct approach, Ben-Gurion laid his cards on the table. The Jews were determined to reestablish their statehood in their ancestral homeland and there was absolutely no room for compromise on this matter, or on the question of immigration, the elixir of life of the prospective Jewish state, he said. At the same time, just as they expected the Arabs to recognize their national aspirations, the Jews were fully prepared to accept the main article of faith of inter-Arab politics since World War I, namely the existence of an Arab nation, and to recognize its "unity and independence." Not only was there no basic contradiction between these two national movements, but they were potentially complementary: "If the Arabs agreed to our return to our land, we would help them with our political, financial and moral support to bring about the rebirth and unity of the Arab people."

Ben-Gurion then proposed that Palestine become an independent Jewish state attached to an Arab federation. This, in his view, would allow the country's Arab inhabitants to avoid a minority status by being linked with millions of Arabs in the neighboring countries. "The Palestinian Arabs will not be sacrificed so that Zionism might be realized," he argued. "According to our conception of Zionism, we are neither desirous nor capable of building our future in Palestine at the expense of the Arabs. The Palestinian Arabs will remain where they are, their lot will improve, and even politically they will not be dependent on us, even after we come to constitute the vast majority of the population."[59]

Ben-Gurion's arguments made little impact, as did parallel attempts at persuasion by other Zionist leaders in a string of meetings with Palestinian Arabs and representatives of Syria, Lebanon, Egypt, and Saudi Arabia.[60] Though Sulh and Abdel Hadi seemed amenable to the envisaged Arab federation, and Alami, who had been "favorably impressed by Ben-Gurion's forthrightness," even agreed on a joint declaration stating that "the complete realization of the aspirations of the Jewish people in Palestine did not conflict with those of the Arab people" and that "cooperation between the two peoples would be of benefit both to Palestine and to the other Arab states," no concrete progress was made.

Informed by Alami of Ben-Gurion's ideas, the Mufti promised to give them due consideration yet claimed that there was nothing he could do since

"Arab public opinion was far removed from such a proposal, and no leader could do anything behind the Arabs' backs. Public opinion had to be changed, a different atmosphere created."[61]

In reality, it was the Mufti who was primarily responsible for the radicalization of Palestinian Arab public opinion. In June 1930, his representatives at the deliberations of the international commission on the future of the Wailing Wall, convened in the wake of the 1929 massacres, refused to recognize any Jewish rights in Palestine (and not only at the Wall),[62] and this recalcitrance was amplified by a pan-Islamic congress held in Jerusalem in December 1931.

This zero-sum approach that assigned to the Jews no national or collective rights whatever gained considerable momentum in the early 1930s as the rival Arab factions and clans vied for political dominance through the creation of new parties. In August 1932, Abdel Hadi established the Palestinian branch of the pan-Arab Independence Party (Istiqlal), followed shortly afterward by the creation of the Youth Congress, headed by Yaqub Ghussein. Two years later, the Party for National Defense was created as the political arm of the Nashashibis, the second most powerful Palestinian Arab clan and the Husseinis' bitterest enemies, and the latter responded in kind by forming, in March 1935, the Arab Palestinian Party headed by Jamal Husseini. These were followed in the same year by the Reform Party, established by Jerusalem's mayor, Hussein Khalidi, and the National Bloc, created by the Nablus notable Abdel Latif Salah – both of which took a neutral stance in the rivalry between their larger counterparts.

This struggle for political pre-eminence was further radicalized by the Nazi seizure of power in Germany. The long-established paper *Karmil* pined for the appearance of "an Arab Hitler" who "will awaken the Arabs and rally them behind his leadership so that they will do what needs to be done," while Jamal Husseini invoked one of Hitler's famous refrains in inaugurating his party's youth organization. "When we began our activity we were six, then we became 6,000 and then 60 million," he quoted the German tyrant before urging the gathered youths to emulate the Nazi example by "toughening their bodies and souls so as to be able to defend the nation's honor and rights in time of need."[63]

It was indeed the Husseinis, the foremost influence in Palestinian Arab politics, who displayed the greatest enthusiasm for Nazism, going so far as to model their youth organization on the lines of the *Hitlerjugend* and temporarily naming it "The Nazi Scouts." Losing no time, the Mufti rushed to the German consul in Jerusalem to tell him that "the Muslims in Palestine and elsewhere were enthusiastic about the new regime in Germany and looked forward to the spread of Fascism throughout the region." In a foretaste of his actual World War II conduct, he endorsed the Nazi Jewish policy and offered to persuade Muslims worldwide to adopt similar measures.[64]

It is hardly surprising therefore that none of the Zionists' Palestinian interlocutors was prepared to put himself on the line, aside perhaps from Tahir Husseini, son of the late Kamil, the Mufti's predecessor, who held his uncle in disdain on account of his poor religious learning and political extremism and who was prepared to provide evidence of Hajj Amin's culpability for the 1929 massacres.

Particularly striking was the abrupt transformation of Hussein Khalidi, scion of a distinguished family that traced its origin to Khalid ibn Walid, Palestine's seventh-century conqueror, whose comparative past moderation had won him the Jerusalem mayoralty on the crest of the Jewish vote. In the spring of 1935, he told his Jewish deputy, future Jerusalem mayor Daniel Auster, of his intention to establish a moderate Arab party and emphasized the need for a negotiated settlement with the Yishuv. "The Jews have come to the country, have taken its citizenship and have become Palestinians, and it is impossible to throw them into the sea," he said. "They have also bought lands and obtained lawful title deeds, and these must be respected. There is no point in ignoring these clear matters."

In a later conversation, shortly after launching his party, Khalidi seemed a different person. Gone was support for a negotiated Arab-Jewish settlement; in its place was advocacy of an Anglo-Arab agreement to be imposed on the Jews. His acquiescence in Jewish land purchases and limited immigration, provided the Jews didn't exceed 40–45 percent of Palestine's population, was similarly replaced by a demand for a ban on land sales to Jews and the country's closure to Jewish immigration for one year in the first instance. "My general impression from the last conversation is that he has moved toward the Arab extremists, and that there is no difference between his attitude toward us and that of the Mufti," Auster gloomily penned his impressions.[65]

When, in mid-April 1936, Palestine slid into anarchy, Khalidi and the rest of the Palestinian leaders unflinchingly jumped on the Mufti's bandwagon, in stark contrast to their privately stated moderation. "National Committees" (NCs) sprang up throughout the country to oversee the rapidly spreading acts of violence, demonstrations, and the nascent anti-Jewish boycott, and on April 25 a ten-member Arab Higher Committee (AHC), headed by Hajj Amin, was established as the effective "government" of the Palestinian Arabs.[66]

For the next few months, a growing number of armed gangs roamed the country, attacking Jewish neighborhoods, British forces, and fellow Arabs who dared defy the anti-Jewish boycott, abstained from striking, or refused to provide the rebels with food and supplies. They were soon joined by

Arab volunteers and trained guerrilla leaders from outside Palestine, notably Fawzi Qawuqji, a Syrian officer who had served with distinction in the Ottoman army during World War I, and who promptly appointed himself "generalissimo" of the rebel forces. Under his leadership the gangs were organized, trained, and armed, which allowed them to conduct several successful attacks on the British forces and to intensify their acts of murder, plunder, and sabotage. The oil pipeline in northern Palestine was repeatedly sabotaged, roads were mined, neighborhoods sniped at, railways frequently damaged, and agricultural plantations and vast stretches of forests set on fire. By the end of September, however, the outbreak had ebbed sharply owing to the arrival of substantial British reinforcements, and was suspended the following month at the request of a number of Arab rulers. Qawuqji and his foreign volunteers were allowed to leave the country.[67]

In July 1937, Arab violence reaped its greatest reward when the Peel commission, appointed eleven months earlier to ascertain the causes of the Arab "revolt" and suggest ways and means for pacifying the country, recommended the repudiation of the terms of the mandate altogether and, instead of "placing the country under such political, administrative and economic conditions as will secure the establishment of the Jewish national home," the partition of Palestine into two states: an Arab state, united with Transjordan, that would occupy some 85 percent of the mandate territory; and a Jewish state in the remainder. Jerusalem, Bethlehem, and a corridor connecting them to the Mediterranean Sea were to remain a British mandatory zone. To reduce future friction between the two communities, the commission proposed a land and population exchange between the Jewish and Arab states, similar to that effected between Turkey and Greece in the wake of World War I.[68]

After a heated debate, the Zionist leadership gave the plan its qualified support. The AHC and the Arab governments dismissed it out of hand, with the sole exception of Emir Abdullah, who viewed the unification between the prospective Arab state and Transjordan, which he had ruled since the spring of 1921, as a steppingstone to the vast pan-Arab empire he had been striving to create throughout his career.

In his evidence given before the commission, the Mufti demanded the abandonment of the Jewish National Home plan; the immediate and complete cessation of Jewish immigration; a total prohibition on land sales to Jews; and the creation of an Arab-dominated unitary state in which the Jews would remain a small minority. When asked by Lord Peel whether he believed that Palestine could "assimilate and digest the 400,000 Jews now in the country," the Mufti responded with a categorical No.

"Some of them would have to be removed by a process kindly or painful as the case may be?" queried Lord Peel.

The Mufti did not demur at this envisaged ethnic cleansing. "We must leave all these things for the future," he commented nonchalantly.

"You complain that there are too many Jews. Would they be safe in an Arab Palestine?" Lord Peel persisted. The Mufti remained non-committal: "That would depend on the Arab government."

"We are not questioning the sincerity or the humanity of the Mufti's intentions and those of his colleagues," the commission noted in its report with quintessential English understatement, "but we cannot forget what recently happened, despite treaty provisions and explicit assurances, to the Assyrian minority in Iraq [where thousands were brutally slaughtered in 1937 by the Iraqi armed forces]; nor can we forget that the hatred of the Arab politician for the National Home has never been concealed and that it has now permeated the Arab population as a whole."

Nor did the Mufti have any qualms about reiterating the old canard about Jewish plans to destroy al-Aqsa and the Dome of the Rock, with British connivance, in order "to reconstruct there the Temple."

"You think they would be able to persuade the Mandatory power to destroy those Mosques and to erect a Temple?" an evidently astounded Lord Peel retorted.

"I know that they have already demolished Mosques in villages which were acquired by them."

"Might I repeat my question," Lord Peel insisted. "It was whether His Eminence thinks that the Jews have so much influence with the Mandatory power that they would be able to persuade them to allow them to pull down, for instance, the Mosque of Aqsa, and to erect a Temple?"

"I do not imagine that the British Government would do that itself," replied the Mufti, "but the people who have persuaded a great Government like Great Britain to adopt a policy like the Balfour Declaration can do many things."

The commission members remained confounded. "We want it quite clear," one of them interceded. "The suggestion is that although the British Government was still the Mandatory and still bound by those Articles of the Mandate, that the power of the Jews would somehow imperil the British Government till the Moslem holy places were desecrated – desecrated or removed?"

"I would like to answer quite frankly. If this question were put to me I would say definitely no. But if I say 'No' now I will not be true to myself because according to my information and experience I know that the Jews have great influence in England," responded the Mufti.

Map 3 The Peel Commission Partition Plan, July 1937

"So the answer is 'Yes'?"

"As far as the resulting consequences are concerned the answer is 'Yes.' "[69]

The uprising was thus renewed with increased ferocity, only now it was primarily directed against the Mufti's Arab rivals and ordinary Palestinian Arabs, many of whom had become deeply disillusioned with the ongoing violence, not only because of the suffering and dislocation it occasioned, but because of the growing extortions of the gang leaders who were lining their own pockets under the guise of rebellion. On June 30, 1937, a week before the publication of the Peel report, Fakhri Nashashibi, the moving spirit of his clan, narrowly escaped an assassination attempt (he was eventually murdered in 1941). So did Hassan Shukri, longtime mayor of Haifa and a prominent champion of Arab-Jewish coexistence, and Jaffa's mayor, Umar Bitar, who miraculously survived a murder attempt at point-blank range.

The acting mayor of Hebron had no such luck. He was murdered, in August 1936, as were the prominent Jerusalemite politician Hassan Sidqi Dajani, the leading Haifa activists Khalil Taha and Ibrahim Khalil, the Jaffa politician Said Shantti, the Tiberias counselor Ibrahim Yusuf, the Jenin notable Abdel Salam Barqawi, the al-Aqsa imam Ali Nur Khatib, and numerous sheiks, *mukhtars*, and heads of smaller localities. Attempts to assassinate a number of Nablus notables, including the mayor, Suleiman Tuqan, were foiled, yet in December 1937 Tuqan fled the country, having first issued a public appeal to the government to suppress terrorism.[70]

The number of Arabs murdered by the gangs thus far surpassed that of Jewish and British victims, as did the acts of repression, extortion, and sheer plunder of the general Arab population, both city-dwellers and villagers, who became increasingly outraged with the senseless violence and the widespread corruption of gang members and leaders. While in 1936, according to official British statistics, 195 Arabs were murdered by their Arab brothers, compared with 37 British and 80 Jews, two years later these figures rose to 503 Arab fatalities, compared with 255 Jewish and 77 British deaths. Fatalities in 1939 remained on a similar level: 414 Palestinian Arabs murdered by Arab gangs, as opposed to 94 Jews and 37 Britons. Some Palestinian Arab sources put the number of murdered Arabs at a staggering 3,000–4,500. In a letter to Abdel Qader Husseini, Hassan Saleme – a native of a village near Lydda who had sold weapons to the Hagana in the early 1930s before becoming the Mufti's henchman and styling himself as "Leader of the Jaffa, Ramallah, and Lydda Area" – informed his fellow gang leader that

> complaints are being received from the villagers of the Jerusalem District as
> a result of pillaging, looting, killing, and torturing committed by some

of the vile people who are wearing the clothing of the holy warriors [i.e., members of "the Holy Jihad," as Abdel Qader's force was called]. . . . I admit that there are among the murdered people some who have been sentenced to death, but what are the faults of the innocent whose money is stolen, whose cattle are looted, whose women are violated, whose jewels are pillaged, and who suffer in many other ways of which you have undoubtedly heard? Our rebellion has become a rebellion against the villages and not one against the Government or the Jews.[71]

Indeed, while many Arabs chose to flee the country in a foretaste of the 1947–48 exodus, others preferred to fight back through the creation of "peace squads," which strove to stamp out the violence, often in collaboration with the British authorities and the Jewish underground defense organization, the Hagana. Still other Arabs sought shelter from the rampaging gangs in Jewish neighborhoods. Even many "rebels" became increasingly disillusioned. "Hajj Amin's activities in the Supreme Muslim Council during eighteen years may be summed up in that he received as proceeds from the Waqf property something like one million pounds [£44 million in today's terms]," read a strongly worded manifesto issued by eight former "regional commanders" from their Damascus hideout.

For the Syrian rebellion, the disturbances of 1929, the reconstruction of the Aqsa Mosque, the Wailing Wall, the relief of the distressed in 1921, 1933 and 1936, and finally the present rebellion in Palestine, he collected as contributions from Arab countries, America and India no less than *two million pounds*. This is in addition to the sums of money which he collected for the Aqsa mosque, and the Muslim Congress and the inestimable sums of money received from foreign powers. These are millions of pounds, but can Hajj Amin point to a single mosque, a school or a hospital he erected during this period? Did he build a shelter or an asylum or a charity cistern from which poor tramps could drink?

There are about 20,000 persons in the country of orphans and sufferers. Will His Eminence, or his responsible adherents, point to us one orphan or one distressed person who has received even one piaster from the relief funds? Can His Eminence or his henchmen say that one piaster has been paid in compensation for the property demolished or blown up by the troops or for the houses and orchards damaged?[72]

The wanton Arab violence shocked the Zionist leadership and drove it to intensify its efforts toward an Arab-Jewish agreement. On April 22, 1936, Ben-Gurion met George Antonius, a Christian of Syrian origin who had settled in Palestine and become a pre-eminent theoretician of pan-Arabism as well as a confidant of the Mufti. Three days earlier, nine Jews had been murdered by rioting Arab mobs in Jaffa in what signified the beginning of the Palestinian Arab "revolt." Thus in their meeting Ben-Gurion wondered whether there were any Arab leaders who were prepared to work for reconciliation. Antonius replied in the negative. The Arabs believed that the Jews were totally indifferent to their views and needs and that they therefore had no recourse but to fight. True, there were a handful of thinkers and intellectuals who held that the Jewish question could not be ignored, but even they doubted whether there was any possibility of mutual understanding. Undeterred, Ben-Gurion reiterated the proposal for a Jewish state attached to a pan-Arab confederation: to no avail.[73]

Moshe Shertok (Sharett), head of the Jewish Agency's political department, or its "foreign ministry," had no more luck in his May–June 1936 meetings with Alami and Abdel Hadi, perhaps the second most influential politician after the Mufti. Yet Shertok would not give up hope. "I regard the matter as highly important," he told a Mapai party leadership meeting on June 21, 1936:

> Not because I expect these talks to culminate in an agreement but because, for the sake of our long-term relations with the Arab people, I attribute the utmost importance to the fact that we should not miss any opportunity or shun any possibility of negotiations with the Arabs, especially now. I consider our activity in this direction one of Zionism's political and diplomatic imperatives. I have also [received] letters and telegrams from Ben-Gurion [then in London] strenuously demanding not to stop the negotiations.[74]

In line with this thinking, in May 1937 Shertok approached Abdel Hadi again and the two met in the latter's home. The Peel commission was likely to recommend the partitioning of Palestine, Shertok said. The Jews were opposed to this option as it would deprive them of most of the National Home's territory, but the Arabs stood to lose even more, and the only way to forestall this adverse development was to reach an Arab-Jewish agreement. Abdel Hadi refused to budge. The Arabs were opposed to partition and would fight it tooth and nail, he said, but they would never accept any agreement that would allow the Jews to grow above their present relative strength: namely, a third of the total population.

But did they not see that the perpetuation of the conflict would inexorably lead to economic ruin? "The Arabs are poor anyway and are not susceptible to economic considerations," Abdel Hadi retorted. "This is a matter of national dignity. The Arabs may well go down, but this shouldn't prevent them from fighting. . . . They have only one choice: victory or defeat."

As he took his leave, a despondent Shertok told his host that he was leading his people to assured destruction.[75] It would be another decade before this stark warning would be fully vindicated.

CHAPTER 2

Pan-Arab Ambitions

"If a common enemy is the prelude to the formation of national unity, one may say that the Palestine problem has hastened this unity."

Hajj Amin Husseini, 1941

Britain's retreat from its mandatory obligation to facilitate the establishment of a Jewish National Home, which culminated in the Peel commission's recommendation to drop the mandate altogether, was not merely a response to the deterioration of Arab-Jewish relations in Palestine. No sooner had the "Palestine question" developed into a pressing international issue than it was picked up by the nascent doctrine of pan-Arabism, which was to dominate Arab politics for most of the twentieth century, as its most celebrated cause.

This, however, had little to do with concern for the wellbeing of the Palestinian Arabs, let alone the protection of their national rights. For one thing, though anti-Zionism formed one of the core principles of pan-Arab solidarity (as it is easier to unite people through a common hatred than through a shared loyalty), its invocation had almost always served as an instrument for achieving the self-interested ends of those who proclaimed it. For another, giving the notion of the territorial nation-state short shrift as a temporary aberration destined to wither away before long, pan-Arabism viewed the Palestinians *not* as a distinct people deserving statehood but as an integral part of a single Arab nation bound by common ties of language, religion, and history, which was destined to substitute a unified Arab state, or rather empire, for the artificial Middle Eastern system created in the wake of World War I. The territorial expanse of this supposed nation has varied among the exponents of the ideology, ranging from merely the Fertile Crescent to the entire territory "from the Atlantic Ocean to the Persian Gulf." But the unity of the Arabic-speaking populations inhabiting these vast territories is never questioned. As the eminent Arab-American historian Philip Hitti told an Anglo-American commission of inquiry in 1946:

There is no such thing as Palestine in history, absolutely not. . . . [It is but] a very small tiny spot there on the southern part of the eastern shore of the Mediterranean Sea, surrounded by a vast territory of Arab Muslim lands, beginning with Morocco, continuing through Tunis, Tripoli and Egypt, and going down to Arabia proper, then going up to Transjordan, Syria, Lebanon, and Iraq – one solid Arab-speaking bloc – 50,000,000 people.[1]

This doctrine was first articulated by a number of pre-World War I intellectuals, most notably the Syrian political exiles Abdel Rahman Kawakibi and Najib Azuri, as well as by some of the tiny Arab secret societies operating in the Ottoman Empire before its collapse. Yet it is highly doubtful whether these early beginnings would ever have amounted to anything more than intellectual musings had it not been for the huge ambitions of the sharif of Mecca, Hussein ibn Ali of the Hashemite family, and his two prominent sons, Abdullah and Faisal. Together, they perpetrated the "Great Arab Revolt" against the Ottoman Empire.

When Hussein proposed to the British that he rise against his Ottoman master, he styled himself champion of "the whole of the Arab nation without any exception" – an incredible claim given that he represented little more than himself. In December 1916, six months after the sharif began his rebellion, a British report found the residents of his home town of Mecca "almost pro-Turks."[2] Even at its height the revolt attracted a fraction of the 8 to 10 million Arabic-speaking Ottoman subjects, most of whom remained loyal to their imperial master to the bitter end, with 100,000–300,000 fighting in the Ottoman army.

Not that this prevented Hussein from demanding the creation of a vast new empire on the ruins of the Ottoman Empire, stretching from Asia Minor (Anatolia) to the Indian Ocean and from Iraq to the Mediterranean.[3] When this grandiose vision failed to materialize to its full extent, the Hashemites quickly complained of being "robbed" of the fruits of victory promised to them during the war. (They were, as it happens, generously rewarded in the form of vast territories several times the size of the British Isles, including the Hijaz, the westernmost part of the Arabian Peninsula that was the birthplace of Islam, Iraq, and Transjordan, latterly Jordan.) Thus arose the standard grievance that Arab intellectuals and politicians leveled at the Western powers, Britain in particular, and thus emerged the pan-Arab ideal with the avowed aim of redressing this alleged grievance.

It was indeed the Hashemites who placed the Palestine question on the pan-Arab political agenda. To begin with, there was the claim that the territory was included in the prospective Arab empire promised to Hussein by Sir Henry McMahon, the British high commissioner for Egypt, in their wartime correspondence preceding the revolt. Actually, McMahon excluded Palestine from such an empire, a fact acknowledged by Hussein in their exchanges and by Faisal shortly after the war.[4] This did not prevent successive generations of pan-Arabists and their Western champions from reiterating the charge. Hussein himself did so in a May 1923 letter to Musa Kazim Husseini, head of the Arab Executive Committee (AEC), the umbrella organization of the Palestinian Arabs until the early 1930s, who in turn used it to inflame local sentiments.[5]

Then there were the grandiose ambitions of Faisal and Abdullah. Already during the war against the Ottoman Empire, Faisal, who had become the revolt's "public face" owing to his close association with T. E. Lawrence ("Lawrence of Arabia"), had begun toying with the idea of establishing his own Syrian empire, independent of his father's prospective regional empire. In late 1917 and early 1918, he went so far as to negotiate this option with key members of the Ottoman leadership behind the backs of his father and his British allies (even Lawrence, who wholeheartedly endorsed the illicit adventure and kept most of its contours hidden from his own superiors, would admit years later that Faisal was "definitely 'selling us' ").[6] As his terms were rejected by the Ottomans, Faisal tried to gain Great Power endorsement for his imperial dream by telling the postwar Paris peace conference that "Syria claimed her unity and her independence" and that it was "sufficiently advanced politically to manage her own internal affairs" if given adequate foreign and technical assistance. When the conference planned to send a special commission of inquiry to the Middle East, Faisal quickly assembled (a highly unrepresentative) General Syrian Congress that would "make clear the wishes of the Syrian people."[7] And by way of leaving nothing to chance, the emir manipulated Syrian public opinion through extensive propaganda, orchestrated demonstrations, and intimidation of opponents.

When all these efforts came to naught, and his position in Syria was increasingly threatened by the French, Faisal allowed the General Syrian Congress to proclaim him the constitutional monarch of Syria "within its natural boundaries, including Palestine," and in political and economic union with Iraq. On March 8, 1920, he was crowned as King Faisal I at the Damascus City Hall, and France and Britain were asked to vacate the western (that is, Lebanese) and the southern (that is, Palestinian) parts of Syria. This resulted in the Jerusalem pogrom of April 1920, which was carried out *not* in the name of Palestine's independence but under the demand for its incorporation into Faisal's kingdom. Hajj Amin, as we have seen, was at the time an ardent supporter of Hashemite-led pan-Arabism, as were most contemporary Palestinian Arab politicians. In an October 1924 report to the League of Nations, the AEC still referred to Palestine as the

unlawfully severed southern part of "the one country of Syria, with its one
population of the same language, origin, customs and religious beliefs, and
its natural boundaries." As late as July 1937, the Arab Higher Committee
(AHC), which succeeded the AEC as the effective "government" of the
Palestinian Arabs, justified its rejection of the Peel partition plan on the
grounds that "this country does not belong only to [the] Palestine Arabs but
to the whole Arab and Muslim Worlds."[8]

Neither did Faisal abandon his Greater Syrian dream after his expulsion
from Damascus by the French in July 1920. Quite the reverse: using his
subsequent position as Iraq's founding monarch, he toiled ceaselessly to bring
about the unification of the Fertile Crescent under his rule. This policy was
sustained, following his untimely death in September 1933, by successive
Iraqi leaders, notably by Nuri Said, Faisal's comrade-in-arms and a longtime
Iraqi prime minister. In the summer of 1936, Said sought to convince
Palestine's Arab and Jewish communities, as well as the British government,
to agree to the country's incorporation into a pan-Arab federation, and seven
years later he published a detailed plan for pan-Arab unification (known as
the Blue Book) which envisaged that "Syria, Lebanon, Palestine, and
Transjordan shall be reunited into one state."[9]

The scheme was vigorously opposed by Abdullah. The brightest and most
politically astute of Hussein's sons and the moving spirit behind the
Hashemite revolt, he deeply resented his marginalization by his younger
brother and resolved to secure himself the largest possible war spoils. Once
Faisal had been driven from Damascus, Abdullah, who had earmarked Iraq
for himself, knew that it was only a matter of time before his brother would
disinherit him from his spoils by substituting this country for his lost Syrian
kingdom. In a bid to forestall this eventuality, at the end of September 1920
the emir led several hundred tribesmen out of Mecca and into the small oasis
town of Maan at the northern tip of the Hijaz, arriving there in mid-
November. Ostensibly, Abdullah was responding to appeals by Syrian
nationalists to help them drive the French out of Syria on behalf of his
deposed brother. In reality, he was establishing himself as a key player in the
scramble for the spoils from the defunct Ottoman Empire.

The ploy had the desired effect. In three meetings with Abdullah in late
March 1921, colonial secretary Winston Churchill agreed to make the emir
Transjordan's effective ruler for a period of six months "to prepare the way
for the appointment, with his consent, at the end of that time of an Arab
Governor under the High Commissioner [for Palestine]," and indicated
Britain's possible acquiescence in Abdullah's eventual domination of Syria.[10]
True, this was a long shot that might or might not pay off. But knowing full
well that he had pressed his luck to its utmost limits, and that there was

absolutely no chance of extracting further British concessions at that particular juncture, the emir was determined to use his temporary rule of Transjordan as a springboard for the creation of a vast regional empire comprising Syria, Palestine, and possibly Iraq and Saudi Arabia.

This was an ambition that Abdullah was to nurture until the late 1940s, when it was dealt a mortal blow by the establishment of the state of Israel and its ability to withstand the pan-Arab assault of May 1948; so intense was his ire with Faisal's parallel ambitions that he lambasted the mourning throughout Palestine that accompanied his brother's premature death on the grounds that Faisal had done absolutely nothing to deserve this adulation.[11]

As a quintessential product of the Ottoman imperial system, where religion constituted the linchpin of the socio-political order of things, Abdullah had no real grasp of Jewish nationalism (or for that matter the general phenomenon of nationalism). He thus viewed Jews, like other non-Muslim minorities, as members of a tolerated religious community (or *dhimmis*), deserving protection and autonomy in the practice of their religious affairs – but not a state of their own; and given his perception of Jews as an influential, affluent, and technologically advanced community, he was keen to incorporate them into his kingdom – as subjects. As Transjordan's prime minister, Samir Rifai, told a senior British official in December 1947: "The enlarged Transjordan State with the support of Jewish economy would become the most influential State in the Arab Middle East."[12]

Abdullah made his first overture to the Zionist movement in the autumn of 1921, indicating his readiness to recognize the Balfour Declaration and to allow Jewish settlement in Transjordan provided the Jews gave up their goal of national self-determination and were integrated into a unified Transjordanian-Palestinian kingdom under his headship. In the meantime, he had a small favor to ask. The £3,500 monthly subsidy from his father was paid through the Zionist-owned Anglo-Palestine Bank in Jerusalem. Would the bank be prepared to advance him £7,000 (£230,000 in today's terms) to be repaid by the remittance from his father? The bank's evasive reply did little to deter the emir. In November 1922, he traveled to London, where at a secret meeting with the head of the Zionist movement, Chaim Weizmann, and a number of Zionist officials, he reiterated his proposal and asked that they use their good offices with the French government to secure the Syrian throne for him.

Though nothing definite was agreed, news of the meeting inflamed Arab and Jewish sentiment in Palestine. Confronted with strong criticism of underhand dealings, if not a sellout that would irrevocably compromise the Jewish national cause, Weizmann denied any wrongdoing and defended the talks with Abdullah. True, the emir wanted to incorporate Palestine into Transjordan, but the idea had been rejected upfront. As for Abdullah's Syrian ambition, "there is nothing wrong in helping him, as this may help improve our relations with him. Still, we haven't made any concrete move on this front either."[13]

This controversy reflected the wider divide within the Zionist movement over the implications of pan-Arabism in general, and the Hashemite grand ambitions in particular, for the Jewish national revival. To some, notably the veteran Max Nordau, the drawing of Palestine into the intricate web of pan-Arabism posed a clear and present danger that could only be neutralized through the accelerated buildup of the Yishuv to an extent that would underscore the merits of Arab-Jewish coexistence and defuse anti-Zionist opposition.[14]

Most Zionist leaders, however, preferred to look on the full half of the glass. Incessant interventionism under the pretense of pan-Arab solidarity could of course complicate Arab-Jewish relations in Palestine, yet it also contained undeniable opportunities. For if all Arabs were members of a single nation that was to be constituted into a unified regional state, then it would be infinitely easier for them to concede a tiny fraction of this vast entity, in return for generous rewards, than it would be for a distinct Palestinian nation to give up a substantial part of its homeland. Besides, if Palestinian Arab leaders were beholden to a higher pan-Arab authority and recognized the indispensability of pan-Arab aid and support, they were likely to be attentive to the interests and desires of their external benefactors.

While contacts between the Zionist movement and some of the secret pan-Arab societies operating in the Ottoman Empire had already been established prior to World War I, it was Weizmann who more than anyone else epitomized the belief in the primacy of pan-Arab-Jewish high politics. A Russian Jewish chemist who in 1904 had settled in Britain, where he obtained a position at Manchester University, Weizmann was a secondary figure in the Zionist movement at the outbreak of World War I. But his personal charm, burning ambition, immense energy, and, above all, his ability to sense a great opportunity and to seize it, catapulted him within a few years to the movement's leadership, not least owing to his important role in the attainment of the Balfour Declaration.

A few months after the issuance of the Declaration, Weizmann led a Zionist commission to the Middle East to explore ways and means for implementing it, including "the establishment of good relations with the Arabs and other non-Jewish communities in Palestine." In Cairo he managed to convince a number of leading Syrians and Palestinians, who at the time lived in the Egyptian capital, that "Zionism has come to stay, that it is far more moderate in its aims than they had anticipated, and that by meeting it in a conciliatory spirit they are likely to reap substantial benefits in the future." He also succeeded in allaying the fears of the Egyptian sultan (later king), Fuad, of Zionism's alleged designs on Islam's holy places, especially its supposed intention to pull down the Dome of the Rock and to re-establish the Jewish Temple on its ruins. But his most important meeting was with Faisal (on June 4, 1918) at the emir's camp near Aqaba, on the northern tip of the Red Sea.

The two struck up an immediate rapport, and Faisal readily acknowledged "the necessity for cooperation between Jews and Arabs" and "the possibility of Jewish claims to territory in Palestine." Yet he refused to discuss any concrete arrangements on the pretext that "in questions of politics he was acting merely as his father's agent and was not in a position to discuss them" and that negotiations about Palestine's future could only be held at a time "when Arab affairs were more consolidated."[15]

When they met again in London in December 1918, Faisal was far more forthcoming. By now he had established a foothold in Syria, under the protective wing of General Sir Edmund Allenby, commander of the Egyptian Expeditionary Force which had driven the Ottoman forces from the Levant, and the emir hoped to expand this opening into a full-fledged empire with US backing and support. "The Arabs had set up some form of government centered in Damascus, but it was extremely weak," he told Weizmann. "It had no money and no men. The army was naked and had no ammunition. His great hope was in America, which he thought would be able to destroy the [1916 Sykes-Picot] agreement." Were the Zionists to help in swinging American public opinion behind his cause, he "was quite sure that he and his followers would be able to explain to the Arabs that the advent of the Jews into Palestine was for the good of the country, and that the legitimate interests of the Arab peasants would in no way be interfered with."

"It [i]s curious there should be friction between Jews and Arabs in Palestine," Faisal added after hearing Weizmann's exposition of Zionist aims. "There was no friction in any other country where Jews lived together with Arabs. He was convinced that the trouble was promoted by intrigues. He did not think for a moment that there was any scarcity of land in Palestine. The population would always have enough, especially if the country were developed." Faisal reiterated this benevolent observation at a dinner held on his behalf by Lord Rothschild, to whom Balfour sent the letter containing his famous Declaration. "No true Arab can be suspicious or afraid of Jewish nationalism," he stated, "and what better intermediary could we find anywhere in the world more suitable than you? For you have all the knowledge of Europe, and are our cousins by blood."

These sentiments were translated, as we have seen, into the January 1919 Faisal-Weizmann agreement endorsing the full implementation of the Balfour Declaration, and for several months the emir seemed to be working to this end. So much so that in April 1919 Weizmann maintained that "between the Arab leaders, as represented by Faisal, and ourselves there is complete understanding, and therefore complete accord," and that Faisal "has undertaken to exercise all his influence towards having his estimate of the Zionist cause and the Zionist proposals as 'moderate and proper' shared by his following." Nearly six months later, Weizmann still considered Faisal a staunch ally who fully understood the immense potential of Arab-Zionist cooperation. "He is ready to take Jewish advisers and is willing, even anxious, to have Zionist support in the development and even administration of the Damascus region," he wrote to Balfour in September.

> We, of course, would be willing to make a very great effort to help Faisal, as it would help us very much towards establishing good relations with the Arabs both in Palestine and Syria. The agitation against us in Palestine is conducted from Damascus. By cooperating with Faisal we would gain the goodwill both of Damascus and of Mecca, we would have peace in Syria and Palestine and, incidentally, get out of the impasse into which the present Anglo-French-Arab negotiations have got.[16]

What this upbeat analysis failed to consider was that no empire or imperial aspirant would willfully relinquish their possessions or expansionist dreams, and pan-Arabism was no exception to this rule. Many Arabs and Muslims to this very day pine for the restoration of Spain and consider their 1492 expulsion from the country a grave historical injustice, as if they were Spain's rightful owners and not colonial occupiers of a remote foreign land, thousands of miles from their ancestral homeland; it is hardly surprising, then, that they had no intention of allowing the Jews to encroach, however minutely, on the perceived pan-Arab patrimony.

And thus it was that within days of Faisal's proclamation as king of Syria and five months after claiming to "understand his mentality and his difficulties fairly well," a disillusioned Weizmann concluded that "in spite of his momentary success, obtained also partly by British gold – [Faisal] is in the long run a broken reed." On March 31, 1920, days before the clamoring for Palestine's annexation to Faisal's newly proclaimed kingdom turned into a murderous pogrom in Jerusalem, Weizmann warned General Sir Louis Bolls, chief military administrator in Palestine, that further appeasement of Faisal could only lead to Palestine's effective annexation by Syria, among other adverse regional consequences. "Two years ago he was a Bedouin sheik, a capable but modest soldier; at present he is attempting to play the role of a Near Eastern Napoleon and to set up an Arab Empire from the Euphrates almost to the Nile," he lamented.[17]

Beggars can't be choosers. With the Mufti steadily undermining Arab-Jewish coexistence, and Palestinian leaders refusing to stand up and be counted, the Jews continued to look to the Arabic-speaking world for a moderating voice: to no avail. Abdullah, who replaced his brother as the Zionist movement's foremost pan-Arab point of reference, did not back down one iota from his desire to annex Palestine to his coveted Greater Syrian empire, and his incessant meddling in the country's domestic affairs did little to boost Arab-Jewish coexistence. Nor did the Zionists manage to persuade any of their Arab interlocutors to accept the idea of Jewish independence even in a wider pan-Arab entity, as Ben-Gurion realized at first hand. In the despairing words of the Peel commission,

> British Ministers, Commissioners of Inquiry, and the spokesmen of Zionism had unanimously re-affirmed the assumption on which the successful operation of the Mandate had rested from the outset, namely, that somehow and at some time Jews and Arabs would cooperate in promoting the peace and welfare of Palestine. Only one voice was missing from the chorus – the Arab voice. Not once since 1919 had any Arab leader said that cooperation with the Jews was even possible.[18]

Only in Egypt did Zionist aspirations seem to garner any genuine sympathy, though for the opposite reasons of those articulated by Zionist champions of the "pan-Arab connection." Given its physical detachment from the eastern part of the Arabic-speaking world on the one hand, and its illustrious imperial past dating back to pharaonic times on the other, Egypt was seen by early pan-Arabists as "not belonging to the Arab race." For their part, Egyptians looked down on the rest of the Arabs, using the term "Arab" in a derogatory fashion to denote a shiftless and uncultured nomad, someone to be viewed with contempt by a people with a millenarian tradition of settled cultivation. "If you add one zero to another, and then to another, what sum will you get?" Saad Zaghlul, the doyen of modern Egyptian nationalism, dismissed the pan-Arab ideal of unity.[19]

During the 1920s and the early 1930s, Egypt was totally indifferent to the Mufti-led anti-Zionist struggle. So much so that a prominent Palestinian Arab journalist, then living in Egypt, recalled in his memoirs how he was asked by ordinary Egyptians who "Mr. Palestine" was, while others thought that Zionism was the name of a certain woman with whom Mr. Palestine had quarreled and whom he therefore hated.

Ziwar Pasha, the governor of Alexandria, was certainly better informed, not that this knowledge prevented him from participating in the celebrations of the local Jewish community upon the issuance of the Balfour Declaration. Eight years later, as Egypt's prime minister, Ziwar sent an official representative to the inauguration of the Hebrew University in Jerusalem, which he applauded as a contribution to humankind; by contrast, the Egyptian government refused to send a delegation to the ceremonies celebrating the restoration of the al-Aqsa mosque, contenting itself with the attendance of its Jerusalem consul. Likewise, no government official bothered to meet the Mufti during his visits to Cairo in 1926–28; on one occasion he was even directly snubbed by the Egyptian prime minister, who would not see him despite staying in the same hotel – this at a time when Weizmann had already conferred with Fuad in 1918 and other Zionist officials met Egyptian counterparts as a matter of course. As late as 1928, the king could still hold discussions on the merits of Zionism with the chief rabbi of the Egyptian Jewish community. Even the charges of a Jewish design to destroy the al-Aqsa mosque attending the 1929 massacres failed to rally the Egyptian masses behind their Palestinian Arab brothers.[20]

This indifference began to change in the mid-1930s. Pan-Arab ideologues came to consider Egypt an integral and important part of the "Arab nation," if not a key player in the quest for regional unity, and this theme struck a responsive chord among educated Egyptians. King Faruq, scion of a non-Arab family that had ruled Egypt since the early nineteenth century, first under Ottoman auspices then as the country's reigning monarchy, invested considerable energies in establishing himself as the leader of all Arabs, if not the caliph of all Muslims. Yet it was the three turbulent years of the Palestinian Arab "revolt" that, more than any other contemporary development, irretrievably insinuated the Palestine problem into the intricate, and ultimately devastating, web of pan-Arab politics.

In a meeting with Abdullah at the Jerusalem King David Hotel in November 1936, seven months after the eruption of violence in Palestine, the Zionist movement's "foreign minister," Moshe Shertok, found the emir lukewarm to his plea for intervention. The Jews had to understand that his difficult position forced him at times to act against their interests, Abdullah argued, and their best hope in the circumstances was to slow down their national enterprise. "He was not feeling himself the boss of the show," Shertok wrote in his report. "His object in coming to Jerusalem had been primarily to ascertain the state of feeling among the Arabs and he had come to the conclusion that it would be useless to try and persuade them to change their mind."

Two months later, at a meeting with the Peel commission in his Amman palace, Abdullah clarified the nature of the envisaged "slowdown." Not a single Arab would agree to Palestine's transformation into a Jewish National Home, he claimed, since the country had been promised to the Arabs well before the Balfour Declaration. This was not to suggest the expulsion of the Jews from Palestine. They could stay if they so wished, or even settle in Transjordan, provided they acted as loyal subjects of the lawful Arab government, remained a permanent minority of less than 35 percent of the total population, and demanded no distinct national or political prerogatives.[21]

In these circumstances, it was only natural for the Zionist leadership to look for additional Arab interlocutors. Capitalizing on Syria's eagerness to mobilize (the perceived) Zionist influence over the French government (headed at the time by the Jewish politician Léon Blum) to facilitate an agreement that would lead to full independence (Syria and Lebanon had been placed under a French mandate after World War I), in the summer of 1936, Zionist officials secretly met with senior Syrian politicians to discuss the situation in Palestine and the possibility of an Arab-Jewish peace.[22] A few months later, two members of the Jewish Agency's political department – the Syrian-born Elias Sasson, head of the department's Arab section, and Arab affairs expert Eliahu Epstein (Elath) – visited Damascus, where they conferred with prime minister Jamil Mardam, defense minister (and future president) Shukri Quwatli, and propaganda minister Fakhri Barudi.

By now the Syrians had secured the coveted agreement with France, and while this had yet to be ratified they no longer felt the need for Zionist good-will. Mardam and Quwatli were thus courteous but non-committal. The government was preoccupied with the country's domestic problems, the prime minister said, but it would restore its peace efforts at the first available opportunity. The conflict between Arabs and Jews was a family affair, rather than a dispute between strangers, which gave room for optimism about its possible resolution, especially since this basic affinity was buttressed by mutual interests. Asked to facilitate an Arab-Jewish agreement, Mardam promised to contact the Mufti and urge him to enter into a serious dialogue with the Zionist movement.[23]

Barudi was more skeptical. The Arab states did not possess the ability to promote peace in Palestine. So long as the country's two communities remained at each other's throat, no Arab ruler or regime would make peace with the Zionist movement and all would be under intense pressure to help their Palestinian brothers. It was up to the Jews to seize the initiative and to appease their Arab compatriots, and what would be a better way to do that than to accept a temporary cessation of immigration?

Weizmann heard a similar argument in his London meeting with Nuri Said on June 9, 1936. The solution to the Palestine problem lay with the creation of a vast pan-Arab federation, in which Jews would enjoy considerable prerogatives short of national self-determination, the then Iraqi foreign minister argued. In the meantime, could the Zionists make a gesture to their Arab compatriots, and the Arab world at large, by voluntarily suspending immigration? To his surprise, Weizmann agreed to propose to the British government a year-long cessation of Jewish immigration so as to help ease the situation.

The importance of this concession cannot be overstated. Immigration (or *Aliya*, "ascent," as it is known in Hebrew) had been the elixir of life of the Jewish national revival from the outset. Enshrined in the League of Nations mandate, which obliged the British "to facilitate Jewish immigration," it was one of the few core issues on which the Zionist leadership would not compromise come what may. Yet here was the movement's elder statesman cavalierly discarding this principle after less than two months of Arab violence. There was absolutely no chance that this gaffe could stand, as Weizmann was swiftly to realize.

Indeed, even before the meeting, he was "strictly warned" by Ben-Gurion, then in London, against entertaining any "heretical ideas." The following day, though still in the dark concerning Weizmann's concrete promises to Said, Ben-Gurion felt sufficiently alarmed to record in his diary: "Yesterday I was under the impression that I had disabused Chaim of his terrifying idea, only to be proven wrong. Today, in our morning session [with a number of leading London Zionists] he reiterated the proposal. . . . Given the seriousness of the situation I instructed Moshe [Shertok] to fly immediately to Egypt and phone me from there [a precaution to evade British monitoring of the conversation]."

On June 11, Ben-Gurion called again on Weizmann. He warned that the suspension of immigration would be tantamount to national suicide, only to be bluntly told that the issue was closed and needed no further discussion. But it was not, for on June 15 Said told the British ambassador to Baghdad, Sir Archibald Clark-Kerr, of the pledge. The ambassador promptly relayed the story to the colonial secretary, William Ormsby-Gore, who for his part approached Weizmann (on June 25) for a clarification.

At a meeting with his Zionist colleagues, an evidently embarrassed Weizmann denied having made any promises and claimed that he had informed Said of the unacceptability of his idea. Ben-Gurion remained unconvinced. "This is a very grave matter. Nuri didn't make it up, and I doubt whether it will be kept a secret," he recorded in his diary on June 27. "Had we not been in a life-or-death situation, I would undoubtedly have made the simple and necessary decision; but at this time an internal schism might undermine our political stance. Still I find it difficult to work with him [i.e., Weizmann]." His skepticism was shared by Mrs. Blanche Dugdale (better known as Baffy), Lord Balfour's niece and Weizmann's confidante, who "found Chaim very depressed, partly because of an indiscretion committed by himself when talking to Nuri Pasha."

The next day Ben-Gurion and Lewis Namier, the eminent British historian and Zionist activist, went to see Weizmann to discuss his reply to Ormsby-Gore (and possibly to Said). "It was a painful conversation," Ben-Gurion recorded. "It's difficult to see a man disgraced in this fashion. . . . Chaim is totally depressed – and so am I." Within hours Weizmann sent his version of events to the colonial secretary, followed a day later by a letter to Clark-Kerr, in which he claimed that Said "never suggested that [the suspension of immigration] should be done 'for a year' " and that "to the best of my recollection, I did not agree to this suggestion, though possibly I did not oppose it as vehemently as I might have done." Undeterred, the indefatigable Said approached Shertok with the same proposal, only to be told that, aside from its general unacceptability, any suspension of immigration, however minute, was certain to be interpreted as a reward for terrorism and would consequently exacerbate, rather than pacify, the situation.[24]

Whether or not Said was convinced, in October 1936 he found himself out of office, and the country, as a military coup toppled the ardent pan-Arabist government in which he served. Taking its cue from modern Turkey's founding father, Kemal Atatürk, who extricated that country from its imperialist legacy and re-established it as a modern nation-state, the new regime was determined to subordinate Iraq's pan-Arab commitments to its national needs and interests. In a visit to Baghdad in February 1937, Sasson and Epstein were repeatedly told that Iraq had already wasted seventeen years (since its creation in 1921) in its futile preoccupation with the Palestine problem and it was time that it concentrated on its pressing domestic issues. In the colorful words of a prominent Iraqi politician:

Neither us nor any other Arab country should carry two watermelons in one hand. Each and every Arab state should concentrate, at least for the next twenty years, on self-consolidation and only then concern itself with the affairs of its neighbors. Our brothers, the Palestinian Arabs, claim that during these twenty years they will be swamped by the Zionists. This may or may not be true, yet one must not sacrifice the interests of the entire Arab east for the sake of a small Arab community totaling some 800,000–900,000 people. Palestine is no dearer to the Arab world than Lebanon, which our Syrian brothers agreed to leave in its Christian character. . . . If the Christians are allowed to form their own government in a small part of the Arab east, surely the Jews have no lesser a right to do so.[25]

In April 1937, as the Peel commission was putting the final touches to its recommendations regarding Palestine's future, Ben-Gurion traveled to Beirut for a three-hour secret meeting with the Lebanon-born Saudi deputy foreign minister Fuad Hamza. For all his great respect for the commission and its members, he doubted whether it could resolve the Palestine problem, which would continue to fester as long as Jews and Arabs failed to reach a mutual agreement, Ben-Gurion told Hamza. Regrettably, with the sole exception of Iraq's late King Faisal, no Arab statesman had grasped the true essence of the problem. Could Ibn Saud, founding monarch of Saudi Arabia, be that great statesman? Would he be able to cut to the heart of a complex issue that was remote from his own world and suggest ways and means for its resolution? This was not an official request for intervention: as a Muslim and an Arab, the king could hardly be expected to be an impartial party. Yet the Jews were anxious to hear what a great personality like Ibn Saud would propose after having familiarized himself with all aspects of the problem, not just the Arab side of things.[26]

As the conversation ended inconclusively (much later the Zionists learned that Hamza's enemies in the royal court used it to undermine his position), in May Ben-Gurion met in London another key advisor of the Saudi monarch: the famous British Arabist, adventurer, author, and one-time colonial official St. John Philby, who had converted to Islam and resided in the desert kingdom. After reminiscing on mutual Palestinian acquaintances and chatting about new archeological discoveries, Philby treated his guest to a lengthy exposition of his thinking on the Arab-Jewish conflict. The fault lay not with the Jews, he argued, but with the British, who had long coveted Palestine and had used the Balfour Declaration as a springboard for transforming the country, which they had no intention of relinquishing, into a crown colony. This left the Arabs with no choice but to fight. For the time being, owing to Ibn Saud's intervention, they had accepted a temporary suspension of hostilities until the issuance of the Peel report. But as soon as this was published the Arab and Muslim worlds would rise in arms for the simple reason that Palestine was not the exclusive possession of its inhabitants but an integral part of the pan-Arab patrimony, unlawfully invaded by the Jews. "The hatred of Jews among all the Arab peoples [is] tremendous, and one could not rule out a slaughter in which all the Jews of Palestine would be annihilated," Philby warned. "The Jews were the victims of the English. England should get out of these countries; this was an Arab country."

"This is our land, this was our land, and this will be our land," Ben-Gurion retorted. "We did not wish to evict the Arabs, nor were we in a position to do so, but we were returning to the country as a matter of right, and if a war should break out we would fight, although our aim was peace and we wished to sign a treaty of agreement with the Arabs."

"On what basis?" Philby asked.

Ben-Gurion explained his three-pronged plan: 1) Jewish immigration unrestricted in numbers or for political reasons, with the exception of the non-eviction of Arabs; 2) the country's independence in internal affairs; 3) ties with an Arab federation or confederation.

This whetted Philby's appetite. Having satisfied himself of Ben-Gurion's seriousness, he quickly drew up a draft agreement envisaging a pan-Arab federation to which the Jews would be allowed to immigrate and in which they would be guaranteed "complete freedom to lead their religious and cultural lives according to their own principles." What the plan ignored, though, was the core Zionist demand for national self-determination, something that Ben-Gurion did not fail to point out. "While your suggestion would, I think, give complete satisfaction to the Arabs – abolition of the Balfour Declaration, termination of the Mandate, independence of Palestine, it ignores completely the rights and claims of the Jews," he wrote to Philby.

> No agreement is conceivable which does not explicitly recognize the right of the Jewish people to establish themselves in Palestine. The Jews coming to Palestine do not regard themselves as immigrants: they are returning as of right to their own historic homeland. This right is limited only by the condition that the Palestine Arabs shall not be displaced. We are fully ready to admit this limitation; but you will not find a single Jew who would consent to the abolition of the Mandate in favor of an agreement with the Arabs which contained no clear recognition of the right of the Jews to enter Palestine and re-establish there their National Home.

Philby did not respond.[27]

In one respect Philby was right. No sooner had the Palestinian Arabs rejected the Peel partition plan and resumed the violence than the Arab states fell into line, albeit not in the Armageddon-like fashion he had predicted. Iraq's prime minister, Hikmat Suleiman, who until then had avoided the Palestine problem like the plague, led the way with such vehemence that Anthony Eden, then secretary of state at the British Foreign Office, reprimanded the Iraqi ambassador in London, saying that this kind of behavior "was not what we should have looked for in an ally."[28]

Suleiman was quickly followed by Ibn Saud, who claimed that the creation of a Jewish state was anathema to the principles of Islam, and by Jamil Mardam, who only a couple of months earlier had pleaded with the Mufti and the prominent Palestinian Arab politician Awni Abdel Hadi to reach a peace agreement with the Jews. In September 1937, a pan-Arab conference met in the Syrian resort town of Bludan, with the participation of some 400 delegates, who discussed practical measures for helping the Palestinian Arabs, urged the abrogation of the mandate and the Balfour Declaration, as well as the banning of Jewish immigration and land purchases, and vowed to "struggle by all legal means for the Arab cause in Palestine until the country is saved and Arab sovereignty established." Even the Egyptian prime minister, Mustafa Nahhas, Zaghlul's disciple and no admirer of pan-Arabism, felt obliged to tell parliament of his "pains to safeguard the rights and interests of the Arabs in the country, in which there existed these holy places to which Egypt was bound by glorious religious and historic memories."[29]

Behind these demonstrations of public solidarity lay ulterior motives. Having been criticized for ignoring the struggle of their Palestinian brothers, the Syrian and Iraqi governments capitalized on the Peel report to redeem their pan-Arab credentials. No less important, the two governments, not to mention those of Egypt and Saudi Arabia, were greatly alarmed by the proposed annexation of the Arab part of Palestine to Transjordan, which would have moved Abdullah closer to his dream of a Greater Syrian empire under his rule.

At a meeting with Ambassador Clark-Kerr, Prime Minister Suleiman explained that his public intervention in the Palestine problem was not intended to inflame an already volatile situation but rather to deflect the public pressure in Iraq to take the lead on the issue. "No Iraqi Government could remain in office that did not give some measure of satisfaction to public hatred for the proposal to partition Palestine," he argued. "Had he not done so [the situation] would have got out of hand and swept him away."

The ambassador was impressed. "I gather that he felt that he had done what was necessary to satisfy public opinion and that he was confident that he could control it," he reported to London, adding that in Suleiman's assessment the partition plan would not be approved by the League of Nations and that "there was therefore no reason for agitation."[30]

When the Mufti asked Nahhas that Egypt increase its support for the Palestinian Arabs, the prime minister unceremoniously referred him to the above parliamentary statement. Likewise, in the summer of 1937 Ibn Saud rejected a request to hold a pan-Arab congress in the holy city of Mecca, and a demand by his religious scholars (*ulama*) to declare a jihad on the Jews, on the grounds that "we wish to avoid as far as possible any further difficulties for our friends, His Majesty's Government." At a meeting with the British ambassador in December 1937, the Saudi monarch criticized those Arab leaders who "were bringing forward schemes for Palestine not from love of Palestine or of the Arabs, nor from friendship toward His Majesty's Government but from personal ambition." In speaking about the Palestine problem, "the king was not violent, or even reproachful, but very anxious about his position," the ambassador reported. "He said more than once, as he had said before, that while he objected to partition as an Arab and a Muslim he objected to it also because he felt it would be ruinous to Britain and therefore dangerous to himself. At one point he said he would rather that the British mandate should last for another century."[31]

In a meeting with the Lebanese president, Émile Eddé, in August 1937, a senior Zionist official was told that, notwithstanding its militant bluster, "Lebanon wanted to live on terms of friendship with its neighbors" and that "he had always believed that the Jews and [the] Lebanese had a common program in the East."[32]

Sasson heard similar reassurances of Syria's unabated support for Arab-Jewish coexistence when he met Mardam a couple of weeks earlier. The Syrian government did not approve of the Palestinian violence and was not arming the insurgents, the prime minister argued: most of the supplied weapons originated in Nazi Germany, Turkey, and Greece and made their way via Lebanon. Nor did Syria allow the insurgents to train on its territory, let alone use it as a base for cross-border attacks. Politically, he had always considered the Bludan conference a big mistake, and most Syrian leaders had retrospectively come to the same conclusion. It had been convened when he was in Paris; had he been in Syria he would not have allowed it, which is why he did not authorize Damascus as the venue of the next pan-Arab summit (which was subsequently convened in Cairo). (This was only partly truthful: Damascus did become a key center for directing and supplying the agitators in Palestine despite the government's strenuous efforts to prevent this development.)

Mardam conceded that the Syrian press was virulently anti-Jewish and anti-British, yet claimed that the situation was far better than in the other Arab countries. The Syrian government was keenly aware of the hazards of fomenting racial hatred and was doing its utmost to keep things in check. Three months earlier it had ordered school headmasters and owners of coffee houses and cinemas, as well as mosque leaders, to avoid propaganda and incitement on the Palestine problem, and the order had been strictly enforced. "Let no Jewish person think that the Syrian government under my stewardship will collude with someone at the expense of the blood of the

Jewish people," pledged Mardam as Sasson was taking his leave. "I never envisaged the Jewish people immersed in such a horrible bloodletting with the Arab people as that in Palestine. The two peoples have no recourse in the world but their intrinsic strength and the belief in their right to exist. Let's not commit collective suicide."[33]

Hafiz Wahba, the Saudi ambassador to London, was no less cordial in his private meeting with Ben-Gurion in August 1938, in complete contrast to his kingdom's public stance. Having listened attentively to his guest's explanation of Zionist objectives, he regretted the reluctance of Palestinian Arabs to meet with their Jewish compatriots for fear of being ostracized as Jewish stooges, noting that he had himself been on the receiving end of such stigmatization after urging that Jerusalem be made a catalyst for peace given its sacredness for the three monotheistic religions, and not merely for Islam.

It was precisely this unhappy state of the Palestinian Arab leadership that had led him to view Ibn Saud as "the only personality in the Arab world strong enough and independent enough to do anything," Ben-Gurion said, adding that the Zionist leaders would be delighted to meet him and discuss the situation. The ambassador conceded the importance of such a meeting but explained that it was easier said than done. The king received no foreigners in his capital of Riyadh, and would only be going to Jeddah, where the meeting could be held, at the beginning of the pilgrimage season, and that was not for another four months. He would, however, inform Ibn Saud about the proposal and would perhaps himself be going to Mecca this year, where he would be able to sound out the king. In the meantime, could Ben-Gurion let him have his address and telephone number in London in the event that he needed to contact him again?[34]

Philby was not the only Englishman who expected the Peel commission to end in tears. When in June 1937 Weizmann told a small group of sympathetic British politicians of his inclination to accept the crystallizing partition plan provided this allowed for the annual immigration of 50,000–60,000 Jews to Palestine, Winston Churchill, then a widely ignored Cassandra warning of the looming Nazi disaster, interposed. "You are wrong, Weizmann," he said:

> Your [envisaged Jewish] state is a mirage. They will not allow you to bring your 60,000 immigrants. . . . The Arabs will revert to provocations, will shoot at you and throw bombs, and you will eventually be blamed for sparking a bloody war. . . . We have a disastrously weak government. . . . Were England to depend on them it would be ruined. . . . But this

situation will not last for long. England will come back to its senses and will defeat Mussolini and Hitler, and then your time will come.[35]

Churchill's words proved prescient. It did not take long for the British government, headed since late May 1937 by the timid Neville Chamberlain, to give in to Arab violence. To be sure, the assassination of the Galilee's acting district commissioner (on September 26, 1937) unleashed a repressive British campaign combining crude force (collective punishments, bombardment of gang-controlled villages, execution of terrorists, etc.) with harsh political measures. On October 1, the AHC and all local national committees were outlawed and the Mufti was sacked from the presidency of the SMC, which was in turn disbanded and replaced by a three-man committee (two Britons and an Arab) for the handling of Muslim religious affairs. Hundreds of Arab activists were arrested and warrants for the arrest of six AHC members were issued; five were detained and deported to the Seychelles Islands. The sixth, Jamal Husseini, evaded arrest and fled the country, as did the Mufti on October 14, 1937.

The British measures failed to achieve the desired result. From his comfortable exile in Lebanon the Mufti continued to direct the Palestine insurgency, with the French turning a deaf ear to repeated British and Jewish pleas to restrain their troublesome guest. The Mufti's home near Beirut became a site of pilgrimage for many Palestinian leaders and a source of regional incitement. Losing no time, Hajj Amin sent Jamal to Berlin for advice and support, where he met Dr. Joseph Goebbels, the minister of propaganda, and other Nazi leaders "from whom he had received certain advice," and with whom he laid the groundwork for Arab-Nazi collaboration. Small wonder that a steady flow of German weapons made its way to Palestine.[36]

True to form, the Chamberlain government opted for appeasement. As Arab violence showed little sign of abating, in October 1938 another commission of inquiry, headed by Sir John Woodhead, recommended dropping the partition plan, and in January 1939, the colonial secretary, Malcolm MacDonald, concluded that "active measures must be taken" to improve Anglo-Arab relations. On May 17, the government issued the Palestine White Paper which provided for "the admission, as from the beginning of April [1939], of some 75,000 immigrants over the next five years. . . . After the period of five years no further Jewish immigration will be permitted unless the Arabs of Palestine are prepared to acquiesce in it." Also imposing severe restrictions on Jewish purchases of land, the White Paper envisaged an independent state in which the Jews would comprise no more than one-third of the total population. To add insult to injury, in July MacDonald announced that all Jewish immigration to Palestine would be suspended from October 1939 until March 1940.[37]

Given the deteriorating position of Europe's Jews and the fact that Jewish immigration had been both the leading symbolic and practical indicator of the permanency and success of the Zionist project, it was hardly surprising that world Jewry responded with vehement indignation to what it saw as the subversion of the Jewish national revival in Palestine and the abandonment of European Jewry to their Nazi persecutors. Chief Rabbi Isaac Herzog of Palestine wrote to the London *Times* that the White Paper was "a sin against the spirit of God and the soul of Man"; Weizmann called it a "liquidation of the Jewish national home," while the American Zionist leader Rabbi Stephen S. Wise denounced it as a policy that "repudiates the letter and the spirit of the Mandate." So did a number of British politicians, including the surviving members of the Peel commission, while the League of Nations' Permanent Mandate Commission asserted in an August 1939 report that "the policy set out in the White Paper was not in accordance with the interpretation which, in agreement with the Mandatory Power and the [League's] Council, the Commission had always placed upon the Palestine Mandate."[38]

Agitating for more, the Arabs dismissed the plan as insufficient, demanding the immediate creation of an Arab state in Palestine, the complete cessation of Jewish immigration, and a review of the status of every Jew who had entered the country after 1918. Only Abdullah and his Palestinian Arab supporters remained aloof, while the Bedouin sheiks and tribal heads of the Negev desert in southern Palestine protested to the high commissioner over the prohibition on land sales, which, they claimed, would further afflict their depressed economic position by denying them an invaluable source of income.[39]

In a meeting with a senior Zionist official, Abdullah's personal envoy, Muhammad Unsi, castigated the Woodhead report as a catastrophic blunder that played into the hands of the extremists since "many Arabs thought it was the Mufti's objection to partition which had prevailed upon the British Government to abandon this policy." "The Emir had acted in accordance with Great Britain's wishes and had controlled all unruly elements and now he had to face the bitter disappointment of his followers," he lamented, while "the Mufti's followers claim a threefold victory. First, the abandonment of partition; second, the recognition of the justice of their struggle and proof that [the] Government was unable to suppress their terrorist activities; third, the joining of the representatives of the Arab States as a potent factor in the Palestine problem."[40]

On May 22, 1939, Churchill addressed the White Paper issue in parliament. As one "intimately and responsibly concerned in the earlier stages of our

Palestine policy," he could not "stand by and see solemn engagements into which Britain has entered before the world set aside." "What will our potential enemies think?" he asked. "Will they not be tempted to say: 'They're on the run again. This is another Munich.' "

Staring straight into the prime minister's eyes, he recalled how twenty years earlier, in the same chamber, Chamberlain had said – he was quoting him directly – "A great responsibility will rest upon the Zionists, who, before long, will be proceeding with joy in their hearts, to the ancient seat of their people. Theirs will be the task to build up a new prosperity and a new civilization in old Palestine, so long neglected and misruled." "Well, they have answered his call," Churchill concluded. "They have fulfilled his hopes. How can he find it in his heart to strike them this mortal blow?"[41]

CHAPTER 3

"The Most Important Arab Quisling"

"Of Germany's victory the Arab world was firmly convinced, not only because the Reich possessed a large army, brave soldiers, and military leaders of genius, but also because the Almighty could never award the victory to an unjust cause."

Hajj Amin Husseini to Adolf Hitler, 1941

The outbreak of World War II threw the nascent struggle against the White Paper into disarray as the Zionist movement rallied to the Anglo-French call to arms. At the Twenty-First Zionist Congress, held in the Swiss city of Geneva in mid-August 1939, Ben-Gurion deplored the White Paper as driving the Jews into a ghetto, yet vowed that "the Jewish people would always remain on the side of Great Britain in an emergency, especially in time of war." In a letter to Chamberlain on August 29, 1939, three days before the German invasion of Poland unleashed the deadliest conflict in human history, Weizmann reaffirmed that Jews worldwide "stand by Great Britain and will fight on the side of the democracies" and offered to give effect to this pledge by entering into immediate arrangements for harnessing Jewish manpower, technical ability, and resources to the war effort.[1]

This is not what happened. Rather, the British realization of the Jewish total lack of choice between the warring parties, coupled with uncertainty over the loyalty of the far larger and strategically important Arab world, meant that the Chamberlain government had no intention of discarding its policy of appeasement after the commencement of hostilities as far as the Middle East was concerned. The gates of Palestine remained closed to the small number of Jewish refugees who could find their way out of Europe, and the land restrictions were significantly tightened by the February 1940 Land Transfer Regulations which prohibited sales to Jews in 63 percent of Palestine, restricted such transactions in another 32 percent, and left a paltry 5 percent of the country fully accessible to Jews. When some 1,400 East European Jewish refugees landed on a Tel Aviv beach on September 2, 1939, they were peremptorily detained by the authorities (apart from 200 who were spirited away by the Hagana). A fortnight later, the colonial secretary, Malcolm MacDonald, rejected Weizmann's plea for the admission of 20,000 Jewish children from Poland into Palestine as part of the White Paper quota, as a life-saving measure. Much as he sympathized with the plight of Polish Jewry, which was just coming under Nazi occupation, MacDonald said he felt unable to admit large numbers of Jewish immigrants beyond those already authorized lest "it would seriously embarrass Great Britain and her Allies in their endeavor to bring the war to a victorious issue."[2]

The Zionist offer of military support (by the end of September 1939, some 100,000 men and 30,000 women, nearly a quarter of the Yishuv's total population, had volunteered for war service) was rejected on similar grounds. It would take Winston Churchill four full years after assuming the premiership on May 10, 1940 to prevail over his commanders and bureaucrats and establish a Jewish Brigade Group that fought as part of the British army in Italy.

To add insult to injury, the mandatory authorities sought to break the Yishuv's military power. In early October 1939, forty-three participants in a secret training course were arrested and handed harsh prison sentences, and the commander of the British forces in Palestine proposed giving the Jewish Agency an ultimatum to disband the underground organizations and surrender their weapons within a given period of time. Should it fail to comply, the authorities would embark on systematic searches of illegal weapons, reduce the size of the Jewish police force, discharge Jewish volunteers who had joined the British army, and forbid military and paramilitary training.[3]

Nor were the Jews appeasement's only victims in Palestine. Members of the anti-Husseini opposition, especially the Nashashibis, the second most important Palestinian Arab clan, which had cooperated with the government in suppressing the 1936–39 violence, and which promptly declared itself on the side of Britain at the outbreak of war, were shunned and at times ostracized and persecuted by the mandatory authorities. Even Arif Arif, one of Palestine's most respected nationalists, who had been indicted for the 1920 pogrom together with Hajj Amin yet subsequently adopted a non-violent form of resistance to Zionism, was reprimanded by the British authorities for attempting to promote Arab-Jewish understanding. Meanwhile the Mufti, who in October 1939 fled to Baghdad with his key advisors after the French authorities in Lebanon increasingly clamped down on their subversive activities, was courted by the British government and offered a full amnesty in return for acquiescence in the White Paper policy.[4]

Appeasement of one's enemies at the expense of friends whose loyalty can be taken for granted is a common if unsavory human trait. So is the propensity of weakness to beget aggression. Just as Britain's shameful betrayal of Czechoslovakia (in the September 1938 Munich agreement) served to whet Hitler's appetite rather than curb his expansionism, so the 1939 White Paper reinforced Arab perceptions of Britain as a spent force at pains to hold its own in the face of the rising Nazi power. In the words of Reader Bullard, the veteran British ambassador to Saudi Arabia: "I suppose that, seeing us in a hole, they propose to take full advantage of the opportunity in order to extract, if possible, their full demands."[5]

In line with this thinking, not only did the Arab states, with the sole exception of Transjordan, refuse to declare war on Germany (Iraq did so in January 1943 after the Nazi threat to the Middle East had been irrevocably defeated at Alamein, while Egypt, Syria, Lebanon, and Saudi Arabia followed suit as late as February 1945, three months before the end of the war), but many Arabs had been looking to the Third Reich for help and inspiration even before the war began. This included, aside from Hajj Amin and other Palestinian leaders who made their pro-Nazi sympathies known within weeks of Hitler's rise to power, such prominent figures as King Ibn Saud, who sought German weapons and ammunition, Iraqi prime minister Hikmat Suleiman (October 1936–August 1937) who plotted a pro-German coup in Baghdad, Hassan Banna, founding head of the militant Muslim Brothers and an unabashed admirer of Hitler and Mussolini, as well as numerous pan-Arab activists in the Middle East and beyond.

That the Nazis were slow to capitalize on these opportunities was due to their limited strategic interest in the Middle East, on the one hand, and a total lack of empathy for Arab hopes and aspirations, on the other. They also viewed most Arab regimes as British lackeys incapable of real change or effective collaboration; were reluctant to antagonize Britain in a secondary arena so as to ensure the continuation of its appeasement policy in Europe; and deferred to their Italian ally, which fancied itself as a key player in the eastern Mediterranean and the Middle East. Yet as his self-confidence grew during the summer and autumn of 1938, especially after the annexation of substantial Czechoslovak territories to Germany, Hitler was increasingly casting his glance eastward. By this time, the Nazis were already financing the Arab "revolt" in Palestine and had initiated arms shipments to the rebels via Iraq and Saudi Arabia, with their governments' consent. In January 1939, the German ambassador to Iraq, Fritz Grobba, visited Saudi Arabia, where he was accredited as envoy to the desert kingdom in addition to his main appointment in Baghdad.

Five months later, Hitler hosted Khalid Hud, Ibn Saud's personal envoy, for a long conversation in his official retreat overlooking Salzburg. He had a strong affinity for the Arab world dating back to his childhood reading,

Hitler told his guest. Now, as head of state, this sympathy was reinforced by
the historic convergence of destinies that pitted both Germans and Arabs
against the same enemies, notably the Jews, and he "would not rest until the
last Jews had left Germany."

This was precisely what the Prophet Muhammad had done, enthused Hud.
"He had driven all the Jews out of Arabia. Only one lived in Saudi Arabia
today, and he had attempted to take the armaments transactions away from the
Government and had been sentenced for three years' imprisonment for this."
"[Imagine] what would have become of Europe if Charles Martel had not
beaten back the Saracens [in 732], but if the latter, imbued with the Germanic
spirit and borne along by Germanic dynamism, had transformed Islam in their
own fashion," Hud fantasized as they continued their conversation at the tea
table. This was a very remarkable line of thought, Hitler concurred. Before
long, this meeting of minds was translated into an arms deal for the supply of
8,000 rifles, 8 million rounds of ammunition, light anti-aircraft guns, armored
cars, and a small munitions factory, to be built in Saudi Arabia.[6]

As the Nazis went from strength to strength, conquering Holland,
Belgium, Norway, and much of France, having routed the French army and
beaten a British expeditionary force into a hasty retreat, their prestige in the
Middle East shot to new heights. In a secret message to Hitler, passed on by
his father-in-law, the ambassador to Tehran, Egypt's King Faruq expressed
"strong admiration for the Führer and respect for the German people, whose
victory over England he desired very sincerely." He also emphasized his determination to withhold support from Britain as demonstrated by his refusal to
declare war on the Axis despite relentless British pressure.

In a meeting with Lt. Colonel James Roosevelt, eldest son of the US president and then attached to the British army headquarters in Cairo, the king
had nothing but praise for Nazism, which in his view had proved its mettle,
unlike the sluggish and inefficient Western democracies. Unimpressed by his
guest's strong objections, Faruq reassured Roosevelt that, notwithstanding
his Nazi sympathies, he was loath to see the United States destroyed, hence
it was advisable for it to stay out of the war.[7]

Even Nuri Said, one of Britain's foremost Arab champions, began hedging
his bets. As prime minister of Iraq, he had succumbed to British pressure and
severed diplomatic relations with Germany upon the outbreak of hostilities
(though refusing to go a step further and issue a declaration of war). A year
later, as foreign minister in a cabinet headed by his political opponent the
staunchly pro-Nazi Rashid Ali Kailani, he sought the Mufti's good offices in
making contacts with the Axis powers.[8]

Hajj Amin, however, felt no gratitude to the person who had welcomed
him to Iraq. Just as in 1921 he had won the post of the Jerusalem Mufti by

pledging to promote Arab-Jewish coexistence, only then to do precisely the opposite, he had no compunction in reneging on his promise to be on his best behavior in Baghdad. Within a fortnight of his arrival, British intelligence sources reported his efforts to revive the dying Palestine "revolt," while later briefs had him forbidding ordinary Palestinians to volunteer for military service, ordering them to keep their weapons and ammunition hidden until needed and urging "more energetic measures" against opposition factions. In the 1940 celebrations of the birthday of the "Prophet Moses" (Nabi Musa) at a shrine bearing his name near Jerusalem, the same event that had sparked the first anti-Jewish pogrom in April 1920, the Mufti's loyalists urged villagers and tribesmen to renew the revolt at the earliest opportunity. Capitalizing on the German successes in France, they also spread a rumor throughout Palestine that Hajj Amin had been promised the headship of a new Palestinian Arab government independent of, but friendly toward, Nazi Germany.[9]

Nor were the Mufti's machinations confined to Palestine. He rapidly immersed himself in Iraq's domestic affairs, fomenting sedition among the Shiite clergy with a view to sparking mass violence in the mid-Euphrates as a steppingstone to a wider anti-British rebellion throughout the Middle East, and seeking to undermine the pro-British elements in government and parliament so as to steer the country in the direction of the Axis.[10] This, however, did not represent the farthest limits of the Mufti's ambitions. Styling himself as spokesman for the entire "Arab nation," in July 1940 he asked the German ambassador to Turkey to inform "the Great Chief and Leader" that "the Arab people, slandered, maltreated, and deceived by our common enemies, confidently expects that the result of your final victory will be their independence and complete liberation, as well as the creation of their unity, when they will be linked to your country by a treaty of friendship and cooperation."

In two visits to Berlin the Mufti's private secretary, Uthman Haddad, sought to cement his master's image as the grandest contemporary Arab statesman. Virtually ignoring the Palestine problem, he told his interlocutors of the establishment of a high-level pan-Arab committee, headed by Hajj Amin, which included Prime Minister Kailani and some of his ministers, senior Iraqi officers, prominent Syrian nationalists, as well as Ibn Saud's private secretary, Yusuf Yasin, and royal counselor Hud, who had met Hitler the previous year. In his account, the committee decided to side with the Axis powers and to give them valuable military, economic, and political support, notably a large-scale anti-British rebellion in the Levant, provided the independence of the Arab states, and their right to form a regional union, or rather an empire, was recognized. "We Arabs hope for the victory of

Germany and are convinced that Germany will be the victor over England, even though difficulties will naturally still have to be overcome and it perhaps might take another year," Haddad argued. "There is no conflict of interests between the Arabs and Germany."

By January 1941, the Mufti felt confident enough to make a direct pitch to Hitler for pan-Arabia. In a lengthy memorandum he treated his admired would-be patron to a detailed exposition on the political history and geostrategic importance of the Arab states before arriving at the question of Palestine, which he presented not as a distinct struggle for statehood but as "a case of creating an obstacle to the unity and independence of the Arab countries by pitting them directly against the Jews of the entire world, dangerous enemies, whose secret arms are money, corruption, and intrigue." In these circumstances, he argued, "the Arabs are disposed to throw their weight into the scales and to offer their blood in the sacred struggle for their rights and their national aspirations."[11]

This resonated with the World War I negotiations between the British and the Hashemites. Then as now, a secondary local potentate pretended to speak on behalf of the entire "Arab Nation" at a time when he represented little more than himself, cleverly substituting feigned concern for a fictional yearning for regional unity for his own grand ambitions; and on both occasions the mightiest power on earth was sufficiently impressed by the audacity of this minor pretender to make far-reaching, albeit highly equivocal, promises of support.[12]

Though skeptical whether "the Arabs are sufficiently mature for such a form of [regional] state" (in July 1941 a senior German official reported, after a study visit to Syria, that he found "no Arab movement there") and reluctant to grant the Mufti "the monopoly of the all-Arabian questions, which he is seeking to obtain," the Nazis saw no downside in conceding his request for a public declaration of support for Arab independence, albeit not for the regional union he had in mind. They were particularly prone to generosity on the Palestine issue, where they "need not promise the Arabs merely a 'tolerable' solution of the Jewish question . . . but can with good conscience make the Arabs any concession in this field."[13]

Even when the Mufti, like the Hashemites in World War I, failed to make good his far-reaching promises, not least the announced revolt in the Levant, and at the end of May 1941 fled to Tehran after the British toppled Kailani's army-propped pro-Nazi government, the Nazis felt obliged to reassure him of their continued support, while the Italian embassy in Tehran went out of its way to induce him (and the deposed Kailani, who had also fled to Iran) to conclude political and military agreements with Rome. When, in August 1941, Anglo-Soviet forces occupied Iran and forced the pro-Nazi Reza Shah to abdicate in favor of his son, the Italians smuggled Hajj Amin out of the country; in October he reached Rome, where he was promptly received by Mussolini for a lengthy conversation about the Arab problem.

In what had by now become his stock pitch, the Mufti styled himself not as a representative of the Palestinian Arabs but as a spokesman for the entire "Arab Nation." He told his host that "his political aim was the independence of [unified] Palestine, Syria and Iraq" and asked for public Italian-German identification with his political endeavors, to which Mussolini gave his consent. Yet when the Mufti met the Italian foreign minister to discuss the details of the proposed statement he ran into an unyielding rejection of a unified Arab empire. Undaunted, Hajj Amin raised the issue with the German foreign ministry upon his arrival in Berlin in early November, stating his eagerness for a personal audience with Hitler, during which the Führer would endorse the proposed statement. The meeting, he argued, "will have a great propaganda effect on the entire Arab world and, beyond that, the Islamic world."

When they met on November 28, 1941, the Mufti again donned his pan-Arab mantle. The Arabs were the Nazis' natural friends because they had the same enemies, namely the English, the Jews, and the communists – thus he tried to whet Hitler's appetite. "They were therefore prepared to cooperate with Germany with all their hearts and stood ready to participate in the war, not only negatively by the commission of acts of sabotage and the instigation of revolutions, but also positively by the formation of an Arab Legion." Such a legion, the Mufti argued, could be easily established. All that was needed was his appeal "to the Arab countries and the prisoners of Arab, Algerian, Tunisian, and Moroccan nationality in Germany [who] would [then] produce a great number of volunteers eager to fight." The Axis could greatly facilitate this effort by publicly endorsing the Arabs' aspirations for independence and unity so that they "would not lose hope, which is so powerful a force in the life of nations."

However wary of pan-Arab unification, Hitler applauded Hajj Amin's political outlook and objectives as fully congruent with the Nazi worldview. "Germany was resolved, step by step, to ask one European nation after the other to solve its Jewish problem, and at the proper time direct a similar appeal to non-European nations as well," he said, sharing with the Mufti his envisaged "final solution" of the Jewish problem. Once this moment came, he would personally "give the Arab world the assurance that its hour of liberation had arrived. Germany's objective would then be solely the destruction of the Jewish element residing in the Arab sphere under the protection of British power. In that hour the Mufti would be the most authoritative spokesman for the Arab world. It would then be his task to set off the Arab operations which he had secretly prepared."[14]

Although this pledge was hardly concrete, Hajj Amin was immensely flattered. "I didn't expect my appointment in the famous chancellery to be a formal event but an ordinary meeting with the Führer," he fondly recalled years later, "yet no sooner had I arrived at the spacious courtyard in front of the great building and disembarked from my car than I was greeted with martial music, with a guard of honor of some 200 German soldiers standing to attention."

The Mufti was no less impressed by the attention lavished on him by Heinrich Himmler, Hitler's murderous henchman, who invited him to his East Prussian estate where he was introduced to senior SS generals and other dignitaries. The two spent hours discussing the political and military affairs of the Arab and Muslim worlds and ruminating on the absolute evil of the Jews, who spread corruption wherever they lived and sparked conflicts and wars with a view to profiting from the victims' suffering. This is what the Jews did to Germany in World War I, Himmler told Hajj Amin sometime in the summer of 1943, which is why Nazi Germany was determined to prevent a repetition of this crime and had thus far exterminated some 3 million of them. He also boasted of the great progress made by the Nazis in the development of nuclear weapons, which would win them the ultimate victory. "There were no more than ten officials in the German Reich who were privy to this secret," the Mufti proudly reminisced.[15]

As Hajj Amin became "the most important Arab Quisling in German hands" (to quote the words of a contemporary British report)[16] – broadcasting Nazi propaganda to Arabs and Muslims worldwide, recruiting Arab prisoners of war and Balkan Muslims for the Nazi fighting and killing machine, and urging the extermination of Jews wherever they could be found – ordinary Palestinians sought to return to normalcy and re-establish coexistence with their Jewish neighbors.

The citrus-growers led the way as early as November 1939, when a joint Arab-Jewish delegation called on the British high commissioner to request government assistance for Palestine's foremost industry. This was followed by a gathering of some 1,000 Arab and Jewish planters, who urged the cancellation of customs duties, the extension of government loans to cultivators for the duration of the war, the regulation of fruit exports, and the remission of land tax.

These appeals did little to alleviate the citrus industry's plight: in 1939–40, exports dropped from 15 million to 7.5 million cases and subsequently became negligible; not until 1943 did they approach the million mark again. Yet other industries and agriculture benefitted from Palestine's loss of foreign imports, with all local produce being absorbed and

Arab-Jewish economic interaction intensified. Large quantities of Arab agricultural produce reappeared in Jewish markets, and this phenomenon
expanded in subsequent years as both communities enjoyed the unprecedented spending and investment boom attending Palestine's incorporation
into the British war effort.[17]

Manifestations of coexistence in other walks of life followed. Land sales
continued as far as possible, with Arabs often acting as intermediaries for
Jewish purchases in the prohibited and restricted zones. Arab and Jewish
soccer teams resumed regular competitions, including in Arab neighborhoods that had for years been out of bounds for Jews. In April 1940, the first
ever Jewish-Arab hockey match was held in Jaffa, to the cheers of a big crowd
of Arab spectators. That same month, on the eve of the Jewish holiday of
Passover, chief rabbis Isaac Herzog and Benzion Uziel visited Hebron at
the head of a large congregation and prayed at the entrance to the Tomb
of the Patriarchs: the first visit of Jews to the city without an escort in four
years. Thousands of Jews made the traditional pilgrimage to Rachel's Tomb,
near Bethlehem, while Jewish students visited this exclusively Arab town
for the Christmas celebrations – inconceivable during the three-year "revolt."
Jews rented accommodation in Arab villages and opened restaurants and
stores with the villagers' consent; the Nablus municipality initiated talks
with senior Zionist officials on linking the city to the Jewish electricity grid;
and former rebel commanders and fighters made their peace with their
Jewish neighbors. By July 1940, the British foreign secretary, Lord Halifax,
could tell parliament, with undisguised satisfaction, that the situation in
Palestine was distinctly quiet. This assertion was confirmed by numerous
intelligence reports by the Hagana, the foremost Jewish underground organization in Palestine. Even the German foreign office grudgingly conceded,
at the end of 1940, that "conditions [in Palestine] are entirely peaceful.
Jewish-Arab conflict is no longer apparent. The people are in need of
tranquility."[18]

This tranquility, however, was not matched by corresponding political
reorganization on the Arab side. Though finding themselves in a theoretically
better position than their Husseini adversaries, whose military backbone
had been broken and whose leaders were out of the country, the Nashashibi-
led opposition failed to seize the moment. Exhausted by years of internecine
strife, lacking a strong organizational infrastructure, and disillusioned with
the mandatory authorities, who seemed keener to placate erstwhile enemies
than to reward loyal friends, they preferred to bide their time while enjoying
the war's economic benefits. They were also deterred by the continued
assassinations of the Mufti's rivals, which culminated in November 1941 in
the murder of Fakhri Nashashibi, the clan's pre-eminent member and

architect of the "peace squads" that had helped suppress the 1936–39 "revolt."

Nor did the lesser opposition factions fare any better. When in 1943 the veteran politicians Awni Abdel Hadi and Rashid Hajj Ibrahim attempted to revive the waning fortunes of the pan-Arab Istiqlal party by re-establishing the Nation's Fund (*Sunduq al-Umma*), the primary Arab instrument for fighting land sales to Jews – a rather ironic measure given that the pair had been involved in such transactions – they quickly ran into an unholy alliance between the Husseinis and the Nashashibis who temporarily papered over their enmity to fight an old-new rival. A vicious campaign of recrimination and defamation ensued, in which all parties sought to discredit their adversaries as corrupt and unpatriotic, with the Husseinis setting up their own organ for "redeeming" the country's lands – the Constructive Enterprise (*al-Mashru al-Insha'i*) – headed by Musa Alami, the Mufti's confidant (and himself a past seller of land to the Zionists).[19]

Into this vacuum again stepped the Arab rulers, and as before they did so not out of concern for the national rights of the Palestinian Arabs but as a means of promoting their own grand ambitions. At a meeting between Abdullah and the Iraqi regent Abdel Illah, who had ruled the country since April 1939 on behalf of his minor nephew Faisal II, whose father, King Ghazi, was killed in a car accident, Nuri Said urged the two Hashemite monarchs to coordinate their endeavors for regional domination rather than exhaust each other in futile squabbles and mutually exclusive ambitions. As Abdullah remained unmoved, Said returned to his eternal dream of a Hashemite-dominated Fertile Crescent empire, which he outlined in some detail in an extended memorandum (the Blue Book) sent in January 1943 to the British minister of state resident in Cairo and widely distributed among British, foreign, and Arab decision-makers and administrators.

In the paper, Said referred to Palestine not as an independent entity but as the smaller part of "Southern Syria" (the larger part being Transjordan), indistinguishable from its northern counterparts (the mandated territories of Syria and Lebanon), from which it had been unlawfully severed by the great powers in the wake of World War I. "The only fair solution, and indeed the only hope of securing permanent peace, contentment and progress in these Arab territories," he argued, lay in their unification into one state, where Jews would be given semi-autonomy in the running of their daily affairs along the lines of the Ottoman "millet system," which allowed the empire's non-Muslim subjects (or *dhimmis*) some leeway in the conduct of their religious and communal affairs in return for legal and institutional inferiority. Should it be possible to establish a wider pan-Arab confederation comprising Iraq,

Syria, Palestine, and Transjordan, to which other Arab states would later adhere, "then a great many of the difficulties which have faced Great Britain and France during the past two decades will disappear."[20]

For his part Abdullah continued to strive doggedly to annex Palestine to the Greater Syrian empire he was seeking to establish. During World War II his favorite envoy, Muhammad Unsi, held no fewer than two dozen meetings with Zionist officials, in which he underscored the merits of Jewish inclusion in his master's coveted empire. So did the emir when he hosted Shertok and Sasson in his Amman palace in November 1942, only to be met with a categorical No.[21]

Nor were these the only contemporary attempts to incorporate Palestine into a regional pan-Arab framework. In November 1939, Ben-Gurion told the Jewish Agency Executive (JAE), the effective government of the Yishuv, of two such proposals. The first, by St. John Philby, envisaged a Jewish state occupying the whole of Palestine within a regional pan-Arab empire headed by Ibn Saud, provided the Jews funded the Saudi monarch to the tune of £20 million (nearly £1 billion in today's terms) and helped him obtain weapons. The second plan, contrived by a group of British dignitaries and officials headed by Arnold Lawrence, brother of the famous "Lawrence of Arabia," foresaw a tiny Jewish entity, roughly along the lines of the Peel plan, as part of a Greater Syrian federation. Perhaps because of his own unproductive experience with Philby, Ben-Gurion deemed his scheme "an interesting curiosity" lacking "a firm political basis" (a view shared by the head of the Jewish Agency's political department, Moshe Shertok); Lawrence's plan he found seriously wanting.[22]

Weizmann, to whom Philby had confided his ideas in the first place, begged to differ. With no authorization from Palestine's Zionist leadership and with the diminishing backing of his London-based colleagues, he capitalized on Churchill's support for a Saudi-Iraqi-Transjordanian kingdom comprising "the Jewish State of Western Palestine [as] an independent Federal Unit" to keep the Philby scheme alive.[23] When British officialdom effectively blocked Churchill's vision, the prime minister urged Weizmann to encourage American interest in the idea, which he dutifully did – with such success that in the summer of 1943 the US administration sent a special envoy, Lt. Colonel Harold Hoskins, to Ibn Saud to explore whether he would be prepared to immerse himself in the Palestine problem and, as a starter, meet with Weizmann. If the king would not meet the Zionist leader himself, would he be willing to appoint a representative who might meet elsewhere than in Riyadh, perhaps even outside the country, in Cairo, for instance, with Weizmann or his representative?

Ignoring the fact that the scheme had emanated from his longtime confidant whom he had done little to discourage, the Saudi monarch subjected his distinguished guest to a self-righteous tirade. His own outstanding qualities were his personal honesty, his Arab patriotism, and his religious sincerity, he argued, and in sending Philby to him with a £20 million bribe the Jews had impugned all three in an attempt to make him "a traitor to his religion and his country." Did they not understand that he had the political sense to realize that, despite his position of leadership in the Arab world, he could not, without prior consultation, speak for Palestine, much less "deliver" it to the Jews, even if for an instant he had been willing to consider such a proposal? He was prepared to receive "anyone of any religion except a Jew," Ibn Saud told Hoskins. "The Jews are a special case, and there is an ancient enmity between them and the Arabs. [He] is suspicious of Jewish treachery and can neither hold discussions with them, nor trust [them]," Hoskins reported.

"What was one, what is one to make of all this?" Weizmann despairingly recalled in his memoirs. "Did Ibn Saud deliberately misrepresent his position to Hoskins? Or had he said something which could be interpreted as a complete reversal of his previous position? . . . How was one to get at the truth – if there was a truth?"[24]

The truth, of course, was that while Ibn Saud would have gladly received a hefty Jewish subvention at a time when his financial resources were in a dire state, he was no more amenable to the idea of Jewish national self-determination – "an injustice unparalleled and unequalled in history," as he put it in a letter to Roosevelt – than any of his Arab peers. "Not only is the gathering of Jews in Palestine based on no historical argument nor on natural right, and is in fact absolutely unjust," he claimed, "but it constitutes at the same time a danger to peace to [the] Arabs and to the Middle East . . . [as] the ambitions of the Jews are not confined to Palestine alone."[25]

And therein, no doubt, lay Zionism's lingering problem. For while there was no shortage of Arab interlocutors who would privately acknowledge the merits of the Zionist enterprise for the wider Arab cause,[26] none would publicly own up to such covert contacts, let alone concede the Jewish right to national self-determination. As Jamil Mardam told Shertok in November 1943: "You won't find a single Arab leader who would voluntarily acquiesce in your becoming the majority in Palestine. Should this be forcefully imposed – it will be a different matter; but there can be no mutually agreed settlement, as no Arab statesman will accept a Jewish majority." While he fully understood the Jewish attachment to Palestine, the then Syrian foreign minister added, the Jews would be much better off redirecting their efforts elsewhere and leaving Palestine to its own devices.[27]

Mardam was not alone in this view. Ben-Gurion got a similar line from the British colonial secretary, Lord Moyne, when they met in London in August

1941. Why did the Jews insist on Palestine, Moyne queried. Wouldn't it be better if the Jewish state were established in East Prussia, whose German inhabitants would be expelled after the war by the victorious allies? "You may be able to expel the Germans," the astounded Zionist leader retorted. "But the Jews will not go there; it will take machine guns to force them to go; the Jews will not settle in a country whose inhabitants have been expelled by you." As Moyne dismissed the view as moralistic naïveté, Ben-Gurion ended the discussion: "We have a country and will settle there."[28]

As a lifelong admirer of Zionism, Churchill drastically diverged from his close friend Moyne regarding the Jewish historical attachment to Palestine. Yet he rarely used his wartime dominance of British politics to help the Zionists (or indeed European Jewry). However appalled by the White Paper, he failed to abolish this "low-grade gasp of a defeatist hour" (to use his own words),[29] refrained from confronting his generals and bureaucrats over the creation of a Jewish fighting force, which he wholeheartedly supported, and gave British officialdom a free rein in the running of Middle Eastern affairs, which they readily exploited to further erode Britain's international obligations to the Jewish national cause and to get the Arab case across to the American public. In November 1943, for example, Freya Stark, the acclaimed author, orientalist, and Arabian adventurer, was sent to the US on a seven-month propaganda campaign aimed at undercutting the Zionist cause and defending Britain's White Paper policy.[30]

That this could happen at the height of the Nazi extermination of European Jewry of which Whitehall was keenly aware offered a stark demonstration of the mindset of British officialdom, which was less interested in stopping genocide than in preventing any potential survivors from reaching Palestine after the war. Such was the depth of the indifference to Jewish suffering and the preoccupation, even obsession, with fighting Zionism during the war, that senior foreign office members portrayed Britain, not Europe's Jews, as the main victim of the Nazi atrocities. So much so that a prominent Syrian politician told a Zionist acquaintance that whenever he discussed Palestine with British officials he was left with the distinct impression that it was they, rather than the Arabs, who were Zionism's main enemies.[31]

This anti-Zionism was promptly adopted by the Labour party, which in July 1945 swept to power in a landslide electoral victory. Only thirteen months earlier the party, which had vehemently opposed the White Paper and had maintained a close relationship with its Zionist labor counterpart, proposed to allow the largest possible number of Jews into Palestine so as to enable them to become the majority, for otherwise "there is surely neither hope nor meaning in a 'Jewish National Home.'" It moreover suggested encouraging the Palestinian Arabs to emigrate to the neighboring states and extending Palestine's existing boundaries, by agreement with Egypt, Syria, or Transjordan, to accommodate the nascent Jewish state. "There was a strong case for this before the War. There is an irresistible case now, after the unspeakable atrocities of the cold and calculated German Nazi plan to kill all Jews in Europe," read the party's proposed program. "Let the Arabs be encouraged to move out as the Jews move in. Let them be compensated handsomely for their land and let their settlement elsewhere be carefully organized and generously financed. The Arabs have many wide territories of their own; they must not claim to exclude the Jews from this small area of Palestine, less than the size of Wales."[32]

No sooner had Labour come to power, however, than these recommendations – some of which, notably encouraging Arabs to leave Palestine, were opposed by the Zionists[33] – were all but forgotten as prime minister Clement Attlee and foreign secretary Ernest Bevin began to take their cue from their bureaucrats. The empathy for the Jewish tragedy in Europe was forgotten, replaced by a belief that the Jews were receiving a disproportionate amount of sympathy at the expense of other victims of Nazi persecution. This was most publicly aired by Bevin, who in November 1945 criticized the supposed Jewish tendency "to get too much at the head of the queue" in demanding help. "Is it 'getting too much to the head of the queue' if, after the slaughter of six million Jews, the remnant of a million-and-a-half appeal for shelter in their homeland?" the mild-mannered Weizmann responded. "What sorry epitaph the new declaration of policy seeks to write over the graves of the six million of our dead!"[34]

Four months earlier, US president Harry Truman, who had considered the White Paper a shameful product of the "Munich mentality," demanded the immediate admission of 100,000 Holocaust survivors into Palestine. To abort the idea, perfectly congruent with Labour's pre-election position but now viewed as "calculated to embarrass the Labour Government," Bevin suggested the establishment of an Anglo-American committee of inquiry "to examine what could be done immediately to ameliorate the position of the Jews now in Europe" and "the possibility of relieving the position in Europe by immigration into other countries, including the United States and the Dominions." The committee was also "to consider how much immigration into Palestine could reasonably be allowed in the immediate future," but the phrasing of this question, let alone the keeping of the White Paper's restrictions (loathed by Labour while in opposition) in place, left little doubt as to the answer Bevin had in mind. "Should we accept the view that all the Jews or the bulk of them must leave Germany?" he cabled Lord Halifax, now ambassador to Washington. "I do not accept that view. They have gone through, it is true, the most terrible massacre and persecution, but on the other hand they have got through it and a number have survived. Now what succour and help should be brought to assist them to resettle in Germany and to help them to get over the obvious fears and nerves that arise from such treatment?"

In public Bevin was considerably subtler, if hardly more accommodating. "The Jewish problem is a great human one," he told the House of Commons on November 13, 1945, in an official policy statement on Palestine. "We cannot accept the view that the Jews should be driven out of Europe and should not be permitted to live again in these countries without discrimination, and contribute their ability and talent toward rebuilding the prosperity of Europe."[35]

Had the foreign secretary genuinely been interested in harnessing Jewish ability and talent to the rebuilding of Europe, let alone in relieving the plight of these survivors, largely congregated in congested camps in the country that had just butchered 6 million of their co-religionists, he could easily have shown the way by seeking their admittance into Britain; after all, a few minutes before being asked to approve the Anglo-American committee, the British cabinet was told of representations from the chief rabbi to admit displaced Jews who had no wish to be settled in Germany. The burden on British society would not have been that onerous: even Truman's proposed 100,000 refugees amounted to a mere 0.2 percent of the existing British population. But Bevin did not give the idea – and for that matter the wishes of these Holocaust survivors, the vast majority of whom wanted to go to Palestine – a fleeting thought: under no circumstances were they to be allowed to complicate Britain's relations with the Arabs by emmigrating to the Promised Land. As he put it in his letter to Halifax: "I think that to fly in the face of the Arabs after all the undertakings that have been given would cause a breakdown at the beginning."[36]

By way of avoiding this breakdown, Bevin unflinchingly flouted Britain's obligations to the Zionist movement. "The mandate for Palestine requires the mandatory to facilitate Jewish immigration and to encourage close settlement by Jews on the land, while ensuring that the rights and positions of other sections of the population are not prejudiced thereby," he asserted in the parliamentary address referred to above, conveniently overlooking the fact that immigration and settlement (draconically curtailed by the 1939 White Paper) were but means to the ultimate end of "putting into effect the declaration originally made on 2 November 1917 by the Government of His Britannic Majesty . . . in favour of the establishment in Palestine of a national home for the Jewish people."[37]

Bevin's omission of the mandate's raison d'être was anything but accidental. In a closed meeting with prominent Labourites a few weeks before making his policy statement, he categorically rejected the idea of a Jewish state; shortly after his parliamentary address, he told members of the press that "the British Government had never undertaken to establish a Jewish State in Palestine."[38]

This blatant misrepresentation of the letter and spirit of the mandate (and effective repudiation of the electoral platform on the crest of which Labour had risen to power) was partly due to Bevin's "egocentric and emotional temperament, [and] his disposition to fight when faced with opposition and not to guard his tongue when angered," and partly to his Baptist upbringing and total ignorance of Jewish history, religion, and culture. A former trade unionist, his only interaction with Jews had been with either like-minded leftist activists scoffing at their own Jewish origins or with ultra-Orthodox constituents, who were similarly dismissive of Zionist aspirations. As a result, Bevin viewed Jews not as a national group deserving of self-determination but as a multitude of religious communities who should resign themselves to a permanent minority status in the respective societies in which they lived.[39]

Given his personal background, it was only natural for the newly appointed foreign secretary to be instantaneously converted to the imperialist creed of British officialdom, which had no empathy for the yearning of subject peoples and communities for national liberation but rather viewed them as thankless natives who failed to appreciate the White Man's "civilizing message."

In the case of Jewish nationalism, this outlook was aggravated by the pervasive anti-Semitism within British officialdom (the last high commissioner for Palestine, General Sir Alan Cunningham, for example, described Zionism as a movement where "the forces of nationalism are accompanied by the psychology of the Jew, which it is important to recognize as something quite abnormal and unresponsive to rational treatment"),[40] and by their frustration with their inability to patronize the Jews in the same way that they condescended to the Arabs. "These officials aren't really anti-Semitic," the prominent British politician Richard Crossman noted after his meetings with British officials in Palestine during his tour of duty on the 1946 Anglo-American committee, "but they certainly are anti-Jewish and they are either pro-Arab or strictly impartial in detesting both sides. . . . Off the record, most of the officials here will tell you that the Jews are above themselves and want taking down a peg."[41]

No empire, let alone imperial administrators and bureaucrats, would readily concede defeat to a national liberation movement. In the immediate post-World War II years, it was Zionism that constituted the foremost anti-imperialist force in the Middle East, steadily driving Britain out of Palestine in a campaign that was to scar Anglo-Israeli relations for many years to come.

As a veteran British diplomat candidly admitted: "Many of us, including myself, who spent the last years of the British Mandate in Palestine, will never recover fully from the shame and humiliation of the dismal retreat in the spring of 1948."[42]

But even if the Jews had been on their best behavior, the government would still have ridden roughshod over their national aspirations owing to the simple fact that, as occupiers of vast territories endowed with natural resources (first and foremost oil) and sitting astride strategic waterways (e.g., the Suez Canal), the Arabs had always been far more meaningful for British imperial (and post-imperial) interests than the Jews. "No solution of the Palestine problem should be proposed which would alienate the Arab states," the chiefs of staff advised the cabinet in July 1946, and seven months later the chief of the air staff told the cabinet that if "one of the two communities had to be antagonized, it was preferable, from the purely military angle, that a solution should be found which did not involve the continuing hostility of the Arabs; for in that event our difficulties would not be confined to Palestine but would extend throughout the whole of the Middle East." Cunningham put the matter in far blunter terms: "Zionism has exhausted its usefulness to Great Britain and has become more of a liability than an asset."[43]

CHAPTER 4

The Road to Partition

*"Should partition be implemented, it will only be achieved over the bodies of
the Arabs of Palestine, their sons, and their women."*

Jamal Husseini, November 1947

*"Through force alone we can neither achieve the vision of Jewish redemption
nor build the Jewish state. We look to peace, peace in the world and peace in
that corner of the world called the Near- or the Middle East."*

David Ben-Gurion, November 1947

Britain's anti-Zionist shift failed to impress the Arabs. Just as they had
rejected the Peel plan of July 1937, which would have established Arab sovereignty over 85 percent of mandatory Palestine, and two years later rebuffed
the White Paper, though its draconian restrictions on immigration and land
sales meant the effective demise of the Jewish national revival, so they
remained indifferent to Labour's instantaneous transformation, after its rise
to power, from a friend to a bitter enemy of Zionism.

Having paid lip service to Bevin's sensitivity to Arab rights in Palestine, the
newly established Arab League attacked his proposed Anglo-American
committee of inquiry as a surrender to Zionist pressure (in fact the Zionists
were far from happy with the committee's formation)[1] and proclaimed an
indefinite boycott on the import of Jewish goods from Palestine to the Arab
countries as "a defense measure against Zionist expansion." Asked whether it
had considered the boycott's possible impact on the wellbeing of the 70,000
Arabs working in Jewish industries in Palestine, the League's first secretary-
general, the veteran Egyptian politician Abdel Rahman Azzam, sarcastically
replied: "I guess the Zionists will be most pleased when 70,000 Arabs are
forced to leave Palestine." When General Sir Alan Cunningham, who in
November 1945 became high commissioner for Palestine, asked for Arab
consent to monthly Jewish immigration of 1,500 during the four mo
the committee's work, a gathering of top Palestinian Arab leaders di

the request out of hand, refusing "to allow even one Jewish immigrant to enter."[2]

In April 1946, the Anglo-American committee submitted its report, which recommended the immediate admission into Palestine of 100,000 Holocaust survivors and the abolition of the restrictions on Jewish purchases of land.[3] Although the British government swiftly ruled out the admission of the refugees to Palestine, an emergency pan-Arab summit convened in Cairo on May 28–29, 1946, vowed to keep Palestine an integral part of the Arab world, and denounced Zionism as "a danger not only to Palestine but to all Arab and Muslim peoples" that had to be met by force of arms. The declaration was backed by secret decisions to provide the Palestinian Arabs with military training, weapons, and financial support, to tighten the economic blockade of the Yishuv, and to take the Palestine problem to the nascent United Nations, where, after the expected admission of Transjordan, which on May 25 assumed full independence as a Hashemite kingdom, the Arab states would represent one-eighth of the total membership. In the event of a political impasse, the Arabs would resort to force.[4]

The following month, yet another extraordinary summit, in the Syrian resort town of Bludan, adopted a series of measures to prevent the creation of a Jewish state. These included the formation of a special committee to oversee all matters relating to Palestine, and reaffirmation of the pledge to arm and train the Palestinian Arabs and to use the regular Arab armies against the Jews should the need arise. No less important was the decision to use political, economic, and cultural sanctions against the United States and Britain, including the abolition of oil concessions, were they to implement the committee's recommendations and introduce 100,000 Jewish refugees into Palestine.[5]

Behind the façade of solidarity and unity lay the perennial web of inter-Arab rivalries, hatreds, and ambitions. Far from fulfilling a historic yearning for regional unity, the establishment of the Arab League in March 1945 was an uneasy compromise among the most unlikely bedfellows that left none fully satisfied. Egyptian prime minister Mustafa Nahhas, the organization's architect, wished to improve his domestic prestige by posing as a leader of the Arab world (in whose affairs he had previously taken little interest), while Egypt's King Faruq, who sacked Nahhas on October 8, 1944, a day after a pan-Arab conference in Alexandria signed a protocol calling for the formation of a league of Arab states, was also driven by ulterior motives, namely the desire to deny his prime minister, imposed on him by British bayonets in February 1942, any political credit.

For his part Ibn Saud resented the "unpractical and unworkable" ideal of pan-Arab unity, which he equated with a Hashemite domination of the

Fertile Crescent that was bound to endanger his own position, yet decided to enter the fray after being assured that the initiative would not assume "a strong political character." His skepticism was shared by the imam of Yemen, by Syria's president, Shukri Quwatli, who subordinated his staunch pan-Arab sentiments to his friendship with the Saudi monarch, and by the government of Lebanon, where the dominant Christian community, wary after the 1860 massacres of its members, was determined to preserve the country's complete independence in order to avoid its absorption in a Muslim bloc.

Nuri Said's resentment of the newly established pan-Arab organization ran even deeper. Though foreshadowed in his 1943 Blue Book, the League was no personal triumph of the Iraqi prime minister, who had envisaged it as a corollary of his Fertile Crescent scheme rather than an independent "super-government," let alone an Egyptian-dominated one. As early as November 1945, he contemplated taking Iraq out of the organization; this sentiment was echoed two months later by Abdullah, who suggested to the Iraqi regent that "in view of the obvious anti-Hashemite attitude of Egypt and Saudi Arabia it is time for Iraq and Transjordan to withdraw from [the] Arab League."

Nor did Said have the slightest esteem for Azzam, whom he considered a highly irresponsible and dangerous man – "not from malice but because he is stupid, unbalanced, and vain" – who misused the organization he headed to promote Egyptian interests. This view was shared not only by Iraqi offi-cialdom and the political elite but also by Musa Alami, the Palestinian dele-gate to the preparatory talks on the League's formation, who accused the secretary-general of "trying to split the Arab League into two factions in order to play off one faction against the other, thereby rendering it easy for Egypt to continue to play the leading role in Arab affairs."

The Lebanese representative at the talks described the ulterior motives of the League's founding members in equally scathing terms. "[T]he various Arab States were not actuated by motives of Arab union but by motives of internal policy," he argued a day after the League's foundation:

> King Faruq was attracted by the idea of being the principal personage in the Arab world. Iraq wanted to have the premier role itself and to unite the Fertile Crescent in a Hashemite Empire. Ibn Saud merely wanted to wreck any northern confederation. Syria was thinking mainly of a republican regime in order to forestall a Hashemite monarchy. The Emir Abdullah was only dreaming of a union of Syria and Transjordan with him as King. . . . The result of all this was division in the League.[6]

Against this backdrop of conflicting objectives and mutual animosities and distrust, it was hardly surprising that Said considered the Egyptian conduct at the Cairo summit as "trying to get 100% and not give 1%," while in Bludan the Iraqi foreign minister proclaimed that "the League had failed in its full duty toward Palestine and that Iraq could not consider her liberty of action as regards Palestine restricted by the procedure agreed upon." He subsequently withdrew his invidious declaration under heavy Syrian pressure, yet such was the extent of mutual distrust at the summit that an Iraqi proposal for an anti-American boycott was seen by Ibn Saud as a devious plot to slash Saudi Arabia's oil revenues. When Egypt, which "wobbled between moderation and extremism," backed a Saudi request for the exhaustion of all peaceful means before any other action was undertaken, it was derided by Iraq for its (supposed) lack of political commitment and military preparedness.

Not that there was any real and abiding Arab enthusiasm for activism. When in April 1946 Jamal Husseini and Hussein Khalidi of the Arab Higher Committee (AHC), the Palestinian Arabs' effective "government," which had been disbanded by the British in October 1937 and reconstituted by the Arab League in November 1945, requested Arab backing for a resumption of violence, they were given the cold shoulder. Jamal's plea (at the June 1946 Bludan summit) for the establishment of a Palestinian government-in-exile that would conduct a sustained struggle against Zionism and would raise a 100,000-strong army to liberate Palestine in its entirety proved equally futile. However impressed by his passion and eloquence, the delegates would commit themselves to nothing beyond a vague promise to take the matter up with their governments. Asked about the possible formation of an Arab League force, Azzam replied that the armies of the Arab states were the League's and a united army could only be formed "if the world unites and is organized and the League is entrusted with the maintenance of peace." If anything, the establishment of the Palestine committee at the summit sent a clear and unmistakable signal that the Arab states, rather than the Palestinian leadership, would be calling the shots on the Palestine problem.[7]

This approach reflected, no doubt, the widespread unease in the Arab world with the person who had led the Palestinian Arabs since the early 1920s and whose war activities in the service of the Nazis were seen as a major liability at this particular juncture. When, in May 1945, the imam of Yemen asked Ibn Saud to join him in an appeal against the Mufti's possible prosecution at Nuremberg alongside his former Nazi masters, the Saudi monarch replied that he knew Hajj Amin's wartime activities all too well to be able to make such an appeal. This sentiment was shared by leftist elements among the Palestinian Arabs who opposed the Mufti's return on anti-fascist grounds, while Awni Abdel Hadi and his followers tried, for their own reasons, "to pull strings to prevent the Mufti's being brought back to Palestine."

Such was the loathing of Hajj Amin by his peers that Arab League secretary-general Azzam and its Washington office director, Cecil Hourani, had no compunction about telling Eliahu Epstein, the Jewish Agency's representative in the US, that "the Mufti is undoubtedly a menace to the general Arab interests" and that his autocratic methods had prevented that social development of the Palestinian Arabs which was so necessary to their cause – both in their confrontation with the Jews and in the establishment of an independent, democratic Palestine. "If a Jewish State is established in Palestine," Hourani told Epstein, "[you] will have to thank the Mufti, who by his utterances and behavior has strengthened the claim that Jews and Arabs cannot live within the same State."

Elias Sasson, head of the Arab section of the Jewish Agency's political department, got the same line from Abdullah and Egyptian prime minister Ismail Sidqi, who derided the Mufti as "a schemer seeking his own personal interest [who] couldn't care less if the entire Arab world were destroyed so long as he achieved his own goals." Even King Faruq, who regarded Hajj Amin's Nazi collaboration as "pro-Arab and anti-Jew but not pro-Hitler," expressed his pity "for any head of state in whose country he might turn up."[8]

When the Mufti escaped on May 29, 1946 from the Paris mansion where he had been held for a year pending a decision on his possible prosecution as a war criminal and arrived in Egypt, Ibn Saud promptly informed the British that "he was not willing to receive the Mufti in Saudi Arabia and would make him leave the country should he arrive," while Sidqi was at a loss over how to treat his unwanted guest. Having discussed the matter with his ministers and solicited Faruq's opinion, the prime minister announced that the Mufti had requested "the protection of the noble royal family" and would "receive from our august sovereign the solicitude and protection worthy of his high position."

"The hour is not for recalling the political mistakes attributed to his Eminence," read the official statement. "It is a question of aid imposed by magnanimity and protection dictated by honor. Oriental nations in general and especially Islamic nations have always distinguished themselves by this unique generosity and hospitality." And to remove any doubts regarding the strings attached to this charitable act, the statement concluded with a thinly veiled threat: "It is known that Egypt is going through a particularly delicate period in her political life, and it is to be hoped that she will reach her goal without hindrance, and in an atmosphere of calm and order. There is no doubt that his Eminence is perfectly aware of this."[9]

Hajj Amin, however, had no intention of playing the role assigned to him by his Egyptian hosts. Ignoring repeated demands to cease his "clear and flagrant breach of the assurances given to King Faruq and the Egyptian

Government,"[10] he turned his Cairo residence into the control center of Palestinian Arab affairs and a buzzing hub of inter-Arab politics frequented by scores of dignitaries visiting the Egyptian capital. Before long his name was linked to the abortive attempt to establish an "Arab People's League" – an alternative pan-Arab organization comprising opposition parties and radical groups (notably the Egyptian Islamist group the Muslim Brothers) designed to goad the Arab governments into a more militant policy. Meanwhile his emissaries were busy persuading the Arab rulers that the Palestine problem could only be resolved by force of arms.[11]

This effort culminated in the fourth session of the Arab League council (which opened in Cairo on October 30, 1946, but adjourned until November 18) where AHC vice-president Jamal Husseini urged the delegates to prepare for war and to support the 30,000-strong force allegedly formed in Palestine. Though this claim was patently false (the Husseinis could hardly claim to have a few thousand militiamen in their Futuwa squads, moribund since the late 1930s), Jamal's plea struck a responsive chord among the delegates, especially the Syrians and the Iraqis, who lambasted Azzam for failing to prevent the fragmentation of Palestinian society and to implement the June 1946 Bludan resolutions. The repressive measures against individuals and bodies involved in land sales to Jews were peremptorily reaffirmed, and the Arab states undertook to contribute £250,000 (£7 million in today's terms) to the capital of a company to be formed for the purpose of "saving the Arab lands in Palestine."[12]

By now the Husseinis had tightened their grip over the AHC, which in January 1947 doubled in size with the entry of five of their stalwarts (Rafiq Tamimi, Muin Madi, Izzat Darwaza, Sheik Hassan Abu Saud, Ishaq Darwish),[13] and had launched a campaign of terror, intimidation, and assassinations against political opponents and alleged "collaborators" that quickly re-established them as Palestine's foremost Arab clan. So much so that Sasson noted that "such is the clamoring for the Mufti in Palestine that anyone who quarrels with his friend – be it a merchant, a lawyer, an activist, or a worker – goes to Cairo to be arbitrated by him."[14]

A steady stream of weapons began flowing into the country as the various militias and groups, including the Muslim Brothers, who in the late 1930s had gained a firm foothold in Palestine, began arming for the looming outbreak of violence. This was accompanied by a constant incitement to violence of the Palestinians and the Arab masses throughout the region. "There is not a single Palestinian Arab in the world who believes in political means," Jamal told a leading Egyptian newspaper on December 27, 1946, shortly after the end of the League's fourth session. "They all know that bloodletting is the only way to resolve the problem, and every one of them is prepared to shed his blood for the holy cause." He reiterated this threat three days later, telling the Husseini paper *al-Wahda* that the Palestinian Arabs would resist partition with all their might since "even the tiniest Jewish state will be a rotten apple in a box of otherwise good apples." Once the last Palestinian Arab had been martyred, the cause would be taken up by the Arab states which would continue the struggle until victory.[15]

This fiery rhetoric was also directed at the Twenty-Second Zionist Congress, the first to convene since the outbreak of World War II, which on December 24 ended its deliberations in the Swiss city of Basle with a categorical rejection of any arrangement "which might postpone the establishment of a Jewish State, based upon full equality of rights for all inhabitants without distinction of religion or race, with every community exercising autonomy in religious, educational, social, and cultural affairs." And while the congress preferred the constitution of the whole of Palestine "as a Jewish state integrated into the structure of a democratic world" (in the words of the May 1942 resolution of an emergency Zionist conference held in the New York Biltmore Hotel), it left the door open to the establishment of a Jewish state "in an adequate area of Palestine" – the policy decided by the Jewish Agency Executive (JAE), the effective government of the Yishuv, four months earlier.[16] As Ben-Gurion put it in a letter to British Foreign Minister Ernest Bevin a few weeks later: "The only immediate settlement possible, with finality, is the establishment of two States, one Jewish and the other Arab (or the Arab area might be joined to Transjordan)."[17]

This, as we have seen, was not what Bevin, Attlee, and their civil and military bureaucrats had in mind, resentful as they were of the idea of Jewish statehood even in a partitioned Palestine (years after Israel's establishment, Attlee would not resign himself to its existence, still referring to it in private as Palestine). On July 31, 1946, the government unveiled its plan (in a parliamentary statement by the Lord President of the Council, Herbert Morrison) for the partition of Palestine into four autonomous (but not independent) entities – a Jewish province (comprising some 17 percent of Palestine's territory), an Arab province (40 percent of the country), and the British-controlled districts of Jerusalem and the Negev (53 percent of Palestine) – and invited the two adversaries for talks in London in September. The Arab states sent their delegates, but the Mufti forbade the AHC to attend – in open defiance of the Arab League – while the Zionists refused to come in protest at the British government's refusal to address the possibility of Jewish statehood. When a Palestinian Arab delegation, headed by Jamal, arrived in London for the renewal of the talks in January 1947, its presence had a radicalizing, rather than a moderating, effect since no Arab representative dared challenge its uncompromising line. A series of meetings between Bevin and colonial secretary Arthur Creech Jones with a group of Zionist officials headed by Ben-Gurion proved equally inconclusive, as the latter would not disavow the demand for immediate statehood.[18]

Foiled and frustrated, Bevin decided to up the ante and on February 18, 1947 told parliament of the government's decision to refer the Palestine question to the United Nations. The driving force behind the Palestine scheme, prepared by his bureaucrats under his close supervision (Morrison was not even supposed to announce the plan that came to bear his name but stepped in for Attlee when he was unable to attend parliament at that particular date), the foreign secretary apparently hoped that the UN would refer this explosive political issue back to Britain with a clear mandate to enforce its trusteeship over Palestine, or, better still, to establish a unitary Arab state (in which the Jews would remain a small minority) that would be either absorbed or dominated by Transjordan. As he told parliament in defense of the government's decision to surrender the Palestine mandate to the United Nations, "We really cannot make two viable States of Palestine, however we may try. We can make one viable State, and, so far as I can see, or as far as any student of the map could see, the only thing we could do would be to transfer the rest to one of the Arab States, but I ask what trouble is that going to cause in the whole of the Arab world?"[19]

This is not what happened. Although at Britain's request the UN General Assembly convened for a special session (April 28–May 15) that appointed the United Nations Special Committee on Palestine (UNSCOP) to study the question and suggest means for its resolution, the committee's report, published at the end of August 1947, was a far cry from British hopes and expectations. Urging the earliest possible termination of the mandate and the granting of independence to Palestine, it diverged over the nature of the envisaged independence. Seven of the committee's eleven members (the representatives of Canada, Czechoslovakia, Guatemala, Holland, Peru, Sweden, and Uruguay) proposed the partition of Palestine into two independent states – one Jewish, the other Arab – linked in an economic union, with Jerusalem internationalized by means of a trusteeship agreement that would designate the UN as the administering authority. Three members (the representatives of India, Iran, and Yugoslavia) proposed the creation of an independent federal state of Palestine (with Jerusalem as its capital) comprising Jewish and Arab districts that would enjoy full powers of local government but not supreme authority over such issues as national defense, foreign relations, immigration, currency, taxation, and transport and communication, which would be vested in the federal government. The eleventh member, Australia, abstained from voting on either scheme.

The British government, however, did not lose hope of subverting this "clear victory for the principle of partition" (in the words of the first UN secretary-general, Trygve Lie). As an Ad Hoc Committee on the Palestinian Question, comprising representatives of the world organization's fifty-seven member states, began deliberating (on September 25) the two UNSCOP reports with a view to submitting final recommendations to the General Assembly's annual session, Britain cajoled and intimidated the smaller members in an attempt to raise wide-ranging concerns over the adverse implications of the creation of a Jewish state. It warned of an Arab oil embargo that would subvert Europe's fledgling economic recovery after the destruction wrought by World War II, and of a violent pan-Islamic backlash against the West. It claimed that the Jewish state was certain to become a Soviet bridgehead in the Middle East and that the only way to contain Soviet expansionism was to establish a bulwark of Arab states – Transjordan, Iraq, Egypt, and Palestine – backed by British forces in the region.

"Why did you agree so readily to the idea of handing over the Palestine problem to the United Nations?" Harold Beeley, Bevin's foremost Middle East advisor, berated a Zionist official. "Look at the Charter of the United Nations and the list of its member nations. To get an affirmative decision, you'll need two-thirds majority of the votes of these members. You can only win a majority if the Eastern bloc and the United States join together and support the same resolution in the same terms. That has never happened, it cannot happen, and it will never happen!"

When this presumption collapsed on November 10, as the United States and the Soviet Union agreed to set the end of the mandate at May 1, 1948 and to establish a special UN commission to oversee the process, the British government took an overtly recalcitrant position. Britain would not be able to complete the withdrawal of its troops from Palestine before August 1, announced the British ambassador to the UN, Sir Alexander Cadogan, but this did not mean that these forces would help enforce any political solution, or that Britain would continue to maintain a civil administration in Palestine until that date. On the contrary, Britain reserved the right to lay down its mandate and end its civil administration at any time after it became evident that the General Assembly had been unable to reach a settlement acceptable to both Jews and Arabs. In the interval between the end of the mandate and the withdrawal of their last troops, the British would confine themselves to the maintenance of order in the residual areas still controlled by their remaining forces. "Great Britain had placed the [Palestine] matter before the Assembly with the declared conviction that agreement between the Arabs and Jews was unattainable," an exasperated Lie recorded in his memoirs. "This did not deter the British representative, Arthur Creech Jones, from informing the Assembly that Britain would give effect only to a plan accepted by the Arabs and the Jews." Cunningham put the matter in a characteristically frank manner, telling Colonial Secretary Creech Jones: "It appears to me that H.M.G.'s policy is now simply to get out of Palestine as quickly as possible without regard to the consequences in Palestine."[20]

The Arab anti-partition campaign was no less vigorous, if far blunter. Contemptuously dismissing UNSCOP's majority and minority recommendations, the Mufti warned that neither of them could be implemented without much bloodshed and suffering for all concerned. "But we Arabs shall not be the losers in the last round," he gloated. "We shall be fighting on our own ground and shall be supported not only by 70,000,000 Arabs around us, but also by 400,000,000 Muslims."

In an informal meeting with British officials, sent to gauge his readiness to accept a partition that would assign most of Palestine to the Arabs, the Mufti was equally adamant. "We do not fear the Jews," he said. "We would have many losses, but in the end we must win. . . . They will eventually crumble into nothing, and we do not fear the result, unless of course Britain or America or some other Great Power intervenes. Even then we shall fight and the Arab world will be perpetually hostile."[21]

This bravado hid serious misgivings regarding the Arab states' commitment to the Palestine cause. In a special session of the Arab League's political committee, convened on September 16–19 in the small resort town of Sofar, outside Beirut, to forge a unified strategy at the General Assembly's annual session, AHC member Emile Ghouri implored the Arab delegates to do their utmost to abort the partition recommendation, which he believed was likely to be endorsed by the UN. The Palestinian Arabs would defend their country to the last man, he stated, and would do so with or without the League's support should it fail to recognize that a Jewish state posed a mortal danger to the entire Arab world rather than to Palestine alone.

Iraq's prime minister, Saleh Jabr, at whose initiative the meeting had been convened, intervened sharply. The Arab states had done practically nothing for Palestine aside from a limited diplomatic effort and it was high time that they owned up to their collective responsibilities, just as his government had done by informing Britain of its determination to arm the Palestinian Arabs. They could, for a start, extend military, financial, and material aid to the Palestinians, including the formation of a pan-Arab volunteer force; and they should all warn Britain and the US that their support for partition would inexorably lead to the sanctions agreed in Bludan three months earlier.

A heated debate ensued. The Syrians argued that the imposition of sanctions had to be preceded by a thorough examination of their implications given the dire economic situation in most Arab countries. The Egyptians claimed that for all their selfless support for the Palestinian Arabs, often at a real cost to their own interests, they could not afford any military adventure at a time when Egypt was locked in a bitter struggle over the evacuation of British forces from its territory. Meanwhile the Saudis maintained that the Bludan resolutions had been issued in response to the Anglo-American committee of inquiry and were no longer of any practical value. Besides, economic sanctions would be a double-edged sword – not merely because the oil-producing countries would be the main losers in such a move but also because the Saudi government was currently able to use the oil companies to lobby the US administration, and this powerful lever would be lost in the event of an oil embargo; indeed, the oil companies would probably retaliate by throwing their weight against the Arabs.

Jabr remained unimpressed. As an oil-producing country, Iraq was in the same boat as Saudi Arabia, he retorted, yet it had already warned the British government four months earlier that it would if necessary cut off its oil supply. If the Saudis were unable to do likewise, they should say so upfront rather than beat around the bush with false pretenses.

This the Saudis would not do. Having consulted his superiors, the Saudi delegate to Sofar acquiesced in a militant communiqué that rejected UNSCOP's majority and minority reports, warned that their execution would endanger the Arab world's peace and security, and promised "to resist with all practical and effective means any measures which fail to ensure the independence of Palestine as an Arab State." Following in Iraq's footsteps, Syria and Lebanon sent virtually identical notes to the British and American governments protesting against the partition scheme.

This public bravura was backed by a string of secret resolutions indicating a growing, though by no means wholehearted, readiness to employ force to prevent the creation of a Jewish state. These included the donation of £1 million (about £26 million in today's terms) to the Palestinian Arabs and the establishment of a technical committee that would determine Palestine's defense needs, coordinate and organize military and material assistance to the Palestinians, and oversee the disbursement of funds provided by the Arab states. No less importantly, and reflecting the League's assessment of the severity of the looming confrontation, the Arab rulers were urged "to open the gates of their respective countries to receive children, women and aged people and to support them in the event of disturbances breaking out in Palestine and compelling some of its Arab population to leave the country."[22]

The Sofar recommendations were approved the following month by the sixth regular session of the League's council, which opened on October 7 in the Lebanese town of Aley (instead of Cairo, which had been hit by cholera).

The Mufti, who came to Beirut to follow the deliberations, was promised a substantial sum of money in the immediate future, assistance in the recruitment and organization of Palestinian armed forces, and pan-Arab intervention in the event of a serious escalation of Jewish attacks – even before the British departure from the country. Last but not least, the Arab states undertook to forgo separate operations in Palestine and to withdraw their forces from the country after the destruction of the Jewish state and its replacement by an Arab one in the whole of Palestine.[23]

This, however, was not exactly what Hajj Amin had expected. For one thing, the rejection of his demand for the formation of a Palestinian Arab government-in-exile, and the creation of the technical committee in which the Arab states called the shots despite the inclusion of a notional Palestinian representative, marginalized the AHC and vested control of the political and military campaign for Palestine in the Arab League, or rather in its member states. For another, the person tipped to command the pan-Arab volunteer force that was to be established in accordance with the Sofar and Aley resolutions – Fawzi Qawuqji, leader of the foreign Arab intervention in the 1936–39 "revolt," who like Hajj Amin spent most of World War II in Nazi Germany – was anathema to the Mufti, who considered him an opportunistic mercenary ready to sell his services to the highest bidder, in this case to Abdullah, who had made no secret of his desire to include Palestine in his coveted Greater Syrian empire. (Ironically, Abdullah was no happier with Qawuqji's appointment for similar reasons.)

Indeed, for all the talk of a unified pan-Arab military effort it was evident to all that the execution of the expedition would fall almost entirely to the Hashemite kingdoms of Transjordan and, to a lesser extent, Iraq. The Egyptian prime minister, Mahmud Fahmi Nuqrashi, made it clear from the outset that the dispatch of troops to the frontier was the utmost limit of his country's participation and that so long as British forces remained in Egypt there could be no question of an Egyptian military intervention in Palestine. Owing to internal problems, the Syrians could do little, and the same applied to Lebanon, though both moved troops to the border in the wake of the Aley summit as a token of their commitment to the Palestine cause.

Above all, none of the Arab rulers expected Abdullah to abide by the pledge to relinquish those parts of Palestine that were to fall under his control. As early as March 1947, Transjordan's prime minister, Samir Rifai, told the Arab League's fifth session, which discussed the implications of the British decision to refer the Palestine question to the UN, that his country reserved the right to pursue an independent policy should the need arise. "We are greatly affected by the developments in Palestine and feel [them] far more strongly [than any other country] as partners in adversity," he argued.

"Should Palestine be lost, we will be next in line whereas the rest of the Arab countries will feel the consequences much later."

Now that the Arab states seemed to be edging toward the military option, Rifai had few qualms about clarifying what this freedom of action meant. "He was thinking in terms of occupying the whole (repeat whole) of Palestine," a member of the Beirut embassy who met the prime minister after the Aley summit reported to London.

> Speed, he said, was essential and plans would have to be made for the completion of operations within three weeks. The Rutenberg hydro-electrical installation (situated on Transjordanian frontier), the Dead Sea potash works (whence Jews obtained raw materials for explosives) and the port of Haifa would be occupied immediately. The Hashemite kingdom of Jordan (comprising Transjordan and Palestine) would then come into being. The Jews would be offered favourable terms on lines of the Arab plan submitted at the London Conference; he would even be prepared, in spite of the probable opposition from [the] Palestinian Arabs, to give them local autonomy and status comparable to that obtaining in Mount Lebanon prior to 1914.

Jabr was equally candid. "He made it abundantly clear that what he had in mind was that when the British withdrawal was effected Transjordan and Iraqi troops would occupy the whole, repeat the whole, of Palestine," a British diplomat reported on his conversation with the Iraqi prime minister on October 10.

> It would be a fait accompli which other Arab States would be bound to recognize and for which they should even be grateful. It would also, he added, be in the interest of the Jews themselves; bloodshed would be avoided and the Jews given the necessary safeguards. If they had any doubts on the latter point, they need only witness Iraq and see how [the] Iraqi Government treated [the] 300,000 Jews living there.[24]

Whether Iraq's treatment of its minorities should have inspired confidence among the Zionists is open to question. Only fourteen years earlier its army had slaughtered thousands of hapless Iraqi Christians and in June 1941 rampaging mobs, incited by army officers, the police, and fascist groups, carried out a murderous pogrom in Baghdad in which some 200 Jews were massacred and thousands more were wounded. Nor for that matter could the Zionists be reassured by the November 1945 slaughter of some 140 Jews in Tripolitania (today's Libya), and the wanton plunder and destruction of Jewish property.[25]

At the same time as Jabr was lauding the Arab world's attitude toward the Jews, Arab spokesmen at the UN were threatening these very communities with wholesale violence. "[I]t should be remembered that there were as many Jews in the Arab world as there were in Palestine, whose positions might become very precarious," Jamal Husseini warned. Even the reputedly moderate Muhammad Hussein Heikal, president of the Egyptian senate and former cabinet minister, who had secretly met Zionist officials on several occasions and now headed his country's delegation to the General Assembly annual session, cautioned that "if a Jewish State were established, nobody could prevent disorders. Riots would break out in Palestine, would spread through the Arab States and might lead to a war between the two races."[26]

These threats were accompanied by a vicious campaign of incitement and de-legitimization. One after another, Arab spokesmen admonished Zionism in the vilest possible terms, combining anti-Jewish bigotry dating back to Islam's early days with the hoariest and most bizarre themes of modern European anti-Semitism. "The Jews are questioning the record of an Arab spiritual leader. Does that properly come from the mouth of a people who have crucified the founder of Christianity?" AHC member Emile Ghouri defended the Mufti's Nazi collaboration at the General Assembly's special session on Palestine (April 28–May 15, 1947), to the shock and disgust of many delegates.[27]

For his part, the Iraqi foreign minister, Fadel Jamali, chose to underscore a modern-day canard, articulated in *The Protocols of the Elders of Zion* (the notorious anti-Semitic tract fabricated by the Russian secret police at the turn of the twentieth century) and taken up by the Nazis, namely that "the homelessness of the Jews was an acquired feeling which was detrimental to their loyalty and destroyed the unity of the countries in which they lived."

Even UNSCOP's proposed economic union between the prospective Arab and Jewish states was derided as a devious Zionist plot for economic penetration, and ultimate domination, of the Arab world rather than the major boon it was for the Arab state (and a corresponding burden on its Jewish counterpart). In the words of Fares Khouri, the chief Syrian delegate to the UN debate: "It was clear that the choice of Palestine to satisfy Zionist aspirations was based not on humanitarian sympathy but on the intention of the Zionists in the United States to launch an economic invasion of the whole eastern world and to achieve that end by creating a bridgehead in Palestine, to be the headquarters of their activities."

Invoking not only the standard conspiratorial thinking regarding Jewish clannish domination of world affairs à la the *Protocols* but also Adolf Hitler's description that a Jewish state would be "a central organization of their international world cheating," Jamal Husseini amplified the claim. "The Zionist organization . . . did not want Palestine for the permanent solution of the Jewish problem nor for the relief of the distressed Jews," he argued. "The Zionist program was a well-calculated policy aimed at the acquisition and domination of the greater part of the Near East and the expansion of its influence over all the Middle East."

Nor did this outpouring of the most outlandish conspiracy theories and blood libels prevent the Arab spokesmen, some of whom had been past admirers and collaborators of Nazi Germany, from making the abysmal equation between the Jews and their Nazi murderers. Thus we have Jamali describing Zionism as "a modern political movement of an aggressive character founded on an association of religion and racial mythology, and using Nazi propaganda methods," and, incredibly, a Syrian delegate telling the General Assembly: "There was a basic similarity between Zionism and Nazism in that they were both based on racism – on distinctions between Jews and Gentiles, between Aryans and non-Aryans – on expansion and acquisition of power, and on violence to secure that expansion. The United Nations, which had been formed through the common endeavor to destroy Nazism, should not support its parallel, Zionism." Were the United Nations to betray its destiny and to force partition upon Palestine, Jamal Husseini threatened, "it would have little chance of permanence in the midst of a strongly aroused and genuinely apprehensive Middle East. The fight would continue, as it had in the Crusades, until the injustice was completely removed. By imposing partition, the United Nations would virtually precipitate Palestine into a bloodbath."[28]

Beyond the General Assembly's discussion halls, especially when addressing their own subjects in their own language, Arab leaders and their media outlets were far more outspoken. Jamal warned that "should partition be implemented, it will only be achieved over the bodies of the Arabs of Palestine, their sons, and their women," while Ibn Saud vowed "to wage war with the same determination and force as during the Crusades," and Mardam pledged that "the Arabs would defend Palestine against Zionism even if this led to the sacrifice of their dearest possessions." Even Azzam, who in his public appearances and private meetings with Western diplomats and politicians went out of his way to underscore Arab peacefulness, was not deterred from telling an Iraqi audience that "the Arabs will use force to help the Palestine Arabs to prevent partition and the establishment of a Jewish State there." This paled in comparison with the standard threat in the Arab media to "wipe the Zionists from the face of the earth."[29]

While the Arabs were steadily escalating their anti-partition campaign, the Zionists were seeking to persuade them to eschew violence and reach a negotiated settlement. During his stay in New York for the General Assembly's special session on Palestine (April 28–May 15), Ben-Gurion heard from Azzam that, although there were Arab leaders who favored an agreement with the Jews, no one dared say so in public. Yet once confronted with the fait accompli of an established and internationally recognized Jewish state, they would readily acquiesce.[30]

One of these leaders was Egyptian prime minister Nuqrashi, whose concern for the Palestinian Arabs was no stronger than that of his predecessors. His overriding preoccupation was to secure the speediest evacuation of British forces from Egypt and the unity of the Nile valley (that is, the annexation of Sudan, under Anglo-Egyptian rule since 1899, to Egypt), and like his immediate predecessor, Ismail Sidqi, he had no qualms about seeking Zionist support in promoting these goals. (Sidqi, in fact, went further than secretly talking to the Zionists. In August 1946, he actually agreed to the creation of a Jewish state in part of Palestine, giving the local Arabs the option to unite with Transjordan or to establish their own separate state, but he subsequently backed down from the offer.)[31]

At the initiative of his UN representative (and future Egyptian foreign minister and prime minister) Mahmud Fawzi, in June 1947 Nuqrashi agreed to meet Eliahu Epstein, the Jewish Agency's US representative whom he had known for some years, only to get cold feet at the last moment. UNSCOP members were in Palestine hearing Jewish and British testimonies (the AHC boycotted its deliberations altogether) and the Egyptian prime minister had no wish to lay himself open to unnecessary charges of betrayal. Yet when Jamal Husseini demanded that the Arab League shun the committee (which was to leave for Beirut on July 21), Nuqrashi dismissed the request as presumptuous and foolish, stating that under no circumstances would Egypt boycott the UN at a time when it was submitting its own case to the organization. "Egypt is not naturally interested in Palestine," commented a veteran British diplomat. "Egyptians not only are not Arabs but they have not the same to fear as have the Iraqis and the Syrians that a Jewish state would be a menace to their own countries. Egypt shows interest in Palestine because Palestine is the one question on which all Arab states are agreed and if Egypt is to continue to dominate the League she must take the lead in this question."[32]

In a meeting with Azzam on June 18, Epstein found the secretary-general totally impervious to his arguments. Gone was the implicit acquiescence in an internationally imposed partition as expressed to Ben-Gurion a few weeks earlier; in its place was an adamant demand for Jewish incorporation into a Mufti-ruled Arab Palestine. Not that Azzam had changed his view of the Palestinian leader ("a hindrance to the general Arab interests") or failed to grasp the problematic nature of such an arrangement. Yet he claimed that "although the first few years may be difficult for the Jews, if they submitted to a peaceable policy of cooperation and proved their good intentions to their Arab neighbors, matters might improve." Reverting to his favorite historical parallel, he predicted that, "even if in accordance with UN recommendation, a Jewish State would be established in Palestine, it would fare no better than did the Crusaders during the 12th and 13th Centuries. Being of an artificial nature – surrounded by hostile Muslims and dependent upon the goodwill of foreign powers – such a State would not last any length of time."[33]

Notwithstanding Epstein's explanation that the comparison had no basis in historical fact because there was little in common between the structure of the Crusaders' society and the National Home that was being built by the Jews, whose attachment to Palestine dated back to antiquity, Azzam invoked it again at a meeting on September 15 with David Horowitz and Aubrey (Abba) Eban, the Jewish Agency's liaison officers with UNSCOP. The following day the General Assembly was to open its annual session, which was to discuss the committee's report, and the Zionists were eager to explore the possibility of a mutually agreed compromise.

Seated in Azzam's sumptuous suite at the London Savoy Hotel, Horowitz and Eban tried to persuade the secretary-general that the majority report provided a fair and lasting basis for Arab-Jewish cooperation and that "once agreement had been reached on a practical compromise such as that suggested by UNSCOP, it should not be difficult to convince the Arab world that it had nothing to fear from Jewish development, and that no threat of Jewish expansion would exist"; and by way of allaying Arab fears of Jewish expansionism, they suggested "to offer a Jewish guarantee, and to accept the guarantees of the Arab League and the United Nations, against any encroachments by the Jews upon the boundaries of other States."

They argued that "the Palestine conflict was uselessly absorbing the best energies of the Arab League, diverting it from the constructive purposes to which it might otherwise address itself" (to which the secretary-general nodded vigorous assent); that both Arabs and Jews would greatly benefit from "active policies of cooperation and development"; and that the Jewish state-to-be was keenly interested in being integrated into processes of regional development, and in certain conditions "would not be averse to joining with the Arab States in a single League."

At this point Azzam reacted strongly. No Middle Eastern league based on diversity could in any way be considered, he said. The Arabs were not afraid of Jewish expansion. They resented Zionism's very presence as an alien organism, which had come without their consent and which refused to be assimilated to their way of life. "For me you may be a fact, but for them you are not a fact at all – you are a temporary phenomenon," he said. "Centuries ago, the Crusaders established themselves in our midst against our will, and in 200 years we ejected them. This was because we never made the mistake of accepting them as a fact."

Without disputing the relevance of this historic memory, Horowitz replied that a modern people had also to apply realistic criteria, which in this particular case meant that the existence of Palestine Jewry, and its refusal to assimilate, must be accepted as facts. Eban followed suit. Though these were recent facts, it did not make them less historic, he said. "Arab statesmanship had to consider, from the viewpoint of its own interests, whether more has to be gained by envisaging its relationship with the Jews in terms of harmony or in terms of conflict."

Azzam remained unmoved. "The Arab world is not in a compromising mood," he said.

> You may easily convince me that the Arabs now have an interest in allowing you to develop your State, and to live at peace with them, but having convinced me of this, you will have achieved nothing, for you have nothing at all to offer which I can take back to my people tomorrow. Up to the very last moment, and beyond, they will fight to prevent you from establishing your State. In no circumstances will they agree to it.

The Jews were profoundly deluding themselves in pinning the slightest hope for peace on the personal attitude of this or that Arab leader, Azzam continued: "They were all entirely governed and directed by historic forces – call them God or call them nature, or call them history – which they could not influence or control. The same impulse would impel Arabs to fight the Jewish foothold whether the fight redounded to their interest or not."

But wasn't it too pessimistic to think of history in terms of biological predestination? Surely there was an element of choice in politics which allowed people to follow the line of their greatest interests, suggested Azzam's interlocutors.

The secretary-general insisted that no such considerations were valid here. He could imagine the emotional forces that had driven the Zionists into their position, and he knew of the forces which lay at the root of the Arab feeling and which precluded any agreement that did not involve the total abandonment of Zionism. Politics were not a matter for sentimental agreement, he said; they were the result of contending forces:

> Nations never concede; they fight. You won't get anything by peaceful means or compromise. You can, perhaps, get something, but only by the

force of arms. We shall try to defeat you. I'm not sure we'll succeed, but we'll try. We were able to drive out the Crusaders, but on the other hand . . . we once had Spain, and then we lost Spain, and we have become accustomed to not having Spain. We once had Persia, and then lost Persia, and we have become accustomed to not having Persia. Whether at any point we shall become accustomed to not having a part of Palestine, I cannot say. The chances are against it, since 400,000 of our brethren will be unwilling citizens of your state. They will never recognize it, and they will never make peace.

"We left the hotel and crossed over into the Strand both stirred and depressed," Horowitz wrote in his memoir. "Azzam had managed to impart something of his spirit and outlook to us. . . . The admiration of force and violence which was evident in his statements seemed to us to be both strange and repugnant, and his description of any attempt at compromise or peace as a naïve illusion left no door of hope open."[34]

In these circumstances the Zionists turned to their longest-standing Arab interlocutor, who by all accounts held the key to any pan-Arab military move. On November 17, Golda Meyerson, acting head of the Jewish Agency's political department (Shertok was at the General Assembly session, seeking to garner support for the partition option), accompanied by Elias Sasson and Ezra Danin, an Arab affairs expert at the department, met Abdullah in the residence of Abraham Rutenberg, director of the hydroelectrical installation in Naharaim, on the Palestine-Transjordan border, in an attempt to persuade the king to accept partition, or at least to shun the envisaged pan-Arab attempt to subvert it by force.

Making no bones about his unwavering commitment to the Greater Syrian scheme, Abdullah lost no time in outlining the place of the Jews in this imperial vision. "Over the past 30 years you have grown in stature and strength and have achieved much," he said.

You cannot be ignored, and it is a duty to compromise with you. There is no conflict between you and the Arabs. The conflict is between the Arabs and the British, for having brought you here; and between you and the British, who have reneged on their promises to you. Now I am convinced that the British are departing and that we will be left face to face. Any clash between us will be to our mutual detriment. We are speaking about partition. I would agree to a partition that will not disgrace me before the Arab world when I come out to defend it. Let me seize this opportunity to suggest to you the idea, for future consideration, of an independent Hebrew republic in part of

Palestine within a Transjordanian state comprising both banks of the Jordan, under my headship, and in which the economy, the army and the legislature will be joint.

Abdullah did not expect an immediate reply but emphasized that this entity would be a stepping stone to the creation of a much larger empire comprising Syria, Lebanon, and Saudi Arabia.

This was not what the Jews had in mind, Meyerson retorted. The Palestine question was presently being discussed by the Ad Hoc Committee, which would hopefully recommend the establishment of two states – one Jewish, the other Arab. Any Jewish-Transjordanian agreement would therefore have to be based on this principle.

In this case, Abdullah asked, how would the Jews regard an attempt by Transjordan to seize the Arab part of the country? "We will view it with favor," Meyerson replied, "provided it will not obstruct the establishment of our state, will not trigger a confrontation between our forces, and will be accompanied by a declaration that the occupation is solely designed to preserve law and order and keep the peace until the United Nations will be able to establish a government in that part [of Palestine]."

The king was taken aback. "But I want that part for myself in order to incorporate it into my state," he protested. "I do not want to create a new Arab state that will disrupt my plans and allow the Arabs to ride on me. I want to be the rider, not the horse."

What then about a carefully engineered referendum that would establish his authority among the Palestinian Arabs?

Ignoring the proposition, Abdullah stressed his strategic importance lest this fact was lost on his interlocutors. The Arab rulers had neither the muscle nor the stomach for war, he argued. They had all acknowledged his military pre-eminence and were unlikely to make a move without his consent. This, however, was not going to be given lightly, as evidenced by his closure of Transjordan to all Arab armies and his refusal to participate in any effort that was not under his complete control and geared toward stabilizing the situation and reaching an understanding with the Jews. The prevailing circumstances necessitated compromise, not war, and he would be happy to meet again with Zionist representatives shortly after the UN had made its decision so as to explore the feasibility of such a compromise.[35]

Abdullah was not being totally candid. It is true that he was reluctant to allow Arab forces to cross his territory en route to Palestine, but this had more to do with his fear and distrust of their intentions than with his concern for Palestine's wellbeing. As he wrote the Iraqi regent, "If we permitted the entrance of forces from our sister Iraq, Saudi Arabia would demand the admittance of her forces also, perhaps even Syria might do so, and then this Kingdom of yours would be occupied before Palestine had been conquered."[36] It is also true that he preferred to achieve his goals in Palestine by peaceful rather than warlike means. Yet this did not prevent him from telling a pan-Arab delegation that visited Amman a month prior to his meeting with Meyerson that Jordan was in a better position than any other Arab country to invade Palestine since it was not a UN member and was therefore likely to attract less international opprobrium; the Arab states could help by bankrolling the intervention and by providing political and diplomatic support, but not much more.

Prime Minister Rifai, who often acted as Abdullah's alter ego, vented this intention in public, telling a Palestinian Arab radio program that "since Transjordan is not a member of [the] UN, she will not be bound by UN decisions and will be able to carry out whatever decisions the Transjordan government takes as regards Palestine. Transjordan is bound only by the decisions of the Arab League."[37]

Not everyone was reassured. Though Nuqrashi, relieved to have another state bear the brunt of the military intervention, agreed to help fund Transjordan's Arab Legion should Britain withdraw its subsidy from the force following an invasion of Palestine, Syrian president Shukri Quwatli feared an Anglo-Transjordanian-Iraqi collaboration to annex Palestine's Arab parts to Transjordan as a prelude to the realization of Abdullah's Greater Syria dream. (Bevin would indeed authorize the invasion in a February 1948 meeting with the Transjordan prime minister.)[38] So did General Ismail Safwat, Iraq's assistant chief of staff and head of the Arab League's newly formed technical committee, while Azzam went out of his way to persuade Abdullah to drop his Greater Syria scheme, at least until the satisfactory resolution of the Palestine problem. "Saladin's reign ended shortly after he had liberated Palestine from the Crusaders but his name lived on for over a thousand years," he appealed to the king's vanity. "Monarchy doesn't last but one's reputation lasts forever."[39]

His words fell on deaf ears: "King Abdullah has in no way discarded his idea of the Greater Syria scheme with Palestine as a dependent state ruled by his son, Prince Talal, as viceroy," read a British intelligence report. Moreover, in his eagerness to dissuade Abdullah from his Greater Syria scheme, Azzam accepted the king's demand to restrain the Mufti's activities and to hold a referendum on Palestine's future after the country's conquest, under Transjordan's auspices and control.[40]

This left Hajj Amin – who was convinced of Abdullah's determination to incorporate Palestine into his kingdom after the British departure, then to

Map 4 The United Nations Partition Plan, 1947

"come to an agreement with the Jews which will satisfy their ambitions for statehood" – impervious to repeated pleas to cooperate with Qawuqji, who began laying the groundwork for the pan-Arab force decided on at the League's summits. Instead he delegated responsibility for the impending violence to his key loyalists: Abdel Qader Husseini, a favorite nephew, was made commander of the Jerusalem district; Hassan Salame of 1936–39 fame, who followed the Mufti to Nazi Germany, was to command the southern front; and Abu Ibrahim, another gang leader in 1936–39, was appointed commander of northern Palestine.

In a secret meeting with Azzam in Beirut, where he remained after the Aley summit, the Mufti demanded the formation of a Palestinian Arab government-in-exile, as if the idea had not already been rejected by the Arab states a few weeks earlier. Meanwhile, he worked assiduously to consolidate his control over the Palestinian Arabs, setting up national committees in Palestinian Arab cities and localities, distributing the substantial quantities of weapons smuggled into the country, collecting a newly imposed poll tax, and eliminating the remaining vestiges of opposition. The assassination of the prominent Haifa moderate Sami Taha on September 12 threw the anti-Husseini camp into disarray and brought a stream of dignitaries to the Mufti's Beirut's residence, including traditional Nashashibi supporters.[41]

Nor were the Zionists reassured by Meyerson's meeting with Abdullah. Rather it underscored Abdullah's vision of the Jews as an autonomous community in a vast Hashemite empire, which he had been articulating since the early 1920s and had most recently repeated in two meetings with Sasson in August 1946.[42] Yet their nagging fears of the king's imperialist designs, let alone concerns over the Mufti's political and military preparations, were temporarily superseded by the immediate goal of securing the UN vote for partition. On November 25, the Ad Hoc Committee approved the idea by a majority of 25 against 13 (with 17 abstentions and 2 absences), and since this would not have sufficed to have the resolution passed at the General Assembly plenum, where a two-thirds majority was required, an epic battle ensued between the Arabs and their supporters, who pressed for an immediate vote, and the Zionists and their friends, who needed a breathing space to canvass for the additional votes.

On November 29, three days after the start of the debate, the General Assembly passed Resolution 181 calling for the partition of Palestine into Jewish and Arab states linked in an economic union, with Jerusalem placed under an international regime. The next day violence came to Palestine.

CHAPTER 5

Kingdoms are Established over Dead Bodies and Skulls

"Palestine is our land. We were born in it, we have lived in it, we shall die in it. We shall then meet the face of Allah with smiles, warm hearts, and satisfied souls."

Arab Higher Committee, November 1947

"If the Arab citizen will feel at home in our state . . . if the state will help him in a truthful and dedicated way to reach the economic, social, and cultural level of the Jewish community, then Arab distrust will accordingly subside and a bridge will be built to a Semitic, Jewish-Arab alliance."

David Ben-Gurion, December 1947

In the early hours of November 30, as Jewish revelers were making their way home after celebrating the UN partition resolution, bus driver Arie Heller set out from the coastal town of Netanya on his way to Jerusalem. After an hour's drive, as he approached the Arab village of Faja, near the town of Lydda, three men signaled him to stop. Mistaking them for passengers, Heller slowed down. When he saw to his horror a submachine gun concealed under the coat of one of them, he accelerated and the men opened fire and lobbed hand grenades at the bus. A woman seated beside the driver was instantly killed, and a number of other passengers were wounded.

Heller swerved to the right and the bus tumbled down a ditch. He and a couple of others managed to get out and took cover behind the vehicle's thick wheels. One of the attackers then entered the bus and took the driver's pouch. Seeing a wounded passenger trying to help his injured wife, the assailant killed him at point-blank range. Having murdered five of the bus's twenty-one passengers and wounded five more (two of them seriously), the gang left the scene on its way to attack another Jerusalem-bound bus, killing one passenger and seriously wounding three.

These were literally the opening shots of what came to be known by Israelis as the War of Independence and by Palestinians and Arabs as *al-Nakba,* "the catastrophe." The killers were hardly a shining example of unadulterated Arab patriotism: it soon transpired that they were hardened criminals driven by monetary concerns rather than a desire for national liberation. Yet political leaders have never shied away from using less savory groups within society for the promotion of extreme goals, and the Mufti and his Arab Higher Committee (AHC) were no exception. They used gang violence during the 1936–39 "revolt" to terrorize the Yishuv and enforce their rule on Arab society, and they had no qualms about repeating this practice now that the Palestine question had reached the moment of truth. Within hours of the bus attacks, another person was murdered in Tel Aviv, while Arab prisoners in Palestine's main prison, in the northern city of Acre, attacked Jewish inmates, who barricaded themselves in their cells until the British authorities managed to restore calm. In the mixed population city of Haifa, shots were fired at Jews passing through Arab neighborhoods, and Jewish residents were attacked in Jerusalem, Jaffa, Safad, and Ramle, among other places.[1]

The next day brought no respite to the violence. Shootings, stonings, stabbings, and riots continued apace. Bombs were thrown into cafés, Molotov cocktails were hurled at shops, a synagogue was set on fire. To inflame the situation further, the AHC proclaimed a three-day nationwide strike to begin the following day. Arab shops, schools, and places of business were closed, and large Arab crowds were organized and incited to take to the streets to attack Jewish targets. "Kingdoms are established over dead bodies and skulls," read an AHC manifesto on November 30. "Palestine is our land. We were born in it, we have lived in it, we shall die in it. We shall then meet the face of Allah with smiles, warm hearts, and satisfied souls." In a single week, from November 30 to December 7, 1947, thirty-seven Jews were killed and many more were injured. By the end of the year another 180 Jews had been murdered.[2]

The first mob attack took place in Jerusalem on December 2, when several hundred Arabs ransacked the new Jewish commercial center, opposite the Old City's walls. In full view of British police they smashed windows, looted shops, and stabbed and stoned whoever they happened upon. The next day Golda Meyerson, acting head of the Jewish Agency's political department, sent the chief secretary of the mandate government photographs showing a British police officer standing and smiling with pleasure at the sight of a gang of Arabs ransacking and burning Jewish stores. By contrast, a Hagana platoon that was rushed to the area to protect civilians was peremptorily stopped and disarmed by the British police, and sixteen of its members were arrested for illegal possession of weapons. Some of the confiscated arms were later found on killed and captured Arab rioters.

From the commercial center the frenzied mob proceeded to City Hall, where they attempted to lynch several Jewish municipal workers and to plunder nearby stores. "For a long time the police did not interfere with this little mob," recollected the city's British mayor, Richard Graves, "and it was heartbreaking to see these young hooligans being given a free hand to destroy the products of man's labours. . . . I remonstrated with the police [who] told me that they had orders not to interfere till they were reinforced."[3]

On December 4, some 120–50 armed Arabs attacked the Efal kibbutz, on the outskirts of Tel Aviv, in the first large-scale attempt to storm a Jewish neighborhood. Four days later a more audacious assault was launched, when hundreds of fighters attacked the Hatikva quarter in southern Tel Aviv. They were followed by scores of women, bags and sacks in hand, eager to carry off the anticipated spoils. "The scene . . . was appalling," recalled one of the Jewish defenders. "Masses of Arabs were running toward the neighborhood. Some of them carried torches while others fired on the fly. Behind them we saw flashes of fire from machine guns covering them as they ran amok." Some 2,500 Jewish residents fled their homes while another 300 were rendered destitute as their properties were burnt down by the rioters. Yet the local Hagana forces held their ground. By the time the fighting was over, the Arabs had been forced into a hasty retreat, leaving behind some 40–45 dead.[4]

This failure notwithstanding, the battle constituted a watershed in the general plunge into war. Planned and executed by Hassan Salame, a prominent Mufti loyalist who had followed him to Nazi Germany during World War II, and using numerous fighters from other Palestinian Arab localities (notably Nablus and Lydda),[5] the operation heralded the transformation of the conflict from mob rioting and local clashes into a more orderly guerrilla and terror campaign.

In doing this, the Arabs took advantage of the Yishuv's awkward geostrategic position. With many Jewish villages situated in predominantly Arab areas, and the Arabs controlling most of Palestine's hill regions and its major road arteries, the 600,000-strong Jewish community was highly vulnerable both to attacks on isolated neighborhoods and to the disruption of communications between different parts of the country. Moreover, Palestine's encirclement by four Arab states – Lebanon and Syria in the north, Transjordan in the east, and Egypt in the southwest – made the Yishuv virtually landlocked and dependent for its very existence on naval and aerial transportation, and the port of Haifa – Palestine's primary naval outlet – was controlled by the British until their departure, while the country's sole international airport was a stone's throw from the Arab town of Lydda.

Three areas were particularly vulnerable to Arab attacks. First there were the thirty-three Jewish localities excluded from the prospective Jewish state and located deep in the territory of the would-be Arab state. Then there was the Negev, that vast and largely unpopulated desert south of the Gaza-Beersheba line, which comprised about 80 percent of the territory assigned to the Jewish state by the partition resolution. The twenty-seven isolated Jewish villages in this area, with their tiny population of a few hundred farmers, were widely seen as an operational liability that should be removed at the first available opportunity; the only reason that this did not happen was David Ben-Gurion's stark determination to hold on against all adversity.[6]

Last but not least was the problem of Jerusalem. By virtue of geography and topography, the city was the most isolated of the Yishuv's urban centers. Lying at the heart of an Arab area with only a handful of neighboring Jewish communities, and with its lifeline passing through hostile Arab territory, Jerusalem's Jewish population could easily fall victim to Arab war plans. To this must be added the extreme difficulty of ensuring security along the 60 km road between Tel Aviv and Jerusalem, nearly half of which wound through rough and hilly country. All the Arabs had to do was to block stretches of road running near their villages, then sit on the overlooking ridges and aim their shots at the trapped Jewish convoys as they attempted to remove the roadblocks.

This is precisely what they did. As early as December 7, Ben-Gurion ran into an ambush as he was making his way to Jerusalem for a meeting with the British high commissioner. "We went ahead of Ben-Gurion's car," recalled the head of his security team.

> Our radiator overheated and a tire went flat. I saw movement on one of the hills and sent two boys to check it out. Three men stayed with me to protect Ben-Gurion and [Moshe] Sneh [a prominent Zionist leader]. As we changed the tire, Ben-Gurion asked to get out. I told him: "Excuse me, sir, but I'm responsible for your safety. You'll sit inside, bent down." The tire was changed. The boys sent up the hills drove off the Arabs.[7]

Yehoshua Globerman, the Hagana's newly appointed commander of the Jerusalem zone, was far less fortunate: he was killed the next day at approximately the same place. Three days later, ten Jewish fighters were killed when a convoy on its way to the Etzion bloc, a cluster of four villages north of Hebron, was ambushed by a large Arab force, and on December 14 yet another relief convoy on its way to the besieged village of Ben Shemen, near Lydda, was attacked by Transjordan's British-controlled Arab Legion, then largely deployed in Palestine. Thirteen people were killed, nine were seriously wounded. Two more Jewish drivers were killed when a convoy was trapped for hours in the Arab village of Yazur, south of Jaffa. On December 23,

Ben-Gurion experienced yet another attack when a convoy from Jerusalem to Tel Aviv in which he was traveling was ambushed in what had by now become a commonplace occurrence.

"The Arabs are beginning to succeed in making the ordinary daily round of the Jews extremely difficult," read a British intelligence report in mid-December.

> Since the beginning of the month there have been numerous attacks on communications, causing considerable concern to the community and in some cases seriously affecting their economy. This, it is thought, may possibly be the plan of the Arab Higher Committee and the Mufti – in other words, not to have a "bloodbath," in which the Arabs would suffer from their inferior armament, but to break the economic life of the Jews and so squeeze them out of business and Palestine.[8]

The attacks on Jewish transportation were accompanied by attempts to occupy Jewish neighborhoods throughout the country. On December 10, a concerted Arab assault on the Jewish quarter of Jerusalem's Old City was rebuffed. So were Arab attacks on the villages of Kfar Yaabetz (December 27), Kfar Uriya (January 11, 1948), Ramat Rahel (January 14), and Ein Zeitim (February 2), as well as on the Jewish quarter in Safad (January 5).[9]

On January 14, the Arabs launched their largest offensive in the war yet, when some 1,000 fighters commanded by Abdel Qader Husseini, the Mufti's favorite nephew and a prominent gang leader in the 1936–39 "revolt," attempted to storm the Etzion bloc. The main assault, involving a battalion of 400 well-trained fighters, was mounted against the bloc's principal village, Kfar Etzion, while diversionary attacks were launched against the neighboring kibbutzim of Masuot Yitzhak and Ein Zurim. The substantial British police and military forces stationed in the neighborhood made no attempt to stop the fighting.

So confident were the Arabs of their success that they brought with them hundreds of non-combatants, men, women, and children, carrying empty bags for the loot. They were to be bitterly disappointed. Anticipating the thrust of the assault, the defenders took up concealed positions along the main route of advance, catching their attackers by surprise. By dusk the Arabs had retreated in disarray, leaving behind some 200 dead and a similar number of wounded, casualties inflicted by fewer than thirty defenders. "In Kfar Etzion you avenged the 1929 massacre of the Hebron Jews," a local Arab told a Jewish correspondent shortly after the battle. "This was the hand of God." Among Hebronites, Abdel Qader's name became synonymous with ignominy. Hardly could it be mentioned in public without attracting the vilest swearing and derision.

Before long, however, the Arabs were to exact their revenge. With Kfar Etzion's meager reserves of arms and ammunition depleted in the battle, a platoon of thirty-five fighters was sent the next day to reinforce the besieged kibbutz only to find itself surrounded by masses of Arabs who had traveled to the area from their villages. Taking positions near the opening of a cave on the local road, the platoon fought to the last man. A British police officer was to tell later how he found the body of one of the fighters with a stone, his last weapon, in his hand. True or not, the death of the thirty-five would take its place in the Israeli collective memory as a symbol of heroism, and in the Arab narrative as a shining military success. As a result, when the Israeli army occupied the area in the 1967 Six-Day War, many Arabs from villages who had participated in the 1948 battle fled their homes for fear of revenge.[10]

Violence was by no means confined to Palestine. Throughout the Arab world Jewish communities were singled out for attack. In British-ruled Aden, seventy-six Jews were slaughtered by rioting mobs, while massacres in the northern Syrian city of Aleppo drove most members of its 10,000-strong Jewish community to flee across the border to Turkey, Lebanon, and Palestine. In Beirut, Cairo, Baghdad, and Alexandria, Jewish houses and businesses were ransacked, and synagogues were torched and desecrated. "When our nation starts a fight it doesn't look forward to its conclusion," Azzam told a large gathering in Cairo. "We will start [the battle] and will not stop until victory has been achieved and our enemy has been thrown into the sea."[11]

Between December 8 and 17, the Arab League's political committee met in Cairo to discuss the Palestine situation. The gathering defined the overarching Arab objective as "obstructing the partition plan, preventing the creation of a Jewish state, and preserving Palestine as an independent unified Arab state," but again rejected the formation of an exile Arab government headed by the Mufti, who was excluded from the discussions at Iraq's and Transjordan's insistence. An Egyptian allusion to Hajj Amin as ruler of the prospective Arab state of Palestine produced an explosion of rage from Iraqi prime minister Saleh Jabr.

General Ismail Safwat, Iraq's assistant chief of staff and head of the League's technical committee, warned that the Palestinian Arabs were incapable of defeating the Jews on their own and made an impassioned plea for an immediate pan-Arab intervention. He was backed by Jabr, who reiterated the call for oil sanctions against the Western powers, but was opposed by the rest of the Arab leaders, who insisted that such a move could not be countenanced so long as the British remained in Palestine, and indeed that "the open use of Arab armies against the Jews even after the end of the mandate was not practical for the present." Instead they adopted a series of measures aimed at supporting the Palestinian Arabs and enticing them to resist violently the partition resolution. These included a pledge for an additional £1 million (some £26 million in today's terms); the dispatch of 10,000 rifles and 5,000,000 rounds of ammunition; intensification of the economic boycott of the Yishuv; maintenance of a strong military presence along the Arab states' borders with Palestine; and the recruitment of 3,000 fighters for the pan-Arab force of Palestinian and Arab volunteers, dubbed the Arab Liberation Army (ALA), that was being established in the southern Syrian town of Qatana.[12]

Safwat was appointed ALA commander-in-chief while Fawzi Qawuqji, of 1936–9 "revolt" fame, became the force's field commander. Taha Hashemi, a retired general and former prime minister of Iraq, assumed the post of inspector general. In deference to the Mufti's relentless pressure to install his protégés in command posts, Safwat divided the country into three military zones: northern Palestine, all the way to Tel Aviv's environs, was placed under Qawuqji's command; the southern zone, south of Gaza, Hebron, and the Dead Sea, was earmarked for an Egyptian commander; while the central front was placed under Abdel Qader's command.[13] As the arrangement failed to satisfy the Mufti, Safwat relented still further and established the Lydda zone under Salame. Abdel Qader became commander of the Jerusalem district and was given special powers.[14]

To the high commissioner for Palestine, General Sir Alan Cunningham, these decisions appeared a recipe for disaster. "I cannot escape the conclusion that the Arab League has no clear idea of the outcome of its present action, and has taken it merely to save face in view of past utterances," he wrote to colonial secretary Arthur Creech Jones.

> An open war to suppress the Jews however undesirable is understandable and leads to a clear cut issue. But it is apparently accepted that partition cannot be prevented. The present policy of the League therefore can only lead to the destruction of Palestine, which will undoubtedly bring much suffering and loss of life to both Palestinian Arabs and Jews, and from which neither can gain any possible benefit either now or in the future. Has the League really got the interests of the Palestinian Arabs at heart?[15]

In the long run, these words proved prophetic. In the short term, and despite its dubious origin as an uneasy compromise reflecting the delicate balance of power, ambitions, and interests among the Arab states, the ALA attracted a much larger number of volunteers than had been envisaged by the Cairo summit. In December 1947, according to British sources, approximately 500

ALA fighters infiltrated Palestine in small groups, dispersing among the villages of the Galilee, and by the end of January 1948 their number had risen to about 3,000. Most of them were concentrated in the Samaria area, where they were reconnoitering the area, collecting intelligence, and seeking to assert strict military control over the local population. A month later their size had grown to 6,000–7,000 and by mid-April, according to Hagana sources, they had reached some 9,000 fighters, organized in six battalions and armed with light weapons, mortars, and guns. Of these, 3,000–4,000 were deployed in Samaria, while another 1,000 camped in the Galilee in groups of 50–100 under a central command. A few hundred fighters were deployed in each of Palestine's primary cities – Jaffa, Haifa, and Jerusalem – in addition to the 500 based in the Jerusalem area and the 100 in the Gaza district. On the night of March 5–6, Qawuqji entered Palestine at the head of a 200-strong contingent to assume direct command of his forces. "Arab history is repeating itself," a Syrian observer was quoted as saying by a foreign journalist. "In the Crusades Saladin had to free Jerusalem from the Infidels. Today Fawzi Bey is our Saladin."[16]

The ALA's growing strength was accompanied by a corresponding boost in self-confidence, and before long it launched its first large-scale attack on a Jewish locality. On January 10, some 250–300 fighters crossed the Syrian border and attacked the Kfar Szold kibbutz. Despite overwhelming inferiority in numbers and equipment, the defenders managed to hold their ground and were eventually saved by a British armored unit sent to their aid. Ten days later, the isolated kibbutz of Yehiam in the western Galilee was attacked by some 400 ALA fighters armed with mortars, machine guns, and rifles, and commanded by Adib Shishakly, a future ruler of Syria.

The kibbutz was completely surrounded and the attack opened simultaneously from all sides. Roadblocks were established at all approaches, and bridges and culverts were made impassable, indicating that the attackers intended to occupy the village at all costs. There being no other means of communication, the defenders managed to request help by heliograph, and police armored cars were sent out from Acre, together with a platoon of soldiers. Having helped the defenders fend off the attack, the force returned to its base. But when the Arabs resumed the attack the next morning, they were unpleasantly surprised to find the kibbutz reinforced by sixty Hagana fighters who had arrived overnight.[17]

Unfazed by this resistance, in the early hours of February 16, the ALA laid down a heavy barrage of mortar shells and machine-gun fire on Tirat Zvi, in the Beisan valley of the eastern Galilee. Shortly afterward, some 500–600 troops advanced on the kibbutz. They succeeded in cutting the perimeter fence at one point but failed to penetrate the inner defenses and were forced into a hasty retreat. Some sixty Arabs were killed in the fighting and about 100 wounded. Having ordered the attack from his Damascus headquarters, Qawuqji refused to accept defeat, at least in imagination. In his memoirs he misrepresented the battle as a shining victory that "greatly disquieted the Jews," saying that they had suffered 112 fatalities and a higher number of wounded: in truth, one Jewish fighter was killed and another wounded.[18]

The outbreak of hostilities did not take the Yishuv by complete surprise, not least since Arabs had long threatened to abort the creation of a Jewish state by force of arms. Ben-Gurion, in particular, had taken these threats at face value and labored under the assumption that upon the termination of the mandate the Yishuv would have to confront the full military might of the Arab world, on top of that of the Palestinian Arabs. "An assault by the Palestinian Arabs doesn't endanger the Yishuv," he told the Twenty-Second Zionist Congress in December 1946, where he assumed the defense portfolio in addition to the chairmanship of the Jewish Agency Executive (JAE),

> but there is a danger that the neighboring Arab states will send their armies to attack and destroy it . . . perhaps not today or tomorrow as the Arab states are not yet ready for such a move; yet [major] developments and vicissitudes lie ahead and we must not await the ripening of the danger but rather start preparing to the best of our technical and financial abilities. This, in my opinion, is Zionism's foremost task at the moment. I will not comment on the relative importance of the challenges confronting us – there are two or three vital and critical issues – but the security problem lies at the heart of the matter since our very existence is endangered. We need an entirely new approach to the problem: greater means, reorganization of our forces and new modes of preparation.[19]

In line with this thinking, in early November 1947 the Hagana underwent a major structural change, aimed at transforming its semi-mobilized units into a national army based on compulsory conscription that would be able to resist an invasion by the regular Arab armed forces. The Palmah (Hebrew acronym for "Shock Platoons"), the Hagana's elite unit comprising some 2,100 men and women on active duty (plus 1,000 trained reservists who had returned to civilian life but could be recalled at a moment's notice), and the 12,000-strong infantry force (2,000 on active service and 10,000 reserves) called the Hish (Heil Sadeh, or field force), were amalgamated into a centrally controlled unified force (the Hail, or army) comprising four brigades and aimed at rebuffing an external invasion. It was supported by the Mishmar (Guard), a garrison force consisting of men and women of twenty-five and over who were declared unfit for combat units and were assigned instead to static defense missions, especially in villages throughout the country.[20]

Yet such was the Jewish yearning for peace and exhilaration at the partition resolution that there was a general reluctance to entertain the possibility of a protracted and bloody conflict. "Apart from a number of isolated attacks, there were no indications of Arab-Jewish tension. Arabs joined in celebrations at settlements, sold their wares in towns and moved about as usual," the *Palestine Post* reported on December 1, a day after seven Jews were murdered and scores wounded in Arab attacks. The paper quoted a Jerusalem Arab textile merchant as saying, "I am not concerned with politics. We want to live in peace and support our families." An Old City sheik was even more pointed: "Without interference from outside Arab nations there will be no trouble in Palestine."[21]

On December 3, the daily newspaper, *Davar*, argued that despite the violent flare-up of the past few days there was little appetite among the Palestinian Arabs for a general conflagration given how fresh were their recollections of the 1936–39 disturbances, which had hit Arab society far harder than its Jewish counterpart. "Jews have already been killed and not inconsiderable damage has been inflicted," the paper argued. "But the Yishuv, which views the acts of violence in exclusively anti-Jewish terms, must not consider itself their direct target. These days, attacking the Jews is but a handy tool within the Arab community. Having failed at the United Nations, and facing an imminent failure in the Arab League, the official Palestinian Arab leadership now attempts to entice its constituents into actions, which it knows have no chance of success."[22] In the same vein, the respected Arab affairs commentator Michael Asaf claimed that the violent demonstrations in Egypt were not primarily a response to the partition resolution but a reflection of deep xenophobic undercurrents within Egyptian society, fanned by militant pan-Arabists and pan-Islamists such as the Arab League's secretary-general, Abdel Rahman Azzam, and the Muslim Brothers' founding leader, Hassan Banna, who constantly preached Arab/Muslim racial and spiritual supremacy. How else could one explain the fact that the rampaging Egyptian mobs targeted British and Greek Orthodox establishments to a greater extent than their Jewish counterparts, though both countries had been staunchly opposed to partition, with Greece voting against the UN resolution?[23]

Even Ben-Gurion, the tireless Cassandra who missed no opportunity to alert his colleagues and the public at large to the gravity of the Arab threat, tried to hit the odd positive note. "The Arabs – both the AHC and spokesmen of the Arab states – have announced their refusal to abide by the UN decision; having lost their case before the supreme forum of free humanity, they threaten that they will try to resolve the Palestine issue by brute violence," he stated on November 25, 1947, four days before the passing of the partition resolution. Such an attack might or might not materialize, he reasoned, but to ignore or minimize this danger was nothing short of national suicide; and while the Jews could defeat an all-Arab assault provided they were properly mobilized and equipped, they should avoid the fatal Arab error of seeing armed force as the be-all and end-all:

> True, without [defensive] force we risk destruction. But through force alone we can neither achieve the vision of Jewish redemption nor build the Jewish state. We look to peace, peace in the world and peace in that corner of the world called the Near- or the Middle East. While making every effort – economically, organizationally, and technically – to enhance our capacity for defense against aggression, from wherever it may come, we must at the same time do our utmost to maintain, strengthen, and deepen friendly and peaceful relations with our Arab neighbors.

Why was there hope of such a momentous development? Because just as "the justice of the Jewish cause and the blessings of its constructive enterprise" enabled Zionism to capture the world's heart and imagination, they would hopefully also allow it to "win the hearts of our Arab neighbors within Palestine and outside its frontiers." This would not be achieved overnight, but neither had the sympathy of the international community been gained in a day. There was thus no reason to despair of winning the trust and friendship of the Arab world. On the contrary:

> Encouraging signs are already discernible on the horizon. Even in the recent days of tension and agitation we have heard other words than those of menace and hostility alone. We should remember that the great mass of the Arab people are still inarticulate; they are deprived of voice and means of political expression, because those who speak in their name today represent neither their feelings nor their needs. The common Arab people are not keen to seek quarrel or battle with those who, some of them feel, are the natural allies of their own welfare and liberation. It would be a dangerous illusion to believe that incitement cannot succeed in inflaming crowds. But the inciter's task is no longer so easy today and it will become even more difficult in the measure that the realization spreads among the Arab people that Jewish strength must be respected and that our sincerity, fairness and integrity can be relied upon.[24]

These were no hollow words. For all his keen awareness of the pan-Arab threat and the pain it could inflict on the Yishuv, or perhaps because of it,

Ben-Gurion was loath to leave any stone unturned in furthering the goal of peaceful coexistence. As Meyerson's mission to Abdullah failed to assure the Jewish leadership of the king's ultimate intentions, and a subsequent peace overture to Azzam elicited no response,[25] Ben-Gurion went out of his way to underscore Zionism's peaceful intentions. In a string of speeches and interviews, widely publicized by the Jewish media, he sought to dispel the pervasive scaremongering about the likely oppression of the Arab citizens of the prospective Jewish state, vowing that the position of this minority would, in law and in practice, be exactly the same as that of its Jewish majority counterpart. "The Arab will enjoy full civic and political equality," he stated time and again. "He will have the franchise on the same terms as the Jews. He will be eligible for membership in all legislative and executive bodies. He will have access to the public services on the same terms as any Jew."

In line with this conception, committees laying the groundwork for the nascent Jewish state discussed in detail the establishment of an Arabic-language press, the improvement of health in the Arab sector, the incorporation of Arab officials into the government, the integration of Arabs within the police and the ministry of education, and Arab-Jewish cultural and intellectual interaction.[26]

Ben-Gurion brushed aside allegations of aggressive and expansionist Jewish designs on the neighboring Arab states as anathema to the very essence of Zionism. "We respect the independence of the other nations of the Middle East, just as we ask them to respect ours," he said.

> We sincerely hope that our neighbors will leave us to do our work in peace, and that their threats were just rhetorical effusions uttered in the heat of debate. If we are attacked we shall take up the challenge. But we sincerely hope that there will be no need for this. Let there be an end to all those threats of force. They only create an unhappy atmosphere to which all parties concerned are bound to suffer.[27]

To prevent this scenario from becoming a self-fulfilling prophecy, Ben-Gurion instructed the Hagana to exercise the greatest possible restraint so as to prevent violence from spiraling out of control. "For two days now the peace in the country has been disrupted by shootings, arsons, and murders in various places by agitated Arabs," ran a typical Hagana flyer on December 3. "We have been holding back for the time being since we aspire to peace, good neighborly relations, quiet work, and mutual happiness. But be warned: should the bloodletting continue we will be forced to take severe measures against the perpetrators of violence and those responsible for the violation of peace." Two days later, a British intelligence report observed that "so far, the Jews have kept themselves fairly well in hand, but if the Arabs continue their attacks retaliation by the dissidents, probably the Hagana too, will be inevitable."

It was only on December 9, as Arab attacks on Jewish transportation across the country began to have a palpable effect and as the Jewish leadership concluded that the Mufti was gaining control over the Arab public, that the Yishuv began to respond in kind. At a closed meeting on December 10, Israel Galili, who four months earlier had been appointed the Hagana's commander-in-chief, enumerated the main components of the tactical shift: attacks on transportation (for the time being without inflicting human casualties) in order to pressure the Arabs to desist from attacks on Jewish transportation; the destruction of the property of inciters, organizers, and perpetrators of violence; strikes against known bases of armed gangs, and villages or localities serving as springboards for anti-Jewish attacks.[28]

One such action took place on December 9, when a Hagana squad infiltrated the southern village of Karatiya, which had been used as a base for attacks on Jewish traffic in the area, and blew up a building after evacuating its residents. Similar attacks were carried out against the villages of Qazaza, in central Palestine, Silwan and Beit Suriq in the Jerusalem area, and Balad al-Sheik near Haifa, among other places; but a retaliatory operation (on December 18) in the Galilee village of Khisas, in response to the murder of a kibbutz member three days earlier, went terribly wrong as sappers miscalculated the amount of explosives needed for demolishing a building, causing the collapse of a neighboring house and eight fatalities. The Hagana promptly expressed its regret, yet this didn't prevent Ben-Gurion from instructing Galili and his head of operations, Yigael Yadin, to up the ante and develop a more proactive "aggressive defense" that would serve as a deterrent without leading to a widening of the conflict.

They complied, and the general principles of the nascent strategy were agreed in a comprehensive discussion on January 1–2, 1948, chaired by Ben-Gurion and with the participation of top Hagana commanders and Arab affairs experts. These provided, most notably, for active defense through retaliation against perpetrators of aggression while sparing places of worship, hospitals, schools, and the like, that had been used in the course of anti-Jewish attacks; a preference for a few decisive and painful counterstrikes over numerous but comparatively feeble retaliatory actions; the avoidance of escalation in areas that had not already been drawn into the fighting; and a serious effort to hit only culpable parties and sites. When Arab snipers used a mosque to fire on Jewish civilians in Jerusalem's Old City, injuring three people (two of them seriously), local Hagana forces were ordered to hold their fire since "shooting at mosques is absolutely forbidden."[29]

The "dissident" underground organizations (as they were called by the mainstream Yishuv) had fewer scruples: if Jews were to be indiscriminately attacked throughout the country, so would Arabs. Thus, hours after the mob attack on the Jerusalem commercial center on December 2, the 2,000–4,000-strong Irgun Zvai Leumi (National Military Organization, or IZL) set fire to a Jerusalem cinema frequented by Arabs. Ten days later it placed a car bomb in Jerusalem's Old City, killing twenty people and wounding another five. Its smaller counterpart, Lehi (Fighters for the Freedom of Israel), comprising some 500–800 members, used the same method to blow up the headquarters of the Jaffa national committee on January 4, 1948.

On December 30, 1947, IZL fighters hurled a bomb at a group of Arab workers outside the Haifa oil refinery, killing six people and wounding others. Within hours, the 2,000 Arab workers at the plant turned on their 450 Jewish colleagues with axes, iron bars, and firearms, killing 39 and injuring many more.[30] In response, the Hagana raided the village of Balad al-Sheik, whence many of the rioters had come, killing some 60 people.[31]

By the end of 1947, then, Palestine was rapidly sliding into anarchy. "Arab-Jewish violence is now diffused over virtually all of Palestine with the exception of the Tulkarm sub-district," Cunningham reported to London on January 3, 1948. "Figures of casualties from 30 November to 31 December are 450 dead and some 1000 injured, nearly half of the latter seriously. Of the dead 204 are Jews and 208 Arabs. Twelve British soldiers and five British police were killed during this period."[32]

At a Mapai central committee meeting a few days later, Ben-Gurion did not mince his words in underscoring the seriousness of the situation. "We recall disturbances that lasted for three years, from 1936 to 1939, as well as those of August 1929, which, though not as protracted, were starker and destroyed an entire community overnight," he told his fellow party members.

But this time we are confronted with something that didn't exist in 1936, 1929, 1921, or any other year for that matter. This time there are no "riots" or disturbances but real war, pure and simple, and a declared one at that. In our generation, as in the past, there have been "undeclared" wars: the war against us is "declared." The Arab delegates have clearly stated in Lake Success [the temporary UN headquaters in New York], in the press, and in the Arab parliaments that they would wage war on the Jews, and this time we shouldn't doubt their words.

Every war is politically motivated, and the political goal of this war is Arab rule over the whole of Palestine. This basic goal has three aspects: a)

Exterminating and destroying the Yishuv. . . . b) Preventing the establishment of a Jewish state – even in part of the country. . . . c) Should these
two objectives not be achieved – with the Yishuv intact and a Hebrew state
established – the war will aim at reducing the territory of this state in the
Negev, the Galilee, and perhaps in Haifa and other places.[33]

This stark prognosis notwithstanding, the Jewish leadership did not lose
hope of containing the war. At the January 1–2, 1948 meeting, the
consensus among the Arab affairs experts was that the Palestinian Arabs were
staunchly opposed to the conflict – "the villager, the merchant, the worker,
and the citrus-grower didn't want [war] and don't want [it] now" – and were
being drawn into the fighting against their will by a small and militant
minority headed by the Mufti.

The experts differed on the actual balance of forces within Palestinian Arab
society and its operational and political implications: some believed that the
Mufti was counterbalanced by a powerful and strengthening opposition,
which was less concerned with the Arab-Jewish dispute than with winning
power in the prospective Arab state, and which was biding its time in anticipation of the right moment to act; others maintained that the Mufti's gains
had exceeded his expectations and that the opposition was both insubstantial
and unsympathetic to the Jewish cause. Yet there was unanimity that the
Mufti had to be crushed before he managed to set the entire country ablaze
and to implicate the Arab governments more deeply in the conflict, and that
this had to be done through a highly discriminate policy that targeted the
culpable and spared the innocent. In Ben-Gurion's summation: "a) Hitting
perpetrators of attacks – be they a clan, a village or a neighborhood; b) under
no circumstances hurting any Arabs who maintain the peace." These principles were further elaborated in a Hagana circular issued on the same day
(January 2):

> The moral principle – that has never ceased to guide us – as well as the
> imperative of political expediency command us to do our utmost to *avoid*
> killing ordinary civilians and to always hit the criminals themselves, the
> bearers of arms, and the perpetrators of attacks. Our present goal is to
> *isolate* the rioters from the Arab masses. We have no desire for the spread
> of the disturbances and the rallying of the entire Arab public – including
> the various opposition groups, the peace seeking elements, the [urban]
> masses and the peasants – behind the Mufti and his gangs.[34]

On January 6, Ben-Gurion told Cunningham that "the Hagana would only
use force for self-defense" and that "even now most of the Arab people do not

wish to follow the Mufti. . . . The felaheen [i.e., rural population] [do] not want trouble and the Jews [a]re not going to provoke them." Indeed, in a report on the situation in Palestine, written on March 23, 1948, ALA commander-in-chief Safwat noted with some astonishment that, despite their overwhelming superiority over the Palestinian Arabs, "the Jews have constantly endeavored to narrow the theater of operations" and "have not attacked a single Arab village unless provoked by it." His explanation: the belief that self-restraint was conducive to eventual Arab acquiescence in the existence of a Jewish state in line with the partition resolution, fear of British military intervention in the event of an Arab collapse, and a desire to preserve Jewish strength for the impending pan-Arab invasion after the British withdrawal.[35]

These observations were not far off the mark. On February 3, 1948, Ben-Gurion told a Zionist gathering that "most of the Palestinian Arabs have refused, and still refuse, to be drawn into the fighting." Three weeks later he argued in a special public message that "we consider those Arabs fighting against us victims of incitement and irredentism rather than an historical enemy." In mid-March, a Jewish Agency spokesman stated that the "provisional cabinet for the Jewish state," approved a few days earlier, was "not considered final because the Jewish authorities still intend to admit representatives of [the] Arabs residing in the Jewish state." This was followed two days later by a statement that the provisional cabinet had no intention of expelling Arabs from the prospective Jewish state but considered them equal citizens, whose interests and livelihood would be safeguarded and who would participate in the government on an equal footing.

As late as April 7, two days after the Hagana had launched its largest operation in the war up to that point, Ben-Gurion told the World Zionist Executive that despite the grievous situation the key principles of the Jewish political program remained unchanged: a) establishment of a Jewish state; b) Arab-Jewish cooperation; and c) reliance on the United Nations and striving for world peace. He conceded that in the present circumstances the prospects of Arab-Jewish cooperation were not particularly high, especially since the conflict had recently assumed far wider proportions with the growing involvement of the *fellaheen* and the working classes in the fighting. Yet he maintained that:

we should not despair of the possibility of mutual understanding provided a Jewish state is established and we prove – through reliance on our own strength rather than on international backing – that we are invincible and indestructible. . . . Once the Jewish people has shown the ability to establish its own state and to defend it – the Arab world will recognize the feasibility and value of Arab-Jewish cooperation. The Arabs need us no less than we need them.[36]

In line with this thinking, on April 1, at Ben-Gurion's personal authorization and guidance, one of his senior Arab experts, Josh Palmon, met with Qawuqji in an attempt to find common ground for the cessation of hostilities. The two had never met before, but a couple of years earlier Palmon had passed on to Qawuqji, via an Arab intermediary, a letter from the Mufti to the Nazi foreign minister, Joachim von Ribbentrop, found in the Nazi archives after the war. In the letter, Hajj Amin, who apparently resented the high esteem accorded by the Nazis to his fellow fugitive, defamed Qawuqji and two prominent Palestinian brothers, who also spent the war years in Germany, leading to their incarceration by the Nazis and the death of one of the siblings.

Grateful for the information, which confirmed his earlier suspicions of the Mufti, Qawuqji had asked to meet Palmon at the time, but their scheduled rendezvous was overtaken by events. Now that they were about to meet at long last, albeit in the presence of other Arab officers as a private meeting would have compromised Qawuqji's position, Palmon hoped that the latter's hatred of, and contempt for, the Mufti would make him amenable to the Jewish peace overture. Indeed, despite the presence of his subordinates at the meeting, Qawuqji was not deterred from disparaging the Mufti's murderous practices and political ambitions, "which are not in the interests of the Arab nation and which any patriotic Arab should oppose." He was no more complimentary of Abdel Qader, who was constantly scheming against him. "I don't care if your people fight him," he told Palmon. "In fact, I hope you do fight him and give him a good lesson. If you do, he is not going to be able to count on me for any help."

As Palmon began to raise his hopes, however, Qawuqji launched into a lengthy diatribe about the supposed evils of Zionism, which in his view was based on "arrogance and unreasonableness." The Zionists sought to dominate the entire Arab world as a bridgehead of Western imperialism, he argued, but the Arabs would never accept this alien implant in their midst and would not hesitate to shed their blood to uproot it. Even if the Jews succeeded in accomplishing their goal in the short term, this would hardly be the end of the story. The Arabs were prepared to continue fighting for decades, just as their ancestors had done in the past, until they prevailed over the latest foreign invader.

Palmon's explanation that Zionism was a constructive and enterprising national liberation movement seeking peaceful coexistence rather than regional domination fell on deaf ears. There was only one way for the Jews to be accepted: abandonment of their claim to statehood and acquiescence in a minority status within the Arab world, as had been the case for a millennium. In such circumstances, they could play a prominent role in the economic and political renaissance of the Arabs commensurate with their natural talents and enterprising spirit. "Do not think for a moment that you will find anyone from among the Arab ranks who will cooperate with you," Qawuqji warned Palmon. "Not a single Arab, not even the king [Abdullah], can do you any good and strengthen your position, if this is to be done against the general will of the Arab world."[37]

The Jewish attempts to bring about a cessation of hostilities took place against a steady escalation in the fighting. Notwithstanding a number of Jewish achievements, notably the destruction of a large arms shipment from Lebanon to Haifa,[38] the intensification of Arab attacks on Jewish transportation to Jerusalem and the Negev during the month of March led to the virtual isolation of these areas. On March 18, a supply convoy on its way to the Hartuv kibbutz, near Jerusalem, was ambushed on its return and eleven fighters were killed. Six days later, a similar attack on a convoy to the outlying neighborhood of Atarot exacted fourteen fatalities and eleven casualties. On the same day, a large Jewish convoy to Jerusalem was forced to turn back at the narrow ravine of Bab al-Wad (Gate of the Valley), where the coastal road sharply ascends toward Jerusalem, leaving behind fourteen burned-out homemade armored cars. Meanwhile the Hagana had to abandon the use of the southern coastal road, which ran through densely populated Arab areas, leaving the Negev totally severed from the rest of the Yishuv. In the north, a convoy from Haifa to the besieged Yehiam kibbutz was ambushed near the Arab village of Kabri. The first few vehicles managed to break through, but the rest of the convoy was trapped and all forty-six crew members were killed and their bodies mutilated.

A particularly painful setback was suffered on March 28, when a large supply convoy (comprising thirty-seven trucks and fourteen homemade armored cars) returning from the Etzion bloc to Jerusalem was trapped at a roadblock south of the city. Leaving their vehicles, the crew took up positions inside a deserted building named after the Prophet Daniel (Nabi Daniel), whence they fought back successive assaults by thousands of armed Arabs. The battle raged for nearly twenty-four hours, by which time the defenders had almost run out of ammunition and had lost all hope of being reinforced. With fifteen dead and scores more wounded (the Arab casualty toll was twenty-five dead and sixty wounded), they were eventually evacuated by the British army to Jerusalem, leaving behind their cars and weapons, which were surrendered to the Arabs.[39]

Since the convoy included most of the Yishuv's reservoir of homemade armored cars that had maintained communication links between Tel Aviv and Jerusalem, their loss meant the effective severance of Jerusalem from the coastal plain. As if to underscore this bitter reality, yet another convoy that tried to break through from the village of Hulda (on March 31) was ambushed and forced back after suffering twenty-four fatalities. In the course of a single week, the Jews lost more than 100 fighters in the battle over the roads. "The supply situation in Jerusalem is horrific after the loss of the Kfar Etzion convoy," the Hagana's Jerusalem command cabled Ben-Gurion on March 28. "An utmost effort must be made without delay to resupply the city already at the beginning of this week." Other telegrams reported rapidly spreading panic and warned of possible food riots, should the city not be immediately resupplied. "We're approaching you with an unreserved demand to mobilize all available armored vehicles for Jerusalem's supply," a senior Jerusalem official wrote to Bernard Joseph, soon to become the city's military governor. "We emphasize most emphatically that Jerusalem is already hungry; if, Heaven forbid, the population's morale is broken, the city's defense may well collapse."[40]

By April 1948, then, the Jewish position had become extremely precarious. True, for all their numerous assaults, the Arabs had failed to occupy a single Jewish neighborhood or village. Nor did they manage to gain the upper hand in the ongoing fighting in Palestine's main urban centers – Jaffa, Haifa, and Jerusalem – which were rapidly emptying of their Arab inhabitants. Yet the Yishuv was beginning to reel from the war's heavy human and material cost, having suffered more than 900 fatalities and 1,858 wounded, compared with 967 and 1,911 Arab casualties, respectively.[41] Given that Palestine's Jewry was roughly half the size of its Arab counterpart, these losses were proportionately twice as heavy as those suffered by the latter.

The impact of this human toll was further exacerbated by the setbacks of late March. There were manifestations of declining morale and growing disorientation, and doubts were voiced about the Yishuv's ability to weather the storm. Most alarmingly, given the siege around Jewish Jerusalem and the attendant shortages in basic commodities, as well as in weapons and ammunition, the possibility of the city's fall could no longer be ignored unless dramatic action was immediately taken. "It is becoming increasingly apparent that the Yishuv and its leaders are deeply worried about the future," read a British report.

The 100,000 Jews of Jerusalem have been held to ransom and it is doubtful whether the Arab economic blockade of the city can be broken by Jewish forces alone. If the Jewish leaders are not prepared to sacrifice the 100,000 Jews of Jerusalem, then they must concede, however unwillingly, that the

Arabs have won the second round in the struggle which began with a Jewish victory in the first round on the 29th November.[42]

"I presume that if you are not doing [more] to help Jerusalem you are not in a position to do so," David Shaltiel, the city's commander, wrote to Ben-Gurion and the Hagana top echelon on March 28. "But it is my duty to inform you that should we fail to vacate the disconnected neighborhoods, should you fail to send real reinforcements – commanders, fighters, weapons, armored cars, and supplies – and should the city remain without food and people capable of organizing its effective distribution (not amateurish apparatchiks), Jerusalem will not hold out even until May 15." "Please accept this letter as an appeal emanating exclusively from a sense of responsibility for Jerusalem and its 100,000 Jews," Shaltiel pleaded. "It is written by a man whom you have known for many years and who, as you know full well, is not a defeatist or a pacifist. . . . [But] I cannot assume responsibility for sustaining the line you assigned me, and, I think, no one in the world can shoulder such a responsibility."[43]

To make matters worse, the US administration seemed to be backtracking from its earlier support for partition. The creation of a Jewish state had always been anathema to American foreign policy and defense department officials. Reluctant to alienate the oil-rich and strategically located Arab states, not to mention the powerful US oil companies, and apprehensive of the possibility of having to send American troops to the rescue of the nascent Jewish state were it to be overwhelmed by its Arab neighbors, they had done their utmost to abort the partition of Palestine – and, failing that, to reduce the territory of the prospective Jewish state to the barest minimum – only to be overruled by President Truman. When secretary of defense James Forrestal reminded the latter of the importance of Arab oil for US strategic interests, Truman said that "he would handle the situation in the light of justice, not oil."[44]

Now that the Palestinian Arabs seemed to be gaining the upper hand, even without the direct intervention of the Arab states, the bureaucrats got their way. On March 19, the United States representative to the United Nations, Warren Austin, announced that since the conflict in Palestine had proved that partition was no longer possible, the country should be placed under a United Nations trusteeship.

In these circumstances, an early operational breakthrough became, literally, a matter of life and death for the Yishuv. As the Hagana's chief of operations, Yigael Yadin, put it in a memo submitted to Ben-Gurion on April 1: "Thus far the course of the fighting has been dictated by the enemy and we have been unable, up to this moment, to influence the strategic and operational course of the confrontation, which has evolved from disturbances to war between semi-regular forces. The only solution is to seize the operational initiative with a view to defeating the enemy."[45]

Already in mid-March the Hagana had adopted a new strategy, codenamed Plan D, which sought to turn the tables on the Arabs by seizing the operational initiative. In line with this thinking, it was decided, at a late-night meeting in Ben-Gurion's Tel Aviv flat on March 31–April 1, to breach the Arab siege of Jerusalem by securing a corridor on both sides of the Tel Aviv-Jerusalem road, ranging in width from 10 km (6 miles) in the coastal plain to 3 km (2 miles) in the mountains. Operation Nahshon, as this particular maneuver was named, constituted a turning point in the Yishuv's conduct of the war, from a defensive to an offensive strategy, and the Hagana's debut as a conventional military force. Until then, its operations had never been above the company level. Now, at Ben-Gurion's insistence, a brigade-size assault was to be mounted, involving some 1,500 fighters organized in three battalions. This in turn necessitated the dilution of Jewish forces elsewhere in the country, but Ben-Gurion saw no alternative. "This is the decisive war now," he warned his commanders as they were deliberating over the operation. "The fall of Jewish Jerusalem can deal the Yishuv a mortal blow. The Arabs understand this and will concentrate large forces in order to sever the transportation [to the city]. We must take all fighters who are not absolutely indispensable in the central sector, in Tel Aviv and in the south, and to send them with their weapons to the Hulda-Bab al-Wad-Jerusalem road."[46]

Launched on April 5, Operation Nahshon was preceded by two subsidiary local actions. The first was the capture, on the night of April 2–3, of the strategic village of Qastel which dominated the approaches to Jerusalem about 8 km (5 miles) to the west of the city. The second, of no less importance, was the blowing up of Salame's headquarters in the city of Ramle in the early hours of April 5. The destruction of this heavily fortified and guarded base, in which some thirty Arab fighters were killed, dealt a powerful blow to Salame's prestige and prevented his forces from playing an active role in the fighting over the Jerusalem road. By April 15, when Operation Nahshon came to an end, the Jewish forces had managed to occupy a number of Arab villages along the Tel Aviv-Jerusalem road and to get three large convoys of food and weapons into Jerusalem.

Fighting was particularly intense around Qastel. The first Arab village conquered by the Jews since the outbreak of hostilities and a highly important one at that, its fall struck the Arab leadership like a bombshell. At a special meeting of the Arab League's technical committee, attended by the Mufti, Azzam, and Lebanon's prime minister, Riyad Sulh, in addition to the committee's regular members, Safwat lambasted the Jerusalem district commander Abdel Qader. "You must recapture Qastel," he said. "But if you consider yourself unequal to the task, do let us know and we'll assign the mission to Qawuqji."

This was too much for Abdel Qader, who had already instructed his deputy, Kemal Erekat, to retake the site. "Qastel is a foreign name meaning a castle, and it is no mean feat to conquer a castle with the few Italian rifles and meager ammunition at our disposal," he retorted. "Give me the weapons I asked for and I'll restore the village." As the committee members remained unimpressed, knowing as they did that Abdel Qader's forces were more numerous and better equipped than he would have them believe, and as Safwat insisted on rushing Qawuqji's artillery to the Jerusalem front, Abdel Qader exploded. "You are all traitors and criminals," he shouted, throwing a map at the Syrian minister of defense. "You will go down in history as those who have lost Palestine. I will recapture Qastel, even if this results in my own death and the death of many of my fighters."

Taking his leave, Abdel Qader arrived in Jerusalem in the early afternoon of April 7. After a short consultation he then left for Qastel to take command of the fighting, only to be killed late that night, or in the early morning of April 8, having accidentally stumbled across a Jewish position. "He lost his way and, at the head of a four-man group, came across a site manned by a squad of ours," Ben-Gurion recorded in his diary. "Our boys immediately hit three of them; Abdel Qader raised his hands and begged for his life; our boys didn't know who he was and shot him. Only upon checking his papers did they realize who he actually was."[47]

The implications of Abdel Qader's death for the Palestinian Arab struggle extended well beyond the loss of a commanding personality or the fall of a strategic village. It led to a widespread loss of purpose and demoralization, with some dignitaries blaming the Mufti for the ongoing bloodshed and mooting the hitherto unspeakable idea of acquiescing in a Jewish state in a small part of Palestine. At the same time a cry for revenge engulfed Arab society as imaginary stories about the decapitation and mutilation of Abdel Qader's body circulated widely. Thousands of mourners paid their respects at the fallen leader's funeral.

In an ironic twist, a figure who had proved highly controversial during his lifetime, whose military record had been far from a success story, and whose recruitment efforts had been spurned by numerous villages and towns (two months before his death Abdel Qader had been widely ridiculed in local coffee houses as "Corporal Qader"),[48] was instantaneously transformed into a national hero by virtue of his death. "The fortunes of the Palestinians are astonishingly mercurial," commented a British intelligence report. "Two weeks ago the Jews were in the depths of despair and the Arabs jubilant. The situation today is completely reversed – but always liable to a further change. The turning point was the Hagana's capture of Qastel and the death of Abdel Qader Husseini, which caused wholesale disintegration in the Jerusalem Arab command."[49]

A further blow to Arab morale was dealt on April 9, the day after Abdel Qader's death, when IZL and Lehi fighters occupied the village of Deir Yasin, on the outskirts of Jerusalem, killing in the process some 100 people, including women and children.[50] Although the IZL categorically denied any massacres, claiming that the casualties had been sustained in the course of heavy fighting,[51] the Jewish Agency and the Hagana immediately expressed their disgust and regret.[52] This failed to satisfy the Arabs. Exacting swift revenge by killing (on April 13) seventy-seven Jewish nurses and doctors en route to the Hadassah hospital on Mount Scopus,[53] they capitalized on the tragedy in an attempt to reap immediate political gains. In subsequent decades, Deir Yasin would become the most effective Arab propaganda tool against Israel. At the time, however, the widely exaggerated descriptions of Jewish atrocities, especially of alleged rapes of women that never took place, spread panic across Palestinian society and intensified the ongoing mass flight.[54]

No less detrimental to the Palestinian war effort was the ALA's abortive attempt to occupy the Mishmar Haemek kibbutz in the western Galilee. Reeling from the humiliating February defeat at Tirat Zvi, where some sixty Arab fighters were killed compared with a single Jewish fatality, Qawuqji viewed the Hagana's preoccupation with Operation Nahshon as a golden opportunity to prove his force's mettle. The choice of Mishmar Haemek could not have been better from a military point of view. Lying in the foothills of Mount Ephraim, opposite the Jezreel valley, the kibbutz was overlooked by a number of Arab villages and flanked by others. Its conquest would have allowed the Arabs to isolate the strategic city of Haifa by blocking the Wadi Milleh valley, through which all Jewish traffic between Tel Aviv and Haifa had to pass following the closure of Jewish transportation on the country's main south-north artery along the Mediterranean. On a broader level, the operation was seen by its planners as inaugurating a nationwide assault on Jewish rural localities that would force the Yishuv to abandon its national aspirations and sue for minority status in an Arab Palestine.[55]

In the early hours of April 4, the ALA launched a heavy artillery barrage on Mishmar Haemek, using seven field guns from Syria. This was followed by an attack by some 1,000 soldiers, which was contained by the defenders at the village perimeter. A second assault, on the night of April 6–7, was stopped the next morning by the British, who mediated a twenty-four-hour ceasefire for the evacuation of women, children, and wounded from the kibbutz. On April 8, the ALA headquarters claimed total victory: "The Arab flag flies over

Mishmar Haemek. The Iraqi commander has forced the Jews to leave their shelters and surrender themselves. The Arab forces are busy counting the captured weapons, equipment, and supplies." Three days later, Qawuqji gloated in a radio broadcast that "after preliminary and sporadic skirmishes I shall give the Zionists a blow from which they will never recover." Yet as the residents of the neighboring Arab city of Jenin began to celebrate the alleged triumph, a Hagana infantry battalion counterattacked and captured several Arab villages and strongholds in the mountains above and to the rear of the kibbutz. For the next five days and nights the two sides battled over these sites, with the Jews taking them by night and the Arabs using their numerical and material superiority to regain them the following day; one stronghold was subjected to no fewer than eleven consecutive Arab attacks.

In his growing desperation, on April 12 Qawuqji mounted yet another large-scale assault on the kibbutz, only to find his forces routed and in danger of encirclement. Realizing that all was lost, he ordered a hasty retreat to Jenin. Meanwhile Hagana forces defeated an attack by a Druze battalion on a neighboring kibbutz aimed at relieving the pressure on the ALA. On April 18, Ben-Gurion recorded in his diary:

> Qawuqji was roundly routed though our units are exhausted (there were no reserve forces whatever). Qawuqji's defeat was caused by: lack of [solid] military thinking and Arab inability to prosecute a [comprehensive] military campaign. We prevailed despite an inferiority of 1:3 in manpower and 1:8 in firepower (Qawuqji had 7 artillery pieces and 12 armored cars). Qawuqji had three battalions of 700–800 fighters each. We had 340 Palmah fighters (including 70 non-fighting personnel), and 300 Hish fighters.[56]

Five months after waging his war of annihilation on the Yishuv, the Mufti's strategy had backfired in grand style. His forces, together with the ALA, had been routed, and Palestinian Arab society had been profoundly shattered, with tens of thousands of terrified and disorientated Arabs taking to the road. On April 18, another milestone in the war was passed when, after a few days of fighting, the Hagana made its first urban gain, capturing the mixed-population city of Tiberias, overlooking the Sea of Galilee, where some 6,000 Jews and about as many Arabs were living.

Ignoring pleas by the local Jewish leadership to stay put, the Arabs – acting on the orders of the Nazareth National Committee and on the advice of local British commanders – chose to leave Tiberias en masse and were evacuated by the British army.[57] The same scenario was to recur within days, on a far wider scale, in the city of Haifa, in a move that was to have a profound impact on the general course of the war.

CHAPTER 6

Fleeing Haifa

"Every effort is being made by the Jews to persuade the Arab populace to stay and carry on with their normal lives, to get their shops and businesses open and to be assured that their lives and interests will be safe."

British district superintendent of police, April 1948

From a marginal site containing some 1,000 people at the turn of the nineteenth century, the smallest of Palestine's twelve significant towns, by 1947 Haifa had developed into a major center of some 145,000 residents – 70,910 Arabs (41,000 Muslims, 29,910 Christians) and 74,230 Jews – second only to Jerusalem in national importance, and in certain respects even superior to it.[1] The city constituted the main socio-economic and administrative center in northern Palestine for both Arabs and Jews. It was one of the primary ports of the eastern Mediterranean, the hub of Palestine's railway system, the site of the country's oil refinery, and a formidable industrial center.

As such, it was evident to all that, though assigned by the UN partition resolution to the prospective Jewish state, Haifa's fate would be sealed by force of arms after the termination of the mandate. No sooner had the UN voted on partition than the city became engulfed in intermittent violence that pitted Arab fighters, recruited locally as well as from neighboring Arab countries, against the Hagana forces. Hostilities would reach their peak on April 21–22, when the Arab war effort collapsed overnight, triggering a mass exodus. But in fact Arab flight from Haifa began well before the outbreak of these hostilities, and even before the UN partition resolution.

On October 23, 1947, over a month earlier, a British intelligence brief was already noting that "leading Arab personalities are acting on the assumption that disturbances are near at hand, and have already evacuated their families to neighboring Arab countries."[2] By November 21, as the UN General Assembly was getting ready to vote, not only "leading Arab personalities" but "many Arabs of Haifa" were reported to be "evacuating their families to neighboring Arab countries in anticipation of the period of disorder they foresee."[3] And as the violent Arab reaction to the UN resolution gathered force, eradicating any hope of its peaceful implementation, this stream of refugees turned into a flood.

By mid-December 1947, some 15,000–20,000 Arabs had fled. A month later, according to Arab sources, this had swollen to 25,000 people, creating severe hardship for those remaining.[4] Economic and commercial activity ground to a halt as the wealthier classes converted their assets into gold or US dollars and transferred them abroad. Merchants and industrialists moved their businesses to Egypt, Syria, or Lebanon, causing unemployment and shortages in basic necessities. Entire areas were emptied of their residents.

The situation was exacerbated by the deep schisms within the Arab populace. Not only did the city's Muslims and Christians lead a mutually antagonistic and largely segregated existence, but both communities were beset by a string of socio-economic and religious divisions – between rich and poor, veterans and newcomers, urbanites and villagers, and so on and so forth. The Christian community, in particular, was fragmented into a colorful mosaic of sects, the largest and most affluent being the Greek Catholics, followed by the Greek Orthodox, the Maronites, and a string of smaller groups such as Protestants, Roman Catholics, and Armenians. This sectarianism prevented the development of an overarching Christian identity, as most groups had distinct religious, social, and educational institutions.

The Muslims fared no better. Though less fractured than their Christian brethren, they were beset by power struggles among prominent families and were deeply alienated from their poor co-religionists who streamed into the city in the 1930s and the 1940s. Unaccustomed to city life, socially and economically attached to their villages, and given a cold shoulder by the Haifa veterans, the new arrivals quickly developed into a distinct underclass that scarcely interacted with the established urbanites, maintaining instead a rural lifestyle buttressed by separate social networks based on their villages of origin. They regularly returned to these villages for seasonal work (notably at harvest times), married spouses from their birthplaces, established their own charitable societies and social venues, and congregated with their kinsmen in both work places and residential areas, so much so that entire neighborhoods in Haifa came to be known by their residents' places of origin.[5]

Thus it was that, when fighting for the city ensued, the Haifa Arabs did not constitute a cohesive entity but rather an amalgam of parallel groups, each with its own interests, institutions, and leaders. The Christians, erecting clear boundaries between themselves and the Muslims, refused to feed the ALA's Syrian, Lebanese, and Iraqi fighters when they arrived to wrest the city from the Jews, asserted their determination not to attack Jewish forces unless attacked first, and established a special guard to protect themselves from

Muslim violence. Added to this was a growing lawlessness, including pandemic looting of deserted properties.[6]

Nor did the public display excessive confidence in either its local leadership or the AHC. Rumors were rife about the sexual exploits of Bishop George Hakim, head of the Greek Catholic Church in northern Palestine, as well as about the ruthless profiteering of the prominent Islamist activist Sheik Muhammad Nimr Khatib, which allegedly compromised his national and religious convictions. The rosy stories emanating from the AHC Cairo headquarters of pan-Arab solidarity and commitment to the Palestine cause were met with skepticism. So was the praise heaped on the anti-Jewish economic boycott: not only did most of the Haifa Arabs continue to shop in Jewish neighborhoods in defiance of the boycott, but, bowing to the inevitable, the local boycott committee authorized this practice wherever certain products were unavailable in Arab areas, at times charging a handsome commission for the issuance of such permits. Moreover, in June 1947 the committee temporarily ceased its activities in a stark admission of its own ineffectiveness and divisions.

Lofty nationalist rhetoric left many unimpressed. The selling of lands to Jews continued, if covertly, despite the Mufti's religious ruling (*fatwa*) prohibiting such acts and the repeated death threats from his loyalists. There was muttering about the need for Arab-Jewish understanding and tacit satisfaction with the renewed activities of the anti-Husseini opposition. Even when the specter of violence began to loom large following UNSCOP's majority recommendation on partition, many Haifa Arabs doubted its prudence and utility given their longtime coexistence with their Jewish neighbors and fears of Jewish military might. When, in August 1947, violent clashes between Arabs and Jews broke out along the Tel Aviv-Jaffa boundary, a special meeting of Haifa's Arab leaders condemned the incidents and instructed the city's imams to urge the public, in their Friday sermons, to exercise the utmost restraint – which they did. Even the Haifa branch of the militant Islamist group the Muslim Brothers sent its leader to Jaffa to convince the religious authorities there to issue a public plea for the cessation of violence.[7]

At the time, the official leadership of the Haifa Arabs was a fifteen-member National Committee (NC), established on December 2, 1947, and headed by Rashid Hajj Ibrahim, a scion of a respected family of North African origin, whose public activity dated back to Ottoman times. Although the Committee strove to curb the mass flight, urging residents to stay put and castigating those who fled – occasionally, these warnings were backed up by the torching of escapees' belongings – its remonstrations proved of no avail.[8]

To be sure, the NC itself hardly constituted a model of commitment or self-sacrifice. Its members seemed to view their participation in the Committee as a hobby or a charitable activity undertaken in one's free time, rather than the critical national endeavor it was supposed to be. Scarcely a meeting was attended by all members, with apologies for absence citing other commitments ranging from business trips, to a convalescence retreat, to participation in a meeting of the Anti-Tuberculosis League. It was only at the NC's twenty-seventh meeting, more than two months after the commencement of its activities, that Ibrahim announced his intention to devote six days a week (apart from Sundays) to its affairs and NC members were gently reminded not to absent themselves from meetings.[9]

Moreover, affluent though they were, NC members, while taking care to reimburse themselves for the smallest expense, rarely contributed financially to the national struggle. Nor did Muhammad Hamad Hunaiti, a young Transjordanian officer who resigned his commission as a lieutenant in the Arab Legion to become the city's commander only after extracting a generous remuneration package from the NC, including a handsome salary, comfortable accommodation, a car, and a telephone. "His terms were harsh," recalled Muhammad Nimr Khatib, the NC's most militant member and Hunaiti's personal friend. "But we accepted them all, anxious as we were for a military commander."[10]

Transcripts of NC meetings do not exactly convey a grasp of the severity of the situation: they tend to be taken up instead with trivialities, from the placement of an office partition, to the purchase of library books, to the payment to a certain individual of £1.29 (£34 in today's terms) in travel expenses, to the return of a typewriter borrowed by the Committee. As late as March 16, the NC was discussing such minor matters as the purchase of chairs (for £34.25), books (with vouchers worth £8), and a typewriter, as well as the mode of payment of the monthly rent on its office. In its last meeting, on April 13, nine days before the fall of Haifa, the NC found the time to approve the purchase of £5.40 worth of stationery.[11]

Even when the committee did try to deal with the endemic violence in which the town was embroiled, its efforts were repeatedly undermined by the sheer number of armed groups operating in defiance of its authority, by infighting between its own moderates and militants, and by the total lack of coordination, if not outright hostility, between the Committee and its parent body, the Cairo-based, Mufti-controlled AHC. Giving his own terrorists free rein in Haifa, the Mufti paid no attention to the NC's requests and recommendations.

Not that the Committee was amenable to Haifa's inclusion within the prospective Jewish state, as envisaged by the partition resolution, or that it eschewed violence as a means to avert this eventuality.[12] When on December 12, 1947, the city's Jewish mayor, Shabtai Levy, suggested the issuance of a joint Arab-Jewish proclamation urging the population to forgo violence, and expressed his readiness, as representative of the Jewish community, to negotiate a ceasefire agreement with an authorized Arab body, the NC rejected his proposal. "We have been toiling day and night to maintain [peace and] quiet and to implement a high, unified Arab policy regardless of the incitement by the Jewish traitors," argued Ibrahim. "There is no way we can negotiate with the Jews. Let them take care of their interests and we'll ensure our security."[13]

Matters came to a head in mid-January 1948 following the bombing of a Jewish commercial center in which eight people were killed and scores of others wounded. Carried out by the Mufti's local supporters, the atrocity brought to an abrupt end the tenuous truce, organized under pressure from the British in late December, and drove a few hundred (mostly Christian) families to flee the city.[14] At the NC's meeting on January 18, Ibrahim left little doubt as to who, in his opinion, was culpable for this recent deterioration. "While we were navigating the ship with your help and maintaining its balance, a sudden storm has thrown us off course," he told his colleagues, insisting that his words be recorded verbatim as evidence for future generations. "And this was done by people claiming association with the AHC and other officials abroad." In Ibrahim's view, the severity of the situation left the NC no choice but to send a delegation to Cairo to ascertain whether the AHC had indeed been behind the latest bombing and to impress upon the Mufti the seriousness of the situation. Were the supreme leader of the Palestinian Arabs to remain impervious to the city's predicament, he was to be warned that, if terrorist activity did not cease, the result would be the eventual disappearance of the entire Haifa community.[15]

The delegates pleaded to no avail. Though evidently shaken by the stark picture they painted, the Mufti decried the request for an armistice as tantamount to surrender. He agreed to the evacuation of women and children from danger zones so as to reduce casualties, but ordered the NC to intensify its efforts to shore up the city's defenses, to stop the mass exodus, and to urge those who had fled to return. As a sweetener, the Mufti denied any connection with the January bombing and endorsed the NC as Haifa's supreme political and military decision-making body, promising to put under its command a soon-to-be-formed 500-strong force.[16]

This failed to impress the Haifa population. Notwithstanding the arrival of fresh arms shipments from Syria, Lebanon, and Egypt, together with military reinforcements, a general sense of foreboding engulfed the city, especially the Christian community. The Mufti's rejection of the delegation's request for emergency food supplies, coupled with the growing lawlessness in the Arab districts, drove many merchants to begin preparations to leave Haifa. Neither did Hajj Amin, for all his feigned affability, change his attitude toward the NC or pressure his Haifa loyalists to cease hostilities. As early as October 1947, he had rejected local requests for funds for the purchase of arms on the pretext that the matter had been entrusted to the Arab League. But when, two months later, the League sent some 600 rifles for the Haifa Arabs, only a fifth reached their destination: the rest were distributed elsewhere at the Mufti's instructions.[17]

When the NC appointed Hunaiti as Haifa's military commander, it was reprimanded by the Mufti's Beirut office for overstepping its authority and informed that an Iraqi officer, at the head of an armed group, was on his way to assume command of the city's defense. Although Ibrahim managed to talk the group into quitting Haifa for the neighboring village of Shafa Amr, the episode eroded the already strained relations between the AHC and the Committee, which correctly interpreted the situation as a show of no confidence in its ability to direct Haifa's military affairs. Phone conversations between Ibrahim and the Mufti, as well as several meetings in Cairo between Khatib and the supreme Palestinian leader, yielded no practical results. Before long Ibrahim was pleading with the Arab League and the Syrian government for weapons and tighter control of the Arab factions in Haifa, especially those dominated by the Mufti, and threatening to resign his post unless these were brought to heel. This act of insubordination did not pass unnoticed, and on January 29 the NC was peremptorily ordered to avoid any contact with the Arab states or the League, as this was the exclusive prerogative of the AHC in its capacity as the effective "government" of the Palestinian Arabs.[18]

Meanwhile, as this power tussle was going on, further waves of Arab residents fled Haifa. Following the demolition of several houses in the Wadi Nisnas area in early February, for instance, the residents complained to Hunaiti of the shortage of guards, only to be told that he would not protect the properties of owners who had fled the country. Since the residents had no intention of being penalized for the actions of their absentee landlords, they unceremoniously fled their homes, shortly to be followed by residents of the Wadi Rushmiya, Wadi Salib, and Halisa neighborhoods.[19] In a revealing incident, Christian residents beat up a group of Arab fighters seeking to use their street for the shelling of Jewish targets. Lawlessness spiraled to new heights, with the foreign irregulars stationed in the city unabashedly exploiting their position to abuse the very people they had been brought in to defend.

The alarmed Mufti instructed the NC to stamp out the burgeoning lawlessness.[20] Yet the Committee's attempt to enforce tighter discipline by prohibiting individual use of weapons and authorizing its militia, the

National Guard, to arrest persons bearing arms in public places and to open fire on undisciplined crowds backfired. The Guard was held in contempt by the Haifa populace on account of its repeated military failures and implication in countless acts of lawlessness and corruption, notably the plundering of deserted properties. Panic spread across the city, with many searching in vain for the few removal vans in the city; those who were fortunate enough to find a vehicle had to pay an exorbitant price for a delivery to the neighboring city of Nazareth; others seeking to flee to the more remote Nablus were informed that the city was already swarming with refugees.[21]

In these circumstances, the NC apparently gave up hope of stemming further flight. Shortly after the return of the delegation from Cairo, a proposal was passed urging improvements in the condition of Palestinian refugees in the Arab states where they now found themselves, and requesting help in settling them there. This was momentous indeed: the official leadership of the second largest Arab community in mandate Palestine was not only condoning mass flight but suggesting that Arab refugee status be, however temporarily, institutionalized. As the months passed and Britain's departure from Palestine neared, such attitudes gained further currency. Even the Mufti, who had warned that "the flight of . . . families abroad will weaken the morale of our noble, struggling nation," was not averse to the evacuation of the non-fighting populace. In March 1948, the AHC evidently ordered the removal of women and children from Haifa; a special committee was established in Syria and Lebanon to oversee the operation, and preparations began in earnest with the chartering of a ship from an Egyptian company.[22]

While the organized evacuation was moving slowly, the flight from the city gained momentum following a further escalation in the fighting. On March 17, the Hagana ambushed a large arms and ammunition convoy from Syria, killing fourteen Arab fighters, including Hunaiti, and destroying the entire shipment. This was a severe blow to Arab morale, not least since it was viewed as largely self-inflicted. During a visit to Muhammad Nimr Khatib in a Beirut hospital where the sheik was recuperating after a Hagana attempt on his life, Hunaiti had been warned not to expose himself, and the convoy, to the unnecessary risks attending land travel, given the densely populated Jewish neighborhoods en route to Haifa; the warning was repeated as the convoy reached Acre. Yet not only did Hunaiti fail to heed the advice, he seemed to do everything within his power to bring about his own demise. Already during his stay in Beirut he had attracted the Hagana's attention to his mission by posing for a local newspaper photographer with the newly acquired weapons under the provocative caption "Where are you, O cowardly Jew?" Then, upon arriving at the border post of Ras Naqura, he phoned his Haifa headquarters to inform them of the convoy's travel plans – a call that was monitored by the Hagana, which quickly organized the ambush.[23]

The Arabs reacted to this setback by exploding a car bomb near a Jewish commercial building, killing six people and wounding twenty-eight. With the Hagana responding in kind a few days later, yet another torrent of people tried to pour out of Haifa. Long queues besieged the Syrian and Lebanese consulates, only to be told that no visas were on offer, especially to men between the ages of sixteen and sixty. Only women, children, and the elderly, as well as officials, holding travel permits from the AHC, were allowed entry. Flight was further hampered by the formidable obstacles to land travel to Lebanon: vehicular traffic had stopped almost completely while the railway line was sabotaged. Those fortunate enough to secure a visa, including a large number of Christian municipal officials, vied for a place on the cramped boats sailing to Lebanon; the less fortunate made their way to the increasingly congested Acre; the rest congregated in what were viewed as the safer parts of Haifa.[24]

By early April 1948, according to Hajj Ibrahim, the city's Arab populace had dwindled to some 35,000–40,000, nearly two-thirds its size four months earlier. A week later a meeting of Haifa's trade, security, and political leaders estimated the remaining population at half its original size (or about 35,000). And "an Arab source," quoted by the Hebrew daily *Haaretz* on April 14, set the number of Arab escapees at 30,000, leaving some 40,000 Arab souls in the city.[25]

Severe shortages in foodstuffs, especially flour and bread, forced the NC to try to enforce an austerity regime, including a ban on the export of victuals from the city. Yet when it attempted to confiscate the lion's share of a flour shipment received in early April from the mandatory authorities on behalf of the ALA forces deployed in the city, it encountered a violent backlash from merchants who argued that these units had to be fed by the Arab states. The Committee's public warning to absentee grocery-owners to return to Haifa immediately lest their stocks be transferred to their competitors who remained in town was similarly ignored.[26]

By now the NC had lost any last vestiges of respect. Most of its members fled the city in late March or early April, with its final session on April 13 being attended by only four of the original fifteen members.[27] In a strongly worded letter to some of the absentees, in late March, Ibrahim had threatened that unless they returned to Haifa immediately, the NC would have to discuss their future;[28] yet he himself left for Egypt shortly after participating in the Committee's meeting of April 1, never to return to the city in whose public life he had been actively involved for decades.

The NC's unceremonious demise epitomized the wider disintegration of the city's Arab institutions. Arab municipal officialdom had practically withered away at a time when power was being devolved from the mandatory government to the local authorities, the absence of the representatives of the latter being further underscored by Mayor Levy's plea to his Arab colleagues to return, widely interpreted in the Arab street as indicating that he had a greater concern for Arab interests than did his Arab peers. The hundreds of ALA fighters (Syrians, Iraqis, Transjordanians) arriving in late March proved more of a liability than an asset, spreading mayhem and lawlessness throughout the city. Relations were particularly acrimonious between the local populace and the Iraqis, who gained notoriety as plunderers, womanizers, and drunkards; their officers were seen as seeking nothing but immediate gratification of their hedonistic impulses. In mid-April, about 100 National Guard troops deserted the city, taking their weapons with them, having failed to receive their salaries.[29]

By way of establishing his military credentials, and arresting the Arab community's rapid fragmentation, Amin Izz al-Din, a former captain in the Transjordan Frontier Force who assumed command over the city's defense in early April, moved on to the offensive. On the afternoon of April 15, a truckload of explosives went off near the Haifa flour mills, killing one person and causing widespread damage; only Jewish suspicions of the truck driver averted a greater loss of life. Jewish vigilance proved more successful the following day, when yet another vehicle loaded with explosives, seeking to infiltrate Hadar Hacarmel, the foremost Jewish neighborhood in Haifa, was stopped and disarmed. These bombing attempts were accompanied by a substantial intensification of the fighting, so much so that on the afternoon of April 16, the British Sixth Airborne Division, in charge of northern Palestine, recorded that "firing in Haifa in general and Sit[uation] appears out of control. Where mil[itary] take action there is temporary quiet but firing soon starts again." And a battalion of the Hagana's Carmeli Brigade, deployed in northern Palestine, reported on the same day that "in Haifa there is a general reinvigoration of enemy activities, manifested in numerous exchanges of fire in downtown Haifa and Hadar, and in a mortar attack. Four Jews were killed and another five wounded."[30]

Two days later one of the Sixth Airborne Division's battalions in Haifa reported that "considerable automatic and mortar fire went on till midnight from both sides with the Arabs mainly on the offensive." In the early hours of April 20, an Arab attack supported by mortar and machine-gun fire managed to penetrate the garden of the police station in Hadar.[31]

It was not long, however, before the Arab offensive backfired in grand style. As early as March 1, Major General Hugh Stockwell, commander of northern

Palestine, had informed Lt. General G. H. A. MacMillan, General Officer Commanding (GOC) the British forces in Palestine, of the inadequacy of the existing Haifa deployment and of the need for reinforcements "to enable the final evacuation [of British forces from Palestine] to be completed without hindrance, and to uphold the British prestige."[32] Now that the Arab offensive aimed at nothing short of penetrating Hadar, Stockwell feared that a general conflagration was in the offing and ordered his forces to deploy in fewer but better-protected strategic points in Haifa by first light on April 21. This was completed by 6 am, and four hours later Stockwell informed a Jewish delegation of the move's rationale and operational ramifications. At 11 am, he delivered the same message to an Arab delegation. Urging the two groups to stop the ongoing clashes, the general stated his determination not "to become involved in any way in these Arab-Jewish clashes." He emphasized the vital importance of the redeployment for the completion of the British withdrawal from Palestine, as well as his resolve to "take such measures as I may deem necessary at any time" to prevent interference by either community with his forces' disposition or with any of the municipal services in Haifa. On a more conciliatory note, Stockwell expressed his readiness "at all times to assist either community in any way they may desire for the maintenance of peace and order." "It is my wish that the withdrawal of the British from Haifa shall be carried out smoothly and rapidly and that our good relations may continue in the future and that we may carry away the respect and comradeship of both Communities," he told his interlocutors.[33]

This is not what happened. No sooner had the two delegations left Stockwell's office than the battle for the city was joined as Arabs and Jews rushed to fill the vacuum left by the British departure.

For quite some time the two communities had been gearing up for the final battle for the city. In late March, at the height of Arab attacks on Haifa's Jewish community, the Hagana's Carmeli Brigade drew up a plan (code-named Operation Scissors) envisaging a series of strikes against enemy bases, forces, and arms depots. But the brigade's involvement in combat operations elsewhere in north Palestine delayed its implementation, which was eventually set for April 22 regardless of the British military presence throughout the city. Once news of the British redeployment broke, Operation Scissors was immediately canceled and an alternative plan quickly implemented, aimed at opening up transport routes to downtown Haifa by capturing Wadi Rushmiya so as to secure the communication link between the city and the north of the country.[34]

These plans were countered by similarly elaborate planning on the Arab side. On March 24, the Haifa NC was instructed by the AHC to draw up a list of people who would administer the city after the completion of the British withdrawal from Palestine. Four days later, the Arab League's technical committee made the district of Haifa an independent operational unit answerable to the supreme command and assigned to it a detailed war plan. This envisaged the disruption of Jewish transportation throughout the district, attacks on Jewish urban and rural neighborhoods, and operations against the Hagana forces, preferably through guerrilla warfare in mountainous areas.[35]

The plan had probably formed the basis of Izz al-Din's offensive of early and mid-April. But when the moment of truth arrived, the commander of Arab Haifa failed to rise to the challenge. Shortly after his meeting with Stockwell on April 21, Izz al-Din sailed out of Haifa, ostensibly to gather reinforcements. He was quickly followed by one of his deputies, Amin Nabhani, while a second deputy, Yunas Nafa, a colorful local activist whose past occupations included partnership in a fish shop and a spell as a municipal sanitary inspector, left hurriedly the next day. "Nafa's considerable weight did not appear to have materially impeded his rate of progress," an Arab informant of the British commented ironically.[36]

Whether these desertions stemmed from cowardice, as claimed at the time by embittered Arab fighters and refugees fleeing Haifa,[37] or from "miscalculation," as suggested later by a Palestinian apologist,[38] they had a devastating impact on Arab morale. News of the flight quickly spread across the city, fanned by the Arabic-language broadcasts of the Hagana, which provided their numerous Arab listeners with real-time information about these desertions, mainly obtained through the interception of phone conversations.

Knowledge of the desertion of the Haifa Arabs by their military commanders was not limited to the Hagana and the Arab community. The British had up-to-date information about this development, as did the American Haifa consulate, and both deemed it the foremost cause of the Arab collapse in Haifa.[39] "There was little unity of command in Haifa and as it transpired, the actual leaders left at the crucial stage," Stockwell wrote on April 24 in his report on the events leading to the Jewish occupation of Haifa. And the American vice-consul in Haifa, Aubrey Lippincott, who had spent the night before the crucial fight with the Arab fighters, reported on April 23 that "they were much too remote from their higher command . . . some fairly reliable sources state that the Arab Higher Command all left Haifa some hours before the battle took place . . . those Arabs who escaped and with whom this officer has talked all feel that they have been let down by their leaders. The blow to Arab confidence is tremendous."[40]

Flight of military commanders at the most critical moment can wreck havoc even on the best of armies; its impact on a weakened and disorientated society can be nothing short of catastrophic. Debilitated by months of fighting, deeply divided along religious, political, and socio-economic lines, and lacking a coherent and accepted leadership, the depleted Arab community remaining in Haifa up to the final battle was simply too demoralized to mount the necessary final effort in its own defense. Describing this phenomenon with typical English understatement, Stockwell reported: "I think local Arab opinion felt that the Jews would gain control if in fact they launched their offensive"; while a fortnightly intelligence report from the headquarters of the British forces in Palestine scathingly observed that "the desertion of their leaders and the sight of so much cowardice in high places completely unnerved the inhabitants." Lippincott put it in far harsher terms:

> The local Arabs are not 100% behind the present effort. Those who are fighting are in [a] small minority. . . . It may be that the Haifa Arab, particularly the Christian Arab, is an exception, but generally speaking he is a coward and he is not the least bit interested in going out to fight his country's battles. He is definitely counting on the interference of outside Arab elements to come in and settle this whole question for him.[41]

It was only a question of time, therefore, before this defeatist mood translated itself into the all-too-familiar pattern of mass flight. In the early morning of April 22, as Hagana forces battled their way to the downtown market area, thousands streamed into the port, which was still held by the British army. Within hours, many of these had fled on trains and buses, while the rest awaited evacuation by sea.[42]

What was left of the local Arab leadership now reconstituted itself as an ad hoc "Emergency Committee" and asked the British military to stop the fighting. When this failed, a delegation requested a meeting with Stockwell "with a view to obtaining a truce with the Jews."[43] Having learned from the general the Hagana's terms for such a truce, the delegates left to consult with their peers, in particular asking the Syrian consul in Haifa to inform his government and the Arab League. Very quickly, the British ambassador to Damascus, Philip Broadmead, was summoned to a meeting with President Quwatli. "An Arab delegation had seen the British Commander of the troops and had asked for intervention in order to stop [the] violent attack of the Jews against the Arabs," said Quwatli.

> The Commander had refused to intervene, to allow Arab help to enter the town or to take measures to stop the killing of Arab women and children unless Arabs conclude a truce with [the] Hagana on conditions explained by the Commander, chief of which was the delivery of all arms to the Jews.

Immediate instructions were asked for in view of the meeting between the
Arab Delegation, [the] British Commander and the Jewish representatives
at 4 p.m.

Quwatli then expressed his bewilderment at the Jewish demand for the
surrender of Arab weapons. Nor could he see what instructions he could
send. What did the ambassador propose to do?

Reminding the president that neither of them was familiar with the real
situation on the ground, Broadmead begged him "to urge moderation and to
take no action which would bring this local Haifa issue on to a wider plane."
To this, Quwatli responded that he "was very nervous concerning public
opinion," yet refrained from any threat of military intervention.[44] Thus, no
instructions from Damascus or the other Arab capitals that were apprised of
the situation seem to have reached the Haifa truce delegation by four o'clock
in the afternoon, when it met its Jewish counterpart at City Hall.

There, after an impassioned plea for peace and reconciliation by Mayor
Levy,[45] the assembled delegates went through the truce terms point by point,
modifying a number of them to meet Arab objections. These included the
retention (rather than the surrender, as demanded by the Hagana) of licensed
arms by their Arab owners, as well as the extension of the deadline for the
surrender of all other weapons from the three hours demanded by the
Hagana to nineteen hours – with a possible further extension to twenty-four
hours at Stockwell's discretion. Most importantly, in view of the adamant
Arab refusal to surrender their weapons to the Hagana, it was agreed that the
confiscated weapons would be "held by the military in trust of the Hagana
and will be handed to them at the discretion of the GOC North Sector not
later than midnight 15/16 May 1948,"[46] when Haifa would become an
integral part of the newly established state of Israel.

At this stage the Arabs requested a twenty-four-hour recess "to give them
the opportunity to contact their brothers in the Arab states."[47] Although this
was deemed unacceptable, a briefer break was agreed and the meeting
adjourned at 5:20.

When the Arabs returned that evening at 7:15, they had a surprise in
store: as Stockwell would later put it in his official report, they stated "that
they were not in a position to sign the truce, as they had no control over the
Arab military elements in the town and that, in all sincerity, they could not
fulfill the terms of the truce, even if they were to sign." Then they offered,
"as an alternative, that the Arab population wished to evacuate Haifa and
that they would be grateful for military assistance."[48]

This came as a bombshell. With tears in his eyes, the elderly Levy
pleaded with the Arabs, most of whom were his personal acquaintances, to

reconsider, saying that they were committing "a cruel crime against their own people." Yaacov Salomon, a prominent Haifa lawyer and the Hagana's chief liaison officer in the city, followed suit, assuring the Arab delegates that he "had the instructions of the commander of the zone . . . that if they stayed on they would enjoy equality and peace, and that we, the Jews, were interested in their staying on and the maintenance of harmonious relations." Even the stoical Stockwell was shaken. "You have made a foolish decision," he thundered at the Arabs. "Think it over, as you'll regret it afterward. You must accept the conditions of the Jews. They are fair enough. Don't permit life to be destroyed senselessly. After all, it was you who began the fighting, and the Jews have won."[49]

But the Arabs were unmoved. The next morning, they met with Stockwell and his advisors to discuss the practicalities of the evacuation. Of the 30,000-plus Arabs still in Haifa, only a handful, they said, wished to stay. Perhaps the British could provide eighty trucks a day, and in the meantime ensure an orderly supply of foodstuffs to the city and its environs? At this, an aide to Stockwell erupted, "If you sign your truce you would automatically get all your food worries over. You are merely starving your own people." "We will not sign," the Arabs retorted. "All is already lost, and it does not matter if everyone is killed so long as we do not sign the document." These fatalistic words were publicly echoed in an ALA radio commentary, broadcast at the same time: "[The] Zionists have not dictated their conditions to us. We will have either to die for Palestine's sake and thus nobody will remain to accept any Jewish conditions or we shall survive and dictate our own terms to the Jews."[50]

Within a matter of days, only about 3,000 of Haifa's Arab residents remained in the city.

What had produced the seemingly instantaneous about-turn from explicit interest in a truce to its rejection only a few hours later? In an address to the UN Security Council on April 23, AHC vice-president Jamal Husseini contended that the Arabs in Haifa had been "presented with humiliating conditions and preferred to abandon all their possessions and leave."[51] But this was not so: not only had the Arab leadership in Haifa and elsewhere been apprised of the Hagana's terms several hours before the meeting on April 22, but, as we have seen, the Arab delegates to the meeting had proceeded to negotiate on the basis of those terms and had succeeded in modifying several key elements.

Later writers have spoken of "a Jewish propaganda blitz" aimed at frightening the Arabs into fleeing. Yet the only evidence offered for this "blitz" is a single sentence from a book by the Jewish writer Arthur Koestler, who was not even in Palestine at the time of the battle for Haifa but (in his own words) "pieced together the improbable story of the conquest by the Jews of this key harbor" about a week after his arrival on June 4 – that is, nearly two months after the event.[52]

As against this isolated second-hand account, there is an overwhelming body of evidence from contemporary Arab, Jewish, British, and American sources to prove that, far from seeking to drive the Arabs out of Haifa, the Jewish authorities went to considerable lengths to convince them to stay.

This effort was hardly confined to Levy's and Salomon's impassioned pleas, reiterated by Stockwell, at City Hall. The Hagana's truce terms stipulated that Arabs were expected to "carry on their work as equal and free citizens of Haifa."[53] In its Arabic-language broadcasts and communications, the Hagana consistently articulated the same message. On April 22, at the height of the fighting, it distributed an Arabic-language circular noting its ongoing campaign to clear the city of all "criminal foreign bands" so as to allow the restoration of "peace and security and good neighborly relations among all of the town's inhabitants." "We implore you again to keep your women, children, and the elderly from dangerous places," read the circular, "and to keep yourselves away from gang bases that are still subjected to our retaliatory action. We do not wish to shed the innocent blood of the city's peace-loving inhabitants."[54]

The following day, a Hagana broadcast asserted that "the Jews did, and do still believe that it is in the real interests of Haifa for its citizens to go on with their work and to ensure that normal conditions are restored to the city." On April 24, another Hagana radio broadcast declared: "Arabs, we do not wish to harm you. Like you, we only want to live in peace. . . . If the Jews and [the] Arabs cooperate, no power in the world will ever attack our country or ignore our rights." Two days later, informing its Arab listeners that "Haifa has returned to normal," the Hagana reported that "between 15,000 and 20,000 Arabs had expressed their willingness to remain in the city," that "Arab employees had been appointed to key posts such as that [of] looking after Arab property, religious matters and other work," and that Arabs had been given "part of the corn, flour and rice intended for the Jews in Haifa." And, on April 27, the Hagana distributed an Arabic-language leaflet urging the fleeing Arab populace to return home: "Peace and order reign supreme across the town and every resident can return to his free life and to resume his regular work in peace and security."[55]

That these were no hollow words was evidenced by, inter alia, the special dispensation given to Jewish bakers by the Haifa rabbinate to bake bread during the Passover holiday for distribution among the Arabs, and by the April 23 decision of the joint Jewish-Arab Committee for the Restoration of

Life to Normalcy to dispatch two of its members to inform women, children, and the elderly that they could return home.[56] In a May 6 fact-finding report to the JAE, Golda Meyerson told her colleagues that while "we will not go to Acre or Nazareth to return the Arabs [to Haifa] . . . our behavior should be such that if they were to encourage them to return – they would be welcome; we should not mistreat the Arabs so as to deter them from returning."[57]

The sincerity of the Jewish position is also attested by reports from the US consulate in Haifa. Thus, on April 25, after the fighting was over, Vice-Consul Lippincott cabled Washington that the "Jews hope poverty will cause laborers [to] return [to] Haifa as many are already doing despite Arab attempts [to] persuade them [to] keep out." And the following day: "[The] Jews want them [to] remain for political reasons to show [the] democratic treatment they will get [and] also need them for labor although [the] Jews claim latter not essential." On April 29, according to Lippincott, even Farid Saad of the Haifa NC was saying that the Jewish leaders "have organized a large propaganda campaign to persuade [the] Arabs to return."[58]

Similarly, the British district superintendent of police reported on April 26 that "every effort is being made by the Jews to persuade the Arab populace to stay and carry on with their normal lives, to get their shops and businesses open and to be assured that their lives and interests will be safe." Two days later he reported that "the Jews are still making every effort to persuade the Arab populace to remain and settle back into their normal lives in the town," while the Sixth Airborne Division recorded in its logbook on May 1 that the "Jews in Haifa [are] now trying to get better relations with [the] Arabs and are encouraging them to return to the town." And a weekly field security report of the same date noted that:

> the Jews have been making strenuous efforts to check the stream of refugees, in several cases resorting to actual intervention by [the] Hagana. Appeals have been made on the radio and in the press, urging Arabs to remain in the town. [The] Hagana issued a pamphlet along these lines, and the Histadrut in a similar publication appealed to those Arabs previously members of their organization to return. On the whole, [the] Arabs remain indifferent to this propaganda and their attitude to the present situation is one of apathetic resignation.[59]

In fact, it was the received wisdom among contemporary observers that the continuation of the Arabs in Haifa, or their return home, would constitute a Jewish victory, whereas their departure would amount to a Jewish setback. As reported by the United Press correspondent in Haifa, Mano Dierkson:

The shooting battle was followed by a political campaign between the Arabs and the Jews. The Arab leaders ordered the town's complete evacuation whereas the Jewish leaders felt that such a development would be a tremendous defeat for them. . . . Should the situation remain calm, there is little doubt that many Arabs will stay despite the evacuation order by the Arab leadership, and one can hear many Arabs expressing their decision to stay. Jewish leaders walked around the Arab quarters today, talking to the Arab leaders who were busy urging their congregation to leave. It would seem today that the Arabs may well lose the political campaign just as they had lost the military campaign last Wednesday.[60]

Meanwhile, as the Jews were attempting to keep the Arabs in Haifa, the Arab Emergency Committee was doing its best to get them out. Scaremongering was a major weapon in its arsenal. Some Arab residents received written threats that, unless they left town, they would be branded as traitors deserving of death.[61] Others were told they could expect no mercy from the Jews. Sheik Abdel Rahman Murad of the NC, who had headed the truce-negotiating team, proved particularly effective at spreading the latter scare story: on April 23, he warned a large group of escapees, who were about to return to their homes, that if they did so they would all be killed, as the Jews spared not even women and children. On the other hand, he continued, the Arab Legion had 200 trucks ready to transfer the Haifa refugees to a safe haven, where they would be given free accommodation, clothes, and food. Likewise, shortly after announcing their intention to remain in their work place, the Christian employees of the British army's northern headquarters began leaving en masse. Asked for the reason for their sudden change of heart, they said that they had been threatened with severe punishment if they did not leave.[62]

The importance of these actions cannot be overstated. The Emergency Committee was not a random collection of self-appointed vigilantes, as some Palestinian apologists would later argue. Rather, it was the successor to the Haifa NC and included two of its members: Farid Saad and Sheik Murad. In other words: the evacuation of the Haifa Arab community was ordered, and executed, by the AHC's official local representatives. The only question is whether those representatives did what they did on their own, or under specific instructions from above.

As indicated earlier, the Haifa leaders had been extremely reluctant to accept or reject the Hagana's truce terms on their own recognizance: hence the initial appeal to their peers, and hence the request for a twenty-four-hour recess to seek the advice of the Arab states. When this was not granted, and the Emergency Committee had to make do with the brief respite granted to it, its delegates proceeded to telephone the AHC office in Beirut for instructions. They were then told explicitly not to sign, but rather to evacuate. Astonished, the Haifa delegates protested, but were assured that it was "only a matter of days" before Arab retaliatory action would commence, and "since there will be a lot of casualties following our intended action . . . you [would] be held responsible for the casualties among the Arab population left in the town."

This entire conversation was secretly recorded by the Hagana, and its substance was passed on to some of the Jewish negotiators at City Hall.[63] In retrospect, it helps explain a defiant comment made at the meeting by the Arab delegates after they announced the intended evacuation – namely, that "they had lost [the] first round but . . . there were more to come."[64] It also sheds light on Meyerson's assessment of the future of Haifa's Arab community in her May 6 report to the JAE. Having told her colleagues of her personal distress at the sight of the Arab exodus, she added: "For my part I think that whether or not the Arabs will remain in Haifa will not depend on our behavior but rather on the instructions they'll receive from their leaders. Until now the Arab leaders have said: 'Leave Haifa, we will bomb it, we will send [our] army there and we don't want you to get hurt.' Should they receive different orders from Damascus and Amman, they will act accordingly."[65] From Yaacov Salomon, one of the Jewish negotiators, we also learn of certain other emotions experienced by his Arab interlocutors:

> The Arab delegation arrived at the evening meeting under British escort, but when the meeting broke up they asked me to give them a lift and to take them home. I took them in my car.
>
> On the way back they told me that they had instructions not to sign the truce and that they could not sign the truce on any terms, as this would mean certain death at the hands of their own people, particularly the Muslim leaders, guided by the Mufti. While therefore they would remain in town, as they thought that would be best in their own interests, they had to advise the Arabs to leave.[66]

What the Hagana had learned by covert means became public knowledge within days. Already on April 25 the American consulate in Haifa was reporting that the "local Mufti-dominated Arab leaders urge all Arabs [to] leave [the] city and large numbers [are] going." Three days later it pointed to those responsible: "Reportedly [the] Arab Higher Committee [is] ordering all Arabs [to] leave."[67] Writing on the same day to the colonial secretary in London, Cunningham was equally forthright: "British authorities in Haifa have formed the impression that total evacuation is being urged on the Haifa

Arabs from higher Arab quarters and that the townsfolk themselves are against it." Yet another contemporary British report asserted that: "Probable reason for [the] Arab Higher Executive ordering Arabs to evacuate Haifa is to avoid possibility of [the] Haifa Arabs being used as hostages in future operations after May 15. Arabs have already threatened to bomb Haifa from the air."[68] Finally, a British intelligence report summing up the events of the week judged that, had it not been for the incitement and scaremongering of the Haifa Arab leadership, most Arab residents might well have stayed:

> After the Jews had gained control of the town, and in spite of a subsequent food shortage, many would not have responded to the call for a complete evacuation but for the rumours and propaganda spread by the National Committee members remaining in the town. Most widespread was a rumour that Arabs remaining in Haifa would be taken as hostages by [the] Jews in the event of future attacks on other Jewish areas: and an effective piece of propaganda with its implied threat of retribution when the Arabs recapture the town, is that [those] people remaining in Haifa acknowledged tacitly that they believe in the principle of a Jewish State.[69]

There, no doubt, lay the reason why the Arab leadership preferred the exiling of Haifa's Arabs to any truce with the Hagana. For, given the UN's assignment of the city to the new Jewish state, any agreement by its Arab community to live under Jewish rule would have amounted to acquiescence in Jewish statehood in a part of Palestine. This, to both the Palestinian leadership and the Arab world at large, was anathema. As Azzam declared shortly after the fall of Haifa to the Hagana: "The Zionists are seizing the opportunity to establish a Zionist state against the will of the Arabs. The Arab peoples have accepted the challenge and soon they will close their account with them."[70]

What the secretary-general failed to mention is that this fiery determination of the Arab peoples to "close their account" with the Zionists had just driven tens of thousands of their hapless fellow Arabs from their homes. Neither did he anticipate that this self-inflicted tragedy would be followed within days by a similarly monumental exodus, this time from Palestine's largest Arab city: Jaffa.

CHAPTER 7

Why Don't You Stay and Fight?

"I do not mind [the] destruction of Jaffa if we secure [the] destruction of Tel Aviv."

Jaffa's Iraqi commander, February 1948

"Ninety percent of the population of Jaffa have just run away, and only some 5,000 now remain. . . . The Mayor has gone, without even saying goodbye, and the remnants of the Liberation army are looting and robbing. This is what the Palestine Arabs get from the assistance provided by the Arab States."

Sir Henry Gurney, May 1948

One of the world's oldest existing cities and a key naval outlet for Palestine, Jaffa has enjoyed fortunes that have alternated dramatically throughout the ages in accordance with the vicissitudes in local and regional power. After a long period of stagnation and decline, the city was demolished in the early fourteenth century by its Mamluk rulers to prevent a possible landing by European Crusaders, and the Ottoman conquest of Palestine (in 1516) brought no respite; to the point that sixty years after the event a European traveler was unable to find a single house in Jaffa. As late as 1726, a German priest described the site as "resembling more a village than a town, with poor and bad houses wherein dwell some Turks, Greeks, Jews and a few Catholic Christians of French nationality." It was only in the nineteenth and early twentieth centuries that a steady flow of foreign and domestic migrants – Egyptian peasants, Lebanese merchants, Algerian refugees, American missionaries, German settlers, Palestinian Arabs, and East European Jews – transformed Jaffa from a 2,750-strong desolate hamlet into a bustling city of some 45,000 residents.[1]

Jewish population growth was particularly impressive – from a paltry sixty souls in the mid-1830s to a 15,000-strong community in 1915, or nearly 40 percent of the city's population (compared to 1 percent in 1835). Since the vast majority of these immigrants arrived in the three decades preceding

World War I not as individuals but as members of a national movement seeking to restore Jewish sovereignty in Palestine, they carried far greater weight than an ordinary group of migrants. As the influx of Jewish manpower and capital, together with the growing number of neighboring agricultural villages, transformed Jaffa (including Tel Aviv, founded in 1909 as a local suburb but rapidly becoming a distinct city) into the effective capital of the Yishuv, the pace of economic activity and social change among the city's non-Jewish population rose dramatically, making Jaffa a front-runner in the modernization of Palestinian Arab society.

Between 1886 and 1913, for example, general exports grew sixfold while the export of oranges, Jaffa's main source of revenue since the late nineteenth century, increased fifteenfold: from 106,000 to 1,609,000 boxes. Likewise, the acute Jewish demand for housing helped stimulate the local economy. Property and letting prices soared as many immigrants were willing to rent the most dismal accommodation: wooden shacks, stables, derelict buildings. Land prices rose even more spectacularly, with a large plot offered in 1894 for less than 400 francs per acre selling a decade later for 6,100 francs an acre. By 1913, the going rate for real estate in central Tel Aviv locations had risen to 32,000–38,000 francs an acre.

Economic development and commercial interaction, however, did not spill over into the social sphere. Up until to the Ottoman collapse in the wake of World War I, religion remained the organizing principle of the socio-political order, with the empire's non-Muslim subjects (*dhimmis*) continuing their separate existence of legal and institutionalized inferiority, humiliating social restrictions, and sporadic violence at the hands of local officials and the Muslim population at large.[2] To this must be added the ethnic and social divisions within Jaffa's non-Muslim communities: between oriental Jews of the "Old Yishuv" and the large number of Ashkenazim streaming into the city, between Arab and European Christians, and between Catholics, Greek Orthodox, and Protestants. Even the majority Muslim community was deeply fractured, with ethnicity overshadowing any sense of religious solidarity. Each ethnic group congregated in its distinct neighborhood, maintained its own way of life and social networks, and often looked down on its Muslim counterparts. Established inhabitants, for instance, would not give their daughters in marriage to dark-skinned Muslims or those of Egyptian origin. Some Muslim communities spoke their own languages, whether Turkish, Afghan, or Farsi, while others (notably Egyptians and North Africans) used the Arabic dialect spoken in their home countries.[3]

These schisms were superficially papered over during the mandate years as anti-Zionism became the main common denominator of local (and national) solidarity and a handy diversion from the Arab society's real problems. In

May 1921, the Arabs of Jaffa launched a murderous attack on their Jewish neighbors and a number of adjacent Jewish villages, killing ninety people, wounding hundreds, and plundering and destroying much property; and while the city played a comparatively secondary role in the 1929 massacres, in which 133 Jews were murdered and hundreds more were wounded, it remained a hotbed of anti-Zionist incitement and the place where the 1936–39 "revolt" began.

Although the sustained incitement and sporadic outbreaks of violence did not tarnish Arab-Jewish daily coexistence, or even prevent incidents of Arab assistance to Jewish victims of aggression,[4] they nevertheless led to growing intercommunal segregation as the Jews retreated to their own neighborhoods and to Tel Aviv, which had gradually eclipsed its parent city both in absolute population numbers and as the center of Zionist activities. Not only did the two communities increasingly lead parallel lives, but Jaffa's Jewish suburbs became to all intents and purposes an integral part of Tel Aviv, looking to the larger city for education, medical care, and social amenities. Yet when the Zionist movement sought to institutionalize this reality by incorporating these neighborhoods into Tel Aviv, Arab municipal leaders dismissed the idea out of hand. There was no need for an official secession, they argued, since Jaffa was prepared to do as much for its Jewish residents as for its Arab inhabitants; if this failed to satisfy the Jews they could move out of the city, which was after all Arabic in history and character. In the end, neither of these scenarios materialized, and in 1947 Jaffa was still a mixed-population city of some 70,730 Arabs (53,930 Muslims and 16,800 Christians) and 30,820 Jews.[5]

As a result, there was no appetite in Jaffa for confrontation as the UN was about to determine Palestine's future. For one thing, the nascent partition plan awarded the city to the prospective Arab state, and the Zionist leadership had no desire to challenge this. For another, with the horrors of the 1936–39 "revolt" still fresh in the minds of many Arabs, and Muslim – Christian relations at a particularly low ebb,[6] a diverse anti-Husseini and pro-Abdullah coalition comprising the city's more moneyed circles and prominent politicians and notables, including Mayor Yusuf Heikal and Muhammad Nimr Hawari, a local lawyer and founding commander of the national Najada militia, tried to prevent Jaffa's slide into anarchy.

The Arab League's boycott of Jewish services and commodities was largely ignored as many Arabs continued to shop in Tel Aviv – where necessary, bribing the inspectors to turn a blind eye to this practice. In August 1947, under pressure from the anti-Husseini coalition, the police arrested a number of boycott inspectors and expelled others from the city, thus dealing a debilitating blow to the anti-Jewish campaign. When Jamal Husseini, overlooking his own family's land sales to the Jews, demanded that sons kill their fathers if they committed such a "crime" and vice versa, Hawari responded derisively: "For twenty years we have been hearing strong words against middlemen and sellers of land to the Jews, while these very people have been occupying the front rows in every Arab national gathering."[7]

Even the foremost eruption of intercommunal violence, in mid-August 1947, when the murder of four Jews in a north Tel Aviv café by an Arab gang triggered widespread clashes along the Jaffa-Tel Aviv fault line, was quickly brought to an end by Mayor Heikal and his Tel Aviv counterpart, Israel Rokah. Armed Najada squads patrolled the streets to prevent anti-Jewish attacks, leaflets stressing the merits of peaceful coexistence were distributed, and reconciliation meetings between Arab and Jewish residents of the border neighborhoods were held. When, on October 3, the AHC declared a national strike in protest at UNSCOP's recommendations, the Mufti's local henchmen were forced to abandon their plans for violence under pressure from the Jaffa opposition.

In the following weeks, Hajj Amin met numerous delegations from the city (and other Palestinian localities) in his Cairo residence in an effort to patch up differences and to lay the groundwork for a nationwide campaign of violence.[8] These meetings seemed to have achieved their objective. The three-day national strike, declared in early December 1947 in response to the partition resolution, quickly escalated into mass violence. Jewish shops and business establishments were torched, while shooting, sniping, and rioting spread rapidly across the Jaffa-Tel Aviv boundary. As the Jewish residents of these neighborhoods fled en masse to Tel Aviv, young Arabs flocked to the AHC's Jaffa office demanding weapons. By the end of the month, more than sixty Jews had been killed in the Jaffa-Tel Aviv area.

Not all Arabs welcomed the violence. Merchants and businessmen yearned for tranquility, while ordinary people were deeply disturbed by the steep rise in the price of essential goods and rapidly growing unemployment. At a meeting of the National Committee (NC), established by the AHC in December as the city's official leadership, Ahmad ibn Laban, a local councilor and prominent grove-owner, demanded the immediate cessation of hostilities, telling the committee's more militant members to "go to the mountains, the Negev, or the Galilee" if they were so eager to fight the Jews.[9]

Appeals were made to the governing institutions to end the strike and anger was vented on the politicians for wreaking havoc on the city; anti-strike demonstrations were held; bakeries and warehouses were plundered by rioting mobs. Before long Arab and Jewish citrus-growers reached a tacit understanding allowing both sides to harvest and market their produce unhindered,[10] and in mid-December leaders of the southern suburb of

Jabaliya accepted a localized ceasefire with the adjacent Jewish city of Bat Yam but were unable to enforce it on the gangs operating in their neighborhood, who went so far as to beat up the Jabaliya *mukhtar*.[11]

In an attempt to end hostilities, Tel Aviv's Mayor Rokah proposed that the two cities make a public appeal for peace and so enable thousands of residents on both sides of the divide to return to their homes and work. Under intense pressure from the local citrus-growers, Heikal agreed to issue the appeal provided the AHC gave the initiative its blessing. This was good enough for the Hagana, which instructed its fighters to withhold fire and to avoid offensive action so long as there were no Arab shootings or attacks on Jaffa's and Tel Aviv's Jewish neighborhoods. The Husseini response to this, however, was a call for "a jihad against the Jews . . . who have launched an aggressive campaign against the Arabs aimed at dispossessing them from their places . . . eradicating [their] holy places, and subjugating [their] future generations."

The distraught Heikal flew to Cairo and Amman to sue for peace, to no avail. King Abdullah would offer no concrete help to his local followers beyond soothing words of support, while the Mufti would hear nothing of a cessation of hostilities. In early December, he appointed his loyal henchman Hassan Salame commander of the Lydda-Jaffa front with the explicit goal of escalating the fighting, and backed this move with a large shipment of arms and the recruitment of volunteers from other Palestinian Arab localities, Nablus in particular. Needing little encouragement, Salame quickly arranged an attack on the Hatikva neighborhood, which constituted an important milestone in the general slide to war. Later that month he foiled an attempt by Hawari, who in early December was appointed Jaffa's military commander, to reach a ceasefire agreement with the Hagana.[12]

As the fighting continued, Jaffa was rapidly losing its Arab residents. Flight from border neighborhoods ensued within hours of the passing of the UN partition resolution in anticipation of a violent backlash, and by the beginning of 1948 about a third of the city's population had fled to a variety of destinations in Palestine and abroad. This included most of the Christian community, but also a substantial number of Muslims. A male member of the family was often left behind to guard property. "The disturbances have changed everything in Jaffa," read a Hagana intelligence report.

The city's hitherto bustling markets are deserted, the cafés are empty, and the cinema houses are closed. Roadblocks and barbed-wire barricades have been erected at the city center, on top of those existing on its borders. The people in Jaffa live in fear of Jewish bombs and internecine Arab attacks.

Many Arabs who lived in borderline neighborhoods (such as Manshiya and Jabaliya) have abandoned their places. It is estimated that in Manshiya alone some 3,000 families have left. Most of these moved to the old city, as well as to Nuzha and [the affluent] Ajami [neighborhood], where they forceably occupied houses, which are now hugely overcrowded with more than ten people living in every room. Many families left for Syria, Lebanon, Transjordan, Cyprus and Egypt, while others went to Gaza, Nablus, Jenin, and Nazareth. It is estimated that some 25,000 have left Jaffa.[13]

On January 4, around noon, two British army-type vehicles manned by Lehi fighters in British uniform drew up beside the NC's headquarters in Clock Tower Square, in the heart of Jaffa. A few moments later, an explosion reduced the building to rubble, killing some seventy people and injuring another hundred. A tidal wave of panic and helplessness engulfed the city. Residents shunned the main boulevards; coastal neighborhoods were abandoned for fear of a naval attack; numerous people were sighted at bus stops, suitcase in hand, waiting to leave town.

"I heard that some families have been vacating their houses in Faisal Street, and most of them have left Jaffa," a local journalist told a friend shortly after the bombing.

"Why Faisal Street? It's a safe place, deep inside Jaffa."

"There are no safe places any more. Every place in Jaffa is dangerous."

"No, it is not. All the entrances to Jaffa are now protected by Arab guards."

"So they say. But I don't believe them."[14]

Even the mayor's wife seemed to have given up on the city run by her husband. Two days after the Lehi bombing, she called the municipality to inquire whether her travel documents had been arranged. She was told that the person in charge was away and that she would have to phone again the next day. "I can't wait for tomorrow," she retorted. "I wanted to leave already today and postponed my departure for this reason alone. I must leave tomorrow. I can't stay here any more. Check what you can do for me." The prodding had an immediate effect. Later that day Mrs. Heikal was seen waiting for a bus to ferry her out of town.[15]

The Jaffa authorities went to great lengths to stem the flight. In late December 1947, the Manshiya refugees were peremptorily ordered to return to their homes or face the suspension of food rations. A month later the NC went a significant step further by prohibiting people from leaving town without a valid permit, and limiting travel abroad to vital purposes directly related to Jaffa's defense. Ostensibly designed to prevent "Jewish infiltration" into the city, the permit's introduction was widely seen as a desperate bid to stop the exodus, as were the exorbitant taxation of evacuees and the prohibition of food exports, supposedly intended "to prevent the Jews from receiving foodstuff[s] from Jaffa."

"I worked in a branch of the [national] committee based in the headquarters of the Muslim Youth Association near the port of Jaffa," recalled the American-Palestinian academic Ibrahim Abu Lughod, then an eighteen-year-old high-school student in Jaffa.

> Our job consisted mainly of harassing people to dissuade them from leaving, and when they insisted, we would begin bargaining over what they should pay, according to how much luggage they were carrying with them and how many members of the family there were. At first we set up the taxes high. Then as the situation deteriorated, we reduced the rates, especially when our friends and relatives began to be among those leaving.[16]

By way of impressing upon the population the seriousness of its intention to fight the exodus and to restore normalcy, the NC made simultaneous use of the stick and the carrot. It threatened to confiscate the property of absentees, while at the same time attempting to revive Jaffa's depressed nightlife. "We cannot understand why people are still afraid to go out in the street after sunset," the Committee stated. "It is not justified since our heroic defenders have the upper hand in all clashes. Our defense organization has taken all steps to ensure security against raids. There is not the slightest danger whatever inside the town."[17]

These measures were stillborn. From the outbreak of hostilities there was no unified leadership in Jaffa and the bitter enmities among the local factions prevented the effective functioning of the city's governing institutions. Although the Husseinis steadily gained the upper hand (by the end of 1947 they had driven Hawari out of Palestine, having smeared him as a "Zionist stooge" and an embezzler) and flexed their military muscle through the influx of rural forces into the city, they never managed to completely call the shots. Their foremost tool, the NC, was not under their exclusive control, and was more than matched in influence by the municipality and the wily Heikal, who successfully implicated the Arab League in the city's defense. So bitter was the enmity between these two centers of power that after the Lehi bombing of the NC headquarters, the municipality prevented the participation of NC officials in the funerals so as to appropriate the tragedy for its own political benefit.[18] "One month has already passed and things are going from bad to worse," lamented an Arabic newspaper. "In Jaffa the National Committee is competing with the municipality for authority . . . people are perplexed and don't know what to do. . . . Everybody is ready to defend his homeland, but we want organization and direction . . . death by fate and destiny is for God – but we don't accept being driven like sheep to the slaughter."[19]

This rivalry was further aggravated by the multiplicity of armed groups which controlled substantial parts of Jaffa. Military affairs in Jabaliya, for example, were largely dominated by Abdel Rahman Siqsiq, a local lawyer who set up a 500-strong militia, while parts of Salama were controlled by the militant Islamist group the Muslim Brothers, which not only insisted on having a free hand in prosecuting the fighting but also tried to stem the Arab exodus by confiscating the passports of those seeking to leave the city. Then there were the ALA fighters and groups of volunteers from other Palestinian localities who arrived in the initial stages of the war, only to get embroiled in squabbles with the local populace and leave the city when the going got tough.[20]

In these circumstances, the public remained at a loss to know who constituted the legitimate authority in Jaffa, not least since both the NC and the municipality were seen as uncaring and corrupt, lacking any compassion for, or affinity with, their constituents.

"What happened to the NC offices?" enquired a journalist after the Lehi bombing in a phone conversation tapped by a Jewish underground organization.

"Let their name and memory be damned," replied his interlocutor. "The Angel of Death doesn't touch its own kind. The dogs came out alive. I wish they had all been killed."

"Two more bombings like this and nothing will be left of Jaffa. Where have all our guards been?"

"Ask the dog, Dr. Heikal, let his name and memory be damned. He was given 50 armed men for the city's defense. Of these he assigned 25 to guard his home, leaving the rest in his generosity to protect the entire city. It is a pity that they [i.e., the Lehi] didn't blow up the house of the great dictator. Or that of Rafiq Tamimi [head of the NC]."[21]

Others had no qualms about openly venting their anger. "The public thinks that we are lining our pockets with the money we've raised," a member of the NC told Tamimi:

> The other day I saw a person standing in front of your house and screaming at the top of his voice: "Here goes all the money you are collecting, you accursed members of the National Committee." Pointing to the iron gate of your home he claimed that all NC members had divided the funds among themselves, installing iron gates [in their residences] and splashing lavish sums of money on hiring guards to protect them.[22]

Foreign Office,

November 2nd, 1917.

Dear Lord Rothschild,

I have much pleasure in conveying to you, on behalf of His Majesty's Government, the following declaration of sympathy with Jewish Zionist aspirations which has been submitted to, and approved by, the Cabinet.

"His Majesty's Government view with favour the establishment in Palestine of a national home for the Jewish people, and will use their best endeavours to facilitate the achievement of this object, it being clearly understood that nothing shall be done which may prejudice the civil and religious rights of existing non-Jewish communities in Palestine or the rights and political status enjoyed by Jews in any other country"

I should be grateful if you would bring this declaration to the knowledge of the Zionist Federation.

[signature]

---

1 On November 2, 1917, the British Foreign Secretary, Arthur James Balfour, informed the Anglo-Jewish dignitary Lord Lionel Walter Rothschild of his government's support for the "establishment in Palestine of a national home for the Jewish people." Two and a half years later, in April 1920, Britain was mandated to implement the resolution under the auspices of the League of Nations.

2 At the outbreak of Word War I, the Russia-born, Manchester-based Chaim Weizmann was a secondary figure in the Zionist movement. But his personal charm, immense energy, and the ability to sense a great opportunity and to seize it, catapulted him within a few years to the movement's leadership.

3 In March 1921 the British excluded Transjordan from the territory of the prospective Jewish national home, making Abdullah ibn Hussein of the Hashemite family its effective ruler. In the following decades Abdullah would tirelessly strive to transform his emirate into a vast regional empire comprising Syria, Palestine, and possibly Iraq and Saudi Arabia.

4 Having promised the British authorities in Palestine to promote Arab-Jewish coexistence, Muhammad Amin Husseini used his appointment as Mufti of Jerusalem and President of the Supreme Muslim Council to launch a relentless campaign to obliterate the Jewish national revival that culminated in the collapse and dispersion of Palestinian Arab society.

5 Throughout the mandate era (1920–48), periods of peaceful coexistence were far longer than those of violent eruptions and the latter were the work of a small fraction of Palestinian Arabs. Here, Arab dignitaries participating in the cornerstone laying ceremony of a new kibbutz in 1937, at the height of the "Arab revolt" in Palestine.

6 Elias Sasson, head of the Arab section of the Jewish Agency's political department. During the 1930s and 1940s he held countless meetings with prominent leaders in Palestine and the neighboring Arab states in an attempt to find common ground for peace.

7 A mass demonstration in Tel Aviv against the May 1939 White Paper, which imposed draconian restrictions on Jewish land purchases in Palestine and confined Jewish immigration to 75,000 arrivals over the next five years, whence it would occur only with Arab consent.

8 Having swept to power in July 1945 in a landslide electoral victory, Clement Attlee's Labour government swiftly dropped its longstanding support for Zionism, becoming an implacable foe to the idea of Jewish statehood. No one epitomized this shift more starkly than Foreign Secretary Ernest Bevin, who in November 1945 criticized the supposed Jewish tendency "to get too much at the head of the queue" in demanding help.

9 and 10 As Britain maintained a tight naval blockade around Palestine after World War II in an attempt to prevent Jewish immigration, the foremost Jewish underground organization, the Hagana, sought to smuggle Holocaust survivors into the country. Many were caught and incarcerated in concentration camps in Cyprus; others were expelled to Europe, notably the 4,500 passengers of the *Exodus 1947*, whose return to Germany generated an international outcry.

11, 12 and 13 As the United Nations deliberated the Palestine question, the Zionist movement sought to persuade the Arab world of the merits of peace. Golda Meyerson (Meir), acting head of the Jewish Agency's political department, held a secret meeting with King Abdullah, and two senior Zionist officials met Arab League Secretary-General Abdel Rahman Azzam, while David Ben-Gurion, soon to become Israel's first prime minister, was busy assuring the Arab citizens of the prospective Jewish state that they would, in law and practice, enjoy the same rights and privileges as their Jewish counterparts.

14 and 15 On November 29, 1947, the United Nations' General Assembly passed a resolution calling for the partition of Palestine into two independent states – one Jewish, the other Arab – linked in an economic union. In Jewish localities throughout Palestine crowds danced in the streets. In the Arab capitals there were violent demonstrations, while in Jerusalem several hundred Arabs ransacked the new Jewish commercial center.

16 and 17 A week after the passing of the partition resolution, the Arab League's political committee met in Cairo and decided to vest Palestine's defense, until the end of the mandate, with the newly-established Arab Liberation Army (ALA). The Iraqi General, Ismail Safwat, was appointed ALA commander-in-chief and Fawzi Qawuqji, a Syrian officer who had served in the Ottoman army during World War I and led the foreign intervention in the 1936–9 Palestinian Arab "revolt," became the force's field commander.

18 Confronted with the distinct possibility of a full-fledged pan-Arab assault, in early November 1947 the Hagana underwent major structural changes aimed at transforming its semi-mobilized units into a national army based on compulsory conscription that would be able to resist an invasion by the regular Arab armed forces.

19 Having been on the defensive during the four months of fighting that followed the partition resolution, in early April 1948 the Hagana moved onto the offensive, and by the end of the month captured the mixed-population cities of Tiberias and Haifa. Jaffa (in photo), the largest Arab city in Palestine surrendered on May 13.

20 Abdel Qader Husseini, the Mufti's favorite nephew and commander of the Jerusalem district, whose death in the battle for the city transformed him instantaneously from a highly controversial figure into a national hero.

21 On the afternoon of May 14, a few hours before the termination of the mandate, the Yishuv leadership gathered at the Tel Aviv city museum, where David Ben-Gurion proclaimed the establishment of the state of Israel, becoming its first prime minister and minister of defence.

22 and 23 Within hours of its proclamation, Israel came under a sustained pan-Arab assault. Tel Aviv was subjected to air attacks while Jewish Jerusalem, reeling from months of war and privation, came under siege by Transjordan's Arab Legion.

24 On June 11, 1948, largely due to the efforts of the UN special mediator, Count Folke Bernadotte, a truce came into effect. In the following months Bernadotte worked assiduously to bring an end to the conflict. His progress report, submitted to the UN Secretary-General on September 16, a day before his assassination in Jerusalem by Jewish zealots, constituted the basis of General Assembly Resolution 194 of December 11, 1948.

25 and 26 As the Arabs resumed fighting on July 9, the IDF turned the tables on the invading armies and in the ten days of fighting before a new UN-imposed ceasefire came into effect, captured the strategic towns of Lydda and Ramle (in photo above) and made significant territorial gains in the Galilee, including Nazareth. In a string of follow up offensives in the autumn, the IDF drove the ALA and a Syrian battalion out of the Galilee, shattered the Egyptian line of the defense, and occupied the city of Beersheba (in photo below).

27 In a visit to Nazareth three months after its conquest, Ben-Gurion was positively surprised by the affability between the authorities and the local population.

28 A local Bedouin speaking to members of kibbutz Negba, then under attack by the Egyptian army.

29 The 1948 war resulted in the total disintegration of Palestinian Arab society. By the end of the British mandate in mid-May 1948, some 300,000–340,000 people had fled their homes; by the end of the year these numbers had swelled to nearly 600,000 as a direct result of the pan-Arab invasion.

30 On September 13, 1993, PLO Chairman Yasir Arafat and the Israeli prime minister, Yitzhak Rabin, signed the Declaration of Principles on Interim Self-Government Arrangements (DOP). It quickly transpired, however, that for the Palestinian leader the agreement was a strategic means not to a two-state solution – Israel and a Palestinian state in the West Bank and Gaza – but to the substitution of a Palestinian state for the state of Israel. Having built an extensive terror infrastructure in the territories under his control, in September 2000 he pitted Palestinians and Israelis in their bloodiest confrontation since the 1948 war, inflicting great damage on Israel and destroying the fragile fabric of civil society that had been developing in the West Bank and Gaza during the decades preceding his arrival.

These grievances were not wholly unfounded. The NC was hardly a model of inspired leadership. On the face of it, Jaffa fared better than other localities in that its NC was headed by an AHC member, which reduced the potential for the sort of friction between these two bodies that largely paralyzed Palestinian Arab activities throughout the rest of the country. Yet Tamimi, an Abdullah supporter turned Husseini stooge, proved weak and indecisive. He failed to push Jaffa's affairs with his superiors who, for their part, seemed surprisingly oblivious to the fate of Palestine's largest Arab city. After the Lehi bombing, Tamimi couldn't even make up his mind whether to inform the Mufti of the disaster. "I don't know what to do," he confided to the NC member who told him of the bombing. "What do you think? Should I contact [the Mufti]?"

"But of course you should; and you should also pressure him to send us immediate help, especially now that there are so many dead and wounded."

"I will contact the Mufti immediately," promised Tamimi. Yet it took him two full hours to do so, only to find his superior totally unmoved. The high death toll, the state of the wounded, the physical carnage, the panic and the attendant flight: all were of no consequence to the Mufti. Instead he questioned why Tamimi, who had been due in Cairo for some time, had not yet arrived. "I sent my passport to the AHC in Jerusalem by mail and it must have been lost with the rest of the items when the train was robbed," Tamimi replied, before timidly asking for financial support. "I have already sent [the money]," an evidently irritated Mufti retorted. "You will probably receive it tomorrow or the next day." As the money failed to arrive, the Jaffa NC contacted the AHC's Cairo headquarters to plead for an immediate disbursement of £10,000 (£250,000 in today's terms). They were told that they were not going to get the requested sum since the Mufti had only authorized a £3,000 installment, and even this was made in repayment of old debts.[23]

If this was the attitude of the supreme leader of the Palestinian Arabs, it was hardly surprising that the local British authorities were no keener to intervene. Asked by an Arab journalist after the Lehi bombing what he proposed to do about the city's security, the police district superintendent erupted. "The Arab public is undisciplined and it is impossible to collaborate with it," he said. "If we were dealing with disciplined people, we could have organized them to defend the [city's] border areas. But every Arab possesses his personal weapon and wants to protect the borderline on his own, which makes it easier for potential attackers to do so."[24]

This was an astute observation. Arab military operations lacked coordination and a corporate sense of purpose. In Jabaliya and Manshiya, fighters refused to go on guard duty because they had not been properly fed, and residents openly defied the NC's authority. "I must tell you that the Manshiya people are no good," Tamimi lamented to a local journalist.

After we took good care of them and gave them 30 rifles, they became highly abusive to our people. We found out that they needed [further] help and sent them another detachment of fifteen fighters, headed by a very important person – a former officer in a British commando unit by the name of Isa Khalili. Upon his arrival he was told that there was no need for him or his men, only for their weapons. When he refused to leave, the local residents pointed a gun at him and threatened to kill him if he didn't depart. What would you say to this?

A few days later Tamimi aired his grievances with one of Manshiya's leaders when the latter contacted him for military support. "Your people are insolent, taking orders from no one and doing as they like," he complained.

"But the rifles we have, 26 in all, are all of French make, and are not satisfactory."

"It makes no difference what make they are," said Tamimi. "A rifle is a rifle. I don't want to interfere in this matter. Contact the National Committee."[25]

Meanwhile the mood in Jaffa was rapidly nearing pandemonium. People stayed indoors for fear of attack by either Jews or Arabs. It was widely believed that owing to its vulnerable geographic location, that is, being surrounded by Jewish neighborhoods, the city was taking excessive punishment from the Jews for acts of hostility elsewhere in Palestine. (In fact, for political reasons the Jews refrained from translating their overwhelming local superiority into a general assault on Jaffa, let alone an attempt to conquer the city: they did not want to challenge the United Nations, which had awarded Jaffa to the prospective Arab state, or to antagonize the British, who were loath to allow the city to fall into Jewish hands.) The flight thus continued apace, with homes of absentees often being plundered or occupied by those who stayed behind. Severe food and fuel shortages became endemic, while companies and factories transferred assets and machinery out of town. There was considerable anger with Tamimi, and the AHC more generally, for failing to attend to the city's needs. When in February Tamimi traveled to Egypt for consultations with the Mufti, the purported aim of the trip was widely seen as a cover for his fleeing the country. Hassan Salame's attempts to enforce a system of central operational control failed miserably as only a handful of people responded to the demand to surrender their private weapons to his headquarters.

To make matters worse, local fighters began selling their ammunition to the highest bidders, telling their commanders that it had been exhausted in the fighting against the Jews. So widespread did this practice become that the NC was forced to send guards to confiscate ammunition from local residents and to issue a public warning that any weapons used for purposes other than defense would be impounded and their owners prosecuted. An AHC member visiting Jaffa on a fact-finding mission was scathing in his judgment of the local leadership. "I discovered numerous irregularities and squabbles among key personalities in the city," he informed the Mufti on January 21. "In my opinion, and for the public good, Rafiq Tamimi should be removed from Jaffa. He and several NC members who are practically doing nothing have unnecessarily wasted a lot of money."[26]

Public morale was boosted in early February by the arrival of some 250 ALA fighters, bringing the city's military strength to about 1,600. Appointed Jaffa's commander by ALA commander-in-chief Ismail Safwat, an Iraqi major by the name of Abdel Wahab Sheik Ali received an almost regal reception. A luncheon, attended by some 200 dignitaries, was held in his honor, and Heikal threw a lavish tea party on his behalf.[27]

This idyll did not last long. Though he introduced a measure of discipline into the local militias and launched a string of successful attacks on Tel Aviv and the Jewish cities of Bat Yam and Holon on Jaffa's southern borders, Sheik Ali failed to assert his authority over the armed gangs operating in the city, and his relations with Heikal soured as the mayor insisted on subordinating military affairs to political objectives. Warned that the escalation of fighting could lead to Jaffa's eventual destruction, he reportedly retorted: "I do not mind [the] destruction of Jaffa if we secure [the] destruction of Tel Aviv."[28]

This was to be Sheik Ali's swan song. Within a fortnight of his arrival, he had already asked to be relieved of his post and to return to Iraq. Shortly afterward, following a successful Hagana attack that totally ruined his reputation, he traveled to Damascus and tendered his resignation, complaining of the fecklessness and divisiveness of the Jaffa people. He was particularly embittered by the machinations of the Mufti's loyalists, notably Salame, who had done their utmost to undermine his position, yet was hardly more complimentary about Heikal.[29]

On February 19, a new Iraqi commander – Lt. Colonel Adl Najim al-Din – arrived in Jaffa at the head of a further 150 Iraqi and Bosnian fighters. Peremptorily conferring with representatives of the municipality and the Muslim Brothers, he informed them in no uncertain terms that he would not tolerate the kind of treatment meted out to his unfortunate predecessor. He knew what he was talking about. No sooner had he arrived in Jaffa than Salame left for Cairo, at the Mufti's demand, reportedly to plot Najim al-Din's downfall.[30]

By late March, the position of Arab Jaffa had become precarious. Successful Hagana operations, and the flight of some Iraqi and Syrian troops, led to a sharp drop in morale among the military. Attempts to recruit fighters from other Palestinian localities came to naught despite the handsome financial rewards offered to potential volunteers. The arrival of some 200 ALA fighters did little to improve the situation, as relations between the foreign troops and the local population continued to deteriorate: so much so that, in the words of a prominent Palestinian Arab leader, "the city's residents came to dread [the foreign troops'] misconduct more than Jewish perfidy." Treating the Jaffa populace as subordinates, the ALA forces, particularly the Iraqis, engaged in widespread extortion and racketeering, imposing "levies" and "taxes" on the hapless residents and confiscating weapons and cars, which they then sold on. Fighting and beatings became commonplace, resulting in a number of deaths and many injuries. Even Salame was beaten up by Iraqi fighters.[31]

Residents began to pine for a ceasefire, or even for a Jewish takeover after the British withdrawal. Heikal rushed to Syria and Transjordan at the head of a local delegation in search of fresh reinforcements and arms supplies. They were cordially received by the Syrian prime minister who promised full support, but were told by the defense minister that Jaffa was militarily indefensible and that its Arab inhabitants should leave the city and return to it later.[32]

The trip to Amman was ostensibly more productive as the delegation managed to extract a pledge from Abdullah, backed by a royal gift of two armored cars, to send the Arab Legion to Jaffa; and while the British announced that they would not allow the Legion to enter the city so long as they remained in Palestine, Abdullah's prestige shot to new heights, not least since Heikal hid the dismal results of his mission from his constituents, instead applauding the pan-Arab determination to rid Palestine of the Zionists, who "threatened the entire Arab nation."

By contrast, the Mufti's stature was diminishing rapidly, especially after it transpired that he had diverted a large consignment of Jaffa-destined rifles to Abdel Qader. Tamimi, who had never carried much weight, could do little to rectify the situation from faraway Cairo, whence he showed no desire to return. Having lost interest in the city he was supposed to represent, he carried out errands for the Mufti vis-à-vis the Arab League on behalf of other Palestinian localities. Likewise, Salame's ability to command one of the most demanding military zones in Palestine was severely compromised, especially after the spectacular bombing of his headquarters by the Hagana in early April 1948.[33]

This last incident, together with the Deir Yasin tragedy, the Arab setbacks in the battle for the Tel Aviv-Jerusalem highway, and the fall of Haifa, reduced morale in Jaffa still further, generating a fresh wave of flight, particularly of women, children, and the remaining members of the leading families.

By the time the Irgun Zvai Leumi (National Military Organization, or IZL), the small militant organization headed by Menachem Begin, future prime minister of Israel, began its offensive in the morning hours of April 25, inaugurating what was to be the final round in the battle for Jaffa, the city's 70,000-strong Arab population had dwindled to about 20,000–30,000 residents.[34] This is not to say that the situation was totally hopeless. On the contrary, with its defenses reorganized by Najim al-Din, who introduced a measure of unity into the disparate forces operating in the city, Jaffa was giving Tel Aviv, Bat Yam, and Holon as good as it got. In the words of a contemporary British report, "As long as mortar bombs are fired from Jaffa at Tel Aviv, life in that city is also precarious." On April 22, three days before the commencement of IZL operations, mortar shells from Jaffa rained on Tel Aviv throughout the entire night. On April 26 and 27, while the offensive was in full swing, Tel Aviv was still under heavy fire, including mortars, from Jaffa.[35]

Yet military might is of little consequence in the absence of inspired and committed leadership. As Jaffa reached its moment of truth, infighting between the municipality and the NC continued, as if the city were not already on the verge of a major catastrophe, while relations between the ALA and the civilian population ebbed still further. Iraqi soldiers punctured the car tires of virtually every dignitary in Jaffa before embarking on a robbery spree that spared few establishments and drove merchants and shop owners to salvage their remaining stock and flee the city. The local law-enforcement agencies were nowhere to be seen: most policemen who were not entitled to pension rights deserted the city with their weapons; others expressed their readiness to fight the municipality if the NC promised to continue their employment after the British withdrawal.

"Jaffa is in its death throes," ALA field commander Fawzi Qawuqji cabled to one of his battalion commanders on the evening of April 25, ordering him to carry out a diversionary attack against the neighboring town of Petah Tikva so as to relieve the pressure on Jaffa. As nothing was done, on April 27 Taha Hashemi, the ALA's inspector-general, rang the alarm bells more loudly. "No contact with Jaffa since yesterday," he cabled Qawuqji. "Establish contact with the city at all costs. Assure us that reinforcements are on their way and that they will fight to the last man." This was soon followed by yet another telegram: "Situation too grave for a delay. Send reinforcements to protect Jaffa whatever the cost." Yet it was not before April 28, when the Hagana followed in the footsteps of its smaller underground counterpart and launched a large-scale operation against Jaffa's surrounding villages, that a 500-strong ALA force arrived from Ramle to help the city's defense.[36]

The incensed Qawuqji peremptorily sacked Najim al-Din, who left town on May 1 at the head of a few hundred Iraqi and Bosnian fighters, carrying off some £8,000 (nearly £200,000 in today's terms) sent for military operations, as well as a substantial quantity of weapons. His successor – a former

Transjordan Frontier Force captain by the name of Mishel Isa – had an even briefer term in office. Having exploited a moment of complacency among the Hagana fighters to dislodge them temporarily from the Tel Arish neighborhood, in southern Jaffa, he reported to Qawuqji on May 2 that his troops had been "infected by panic flight." Shortly afterward he fled the city himself with a few members of the NC, followed by 350–400 Yemeni and Egyptian fighters. "The situation in Jaffa is extremely complicated, and most of the 2nd company's soldiers have dispersed by land and sea in all directions," the unit's commander reported to the ALA headquarters. "Of the entire company, only 10 soldiers have remained and it is inconceivable that we'll manage to hold out [for much longer]."[37]

Told by the Lydda mayor of the arrival of these troops in his city, Heikal exploded: "They are dogs. Take their weapons. They fled after having been paid their salaries." Yet he had only himself to blame. Instead of boosting public morale and bracing his constituents for the mortal fight confronting them, Heikal exacerbated panic by consistently underplaying the seriousness of the situation, then spreading the fabrication that "hundreds of Arab men and women had been trapped in the Manshiya [neighborhood] and then ruthlessly slaughtered by the Jews."

The mayor must have considered this lie a clever ploy to garner support for his city, especially as Jaffa was being attacked by the same underground movement that had perpetrated the Deir Yasin carnage, yet the move backfired disastrously. "I never found the slightest shred of evidence to support this contention and I examined Manshiya carefully just after the battle," wrote the renowned American journalist Kenneth Bilby. "But the fact was that Heikal's story had spread like sage fire among the Arabs of Jaffa and they needed no urging to get out."[38]

By now, the British had become Jaffa's main protectors. "After [the] defeat at Haifa in order to excuse their own ineptitude [the] Arab leaders accused us of helping [the] Jews and hindering [the] Arabs although it was actually due to [the] inefficient and cowardly behaviour of Arab Military Leaders and their refusal to follow our advice to restrain themselves," read a special situation report submitted to the British cabinet and military leadership. Yet the British authorities felt unable to ignore the Arab leaders' baseless criticism since the "position of Jaffa, surrounded as it is by [the] Jews and being [the] most important Arab Town in Palestine has always been [the] subject of acute anxiety to leaders including King Abdullah."[39]

An ultimatum was thus relayed to the Tel Aviv mayor to call off the offensive, which by April 27 had broken through the Arab line of defense, or face a harsh British retaliation. As the threat failed to have an impact, some

4,500 troops, supported by tanks, armored cars, and field artillery were rushed to Jaffa, where they clashed with IZL fighters, while Spitfire aircraft strafed Jewish positions and two Royal Navy destroyers waited offshore ready to engage if needed.

On April 29, High Commissioner Cunningham reported with satisfaction that "by intervention of British troops and air force and the threat of using the air against Tel Aviv Jaffa has just been saved from being overrun by [the] Jews." He elaborated the following day: "After some heavy fighting (in which a British tank commander was killed) and an air strike against Jewish strong points at Bat Yam and Holon, the badly shaken Jews retired to their original positions and requested a truce."[40]

This is true as far as it goes, yet one can only help those who are prepared to help themselves. In no time Cunningham's upbeat mood gave way to stark pessimism, and by the end of the month he seemed to have lost all hope of shoring up the Arab campaign. "Wherever the Arabs are in contact with the Jews their morale has practically collapsed and we are finding increasing difficulty in bolstering them up," he reported to the colonial secretary.

> Jaffa is rapidly emptying of all its inhabitants and I am told that the Iraqis with the ALA there are also threatening to leave. . . . We are in a weak position in attempting to discourage evacuation because whatever counter-operations we might take against the Jews we cannot guarantee safety of [the] Arabs in a fortnight's time . . . [although] the Jewish Agency have today undertaken that if Iraqi and other foreign troops who remain in Jaffa are withdrawn there will be no (R[epeat]) no further Jewish attack on the town.[41]

Cunningham had little doubt as to who was culpable for the unfolding tragedy: "Perhaps it could be explained that this disaster at Jaffa is the fruit of premature military action against which [the] Arab governments have been repeatedly warned and that further premature action on their part will only add to the suffering of the Arabs of Palestine."[42]

Sir Henry Gurney, chief secretary to the Palestine Mandate Government and a harsh critic of Zionism, was even more scathing. "Really the Arabs are rabbits," he recorded in his diary on May 5:

> Ninety per cent of the population of Jaffa have just run away, and only some 5,000 now remain. Yesterday the municipal engineer locked the door of the water supply pumping station, and walked off. The [British] army have taken it on. The Mayor has gone, without even saying goodbye, and the remnants of the Liberation army are looting and robbing. This is what the

Palestine Arabs get from the assistance provided by the Arab States. Perhaps our warnings to the States not to indulge in such premature military action were not always enough.[43]

Thus it was that instead of stemming the Arab exodus the British forces in Jaffa found themselves facilitating an accelerated flight. On April 25 alone, some 4,000 people left by sea, while hundreds more fled by land to the neighboring village of Yazur, followed the next day by a large convoy of trucks, under British escort, carrying women and children. Two days later, in the morning hours of April 28, Hagana observation posts reported a heavy traffic of trucks, buses, cabs, and private cars in the direction of Jerusalem – all loaded to capacity with people and personal belongings; in the afternoon, a ship full of escapees was spotted in the port while an armada of boats was busy delivering refugees in the direction of Gaza. The flight continued unabated in the following days, with scores of people leaving on foot and with vehicular convoys departing from Jaffa every single day, often under British protection: at least 100 trucks left on April 29, over 130 trucks on May 1, and some 200 trucks, as well as tens of cabs and private cars, on May 3 and 4 carrying some 2,000 people. These were followed on May 5 by at least 4,000 Arabs, and a day later by yet another 1,000 evacuees.[44]

Having failed to protect its constituents, the municipality was reduced to organizing their departure by both land and sea. In mid-April, for example, a special convoy for the transfer of all municipal officials to Amman was organized.[45] At the same time the municipality approached the British authorities for assistance in the evacuation of the city's residents. "Jaffa Municipality has asked that arrangements be made for evacuation of Arab civilians by sea from Jaffa to Beirut," Cunningham reported to London on May 1:

It is believed that shipping firms [whose] telegraphic addresses are shown below now have ships in or near Tel Aviv and would be prepared to effect [the] necessary lift.

    (a)   Unexpected, Beirut.
    (b)   Adriamare, Venice.
    (c)   Armenlauro, Naples.

2. Numbers of deck passengers offering probably two thousand.

3. Grateful if request could be conveyed through firms to captains of any suitably placed ships to proceed [to] Jaffa soonest possible. Failing clear instructions ships which may be in Tel Aviv are likely to be kept there by [the] Jews.[46]

The request seemed to have the desired effect. Later that day two passenger ships arrived in Jaffa and began embarking Arab residents anxious to flee the city. The following day, two more ships ferried away the wealthier residents who had hitherto failed to flee the city, while the lower classes had to make do with the boat service to Gaza.[47]

By May 1, according to British sources, Jaffa's Arab population had dwindled to some 20,000. Two days later, speaking from the upmarket Philadelphia Hotel in Amman, where he had temporarily settled, Heikal claimed that "every Arab has now left Jaffa. It is a ghost town." By May 8, according to various estimates, the city had virtually emptied, with a mere 3,000–5,000 Arabs remaining in situ. Many of them were making a living by looting abandoned shops and shipping the merchandise to Gaza and Nablus, and there were widespread fears that deserted homes were next in line. Municipal departments were shut, as were other public services and institutions such as banks and the city hospital. ALA forces had all but vanished, leaving the city to a few hundred armed gangsters who roamed the streets exchanging fire and plundering whatever they could lay their hands on.[48] But as far as fighting the Jews was concerned, the struggle was over. At 3:30 pm on Thursday, May 13, 1948, after brief but intensive negotiations, the remaining members of Jaffa's Arab leadership sat down with Hagana representatives to sign an agreement on the city's capitulation. "This is not a time to rejoice," read a special Hagana communiqué issued to mark the momentous event. "The city of Jaffa is almost empty. We promised the [remaining] residents a peaceful and dignified life and it is incumbent on each and every one of us to uphold this commitment; this is a matter of honor and the hard moral core of our army."[49]

Some of Jaffa's former Arab residents were no less contemplative of the city's last moments. "There was a Belgian ship," recalled Ibrahim Abu Lughod, who fled Jaffa for Beirut ten days before its surrender, "and one of the sailors, a young man, looked at us – and the ship was full of people from Jaffa, some of us were young adults – and he said: 'why don't you stay and fight?' I have never forgotten his face and I have never had one good answer for him."[50]

CHAPTER 8

Jerusalem Embattled

*"Jerusalem is lost. No one is left in Qatamon; Sheik Jarrah has emptied; even
the Old City is being deserted. Everyone is leaving. Anyone who has a check or
some money – off he goes to Egypt, off to Lebanon, off to Damascus."*
Hussein Khalidi, January 1948

Of all the partition's failings, none was more galling for the Zionist
movement and Jews worldwide than the UN decision to internationalize
Jerusalem, or Zion. The city had been Judaism's holiest site since biblical
times and had become the focus of the millenarian Jewish yearning for a
return to the ancestral homeland. Its exclusion from the territory of the
prospective Jewish state placed in question not only the success of Zionism
but also the historical Jewish attachment to Palestine to which the Balfour
Declaration and the League of Nations mandate had granted international
recognition. Besides, if existing population distribution were the main crite-
rion for the partitioning of Palestine, then Jerusalem was the place that had
been predominantly and increasingly Jewish in population since well before
the birth of the Zionist movement in the 1880s. If in the name of this principle Jaffa could remain an Arab enclave in the heart of the Jewish state, it
was only fair that Jerusalem, where Jews outnumbered the Arabs by a large
margin, should be included in Israel.[1]

Being the astute political realists that they were, many Zionists realized as
early as the mid-1930s that partition offered the only viable opportunity for
the creation of a Jewish state and that the attainment of this goal was linked to
the internationalization of Jerusalem. This manifested itself in a (begrudging)
acquiescence in the 1937 Peel plan, which confined the prospective Jewish
state to a small fraction of Palestine and excluded Jerusalem from its territory,
and in the far more enthusiastic acceptance of the partition resolution a decade
later. What apparently made internationalization somewhat more palatable
was the awareness that, whatever Jerusalem's political status, with its 100,000-
strong community, about one-sixth of the Yishuv's total population, the city

was bound to play a pivotal role in the life and development of the nascent Jewish state. In Ben-Gurion's words: "Jerusalem was not assigned as the capital of the Jewish state, but Jerusalem has been, and must remain, the heart of the Jewish people."[2]

This, however, was easier said than done, not least since the city's physical isolation and heavy dependence on outside supplies made it vulnerable to Arab whims. No sooner had the UN voted on partition than Jewish Jerusalem came under sustained attack and a prolonged siege that was broken only after months of bitter fighting that exacted heavier casualties than any other campaign of the war.

Within a week of the start of hostilities, Jerusalem's Jewish community was short of dairy products and vegetables and had no supply of fresh milk. By the end of January 1948, it possessed only about a fortnight's supply of flour and a month's sugar. The supply of eggs was down by 35 per cent, milk by 65 per cent, while food standards in Jewish Jerusalem had fallen by about a third in quantities consumed, and even lower in nutritional terms because of the lack of protein in the diet. A month later the community was left without basic food products including meat, fish, eggs, milk (except for children), vegetables, and butter – in stark contrast to the city's Arab population, which could rely on the hinterland of surrounding towns and villages for a regular supply of food and other vital commodities.

"Arab markets are glutted with food supplies . . . poultry, fresh vegetables and fruits are particularly abundant," read a February 1948 report by the US Jerusalem consulate, while a Hagana brief (in late March) told of an "excellent" state of supply in Arab Jerusalem. "Vital food products are plentiful and cheap," it wrote. "Geared to supplying the needs of its Jewish counterpart, the Arab market has been left with a large food surplus. To this must be added the [endemic] train robberies, which have filled Arab warehouses, as well as the importation of certain products from Transjordan, which, owing to low customs, are cheaply sold." In December 1947 alone, according to official British figures, Arab train robbers seized 120 tons of wheat and barley, 30 tons of rice, 190 tons of flour, 15 tons of sugar, 20 tons of oranges, and 43 cows, in addition to 100 tons of wood, 190 tons of cement, and 100 tons of miscellaneous goods. This at a time when, in the words of a British intelligence report, the Jewish population was "desperately short of food and other essential domestic commodities."[3]

The prominent Zionist official Bernard Joseph, in charge of the affairs of Jewish Jerusalem for most of the war, recalled the difficult dilemma confronting many of the city's Jewish employees in the mandate administration as regards food supplies for their families:

The Arab officials, who had plenty of food that came in freely from the hinterland, used to offer them eggs, bananas and other tempting items which they would have been eager to take home for their children. The Arabs wished in this way to prove how badly off the Jewish population were. The Jewish officials soon realized this and agreed that as a matter of principle none of them would accept any such food, even from Arab friends.

To tackle this predicament, the Jewish authorities enforced a strict austerity regime, maintaining tight control over the stockpiling, distribution, and pricing of basic commodities. A systemic effort was launched to clean and repair cisterns, used since biblical times for storing water; people were encouraged to plant vegetables in their gardens and to use their waste water to this end; and rationing was imposed on petrol for both public and domestic consumption. Even with these measures in place, residents were reduced to cooking in their gardens and back yards over campfires of sticks and left-over bits of wood. In late March, bread rationing was introduced, with every resident receiving 200 g (14 oz) per day (about four slices of this staple). By mid-April, the Jewish community was drawing on its last rations of flour after ten days without any meat, fish, eggs, or milk, except for children.[4]

Nor could the city's Jewish community bring to bear its numerical superiority over its Arab counterpart, about two-thirds its size, both because of its aging population and socio-economically weak composition and because of its dispersion in noncontiguous suburbs, many of them surrounded by Arab neighborhoods. To the west of the city, Beit Hakerem and Bait Vegan were separated from the rest of the city by the Arab suburbs of Sheik Bader, Lifta, and Romema, and the Arab lands west of the affluent Jewish neighborhood of Rehavia. To the north, Mount Scopus, home to the Hebrew University and the Hadassah hospital, was cut off by Wadi Juz, Sheik Jarrah, and the American colony. In the southeast, Talpiot was flanked by Qatamon, Baq'a, and the Greek and German colonies, as was the outer suburb of Mekor Haim, which also faced the Arab village of Beit Safafa. The position of the Jewish quarter in the Old City, where some 1,500 Jews lived among 22,000 Arabs, was particularly dire. Communication between this area and the other Jewish neighborhoods had been precarious even at the best of times, and subject to regular disruption by Arab mobs, especially on Muslim religious festivals. Once hostilities broke out, the quarter came under immediate siege and repeated attacks, as did the adjacent Yemin Moshe, the first Jewish neighborhood built outside the Old City's walls, in the 1860s.[5]

The problem of defense was further compounded by the massive British military presence in the city, which prevented the Hagana from operating freely, and by the draconian measures it imposed, notably the cordoning off of about one-third of new Jerusalem in security zones, which were largely closed to Jews but open to armed Arabs who roamed them with impunity. "There is probably some reason for the Jewish complaint that the British are favoring the Arabs," wrote the US consul-general in Jerusalem, Robert Macatee, in December 1947. "Requests from Jews for authorization to organize their own protection against the Arabs are refused. [By contrast] police arrests and searches among Jewish personnel and settlements are the order of the day." Two months later, the consul-general was much blunter. "The Police have no sympathy for the Jews, and state freely their opinion that the latter will 'collect a packet' from the Arabs once the British relinquish the mandate," he wrote. "Many Police add that in their opinion the Jews have 'asked for it.'" Even High Commissioner Cunningham conceded, with quintessential English understatement, that "on the whole more Jewish attacks on Arabs have been prevented [by British forces] than vice versa."[6]

But the story doesn't end there. British security personnel were also implicated in a series of anti-Jewish outrages in Jerusalem, from the distribution of weapons to Arab rioters in early December, to the bombing of the building of the moderate English-language newspaper the *Palestine Post* on February 1, to the surrender twelve days later of four unarmed Hagana men to a rampaging Arab mob, which murdered them in cold blood, to the February 22 bombing of Ben Yehuda Street in central Jerusalem, in which fifty-two people were killed and another 123 wounded, to shootings on civilian Jewish targets in the Old City, to armed provocations aimed at inflaming Arab – Jewish relations.[7]

Jewish anger with the British boiled over as a result of the latter's total passivity during the attack on a Hadassah-bound convoy on April 13. A British military post, less than 200 m (600 ft) from the incident, did nothing to stop the carnage, which raged for over five hours, and the authorities dissuaded the Hagana from sending reinforcements to the area. At 9:45 am, some ten minutes after the start of the attack, Lt. General Gordon MacMillan, commander of the British forces in Palestine, passed nearby in his car but did nothing to stop the bloodletting. Twice subsequently, at 1 pm and 2 pm, British military cars passed and were hailed by Dr. Haim Yassky, the hospital's director who was trapped in the convoy; neither stopped. At 1:45, Dr. Judah Magnes, president of the Hebrew University, telephoned MacMillan with a desperate plea for help, only to be told that British forces were on their way. An hour later, with no sign of the promised help in sight, two of the convoy's buses were set on fire and most of the passengers who had not been killed already were burned alive. By the time the Arabs were finally driven away around 4:40 pm, seventy-seven doctors, nurses, and scientists had been killed, including Dr. Yassky, though it took some time to identify the bodies, many of which had been burned to ashes. "They're bringing them out now, all that. This is the twenty-seventh, I think," a British police constable reported in a wireless message intercepted by the Hagana, before losing his calm and yelling at his superior: "If you'd have [had] us move from this spot when I asked you, we could have got them all out safe." The Arab commander of the massacre had a different complaint, namely that "had it not been for Army interference, not a single Jewish passenger would have remained alive."[8]

Ironically, though not unlike other Arab settlements, Jerusalem's Arab commu- nity unraveled rapidly despite the fact that its circumstances were relatively good. As early as November 30, Arabs began vacating not only borderline neighborhoods (as did some of their Jewish counterparts) but also the Old City, where they were far more numerous than the Jews, and the strategically located (and predominantly Arab) suburb of Romema, which controlled the western approach to the city via the Tel Aviv-Jerusalem road. They were shortly followed by residents of Qatamon and Lifta and by children from the Government House area, in the southeastern part of the city. In some instances, evacuees were ordered out by armed gangs who transformed the vacated sites into bases for attacks on adjacent Jewish neighborhoods.[9]

By the end of the year, Romema and Lifta had largely emptied of their Arab residents. So had the northern village of Qalandiya, from which even the livestock had been removed, while in Qatamon and Sheik Jarrah the flight gained momentum as the fighting intensified. Particularly disorien- tating was the January 5 bombing of the Semiramis hotel in Qatamon, which served as a military headquarters and an arms cache.[10] Though gener- ating an international rebuke, as a Spanish diplomat who resided in the hotel was one of the bombing's fourteen fatalities, the attack also heightened the Arab sense of vulnerability and triggered a fresh wave of evacuees. "Many of those who had been pontificating about the Palestine problem and vowing to defend the country to their last drop of blood now keep their heads down, timidly avoiding eye contact with their friends," reported a Hagana intelli- gence source. "They say that if the Jews succeeded in penetrating Qatamon and blowing up such a huge building and its occupants, there is nothing left to do here. Many families are making preparations for leaving the place."

Arab threats to burn evacuees' belongings and to expropriate their property failed to stem the flight; warnings to punish young evacuees who refused to return were ignored. Nor did the deployment in Qatamon and Sheik Jarrah of some sixty guards, rushed from the neighboring town of Bethlehem, have any perceptible impact. Many residents put the blame for the deteriorating security situation on the Husseinis, who had allegedly deployed small armed gangs in Sheik Jarrah which engaged in anti-Jewish hit-and-run attacks and left the population exposed to retaliatory actions. By mid-January, these suburbs had been largely deserted (though a few families did later return home). The same was true of the Shneler and Sheik Bader areas in central Jerusalem, as well as Beit Safafa, which was abandoned by most of its residents after their repeated pleas to stop using the village as a springboard for attacks on Mekor Haim had been ignored by the AHC and the local gangs. By mid-March, the village had been totally vacated by residents and placed under the control of Iraqi fighters. In the Old City families left for Bethlehem, Ramallah, and neighboring villages, while in Musrara many families were forcibly turned back by Arab guards. Conversely, in Wadi Juz, residents were ordered out of the village to allow for its use as a base for an assault on the Hebrew University and the Hadassah hospital; the same occurred in the eastern suburb of Deir Abu Tur, which became a hub of gang activity.[11]

Even Talbieh, an affluent quarter where Jews and (mainly) Christian Arabs had lived side by side in peace and harmony, was rapidly emptying of its Arab residents. Reluctant to succumb to the mounting pressure to take on their Jewish neighbors, and fearful of threats of revenge for their alleged betrayal of the Arab cause, many families chose to leave for the alluring safety of the neighboring Arab countries. In late January, the Hagana's Jerusalem commander estimated that Talbieh "is increasingly becoming Jewish, though a few Arabs have remained."[12]

Matters came to a head in mid-February, following a spate of Arab attacks in neighboring areas. On the afternoon of February 11, a day after the defeat of a major Arab attack on Yemin Moshe, a Hagana van with a mounted loudspeaker toured Talbieh and warned the residents "to avoid provocative acts." Although the van was peremptorily intercepted by the British police, which arrested its three occupants, and despite assurances by their Jewish neighbors that no harm would be visited upon them, some 60–70 Arab families fled the quarter later in the day to the exasperation of the Arab leadership. Unlike Sheik Jarrah and Qatamon, which continued to serve as military strongholds after their evacuation, it was widely feared that Talbieh would be transformed into a springboard for Jewish attacks. To prevent such an eventuality, the AHC decided to expropriate the abandoned properties and to man them with fighters, while the British incorporated Talbieh into their security zone. This still failed to stem the flight, and in the following weeks most of the remaining families left the neighborhood.[13]

For Hussein Khalidi, AHC secretary and its most senior member in Palestine, the situation was too much to handle. "I don't understand," he lamented in a phone conversation secretly recorded by the Hagana. "In 1936 there were 60,000 [British] troops [in Palestine] and the Arabs were fearless. Now we deal with 30,000 Jews and they are trembling in fear." In another phone conversation with the Mufti, Khalidi made an impassioned plea for the immediate return of his AHC colleagues to Jerusalem. "If the brothers who are with you [in Cairo] don't come back, I won't be able to hold on. The situation is very serious. What are these people doing over there? Emile [Ghouri], Sheik Hassan [Abu Saud], what are they doing? Send Rajai [Husseini]. The AHC has not a single official [in the mandatory administration]."[14]

As the Mufti remained impervious to his pleas, Khalidi rapidly lost heart. "Our situation in Jerusalem is dire," he confided to a Haifa colleague on January 8. "Qatamon has been vacated. Sheik Jarrah has been deserted, half of the Musrara [residents] are gone. No money or people have been sent – we are sitting here as if in transit. For a month I have been phoning [the Mufti in] Egypt. I am going out of my mind."

Two days later, Khalidi was in the throes of despair. "It's forty days since the declaration of jihad and I am completely overwrought," he bemoaned. "Everyone has abandoned me. Six [AHC members] are in Cairo, two are in Damascus – I won't be able to hang on for much longer. . . . Jerusalem is lost. No one is left in Qatamon; Sheik Jarrah has emptied; even the Old City is being deserted. Everyone is leaving. Anyone who has a check or some money – off he goes to Egypt, off to Lebanon, off to Damascus."

But were there not enough young Jerusalemites who could prosecute the fighting, inquired the astonished interlocutor. "They are not worth a penny," retorted Khalidi. "Hassan [Salame] was here for three days and ran away. Emile [Ghouri] left for 48 hours and hasn't been heard off for 15 days." As for the Mufti's top commander, Abdel Qader Husseini, who arrived in Jerusalem in mid-December to take control of the district – he was nothing but trouble, "causing expenses and big problems to the national committees in their respective jurisdictions" while keeping them in the dark about his plans and activities. This resulted in total disarray in the Arab camp, with no central authority in charge of planning and coordinating political and military affairs.[15]

Khalidi was not alone in making his indictment. According to a British intelligence report, Abdel Qader "has not created a very good impression. Sources state that when he visited the Nablus area . . . it cost the local inhabitants £1500 [£36,500 in today's terms] in entertainment expenses alone."[16] Worse, unlike other cities and rural settlements which established National Committees (NCs) prior to, or immediately after, the passing of the partition resolution, it was only on January 27, 1948, that such a body was formed in Jerusalem after lengthy haggling between the AHC and representatives of the various Arab quarters. Even then, the AHC resented the exclusion of some staunch Husseini supporters from the NC and constantly attempted to undermine the body that was officially answerable to it.[17]

By way of boosting his prestige and overcoming the growing reluctance of the middle and upper classes to contribute to the national effort, the Mufti donated his Jerusalem house to the war chest in what was lauded by the AHC-dominated media as a shining example of sacrifice for the greater good. Many Arabs, however, remained unimpressed as it was evident that the house would in all probability be returned to the Mufti at a later date, which made his generosity seem less than sincere.

Public perceptions of the AHC thus remained profoundly negative. Its members were widely seen as corrupt if not extortionist, having cowed ordinary people into contributing to the war effort only to pocket the money for their own purposes. Thefts by the National Guard from the people it was supposed to be protecting did little to endear the AHC to its constituents, despite the draconian punishments meted out by Abdel Qader to suspected thieves, including amputations and summary executions. Every Jewish attack generated a violent backlash against the AHC; even the Semiramis bombing was blamed on this body for having allegedly implicated the Jerusalem Arabs in a fight that was not theirs between the Jews, on the one hand, and the British and the Husseinis, on the other. So low had the AHC's prestige plunged that Khalidi dreaded appearing in public. "You should hear the curses in the streets," he confided to a colleague. "I cannot cross the road. They have eaten me [alive]." After a typical anti-AHC outburst, he reported to the Mufti how the agitated residents "came to our homes, attacking and swearing on all sides."[18]

In these circumstances, it was hardly surprising that many Arab neighborhoods continued to manage their own affairs regardless of the NC's instructions. In the Old City, residents not only set up their own local committee, against Khalidi's strong objection, but also established a movement supporting Palestine's incorporation into the Hashemite kingdom of Transjordan. In upper Baq'a, the Greek Orthodox Christians decided to form their own guard and to purchase their own weapons – not out of fear of the Jews, whose rule they openly preferred, but rather for dread of their Muslim brothers, who vowed to slaughter the "treacherous Christians."[19]

In Qatamon, the remaining residents formed a local committee to attend to the suburb's security needs. "We decided to undertake the guarding of our neighborhood," the prominent educationalist Khalil Sakakini proudly recorded in his diary in the first week of January 1948. "We held prolonged meetings, checked the inventory of arms in our possession, raised money for

buying weapons and hiring security personnel for guard duties around the
clock, and placed soil-filled barrels at the entrance to the neighborhood. . . .
In short, we have transformed our suburb . . . into a fortified castle that
dwarfs the forts of Sebastopol, Firdan, and Gibraltar!"

By mid-March, this buoyant mood had given way to deep depression. "By
God, I have no idea how we can withstand the Jewish aggression," Sakakini
wrote. "They are trained, organized, united and armed with the most modern
weapons, while we have nothing. Isn't it time for us to understand that unity
triumphs over factionalism, organization over anarchy, and preparedness over
neglect?"

A meeting with Khalidi and his AHC colleague Ahmad Hilmi failed to
allay Sakakini's fears. "We asked for weapons and they said: 'We have no
weapons,' " he recalled:

> We asked for guards and they said: "We have no guards." "What shall we
> do then?" we asked. "Buy arms and defend yourselves," they replied. "We
> don't have weapons, and should we buy ones, we don't have anyone who
> can use them," we said. "After the Semiramis bombing and the demolition
> of a number of buildings, how can we be sure that we will not be attacked
> again? It is your duty – as the Arab Higher Committee – to provide us with
> arms and fighters. Where are the trained volunteers [from the Arab states]?
> Where are the funds collected in the Arab and Muslim countries?

An emergency visit to Abdel Qader's headquarters in the neighboring village of
Birzeit proved equally futile. Having been kept waiting for two full hours only
to receive vague promises of support, the delegation returned to Qatamon
deeply disillusioned. "It is hardly surprising that residents consider moving to
other neighborhoods, or other cities, in order to free themselves of this lingering
anxiety and the daily danger they confront," Sakakini wrote. "This is why many
of our neighbors have moved – to the Old City, to Beit Jalla, to Amman, Egypt,
and other places. Only a handful of affluent people [have] remained."[20]

Sakakini was not being fully truthful with himself. The Qatamon
committee was no model of operational efficiency and national commitment. Its first military commander, Shafiq Uwais, quickly wasted the
substantial sum of money received for military operations in futile shootings
on adjacent Jewish neighborhoods. His successor, Ibrahim Abu Dayyeh, a
celebrated associate of Abdel Qader lauded by Sakakini as "a lion,"
temporarily restored local morale but deserted his fighters at the height of the
battle for Qatamon in late April.[21]

Nor was there any shortage of fighters, weapons, or ammunition in Arab
Jerusalem. Quite the contrary: in late February and early March, most

suburbs were reinforced by no fewer than 1,200 ALA troops, as well as fighters from Hebron and Bosnian mercenaries, who helped introduce a measure of law and order and improved local security. Several hundred fighters were placed in Baq'a, while the rest were deployed in the Old City, Sheik Jarrah, Wazi Juz, Musrara, Beit Safafa, and the Greek and German colonies. Qatamon itself was reinforced by some 175 well-armed and organized Iraqi troops (who were later replaced by a similar number of Hebronites), bringing the overall number of fighters in the suburb to at least 400 and boosting public morale.[22]

An effort was also made to improve Muslim-Christian relations after a wave of anti-Christian violence, including attacks on a number of monasteries and the murder of monks, triggered an official complaint [Greek government] to the Mufti. Meetings between the AHC and representatives of most Christian denominations were held in Jerusalem, after which leaders of eleven Christian communities issued a statement expressing complete solidarity with the Muslims and urging the annulment of the partition resolution "in the interests of peace."[23]

Whether the statement reflected a genuine (however transitory) sentiment or an attempt to fend off the common Muslim accusation of treachery, as intimated by a senior Christian government official to a Jewish colleague, Arab interdenominational tensions were temporarily superseded by a surge of euphoria following a string of diplomatic and military gains, notably the apparent withdrawal of US support for partition and successful attacks on Jewish convoys throughout the country. Many Arabs found the Jerusalem bombings, especially the March 11 attack on the Jewish Agency building in which thirteen people were killed and another hundred wounded, particularly uplifting.

Eager to bask in the perceived glow of the atrocities, the AHC reneged on its condemnation of the Ben Yehuda bombing, instructing Abdel Qader to take responsibility for the massacre. While Ben-Gurion was telling the British high commissioner of his eagerness "to have an agreement that everybody in Jerusalem should go freely about their business," Khalidi rejected any cessation of hostilities unless the Jews gave up their hope of independence. "The Arabs will never accept [a truce] because they have nothing to gain thereby," he stated emphatically. "The Jews are the only ones to welcome it, because they would like to see [the] 100,000 Jews in the Sacred City in perfect security so that the Hagana gangs would not have to worry about them."[24]

The daily newspaper *Filastin* was far more blatant. "What happened to the Hagana, [its elite unit] the Palmah and the IZL, lauded in so many superlatives?" it gloated. "Your bluff has been called and you have become ordinary

Jews again, dependent on others' protection even when armed with heavy machineguns."[25]

This euphoria proved short-lived. When in early April the Hagana launched Operation Nahshon in an attempt to break the siege of Jerusalem, some Arabs in the city contrasted the fall of a string of villages along the Tel Aviv-Jerusalem road with their own failure to conquer a single Jewish neighborhood and demanded a response in kind. When this failed to materialize, panic spread, leading to the rapid disintegration of Arab economic life throughout the city – not so much because of the lack of vital products but as a result of massive hoarding. Shortages of petrol and other types of oil were particularly crippling. Like their Jewish counterparts, Arab residents were now reduced to cooking on campfires; public transport services, both inside Jerusalem and with other localities, were greatly reduced, while many taxi drivers were left unemployed; squabbles at petrol stations became a common sight. Still, by early May there was an ample supply of vegetables, whose price dropped sharply. Eggs and butter were readily available, as were beef and pork. Rice was plentiful in the Old City and the German colony, while fish from Jaffa could be obtained two or three times a week. Bread was rationed but of good quality.[26]

In an attempt to slow down the intensifying flight, the Jerusalem branch of the Arab physicians' association threatened to shame escapees by publishing their names – to no avail.[27] Already in mid-March the AHC had allowed women, children, and the elderly to leave the city for Transjordan and Lebanon in a tacit acknowledgment of its inability to stem the exodus.[28] Now that the Jews had loosened the Arab stranglehold on Jerusalem and the Mufti had lost his foremost commander, Abdel Qader Husseini, in the battle for the city, the AHC and the NC were rapidly becoming an irrelevancy. Abdel Qader's successor, the firebrand Ghouri, did little to boost morale: such was his lack of military experience and public standing that most people simply ignored his promotion and regarded Salame and Fadl Abdullah Rashid, the city's Iraqi commander, as Abdel Qader's rightful heirs; even Ghouri's Christian co-religionists resented the appointment for fear that it would antagonize the Muslim majority and aggravate interdenominational relations.

If these fears were not realized Ghouri nonetheless proved a weak and indecisive leader, unequal to the mammoth task with which he had been entrusted. His desperate plea to Sir Henry Gurney to help stem the Arab flight, which starkly contrasted with his public bravado, was curtly rebuffed, as the chief secretary asserted with uncharacteristic forthrightness that the authorities had done everything in their power to help the Arabs and that it was now up to the Arabs to help themselves. While this encounter was not made public, it nevertheless exacerbated the demoralization of the local leadership and the upper classes who clamored to leave the city, many of them with AHC approval.

In no time the Egyptian consulate was flooded with hundreds of visa applications (including a few dozen requests from the Khalidi family) to be processed prior to the end of the mandate in mid-May. Ignoring his government's order to withhold the award of new entry permits, the Lebanese consul sold up to a thousand for a large sum of money. Scores of officials who lost their jobs following the dismantling of the mandatory administration fled to Jericho en route to Transjordan and other Arab countries, where they hoped to obtain gainful employment. By mid-April, NC chairman Ghaleb Khalidi had left for Egypt, though his flight was kept secret for fear of reducing Arab morale still further. So was the departure of the AHC's most senior member – Hussein Khalidi – in the latter part of April, and the Mufti's efforts to obtain Egyptian visas for members of his family.[29]

Not that the masses needed specific reasons to flee. Panic grew by the day, especially after the fall of Qastel and the Deir Yasin tragedy. People slept in their clothes for fear of a Jewish attack; any intensification of the fighting, or rumor thereof, sent many more from their homes. As early as April 2, Musrara had virtually emptied and only a few families remained in Qatamon. By the end of the month they were all gone, as were the residents of many Jerusalem suburbs and outlying villages, including Malha, Ein Karim, Baq'a, Wadi Juz, the Greek colony, and the few remaining families in Talbieh.

In a desperate bid to stem the exodus Fadl Abdullah Rashid ordered residents to stay put, forbidding them even to move from one Jerusalem neighborhood to another. But these were hollow words: there was no one to lead by example. Instead the AHC authorized the evacuation of women and children from border neighborhoods and gave a special dispensation to members of prominent families to leave the country.

Thousands of refugees streamed to Bethlehem and Hebron, while others crossed the Jordan River en route to Amman. "Arabs are now leaving Jerusalem in large numbers," Gurney recorded in his diary.

> Large residential areas like Baq'a and upper Qatamon have been almost evacuated . . . driving through the German Colony, we saw lorry after lorry loaded with household effects, people and baggage on the way out of Jerusalem. Others have gone into the Old City for refuge. Many of the rich have suddenly discovered that they have pressing assignments in Cairo or Beirut. This is Arab fecklessness at its worst, with black market exploitation and throwing of the blame on somebody other than themselves, i.e., the British.[30]

Gurney's harsh words reflected a deep sense of frustration with the course of events. No friend of Zionism (which he believed to be built "upon a foundation of lies, chauvinism, suspicion and deception") or of Jews ("You know, Mrs. Meyerson," he once said, "if Hitler persecuted Jews, there must be some reason for it"), the chief secretary was effectively exhorting the Arabs, with whom the British had "a sort of Robin Hood relationship . . . that no amount of toughness on either side seems to affect," to get their act together. Not all was lost, he reassured himself, the Arabs "would probably win [the] struggle if they kept cutting lines [of] communication."[31]

Indeed, Operation Nahshon's impressive gains notwithstanding, the Jews were nowhere near conquering Arab Jerusalem. Their suburbs were taking no less of a battering than Arab areas, especially the outlying neighborhoods of Neve Yaacov and Atarot, which were undergoing sustained assaults. The siege, though temporarily broken with the arrival of several large convoys, was quickly re-established as the Arabs blocked the Tel Aviv-Jerusalem road. "The Jews have their troubles," High Commissioner Cunningham reported to London on April 30. "In Jerusalem they are short of many supplies including oil of all kinds; and it is difficult to believe their assertion that recent convoys have brought up stores of food sufficient for many weeks. They have little immediate prospect of getting more; for the Arabs have blown down tons of cliff on the Jaffa road at Bab al-Wad and firmly intend to keep that road closed."

To Alexander Heinz, headmaster of a youth institute in the Jewish suburb of Arnona, which in early May became the target of artillery bombardments, together with the Romema, Givat Shaul, and Shneler neighborhoods, this general prognosis was very real. "The security situation in the Talpiot-Arnona-Ramat Rahel front has deteriorated in the past few weeks to such an extent that any child can be hit by a bullet upon leaving home," he wrote to the Hagana local command. "We have actually been on the receiving end of snipers from Sur Bahr and the Bethlehem road . . . [to the extent that] we cannot provide sufficient food to our students."[32]

Fresh Arab reinforcements poured into Jerusalem and the neighboring villages, some of which were evacuated and transformed into military strongholds.[33] On April 15, some 300 fighters arrived in A-Tur, followed by 750 former members of the Transjordan Frontier Force, disbanded by the British a few weeks earlier. About 500 ALA fighters were deployed in Ein Karim and a 600-strong contingent of well-trained Iraqis, armed with heavy mortars and machine guns, arrived in the Old City with a view to invading Jewish neighborhoods to "avenge" the Haifa debacle. All in all, some 3,000 Arab fighters were estimated to have arrived in Jerusalem in the second half of April.[34]

In these circumstances the Arabs showed no intention of stopping the fighting, regardless of the mass exodus. On April 25, Cunningham reported to the British delegation at the UN headquarters in Lake Success, New York, where desperate attempts were being made to arrange a ceasefire, that he was yet to hear back from the Arab side, whose local leadership had all but vanished, and added that the military situation was very much under the control of the foreign forces. "Activities of these leaders are quite uncoordinated by either [the] Arab Higher Committee of which only one effective member is here or [the] local Arab National Committee," he wrote. "[The] Supreme Muslim Council is virtually not functioning, all members except one having left. Arab thieves are now engaged in looting Government property and shooting British police to get their arms. Numbers of Arab temporary police having been paid have now deserted."

The US consulate, which also threw its (far less substantial) weight behind the effort to end the fighting, reported despairingly to Washington: "Most representative Arabs have fled to [the] neighboring countries and Arabs of authority are found only after [the] most diligent searching. Consequently truce and ceasefire talks are greatly hampered and slowed down."[35]

Anxious to prevent a repeat of the Haifa episode, where they had unjustly been accused of surrendering the city to the Jews, the British tried to shore up the Arab military position, as they also did in Jaffa, forcefully dislodging the Hagana from Sheik Jarrah, which it occupied on April 24, on the pretext that the area was vital for the army's projected evacuation route. "For armed Arab bands to hold it is permissible, apparently, but not armed Jews," commented an embittered Jewish journalist.

> Sheik Jarrah is one of the strategic key-points of the city. Through it Arab bands have been pouring into Jerusalem without check. Itself, it was a poison spot long before the massacre of the Hadassah convoy. The Government did nothing to neutralize it. When the Hadassah passengers were massacred, Government just stood by. Now, finally, the Jews themselves clean it up – and Government promptly drives them out. What sickness has hold of the British?[36]

Sheik Jarrah proved the army's swan song in Jerusalem. When the battle for Qatamon was finally joined on the night of April 29, Cunningham refrained from intervening, underscoring the limits of British military power and pleading that pressure be brought to bear on Jamal Husseini and Moshe Shertok – the Arab and Jewish representatives in Lake Success – to extend the temporary ceasefire, agreed earlier that day for the Old City, to the whole of Jerusalem. "[W]e have only enough troops in Jerusalem to intervene when our own communications are threatened and hence cannot always stop these battles outside the communication areas quite apart from the undesirability of using artillery and air in Jerusalem," he wrote to Colonial Secretary Creech Jones. "Furthermore, it is now clear that in this type of house to house fighting the Jews win every time. There seems therefore every advantage to the Arabs to accept the proposal."[37] The next day, as the Arab military position in Qatamon was rapidly nearing breaking point, Cunningham added: "It may interest you to know that the Arab in command of the Qatamon battle also left in the middle. The Arabs had been shooting at the Jews from this quarter for weeks and really brought the attacks on themselves."[38]

This was not what the local Arab leadership thought. In a special proclamation, broadcast simultaneously by the Jerusalem and Damascus radio stations, the NC blamed the British authorities for the fall of Qatamon – they had allegedly lured the Arabs forces to stop fighting so as to allow the Jews to prosecute their offensive with impunity – and urged the Arab states "to save the holy places from the Zionists." In fact, it was the Jewish leadership that was amenable to the idea of a ceasefire. On May 2, as Hagana forces were consolidating their hold on Qatamon, Cunningham met Eliezer Kaplan, the Jewish Agency's treasurer (and Israel's first finance minister), who "earnestly desired a truce for Jerusalem with only one condition namely [the] opening of the road from Tel Aviv to the Old City." Cunningham's explanation: "Recent Jewish military successes have tended to obscure the fact that with [the] Jerusalem-Latrun road still blocked [the] supply situation of Jews in Jerusalem will soon become serious again. But Kaplan who is personally confronted with these economic difficulties recognizes this, and on the Jewish side here agreement to a truce in Jerusalem now depends simply upon the opening of this road."[39]

This, however, was not to be. On the same day that Cunningham met Kaplan, Gurney saw Ahmad Hilmi, the only remaining AHC member in Jerusalem, and NC secretary Anwar Nusseibeh, and demanded a ceasefire in Qatamon. "They demurred but I told them it just had to happen," he recorded in his diary.[40] He might have added that his forceful words were totally pointless. When five days later he joined Cunningham for a meeting with Abdel Rahman Azzam in Jericho, they found the Arab League's secretary-general in no mood for compromise. While agreeing to allow food into Jerusalem provided nothing else was brought in, since it was against the principles of Islam to starve women and children, he would not concede to the opening of the Tel Aviv-Jerusalem road. Told that such a move could lead to the withdrawal of Jewish forces from Qastel, Qatamon, and other Arab settlements occupied in April, Azzam replied that he was not interested in the villages along the road. "I am fighting for a country and villages do not matter," he stated dismissively.

But the Jews insisted on the free use of the Tel Aviv road, Cunningham said. "Let the Jews say that to the world," retorted Azzam. "It will mean the destruction of Jerusalem and theirs will be the blame . . . it was not of any great disadvantage to the Arabs if the Jews took all Jerusalem. It was no center of their resources or manpower. If the Jews insisted on putting it to flames theirs would be the blame."

Azzam then treated his British interlocutors to a lengthy monologue on Jewish bellicosity and Arab peacefulness. "We are not seeking to put the country into anarchy, we did not want to start this fight, it was against our will and against that of the Mufti," he argued. "The Jews had been long prepared and their villages were forts while ours were open." Now that they had succeeded in setting Palestine ablaze, the Jews were constantly fanning the flames, in this case by preventing a truce in Jerusalem, to which the Arabs were agreed in principle, by making unreasonable demands. "There are other roads that will be open but not necessarily this road."

When Cunningham stressed again the Jewish insistence on the opening of the Tel Aviv road, the foremost lifeline to Jerusalem, Azzam dismissed the idea out of hand. He reckoned that the Arabs had been routed in Jerusalem yet he "preferred defeat than to bow to Jewish dictation."

Did he not want the Arab refugees to return to their homes?

Azzam replied that he "did not know whether he wanted the Arabs back in Qatamon as they may be massacred when they went . . . every man must decide for himself whether he wishes to return."

But what about the conquered Arab villages along the Tel Aviv-Jerusalem road – did the Arabs not wish to regain them?

"If it is in the Jewish military interest to keep these villages, let them keep them," Azzam retorted nonchalantly.[41]

CHAPTER 9

All Fall Down

"Jewish victories in Tiberias, Haifa, Jaffa and Qatamon have reduced Arab morale to zero and, following the cowardly example of their inept leaders, they are fleeing from the mixed areas in thousands."
British intelligence report, April 1948

Not everyone shared Azzam's indifference to the loss of Arab villages. The renowned Palestinian intellectual Hisham Sharabi, who in December 1947 left Jaffa for the United States, viewed rural Palestine as the lifeblood of the country's Arab nationalism and the standard-bearer of the anti-Jewish struggle. Three decades later he asked himself "how we could leave our country when a war was raging and the Jews were gearing themselves to devour Palestine." His answer: "There were others to fight on my behalf; those who had fought in the 1936 revolt and who would do the fighting in the future. They were peasants . . . [whose] natural place was here, on this land. As for us – the educated ones – we were on a different plane. We were struggling on the intellectual front."[1]

In fact, the Palestinian Arab peasants proved no more warlike or steadfast than the educated classes. Just as they had not risen in revolt against Zionism or the British in 1936–39 but were rather the hapless pawns of the Mufti's political machinations and helpless against the rapacity of the armed gangs that roamed the Palestinian countryside, so a decade later they did not stay behind and fight to prevent the creation of a Jewish state. On the contrary, fearful that the AHC's violent response to the UN resolution might wreak greater havoc, suffering, and dislocation than the 1930s disturbances, many villagers opted to stay out of the fight.

This mindset was not lost on the Jewish leadership. In a special communiqué to Arab villagers, circulated in the Jerusalem area in December 1947, the Hagana went out of its way to underscore its interest in peace while warning of harsh retribution should the Arabs choose the path of war. "We wish no harm to you or to any other Arabs," the statement read.

We prefer buildup and development to mayhem and destruction; we desire peace and not confrontation. But inciters and warmongers within your camp immersed both of us in this regrettable and painful bloodletting, and it is they who must be held culpable, before God and Man, for the Jewish and Arab blood that has hitherto been spilled.

We know that these warmongers seek to push you to the abyss through lies, propaganda, intimidation, and terror. We therefore implore you to deny them the use of your villages, homes, and fields for the establishment of centers, shelters, or bases so as to spare us the need to enter your villages – in self-defense – and harm you and your property. Should you get involved, we will have no choice but to respond in kind to any attack emanating from your villages.

"You have hereby been warned," the communiqué concluded. "We hope that you'll help to restore peace, quiet and tranquility to the country as a whole and to all its inhabitants. It is our hope that you'll deny the agitators and bloodletters any help that will enable them to perpetrate their machinations and continue their crimes."[2]

This warning seemed to have the desired effect. On December 24, a memo by the Hagana's Jerusalem headquarters recounted peace overtures made by Arab villages to adjacent Jewish neighborhoods and forbade any military operations in these areas without prior consultation with local dignitaries on both sides of the divide. Specifically, commanders were told that a peace agreement had been signed with Qastel, which was consequently struck off the list of villages patrolled by the Hagana, as was the village of Suba, which was about to sign a similar pact. A peace agreement was also reached with Sur Bahir, and the villages of Qatanna, Maliha, and Ein Karim indicated their interest in taking the same route.[3]

With the rapid expansion of hostilities, such agreements became a commonplace. In the Jerusalem area, Maliha was given immunity from Hagana retaliation, while Abu Gosh reached a peace agreement with the adjacent kibbutz of Qiryat Anavim, Deir Yasin with the Givat Shaul suburb, and Beit Hanina with the outlying neighborhood of Neve Yaacov.[4] On Tel Aviv's northern border, the large villages of Sheik Muwannis, Jammassin, and Abu Kishk, together with their smaller neighbors of Sumeil and Jalil, sought and received Hagana protection.[5] In the Sharon Plain, Wadi Hawarith, Shumali, Mansuriya, and Habla approached their Jewish neighbors with offers of peace, stressing their determination to prevent military operations in their areas. Similar overtures were made by Ard Saris, north of Haifa, by Kafr Qara, in the Samaria district, by Aqir, in the southern coastal plain, and by a string of villages in the Tiberias sub-district, including Sejera, Ma'dhar, Ulam, Hadatha, Kafr Sabt, and Ghuweir Abu Shusha.[6]

The Arabs made good their promise. In Sheik Muwannis, the *mukhtars* rejected a demand by the Jaffa National Committee (NC), to which they were officially subordinate, to form an NC in the village, claiming that their friendly relations with the Jews precluded the need for such a move. Abu Kishk used the same justification to deny the use of its territory to an armed gang, and Aqir deflected pressure from the Ramle NC to introduce 100 fighters to the village, arguing that it was perfectly capable of defending itself. Abu Gosh, Ein Karim, Deir Yasin, and Qastel did likewise, preventing, at times through the use of force, repeated attempts to exploit their territory for attacks on Jewish targets. In Maliha, the *mukhtar* went so far as to order villagers to open fire on all foreigners trying to enter the site, be they Arabs, Jews, or British, while the Qastel *mukhtar* gave a Jewish acquaintance early warning of an impending attack. Beit Hanina took this practice a step further by regularly informing Neve Yaacov of military movements in its vicinity. In the Haifa district, relations between Qannir and adjacent Jewish communities were so cordial that Arab gangs plotted their disruption by attacking the village and putting the blame on the Jews.[7]

The refusal to join the fighting, or to serve as bases for anti-Jewish attacks, was by no means limited to those villages that enjoyed the benefit of signed agreements. Numerous Arab settlements throughout the country acted in the same way, regardless of the formal state of their relations with the Jews. In late December, village *mukhtars* in the south of the country warned their constituents to forgo acts of violence unless provoked by the Jews. The following month, delegates from the Jerusalem district villages of Beit Safafa, Battir, Khirbat Lauz, Sataf, Walaja, and Sharafat agreed to preserve the peace and to prevent warlike activities in their respective jurisdictions. A similar decision was reached by representatives of Qaluniya, Beit Surik, Beit Iksa, and Beit Inan. Other villages in the district, including Beit Naqquba, Qatanna, Lifta, Qalandiya, and Silwan, averted gang attempts to use, or even to cross, their territory for attacks on neighboring Jewish targets.

Nor did ordinary Palestinians shrink from quietly defying their supreme leadership. In numerous tours throughout the Jerusalem district, Abdel Qader Husseini found villagers indifferent, if not hostile, to his repeated calls to arms. In Qastel, he encountered adamant rejection of greater military activism; in Shu'fat, his order to attack Neve Yaacov was flatly refused. So were his demands that Maliha attack the Jewish suburbs of Mekor Haim and Bait Vegan, that Deir Yasin provide volunteers for the war effort, that Suba allow fifty fighters into the village, that Qatanna join the attacks on Jewish convoys on the Tel Aviv-Jerusalem road, and that Battir and other villages along the railway line agree to the deployment of fighters in their territory and its use as a base for attacks. In Beit Safafa, Abdel Qader suffered the ultimate indignity, being driven out by angry residents incensed by their village's transformation into a hub for anti-Jewish attacks.[8]

In central Palestine, the villages of Tira, Taiyiba, Zir'in, Arab Jalad, Bashshit, Sabbarin, and Tel Safi rebuffed similar pressure, and occasional physical attempts, to implicate them in attacks on neighboring Jewish localities, as did Shafa Amr, Zib, Tarshiha, Kababir, Daliyat al-Karmil, and Usfieh in the north, among others. A kibbutz member who (in mid-January 1948) entered the village of Yajur, just outside Haifa, while towing a couple of broken-down cars, was mobbed by inhabitants professing their friendship and peaceful intentions. Several women kissed his hands, tearfully begging him "not to do to us what has been done to Balad al-Sheik" (where some sixty people had been killed in a Hagana retaliatory strike a fortnight earlier). Even in faraway Gaza, a prominent tribal head urged his peers to cease hostilities and to maintain the peace for fear of Jewish retribution.[9]

There was an economic aspect to this peaceableness. The outbreak of hostilities led to a sharp drop in trade and an accompanying spike in the cost of basic commodities, driving many villagers to try to salvage their crops by staying out of the fighting. The peace overtures of Tarshiha, Baqa Gharbiya, Miska, Faja, Yasur, and Arab Quz, among others, were explicitly intended to allow these villages to harvest their crops unhindered.

Then there were the numerous villages, dependent for their livelihood on the Jewish or mixed-population cities, that saw no point in supporting the AHC's explicit goal of starving the Jews into submission. Sur Bahir's nonviolent disposition, for example, was largely induced by the destitution attending the village's severance from Jerusalem's Jewish markets, which had hitherto provided most of its merchandise. Likewise, Kafr Saba continued to market its agricultural produce to the neighboring city of Tel Aviv. So prevalent was this maintenance of Arab-Jewish economic interaction that the Jaffa NC prosecuted villagers who continued to trade with Jews; a prominent merchant was even beaten up and his merchandise spoiled.[10]

Abdel Rahman Azzi, head of the large village of Zeita in the central coastal plain and the towering Arab figure in the area, had close and diverse economic and commercial relations with the neighboring Jewish localities. When an armed gang sought to implicate Zeita in a fight with an adjacent kibbutz, Azzi expelled it from the village, warned his Jewish neighbors of the imminent attack, and offered to send 100 fighters to help the kibbutz. A loyalist of King Abdullah, he regarded the AHC's warmongering as totally self-serving and aimed at promoting the interests of the Husseinis (by

enabling them to assert their rule over the Palestinian Arabs) and the British
(by providing them with a pretext to stay in the country). With this in mind,
Azzi resisted pressure to attack the Jewish localities of Gat, Galon, Qedma,
and Kfar Menahem. Were the Arabs to succeed in expelling the Jews from
Palestine, he would have no compunction about helping expel his Jewish
neighbors, he argued; until then, he would rather coexist than fight.[11]

This is not to deny the active participation of villages in the fighting from
the beginning. Balad al-Sheik, Tira, Ijzim, Jaba, Ein Ghazal, Sa'sa, Kafr
Kanna, Lubiya, and Saffuriya in the Galilee district, and Salame, Yazur,
Qula, Majdal Sadiq, Mazra'a, Deir Tarif, Beit Nabala, Deir Muheisin, and
Khulda in the Lydda district needed little encouragement to attack the Jews.
Yet these, and likeminded villages, were the exception that proved the rule.
Not only did most villagers prefer to stay out of the fighting but the few who
answered Abdel Qader's call did so, by and large, in order to obtain free
weapons for their own personal protection and then returned home.[12]

Such was the lack of appetite for war among rural Arabs that as late as
January 21, 1948, nearly two months after the outbreak of hostilities, Ben-
Gurion noted that "most of the Palestinian Arabs – the fellaheen – have so
far refused to take part in the war and still do." A fortnight later, he was even
blunter, stating that "so far most of the Palestinian Arabs have refused to join
the war despite the growing pressure and the plethora of Nazi coercive measures to which they are subjected: racist and religious incitement, lies and
falsehoods, atrocious propaganda, appeals to the basest instincts, promises of
booty, and threats and terror." As late as February 3, Ben-Gurion maintained
that "the villages, in most part, have remained on the sidelines."[13]

These attitudes, in Ben-Gurion's opinion, could be explained by a deep-
seated distaste for violence dating back to the bitter experience of the
1936–39 disturbances. Yet he was painfully aware of the fragility of the situation. Just as in the preceding decades ordinary Arabs had reluctantly been
drawn into the fighting by their bellicose leaders, so it could well be that "the
incitement, the gang pressure, especially by the foreign bands infiltrating the
country [i.e., the ALA], the promise [of booty], and perhaps certain Jewish
setbacks will eventually change the situation and implicate the villagers in the
fighting."[14]

This is indeed what happened. Some villages were drawn into the conflict
at an early stage by the local gangs, or the Mufti's forces, causing suffering
and dislocation, and, at times, total depopulation as frightened inhabitants
fled their homes to safer places. The locations of Qastel and Suba,
for example, were too important stategically for the disruption of the Jewish
lifeline to Jerusalem to allow them to remain aloof. By the end of March

Suba had been drawn into the conflict, while the fighting in the vicinity of Qastel had driven its inhabitants to vacate the village.[15]

Yet even those villages that managed to withstand local pressure found it infinitely more difficult to resist the ALA's influence. As the Arab League's official force, buttressed by the implicit weight of the entire Arab world, the ALA's legitimacy and prestige far exceeded that of the Mufti and his unpopular top men, Salame and Abdel Qader, let alone the AHC – most of whose members stayed outside Palestine at this critical moment. With its superior and much larger forces, moreover, the ALA was better positioned than the local gangs to impose its will on the Palestinian Arabs. Its detachments were deployed in numerous villages in the Samaria and Galilee districts, taking control of the local population and gradually drawing it into the fighting. Private arms were registered and villagers were enlisted for military training; Arabs who interacted with Jews were court-martialed and handed prison sentences or press-ganged into joining the pan-Arab force; ALA groups toured the countryside in an attempt to incorporate villages into the war effort and to identify locations that could be transformed into springboards for anti-Jewish attacks.

These pressures did not pass unopposed. In the Galilee, the largely Druze village of Meghar rejected a demand by Adib Shishakli, ALA commander of the Safad-Tiberias sub-districts and future dictator of Syria, to provide 100 fighters for military operations. In the Tulkarm sub-district, villagers dodged training sessions and failed to disclose their arms holdings so as to prevent their registration; others simply left their homes, only returning after the pressure for military involvement had receded. Yet most settlements succumbed to the demand to admit foreign troops. Take the villages of Sabbarin, Sindiyana, and Bureika in the Haifa district. All three maintained friendly relations with their Jewish neighbors, yet were forced to stop this interaction (some villagers refusing to do so were flogged, others were sent to Tulkarm for punishment), to deploy some 300 ALA fighters in their territory, and to prepare lists of all able-bodied men for recruitment purposes. Similarly, Qannir, which had gotten along famously with its Jewish neighbors, was drawn into the fighting in January, when local gangs began using its territory for anti-Jewish attacks. In early February, an ALA platoon of some thirty Syrians arrived in the village, reinforced by the end of the month by 300–400 fighters. Likewise, Idnibba, near Ramle, which had made a handsome living by selling stolen weapons to the Jews, was left largely deserted in early March after a contingent of Iraqi troops raided the village, confiscating a substantial ammunition cache and arresting one of its *mukhtars* and several other residents.[16]

Or consider the case of Ein Karim. Notwithstanding its elders' efforts to keep the village out of trouble, as early as December 19 Hagana observation posts identified some 200 fighters preparing for an attack on Bait Vegan. In the end the attack failed to materialize (though shots were fired from the village on the Jewish suburb), but the following month many villagers, and some foreigners, underwent military training, bringing the number of local recruits to about 300. These were reinforced in February 1948 by a well-armed ALA force of mainly Syrian fighters, and on March 10 a substantial Iraqi detachment arrived in the village, followed within days by some 160 Egyptian fighters, with a view to attacking Jewish convoys on the Tel Aviv-Jerusalem road. On March 19, the villagers joined their foreign guests in such an attack.

By early April, Ein Karim (and the adjacent Maliha) seemed to have abandoned all restraint. Though refusing to participate in the attempt to recapture Qastel, the two villages attacked Jewish targets in their neighborhood and made strenuous preparations for a large-scale attack on Bait Vegan, including the evacuation of women, children, and the elderly from their territory.[17]

Indeed, the deliberate depopulation of Arab villages and their transformation into military strongholds were marked corollaries of the Arab campaign from the onset of hostilities. As early as December 1947, an unspecified number of villagers throughout Palestine were ordered out of their homes by the local leaderships (notably in the Tulkarm sub-district), and this phenomenon gained momentum after the ALA's infiltration into the country. Within weeks, rumors were circulating of secret instructions to Arabs in predominantly Jewish areas to vacate their villages so as to allow their use for military purposes and to reduce the risk of falling hostage to the Jews.[18]

In mid-January 1948, Hagana intelligence briefs reported that villages in the Hula valley, north of the Sea of Galilee, had been partly emptied to accommodate local gangs and newly arrived ALA forces.[19] By February, this phenomenon had expanded to most parts of the country. In the central coastal plain, for example, villagers in Mirr and Wadi Hunein were ordered to leave their homes; further to the east, residents of Wadi Hawarith were "advised" to evacuate women and children to purely Arab areas, while Dannaba was abandoned and turned into an ALA training camp. In Jalama, the *mukhtar* was visited by ALA representatives who gave him three days to move all residents to Kafr Qasim; anxious to keep the village out of the fighting, the *mukhtar* quickly informed the Hagana of the demand.[20]

The following month saw the evacuation of the Jerusalem villages of Beit Safafa and Isawiya, which were placed under ALA control. In a desperate bid to save their village the Isawiya residents attempted to return home, only to be ordered to leave yet again.[21] A similar fate befell Bureika, whose residents were ordered out by the AHC to allow the village's transformation into a base for attacks on Jewish transportation to Haifa. They were followed by the Galilean settlements of Ulmaniya, Khisas, and Qumiya, where villagers bade an emotional farewell to their Jewish neighbors before departing. Even Sarkas, some 40 km (25 miles) south of Haifa, which had ignored three distinct orders by the AHC to evacuate its women and children, succumbed to ALA pressure and in late March or early April transferred its non-combatant inhabitants to neighboring Arab localities. It was subsequently made into a military base.[22]

This phenomenon gained considerable momentum in April and May as ALA and AHC forces throughout Palestine were comprehensively routed. On April 18, the Hagana's intelligence branch in Jerusalem reported a fresh general order to remove the women and children from all villages bordering Jewish localities. Twelve days later, its Haifa counterpart reported an ALA command to evacuate all Arab villages between Tel Aviv and Haifa in anticipation of a major new offensive. In early May, as fighting intensified in the eastern Galilee, local Arabs were ordered to transfer all women and children from the Rosh Pina area.[23]

These reports highlighted the tremendous scope of Arab-ordered evacuations during April, which not only included the tens of thousands evicted from Haifa and Tiberias by their own leaders but also scores of villages throughout the country that were partly or completely depopulated. These included Ulam, Hadatha, Sirin, and Ma'dhar in the eastern lower Galilee,[24] Fajja, Abu Fadl (Arab Sautriya), and Sarafand Kharab in central Palestine, Qannir in the Haifa district, and the remaining residents in the Jerusalem villages of Beit Hanina, Eizariya, Abu Dis, Isawiya, and Tur.

In early May, it was the turn of the villagers of Ein Dor, Nein, Dahi, and Shuna, in the Galilee, to be evicted by the ALA or local gangs. At the same time, Transjordan's Arab Legion entered the rural town of Beisan (of about 5,000 inhabitants), south of the Sea of Galilee, whence many residents had already fled, ordered the remaining women and children out, and barricaded itself inside. In the Jerusalem area, the Legion ordered the emptying of a string of villages, including Beit Haninna, Shu'fat, Judeira, Bir Nabala, Jib, and Rafat. At times there was no need to order an evacuation. The mere fear of ALA occupation was sufficiently alarming to spark flight, as happened with the Arab Zubeidat tribe, north of Haifa, which in mid-April removed its women and children for fear of the use of its territory by Arab forces.[25]

Fear was indeed the foremost catalyst in the rapid unraveling of rural Palestine, as villagers followed in the footsteps of city-dwellers and took to the road. As early as November 30, 1947, a day after the passing of the partition resolution, women, children, and the elderly were transferred from Jammasin and Sumeil, followed the next day by villagers from Sheik Muwannis and families from the Samarian village of Beit Lid, east of Netanya. By December 25, Sumeil had virtually emptied and a week later many Jammasin villagers fled in fear of retaliation for attacks on Jewish traffic in the neighborhood. The remaining residents left on March 17, 1948, and a fortnight later Sheik Muwannis was fully vacated, together with the neighboring Abu Kishk, which held a farewell feast for its Jewish neighbors, to whom it also sold its livestock. For their part, a number of Sheik Muwannis dignitaries bade farewell to Jewish friends in Ramat Hasharon, on Tel Aviv's northeastern border, leaving their personal belongings for safe keeping with the municipality head. An official Jewish delegation pleading with the village sheik to stay were told that "we are going . . . the big war will begin shortly and we are scared."[26]

In mid-December, Hagana intelligence sources recounted that an "evacuation frenzy . . . has taken hold of entire Arab villages." Before the month was over, many Arab cities were bemoaning the severe problems created by the huge influx of villagers and pleading with the AHC to help find a solution to the predicament. Even the Syrian and Lebanese governments were alarmed by this early exodus, demanding that the AHC encourage Palestinian Arabs to stay put and fight.[27]

As no such encouragement was forthcoming, either from the AHC or anywhere else, villagers fled their homes at an ever-growing rate. Mukheizin, Mansura, Arab Balawana, and Arab Satriya in the coastal plain, as well as Khirbat Azzun in the Sharon, among others, were emptied in part or in total in December.[28] So were scores of other villages throughout the country in the following months, including Beit Safafa, Maliha, Eizariya, Abu Dis, Beit Sahur, and Qalandiya in the Jerusalem sub-district; Balad al-Sheik, Hawsha, Arab Ghawarina, Yajur, and Ard Saris in the Haifa district; Shauka, Khiyam Walid, Maghar, Bawati, and Ubeidiya in the Galilee; and Qisariya, Yazur, Kabara, Arab Malaliha, Saiduna Ali, Arab Huweitat, Arab Rumeilat, and Abu Rizk in the central coastal plain.[29]

By early April, according to British figures, some 15,000 Arab villagers had fled their homes (with thirty-one villages totally abandoned), though the actual number was apparently more than twice as high. This amounted to nearly a fifth of the rural Arab population in the prospective Jewish state – about half of them in the 96 km (60-mile) coastal strip between Tel Aviv and Haifa where "the Arabs have almost completely evacuated [the predominantly] Jewish areas."[30]

The astounding Jewish victories of April and May opened the floodgates and removed all remaining inhibitions about fleeing. Wherever battle was joined, mass flight ensued. In the six weeks from the launch of Operation

Nahshon to the proclamation of the state of Israel on May 14, about 115,000–130,000 villagers (and some 100,000 city-dwellers) fled their homes.

The fighting along the Tel Aviv-Jerusalem road, for example, sent people fleeing the targeted villages and accelerated an exodus that had already been going on for months. Even the neighboring city of Ramallah and its outlying villages, which had not been embroiled in the fighting, were seized by flight frenzy. So much so that the ALA warned that "those who fail to participate in [the] defense of their villages will be liable to confiscation of weapons. If one deserts a village, one's house will be destroyed and crops will be set afire."

For its part the Jerusalem NC announced that all villages abandoned without AHC authorization would be severely punished and stripped of their rights. Few paid any heed. Jerusalem itself was emptying at a hectic pace and its NC, most of whose members had already fled, was hardly viewed by its constituents as the epitome of national commitment.[31]

The Mishmar Haemek defeat in early April triggered a general flight from adjacent villages, including Umm Zinat, Rihaniya, Khubbeiza, Abu Shusha, Daliyat Ruha, Buteimat, Ghubaiyat, Shafa Amr, Kafrin, and Rummana, as well as by the Arab Sawaid tribe. The fall of the large cities had a similar effect. "Jewish victories in Tiberias, Haifa, Jaffa and Qatamon have reduced Arab morale to zero and, following the cowardly example of their inept leaders, they are fleeing from the mixed areas in thousands," read a British intelligence brief. Hagana forces entering Yazur, Salama, Kafr Ana, Kheiriya, Yahudiya, and Saqiya as part of the offensive against Jaffa's rural hinterland ("Operation Hametz") found the villages virtually empty of civilians. Likewise, the fall of Haifa sparked a mass exodus from Arab areas in northern Palestine, including the cities of Nazareth, Safad, and Beisan, where every fresh rumor generated large waves of escapees. The villages of Balad al-Sheik, Hawsha, and Yajur, which had been gradually emptying in the preceding months, were swiftly deserted; in Tira, Arab Legion trucks were busy removing women and children, while Fureidis was largely abandoned on ALA orders and transformed into a military stronghold; Sarafand and Kafr Lam were totally deserted, and in Ein Ghazal, Ijzim, Umm Zinat, and Ibilin many villagers fled in fear. Even the collapse of Tiberias's small community, less than 6,000-strong, triggered a flight from neighboring villages, including Kafr Sabt, Ma'dhar, Majdal, Nasr al-Din, Samakh, Samra, and Shajara.[32]

Within days of the fall of Haifa, Damascus was rife with rumors that the Jews had turned the Galilean town of Safad into a "second Deir Yasin." In a late-night meeting on May 3 with the British ambassador, Philip Broadmead, the Syrian minister of the interior warned that "if [an] immediate stop was not put to Jewish aggression the Syrian forces would have to walk in." No sooner had Broadmead passed the warning on to London than he was yet again summoned to the minister who, "in a very agitated state," told him that 2,000 refugees had just crossed over into Syria as a result of Jewish attacks, and asked for advice on the matter. Unhesitatingly the ambassador warned "not to send the Syrian army in." Yet he was sufficiently alarmed to inform his superiors that "while I fully realize the difficulties confronting our military authorities in Palestine I feel we must keep in mind that [the] Jewish occupation of Acre and Safad and any other Arab center would be calculated to have a most deplorable effect here."[33]

To Chief Secretary Gurney these fears seemed far-fetched. "All sorts of alarmist stories are now flying about Damascus and Amman," he recorded in his diary, "and we can scarcely keep up with the job of telegraphing all round the world that Safad is not threatened with another Deir Yasin Massacre . . . that all the Arab villages in the Hula are not being attacked, and that it is not unsafe for Arabs to return to Haifa." General Hugh Stockwell, commander of the British forces in northern Palestine, concurred. If part of the Safad population was in imminent danger, he reckoned, it was the tiny Jewish community, less than a quarter of the size of its Arab counterpart, rather than the other way around.[34]

Scions of an illustrious community dating back to biblical times, the mostly ultra-Orthodox Jews of Safad had long lived on the whimsical sufferance of their Muslim neighbors, well before they were reduced to a minority in the 1920s or 1930s. When in 1834 Arab peasants revolted against the military conscription imposed by the Egyptian authorities then in control of Palestine, the Jews of Safad (about half the city's population) were slaughtered; nearly a century later, in the summer of 1929, scores of Jews were again massacred by their Arab neighbors.[35] Now that the country was rapidly sliding into anarchy, there was a palpable fear of repeat atrocities. On December 2, 1947, Ben-Gurion was informed of "panic" in the city; three weeks later he was told of "great fear in Safad and difficulty in controlling the public. Even the leaders are petrified. Were there to be free movement [from Safad], many will leave. The Hagana activists are getting destitute, having to spend half of their time on guard duties. They ask for a 100-strong reinforcement for Safad. This is psychologically necessary." By mid-February 1948, the situation had worsened further and the local Jewish leadership demanded the dispatch of 500–600 fighters, in addition to the fortification of the Jewish quarter and a sustained relief effort comprising vast supplies of food and petrol, on the one hand, and the creation of new working areas, so as to stop people from leaving, on the other.[36]

In these circumstances, the Arabs were in no mood for compromise. From the outbreak of hostilities in November 1947, Safad had been the source of much of the violence in the eastern upper Galilee while being careful to keep itself out of the fighting so as to avoid Jewish retaliation against its profitable communication links with Syria and Lebanon. Yet with the British withdrawal from Palestine in full swing, thousands of ALA fighters deployed throughout the country, and with the Arab states poised to invade Palestine upon the termination of the mandate, the coming of war to Safad seemed to be only a matter of time. When, on April 12, Stockwell attempted to engineer a local truce, he was told that the Arabs would accept a brief ceasefire until the British departure from the city if the Hagana abandoned some key strongholds and stopped fortifying others; an enduring truce, however, would require the complete withdrawal of Hagana forces from Safad and the surrender of all weapons held by the Jews, whose "lives and property" would in turn be guaranteed by the ALA. As these terms were rejected by the Jews, on April 16 British forces hurriedly left Safad, to the deep dismay of the Jewish community. "With 55 troops in two isolated billets in Safad town, and the possibility of all communication being cut," the regional commander explained the move, "I could not control or influence a battle between three or four thousand armed Arabs and one thousand or so Hagana."[37]

Convinced that a swift victory would ensue, the Arabs followed the withdrawal with a heavy assault on the Jewish neighborhoods. "Upon the British evacuation on April 16, we occupied all the city's strategic positions: the Citadel, the Government House, and the police post on Mount Canaan," recalled a local fighter. "We were the majority, and the feeling among us was that we would defeat the Jews with sticks and rocks."[38]

What this prognosis failed to consider was the Jewish resolve to hold on to Safad, awarded by the partition resolution to the prospective Jewish state, on the one hand, and the intensity of the flight psychosis, on the other. As tens of thousands of Arabs streamed out of Tiberias and Haifa within days of the British evacuation of Safad, members of the city's leading families and ordinary residents alike decided that now was the time to escape. In the words of a British intelligence report, "such is their state of fear [that] Arabs are beginning to evacuate Safad although the Jews have not yet attacked them."[39]

To make matters worse, the acrimonious relationship between Safad's two commanders – Hassan Bey and the newly arrived Sari Fnaish, a former officer in the Arab Legion turned soldier of fortune – prevented the adoption of a coherent strategy and led to internecine clashes and several deaths. Hassan's departure in late April did little to boost morale, already dampened by the fall of a string of villages around Safad and the eastern Galilee, including Ein Zeitun, Biriya, Zuk Tahtani, Tuleil, Jauna, and Zanghariya. As a former militiaman put it:

We could not defend the city, nor did we count on the Arab forces to protect it. Rumors spread that the Jews had been given Ein Zeitun. . . . The fall of this village left the city besieged from the south, east and north. We felt that the Arab forces did not try to prevent this situation. . . . If Sari Fnaish and his men did not protect Ein Zeitun, what would make you think he would protect Safad . . .?

In a desperate bid to shore up the situation, a delegation of local notables traveled to Damascus, only to be reprimanded by ALA commander-in-chief Ismail Safwat for fleeing the battlefield and ordered to keep on fighting. A subsequent visit by mayor Zaki Qadura to the royal court in Amman was a far more affable occasion yet equally inconclusive. While Abdullah was evidently moved by Qadura's pleas, he argued that there was nothing he could do before the termination of the mandate on May 15 and that the mayor had better return to Damascus and put his case to President Quwatli, who would then urge the ALA into action. Qadura dutifully complied, and following his visit to Damascus some 130 fighters were sent to Safad, arriving in the city on May 9.

This, however, was too little too late. As fighting intensified in early May, the trickle of escapees turned into a hemorrhage. On May 2, following the bombing of the Arab quarter by the deafening albeit highly ineffective home-made "David's mortar," scores of Arabs fled Safad en route to the Jordan valley, accompanied by a substantial number of ALA fighters. Four days later, ALA regional commander Shishakli reported that "the majority of the inhab-itants have left [Safad's neighboring] villages. Their morale has collapsed completely." Heavy artillery bombardments of Jewish neighborhoods failed to do the trick, and as the final battle for the city was joined on the night of May 9 a mass flight ensued. By the time fighting was over the next morning, Safad's entire Arab population had taken to the road; a day later, Hagana patrols reported that "the [Arab] quarter had emptied to a man," with evac-uees leaving behind "a huge quantity of weapons and ammunition." They were followed by the Hula villages and "a great number of villagers in the Eastern Galilee."[40]

Having boasted of glowing successes for some time, the Arabs were loath to reconcile themselves to the fall of Safad. As late as 8 pm on May 9, Jerusalem's Arabic radio reported that the royal cabinet in Amman had been reassured by "the commanding artillery officer in Safad" that the city had not fallen as had been erroneously announced and that the enemy had been repulsed with enormous losses. Greatly relieved, Abdullah replied that "we are very pleased with your telegram and this is what we expect of you. The day [of pan-Arab invasion of Palestine] is approaching." It was only the next

day that the Arab media grudgingly conceded that "our forces had to withdraw from Safad at 6.45a.m., after inflicting heavy losses on the enemy." So
traumatic was the city's fall that Fnaish was summarily tried and publicly
executed for having allegedly surrendered Safad to the Jews for a handsome
financial gain.[41]

The knock-on effect of the Jewish military exploits extended well beyond
their immediate domain. Purely Arab areas, non-contiguous with Jewish
neighborhoods, or areas that had hardly been touched by the fighting, were
also overwhelmed by flight hysteria. In the Samaria district, entire areas were
being deserted while others sought accommodation with the Jews, mainly for
fear of losing their crops. In the southern coastal plain, the city of Ramle was
swamped by refugees from neighboring villages; further to the south, the
small, sleepy town of Beersheba (6,500 residents) was rapidly emptying,
while the district of Gaza was reeling from the arrival of up to 30,000
refugees from all over the country, desperate to get as far away from the
fighting as possible.

Already in February, many villagers in the district had voiced their reluctance to get involved in the fighting in anticipation of the harvest season, and
their preference for a ceasefire or even reconciliation with the Jews. Now that
Gaza was struggling to come to terms with the severe shortages of food,
petrol, and other basic commodities attending the tidal wave of refugees, the
general population seemed to have lost all appetite for fighting. This defeatist
mood was further reinforced by a successful Jewish attack on the ALA camp
in Gaza City in mid-April. In the words of a Hagana intelligence brief: "It
can be stated with certainty that the Palestinian Arabs in the south and the
Negev are done with the war, and would undoubtedly be happy to acquiesce
in sovereign Jewish rule should they be able to get rid of the foreign forces
that keep on pouring into the area from Egypt at an ever growing pace."[42]

CHAPTER 10

The Scramble for Palestine

"The most likely arrangement seems to be Eastern Galilee to Syria, Samaria and Hebron to Abdullah, and the South to Egypt, and it might well end in annexation on this pattern, the centre remain uncertain."
General Sir Alan Cunningham, February 1948

"Abdullah was to swallow up the central hill regions of Palestine, with access to the Mediterranean at Gaza. The Egyptians would get the Negev. The Galilee would go to Syria, except that the coastal part as far as Acre would be added to the Lebanon if its inhabitants opted for it by a referendum (i.e. the inhabitants of the said coastal strip). In Jewish-controlled areas (including Haifa) the Jews would get some measure of autonomy."
Abdel Rahman Azzam, March 1948

The astounding Jewish victories of April and May 1948 in general, and the fall of Haifa, Jaffa, and Arab Jerusalem in particular, drew the reluctant Arab regimes ever more deeply into the conflict. As we have seen, the lack of genuine interest in the fate of the Palestinian Arabs, together with the fear of direct confrontation with Britain, on the one hand, and of the annexation of Palestine, or parts of it, to Transjordan, on the other, resulted in a wide gap between the Arab states' rhetoric and their actual disinclination, in the words of a British intelligence report, "to involve themselves wholeheartedly in any struggle to assist the Palestine Arab cause." Even Iraq's prime minister, Saleh Jabr, the foremost champion of pan-Arab activism, had privately conceded that "the majority of the Army is against fighting; amongst the tribesmen [who, he had boasted, would send 2 million fighters to Palestine] only about 1,000 are at all interested and even less than that number would actually carry on to the bitter end."[1]

When, in December 1947, the Arab League's political committee refused to task Transjordan (and Iraq) with the post-mandate invasion of Palestine, the two prime ministers angrily left the summit prior to its final session and shortly afterward Abdullah proclaimed that "the creation of a Greater Syria is the only solution to the Palestine question."[2] The other Arab rulers were unimpressed. At the seventh session of the League's council, held in Cairo on February 7–22, 1948, Abdullah not only failed to receive the coveted green light for the "liberation" of Palestine once the mandate had ended but his arch-enemy, the Mufti, was permitted for the first time to attend the council at the head of an AHC delegation.

Not that Hajj Amin had finally endeared himself to his Arab peers. Only a few months earlier Abdel Rahman Azzam had lamented that the Mufti "had learnt very little" during his years in exile and that his extremism was "at least, if not more, harmful to the Arabs as to the Jews." Yet knowing full well that the Palestinian leader "had captured the imagination of the Arab masses and the League could not, therefore, drop him,"[3] the secretary-general would rather have him fight his battles inside the League than sabotage its activities from the outside.

To judge by the official communiqué issued at the end of the League's session, which treated the Palestine question rather inconspicuously, this strategy seemed to be working. Rejecting yet again the Mufti's demand for the immediate formation of a Palestinian government-in-exile, the Arab delegates marginalized the AHC still further by setting up a new committee (headed by Azzam) to direct military and civil affairs until a Palestinian Arab administration could be established. At the same time, they did everything in their power to prevent such an eventuality, refusing to appoint an AHC representative to oversee the social and political affairs of the Palestinian Arabs or to authorize the newly established National Committees throughout Palestine to take over from the British upon the termination of the mandate. A request for financial support for the creation of a Palestinian Arab administration was unceremoniously declined, as was a plea for the recompense of war victims. The pretext: the Palestinians had to help themselves before asking others to help them.

Nor was the Mufti the only one to be bitterly disappointed with the lack of pan-Arab commitment to the Palestinian Arab cause. Having threatened to resign his post unless the Arab states defined their war aims, formulated a coherent war strategy, and agreed to send their armies to Palestine at the earliest possible opportunity, ALA commander-in-chief Ismail Safwat was obliged to bide his time until mid-March, when the Arab chiefs of staff would meet to discuss a coordinated pan-Arab strategy.[4]

In the event, the meeting failed to materialize owing to Egyptian opposition, on the one hand, and growing Arab complacency following a string of Jewish military and political setbacks, notably the American declaration that since partition was no longer possible the country should be placed under a

United Nations trusteeship, on the other. Though the proposal was peremptorily rejected by the AHC and the Arab states, America's apparent retreat
from partition was seen as effectively signaling the demise of the idea and a
huge step toward the ultimate goal of Palestine's immediate transformation
into an Arab state. If three months of indigenous Palestinian resistance,
supported by an irregular pan-Arab force, had so profoundly influenced the
position of the world's pre-eminent power, it was reasoned, surely there was
no need for direct intervention by the regular Arab armies: the ALA was
already strong enough to counterbalance the organized Jewish forces in
Palestine and would be even better placed to do so once its armaments were
enhanced with heavy artillery.

In their address to the newly established Palestine committee on March 16,
the Lebanese and Syrian prime ministers, Riad Sulh and Jamil Mardam,
declared a clear Arab victory in the first round of the war. So did Jamal
Husseini, who claimed that the Jews' overstretched military resources had left
Tel Aviv wide open to an Arab assault that would destroy the Zionist project
once and for all. A warning by Taha Hashemi, the ALA's inspector general,
that this self-congratulatory mood was largely premature, given that the Arabs
had failed to conquer a single Jewish neighborhood and that the Jews had not
yet shown their hand but were rather preserving their forces for the final
confrontation after the British departure, fell on deaf ears. An exhaustive
report by Safwat, the Arabs' tireless Cassandra, which stated that the
Palestinian forces and the ALA were incapable of defeating the Jews on their
own and that victory could only be achieved through a full-fledged intervention by the Arab armies, was similarly ignored. On March 21, the League's
political committee ended its session with the public boast that the first phase
of the political and military struggle had been won outright.[5]

In these circumstances, the buoyant Arabs rejected UN attempts to bring
about the cessation of hostilities. Azzam warned that a truce that did not
include the total ending of Jewish immigration and the disbanding of the
Hagana "was itself a threat to Arab existence in Palestine," while the League
instructed the AHC's UN representative to declare that the Arabs would only
cooperate with the world organization "on the basis of the annulment of the
partition resolution and the establishment of a democratic Arab state in
Palestine with minority rights guaranteed."

The AHC needed no such reminder, having just announced its own terms
for a truce: the expulsion of all "terrorist Jews" from Palestine, the disbanding
of the Jewish underground organizations, the total cessation of immigration,
and the repatriation of all Jews "smuggled into Palestine."

Since the AHC had always regarded all Jews arriving in the country after
the Balfour Declaration as alien invaders, the implications of its truce terms

were clear and unequivocal: the obliteration of the Jewish national cause and the ethnic cleansing of most of the Yishuv. In the words of Emile Ghouri: "The blood now being shed in Palestine is the result of the policy of establishing a Jewish national home in Palestine. Should the idea of partition and of the establishment of a Jewish national home be abandoned, peace would reign in Palestine." AHC secretary Hussein Khalidi put the idea in somewhat subtler terms. "The present disturbances were merely the effect," he said, "and before a truce could be negotiated the cause would have to be removed."[6]

While the Arab states were holding out the hope of avoiding a total confrontation, the two main contenders for Palestine were not idle. Having set the country ablaze and thrown his Arab opponents into disarray, the Mufti was assiduously working to establish control of the prosecution of the war despite his feigned deference to the League. In Safwat's scathing words: "Contrary to the specific orders of the Palestine committee, which made all forces in Palestine answerable to the [ALA's] commander-in-chief, the Mufti's henchmen continue to carry out independent war operations, in total disregard of the supreme command, thus spreading anarchy and chaos."[7]

For his part, King Abdullah, aside from consolidating his support base in Palestine, sought to rally Britain, still the paramount power in the Middle East, behind his Palestinian ambitions. As early as October 29, 1947, Sir Alec Kirkbride, the influential ambassador to Amman, warned foreign secretary Ernest Bevin that "Transjordan should not be penalized for being an ally of Great Britain if as may well be the case there is a general scramble for [the] Arab areas of Palestine as a result of our abandoning the mandate and marching out." "A greater Transjordan would not be against our interests, it might even be in their favour," he added, "so even if we are not prepared to help I see no reason why we should place obstacles in the way of Transjordan. [The] alternative of a non-viable Palestine Arab State under the Mufti is not attractive."

This prognosis was supported by the Cairo Middle East office and the Iraq embassy, which opined that "an extension of Abdullah's influence was a small price for successfully containing the Jewish state"; while a senior foreign office bureaucrat argued that, although Transjordan's annexation of parts of Palestine would be resented by Syria, Lebanon, and Saudi Arabia and might well cause some deterioration in Britain's relations with these countries, this temporary setback would be more than compensated by the move's geopolitical merits: "It would establish in a strategic and central position a state stronger than the Transjordan as it now exists, but bound to us by ties not merely of friendship and obligation but also of dependence. The alternative . . . would be a puny Arab Palestine dominated by the unreliable Mufti, incapable of maintaining its independence and a sure source of unrest and even war."[8]

Bevin needed little encouragement: as early as July 1946 he had suggested to the cabinet the idea of "assimilating" most of the Arab areas of Palestine in Transjordan (and Lebanon). He thus complimented Kirkbride on the considerable force of his argument, while asking Abdullah to tone down his Greater Syria rhetoric and to avoid precipitate moves on the Palestine question so long as it was still being discussed by the UN. "Your Majesty may nevertheless rest assured that your interest in this problem is fully recognized by H.M.G.," he wrote to the king, "and that, so soon as they feel that the situation has sufficiently crystallized to permit of their coming to a further decision, they will consult with Y.M. about the policy to be followed."

Arriving in Amman in late November, Bevin's letter allowed Kirkbride to persuade Abdullah ("one of the least patient people I have ever met") to forgo his plan to confront the forthcoming Cairo summit with Transjordan's claim to the Arab areas of Palestine after the Jewish state had been established. This, however, did not prevent prime minister Samir Rifai, during the summit, from trying to win British support for this very option. The idea was not to proclaim any form of annexation or formal government in the occupied territories, he argued, but to impose military administration for a year or two, by which time the Yishuv would have been brought to its knees through a relentless guerrilla campaign and would have no choice but to become an autonomous province of an expanded Hashemite kingdom straddling both banks of the Jordan River. A similar message was passed to London by Abdullah's personal envoy, Umar Dajani, who envisaged Transjordan's Arab Legion marching "into the whole of Palestine" and "containing the Jews" in the coastal plain until they agreed to come to terms.[9]

By way of making an informed decision on the issue, Bevin asked his ambassadors to the Arab states for an appreciation of the likely regional response to Transjordan's occupation of Palestine, in whole or in part. The general gist of the replies, in the words of Harold Beeley, Bevin's chief Middle East advisor, was that "King Abdullah can count on a large measure of support in the Arab world, if his action involves defiance of the United Nations and invasion of the territory assigned by them to the Jewish State. But if he confines himself to occupying what the Arabs have already been given, his action will be interpreted as personal aggrandizement and will isolate him from his neighbors and from Arab opinion generally."[10] Rather than reassure the foreign secretary, this prognosis only served to complicate his dilemma. "For your own information," he wrote Kirkbride, you should know that we hope (a) to see the trouble in Palestine localized and over as soon as possible; (b) that no situation will arise which might call for Security Council action (where it is very unlikely that we should feel able to use our veto to protect an Arab aggressor); (c) that King Abdullah will take no action that might isolate him from the other Arab States and thus give rise to the accusation that we are using him to engineer our re-entry into Palestine and to the possibility that he might unite the rest of the Arab world against him.

So far as we can see at present, it should be possible to satisfy (a) & (b) above, if King Abdullah occupied certain Arab areas of Palestine and refrained from sending the Arab Legion into the areas allotted to the Jewish State by the United Nations. This would however not satisfy (c) above, and it is hardly possible at present to think of any course of action which would satisfy all three requirements.[11]

A meeting between Bevin and Transjordan's newly appointed prime minister, Tawfiq Abul Huda, on February 7 did not dispel these doubts, although it resolved the issue as far as the foreign secretary was concerned. Keenly aware that Britain "might be held morally responsible vis-à-vis the United Nations and world opinion for what the Arab Legion might do," Abul Huda went out of his way to reassure Bevin that this British-financed, armed, and led force would scrupulously concentrate on law enforcement and peacekeeping operations, which would in turn win Transjordan international gratitude rather than censure. Yet he kept the door open to the possibility of an assault on the prospective Jewish state if the Jews "invaded Arab areas" – a rather flexible phrase given that the state was to include numerous Arab localities. He also predicted that "the Jews would find that they had opened their mouths too wide and that the United Nations would come to a similar conclusion" and abolish the partition resolution.

According to Brigadier John Bagot Glubb (Glubb Pasha), the Arab Legion's British commander who acted as interpreter during the meeting, Bevin endorsed Transjordan's invasion of Palestine after the termination of the mandate as "the obvious thing to do" but warned against invading the territory awarded by the UN to the Jews. Declassified British documents, however, show that Bevin made no such warning.[12] And why should he have done so? As an implacable enemy of the idea of Jewish statehood, who had fought tooth and nail to forestall the partition resolution and to prevent its subsequent implementation,[13] it made no sense whatever for the foreign secretary to seek to secure the state whose existence he had opposed in the first place, not least since such a move would have hopelessly isolated Britain's most loyal Arab ally.

Indeed, after the meeting with Abul Huda, Bevin told his advisors of Transjordan's possible invasion of Palestine, following which Bernard Burrows, head of the foreign office's eastern department, circulated a top-secret memorandum which was to be shared with the US administration. "It is tempting to think that Transjordan might transgress the boundaries of the United Nations Jewish State to the extent of establishing a corridor across the Southern Negev joining the existing Transjordan territory to the Mediterranean and Gaza," he wrote. "This would have immense strategic advantages for us, both in cutting the Jewish State . . . off from the Red Sea and by extending up to the Mediterranean the area in which our military and political influence is predominant by providing a means of sending necessary military equipment etc. into Transjordan other than by the circuitous route through Aqaba."[14]

More forthrightly, Michael Walker of the eastern department suggested that Jewish territories be awarded not only to Transjordan but to other Arab states as well. "It is obvious that the Arab Legion cannot hope to control all the Arab areas," he wrote after the Bevin-Abul Huda meeting. "The assistance of Iraq and Syria would therefore be essential and the northern areas of Palestine might well be their responsibility." That the "Arab areas of Palestine" were not seen as identical to those laid down by the UN is evidenced by a later memorandum by Walker: "I think from the talk with the Transjordan Prime Minister . . . that King Abdullah is determined to acquire the Arab areas of Palestine, either as defined by the United Nations or those areas with an Arab majority, except perhaps the north-west corner. Whatever reason may be given for the return of the Arab Legion to Palestine, the ultimate intention will be to obtain new territory for King Abdullah."[15]

Though Bevin refrained from speaking his mind to Abul Huda, his failure to warn him off an invasion was interpreted by the prime minister (as well as by foreign office officials) as acquiescence in Abdullah's territorial ambitions in Palestine, which extended well beyond the country's Arab areas. "Today I had a personal meeting with Mr. Bevin in my capacity as Minister of Defense and pure military questions were discussed," Abul Huda telegraphed to his master. "I am very pleased at the results and am proud to say that it is due to His Majesty that these results have been attained."[16]

The collapse of the Palestinian Arab war effort shook the Arab regimes out of their short-lived complacency and made the tacit Anglo-Transjordan understanding highly topical. As tens of thousands of petrified Arabs fled their homes (or were driven out by their leaders and military commanders), Abdullah was increasingly seen as Palestine's only conceivable savior, an image he embraced with alacrity. "Dissatisfied with their own military leaders and with their manifest inefficiency, the Arabs of Palestine are turning more and more to King Abdullah to rescue them from the consequences of intrigue and chicanery," High Commissioner Cunningham reported to London in late April. "If they are to succeed in a war of attrition they will need better leaders than they have now."[17]

Having listened to a Tiberias deputation on April 19, the king ordered the Legion to facilitate the ongoing evacuation of the city's Arab residents and announced a £3,000 (£75,000 in today's terms) aid package for the refugees. Four days later, after the collapse and dispersion of the Haifa Arab community, he sent a highly publicized cable to Cunningham warning that Arab anger over the latest developments in Palestine "could only be appeased by justice" and that the Jews had to stop harming Palestine on the pretext of building their National Home and agree to live in an Arab Palestine as a protected minority.

In a meeting with a group of prominent Palestinian Arabs who came to plead for his takeover of the country, Abdullah brimmed with militancy. "Were Iraq and the other Arab countries to join the Palestine campaign we shall forge ahead and, with God's help, drive away the Jews in less than ten days," he told the delegates, his eyes filled with tears. "Should they remain aloof because of their UN obligations, I'll be willing to enter the war on my own, putting my trust in Allah . . . and will either triumph or be martyred." In the meantime the king threw open the gates of Transjordan to the inpouring Palestinian refugees, waiving the need for entry visas (at a time when Syria and Lebanon were enforcing harsher restrictions) and giving his army carte blanche to carry out evacuations at its own discretion.[18]

Abdullah had good reason to be satisfied. In its emergency session in Cairo on April 10–22, the League's political committee at long last accepted his offer to undertake the rescue of Palestine with the Arab Legion, albeit not before King Faruq clarified that any pan-Arab invasion of Palestine should be considered "a temporary solution, devoid of any occupation or partition characteristic, and that after it is completely liberated it be handed over to its owners, who will rule it as they may please."

Safwat was thus sent to Amman with a personal letter from Azzam, thanking Abdullah most profusely for his offer and asking him to coordinate his moves with the other Arab states. Meanwhile the secretary-general confided to a senior British journalist that since it had been evident for some time that Qawuqji was no good and that the Arab states were unable to shore up the ALA and the Palestinian forces, it had become necessary for Transjordan "to do the job on condition that Palestine must be taken over as a whole and remain an Arab State." Even Ibn Saud, who a few months earlier had threatened "to go to war" to prevent Abdullah from occupying Palestine, wrote to the Hashemite monarch to express support for his prospective conquest of the whole of the country.[19]

This was music to Abdullah's ears, and he instructed his representative to the Cairo talks to reassure Faruq and the Arab delegates that the Arab Legion "will adopt, after the termination of the British mandate over Palestine, an attitude dictated by the requirements of pure Arabism" and that Transjordan "will cooperate with other sisterly Arab Governments closely and completely in this respect."

In his meeting with Safwat, the king explained the essence of this "close and complete cooperation": putting the irregular forces operating in Palestine under Transjordan's command (rather than making the Legion answerable to Safwat as the latter assumed); making the Hashemite monarch supreme commander of the impending pan-Arab invasion; giving Transjordan whatever military and financial support it deemed necessary; and allowing the Legion to prosecute the war as it judged fit.[20]

Without awaiting a formal reply, Abdullah arranged for the Iraqi ambassador to Amman to go to Baghdad with a request that one Iraqi division with full equipment and aircraft come to Transjordan in accordance with the bilateral treaty between the two Hashemite monarchies. On April 22, the Iraqi government acquiesced in the king's request and the following day Abdullah's nephew, the regent Abdel Illah, who had ruled Iraq since April 1939 on behalf of the minor Faisal II, arrived in Amman with his chief of staff and ministers of defense and finance. They were then joined by Azzam, Sulh, and the Lebanese and Syrian ministers of defense for two days of intensive discussions with Abdullah and his top political and military officials. The decision to invade Palestine after the end of the mandate was reaffirmed and the Arab chiefs of staff were instructed to come to Amman the following week to work out the operational plan. Abdel Illah promised that the Iraqi detachments would arrive in Transjordan within a matter of days, and the dignitaries left for Cairo, where the Arab League's political committee met again and decided to extend to the invading armies all necessary support, including an immediate £1.5 million grant (£37 million in today's terms) to the Arab Legion.

On April 26, the Transjordan parliament approved the forthcoming invasion. A general mobilization was proclaimed and the army was ordered to begin preparations in earnest. "I personally believe that not a single Arab State can resist the desire of the Arab Nations to offer military aid to Palestine," Abdullah told a press conference as the Legion deployed in a number of Palestinian Arab cities (including Jericho, Hebron, and Bethlehem). "The Arabs had expected justice from the UN but have lost all hope. It is not for me to speak on behalf of the other Arab states, but my personal viewpoint is that it is for me to place myself at the disposal of Palestine, and it will be a great pleasure and honor for me to work for its rescue." Claiming to have been appointed by the League to command the invading Syrian and Lebanese forces, the king gave the Zionist movement a last chance to discard its national aspirations or forever be damned. "I have advised the Jews to accept the rights of citizens in a free Arab State, and I am awaiting the Jewish reply to this advice," he publicly stated. "If they do not accept this and do not agree, then I, as the Arab king of an Arab State with an Arab Army, will do what I consider suitable."[21]

While Abdullah was gearing up for war, Bevin and Attlee were busy shielding their loyal protégé from international censure. "What was Abdullah to do?" they asked the US ambassador to London, Lewis Douglas, who protested the Arab Legion's imminent invasion of Palestine:

> First of all, he had never been admitted to the United Nations. His application had been vetoed by the Russians each time, and therefore how did the Charter of the United Nations apply to him? Secondly, were the Jews to be allowed to be aggressors on his co-religionists and fellow Arabs in the State of Palestine while he had to stand idly by doing nothing? . . . What really was Abdullah to do?

Coming from the politicians who had acquiesced in Abdullah's invasion of Palestine and who were scheming to divide the Arab (and Jewish) parts of Palestine between Transjordan and Egypt, and possibly other Arab states, this sudden interest in the fate of the Palestinian Arabs was hardly credible. Yet Bevin and Attlee sustained their duplicitous line of argument. "It seemed to me that the United States policy was to allow no Arab country to help their fellow Arabs anywhere, but for the U.S. themselves to assist the Jews to crush the Arabs within Palestine and to allow the slaughter to go on, and then to ask the British Government to restrain Abdullah," Bevin claimed, ignoring the fact that the Jews had received no weapons from the United States owing to an American arms embargo in the Middle East, while the Arab armies, notably the Legion, were armed, trained, and led by the British:

> Did this not seem a very illogical position? . . . How was such a position to be met unless the U.S. put strong pressure on the Jews, who appeared to us to be aggressive and arrogant, and disregarded all the appeals that had been made by the United Nations . . . the number of Arabs who had infiltrated into Palestine was not large and any acts they had committed had been exaggerated. After all, Palestine was an Arab country.

Attlee took over from his foreign secretary. "What was aggression?" he asked. "Was it aggression for Arabs to come into Palestine from their own countries, and non-aggression for Jews to come in by sea to the tune of thousands?" To the ambassador's reply that the Jews were coming in unarmed and were not fighting men, Attlee gave the "winning argument." "That was just Hitler's method," he retorted. "He put people in as tourists, but they were soon armed once they got in. The Jews would put them in as immigrants but they would soon become soldiers, and it was known that they were already being drilled and trained."[22]

Whether or not Douglas was impressed by the equation of Holocaust survivors trying to reach their ancestral homeland with their Nazi tormentors, Britain's staunch support for Abdullah, underscored by the revised Anglo-Transjordan treaty of alliance of March 1948, was hardly reassuring for his Arab peers. Contrary to Abdullah's public pretense, the Syrians remained deeply unhappy about the decision to put Transjordan in the driving seat of the pan-Arab campaign. Having learned in late April of the Abul Huda-Bevin understanding, President Quwatli promptly wrote to Faruq to warn of an Anglo-Transjordan plan to use the invasion as a catalyst for the implementation of a Greater Syria scheme that would destroy the independence of Syria – "the beating heart of Arabism" and a relentless thorn in Britain's side. Taking their cue from their president, senior Syrian officials cautioned that the king's prospective leadership of the invasion "amounts to a British-directed implementation of the partition plan." They added: "The Jewish State is now assured. Abdullah will secure only the Arab portion of Palestine. That is all his British masters will permit."

The charge struck a responsive chord in Egypt. As shown earlier, Faruq's distrust of Abdullah had been demonstrated by his public insistence on restoring Palestine to its Arab inhabitants after the defeat of the Jews. Yet since he had serious doubts whether this would actually happen, regardless of Transjordan's emphatic reassurances, the Egyptian monarch decided to send his army into Palestine alongside the Legion so as to prevent the country from falling under Hashemite sway and give Egypt the largest possible say in its future; and if Prime Minister Nuqrashi were to oppose this move he would be forced to resign like his immediate predecessor.

This is what Syria's Prime Minister Mardam heard in Cairo, while participating in the political committee's session, first from Azzam, then from the chief of the royal court to whom he submitted Quwatli's letter. A few days later, on April 26, he was told by the Egyptian foreign minister, Ahmad Khashaba, that Nuqrashi had been won over to the idea of war and that the army had been instructed to plan an invasion.

"The Arab states' official military intervention in Palestine, should it at all happen," the head of the Arab section of the Jewish Agency's political department, Elias Sasson, reported on April 18 to Moshe Shertok, soon to become Israel's first foreign minister, "stems not from concern for the fate of the Palestinian Arabs or opposition to the creation of a Jewish state in a partitioned Palestine, but from fear of a unilateral invasion by Transjordan that would conquer the country's Arab areas and improve the prospects of the realization of the Greater Syria scheme."[23]

This fear was much in evidence at the political committee's meeting in Amman (April 30–May 1), which sought to finalize the Cairo decisions of two weeks earlier. Amidst public clamors for war and equally militant declarations by leaders and politicians throughout the Arab world, the delegates sought to shift the military burden to their counterparts while attempting to limit their own countries' involvement to the barest minimum: the Syrians claimed that they needed the best part of their armed forces at home to fend off Turkey's aggressive designs, while the Iraqis made the same excuse with regard to the Soviet threat and the Egyptians on account of domestic instability. All agreed that Transjordan should do the lion's share of the fighting, with Azzam pressing for an invasion prior to the end of the mandate, yet were reluctant to concede Abdullah's demand for unqualified supreme command. The conclusion of the Arab chiefs of staff, who met in Amman at the same time, that the invasion would necessitate a unified force of at least five divisions and six squadrons of fighting aircraft was similarly rejected as fanciful.

In the end, a compromise was devised that allowed most participants to have their cake and eat it too. The invasion, set for May 15, was to be directed by a unified command that would be formed in Amman under the headship of the Iraqi general Nureddin Mahmud. It would be led by the Transjordanian and Iraqi armies and the Arab states bordering Palestine would be free to carry out their own separate operations if they so chose. Non-contiguous Saudi Arabia would send a contingent that would operate as part of the Egyptian army and under its command. No country would be allowed to annex the conquered parts of Palestine, but Transjordan would be given the opportunity to resolve its claim to the country through a referendum: an effective carte blanche to annexation as no one had the slightest doubt regarding the outcome of this pseudo-democratic exercise. Azzam put a shining gloss on the summit: "The Arab countries unanimously agreed to repulse the Zionist danger in Palestine. The Jews, when they decided to establish a Jewish State by force of arms, pronounced a death sentence against themselves."[24]

In private Azzam was far more candid about the ulterior motives of the pan-Arab invasion. "[T]he Arab armies were poised, ready for entry into Palestine," he told a senior member of the US embassy in Cairo shortly after the Amman talks; "if they should fail to do so on May 15, these forces might gradually disintegrate so that they would no longer be really effective at a later date." Having whipped their subjects' passions into an uncontrollable frenzy, the secretary-general added, the Arab rulers had no choice but to invade Palestine, since failure to do so "might lead to dissatisfaction and mutual recriminations among the Arabs. . . . There was also apparently a fear that some of the Arab governments themselves might be overthrown as a result of rising passions among the Arab populations."[25]

Abdullah's rising fortunes were viewed by the Zionists with mixed feelings. As their longest and most persistent interlocutor, who had kept the relationship going even in the direst moments of the conflict and had never shared the Mufti's vision of a Jew-free Palestine, the Hashemite monarch was the best conceivable peace partner in the Arab world. Yet for all his affability, Abdullah was no more accepting of Jewish national aspirations than any other Arab leader in that he had always envisaged the Jews as a tolerated minority in the Arab empire he was striving to establish in line with the traditional *dhimmi* paradigm in the House of Islam. This is what he had invariably offered the Zionists from the beginning of their interaction in the early 1920s up until his November 1947 meeting with Golda Meyerson, which left the Jewish leadership deeply suspicious of his intentions.

On November 16, 1947, a day before the meeting, Ben-Gurion warned his colleagues of the dangers attending the Legion's continued presence in Palestine, reiterating his apprehensions a few weeks later. "The [British] government claims that this is their force," he reported of a meeting with Cunningham, in which he protested on this point. "But this is an Arab Legion." On January 1, 1948, Ben-Gurion recorded in his diary:

> It is said that the Arab Legion will operate [in Palestine] and that the neighboring Arab states will send a symbolic force. This may be correct. According to this information, the Legion will occupy *the whole* of Palestine, though without entering the populated areas, and will force the Jews to negotiate on the [Arab] League's terms: autonomy for the Jewish community under a single [Arab] regime for the whole country; Palestine within the League. Sasson recalled what [Abdullah] said during the [November 1947] meeting in Naharaim: "A partition that will not disgrace me in front of the Arabs. How about a small republic [in my kingdom]?" This proves that the idea resides in the king's heart and is not of recent origin.[26]

Now that Abdullah had been placed at the forefront of the anti-Jewish campaign, the Zionist leadership made simultaneous use of the stick and the carrot to prevent the expansion of the conflict. Thus, for example, Shertok proposed to warn Abdullah that "if [the] Legion go into action, we have [the] means [to] wipe out whole units, [and] shall use them." At the same time, the Jewish Agency wrote to the king to express its shock and disgust at the Deir Yasin carnage, which it condemned as a brutal and barbaric act that contradicted Jewish moral values, only to be accused of overall responsibility for the incident, since "it is common knowledge that the Agency oversees all Zionist activities, both in Palestine and abroad, and acts as Zionism's representative and spokesman anywhere in the world; hence it is to be expected that no Jew will act contrary to its policy."[27]

A cable from Sasson to Abdullah on April 26, protesting his belligerent statement of the same day and insisting that the future of Palestine could not be decided by unilateral decisions or threats but only by bonafide negotiations, "guided by true willingness to guarantee the aspirations, rights, and independence of both Arabs and Jews," was similarly snubbed. "I found nothing in your telegram that merits sharing it with His Majesty, since the contents of HM's statement was perfectly unequivocal," the chief of the royal court wrote to Sasson. "Your personal services are acceptable if you follow the royal statement that the Arabs' sovereignty over their own country is not disputed and that the Jewish community exercise citizenship rights in a state similar to those of the Arabs with a decentralized administration in the areas where the Jews are in a majority."

To add insult to injury, the Legion attacked the Gesher kibbutz, south of Tiberias, and a week later Abdullah reiterated his public renunciation of the Jews' right to statehood. "If they ask for peace," he stated, "they will obtain from us decentralized administration in settlements where they are forming a clear majority, but within a frame of Arab states."[28]

Still the Zionists strove to establish a dialogue that would keep Transjordan out of the war and, it was hoped, avert the pan-Arab invasion altogether. On May 2, a high-ranking Hagana commander met a senior British Legion officer in an attempt to find ways and means to reduce the scope of the looming confrontation. The previous day, a skeptical Ben-Gurion had approved Meyerson's request for a second meeting with Abdullah prior to the expiration of the mandate, and on May 10 the acting head of the Jewish Agency's political department met the king in his Amman palace.

The two had agreed at the end of their previous conversation to meet again shortly after the passing of the UN resolution to explore the possibility of an agreement; and Abdullah's subsequent evasiveness had exacerbated Jewish suspicions with regard to his intentions. Now that the meeting had materialized at long last, Meyerson found the king no more receptive to the idea of Jewish statehood than he had been six months earlier, and his private stance no different from his militant public statements of the past few weeks.

"Why are you in such a hurry to proclaim an independent state?" he asked. "Why don't you wait a few years? I will take over the whole country and you will be represented in my parliament. I will treat you very well and there will be no war." Meyerson's reply that a 2,000-year wait was hardly evidence of impatience failed to impress the king. He had always been for peace, but the only way to avert war at this particular juncture was to accept his proposed solution: an undivided Palestine in which the Jews would have autonomy in the areas where they constituted the majority, such as Tel Aviv. This arrangement would remain in force for one year, after which the country would be incorporated into Transjordan.

While these conditions, which had been conveyed in advance, were totally unacceptable as a basis for negotiations, Meyerson retorted, the Jews had nevertheless decided to make this last-ditch effort to prevent a futile and unnecessary escalation that was liable to be disastrous to all sides. During the past five months they had routed both the ALA and their Palestinian Arab adversaries, and they were perfectly capable of rebuffing the impending invasion; and however committed to honoring the UN-sanctioned frontiers so long as there was peace, they would not feel beholden to these terms if they were subjected to concerted pan-Arab aggression.

Abdullah agreed that the Jews would have to repel any attack but insisted that the disintegration of Palestinian society and the collapse of its military effort made it impossible for the Arab states to remain aloof, and that there was nothing he could do about it. "I was then alone but now I am one among five," he said. "I have no alternative and I cannot act otherwise."

But didn't the king realize that, despite his recent regional pre-eminence, the Jews were his only true friends? Abdullah unhesitatingly agreed. He knew full well the real motives of his Arab peers and had no illusions regarding their dependability, just as he firmly believed that

> Divine Providence has restored you, a Semitic people who were banished to Europe and have benefitted by its progress, to the Semite east, which needs your knowledge and initiative. It is only through your help and guidance that the Semitic peoples will be able to regain their lost glory. The Christians will not do this because of their aloof and contemptuous attitude toward the Semites. If we do not help ourselves by our joint efforts, then we shall not be helped. All this I know and I have a profound belief in what I have said. But the situation is grave, and we must not err through hasty action. Consequently I beg of you again to be patient.

"We do not wish to delude you," Meyerson replied, "but we cannot consider your proposal at all. It would not only be rejected by the responsible institutions, but there are not even ten responsible Jews who will be ready to support such a plan. The answer can be given at once: it is unacceptable. If you give up the argument and want war, then we shall meet *after* the war."

The king remained unmoved. Even as the Jewish representative leader was taking her leave, he reiterated his request to consider his offer, "and if the reply were affirmative, it had to be given before May 15. He would invite his Palestinian backers and the moderate Arabs, and ask us [i.e., the Jews] to send moderate representatives too – and then the matter could be settled. He also said: 'There is no need to fear that the government will include extremist Arabs, Jew-haters, but only moderate Arabs.' " "In [the] course [of a] secret conversation [between] Meyerson and Meir [Abdullah's codename] last night," Ben-Gurion telegraphed the next day to Aubrey Eban at the UN, "he made it clear [that an] Arab invasion with his forces [as a] spearhead will begin on termination of Mandate. Invasion expected [on] Friday or Saturday."[29]

As in his previous meeting with Meyerson, Abdullah was not being fully truthful. Just as in November 1947 he had inflated his military might and his status in the Arab world in an attempt to persuade the Jews to accept his protection, so his feigned helplessness as "one among five" was patently false, for the simple reason that it was his imperial ambitions that had driven the reluctant Arab states to the brink of war in the first place: not to save the Palestinian Arabs but to prevent the annexation of Palestine, in whole or in part, to Transjordan; and it was he who had been pressuring them from the onset of hostilities in November 1947, and most vigorously since April 1948, to let his army spearhead the post-mandate invasion. Had Abdullah discarded his Palestine (and Greater Syria) ambitions and played a less prominent role in the Palestine conflict, the Arab states might well have contented themselves with political posturing and military support for the Palestinians and the ALA and eschewed the idea of direct military intervention altogether.

This state of affairs was vividly illustrated during the fortnight between the Amman summit and the end of the mandate, when, far from being a reluctant member of an eager war coalition, Abdullah was highly instrumental in spurring on the invasion and obstructing international attempts to broker a truce. So much so that on May 1 the three-man UN consular truce commission in Jerusalem warned him "in the strongest terms" that "any warlike decisions or action on the part of Transjordan will undoubtedly be the cause of the gravest censure by the Security Council and the entire UN as a possible threat to peace."

Dismissing the warning out of hand, Abdullah blamed Jewish national aspirations for the ongoing bloodshed in Palestine and urged the Security

Council "to compel them to stop their aggression and give up the idea of a Jewish State, so that peace may be maintained." And by way of underscoring the seriousness of his intentions, on May 2 he ordered his troops to brace themselves for the imminent "liberation of Palestine." "You should be prepared for a struggle of honor," read the Order of the Day. "Advance under God's protection to join your brothers who are struggling in the Holy War and join the forces of our sister Arab countries!" Four days later, the king rejected the cessation of hostilities as a humiliating capitulation to Zionist demands and reiterated his resolve to invade Palestine. On May 13, together with Azzam, he met the consular commission in his Amman palace and repeated his rejection of their truce conditions.[30]

By now the League had appointed Abdullah commander-in-chief of both the invading armies and the Arab forces already operating in Palestine. The embittered Safwat resigned his post and was promptly replaced by Nureddin Mahmud, who became Abdullah's deputy and chief of operations. The king then pressured an emergency summit, held in Damascus with the participation of Azzam, Mardam, Sulh, and Arab military leaders, to reject the UN truce proposals and to reaffirm their commitment to the Amman decisions. On May 6, the Syrian and Lebanese prime ministers left for Riyadh, where they obtained Ibn Saud's support for "all resolutions adopted at meetings of the Arab nations concerning Palestine" and his agreement to participate in the pan-Arab campaign "to defend Palestine." Four days later Abdullah cabled the Saudi monarch to reassure him that the catastrophic situation in Palestine would improve before too long. At the same time he pointed a finger at what he considered to be the main culprit in the unfolding tragedy: the AHC. In a statement from the royal palace, Abdullah accused the Mufti-led body of bringing "misery" to Palestine and ordered it to cease interfering in Palestinian affairs since it "no longer satisfies the entire people of Palestine." The AHC delegates at the UN headquarters in Lake Success were likewise ordered to regard themselves as "no longer representing the Palestine Arabs."

That Abdullah was not merely voicing his own personal view was evidenced by statements from senior League officials, including Azzam, who revealed that the organization had voted down a proposal to set up an independent Palestinian state upon the end of the mandate, thus leaving the country's future open-ended. "We accepted the presumption that the Jews would establish a state [on] May 15," the secretary-general said, "and we agreed to set up an Arab civil administration under the Arab League, to function in cooperation with the occupying Arab forces."[31]

In a desperate bid to forestall the invasion, the Zionist leadership sought to heighten inter-Arab distrust by publicizing the squabbles at the latest League sessions as well as Abdullah's conversation with Meyerson (albeit without revealing her identity). "Rumors are now circulating to the effect the King Abdullah contacted responsible Jewish circles asking for conclusion of a treaty with the Jews and expressing his readiness to recognize a Jewish State," argued the Hagana's Arabic-language broadcasts, widely listened to by the Arabs of Palestine and beyond, a day after the meeting. "Transjordan's Army will occupy the Arab part of Palestine surrounding the Jewish State's territories, and the King will conclude a military alliance with the Jewish state after annexing the Arab part of Palestine to his kingdom. It is reported that important talks were carried out in Amman in this connection during the past few days." "It is no longer a secret," ran another broadcast,

> that there is no aim to the talks carried out between Amman, Damascus, Jeddah, and Baghdad, as they will all not lead to any joint plan for the Arab countries, but contrariwise, as disagreements and difference of opinions, aims and objectives have started to increase.
>
> It is obvious that the Arab countries have been knocking at the door of King Abdullah following the defeat and failure of the Arab Liberation Army, which was originally created in Syria. Yet these countries have not lost their fear and distrust of each other, even under these awkward and critical circumstances, though they all agreed in Amman that King Abdullah and his Army should lead the snipers' march on Palestine.
>
> Even after taking this final decision, the Arab countries were unable to agree upon the drafted plan which they all approved in general. The reason is that Syria and Lebanon, for example, did not agree to the Transjordan Army occupying the Galilee area at their frontiers, fearing that a situation might develop which would bring about the realization of the Greater Syria plan. Egypt also does not approve of King Abdullah's entrance into the Negev.[32]

Rather than slow down the march to war, the circulation of this information and the rumors of Abdullah's readiness to strike a deal with the Jews only served to expedite the invasion, so as to prevent him from carrying out this purported design and, for that matter, from conquering the whole of Palestine. On May 9, the Egyptian government approved a credit of £4 million (£100 million in today's terms) to cover "additional expenditure required by the Egyptian Army stationed on the border between Egypt and Palestine." Two days later, Azzam warned Foreign Minister Khashaba that unless the Egyptian government immediately decided on intervention, Abdullah would march into Palestine on May 15, seize its Arab areas, and put the blame for the loss of the rest of the country on the other Arab states.

On the same day, after a lengthy closed session in which Prime Minister Nuqrashi made an impassioned plea for war, parliament approved the proposal that the Egyptian army "shall with other Arab armies enter Palestine at a suitable time to restore stability and prevent massacres in Palestine." In an interview with the *New York Times*'s Cairo correspondent, Faruq declared that he "cannot and will not tolerate a Zionist state in the Middle East, close to Egypt's borders."

The only figure of note to oppose the cataclysmic slide to war was Nuqrashi's immediate predecessor, Ismail Sidqi. He found it mind-boggling that the prime minister should ask parliament to approve a position that he had adamantly opposed just a few days earlier, not least since the required decision involved the most critical aspect of the national interest: war.[33] "The Palestine problem has been on our agenda for a couple of years and not once were we summoned to discuss it," Sidqi continued.

> Now we are being asked to form our opinion just twenty-four hours before the outbreak of war, and I can't grasp the reason for the rush and zeal of these last hours. Before this session I met with at least ten members of the parliamentary committee [which discussed the issue behind closed doors prior to the general session] and all of them opposed the invasion. Now they are all enthusiastic supporters and I can't figure out the reason [for this U-turn]. I was prime minister a year ago and I know the state of readiness of the Egyptian army in terms of equipment and ammunition. I therefore find it odd to hear the prime minister tell us that the army is equipped for fighting three full months. . . . What has happened? From where have we received the alleged war materiel?

Sidqi didn't confine his criticism to the parliamentary chamber. "I regret the position in which the country is placed in the eyes of nations," he told the influential Egyptian weekly *al-Akhbar*. "It could not resist the very strong current, but I did not fail to warn the responsible persons. I told Prime Minister Nuqrashi Pasha: 'Before obliging us to go to war, try to approve a truce. You will gain three months this way. Who knows what will happen in three months?'" Sidqi concluded: "I know that my words will displease, but I am telling the truth."[34]

His remained a lonely voice. Once decided on war, Arab leaders throughout the region were carried away by euphoria. "The Palestine operations will not exceed ten days," Abdullah boasted. "The Zionist fortress will fall in the first attack, and the Jews will extend the hand of peace to the Arabs." Following the proclamation of the Jewish state on May 14, the king issued a militant communiqué. "The ending of the British Mandate means the termination and abrogation of the promises contained in the Balfour Declaration," it read. "The Jews have no rights in Palestine; the Jews have no rights to local self-independence as they rejected my previous proposals; I repeat my promise that Palestine inhabitants will freely determine their future."[35]

Even the normally cautious Hashemi could not resist the intoxicating smell of victory. "The Jews are weaker than the regular Arab armies," he told Azzam on May 13.

> They are superior to the militias, which are armed with rifles and a number of machine guns . . . but their position is bound to be difficult when confronted with the regular armies – should these operate in a unified and coordinated fashion. This will in turn enable the thwarting of partition, as the mechanized forces will rapidly conquer the Galilee and the Jezreel Valley all the way to Afula, while the Egyptian forces will reach the Jaffa area, lay siege to Tel Aviv, and attack the city when the moment is right.

Buoyed up by the prognosis of his foremost military advisor, Azzam brushed aside Kirkbride's query about the size of the Jewish forces. "It does not matter how many there are," he said. "We will sweep them into the sea!" At a Cairo press conference on May 15 he was no less forthright. "This will be a war of extermination and momentous massacre which will be spoken of like the Mongolian massacre and the Crusades," he predicted as the invading Arab forces were forging through Palestine.[36]

CHAPTER 11

Shattered Dreams

*"Sooner or later the Jewish State would disappear. The war would flare up
again, the Arabs would destroy the State of Israel."*
Abdel Rahman Azzam, September 1948

*"At the moment there are apparently no Arab factors ready to reach an agree-
ment with the Jews. But should the possibility arise . . . I'll be prepared to ask
the government and the Jewish people to content themselves with much less. . . .
For in my view there is hardly a price that is not worth paying for peace."*
David Ben-Gurion, September 1948

This was not quite the war of extermination and momentous massacre
promised by Azzam. Rather than sweep the Jews into the sea as he had confidently predicted, the pan-Arab invasion confirmed the collapse of Palestinian
Arab society, exacerbated the mass exodus, and allowed Israel to capture
wider territories than those assigned to it by the UN resolution. Had the
Arab states forgone the invasion, a Palestinian Arab state would have been
established at the end of the British mandate alongside Israel and many of
the 300,000–340,000 people who had fled their homes might have been able
to return. Instead, by the end of the year these numbers had swelled to nearly
600,000 as a direct result of the fighting, and Israel's readiness to repatriate
them had been significantly reduced.

To be sure, despite their lack of full operational coordination owing to
mutual animosities and distrust, the far better equipped Arab armies checked
the relentless succession of Jewish victories, threw the nascent state of Israel
onto the defensive, and forced it to fight for its very survival. At its first
session on May 16, the provisional Israeli government heard prime minister
and minister of defense David Ben-Gurion offer a stark survey of the military situation.[1] "The number of [Jewish] recruits has exceeded 30,000, but
only 40% of them are armed due to the lack of rifles," he told his colleagues.
"The [Arabs] are using artillery, aircraft and tanks, while we have a single

tank and a number of [captured] British armored cars." Ben-Gurion was confident that Israel would be able to turn the tables on the invading armies after the arrival of newly bought weapons. Until that happened, he anticipated a period of great uncertainty. "In my opinion we'll be able to teach them a lesson they'll remember for generations," he said. "But for the time being the situation is extremely serious."[2]

Many Israeli villages, especially in the Galilee and the Negev, which was effectively severed from the rest of the country by the Egyptian army, found themselves totally isolated and forced to rely on their own tenacity and meager resources. Jerusalem's Jewish suburbs, reeling from months of war and privation, came under siege once more, this time by Transjordan's Arab Legion, and were subjected to heavy bombardments. In the fortnight after the invasion, 250 Jerusalemites were killed and another 1,100 were wounded, 300 of them seriously; by the time the first UN-mediated truce came into effect on June 11, the city's Jewish populace was on the verge of starvation.[3] Still they held their ground, repelling successive penetration attempts, often in hand-to-hand fighting.

So did other Jewish localities throughout the country. Not only did the Arab states fail to achieve their overarching goal of destroying the Jewish state at birth, but at the time of the first truce Israel was in control of some 700 sq km (270 sq miles) assigned by the partition resolution to the prospective Arab state, compared with the 350 sq km (135 sq miles) of its own territory that had been conquered by the Arab armies. Only one Israeli kibbutz (Mishmar Hayarden, near the Sea of the Galilee) fell to the invading forces, compared to the fifty-odd large villages, and numerous smaller settlements, captured by the Israelis in the Arab-assigned part of Palestine.[4]

As in the previous months, the fighting produced its share of evacuees. Jewish women and children were temporarily moved from some sites in the battle zone, while all residents of the Jewish localities in the prospective Arab state that were conquered by the invading armies, together with those of Old Jerusalem's Jewish quarter, were "ethnically cleansed." In Kfar Etzion, occupied by Transjordan's Arab Legion on the eve of Israel's proclamation, more than a hundred surrendering defenders and residents, including an Arab family that lived on the kibbutz, were summarily slaughtered and their bodies mutilated.

On the Arab side, fear and disorientation, its own operations and ordered evacuations, as well as Israeli successes, generated a fresh influx of refugees. Within a week of the invasion, the villagers of Julis, Beit Affa, Ibdis, Karatiya, Jaldiya, Juseir, and Sumeil in the Gaza district fled en masse to escape the fighting. They were followed by the residents of Ghabisiya, Kabri, Manshiya, Nahr, and Umm Faraj in the Acre sub-district, the remaining villagers in Umm Zinat in the Haifa district, and the 5,000-strong village of Hamama (Gaza district), whose residents fled to the neighboring rural town of Majdal in response to a purported Jewish attack (that never took place). In Tantura (Haifa district), Abu Shusha, Zarnuqa, and Yibna (Ramle sub-district), the Israeli forces detained young men of fighting age and expelled the remaining residents.[5]

On the whole, however, the scope and pace of the Arab exodus ebbed drastically during this period, from the hundreds of thousands of the preceding two months to a few thousands. Having been comprehensively routed by their Jewish adversaries (only twelve villages inside Israel put up further armed resistance),[6] the Palestinian Arabs effectively ceased to be a factor in the fighting, which was transformed from guerrilla-type warfare between two rival communities into a conventional war between the Arab states and Israel (with the ALA playing a secondary, if significant, role in the Galilee). This in turn left a far smaller number of civilians directly affected by the conflict, especially since the country's main population centers had already emptied before the end of the mandate. Even Jerusalem, earmarked for internationalization by the partition resolution, had lost nearly half of its 60,000-strong Arab community by mid-May, while Acre, assigned to the prospective Arab state, had largely been deserted. By the time of its fall on May 18, after two days of heavy fighting, only 2,000 of the city's 13,500-strong population were still in residence, alongside a few thousand refugees from other settlements.[7]

Had the truce been extended, let alone transformed into an enduring peace, the Arabs might have emerged from the conflict with tangible gains, not least since Count Folke Bernadotte, the UN mediator who arrived in the region in late May, was well disposed to their cause. Described by his able assistant, Ralph Bunche, as decent and hard-working but not very bright (the first US special representative turned ambassador to Israel, James McDonald, found him "charming, public-spirited, wholly devoted but not unusually able or perceptive"),[8] the Swedish aristocrat considered the partition resolution a grave error that had to be rectified at the first available opportunity.[9] With no first-hand knowledge of the Middle East, he quickly fell under the spell of British officialdom, which for its part viewed the war as a golden oppor-tunity to undo the resolution and reduce Israel to approximately the size envisaged by the 1937 Peel plan: with less than half the land allotted to it by the UN. This included inter alia the surrender of the Negev to Transjordan and Egypt;[10] the prevention of a Jewish land corridor between the coastal plain and Jerusalem; the cession of some territory in the eastern Galilee to Syria;[11] and the creation of a substantial UN-controlled enclave in the Haifa harbor that would serve as a "free port" for the transfer of goods to the neigh-boring Arab countries and Iraq. In other words, Israel was to make its primary port, vital economic installations, and national transport infrastruc-ture available to the strategic and economic needs of its enemies.[12]

It is true that as part of their vision of a "Smaller Israel" the British were prepared to acquiesce in Israel's conquest of the western Galilee, awarded to the prospective Arab state by the partition resolution. Yet they did so, still most reluctantly, because the area was far smaller and less significant for British and Arab interests than the Negev, and because there was no Arab that could dislodge Israel from this area and stake a credible claim to its effec-tive control. Above all, British policymakers feared that if their ideas were not promptly imposed on the belligerents under the guise of the mediator's plan, Israel would defeat the Arab states and regain the Negev, at the time severed from its territory by Egypt, while also retaining the western Galilee (which is what actually happened).

Nor was the British vision of "Smaller Israel" confined to the territorial sphere. Having done its utmost to prevent the remnants of European Jewry from arriving in Palestine during the mandate's final years by keeping the 1939 White Paper's draconian restrictions intact, maintaining a tight naval blockade on Palestine, and herding those Holocaust survivors attempting to brave it into congested concentration camps in Cyprus, the British govern-ment sought to stunt the Jewish population of the newly born state.

In a memorandum detailing various options to be suggested to Bernadotte, Michael Wright of the foreign office's eastern department opined that Israel's territorial diminution "might result in the Jewish authorities themselves having to limit immigration" and that the Arab governments would never reconcile themselves to the existence of an independent Jewish state unless "there should be international agreement to accept numbers of Jewish displaced persons elsewhere than in Israel, and conceivably also to limit immigration to Israel."

Foreign Minister Bevin echoed these ideas at a meeting with the US ambassador to London. "It seemed to us that if the Arabs were to be brought to acquiesce in the establishment of a Jewish State a factor which would weigh heavily in the balance would be immigration," he argued.

It might be necessary not only for the Jews and the Arabs to make a contribution and sacrifices to achieve this but for other Powers to join in making contributions also. If there could be some fresh international attempt or agreement, perhaps sponsored by the Security Council, for the absorption of larger numbers of Jewish displaced persons elsewhere than in Palestine this might have a decisive effect upon the negotiations. The numbers were not really so large if they were divided among the different countries.[13]

Bernadotte was duly impressed. In his framework for peace, presented to Israel and the Arab states on June 27, he proposed the abandonment of partition in favor of a union comprising two members, one Arab and one Jewish, that would be established in the whole of mandatory Palestine, including Transjordan. The union was to constrain the sovereignty of its constituent members in certain key aspects, notably immigration, and to reduce the size of the Jewish state to some 15 percent of western Palestine as the Negev, or parts of it, would be ceded to the Arab state, together with the city of Jerusalem. Haifa bay was to be placed under international control.[14]

The plan was peremptorily rejected by both Arabs and Jews, albeit for diametrically opposed reasons. While the Israelis resented Bernadotte's reneging on the partition resolution, the surrender of Jerusalem to Arab rule, and the proposed encroachments on their sovereignty and territorial integrity, the Arabs felt that the mediator failed to dissociate himself from the resolution by accepting the principle of Jewish statehood, in however limited and truncated a form. "[The] establishment of [a] Jewish State in [the] country lies at [the] root of [the] present dispute," the Arab League explained its rejection of the mediator's proposals and its refusal to extend the truce by another month (to which Israel agreed). "Therefore, the suggestion to accept [the] status quo as [a] basis for discussions to arrive at [a] peaceful and permanent solution of [the] problem undoubtedly proves to be inconsistent with [the] principles of justice and democracy and detrimental [to the] permanent interests of [the] country's inhabitants."[15]

In their meetings with Bernadotte, the Arab leaders made no bones about their categorical rejection of the formation of a Jewish state, even as a less than independent member of an Arab-Jewish union. The Arab world would rather go under than give up the fight, the League's secretary-general, Azzam, told the mediator, adding that "if a part, even though only a small part, of the Arab body were infected, that part must be cut away to allow the whole to recover."

Only Abdullah preferred to look at the full half of the glass. In 1937 he had endorsed the Peel plan, which envisaged the annexation of the Arab parts of Palestine to his kingdom; Bernadotte's strikingly similar scheme (with the added boon of placing Jerusalem under Arab rule) promised to fulfill this long-held ambition for him. Having invited the mediator to his Amman palace shortly before the expiry of the truce, the king urged him to rush to the UN headquarters in Lake Success, New York, to give a personal account of the situation and to put forward his peace proposals. In an interview with a

Western journalist, Abdullah argued that the only solution to the Palestine problem was the country's transformation into an Arab state in which the Jews would enjoy local autonomy, and he expressed his readiness to annex this Arab Palestine. Confronted with an angry retort by his Arab peers, the king quickly disowned the interview and, after a last-ditch attempt to convince the Arab League to extend the truce, joined the renewed pan-Arab attack on Israel.[16]

This proved to be a catastrophic blunder. In the ten days of fighting (July 9–18) before a new UN-imposed ceasefire came into effect, the nascent Israel Defense Forces (IDF), having used the truce period to absorb major new weapon systems, turned the tables on the invading armies. They removed the threat to Tel Aviv and its environs, consolidated the vital land corridor between Jerusalem and the coastal plain, captured the country's international airport near Lydda, and made significant territorial gains in the Galilee, including Christendom's holy city of Nazareth. All in all, Israel won another 600 sq km (230 sq miles) of what should have been territory of the Arab state, triggering in the process a wave of Arab evacuees, most notably from Lydda, Ramle, and their environs.

Assigned by the partition resolution to the prospective Arab state, the two strategically located cities threatened the Israeli heartland and could easily disrupt the vital Tel Aviv-Jerusalem artery. In the weeks attending the pan-Arab invasion, Ben-Gurion repeatedly prodded his commanders to take action against them, but little was attempted by the overstretched Israeli forces beyond a few haphazard attacks. "The Lydda people are the only ones fighting the Jews in the district and none of its residents have fled," the local Arab commander proudly reported. "The city is safe from the Jewish enemy owing to the forces deployed there . . . and is the only protector of Ramle and neighboring settlements, as well as the international airport and the railway hub."[17]

Now that fighting was resumed, a major offensive, codenamed Operation Danny and headed by the youthful general Yigal Allon, closed on the two cities as a stepping stone to the conquest of the Arab Legion's heavily fortified garrison in Latrun, at the foot of the Judean hills overlooking the Tel Aviv-Jerusalem road, and subsequently Ramallah, with a view to breaking the siege of Jerusalem. Having seized a dozen neighboring villages, on July 11 the IDF occupied Lydda after intense fighting, and Ramle surrendered the next day after a brief engagement.

Teeming with evacuees from other Arab settlements, especially Jaffa, the two cities nearly doubled their 35,000-strong original population (18,250 in Lydda, 16,380 in Ramle).[18] As Israeli forces edged toward their latest haven, many of these refugees hit the road again, together with an unspecified number of local residents;[19] the remaining population left a couple of days after the cities' fall, mostly under Israeli orders.[20]

This was the first, indeed the *only*, instance in the war where a substantial urban population was driven out by Jewish or Israeli forces. Small wonder that it was to become a central plank of the Arab claim of premeditated and systematic dispossession. In fact, the exodus emanated from a string of unexpected developments on the ground and was in no way foreseen in military plans for the cities' capture or reflected in the initial phase of their occupation. It was only when the occupying forces in Lydda encountered stiffer resistance than expected that they decided to "encourage" the population's departure to Arab-controlled areas, a few miles to the east, so as not to leave a hostile armed base at the rear of the Israeli advance and in order to clog the main roads in order to forestall a possible counterattack by the Arab Legion.

"Our plan is to conquer the cities only for the sake of self-defense," read an Arabic-language leaflet signed by Allon and dropped from the air by the thousands on July 10. "We have no intention of harming anyone or inflicting material damage. Those who choose to resist will die. Those who choose life should surrender and save themselves and their families. My commanders are ready to meet with your delegates to discuss surrender. The Ramle delegates can come to Barriya by foot in the morning, bearing a white flag. The Lydda delegates should arrive the same way to Jimzu."[21]

A day later, the commander of the Israeli battalion that had gained tenuous control of most of Lydda met a group of local notables headed by the mayor, Muhammad Ali Kajala, who came to offer the city's surrender. Seated at the home of the Greek Orthodox archimandrite who had arranged the meeting, sipping coffee and chatting with the delegates, the Israeli officer accepted the offer, on the proviso that all fighting personnel surrendered and all arms were handed over within twenty-four hours, and suggested that the municipality put its employees to work so that the residents could have water and electricity without delay. Asked whether the inhabitants would be able to stay if they so wished, the commander answered that "yes, they may, if they live here peacefully."

The delegates then left to inform their constituents of the agreement and to persuade them to hand in their arms. Three of the four remaining pockets of resistance agreed to lay down their weapons, and the mayor and some notables headed to the last defensive bastion – the fortified police station manned by some 100–150 Legionnaires and local fighters – to plead for peace. They had reached the front gate when a hail of bullets from inside the station killed the mayor and seriously wounded another person.[22]

By the next morning little was left of the surrender agreement. With no trace of the weapons that were supposed to be handed over, the battalion braced itself for a possible attack by the Legion. This came at 11 am in the form of three armored cars that dashed through the city spraying shots in all directions before disappearing as swiftly as they had arrived. Within minutes the entire city was ablaze. Viewing the incursion as the harbinger of an Arab counteroffensive, many inhabitants reached for their concealed weapons and attacked their vastly outnumbered conquerors. It took the Israelis three hours of bitter fighting, in which some 250 Arabs were killed, to regain control of the city.[23]

The conflagration sealed the city's fate. Had the surrender agreement been implemented in an orderly fashion, no exodus would have ensued. Quite the contrary: on the morning of July 12, the commander of the Yiftach brigade to which the occupying battalion belonged cabled Operation Danny headquarters for a competent administrator and further personnel to come and run the affairs of the civilian population.[24] Now that its tenuous grip on the city had been glaringly exposed, the IDF felt unable to leave a potential hotbed of armed resistance at its rear which might disrupt the ongoing offensive at a time when the Legion was recuperating after its initial surprise and counterattacking in neighboring villages.

Already at the height of the Lydda conflagration, Israeli officers had sought to impress upon the local notables the seriousness of the situation. "As you can see the city has not surrendered and the fighting is still raging," they warned against misconstruing their eagerness to restore normalcy as weakness. "[The city] is rife with weapons and if you can't hand them over, we'll be forced to do this ourselves."

The notables were unimpressed. With their hopes for a reversal of fortune suddenly rekindled, they displayed little of the previous day's submissiveness. It was only after the swift suppression of the uprising that they reverted to their earlier stance and agreed to send a representative throughout the city to order the residents to surrender their arms or risk harsh retribution. This proved unavailing. Not a single weapon was surrendered during the day.[25]

Meanwhile, at the Operation Danny headquarters in the neighboring village of Yazur, commanders were busy explaining the situation to Ben-Gurion and other senior officers and officials. There is no official record of the meeting, and Ben-Gurion's description of it in his diary is extremely laconic, noting the arrival of "a strong Legion column to help Lydda and Ramle" and the insistence of the armored brigade commander that his unit could not be diverted from Operation Danny to help contain the Egyptians in the south.[26]

The most detailed account of the meeting was offered in 1979 by Yitzhak Rabin, who two years earlier had resigned his post as Israel's prime minister and who had acted as the Danny chief of operations. "While the fighting was still in progress, we had to grapple with a troublesome problem, for whose solution we could not draw upon any previous experience: the fate of the civilian population of Lod [Lydda] and Ramle, numbering some 50000," Rabin recalled.

> Not even Ben-Gurion could offer any solution, and during the discussions at operational headquarters he remained silent, as was his habit in such situations. Clearly, we could not leave Lod's hostile and armed populace in our rear, where it could endanger the supply route to Yiftach, which was advancing eastward.
>
> We walked outside, Ben-Gurion accompanying us. Allon repeated his question: "What is to be done with the population?" B.G. waved his hand in a gesture which said, "Drive them out!"
>
> Allon and I held a consultation. I agreed that it was essential to drive the inhabitants out. We took them on foot toward the Bet Horon Road, assuming that the legion would be obliged to look after them, thereby shouldering logistic difficulties which would burden its fighting capacity, making things easier for us.[27]

Whatever Ben-Gurion meant by what was to become the most famous gesture in the history of the Arab-Israeli conflict, at 1.30 pm the Operation Danny headquarters peremptorily instructed the Yiftach brigade to expel the Lydda population in the direction of the neighboring village of Beit Nabala. In a more elaborate order given eleven hours later, the headquarters informed the forces in Lydda and Ramle that all residents of the two cities could leave except those whose departure was to be delayed (for military reasons); that women and children, as well as sickly and elderly persons, must not be forced to leave; that monasteries and churches were not to be touched; and that the IDF would not be responsible for feeding those who stayed behind.[28]

By this time, the Lydda populace needed little encouragement to leave. Fearful of reprisals for the failed uprising, and despondent over the flight of the police fortress defenders on the night of July 12–13 which removed all remaining hope of an imminent Arab rebound, many inhabitants were eager to get as far as from the beleaguered city as they could. On the morning of July 13, the notables informed their Israeli interlocutors of their inability to ensure peace and quiet before asking whether residents who wished to leave would be allowed to do so. Told that this was indeed the case, they requested that an edict be issued to this effect so as to let the inhabitants, many of whom were anxious to depart, know where they stood. "Your wish is our wish," the Israeli liaison officer, Shmarya Guttmann, concurred. "Here is the edict: all leave town today."

"But what about the thousands of [male] detainees at the mosque and the church?" the notables implored. "How can the city be evacuated while the heads and providers of so many families are being detained?"

"Let me assure you," Guttmann retorted. "According to my instructions, all residents should leave town today. We'll shortly send an announcer to inform the inhabitants that whoever wishes to depart should follow the directions we've assigned." The Israeli liaison officer then went to the main mosque, where most of the detainees were held, to break the news to them. Having feared a prolonged separation from their families, if not far worse, the detainees were greatly relieved by their unexpected release, and indeed by the prospect of getting away from the battle zone. Within hours the city had emptied, apart from a few hundred residents who chose to stay put, as an endless stream of civilians slowly made their way toward neighboring Arab villages. In Ramle, where the surrender agreement of July 12 allowed all inhabitants who were not of fighting age to leave town at their discretion, the population was bused to Latrun, whence they were evacuated by the Legion.[29]

Watching the Lydda exodus from the top of the great mosque, Guttmann found the episode reminiscent of the Jewish exilic experience of some 2,000 years earlier: "True, the Arabs were neither chained, nor forcefully evicted, nor driven to detention camps. They left of their free will, fearful to remain in the battle zone, in order to join their own people; but their fate was nevertheless one of exile."

Far less sentimental and biblically minded, Rabin was nonetheless similarly scarred by the event. "Psychologically, this was one of the most difficult actions we undertook," he was to recall. "Soldiers of the Yiftach Brigade included youth-movement graduates, who had been inculcated with values such as international brotherhood and humaneness. The eviction action went beyond the concepts they were used to."[30]

That this episode reflected no new general pattern of expulsion was evidenced by the fact that inhabitants of localities that peacefully surrendered to the Israeli forces during the same period were allowed to remain in situ. These included, among others, the Galilean villages of Shafa Amr, Bu'eina, Uzeir, Ilut, Kafr Kanna, Kafr Manda, Rummana, Ein Mahil, Tur'an, Iksal, Dabburiya, and Reina, which surrendered on July 14–18, together with the sub-district capital of Nazareth.[31]

Like Lydda and Ramle, Nazareth became a major sanctuary, its resources growing increasingly overstretched as successive waves of evacuees from Tiberias, Haifa, Safad, and neighboring villages poured into the city. By mid-June, with some 30,000 refugees camped in Nazareth, twice the city's original population, there were severe shortages of accommodation, food, and clothing. The situation was hardly eased by the excesses of the local gangs, which welcomed the destitute new arrivals with extortionist "levies" and "taxes."

As a large-scale Israeli offensive (codenamed Operation Dekel, or "Palm Tree") sought to clear the ALA from the central Galilee, General Moshe Carmel (Zelitzki), commander of the northern front, was instructed by Ben-Gurion to warn his troops in the strongest possible terms against any possible misconduct during the battle for Nazareth. "You are about to enter the city used by Qawuqji for unholy purposes, but it is Christianity's birthplace, a holy site to millions of people," read the statement issued by Carmel.

> Upon entering the city our soldiers will fight the invaders [i.e., the ALA] and the gangs, should they choose to resist, but will strictly refrain from damaging or desecrating holy places. Our soldiers will not enter churches, will not use them for fighting purposes, and will not barricade themselves inside them, unless forced to do so in extreme circumstances, and even then – only when specifically ordered to do so. No soldier will loot the smallest item in the city. . . . Our soldiers are civilized and cultured and will show respect to others' religious sentiments. Should there be any offenders, they will be swiftly prosecuted and severely punished.

Carmel nonetheless recommended after the city's fall that its inhabitants be expelled, with the exception of the clergy. Ben-Gurion would have none of it. "No people are to be moved from Nazareth," he wrote on the telegram sent by the operation's headquarters.

In line with this order, the surrender agreement stipulated that "the Israeli government, as represented by the military commander, recognizes the equal civil rights of the Nazareth inhabitants, on a par with those of Israel's citizens, without any discrimination on the basis of faith, ethnicity, or language." That these were no hollow words was evidenced by the prompt return of many evacuees to Nazareth and neighboring villages. In a visit to the city three months later, Ben-Gurion was positively surprised by the affability evident in relations between the authorities and the local population.[32]

By contrast, thousands of refugees from other localities, who had been decamping to the area, fled to Lebanon during Operation Dekel. This scenario recurred following the IDF's large autumn offensives: Operation Yoav (mid-October–early November), which shattered the Egyptian line of the defense, trapped an entire brigade in the "Faluja pocket," and occupied the city of Beersheba; and Operation Hiram (October 28–31), which drove the ALA and a Syrian battalion out of the Galilee before sweeping into Lebanon, capturing a few border villages, and reaching as far as the Litani River.[33]

According to UN relief officials in Amman, the fighting in the south sparked the flight of some 30,000 Arabs, thousands of whom crossed into Transjordan. Red Cross representatives who visited South Lebanon and discussed the situation with the local authorities set the number of refugees entering the country as a result of the autumn operations at 25,000; 5,000 of these were sent to Syria and the remainder were moved to a new camp that was being built in the southern port town of Tyre. At the same time, as during the summer fighting, scores of villages that surrendered peacefully to the IDF (e.g., Sakhnin, Hurfeish, Fasuta, Deir Asad, Deir Hanna, Sajur, Rama, Nahf, Jish, Majd Kurum), or even settlements seized after heavy fighting (such as Tarshiha), were left intact.[34]

Such was the panic caused by the Israeli offensives that Lebanese officers moved their families from the southern part of the country to Beirut, while residents of the Syrian city of Quneitra, on the Golan Heights, fled in fear and merchants transferred their establishments to Damascus. In Bethlehem, some 10 km (6 miles) south of Jerusalem, the entire population would have fled had it not been for the appearance of an Arab Legion force, and in the large Samarian city of Nablus the pro-Hashemite mayor, Suleiman Tuqan, was steeling himself for the IDF's imminent arrival. Gaza's Egyptian governor meanwhile sought to stem the flight in southern Palestine by issuing a special communiqué imploring the population to stay put. "How is it that I see the confounded people pack their belongings and travel long distances in search of foreign lands, hastily deserting their cities, lands, homes and relatives and turning southward, where they have no shelter or refuge?" read the statement. "I can assure you that Gaza is a safe haven, protected by the Egyptian army against all enemies. I promise that our forces will not withdraw one iota from Gaza and will maintain their deployment there, and in the neighborhood, with a view to defending the area and its existence come what may."

By contrast, the Syrian president, Shukri Quwatli, opined that the Egyptian army was "broken" and that the Jews were on the threshold of victory. "What could the Security Council do?" he lamented to a British diplomat. "Even if sanctions were imposed on arms . . . [these] would continue to flow to Palestine. The Arabs would soon be driven out of Jerusalem and Nablus and the whole of Palestine would become a Russian controlled base."[35]

Exacerbating the exodus and enabling Israel to gain vaster territory than that envisaged by the UN resolution were not the only, or even the most adverse, consequences of the pan-Arab invasion. By far the most significant result was the diminution in the likelihood of the refugees' eventual repatriation.

As we have seen, far from orchestrating the Arab debacle, the Yishuv was astounded by the magnitude and pace of the exodus, so much so that some

Jewish leaders initially viewed it as a possible ploy to enhance the Arab military position. "There is a danger, which apparently doesn't comprise the entire country but is underway in certain parts," Ben-Gurion told his top security officials on January 9. "That is: the removal of Arab women and children from the country, thus leaving only men [in the evacuated sites] and effectively turning them into garrisons." Three months later he was still uncertain about the real causes of the exodus, telling a meeting of the Zionist Executive that "the Arabs are presently evacuating many villages in the area between Tel Aviv and Zichron Yaacov [some 30 km (19 miles) south of Haifa]. This may be done under pressure of gang commanders for strategic reasons – removing women and children and introducing fighting units – but it may also be caused by fear."[36]

Indeed, at the request of the Hagana commander-in-chief, Israel Galili, in early April a Jewish delegation comprising top Arab-affairs advisors, local notables, and municipal heads with close contacts with neighboring Arab settlements traversed Arab villages in the coastal plain, then emptying at a staggering pace, in an attempt to convince their inhabitants to stay put. Later that month, the Jewish leaderships of Haifa and Tiberias famously pleaded with their Arab counterparts to stay put, while Moshe Shertok, soon to become Israel's first foreign minister, sought to stem the flight by suggesting a public warning to the effect that those who fled could not be assured of return. A month later, at the height of the war, the minister of minority affairs, Bechor Shalom Shitrit, told the cabinet to expect a mass return of Arabs after the termination of hostilities, and insisted that the returnees should enjoy "the same public services as the Jews since they will be the state's citizens, and as such must not suffer any discrimination." No minister disputed this proposal.[37]

Yet as Israel fought for its survival against the combined might of the Arab world, the military and political leaderships became increasingly apprehensive of the return of a hostile and potentially subversive population during the war, as demonstrated by orders to local commanders to prevent this eventuality in their respective areas. At the cabinet meeting of June 16, five days after the first truce had entered into force and a day before meeting with Bernadotte, who had made no bones about his desire to see the refugees repatriated as quickly as possible, Shertok categorically rejected this option, in stark contrast to his position a few weeks earlier. The Palestinian Arab exodus was one of those cataclysmic phenomena which, according to the experience of other countries, changed the course of history, he argued. Had someone suggested in advance that this community be expelled, it would have been sheer lunacy. But since it had happened as a direct result of the annihilationist war waged by the Palestinians and the Arab states, they must bear the full consequences of their actions.

While sharing his foreign minister's broad outlook, Ben-Gurion preferred to focus on the immediate task of preventing a refugee return during the war. "Should the fighting resume, it will be a matter of life and death for us," he said.

> We are not going to destroy the Egyptian or the Syrian peoples . . . but if we fall, we'll be destroyed. . . . This will be a war of life and death and they must not be able to return to the abandoned places. . . . We did not start the war. They made the war. Jaffa waged war on us, Haifa waged war on us, Beisan waged war on us. And I do not want them again to make war. That would not be just but foolish. . . . Do we have to make the war, which is already fought in inhuman conditions, even more difficult for us? Will it be easier for us if, while fighting the Arab Legion in Nablus, we will also have to fight Arabs near Tel Aviv? This is madness. . . . No! You made war [and] you lost.[38]

There was no discussion of the issue, let alone a decision, at the cabinet meeting and the only other member to refer to the matter was agriculture minister Aharon Tzisling, from the left-wing Mapam party, who favored general repatriation after the war. Yet in his meeting with Bernadotte the next day, Shertok refused to discuss the refugee problem while the war lasted, arguing that the matter would have to be addressed in the context of a peace settlement. He could give no assurance at this stage whether the Arabs who had fled would be allowed to return, but promised that proprietary rights would be respected.

On July 28, at Shertok's request, the cabinet officially approved (by a majority of nine to two) the hitherto informal line opposing wartime repatriation apart from special cases, and four days later the foreign minister conveyed the decision to Bernadotte. "[W]e are not unmindful of the plight of the Arabs who, as a result of the present war, find themselves uprooted from their homes and cast adrift," he wrote.

> If, nevertheless, we find ourselves unable to agree on their readmission to the Israel-controlled areas, it is because of overriding considerations bearing on our immediate security, the outcome of the present war, and the stability of the future peace settlement. We feel convinced that any measure of repatriation undertaken solely on humanitarian grounds, in disregard of the military, political and economic aspects of the problem, would prove to have been falsely conceived: it would defeat its purpose and result in graver complications than those which already exist.

"The root cause of the present conflict – of which the mass flight of Arabs and their consequent suffering are mere corollaries – is the refusal of the Arab

League to accept the State of Israel either as a matter of right or an accomplished fact," Shertok continued.

> As long as this intransigence persists, any attempt to tear the problem of Arab refugees out of its context and treat it in isolation can only, as already stated, aggravate the issue: it will render rightful defense more difficult and lend further encouragement to wanton aggression. . . . When the Arab States are ready to conclude a peace treaty with Israel, this question will come up for constructive solution as part of the general settlement.

The foreign minister enumerated a string of additional conditions that would have to be taken into account as part of the "general settlement." These included an Israeli counterclaim in respect of the destruction of Jewish life and property; the long-term interests of the Jewish and Arab populations; the stability of the state of Israel and the durability of the basis of any peace between it and its neighbors; the actual position and fate of the Jewish communities in the Arab countries; and the responsibility of the Arab governments for their war of aggression and their liability for reparations. "For such a comprehensive and lasting peace settlement the Provisional Government is ever ready," Shertok concluded, "but it holds that it cannot in fairness be required to carry through unilateral and piecemeal measures of peace while the other side is at war."[39]

By way of underscoring the seriousness of this position, the foreign minister asked Bernadotte to transmit to the Arab governments Israel's official offer of direct peace negotiations, which the mediator dutifully did – only to receive their negative replies. At the same time Israeli officials were quietly sent to Paris, where the UN General Assembly convened for its annual session and where they conveyed to their Arab interlocutors Israel's readiness for far-reaching concessions in the context of direct peace negotiations.[40] On August 10, in yet another meeting with the mediator, Shertok reiterated Israel's readiness for substantial concessions for the sake of peace. Notwithstanding the merits of resettling the refugees elsewhere, he said, should the Arab states be ready to recognize Israel (something that might prove beyond the realm of the possible), the territorial or population aspect would not be an insuperable obstacle.[41]

Ben-Gurion was similarly upbeat about the implications of a peace settlement, telling US Special Representative McDonald that large-scale repatriation was a distinct possibility in the context of a stable and lasting peace.[42] At a session of the Provisional State Council (the Knesset's predecessor) on July 22, three days after the second truce had come into effect, Ben-Gurion told the gathered parliamentarians that while the IDF's impressive victories during the last round of fighting proved beyond a shadow of a doubt its ability to defeat the Arab armies, Israel had to vigorously seek an agreement with its Arab neighbors. "Only through an alliance with the State of Israel and the Jewish People will the Arab world be able to free itself from its overt and covert subservience and reliance on oppressive and exploitative foreign forces, and only through collaboration with the neighboring [Arab] states will we be able to stabilize the peace in our state and country," he argued. "I don't know whether the time is ripe, and whether the present Arab generation is ready for Arab-Jewish cooperation on equal footing, but this cooperation is a historical necessity. Having demonstrated our military prowess to both friends and foes, we must not miss any possible opportunity for laying, through direct contact with the Arab nations, a foundation for Arab-Jewish cooperation, for cooperation between the Israel and the Arab states."[43]

The prime minister reiterated this position at the September 12 cabinet meeting. "At the moment there are apparently no Arab factors ready to reach an agreement with the Jews," he said.

> But should the possibility arise – and given the matter's importance we must not preclude such an eventuality – then I'll be prepared to ask the government and the Jewish people to content themselves with much less than this [political and territorial] program. For in my view there is hardly a price that is not worth paying for peace. . . . Should we be able to have direct talks with the Arabs that will culminate in peace – we will return the refugees. Should the [postwar] settlement fall short of peace with the Arabs – we will not allow their return.[44]

A month later, at the Provisional State Council's foreign affairs committee, Ben-Gurion rejected a suggestion for an official Israeli demand for the resettlement of the refugees in the neighboring Arab states. He was a Zionist allright, he said, yet he thought that those Arabs who wished to live in Israel should be allowed to return. "We will not close the door to them."[45]

Even Bernadotte seemed to have second thoughts. In his peace plan of June 27, he demanded that "recognition be accorded to the right of residents of Palestine who, because of conditions created by the conflict there, have left their normal places of abode, to return to their home without restriction and to regain possession of their property."[46] He kept on pressing the demand in his meetings with Israeli officials, insisting that the problem be addressed as a humanitarian rather than a political issue and dismissing Israel's fears of the adverse security and economic implications of an immediate refugee return.

Yet his gradual realization of the deep-rooted and permanent complications attending comprehensive repatriation drove the mediator to seek Israeli political and humanitarian gestures while thinking of resettlement elsewhere as the principal solution to the problem.[47]

This shift was vividly illustrated in Bernadotte's progress report, submitted to the UN secretary-general on September 16, a day before his assassination in Jerusalem by Jewish zealots. While underscoring "the right of the Arab refugees to return to their homes in Jewish-controlled territory at the earliest possible date," the report also considered the possibility of resettlement outside Palestine, with those who chose not to return being adequately compensated for their lost property. "It must not . . . be supposed that the establishment of the right of refugees to return to their former homes provides a solution to the problem," the report read.

> The vast majority of the refugees may no longer have homes to return to and their resettlement in the State of Israel presents an economic and social problem of special complexity. Whether the refugees are resettled in the State of Israel or in one or other of the Arab States, a major question to be faced is that of placing them in an environment in which they can find employment and the means of livelihood. But in any case their uncondi-tional right to make a free choice should be fully respected.[48]

This principle was duly incorporated into General Assembly Resolution 194, passed on December 11 after a three-month deliberation of the mediator's report, which placed repatriation on a par with resettlement elsewhere. It advocated, in its own words, that "the refugees wishing to return to their homes and live at peace with their neighbors should be permitted to do so at the earliest practicable date," but also that efforts should be made to facilitate the "resettlement and economic and social rehabilitation of the refugees."

In tacit acceptance of the Israeli position, the resolution did not treat the refugee problem as an isolated issue but as part of a comprehensive settle-ment between Israel and its Arab neighbors. All of its fifteen paragraphs deal with the facilitation of peace, including the single paragraph that alludes to refugees in general – not "Arab refugees" – in language that could as readily apply to the thousands of Jews driven from their homes in the prospective Arab state and Jerusalem by the invading Arab armies. Moreover, the resolu-tion expressly stipulated that compensation for the property of those refugees choosing not to return "should be made good by the governments or the authorities responsible," indicating that the Arab states, as well as Israel, were seen as instigators of the refugee problem, be it Arab or Jewish.[49]

It was just these clauses in Resolution 194 that made it anathema to the Arabs, who opposed it vehemently and voted unanimously against it.[50] Equating return and resettlement as possible solutions to the refugee problem; placing on the Arab states some of the burden for resolving it; and, above all, linking the resolution of this issue to Arab acquiescence in the existence of the state of Israel and the achievement of a comprehensive Arab-Israeli peace were seen, correctly, as rather less than useful to Arab purposes.

Not that the Palestinian leaders were eager to see their hapless constituents return to their homes, lest this be interpreted as implicit recognition of Israel. On September 12, a few days before the submission of Bernadotte's report, Hajj Amin argued that repatriation could only be achieved through the expulsion of the Jews from Palestine. So did his AHC colleague Emile Ghouri. "It is inconceivable for the refugees to return to their homes, for the Jewish occupiers will capture and torture them," he told the Beirut *Telegraph*. "The very suggestion to do so is an attempt by those culpable for the problem to shun responsibility, and will serve as a first step to Arab recognition of the state of Israel and the idea of partition."[51]

In the discussions of Bernadotte's report at the General Assembly's annual session in Paris, AHC delegate Henry Cattan derided the mediator's proposals as "aimed at the political and economic destruction of the Arabs of Palestine for the benefit of a foreign minority." The war that was being waged in Palestine could be stopped only by the removal of its causes, he argued, namely by rejecting the principle of partition, substituting a unified Arab state in the whole of Palestine for the artificial state of Israel ("the greatest treachery in the history of the world"), and expelling "all the terrorist Zionists who had entered the Holy Land." "Arab opposition to the creation of a Jewish state in Palestine followed a law of nature which could be likened to the resistance of the human body to a cancerous growth," Cattan concluded on a defiant note. "That opposition would continue until the cancer was destroyed."[52]

The Arab states played a somewhat subtler game, advocating the quick repatriation of the refugees so as to relieve the heavy burden they placed on the host societies, while avoiding any accompanying recognition of the Jewish state. As Sir Raphael Cilento, the director of UN disaster relief operations in Palestine, who worked closely with Bernadotte in easing the plight of the Palestinian Arab refugees, warned in October 1948:

> the attitude of the Syrian and Lebanese Governments was hardening and was now following a policy of concentrating refugees in their territories in as small an area as possible, in order to be able to get rid of them quickly as soon as U.N.O. [United Nations Organization] was made responsible.

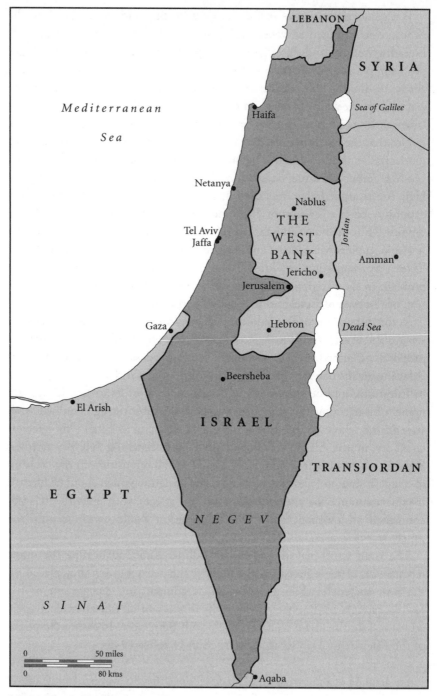

Map 5 The 1949 Armistice Lines

They were totally convinced that U.N.O. ought to take this responsibility and if it did not it was quite possible that the Arab Governments would simply allow the refugees to die.[53]

In his final round of talks with heads of Arab states in Alexandria (on September 6–7), Bernadotte was told by Syria's prime minister, Jamil Mardam, that the return of the refugees was "an indispensable condition for eventual acceptance of a truce and further negotiations." What the mediator was to make of the ultimate purpose of these future negotiations was hardly eased by Azzam's confident prediction that "sooner or later the Jewish State would disappear. The war would flare up again, the Arabs would destroy the State of Israel." In his opinion, this war of destruction would not be fought by the Arab states alone as "it should be easy, among the hundreds of thousands of Arab refugees from Palestine, to form an irregular army that would be in a position to cause a great deal of inconvenience to the Jews by acts of sabotage."

The League's secretary-general did not elaborate whether the refugees would conduct this warfare from their present locations in Arab-controlled territories or as fifth columnists after their envisaged return to Israel. Yet he deemed the Arabs to be in a win-win situation since repatriation would place Israel in an impossible position whereas failure to do so would convince world public opinion that the Jews were little more than terrorists whose methods were cruder and more brutal than those of the Nazis and the Fascists.

As the prominent Egyptian politician Muhammad Salah al-Din, soon to become his country's foreign minister, wrote in the influential Egyptian daily *al-Misri* in October 1949: "in demanding the restoration of the refugees to Palestine, the Arabs intend that they shall return as the masters of the homeland and not as slaves. More specifically, they intend to annihilate the state of Israel."[54]

CHAPTER 12

A Self-Inflicted Catastrophe

"The Arabs failed their fateful test not because of numerical or material inferiority – for the Jews had no edge in either category. They failed because of the spirit that had guided them for quite some time and continues to do so. . . . A spirit of laziness, neglect, incompetence, indecision, divisiveness, delusion, humbug . . . lack of seriousness, willingness to sacrifice, and solidarity . . . and no true belief in the cause for which they are fighting."

Muhammad Izzat Darwaza, 1972[1]

Why did Palestinian Arab society collapse and disintegrate during the fateful five-and-a-half months of fighting that followed the passing of the partition resolution? Why did vast numbers of Palestinians take to the road while their Jewish adversaries, who were facing the same challenges, dislocation, and all-out war, and who paid a comparatively higher human cost, stayed put?[2]

To many contemporary Arabs the answer was clear and unequivocal: the Palestinians were an unpatriotic and cowardly lot who had shamefully abdicated their national duty while expecting others to fight on their behalf. "Fright has struck the Palestinian Arabs and they fled their country," commented Radio Baghdad on the eve of the pan-Arab invasion of the newborn state of Israel in mid-May. "These are hard words indeed, yet they are true." Lebanon's minister of the interior (and future president) Camille Chamoun was more delicate, intoning that "The people of Palestine, in their previous resistance to imperialists and Zionists, proved they were worthy of independence, but at this decisive stage of the fighting they have not remained so dignified."[3]

In two reports to the Arab League's Palestine Committee, ALA commander-in-chief Ismail Safwat lamented that only 800 of the 5,000 volunteers trained by the ALA had come from Palestine itself, and most of these had deserted their units either before completing their training or immediately afterward. This, in his view, reflected a wider malaise of Palestinian Arab society, which remained embroiled in internal squabbles at a time when its corporate existence was in mortal danger. "I have done everything in my power to over-come this regrettable state of affairs, to no avail," he reported to the Arab League. "The situation is deteriorating by the day and the continuation of this trend is certain to entail dire consequences." Fawzi Qawuqji, the local commander of ALA forces, was no less scathing, having found the Palestinian Arabs "unreliable, excitable and difficult to control, and in organized warfare virtually unemployable."[4]

Contempt for the Palestinians only intensified with time. There were repeated calls for the return of the refugees to Palestine, or at the very least of young men of military age, many of whom had arrived in the Arab coun-tries under the (false) pretense of volunteering for the ALA. As the end of the mandate loomed on the horizon, the Lebanese government refused entry visas to Palestinian males aged between eighteen and fifty and ordered all "healthy and fit men" who had already entered the country to register offi-cially or be considered illegal aliens and face the full weight of the law.

The Syrian government took an even more stringent approach, banning from its territory all Palestinian males aged between sixteen and fifty. In Egypt, a large number of demonstrators marched on the Arab League's Cairo head-quarters and lodged a petition demanding that "every able-bodied Palestinian capable of carrying arms should be forbidden to stay abroad." "Why should we go to Palestine to fight while Palestine Arab fighters are deserting the cause by flight to Egypt [?]," was the local reaction in Alexandria upon the arrival of several refugee ships from Haifa in late April 1948. Such was the extent of Arab resentment toward the Palestinian refugees that the rector of Cairo's al-Azhar institution of religious learning, probably the foremost Islamic authority, felt obliged to issue a ruling that made the sheltering of Palestinian Arab refugees a religious duty.[5]

The Palestinians did not hesitate to reply in kind. In a letter to Fares Khouri, head of Syria's UN delegation, AHC vice-president Jamal Husseini argued that "the regular [Arab] armies did not enable the inhabitants of the country to defend themselves, but merely facilitated their escape from Palestine." His AHC colleague Emile Ghouri was even more forthright, blaming the Arab states for the creation of the refugee problem in the first place and demanding that they reconquer Palestine and repatriate its inhab-itants – a demand repeated by the Nablus mayor, Suleiman Tuqan, as well as thousands of demonstrators in east Jerusalem, Ramallah, Nablus, Jenin, and Tulkarm on the first anniversary of Israel's establishment.[6]

The prevailing conviction among Palestinians that they were the victims of their fellow Arabs rather than of Israeli aggression was grounded not only in experience but in the larger facts of inter-Arab politics. Had the Arab states pressured the AHC to accept the partition resolution rather than to abort it by force of arms, or forgone their own attempt to destroy the Jewish state at birth, the Palestinian tragedy would have been averted altogether. Had they been truly interested in the Palestinians' right to national self-determination, Egypt and Transjordan could have readily established independent Palestinian entities in the parts of Palestine that they conquered during the 1948 war — respectively, the Gaza Strip and the West Bank.

Instead, no sooner had his army attacked the nascent state of Israel than King Abdullah moved to erase all traces of corporate Palestinian Arab identity in the occupied territories, a process that culminated in their formal annexation in April 1950. And while Egypt stopped short of annexing the Gaza Strip, this did not imply support of Palestinian nationalism or of any sort of collective political awareness among the Palestinians. The local population was kept under oppressive military rule, was denied Egyptian citizenship, and was subjected to severe restrictions on travel. As an Egyptian diplomat told a British journalist in June 1949: "We couldn't care less if all the refugees die. There are enough Arabs around."[7]

This total lack of empathy was grounded in the wider perception of the Palestine problem as a corollary of the pan-Arab ideal rather than a distinct issue in its own right: not only by the Hashemite monarchs of Iraq and Transjordan and their erstwhile henchmen (notably Nuri Said), who viewed Palestine as simply another province in the vast empires they sought to establish, but also by numerous other rulers and politicians. As we have seen, in September 1947 the Arab League secretary-general, Abdel Rahman Azzam, presented the rejection of Jewish statehood as aimed at fending off a perceived encroachment on the pan-Arab patrimony, while Fares Khouri told the UN General Assembly that "had it not been for the Balfour declaration and the terms of the mandate, Palestine would now be a Syrian province as it used to be."[8]

It was indeed common knowledge at the time that the pan-Arab invasion was more of a scramble for Palestine than an attempt to secure Palestinian national rights, and that if the Arab states had succeeded in defeating the Jews and destroying their nascent state, its territory would not have been handed over to the Palestinians but rather divided among the invading forces. In December 1947, the British mandatory authorities commented that "it does not appear that Arab Palestine will be an entity, but rather that the Arab countries will each claim a portion in return for their assistance, unless King Abdullah takes rapid and firm action as soon as the British withdrawal is completed." Two months later, High Commissioner Cunningham informed the colonial secretary, Arthur Creech Jones, that "the most likely arrangement seems to be Eastern Galilee to Syria, Samaria and Hebron to

Abdullah, and the South to Egypt, and it might well end in annexation on this pattern; the center remain uncertain." Meanwhile Sir Alec Kirkbride, the influential British ambassador to Amman, assessed that "if Transjordan did not occupy [the] Western Galilee immediately someone else would do so."[9]

In a private conversation in late March 1948, Azzam disclosed the existence of a British-mediated understanding between the Arab League and Transjordan whereby:

> *Abdullah was to swallow up the central hill regions of Palestine, with access to the Mediterranean at Gaza. The Egyptians would get the Negev. [The] Galilee would go to Syria, except that the coastal part as far as Acre would be added to the Lebanon if its inhabitants opted for it by a referendum (i.e. the inhabitants of the said coastal strip). In Jewish-controlled areas (including Haifa) the Jews would get some measure of autonomy.*

At the same time, Egypt's King Faruq blocked the Mufti's attempt to form a provisional Palestinian Arab government that would assume authority on May 15, turning down his request to enter Palestine by way of Gaza, along the trail of the Egyptian army's line of communications, lest this gave the false impression that Egypt acknowledged Hajj Amin's leadership.[10]

In the autumn of 1948, as the UN General Assembly discussed Bernadotte's report, which recommended inter alia to sever the Negev from Israel, a special envoy of King Faruq informed Sasson of Egypt's interest in the southern areas awarded to the Arab state by the partition resolution. The Egyptian foreign minister passed on similar messages to Harold Beeley, Bevin's foremost advisor on Palestine, and to Ronald Campbell, the British ambassador in Cairo, emphasizing that "it would be dangerous for the Arabs to permit the establishment of an independent state in the Arab parts of Palestine."

As the Israelis remained unimpressed, the Egyptians asked UN acting mediator Ralph Bunche to secure southern Palestine for them as far north as Majdal, some 48km (30 miles) south of Tel Aviv, though they subsequently modified their bid to the Gaza enclave of the original partition scheme, about twice the size of what was to become the Gaza Strip. (Saudi Arabia's founding monarch, Ibn Saud, was reportedly amenable to Egypt's annexation of the Negev.)

As late as June 1949, a few months after the end of the war and the signing of armistice agreements between Israel, Egypt, Transjordan, and Lebanon (with Syria joining a month later), Israeli officials were told by Arab interlocutors, with whom they carried on covert talks in Paris, that any territories surrendered by the Jewish state would be handed over to Transjordan, Egypt, and Lebanon rather than to a prospective Palestinian state.[11]

"What concerned [the Arab states] most and guided their policy was not to win the war and save Palestine from the enemy, but what would happen after the struggle, who would be predominant in Palestine, or annex it to themselves," the prominent Palestinian Arab politician Musa Alami wrote in October 1949. "Their announced aim was the salvation of Palestine, and they said that afterward its destiny should be left to its people. This was said with the tongue only. In their hearts all wished it for themselves; and most of them were hurrying to prevent their neighbors from being predominant, even though nothing remained except the offal and bones."[12]

In contrast to Arab designs on Palestine, the Zionist movement's acceptance of the partition resolution underscored its continued commitment to the "two-state solution," which it had officially accepted a decade earlier when proposed by the Peel commission. In her November 1947 meeting with Abdullah, Golda Meyerson rejected Transjordan's annexation of western Palestine, insisting on the creation of a Palestinian Arab state in accordance with the impending UN resolution, and this position remained intact after the pan-Arab attack on Israel in which the Hashemite monarch played a prominent role. As Foreign Minister Shertok told the Israeli cabinet on June 16, 1948:

> I presume that it is our unanimous view that an Arab Palestine is here to stay. . . . If Arab Palestine goes to Abdullah, this means unification with Transjordan and a possible linkage with [Hashemite] Iraq. And if this Palestine is a separate state, standing on its own: it is a wholly different matter. . . . We undertook to associate ourselves with a specific partner [i.e., the Palestinian Arabs] and we are prepared to negotiate with it. But not with another partner.[13]

Asked by Bernadotte whether Israel would prefer an independent Palestinian state or would rather have the country's Arab parts annexed to Transjordan or divided among the neighboring states, Shertok expressed an unequivocal preference for a separate state, with the breaking up of the territory into fragments, each to be annexed by one of the neighboring states, being in his view the worst possible eventuality, which Israel would in all probability fight to prevent. While Arab Palestine in its present state was no political entity at all and had no leadership, he told the mediator, "efforts might be made to find out whether a group of people could not be welded together to serve as a center for a separate State." "While we would not fight to prevent the joining of Arab Palestine with Transjordan," he said, "we are very much disillusioned by King Abdullah's misguided truculence, and, anyway, a smaller and a weaker neighbor was preferable to a bigger and stronger one. Transjordan and Iraq belonged to the same dynasty and might, in the course of time, be bracketed together under a common crown. The prospects of having the Iraqi Empire right on our doorstep was not one which we could relish."[14]

Prime Minister Ben-Gurion was equally forthright. "We will not be able to agree lightly to the annexation of [the Arab] parts of Palestine to Transjordan for the following reasons," he told a meeting of foreign policy and Arab affairs experts on December 18, 1948: "1) Israel's security: an Arab state in western Palestine is less dangerous than a state that is tied to Transjordan, and tomorrow – probably to Iraq; 2) Why should we unnecessarily antagonize the Russians? 3) Why should we do this [i.e., agree to Transjordan's annexation of western Palestine] against the [wishes of the] rest of the Arab states?"[15] Even when, in September 1948, the Arab League approved (against Abdullah's violent opposition) the formation of a Gaza-based, Mufti-dominated government for the whole of Palestine, Israel refrained from opposing the move so as to keep the door open to an independent Arab state in part of Palestine (presumably under a friendlier leadership).[16]

As for the Arab inhabitants of the Jewish state that would be born with the termination of the British mandate, all Zionist deliberations were based on the assumption that they would be equal citizens who would participate on an equal footing in all sectors of the country's public life. In Ben-Gurion's words: "In our state there will be non-Jews as well – and all of them will be equal citizens; equal in everything without any exception; that is: the state will be their state as well."[17]

In line with this conception, the Hagana's plan for rebuffing the anticipated pan-Arab invasion (Plan D) was predicated, in the explicit instructions of commander-in-chief Israel Galili, on "the Arab policy of the Zionist movement, that is: acknowledgement of the full rights, needs, and freedom of the Arabs in the Hebrew state without any discrimination, and a desire for coexistence on the basis of mutual freedom and dignity."[18] And if this was the official attitude toward the Arab minority in the nascent Jewish state, it is hardly surprising that Plan D never envisaged the conquest of the Arab state that was to be established in the other half of mandatory Palestine, not to mention the dispossession of its population. Rather, its overarching strategic goal was purely defensive: "To secure the territorial integrity of the Jewish state and to defend its borders, as well as the blocs of Jewish settlement and such Jewish population as were outside those boundaries, against regular, semi-regular, and guerrilla forces operating from bases outside or inside the Hebrew state."

The plan did envisage the possible destruction of villages and "the expulsion of [their] population outside the border of the [Jewish] state," that is:

expulsion to the Palestinian Arab state. Yet these were ad hoc tactical measures dictated exclusively by military necessity rather than political considerations, let alone a premeditated plan of dispossession, and applied only to
sites that served as bases for attacks on Jewish targets (particularly key transportation arteries) which could not be kept from enemy forces after their
conquest due to the unavailability of local forces for their retention.
Wherever one or more of these conditions did not apply, no harm was to be
visited on Arab settlements and their inhabitants, who were to be incorporated into the nascent Jewish state as full and equal citizens – as stated by
Plan D itself and a series of orders for the running of captured Arab territories, which obliged "front commanders and military governors to ensure the
strict observance of civil and individual rights in the conquered areas
and instruct their troops to treat the civilian population courteously and
respectfully."

On March 18, shortly after the launch of Plan D, the Jewish Agency
denied any intention to expel the Arab population of the prospective Jewish
state, emphasizing instead that it "considered them as citizens, safeguarded
their interests and livelihood and intended that they should participate in the
Government provided they were not implicated in incidents or let by
saboteurs."[19]

The same principle was enshrined in Israel's Declaration of Independence,
issued on May 14, 1948, which undertook to "uphold absolute social and
political equality of rights for all its citizens, without distinction of religion,
race, or sex." In particular, Arab citizens were urged "to take part in the
building of the state on the basis of full and equal citizenship and on the basis
of appropriate representation in all its institutions, provisional and permanent." For those Arab citizens who did not speak Hebrew, the declaration
was read in Arabic on the official Israeli state radio, with an Arabic-language
précis broadcast on May 16, a day after the beginning of the pan-Arab assault
on the newborn Jewish state:

> Although we have been forced into a fierce war, we should not forget that
> within our boundaries members of the Arab people should enjoy the rights
> of citizens and that most of them hate this war. We should maintain their
> rights on an equal footing with those of all citizens. We look forward to
> peace and stretch out our hand for their collaboration in constructing the
> homeland. Citizens, let us maintain the integrity of our young
> Fatherland![20]

In its first meeting on the same day, the provisional Israeli government
discussed a basic law regulating the nascent state's ruling institutions and

practices, which ensured inter alia the right of Arab citizens to be elected to parliament and to serve as cabinet ministers, as well as the continued functioning of the autonomous Muslim (and Christian) religious courts that had existed during the mandate. Four months later the government decided that Arabic, alongside Hebrew, would serve as the official language of Israel in all public documents and certificates.[21]

But even if the Yishuv *had* instigated a plot to expel the Palestinian Arabs, which it most certainly did not, the extensive British military presence in Palestine until the end of the mandate, which severely constrained Jewish military capabilities (from the prohibition of the bearing of arms and the confiscation of weapons and arrest of fighters, to the restriction of movement and repeated military interventions on the Arab side), would have precluded the slightest possibility of systematic "ethnic cleansing."

And so it was that in the four months of fighting that followed the passing of the partition resolution vast numbers of Palestinian Arabs fled their homes even though the Jews were still on the defensive and in no position to drive them out. Even before the outbreak of hostilities, many Arabs had already escaped, and still larger numbers left before war reached their own doorstep.[22] By April 1948, some 100,000 had gone, and by the time of Israel's Declaration of Independence the number had more than trebled. Even then, none of the 170,000–180,000 Arabs fleeing urban centers, and only a handful of the 130,000–160,000 villagers who left their homes, had been forced out by the Jews.

The exceptions occurred in the heat of battle and were uniformly dictated by ad hoc military considerations.[23] They were, moreover, matched by efforts to prevent flight and/or to encourage the return of those who had fled – at a time when huge numbers of Palestinians were being actively driven from their homes by their own leaders and/or by Arab armed forces, whether out of military considerations or in order to prevent them from becoming citizens of the prospective Jewish state.

In the largest and best-known example, tens of thousands of Arabs were ordered or bullied into leaving the city of Haifa on the AHC's instructions despite strenuous Jewish efforts to persuade them to stay. Only days earlier, Tiberias's 6,000-strong Arab community had been similarly forced out by its own leaders, against local Jewish wishes (a fortnight after the exodus, Cunningham reported that the Tiberias Jews "would welcome [the] Arabs back").[24] In Jaffa, Palestine's largest Arab city, the municipality organized the transfer of thousands of residents by land and sea; in Jerusalem the AHC ordered the transfer of women and children, and local gang leaders pushed out the residents of several neighborhoods; while in Beisan the women and children were ordered out as Transjordan's Arab Legion dug in. And then there were the tens of thousands of rural villagers who were likewise forced out by order of the AHC, local Arab militias, the ALA, and the Arab Legion.[25]

"The Arab mass flight that we have recently witnessed throughout the country – in Tiberias, Haifa, and other places – is probably not exclusively related to fear and weakness," Sasson wrote to Shertok on April 25.

> It is organized by the Husseini stalwarts in collaboration with the foreign "fighters" with a view to: a) deriding the Jews and casting them as usurpers bent on dispossessing the Arabs from their homeland; b) goading the Arab states to direct military intervention; c) laying the groundwork in the Arab world, and the international community at large, for portraying the imminent invasion of the regular Arab armies as a move to protect the persecuted Palestinians rather than the violation of international conventions [that it would actually be]. The fact that foreign commanders tend to disappear at the beginning of every serious engagement on the pretext of calling reinforcements, leaving the local inhabitants and the "fighters" on their own, indicates the existence of higher orders to introduce chaos and anarchy into the Arab camp with the inevitable result of flight and prompt evacuation.[26]

It is true that neither the AHC nor the Arab states envisaged the magnitude of the exodus and that both sought to contain it once it began spiraling out of control. In the second half of January, a British report noted that "The Arab Higher executive are becoming very perturbed at the large number of Arab families which are leaving the Arab areas. On the instructions of the Mufti they are being ordered to return and, if they refuse, their houses will be occupied by other Arabs sent to reinforce the areas."[27]

But it is no less true that it was the actions of the Arab leaders that condemned hundreds of thousands of Palestinians to exile. As we have seen, the pan-Arab Sofar summit of September 1947 urged the Arab states to open their gates to Palestinian Arab refugees in the event of disturbances, and this recommendation was endorsed the following month by a gathering of Haifa's Arab leadership, which decided to draw up plans for "the evacuation of women and children to neighboring Arab countries." The idea was reiterated by the Mufti and his foremost commander, Abdel Qader Husseini, in January 1948, while King Abdullah promised, in late November or early December 1947, that "if any Palestine Arabs should become refugees as a result of the Husseini faction's activities, the gates of Transjordan would always remain open to them."[28]

The logic behind this policy, in Azzam's Words, was apparently that "the absence of the women and children from Palestine would free the men for fighting." As late as the end of April, when the Palestinian Arab war effort had all but collapsed, the ALA's radio station argued that "the evacuation of Arab women and children from Jaffa [i]s but a temporary military measure." Likewise, it was widely believed in the north Samarian town of Jenin that the mayhem and dislocation had been deliberately engineered by the Palestinian Arab leaders. "Let the blood flow in the streets," ran the defiant argument. "Our goal is to destroy everything. We're emptying all mixed-population localities – suburbs, villages, and cities – so that when the blow comes, it will be powerful and sustained."[29]

This thinking backfired disastrously. Far from boosting morale and freeing the men for fighting, the mass departure of women and children led to the total depopulation of cities and villages as the men chose to join their families rather than to stay behind and fight. In recognition of its mistake, in early March 1948 the AHC issued a circular castigating the flight out of the country as a blemish on "the jihad movement and the reputation of the Palestinians" and stating that "in places of great danger, women, children, and the elderly should be moved to safer areas" within Palestine. But only a week later it was evidently allowing those same categories of persons to leave Jerusalem for Lebanon, and was also ordering the removal of women and children from Haifa. In early March, there were reports of a plan to evacuate Haifa's entire Arab population and to leave only fighters in the city. Again, the AHC attempted to stem the flood by restricting the availability of permits needed to leave the country; yet not only was this haphazardly applied, with AHC relatives and friends given free rein to leave, but it also generated a thriving black market where such permits could be readily obtained for a handsome price. By late April, nothing remained of the AHC's stillborn instruction as Transjordan threw its doors open to the mass arrival of Palestinian women and children and the Arab Legion was given a free hand to carry out population transfers at its discretion.[30]

"The opening of the gates by the Arab states bordering Palestine in order to facilitate the Palestinian migration was among the worst mistakes [of the war]," the Mufti lamented in his memoirs. Muhammad Nimr Khatib, a prominent Palestinian Arab leader during the mandate, expressed a similar sentiment: "The Palestinian Arabs had neighboring Arab states which opened their borders and doors to the refugees, while the Jews had no alternative but to triumph or to die."[31]

This is true enough of the Jews, but it elides the reasons for the collapse of Palestinian Arab society: the total lack of national cohesion or willingness to

subordinate personal interest to the general good. The rural sector, comprising
the vast majority of the country's Arab population, did its utmost to stay out
of the fighting – evading conscription, obstructing military operations,
reaching localized deals with the Jews, forewarning Jewish neighbors of imminent Arab attacks, and even supplying them with invaluable operational intelligence. But the situation was equally bleak in the cities, where conflicting
economic interests, political differences, and social and interdenominational
schisms diminished the appetite for fighting, generated successive waves of
evacuees, and prevented national cooperation. There was no sense of an overarching mutual interest or shared destiny. Cities and towns acted as if they
were self-contained units, attending to their own needs and eschewing the
smallest sacrifice on behalf of other localities. Many National Committees
forbade the export of food and drink from well-stocked cities to needy
outlying towns and villages. Haifa's Arab merchants refused to alleviate a
severe shortage of flour in Jenin, while Gaza refused to export eggs and
poultry to Jerusalem; in Hebron, armed guards checked all departing cars;
Jerusalem retaliated by sabotaging a flour shipment to Hebron. At the same
time there was extensive smuggling, especially in the mixed-population cities,
with Arab foodstuffs going to Jewish neighborhoods and vice versa. Even
Transjordanian manufacturers preferred to export their textile products to the
Yishuv rather than to the Palestinian Arabs, and the AHC gave grudging
approval to this practice under pressure from Abdullah.[32]

The lack of communal solidarity was similarly evidenced by the abysmal
treatment meted out to the hundreds of thousands of evacuees scattered
throughout the country. Not only was there no collective effort to relieve
their plight, but many refugees were ill-treated by their temporary hosts and
subjected to ridicule and abuse for their supposed cowardice. In the words of
a Jewish intelligence report: "The refugees are hated wherever they have
arrived."

Some Palestinian Arab localities flatly refused to accept refugees at all, for
fear of overstraining existing resources. In Acre, the authorities prevented
Arabs fleeing Haifa from disembarking; in Ramallah, the predominantly
Christian population organized its own militia – not so much to fight the
Jews as to fend off the new Muslim arrivals. Many exploited the plight of the
refugees unabashedly, especially by fleecing them for such basic necessities as
transportation and accommodation. A taxi ride to Beirut cost as much as
£4–£5 – about an average month's pay – while the going monthly rent for
an unfurnished room in Bethlehem amounted to £7; and if such was the
treatment of Palestinians by their own brothers, small wonder that in
Amman refugees were charged an exorbitant £300–£400 in advance for a
one-or two-year rental.[33]

Even the survivors of Deir Yasin did not escape their share of indignities. Finding refuge in the neighboring village of Silwan, many were soon at loggerheads with the locals, to the point where on April 14, a mere five days after the tragedy, a Silwan delegation approached the AHC's Jerusalem office demanding that the survivors be transferred elsewhere. No help for their relocation was forthcoming.[34]

Deir Yasin was the most obvious example of yet another catastrophic blunder on the part of the Palestinian Arab leadership, from the AHC to National Committees to local elites: namely, the pervasive use of (commonly false) tales of atrocities perpetrated by the Jews.

It is perhaps an inevitable consequence of intercommunal strife, with guerrilla forces and terror groups active in a country's population centers, that noncombatants no less than fighting units are drawn into the conflict. So it was in Palestine, where civilians on both sides could not be readily distinguished from active participants in the war who operated from among them. Shootings, sniper attacks, ambushes, bombings, which in today's world would be condemned as war crimes, were daily events in the lives of Jews and Arabs. "[I]nnocent and harmless people, going about their daily business," wrote the US consul-general in Jerusalem, Robert Macatee, in December 1947, "are picked off while riding in buses, walking along the streets, and stray shots even find them while asleep in their beds. A Jewish woman, mother of five children, was shot in Jerusalem while hanging out clothes on the roof. The ambulance rushing her to the hospital was machine-gunned, and finally the mourners following her to the funeral were attacked and one of them stabbed to death."[35] As the fighting escalated, Arab civilians suffered as well, and the occasional atrocity sparked cycles of larger-scale violence. Thus, the December 1947 murder of six Arab workers near the Haifa oil refinery by the small Jewish underground group the IZL was followed by the immediate slaughter of thirty-nine Jews by their Arab coworkers, just as Deir Yasin was "avenged" within days by the killing of seventy-seven Jewish nurses and doctors en route to the Hadassah hospital on Mount Scopus.

Yet while the Jewish leadership and media described these gruesome events for what they were, at times withholding details so as to avoid spreading panic and to keep the door open for Arab-Jewish reconciliation, their Arab counterparts not only inflated the toll to gigantic proportions but invented numerous nonexistent atrocities. The fall of Haifa, for example, gave rise to totally false claims of large-scale slaughter, which circulated throughout the Middle East and reached Western capitals, to the point that Cunningham felt obliged to inform London that the "Jewish attack in Haifa was a direct consequence of continuous attacks by Arabs on Jews in Haifa over [the] previous four days. [The a]ttack was carried out by [the] Hagana and there was no 'massacre.' "

Similarly false rumors were spread after the fall of Tiberias, where Jewish fighters were accused of wreaking havoc and raping local women, during the battle for Safad, and in Jaffa, where, as we have seen, the mayor fabricated a massacre of "hundreds of Arab men and women." Accounts of the Deir Yasin tragedy in the Arab media were particularly lurid, describing supposed hammer-and-sickle tattoos on the arms of IZL fighters and making accusations of rapes which had never taken place. According to a senior Palestinian Arab journalist in 1948, it was none other than AHC secretary Hussein Khalidi who drafted the influential radio broadcasts on Deir Yasin, despite being well aware of their falsehood.[36]

This scaremongering was undoubtedly aimed at garnering the widest possible sympathy for the Palestinian Arab plight and at presenting the Jews as brutal predators. As Azzam told the British ambassador to Cairo, the (non-existent) Haifa massacre was "part of a Jewish military plan designed to terrorize the Arab population inside the Jewish state so that by May 15th they would be released of having to deal with any fifth column and be able to concentrate their whole energy on action against regular Arab forces which they believed would then enter Palestine from outside."[37]

Like other pillars of the Arab strategy, however, this thinking proved disastrously misconceived. Rather than boost the fledgling Arab struggle, the "atrocity factor" spread panic within an already disorientated Palestinian society and accelerated the mass flight.[38]

As for the Palestinian Arab leaders themselves, who had placed their reluctant constituents on a collision course with Zionism in the 1920s and 1930s and who had now dragged them helpless into an all-out conflict, they hastened to get themselves out of Palestine and to stay out at the most critical moment. Taking a cue from their higher-ups, local leaders similarly rushed en masse through the door. In the words of Sir Henry Gurney, chief secretary to the Palestine Mandate Government: "It is pathetic to see how the Arabs have been deserted by their leaders, and how the firebrands all seek refuge in Damascus, Amman and elsewhere when the real trouble starts."[39]

This desertion was not confined to the political and civilian echelons. As we have seen, the Haifa military leaders were the first to flee when the battle for the city was joined; some of them escaped to Acre, where they helped organize the local resistance, only to flee to Beirut in a large motorboat once the going got tough, taking with them some of the city's weapons. ALA commanders fled Jaffa at the head of their troops, in the Jerusalem suburb of

Qatamon the commander left in the midst of the battle, and the substantial ALA forces in Nazareth took off ahead of the advancing Israeli forces, together with the city's political and economic leadership. Likewise, the Beisan commander fled the city a day before its surrender, having helped himself to £9,000 (£220,000 in today's terms) from the municipal coffers, while in Samakh the local political and military leadership left town, having reportedly been bribed by the Jews into such a move.[40]

Arif Arif, a prominent Arab politician during the mandate era and the doyen of Palestinian historians, described the prevailing atmosphere at the time: "Wherever one went throughout the country one heard the same refrain: 'Where are the leaders who should show us the way? Where is the AHC? Why are its members in Egypt at a time when Palestine, their own country, needs them?' "[41]

Epilogue

"[I] would prefer the land to remain poor and desolate even for another hundred years, until the Arabs themselves were capable of developing it and making it flower."

Musa Alami, 1934

"Netanyahu will have to wait 1,000 years before he finds one Palestinian who will go along with him."

Saeb Erekat, June 2009

On the afternoon of June 17, 1948, Count Folke Bernadotte and his senior aides called on Moshe Shertok in his Tel Aviv office. A truce between Israel and its Arab attackers had just entered into force and the UN mediator, who was about to submit his proposals for a lasting settlement, was seeking to sound out the foreign minister regarding his government's position. Would Israel be prepared to discuss some frontier modifications, he asked. This would certainly be in its best interests as the present lines were militarily difficult to defend and possibly other boundaries might prove preferable from the Jewish point of view.

Keenly aware that Bernadotte's idea of border changes involved the reduction of Israel's territory to about a third of the size awarded to it by the United Nations, Shertok said that while he was not averse to slight frontier adjustments, the border question was a corollary of the conflict rather than its root cause. "The Arabs had rejected the settlement of November 29 not on account of the boundaries it laid down, but because of the principle of the thing," he argued, and as long as they persisted in their rejection of the idea of Jewish statehood any discussion of any boundary modification would be meaningless: "The continued existence of the State of Israel was a matter that was irreducible. Peace was conceivable only in terms of the Jewish State as a neighbor of the Arab States, and not in terms of a Jewish community endowed with some forms of 'autonomy' and existing as a tolerated minority within an Arab State. The first step toward peace was the State of Israel itself."[1] Little did the foreign minister expect that nearly a century after the League of Nations had recognized the right of the Jews to statehood in their ancestral homeland, and more than sixty years after the League's successor, the United Nations, realized this right by an internationally recognized act of self-determination, Israel would remain the only state in the world whose right to exist is constantly debated and challenged.

Peace, according to the great seventeenth-century philosopher Baruch Spinoza, is not merely the absence of war but rather a state of mind: a disposition to benevolence, confidence, and justice. From the birth of the Jewish national movement in the late nineteenth century, that disposition has remained conspicuously absent from the minds of Arab and Palestinian leaders. Even Abdullah ibn Hussein, founding monarch of Transjordan (later Jordan), whose thirty years of contacts with the Zionists would only be surpassed by the extensiveness of those of his grandson, King Hussein, had no qualms about publicly stating that "history has proved that no nation can live with the Jews as neighbors because it then loses everything it has as a result of the Jews' cheating and fraud." Likewise, Egyptian president Anwar Sadat, the first Arab leader to sign a peace treaty with Israel, could tell his foreign minister shortly before the event that "we are dealing with the lowest and meanest of enemies. The Jews even tormented their Prophet Moses, and exasperated their God."[2]

Against this backdrop, it is hardly to be wondered that, for many Arabs, the primary instrument for opposing Jewish national aspirations was violence, and what determined their politics and diplomacy was the relative success or failure of that instrument in any given period. After Arab violence backfired spectacularly in 1948, inter-Arab politics in the decades to come would be driven by a determination to undo the consequences of that defeat, duly dubbed *al-Naqba*, "the catastrophe," and to bring about Israel's demise. This phase culminated in June 1967 in yet another major war that was irretrievably to change the course of Middle Eastern history.

It was, indeed, the magnitude of the Israeli victory in the Six-Day War of 1967 that punctured the bubble of denial and forced at least some Arabs to confront the reality of Jewish statehood. On June 4, 1967, the ecstatic Arab leaders were confidently predicting Israel's imminent demise and promising their subjects the spoils of victory. A week later they were reconciling themselves to the routing of the Egyptian, Syrian, Jordanian, and Iraqi armies, and to the extension of Israeli control over vast Arab territories about five times its own size, from the Suez Canal to the Jordan River and the Golan Heights. Even Egypt's president, Gamal Abdel Nasser, the high priest of pan-Arabism and champion of the 1967 Arab campaign, now seemed to recoil from the

ideals he had preached for so long. A few days before the outbreak of hostilities on June 5, Nasser had proudly prophesied that "the battle will be total
and our basic aim will be the destruction of Israel." A couple of years later,
still shaken by defeat, he was scolding the Arab leaders who were continuing
to urge Egypt to resume hostilities: "You issue statements, but we have to
fight. If you want to liberate, then get in line in front of us."[3]

The trauma of the 1967 war thus suggested to the Arabs that military force
had its limits, and that the destruction of Israel might have to be pursued in
other ways. If the 1967 war was fought with a view to destroying the state
physically, the next war, in October 1973, launched by Nasser's successor,
Anwar Sadat, had the far narrower objective of triggering a political process
that would allow Egypt to regain the territories lost in 1967. Israel's remarkable military recovery from the surprise Egyptian-Syrian attack, which
deprived the Arab armies of their initial gains, encircled a sizeable Egyptian
force (which was eventually freed through American mediation), and placed
the Egyptian and Syrian capitals under direct military threat, further reinforced Sadat's determination to abandon the path of outright violence, and
culminated in the Egyptian-Israeli peace treaty of March 1979.

Yet this hardly reflected a fundamental acceptance of Israel's legitimacy.
While one can only speculate about Sadat's own ultimate intentions – he was
assassinated in October 1981 by an Islamist zealot – there is little doubt that
his successor, Husni Mubarak, has never had any desire to transform the
formal Egyptian peace with Israel into a genuine reconciliation. For
Mubarak, peace is of no value in and of itself; rather, it is the price Egypt has
had to pay for such substantial benefits as US economic and military aid. As
he candidly explained the nature of the Egyptian-Israeli relationship:

> Against us stood the most intelligent people on earth – a people that
> controls the international press, the world economy, and world finances.
> We succeeded in compelling the Jews to do what we wanted; we received
> all our land back, up to the last grain of sand! We have outwitted them, and
> what have we given them in return? A piece of paper! . . . We were
> shrewder than the shrewdest people on earth! We managed to hamper their
> steps in every direction. We have established sophisticated machinery to
> control and limit to the minimum contacts with the Jews. We have proven
> that making peace with Israel does not entail Jewish domination and that
> there is no obligation to develop relations with Israel beyond those we
> desire.[4]

Over the decades, Mubarak has reduced interaction with Israel to the
minimum level, demonstratively refraining from paying a single official visit

to the Jewish state (his only appearance there was to attend prime minister Yitzhak Rabin's funeral in November 1995). At the same time, he has transformed the Egyptian army into a formidable modern force and turned a blind eye to the massive flow of arms and war materiel from Egyptian territory to the Palestinian terrorist organizations in the Gaza Strip. He has also fostered a culture of virulent anti-Semitism in Egypt, a culture whose premises he himself evidently shares, turning his country into the world's most prolific producer of anti-Semitic ideas and attitudes.

The traditional "blood libel," that medieval fabrication according to which Jews use Gentile blood, and particularly the blood of children, for ritual purposes, is still in wide circulation in Egypt, together with a string of other canards whose tenor may be glimpsed in the title of an 1890 tract recently reprinted by the Egyptian ministry of education: *Human Sacrifice in the Talmud.* Jews have been accused of everything from exporting infected seeds, plants, and cattle in order to destroy Egyptian agriculture, to corrupting Egyptian society through the spread of venereal diseases and the distribution of drugs. No less popular is *The Protocols of the Elders of Zion*, a virulent anti-Semitic tract fabricated by the Russian secret police at the turn of the twentieth century, which may be in wider circulation in Egypt than anywhere else in the world. In 2002, during the holy month of Ramadan, the state-controlled Egyptian television ran a drama series based on the *Protocols*. A few months later, a copy of the *Protocols* was prominently displayed alongside a Torah scroll in an exhibition at the new Alexandria Library.

If this is "peaceful coexistence" as practiced by the largest and most powerful Arab state, which has been at peace with Israel for over three decades, other Arab players, with the partial exception of Jordan, have never felt even the need to acknowledge the Jewish state's legitimacy, and have declined even the most tempting offers in exchange for normalized relations. During the 1990s, four successive Israeli prime ministers, from Yitzhak Rabin to Ehud Barak, were willing to return the Golan Heights to Syria in exchange for peace. President Hafez Assad rejected every proposal. He did so not because of petty squabbles over a few hundred yards of territory around the Sea of Galilee, as was widely believed at the time, but because of a fundamental reluctance to acquiesce formally in the very existence of the "neo-Crusader state," whose fate, Assad never tired of reiterating, would eventually be as stark as that of the medieval Crusader kingdom that came before it.[5]

This recalcitrance had nothing to do with a concern for Palestinian rights. Just as the Arab states' interventionism in Palestine from the 1920s to the late 1940s, especially their concerted attack on the nascent state of Israel in mid-May 1948, had been driven by ulterior motives, so they unabashedly manipulated the Palestinian national cause to their own ends during the decades of Palestinian dispersal. Between 1949 and 1967, Egypt and Jordan ruled the Palestinians of Gaza and the West Bank respectively. Not only did they fail to put these populations on the road to statehood, but they showed little interest in protecting their human rights or even in improving their quality of life. Nasser cloaked his hegemonic goals by invoking the restoration of "the full rights of the Palestinian people."[6] Likewise, Saddam Hussein disguised his predatory designs on Kuwait by linking the crisis caused by his invasion of that country in the summer of 1990 with "the immediate and unconditional withdrawal of Israel from the occupied Arab territories in Palestine."[7]

Assad himself, who as late as 1974 described Palestine as "a basic part of southern Syria,"[8] was a persistent obstacle to the Palestinians' right of self-determination. He pledged allegiance to any solution amenable to the Palestine Liberation Organization (PLO) – appointed by the Arab League in October 1974 as the "sole legitimate representative of the Palestinian people" – so long as it did not deviate from the Syrian line advocating the destruction of the state of Israel. Yet when in November 1988 the PLO appeared to accept the 1947 partition resolution (and by implication to recognize Israel's existence) so as to end its boycotting by the US, Syria immediately opposed the move.[9] When the PLO took its pretense a step further by signing the September 1993 Declaration of Principles on Interim Self-Government Arrangements (DOP) with Israel, which provided for Palestinian self-rule in the entire West Bank and Gaza Strip for a transitional period not to exceed five years, during which Israel and the Palestinians would negotiate a permanent peace settlement, it was strongly condemned by the Syrian regime, while the Damascus-based Palestinian terrorist Ahmad Jibril threatened PLO chairman Yasir Arafat with death.[10]

Assad's apprehensions were wholly unwarranted. Arafat, who dominated Palestinian politics from the mid-1960s to his death in November 2004, was no more accepting of the Jewish right to statehood than his extremist predecessor Hajj Amin Husseini, who first put the Palestinian Arabs on the catastrophic collision course with their Jewish counterparts. As early as 1968, Arafat defined the PLO's strategic objective as "the transfer of all resistance bases" into the West Bank and the Gaza Strip, occupied by Israel during the June 1967 war, "so that the resistance may be gradually transformed into a popular armed revolution." This, he reasoned, would allow the PLO to undermine Israel's way of life by "preventing immigration and encouraging emigration . . . destroying tourism . . . weakening the Israeli economy and diverting the greater part of it to security requirements . . . [and] creating and maintaining an atmosphere of strain and anxiety that will force the Zionists to realize that it is impossible for them to live in Israel."[11]

The Oslo Process of the 1990s (as the Israeli-Palestinian talks were known, after the Norwegian capital where the DOP had been negotiated) enabled the PLO to achieve in one fell swoop what it had failed to attain through many years of violence and terrorism. Here was Israel, just over a decade after destroying the PLO's military infrastructure in Lebanon, asking the Palestinian organization, at one of the lowest ebbs in its history, to establish a real political and military presence – not in a neighboring Arab country but right on its doorstep. Israel was even prepared to arm thousands of (hopefully reformed) terrorists who would be incorporated into newly established police and security forces charged with asserting the PLO's authority throughout the territories. As the prominent PLO leader Faisal Husseini, widely considered a moderate, famously quipped, Israel was willingly introducing into its midst a "Trojan Horse" designed to promote the PLO's strategic goal of a "Palestine from the [Jordan] river to the [Mediterranean] sea" – that is, a Palestine in place of Israel.[12]

Arafat admitted to such a goal as early as September 8, 1993, five days before signing the DOP, when he told an Israeli journalist who came to interview him in his Tunis headquarters: "In the future, Israel and Palestine will be one united state in which Israelis and Palestinians will live together" – that is, Israel would no longer exist.[13] And even as he shook prime minister Yitzhak Rabin's hand on the White House lawn, Arafat was assuring the Palestinians in a pre-recorded Arabic-language message broadcast on Jordanian TV that the DOP was merely an implementation of the PLO's "phased strategy" of June 1974. This stipulated that the Palestinians should seize whatever territory Israel was prepared or compelled to cede and use it as a springboard for further territorial gains until they achieved the "complete liberation of Palestine."[14]

During the next seven years, until the September 2000 launch of his terrorist war, euphemistically titled the "al-Aqsa Intifada" after the mosque in Jerusalem, Arafat played an intricate game of Jekyll-and-Hyde politics. Whenever addressing Israeli or Western audiences, he would habitually extoll the "peace of the brave" he had signed with "my partner Yitzhak Rabin." At the same time, he depicted the peace accords to his Palestinian constituents as transient arrangements required by the needs of the moment. He made constant allusions to the "phased strategy" and repeatedly insisted on the "right of return," a standard Palestinian and Arab euphemism for Israel's destruction through demographic subversion.

The twentieth century witnessed scores of well-documented incidents of mass displacement no less sizeable than the 600,000-strong Palestinian Arab exodus: for instance, the 18 to 20 million Germans forced out of their homes in Poland and Czechoslovakia after World War II; the millions of Muslims and Hindus fleeing the newly established states of India and Pakistan during the partition of the Indian subcontinent in 1948; the millions of Armenians, Greeks, Turks, Finns, and Bulgarians, among others, driven from their lands. All these refugees were resettled elsewhere and incorporated into their new societies as full and equal citizens. By contrast, the Palestinian refugees were kept in squalid, harshly supervised camps across the Arab world as a means of tarnishing the image of Israel in the West and laying the groundwork for its ultimate subversion. "The Palestinians are useful to the Arab states as they are," President Nasser, widely considered the champion of the Palestinian cause, candidly responded to an inquiring Western reporter at a time when Egypt controlled the fate of Gaza. "We will always see that they do not become too powerful. Can you imagine yet another nation on the shores of the eastern Mediterranean!"[15]

In 1949, Israel offered to take back 100,000 Palestinian refugees, and even to annex the Gaza Strip, with its 250,000-strong Arab population. Entrenched in their "all or nothing" approach, the Arabs dismissed these proposals out of hand, though UN Resolution 194 of December 1948 envisaged only partial refugee repatriation, and though such a move would have saddled Israel with a large Arab minority. Of the 750,000 Arab residents of the territory that came to be Israel, only 160,000 were still resident at the end of the 1948 war, or 13.6 percent of the total population. But these numbers did not stay low for long. Thanks to a remarkable fertility rate of 4.2 percent a year, and despite successive waves of Jewish immigration into Israel, the proportion of Arabs grew steadily over the decades. By the end of 2007, Israel's Arab minority had leapt ninefold in number to 1.45 million, or 20 percent of the state's total population; by 2020, according to official Israeli estimates, nearly one in four Israelis will be an Arab.[16] Were millions of refugees to pour into Israel as part of a "right of return," the Jewish state would instantaneously be transformed into one more Arab state.

To further discredit the idea of peace with the Jewish state, Arafat's Palestinian Authority (PA) launched a sustained campaign of racial hatred and political incitement. Israelis, and Jews more generally, were portrayed as the source of all evil, a synonym for iniquity, corruption, and decadence, and responsible for every problem, real or imaginary, in the West Bank and Gaza. Palestinians were not only indoctrinated in the illegitimacy of the state of Israel and the lack of any Jewish connection to the land, but were also told of the most outlandish Israeli plots to corrupt and ruin them, wholly congruent with the medieval myth of Jews as secret destroyers and well-poisoners.

Arafat himself led the way in this campaign, charging Israel with killing Palestinian children to get their internal organs, masterminding the suicide bombings of its own civilians, and flooding the territories with weapons in order to precipitate a Palestinian civil war. The PA's minister of health accused Israeli doctors of using "Palestinian patients for experimental medicines," while the Palestinian representative to the UN's Human Rights Commission in Geneva charged Israel with injecting Palestinian children with the AIDS virus. The director of the PA's committee for consumer protection accused Israel of distributing chocolate infected with "mad cow disease" in the Palestinian territories. The minister of ecology indicted Israel for "dumping liquid waste . . . in Palestinian areas in the West Bank and Gaza." Yasir Arafat's wife, Suha, famously amplified one such charge when, in the presence of Hillary Clinton, she told an audience in Gaza in November 1999 that "our people have been subjected to the daily and extensive use of poisonous gas by the Israeli forces, which has led to an increase in cancer cases among women and children."[17]

Nor did Yasir Arafat confine himself to simply disparaging the Oslo accords and his peace partner. Embracing violence as the defining characteristic of his rule, from the moment of his arrival in Gaza in July 1994 after his years of exile in Tunisia, he set out to build an extensive terrorist infrastructure in flagrant violation of the accords, and in total disregard of the overriding reason he had been brought to the territories: namely, to lay the groundwork for Palestinian statehood. Arafat refused to disarm the Islamist terror groups Hamas and Islamic Jihad as required by the treaties, and tacitly approved their murdering hundreds of Israelis. He created a far larger Palestinian army (the so-called "police force") than was permitted by the accords. He reconstructed the PLO's old terrorist apparatus, mainly under the auspices of the Tanzim, which is the military arm of Fatah (the PLO's largest constituent organization and Arafat's own alma mater). He frantically acquired prohibited weapons with large sums of money donated to the PA by the international community for the benefit of the civilian Palestinian population and, eventually, resorted to outright mass violence. He did so for the first time in September 1996 to discredit the newly elected Israeli prime minister, Benjamin Netanyahu, and then again in September 2000 with the launch of his terror war shortly after Netanyahu's successor, Ehud Barak, had offered the creation of an independent state in 92 percent of the West Bank and the entire Gaza Strip, with East Jerusalem as its capital.[18] "Since [the caliph] Omar and Saladin we haven't given up our original rights in Jerusalem and al-Aqsa, our Jerusalem, our Palestine," ran a typical commentary by the official Palestinian television station, placing the conflict in a broader historical context. "If time constitutes the [criterion of] existence, then Israel's temporary existence is only fifty-two years long while we, the Palestinian Arabs, have lived here for thousands of years, and we, the indigenous population, will eventually expel the invaders, however long it takes."[19]

Had Arafat chosen to accept the Israeli concessions, a Palestinian state could have been established within the very near future. But then, for all his rhetoric about Palestinian independence, Arafat had never been as interested in promoting this goal as in destroying the Jewish state. As far back as 1978, he told his close friend and collaborator the Romanian dictator Nicolae Ceausescu that the Palestinians lacked the tradition, unity, and discipline to become a formal state, and that a Palestinian state would be a failure from the first day.[20] Once given control of the Palestinian population in the West Bank and Gaza as part of the Oslo Process, he made this bleak prognosis a self-fulfilling prophecy, establishing an oppressive and corrupt regime in the worst tradition of Arab dictatorships and pitting Israelis and Palestinians in their bloodiest and most destructive confrontation since the 1948 war.

Indeed, with the exception of Hajj Amin Husseini, Arafat did more than any other person in modern Middle Eastern history to retard the development of Palestinian civil society and the attainment of Palestinian statehood. Had the Mufti chosen to lead his people to peace and reconciliation with their Jewish neighbors, as he promised the British officials who appointed him to his high rank in 1921, the Palestinians would have had their independent state over a substantial part of mandatory Palestine by 1948, if not a decade earlier, and would have been spared the traumatic experience of dispersion and exile. Had Arafat set the PLO from the start on the path to peace and reconciliation, instead of turning it into one of the most murderous terrorist organizations in modern times, a Palestinian state could have been established in the late 1960s or the early 1970s; in 1979 as a corollary to the Egyptian-Israeli peace treaty; by May 1999 as part of the Oslo Process; or at the very latest with the Camp David summit of July 2000.

Instead, the two leaders allowed their anti-Jewish hatred and obsession with violence to get the better of them, dragging their reluctant constituents into disastrous conflicts that culminated in their collective undoing. As was the case in 1948, most ordinary Palestinians in the West Bank and Gaza over the last few decades have not welcomed war, being better disposed to a two-state solution than the Palestinian Diaspora spearheaded by the PLO. According to Palestinian public opinion polls in September 1993, 65 percent of residents in the territories supported the peace process, with 57 percent amenable to revising the Palestinian National Covenant, which called for Israel's destruction, as promised by Arafat to Rabin in the same month;

among Gaza and Jericho residents, who were to be the first beneficiaries of the process, support ran even higher, at 70 and 75 percent respectively.

By January 1996, when Israel transferred responsibility for the West Bank's Palestinian population to Arafat's PA, support for the peace process had risen to 80 percent, while endorsement of terrorist attacks had dropped dramatically to about 20 percent. Even after the tension of the first Netanyahu years (1996–99), support for the peace process remained as high as 60 percent.[21]

These findings are all the more significant given that support for peace, and opposition to terrorism, was strongest among those less-educated parts of Palestinian society – representing the vast majority of the population – whereas the greatest sympathy for violence was exhibited by the best-educated strata. For example, some 82 percent of the less educated favored the Interim Agreement of September 1995 (providing for Israel's withdrawal from Arab-populated areas in the West Bank) and 80 percent opposed terror attacks against Israeli civilians, compared to 55 and 65 percent respectively among university graduates. Even on the thorniest issue of the Palestinian-Israeli dispute, and the one central to the PLO's persistent effort to destroy Israel through demographic subversion, namely, the "right of return," residents of the territories had been far less dogmatic than their PLO and PA leaders. In a survey of March 1999, two months before the official deadline for the completion of the final-status negotiations, less than 15 percent of respondents viewed the refugee question as the most important problem facing the Palestinian people.

Within less than a year of the establishment of the PA in Gaza, more than half of the Strip's residents claimed to have been happier under Israeli rule than under the Arafat-controlled administration. In December 1996, three months after Arafat used the opening of a new entrance to an archeological tunnel in Jerusalem to instigate a violent confrontation in which fifteen Israelis and fifty-eight Palestinians lost their lives, 78 percent of Palestinians in the West Bank and Gaza rated Israeli democracy as very good or good, compared to 68 for the United States, 62 for France, and 43 for the PA. Only 6.9 percent of Palestinians had a negative opinion of Israeli democracy. "I'll never forget that day during the [1982] Lebanon War," marveled a Ramallah resident, "when an Arab Knesset member got up and called [prime minister Menachem] Begin a murderer. Begin didn't do a thing. If you did that to Arafat, I don't think you'd make it home that night."[22]

What makes this state of affairs all the more galling is that, far from being unfortunate aberrations, Hajj Amin and Arafat were quintessential representatives of the cynical and self-seeking leaders produced by the Arab political system. Just as the Palestinian Arab leadership during the mandate had no qualms about inciting its constituents against Zionism and Jews while lining its own pockets from the fruits of Jewish development and land purchases, so PLO officials used the billions of dollars donated by the Arab oil states and, during the Oslo era, by the international community to finance their luxurious lifestyle while ordinary Palestinians scrambled for a livelihood. Nor were the heads of the Arab states any better. Just as the Mufti's position as leader of the Palestinian Arabs had allowed him to weather the pervasive contempt in which he was held by his Arab peers, so notwithstanding the widespread loathing of Arafat in the Arab world (he had been persona non grata in Syria since the early 1980s and in the Gulf states after the 1990–91 Kuwait crisis, while a few years later Mubarak addressed him as a "dog" at a public event that was covered worldwide), none of the Arab leaders dared criticize the "al-Aqsa Intifada" in public lest they seemed disrespectful of the Palestinian cause.

Nor was Arafat alone in his political philosophy. The rejection of the Jewish national revival and the need for its violent destruction have become constants within the Palestinian political elite since their enunciation by the Mufti in the early 1920s. The PLO's hallowed founding document, the Palestinian Covenant, adopted in 1964 and revised four years later to reflect the organization's growing militancy, has little to say about the Palestinians themselves and devotes about two-thirds of its thirty-three articles to the need to destroy Israel, designating "armed struggle" as "the only way to liberate Palestine." Despite signing no fewer than five peace agreements with Israel during the 1990s within the framework of the Oslo Process, the PLO has failed to abolish its Covenant as promised and has in fact never shed its total rejection of the Jewish state.[23]

An offshoot of the Egyptian-born Muslim Brothers, Hamas sees the struggle for Palestine as neither an ordinary political dispute between two contending nations (Israelis and Palestinians), nor as a struggle for national self-determination by an indigenous population against a foreign occupier, but as a battle in a worldwide holy war to prevent the fall of a part of the House of Islam to infidels. In the words of the senior Hamas leader Mahmoud Zahar: "Islamic and traditional views reject the notion of establishing an independent Palestinian state. . . . In the past, there was no independent Palestinian state. . . . [Hence,] our main goal is to establish a great Islamic state, be it pan-Arabic or pan-Islamic."[24]

Hamas's Covenant not only promises that "Israel will exist until Islam will obliterate it," but presents the organization as the "spearhead and vanguard of the circle of struggle against World Zionism [and] the fight against the warmongering Jews." The document even incites anti-Semitic murder, arguing that "the Day of Judgment will not come about until Muslims fight Jews and kill them. Then, the Jews will hide behind rocks and trees, and the rocks and trees will cry out: 'O Muslim, there is a Jew hiding behind me, come and kill him.' "

The extreme belief that a perpetual state of war exists between it and anyone, either Muslim or non-Muslim, who refuses to follow in the path of Allah does not permit Hamas to respect, or compromise with, cultural, religious, and political beliefs that differ from its own. Its commitment to the use of violence as a religious duty means that it will never accept a political arrangement that does not fully correspond to its own radical precepts. In the words of the covenant: "The day that enemies usurp part of Muslim land, Jihad becomes the individual duty of every Muslim. . . . Since this is the case, liberation of Palestine is then an individual duty for every Muslim wherever he may be. . . . There is no solution for the Palestinian question except through Jihad. . . . The Islamic nature of Palestine is part of our religion and whoever takes his religion lightly is a loser."[25]

In these circumstances, it is hardly surprising that when, in January 2006, Hamas replaced the PLO at the helm of the PA, having won a landslide victory in the Palestinian parliamentary elections, Western chancelleries quickly embraced the fallen organization as the epitome of moderation, conveniently overlooking the fact that there was no fundamental difference between the ultimate goals of Hamas and the PLO vis-à-vis Israel: neither accepts the Jewish state's right to exist and both are committed to its eventual destruction.

Such views apply not only to "hardline" elements within the PLO, such as its perpetual "foreign minister," Farouq Qadoumi, but are also a commonplace among supposed moderates. Yasir Abd Rabbo, a cosignatory to the 2003 "Geneva Accords" with a group of leftist Israeli politicians and intellectuals, persistently denied the Jewish attachment to the Temple Mount, and by extension to the Land of Israel, and vowed to regain "all of Palestine." So did Nabil Shaath, another supposed moderate and dedicated advocate of the Oslo Process, and Ahmad Qureia (Abu Ala), chief negotiator of the original Oslo accord. "We did not sign a peace treaty with Israel, but interim agreements that had been imposed on us," he said in June 1996. "When we accepted the Oslo agreement, we obtained territory but not all the Palestinian territory. . . . We did not and will not relinquish one inch of this territory or the right of any Palestinian to live on it with dignity."[26]

Even Mahmoud Abbas (Abu Mazen), Arafat's second-in-command and successor, perhaps the foremost symbol of supposed Palestinian moderation, has not only reverted to standard talk of Israel's illegitimacy but devoted years of his life to giving ideological firepower to the anti-Israel and anti-Jewish indictment. Since the Holocaust is widely considered to be the most powerful modern-day justification for the existence of a Jewish state, and one that overshadows the carefully nurtured image of Palestinian victimhood, Abbas endeavored to prove in a doctoral dissertation, written at a Soviet university and subsequently published in book form, the existence of a close ideological and political association between Zionism and Nazism. Among other things, he argued that fewer than a million Jews had been killed in the Holocaust, and that the Zionist movement played a role in their slaughter.[27]

In the wake of the failed Camp David summit of July 2000 and the launch of Arafat's war of terror two months later, Abbas went to great lengths to explain why the "right of return" was a non-negotiable prerequisite for any Palestinian-Israeli settlement. "Peace will not be achieved without the refugees getting back their sacred rights, which cannot be touched," he argued. "It is the individual right of every refugee, and no one can reach an agreement in this matter without his consent." To dispel any doubt about the nature of this "right," he emphasized that "the right of return means a return to Israel, not to a Palestinian state."[28]

For all their drastically different personalities and political styles, Arafat and Abbas are warp and woof of the same fabric: dogmatic PLO veterans who have never eschewed their commitment to Israel's destruction and who have viewed the "peace process" as the continuation by other means of their lifelong war. As late as July 2002, Abbas described Oslo as "the biggest mistake Israel ever made," enabling the PLO to obtain worldwide acceptance and respectability while hanging fast to its own aims. Shortly after Arafat's death in November 2004, in his address to a special session of the Palestinian Legislative Council in Ramallah, he swore to "follow in the path of the late leader Yasir Arafat and . . . work toward fulfilling his dream. . . . We promise you that our hearts will not rest until the right of return for our people is achieved and the tragedy of the refugees is ended."

Abbas made good his pledge. In a televised speech on May 15, 2005, on the occasion of Israel's Independence Day, he described the proclamation of the State of Israel as an unprecedented historic injustice and vowed his unwavering refusal to ever "accept this injustice."[29] Two-and-a-half years later, at the US-sponsored peace conference in Annapolis, the Palestinian president rejected prime minister Ehud Olmert's proposal of a Palestinian Arab state in 97 percent of the West Bank and the entire Gaza Strip and dismissed out of hand the request to recognize Israel as a Jewish state alongside the would-be Palestinian state (as stipulated by the partition resolution of November 1947), insisting instead on the full implementation of the "right of return" – the Palestinian and Arab euphemism for Israel's destruction. He was quickly followed by his supposedly moderate colleagues – from Ahmad Qureia to chief peace negotiator Saeb Erekat to prime minister Salam Fayad – while the PA's television station broadcast an information clip produced by the PA's Central Bureau of Statistics showing a map in which Israel was painted in the colors of the Palestinian flag, symbolizing its transformation into a Palestinian Arab state.[30]

Abbas was equally recalcitrant when a demand for Israel's recognition was raised in April 2009 by its newly elected prime minister, Benjamin Netanyahu. "A Jewish state, what does that suppose to mean? [sic]" he asked in a speech in the West Bank's political capital of Ramallah. "You can call yourselves as you like, but I don't accept it and I say so publicly."[31]

Even when, on June 14, 2009, in an abrupt departure from his Likud Party's foremost ideological precept, Netanyahu agreed to the establishment of a Palestinian Arab state provided the Palestinian leadership responded in kind and recognized Israel's Jewish nature, the Arab world exploded in rage. President Mubarak, whose country had been at peace with the Jewish state for thirty years, deplored the request as "scuppering the possibilities for peace" and proclaimed that "no one will support this appeal in Egypt or elsewhere." Saeb Erekat warned that Netanyahu "will have to wait 1,000 years before he finds one Palestinian who will go along with him," while Fatah's sixth general congress, convened in Bethlehem in August 2009, reaffirmed its long-standing commitment to the "armed struggle" as "a strategy, not tactic . . . in the battle for liberation and for the elimination of the Zionist presence. This struggle will not stop until the Zionist entity is eliminated and Palestine is liberated."[32]

And so it goes on. More than six decades after the Mufti and his followers condemned their people to statelessness by rejecting the UN partition resolution and waging a war of annihilation against their Jewish neighbors, their reckless decisions are still being re-enacted by the latest generation of Palestinian leaders. For to refuse to recognize Israel's right to exist, long after the acceptance of this right by the international community, and to insist on the full implementation of the "right of return" at a time when Israel has long agreed to the creation of a Palestinian state roughly along the pre-1967 lines, indicates that in the Palestinian perception peace is not a matter of adjusting borders and territory but rather a euphemism for the destruction of the Jewish state. Only when Palestinian and Arab leaders change these dispositions and eschew their genocidal hopes will the refugees and their descendants be able to leave the squalid camps where they have been kept by their fellow Arabs for decades, and will the Palestinians be able to look forward to putting their self-inflicted "catastrophe" behind them.

Dramatis Personae

Arab League

Abdel Rahman Azzam, Secretary-General
Cecil Hourani, Head, Washington Office

Arab Liberation Army

Abdel Wahab Sheik Ali, Jaffa Commander
Adl Najim al-Din, Jaffa Commander
Sari Fnaish, Safad Commander
General Taha Hashemi, Inspector General
Hassan Bey, Safad Commander
Mishel Isa, Jaffa Commander
Fawzi Qawuqji, Palestine Field Commander
General Ismail Safwat, Commander-in-Chief
Adib Shishakli, Commander, Safad-Tiberias Sub-Districts

Britain

General Sir Edmund Allenby, Commander, Egyptian Expeditionary Force
Clement Attlee, Prime Minister
Arthur James Balfour, Foreign Secretary
Harold Beeley, Foreign Office Official
Ernest Bevin, Foreign Secretary
Philip Broadmead, Ambassador to Damascus
Reader Bullard, Ambassador to Saudi Arabia
Bernard Burrows, Head, Foreign Office Eastern Department
Neville Chamberlain, Prime Minister
Winston Churchill, Colonial Secretary; Prime Minister
Archibald Clark-Kerr, Ambassador to Baghdad

Brigadier Gilbert Clayton, Chief Political Secretary, Palestine
General Sir Alan Cunningham, High Commissioner for Palestine
Arthur Creech Jones, Secretary of State for Colonies
Henry Gurney, Chief Secretary, Palestine Mandate Government
Lord Halifax, Foreign Secretary; Ambassador to Washington
Alec Kirkbride, Ambassador to Amman
Malcolm MacDonald, Colonial Secretary
General Gordon MacMillan, Commander, British Forces in Palestine
Henry McMahon, High Commissioner for Egypt
Herbert Morrison, Lord President of the Council
Lord Moyne, Colonial Secretary
William Ormsby-Gore, Colonial Secretary
Lord Peel, Head, Palestine Royal Commission
Herbert Samuel, High Commissioner for Palestine
Freya Stark, Author; Orientalist
General Hugh Stockwell, Commander, Sixth Airborne Division, Palestine
Ronald Storrs, Governor of Jerusalem
John Troutbeck, Head, British Middle East Office, Cairo
John Woodhead, Head of the Woodhead Commission

Egypt

Hassan Banna, Founder, Muslim Brothers Society
Faruq I, King
Fuad I, Sultan, Later King
Muhammad Hussein Heikal, Minister of Education; Senate Speaker
Taha Hussein, Author
Ahmad Khashaba, Foreign Minister
Husni Mubarak, President
Mustafa Nahhas, Prime Minister
Gamal Abdel Nasser, President
Mahmud Fahmi Nuqrashi, Prime Minister
Anwar Sadat, President
Ismail Sidqi, Prime Minister
Saad Zaghlul, Prime Minister; Doyen of Modern Egyptian Nationalism
Ahmad Ziwar, Prime Minister

Germany

Joseph Goebbels, Minister of Propaganda
Fritz Grobba, Ambassador to Iraq and Saudi Arabia

Heinrich Himmler, SS Reichsführer; Interior Minister
Adolf Hitler, Führer

Hijaz

Hussein ibn Ali, Sharif of Mecca; Perpetrator of "Great Arab Revolt"; King of Hijaz

Iraq

Abdel Illah, Regent
Faisal I, Founding Monarch
Saleh Jabr, Prime Minister
Fadel Jamali, Foreign Minister
Rashid Ali Kailani, Prime Minister
Nuri Said, Prime Minister; Foreign Minister
Hikmat Suleiman, Prime Minister

Israel (see also Zionist Movement)

David Ben-Gurion, Prime Minister; Minister of Defense
Eliezer Kaplan, Finance Minister
Moshe Shertok (Sharett), Foreign Minister
Bechor Shalom Shitrit, Minister of Minority Affairs
Aharon Tzisling, Agriculture Minister
Yigael Yadin, Head of Operations, IDF

Italy

Galeazzo Ciano, Foreign Minister
Benito Mussolini, Duce

Lebanon

Camille Chamoun, Interior Minister
Émile Eddé, President
Riad Sulh, Prime Minister

Palestinian Arabs

Mahmoud Abbas (Abu Mazen), President, Palestinian Authority
Awni Abdel Hadi, Head, Istiqlal Party; Member of the AHC
Ibrahim Abu Lughod, Jaffa Resident

Sheik Hassan Abu Saud, AHC Member
Musa Alami, Politician
Yasir Arafat, Chairman, PLO; President, Palestinian Authority
Arif Arif, Politician; Historian
Muhammad Izzat Darwaza, Pan-Arab Activist; AHC Member
Emile Ghouri, Politician; AHC Member
Yaqub Ghusseun, Head, Youth Congress; AHC Member
George Hakim, Bishop, Greek Catholic Church
Muhammad Nimr Hawari, Founding Commander, Najada Militia
Yusuf Heikal, Jaffa Mayor
Ahmad Hilmi, Banker and Politician; AHC Member
Muhammad Hamad Hunaiti, Haifa Military Commander
Abdel Qader Husseini, Military Commander
Hajj Amin Husseini, Jerusalem Mufti; President, Supreme Muslim Council;
  AHC President
Jamal Husseini, AHC Vice-President
Kamil Husseini, Jerusalem Mufti
Musa Kazim Husseini, Jerusalem Mayor; Head, Arab Executive Committee
Rashid Hajj Ibrahim, Chairman, Haifa National Committee
Ghaleb Khalidi, Chairman, Jerusalem National Committee
Hussein Khalidi, Head, Reform Party; Jerusalem Mayor; AHC Secretary
Yusuf Zia Khalidi, Politician
Muhammad Nimr Khatib, Islamist Politician
Muin Madi, Politician; AHC Member
Fakhri Nashashibi, Politician
Ragheb Nashashibi, Politician; AHC Member
Anwar Nusseibeh, Secretary, Jerusalem National Committee
Khalil Sakakini, Educationalist
Hassan Salame, Military Commander
Sami Taha, Trade Unionist; Politician
Rafiq Tamimi, AHC Member; Chairman, Jaffa National Committee
Suleiman Tuqan, Mayor of Nablus

Saudi Arabia

Abdul Aziz Ibn Saud, Founding Monarch
Fuad Hamza, Deputy Foreign Minister
Khalid Hud, Royal Envoy
St. John Philby, Royal Advisor
Hafiz Wahba, Ambassador to London
Yusuf Yasin, Ibn Saud's Private Secretary

Syria

George Antonius, Pan-Arab Ideologue
Shakib Arslan, Pan-Arab Politician
Najib Azuri, Pan-Arab Ideologue
Fakhri Barudi, Minister of Propaganda
Faisal ibn Hussein, King
Abdel Rahman Kawakibi, Pan-Arab Ideologue
Jamil Mardam, Prime Minister; Foreign Minister
Shukri Quwatli, President

Transjordan

Abdullah ibn Hussein, Founding Monarch
Tawfiq Abul Huda, Prime Minister
Umar Dajani, Royal Envoy
John Bagot Glubb (Glubb Pahsa), Commander, Arab Legion
Samir Rifai, Prime Minister
Muhammad Unsi, Royal Envoy

United Nations

Warren Austin, US Representative
Folke Bernadotte, Mediator on Palestine
Ralph Bunche, Acting Mediator on Palestine
Alexander Cadogan, UK Representative
Henry Cattan, AHC Representative
Raphael Cilento, Director, Disaster Relief Operations in Palestine
Aubrey (Abba) Eban, Israeli Representative
Fares Khouri, Syrian Delegate
Trygve Lie, Secretary-General

United States

Lewis Douglas, Ambassador to London
Harold Hoskins, Special Envoy
Aubrey Lippincott, Vice-Consul, Haifa
Robert Macatee, Consul-General, Jerusalem
James McDonald, Special Representative (Later Ambassador) to Israel
Harry Truman, President

Zionist Movement (see also Israel)

Yigal Allon, Military Commander

Haim Arlosoroff, Head, Political Department

Daniel Auster, Jerusalem Deputy-Mayor/Mayor

Menachem Begin, Head, Irgun Zvai Leumi (IZL)

David Ben-Gurion, Labor Politician; Chairman, Jewish Agency Executive (JAE)

Moshe Carmel (Zelitzki), Military Commander

Ezra Danin, Arab Affairs Expert

Aubrey (Abba) Eban, Liaison Officer to UNSCOP

Eliahu Epstein (Elath), Jewish Agency's Political Department; US Representative

Gad Frumkin, Supreme Court Justice, Palestine

Israel Galili, Hagana Commander-in-Chief

Asher Zvi Ginsberg (aka Ahad Ha'am), Author and Thinker

Theodor Herzl, Founding Father of Political Zionism

Isaac Herzog, Chief Rabbi, Palestine

David Horowitz, Liaison Officer to UNSCOP

Ze'ev (Vladimir) Jabotinsky, Founder of the "Revisionist Movement" – Forebear of Today's Likud Party

Bernard (Dov) Joseph, Politician; Jerusalem Military Governor

Frederick Kisch, Head, Political Department

Shabtai Levy, Mayor of Haifa

Golda Meyerson (Meir), Acting Chair, Jewish Agency's Political Department

Max Nordau, Politician

Josh Palmon, Arab Affairs Expert

Yitzhak Rabin, Military Commander

Israel Rokah, Mayor, Tel Aviv

Arthur Rupin, Head, Palestine Office

Yaacov Salomon, Hagana Chief Liaison Officer, Haifa

Elias Sasson, Head of Arab Section, Jewish Agency's Political Department

David Shaltiel, Jerusalem's Military Commander

Moshe Shertok (Sharett), Head, Jewish Agency's Political Department

Chaim Weizmann, President, Zionist Movement

Yigael Yadin, Head of Operations, Hagana

Yassky Haim, Director, Hadassah Hospital, Jerusalem

How Many Palestinian Arab Refugees Were There?

The extraordinary coverage of the 1948 war notwithstanding, the birth of the Palestinian refugee problem during the five-and-a-half months of fighting, from the partition resolution to the proclamation of the state of Israel, passed virtually unnoticed by the international community. Nor for that matter did the Arab states, burdened as they were with a relentless flow of refugees, or even the Palestinian leadership itself, have a clear idea of the dispersal's full magnitude, as demonstrated by Emile Ghouri's mid-June 1948 estimate of the number of refugees at 200,000 – less than two-thirds of the actual figure. A few weeks later, after thousands more Arabs had become refugees, a Baghdad radio commentator was still speaking of 300,000 evacuees "who are forced to flee from the Jews as the French were forced to flee from the Nazis." Taking their cue from these claims, W. de St. Aubin, delegate of the League of Red Cross Societies to the Middle East, estimated the number of Arab refugees (in late July) at about 300,000, while Sir Raphael Cilento, director of the UN Disaster Relief Project (DRP) in Palestine, set the number at 300,000–350,000 (in early August).[1]

Paradoxically it was the Israelis who initially came up with the highest, and most accurate, estimates. In early June 1948, Ben-Gurion was told by Yossef Weitz of the Jewish National Fund (JNF) that:

> some 123,000 Arabs left 155 villages in the Jewish state's territory; another 22,000 left 35 villages outside the Jewish state: a total of 145,000 evacuees and 190 villages. Seventy-seven thousand Arabs left five cities in the Jewish state's territory (Haifa, Beisan, Tiberias, Safad, Samakh). Another 73,000 left two cities [designed to remain] outside the state (Jaffa and Acre). Forty thousand Arabs left Jerusalem: a total of 190,000 from eight cities. All in all, 335,000 Arabs fled (including 200,000 from the UN ascribed Jewish territory).[2]

A comprehensive report by the Hagana's intelligence service, comprising a detailed village-by-village breakdown of the exodus, set the number of

Palestinian Arab evacuees in the six-month period between December 1, 1947 and June 1, 1948 at 391,000: 239,000 from the UN-ascribed Jewish state, 122,000 from the territory of the prospective Arab state, and 30,000 from Jerusalem. Another exhaustive Israeli study set the number of refugees in late October 1948 at 460,000, almost evenly divided between the rural and urban sectors.[3]

This estimate was substantially higher than the 360,000 figure in Bernadotte's report, submitted to the UN General Assembly on September 16, or Cilento's revised estimate of 400,300 a couple of weeks later, and was virtually identical to that in the supplementary report submitted on October 18 by Bernadotte's successor, Ralph Bunche, which set the number of refugees at 472,000 and anticipated the figure to reach a maximum of slightly over 500,000 in the near future.[4]

By now, however, the Arabs had dramatically upped the ante. In a memorandum dispatched to the heads of the Arab states and Arab League secretary-general Abdel Rahman Azzam in mid-August, the Palestine Office in Amman, an organization operating under the auspices of the Transjordan government, estimated the total number of refugees at 700,000, of whom 500,000 were in Palestine and the rest in the neighboring Arab states. The memo struck a chord, for in October the League set the number of refugees at 631,967, and by the end of the month official Arab estimates ranged between 740,000 and 780,000. When the newly established United Nations Relief for Palestine Refugees (UNRPR) began operating in December 1948, it found 962,643 refugees on its relief rolls.[5]

In conversations with British diplomats in early October, Cilento described the figures supplied by the Arab authorities as unreliable, claiming that they increased from week to week in all areas irrespective of known movements of refugees from place to place. A large number of refugees had, for example, moved from the Nablus area to the Hauran in Syria while others from Jericho, Jerusalem, and Transjordan had moved to Gaza. Similarly, at least 2,000 refugees had recently moved from the Egyptian port town of Kantara, on the Suez Canal, to Gaza. Yet the number of refugees in the areas from which these movements had taken place was in all cases reported as increasing instead of decreasing. Similar exaggerations were made in Syria where, according to Bunche's October report, the authorities claimed the existence of 30,000 refugees whereas the actual figure was no more than half that size.

Cilento expected as many as 400,000 Arabs to apply for UN relief in the coming winter, on top of the 360,000–390,000 registered refugees, though these were not genuine refugees in the sense that they were living in their own homes and had not been "displaced." This, however, did not prevent him, when the prediction was vindicated before the end of the year, from raising the number of refugees to 750,000. St. Aubin, who in September 1948 became the DRP's director of field operations, went a step further by placing the figure in July 1949 at "approximately one million."

Admitting to having "some difficulty in separating out the real refugees from the rest, and in explaining the reasons for doing so to the Arab authorities," Cilento attributed this chaotic situation to a number of reasons:

Refugees were registered on arrival and fed, but their names were not struck off the list if they moved or died;

refugees moving from one area to another would check in and be fed at several points en route and at each would be added to the list of refugees in the area. In this way numbers increased on paper in areas vacated as well as at final destination;

local destitute persons were included in numbers, although they were not properly refugees;

fraud and misrepresentation by officials and others in order to utilize supplies, etc.;

there were people who left their homes owing to disturbed conditions but returned to them shortly afterward, yet were briefly registered as refugees and the records remained.[6]

Sir John Troutbeck, head of the British Middle East office in Cairo, got a first-hand impression of this pervasive inflation of refugee numbers during a fact-finding mission to Gaza in June 1949. "The Quakers have nearly 250,000 refugees on their books," he reported to London.

They admit however that the figures are unreliable, as it is impossible to stop all fraud in the making of returns. Deaths for example are never registered nor are the names struck off the books of those who leave the district clandestinely. Some names too are probably registered more than once for the extra rations. But the Quakers assured me that they have made serious attempts to carry out a census and believe they have more information in that respect than the Red Cross organizations which are working in other areas. Their figures include Bedouin whom they feed and care for just like other refugees. They seemed a little doubtful whether this was a right decision, but once it had been taken it could not be reversed, and in any case the Bedouin, though less destitute than most of the refugees proper, are thought to have lost a great part of their possessions. They and the other refugees live in separate camps and in a state of mutual antipathy.[7]

This was hardly a novel phenomenon. Population figures of Palestinian Arab society, especially of rural Muslim communities, were notoriously unreliable, based as they were on information provided by rural and urban headmen (*mukhtars*) that was deliberately inflated in order to obtain greater government support, especially food rations.[8] As explained in the preface to the mandatory government's *Village Statistics 1945*, for all the "very detailed work" invested in this comprehensive compendium of rural Palestine, its estimates "cannot . . . be considered as other than rough estimates which in some instances may ultimately be found to differ even considerably, from the actual figures."[9]

The supplementary volume to the government's *Survey of Palestine* (1946), compiled in June 1947 for the information of UNSCOP, elaborated on the problematic nature of official demographic statistics:

> For the years 1943–46 an investigation recently carried out by the Department of Statistics revealed that many cases of death, especially in rural areas, have not been reported. These omissions (which are mainly due to the attempt to obtain food rations of deceased persons) seriously impair the reliability of the death rates (particularly infant mortality rates) and that of the rate of natural increase. On the other hand, they are not of such magnitude as to effect seriously the estimates of total population.[10]

This may well have been the case. But then, accepting the supplement's estimate of 1.3 million Palestinian Arabs at the end of 1946 (the actual figure was most probably 10 percent lower), the number of refugees could by no stretch of the imagination approximate the million mark for the simple reason that some 550,000–600,00 Arabs who lived in the mandatory districts of Samaria, Jerusalem, and Gaza (which subsequently became the West Bank and the Gaza Strip after their respective occupation by Transjordan and Egypt) remained in situ, while another 160,000 Arabs remained in, or returned to, Israel. This, in turn, puts the number of refugees at 540,000–590,000. Likewise, according to an extrapolation of the *Village Statistics 1945*, the non-Jewish population of the area that was to become Israeli territory at the end of the war amounted, in April 1948, to some 696,000–726,800. Deducting Israel's 160,000-strong postwar Arab population from this figure would leave 536,000–566,800 refugees beyond Israel's frontiers.[11]

As can be seen below, my own calculation, based on British, Jewish, and to a lesser extent Arab, population figures of all identified rural and urban localities abandoned during the war, amounts to 583,000–609,000 refugees.

The Palestinian Arab Exodus, 1947–48

CITIES[12]

Acre – 13,510 (3,885 remained).[13]
Beersheba – 6,490.
Beisan – 5,540.
Haifa – 70,910 (5,000 remained).[14]
Jaffa – 70,730 (4,000–5,000 remained).[15]
Jerusalem – 65,010 (some 30,000 fled).[16]
Lydda & Ramle – 35,078 (2,500 remained).[17]
Majdal – 10,900.
Safad – 10,210.
Tiberias – 5,770.
Total: 247,403 – 248,403.

VILLAGES[18]

Galilee District[19]

Acre Sub-District
Amqa – 1,240, July 9, 1948.[20]
Arab Samniya – 200, late Oct. 1948.
Bassa – 2,950–3,140 (includes Ma'sub), May 14, 1948.[21]
Birwa – 1,460, June 11, 1948.[22]
Damun – 1,310, July 14–18, 1948.[23]
Deir Qasi – 1,190 (including Mansura), Oct. 30, 1948.[24]
Ghabisiya – 690–740, May 22, 1948.[25]
Iqrit – 490–520, Apr. 26–Oct. 30, 1948.[26]
Kabri – 1,530–1,640, May 5–22, 1948.[27]
Kafr Inan – 360, Oct. 30, 1948.[28]
Khirbat Iribbin – 360 (including Jurdeih & Khirbat Idmith), probably in late Oct. 1948.
Kuweikat – 1,050, July 9, 1948.[29]
Manshiya – 810–1,140, May 17, 1948.[30]
Mansura – *see* Deir Qasi.
Mi'ar – 770, Oct. 30, 1948.[31]
Nabi Rubin – *see* Tarbikha.
Nahr – 610, May 22, 1948.[32]
Ruweis – 330, July 18, 1948.[33]
Suhmata – 1,130, Oct. 29–30, 1948.[34]
Sumeiriya – 760–820, May 14, 1948.[35]
Suruh – *see* Tarbikha.
Tell – May 14, 1948.[36]
Tarbikha – 1,000 (including Nabi Rubin & Suruh), Oct. 30, 1948.[37]
Umm Faraj – 800, May 22, 1948.[38]
Zib – 1,910–2,050 (including Manawat), May 14, 1948.[39]

Beisan Sub-District
Arida – 150, May 20, 1948.
Ashrafiya – 230, May 12, 1948.[40]

Bashatiwa – 1,000–1,560, May 16, 1948.
Bawati – 520–700, Mar. 30, 1948.
Bira – 220–500, May 16, 1948.[41]
Danna – 160–400, May 16–28, 1948.
Farawna – 330–350, May 11, 1948.
Ghazawiya – 1,020, late May 1948.
Hamidiya – 220–300, Apr. 6–May 12, 1948.[42]
Hamra, 730, May 1, 1948.
Jabbul – 250–370, May 1–18, 1948.[43]
Kafra – 400–700, May 16, 1948.[44]
Kaukab Hawa – 30–600, May 14, 1948.[45]
Khuneizir – 260–400, May 20, 1948.
Masil Jizl – 100, mid-May 1948.
Murassas – 460–600, May 16, 1948.
Qumiya – 320–440, Mar. 30, 1948.[46]
Safa – 650, May 20, 1948.
Sakhina – 200–530, May 16, 1948.
Samiriya – 250–500, May 12–27, 1948.
Sirin – 600–820, Apr. 24, 1948.[47]
Tell Shauk – 120, probably in mid-May 1948.
Tira – 120–150, Apr. 15, 1948.[48]
Zab'a – 170, May 12, 1948.[49]
Yubla – 150–250, May 16, 1948.[50]
Zir'in – 1,300, May 1, 1948.[51]

Nazareth Sub-District
Indur – 620, May 17–24, 1948.[52]
Ma'lul – 690, July 15–18, 1948.[53]
Mujeidil – 1,600–1,900, July 15–18, 1948.[54]
Saffuriyya – 4,320–4,330, July 15–16, 1948.[55]

Safad Sub-District
Abil Qamh – 230–330, May 10, 1948.[56]
Abisiya – 830–1,220, May 25, 1948.[57]
Akbara – 390–410, May 10, 1948.
Alma – 950, Oct. 30, 1948.[58]
Ammuqa Tahta & Fawqa – 140, May 24, 1948.
Arab Shamalina – *see* Buteiha.
Arab Zubeid – Apr. 20, 1948.
Azaziyat – 390, Apr. 30–May 1, 1948.
Beisamun – 20, May 25, 1948.
Biriya – 240, May 2, 1948.
Buteiha – 650 (including Arab Shamalina), May 4, 1948.[59]
Buweiziya – 510–540, May 11, 1948.[60]
Dahariya – 350, May 10, 1948.
Dallata – 360, Oct. 30, 1948.[61]
Darbashiya – 310, early May 1948.
Dawwara – 700, May 25, 1948.

Deishum – 590, May 9, 1948–Oct. 30, 1948.[62]

Dirdara – July 9–10, 1948.[63]

Ein Zeitun – 620–820, May 2, 1948.

Fara – 820, Oct, 30, 1948.[64]

Farradiya – 670, Oct. 30–Nov. 6, 1948.[65]

Fir'im – 740, May 2–26, 1948.[66]

Ghabbatiya – 60, probably in late Oct. 1948.

Ghuraba – 220, May 1–28, 1948.

Hamra – May 1, 1948.

Harrawi – May 25, 1948.

Hunin – 1,620, May 3–5, 1948.[67]

Husseiniya – 340 (including Tuleil), Apr. 21, 1948.

Jahula – 420, not known.

Jauna – 1,150, May 9, 1948.

Jubb Yusuf – 170, early May 1948.

Kafr Bir'im – 710, Oct. 30, 1948.[68]

Khalisa – 1840, May 11, 1948.

Khirbat Muntar – n.a., May 7, 1948.[69]

Khisas – 470–530, Mar. 26–May 24, 1948.[70]

Khiyam Walid – 210–280, Mar. 29–May 1, 1948.

Kirad Baqqara – 360, Apr. 22, 1948.

Kirad Ghanama – 350, Apr. 22, 1948.

Lazzaza – 230, May 21, 1948.

Madahil – 410, Apr. 7–30, 1948.[71]

Malikiya – 360, May 15–Oct. 30, 1948.[72]

Mallaha – 890, May 25, 1948.

Mansura – 360, May 25, 1948.

Mansurat Kheit – 200–900, Jan. 18, 1948.

Marus – 80, May 26, 1948.

Meirun – 290, May 29–Oct. 29, 1948.[73]

Mughr Kheit – 490, Jan. 18, 1948.

Muftakhira – 350, May 1–16, 1948.

Nabi Yusha – 70, May 16–17, 1948.

Naima – 1,240–1,310, May 14, 1948.

Qabba'a – 460, May 2, 1948.[74]

Qadas – 320–390, May 28, 1948.

Qaddita – 240, May 11, 1948.

Qeitiya – 940, May 2–19, 1948.

Qudeiriya – 390, May 4, 1948.

Ras Ahmar – 620, Oct. 30, 1948.[75]

Sabalan – 70, apparently in late Oct. 1948.

Safsaf – 910, Oct. 29, 1948.[76]

Saliha – 1,070, Oct. 30, 1948.[77]

Salihiya – 1,520, May 25, 1948.

Sammui – 310, May 12–Oct. 30, 1948.[78]

Sanbariya – 130, not known.

Sa'sa – 1,130, Oct. 29–30, 1948.[79]

Shauka Tahta – 200, Feb. 2–May 14, 1948.

Shuna – 170, not known.

Teitaba – 530, Oct. 30, 1948.[80]

Tuleil – *see* Husseiniya.

Ulmaniya – 260, Feb. 25–Apr. 20, 1948.

Weiziya – not known.

Yarda – not know, July 10, 1948.[81]

Zanghariya – 840, May 4, 1948.

Zawiya – 760, May 24, 1948.

Zuk Fauqani & Zuk Tahtani – 1,050, May 11–21, 1948.

Tiberias Sub-District

Dalhamiya – 410, probably late Apr.

Ghuweir Abu Shusha – 1,240, Apr. 21–28, 1948.

Hadatha – 520–550, Mar. 30–May 12, 1948.[82]

Hittin – 1,190, July 17, 1948.[83]

Kafr Sabt – 480, Apr. 22, 1948.

Khirbat Qadish – 410, Apr. 19–20, 1948.[84]

Khirbat Wa'ra Sauda – 1,870 (including Mawasi & Wuheib), not known.

Lubiya – 2,350, July 17, 1948.[85]

Ma'dhar – 480–510, Apr. 16–May 12, 1948.[86]

Majdal – 240–360, Apr. 22, 1948.

Manara – 490, Apr. 10, 1948.[87]

Mansura – 360, May 25, 1948

Nasr al-Din – 90, Apr. 12, 1948.[88]

Nimrin – 320, July 17–18, 1948.[89]

Nuqeib – 290–320 (including Samra), Apr. 23–24, 1948.[90]

Samakh – 3,460–3,660, Apr. 29, 1948.[91]

Samakiya – 380, May 4, 1948.

Samra – see Nuqeib.

Shajara – 720–770, Apr. 21–May 6, 1948.

Tabigha – 330, May 1, 1948.

Ubeidiya – 870–920, Mar. 5–Apr. 21, 1948.[92]

Ulam – 720, Mar. 30–May 12, 1948.[93]

Yaquq – 210, July 18, 1948.[94]

Haifa District

Haifa Sub-District

Abu Shusha – 720, Apr. 9–12 1948.[95]

Abu Zureik – 550, Apr. 12, 1948.[96]

Arab Fuqara – 310–40, Apr. 10, 1948.[97]

Arab Nufeiat – 820–910, Mar. 30–Apr. 10, 1948.

Atlit – 150, not known.

Balad Sheikh – 4,120–4,500, Jan. 7–Apr. 25, 1948.

Bureika – 290, Mar. 6–Apr. 26, 1948.[98]

Buteimat – 110, Apr. 12–May 13, 1948.[99]

Daliyat Ruha – 280–310, Apr. 12, 1948.[100]

Dumeira – 620, not known.

Ein Ghazal – 2,170–2,410, Apr. 25–July 26, 1948.[101]

Ein Haud – 650, July 17, 1948.[102]

Ghubaiyat – 1,130–1,260 (including Naghnagiya), Apr. 9–13, 1948.[103]
Hawsha – n.a., Apr. 4–19, 1948.[104]
Ijzim – 2,970, Apr. 25–July 26, 1948.
Jaba – 1,140, July 25, 1948.[105]
Jalama – n.a., June 1, 1948.[106]
Kabara – 120, apparently late Apr.-early May 1948.
Kafr Lam – 340–380, May 13–15 & July 16, 1948.[107]
Kafrin – 920, Apr. 12, 1948.[108]
Khirbat Damum – 340, late Apr. 1948.
Khirbat Kasayir – n.a., Apr. 27, 1948.
Khirbat Lid – 640, mid-April–mid-May, 1948.[109]
Khubbeiza – 290, apparently in mid-May 1948.
Mansi – 1,200, Apr. 12–15, 1948.[110]
Mazar – 210, May 17, 1948.[111]
Mazra'a – 460, Feb. 6, 1948.
Naghnagiya – see Ghubaiyat.
Qannir – 750, Apr. 5–25, 1948.[112]
Qisariya – 930–1,240, Jan. 12–Feb. 15, 1948.[113]
Rihaniya – 240–340, Apr. 12, 1948.[114]
Sabbarin – 1,700–1,880, May 14, 1948.
Sarafand – 290, early May 1948–July 17, 1948.[115]
Sarkas – Apr. 15–26, 1948.
Sindiyana – 1,250–1,390, May 2–14, 1948.
Tantura – 1,490–1,650, May 6–21, 1948.
Tira – 5,270, Apr. 22–July 16, 1948.[116]
Umm Shauf – 480, May 14, 1948.
Umm Zinat – 1,470, Apr. 26–May 15, 1948.[117]
Wadi Ara – 260, Feb. 27, 1948
Yajur – 610, Feb. 18–Apr. 25, 1948.

Samaria District

Jenin Sub-District
Ein Mansi – 90, not known.
Kufeir – 140, Apr. 27, 1948.
Lajjun – 600, Apr. 16–May 30, 1948.[118]
Mazar – 270–350, May 30, 1948.[119]
Nuris – 570–700, May 30, 1948.[120]
Zir'in – 1,300–1,420, May 28, 1948.

Tulkarm Sub-District
Arab Balawina – Dec. 31, 1947.
Arab Huweitat – Mar. 15, 1948.
Arab Zubeidat (Kafr Zibad) – 1,590, Apr. 16, 1948.
Kafr Saba – 1,270–1,370, May 15, 1948.
Khirbat Azzun (Tabsur) – 50, Dec. 21, 1947–Apr. 3, 1948.

Khirbat Beit Lid – 460–500, Mar. 20–Apr. 5, 1948.
Khirbat Jalama – 70, early Feb. 1948.[121]
Khirbat Manshiya – 260–280, Apr. 15, 1948.
Khirbat Zalafa – 210–370, Apr. 15, 1948.
Miska – 650–880, Apr. 15, 1948.
Qaqun – 1970, May 4 & June 4, 1948.[122]
Umm Khalid – 970–1,050, Mar. 20, 1948.
Wadi Hawarith – 1,330–1,440, Mar. 15, 1948.

Jerusalem District

Hebron Sub-District
Ajjur – 3,720 (including Khirbat Ammuriya), Oct. 22–24, 1948.[123]
Barqusiya – 330, July 9–10, 1948.[124]
Beit Jibrin – 2,430, July 13–Oct. 27, 1948.[125]
Beit Nattif – 2,150, Oct. 22, 1948.[126]
Dawayima – 3,710, Oct. 29, 1948.[127]
Deir Dubban – 730, Oct. 22–23, 1948.[128]
Deir Nakh-Khas – 600, Oct. 29, 1948.[129]
Kidna – 450, Oct. 22–24, 1948.[130]
Mughallis – 540, July 16, 1948.[131]
Qubeiba – 1,060, Oct. 28, 1948.[132]
Ra'na – 190, Oct. 22–23, 1948.[133]
Tell Safi – 1,290, July 9, 1948.[134]
Zakariya – 1,180, July 22–Oct. 24, 1948.[135]
Zeita – 330, July 9–18, 1948.[136]
Zikrin – 330–960, Oct. 22–24, 1948.[137]

Jerusalem Sub-District
Allar – 440, Oct. 22, 1948.[138]
Aqqur – 40, July 13, 1948.[139]
Artuf – 350, July 17–18, 1948.[140]
Beit Itab – 540, Oct. 21, 1948.[141]
Beit Mahsir – 2,400, May 10, 1948.[142]
Beit Naqquba – 240, July 8, 1948.[143]
Beit Thul – 260, not known.
Beit Umm Meis – 70, July 15, 1948.[144]
Bureij – 720, July 15–16, 1948.[145]
Deir Aban – Oct. 19, 1948.[146]
Deir Amr – 10, July 14, 1948.[147]
Deir Hawa – 60, Oct. 19, 1948.[148]
Deir Rafat – 430, July 17–18, 1948.[149]
Deir Sheikh – 220, Oct. 21, 1948.[150]
Deir Yasin – 610–650, Apr. 9–10, 1948.
Ein Karim – 3,180–3,390, Apr. 10–21 & July 10–17, 1948.[151]
Ishwa – 620, July 10–18, 1948.[152]
Islin – 260, July 10, 1948.[153]
Jarash – 190, Oct. 21, 1948.[154]
Jura – 420, late July 1948.[155]
Kasla – 280, July 14, 1948.[156]
Khirbat Ismallah – 20, not known.
Khirbat Lauz – 450, July 13–14, 1948.[157]

Khirbat Umur – 270, Oct. 21, 1948.[158]
Lifta – 2,550–2,730, Dec. 31, 1947–early Jan. 1948.
Maliha – 1,940–2,070, Apr. 21–May 6, 1948 & July 14, 1948.[159]
Nataf – 40, Apr. 15, 1948.[160]
Qabu – 260, Oct. 21, 1948.[161]
Qaluniya – 910–970, Apr. 10–May 3, 1948.
Qastel – 90–100, late Mar.–May 3, 1948.[162]
Ras Abu Ammar – 620, Oct. 21, 1948.[163]
Sar'a – 340, July 10–14, 1948.[164]
Saris – 560–600, Apr. 16–May 3, 1948.[165]
Sataf – 540, July 13–14, 1948.[166]
Suba – 620, July 12–13, 1948.[167]
Sufla – 60, Oct. 21, 1948.[168]
Walaja – 1,650, Oct. 21, 1948.[169]

Lydda District

Jaffa Sub-District
Abbasiya – see Yahudiya.
Abu Kishk – 1,900, Mar. 30, 1948.
Beit Dajan – 3,840, Apr. 25–May 1, 1948.[170]
Biyar Adas – 300, Apr. 12, 1948.
Fajja – 1,200–1,570, Mar. 17–May 15, 1948.[171]
Haram – see Saiduna Ali.
Jalil – 600–1,020, Mar. 23–Apr. 3, 1948.[172]
Jammasin – 1,810–2,050, Jan. 7–Mar. 17, 1948.
Jarisha – 190, apparently in mid-May 1948.
Kafr Ana – 2,000–3,020, Apr. 17–25, 1948.
Kheiriya – 1,420–1,600, Apr. 25, 1948.
Mas'udiya – 850, Dec. 25, 1947.
Mirr – 170–190, Feb. 3–15, 1948.
Muweilih – 360, July 9, 1948.[173]
Rantiya – 590, Apr. 28–May 13, 1948.[174]
Safiriya – 3,070, apparently in late Apr. 1948.
Saiduna Ali – 520–880, Feb. 3, 1948.[175]
Salama – 6,730–7,610, Apr. 25, 1948.
Saqiya – 1,100–1,240, Apr. 25, 1948.
Sawalima – 800, Apr. 20, 1948.
Sheik Muwannis – 1,930–2,000, Dec. 1, 1947–Mar. 30, 1948.
Sumeil – see Mas'udiya.
Yahudiya – 5,650–6,560, May 4–July 10, 1948.[176]
Yazur – 4,030, May 1, 1948.

Ramle Sub-District
Abu Fadl (Sautariya) – 510, Apr. 7–May 9, 1948.
Abu Shusha – 870–950, May 14–20, 1948.
Aqir – 2,480–2,710, May 4–6, 1948.[177]
Barfiliya – 730, July 15–17, 1948.[178]

Barriya – 510, May 1–July 10–11, 1948.[179]
Bashshit – 510–1,770, May 12–13, 1948.[180]
Beit Jiz – 550–600, Apr. 20, 1948.
Beit Nabala – 630–2,310, May 13, 1948.
Beit Shanna – 210, not known.
Beit Susin – 210, Apr. 20, 1948.
Bir Ma'in – 510, July 15–16, 1948.[181]
Bir Salim – 410–950, May 9, 1948.
Burj – 480, July 15–16, 1948.[182]
Daniyal – 410, July 9–10, 1948.
Deir Abu Salama – 60, July 13, 1948.[183]
Deir Aiyub – 320, May 16, 1948.[184]
Deir Muheisin – 460–500, Apr. 7–20, 1948.[185]
Deir Tarif – 1,750, July 9–11, 1948.[186]
Haditha – 760, July 10–12, 1948.[187]
Idnibba – 490, July 9–16, 1948.[188]
Innaba – 1,420, July 10–16, 1948.[189]
Jilya – 330, July 16, 1948.[190]
Jimzu – 1,510, July 10, 1948.[191]
Kharruba – 170, July 11, 1948.[192]
Kheima – 190, July 16, 1948.[193]
Khirbat Beit Far – 300, not known.
Khirbat Buweira – 190, not known.
Khirbat Dhuheiriya – 100, July 10–11, 1948.[194]
Khirbat Zakariya – not known.
Khulda – 260–300, Apr. 7–21, 1948.[195]
Latrun – 190, May 16, 1948.[196]
Majdal Yaba – 1,520, July 12, 1948.[197]
Mansura – 90–100, Dec. 22–29, 1947–Apr. 20, 1948.[198]
Mughar – 1,740–1,900, May 15–18, 1948.[199]
Mukheizin – 200–310, Dec. 29, 1947.[200]
Muzeiri'a – 1,160, July 16–18, 1948.[201]
Na'ana – 1,470–2,270, May 14–June 12, 1948.[202]
Nabi Rubin – 1,420, June 1, 1948.[203]
Qatra – 1,210–1,320, May 17, 1948.
Qazaza – 940, Apr. 17–July 16, 1948.[204]
Qubab – 1,980–2,160, Apr. 20–June 4, 1948.[205]
Qubeiba – 1,720–1,870, May 27–July 9–10, 1948.[206]
Qula – 1,010, July 11–18, 1948.[207]
Sajad – 370, July 9–10, 1948.[208]
Salbit – 510, July 16–17, 1948.[209]
Sarafand Amar – 1,950, probably in mid-May 1948.
Sarafand Kharab – 1,040–1,130, Apr. 20, 1948.[210]
Seidun – 210–230, Jan. 1, 1948.[211]
Shahma – 280–310, May 14, 1948.
Shilta – 100, July 17–18, 1948.[212]

Tina – 750, July 9–10, 1948.[213]
Tira – 1,290, July 10, 1948.[214]
Umm Kalkha – 60, not known.
Wadi Hunein – 1,620–1,770, Jan. 5–Apr. 17, 1948.[215]
Yibna – 5,400–5,920, June 4–5, 1948.[216]
Zarnuqa – 2,380–2,600, May 27, 1948.[217]

Gaza District

Gaza Sub-District
Arab Sukreir – 390–430, Jan. 25, 1948.
Barbara – 2,410, Nov. 30, 1948.[218]
Barqa – 890–980, May 13, 1948.
Batani Sharqi – 650–710, May 11–13, 1948.[219]
Batani Gharbi – 980, June 10–11, 1948.[220]
Beit Affa – 700, May 23–Nov. 10, 1948.[221]
Beit Daras – 2,750–3,010, May 11–12, 1948.
Beit Jirja – 940, Nov. 5, 1948.[222]
Beit Tima – 1,060, May 29–31, 1948.[223]
Bi'lin – 180, July 9–10, 1948.[224]
Bureir – 2,740–4,000, May 12, 1948.
Deir Suneid – 730, late Oct. – early Nov. 1948.
Dimra – 520, late Oct. – early Nov. 1948.
Faluja – 4,670, Oct. 16, 1948.[225]
Hamama – 5,000, June 9–Nov. 30, 1948.[226]
Hatta – 970, July 17–18, 1948.[227]
Hirbiya – 2,240, Nov. 5–30, 1948.[228]
Huj – 800–810, May 28, 1948.
Huleiqat – 420, May 12–Oct. 29, 1948.[229]
Ibdis – 540, May 23, 1948.[230]
Iraq Manshiya – 2,010, Oct. 16–17, 1948.[231]
Iraq Suweidan – 660, July 9–Nov. 10, 1948.[232]
Isdud – 4,620, Nov. 30, 1948.[233]
Jaladiya – 360, May 23–July 9–10, 1948.[234]
Jiya – 1,230, Nov. 5–30, 1948.[235]
Julis – 1,030–1,130, May 23–June 10–11, 1948.[236]
Jura – 2,420, Nov. 5, 1948.[237]
Juseir – 1,180, late May or early June 1948.[238]
Karatiya – 1,370, May 23, 1948.[239]
Kaufakha – 500, Aug. 16–Sept. 24, 1948.[240]
Kaukaba – 680, May 12–Oct. 18, 1948.[241]
Khirbat Khisas – 150, Nov. 30, 1948.[242]
Masmiya Kabira – 2,520, July 9–10, 1948.[243]
Masmiya Saghira – 530, July 9–10, 1948.
Muharraqa – 580–1,100, May 25–28, 1948.[244]
Najd – 600–620, May 12, 1948.
Ni'ilya – 1,310, Nov. 5–30, 1948.[245]

Qastina – 890, July 9–10, 1948.[246]
Sawafir Gharbiya – 1,000–1,030, May 15–18, 1948.[247]
Sawafir Shamaliya – 680, May 11–18, 1948.[248]
Sawafir Sharqiyya – 970, May 15–18, 1948.
Sumsum – 1,200–1,360, May 12, 1948.
Summeil – 950, July 9–10, 1948.[249]
Tell Turmus – 760, July 9, 1948.[250]
Yasur – 1,070, June 10–11, 1948.[251]

Beersheba Sub-District
Bir Asluj – not known, June 11, 1948.[252]
Jammama – 150, May 22, 1948.[253]

Galilee District

Acre Sub-District	20,950–21,860
Beisan Sub-District	9,960–13,640
Nazareth Sub-District	7,230–7,540
Safad Sub-District	34,320–36,030
Tiberias Sub-District	17,430–17,940

Haifa District

Haifa Sub-District	35,290–37,120

Samaria District

Jenin Sub-District	2,970–3,300
Tulkarm Sub-District	8,830–9,570

Jerusalem District

Hebron Sub-District	19,040–19,670
Jerusalem-Sub-District	22,260–22,930

Lydda District

Jaffa Sub-District	39,060–43,670
Ramle Sub-District	47,940–54,410

Gaza District

Gaza Sub-District	58,850–61,400
Beersheba Sub-District	150

Villages Total	324,280–349,230
Cities Total	247,403–248,403
Negev Bedouins	30,510[254]
Refugees Settled in Israeli Localities Other Than Their Original Sites	19,072[255]
Palestine Grand Total	583,121–609,071

Abbreviations

AEC	Arab Executive Committee
AHC	Arab Higher Committee
ALA	Arab Liberation Army
BGA	Ben-Gurion Archive
BGD	Ben-Gurion's Diary
BMEO	British Middle East Office (Cairo)
CBI	Central Bureau of Statistics (Israel)
CO	Colonial Office (Britain)
CZA	Central Zionist Archives
DGFP	Documents on German Foreign Policy
FBIS	Foreign Broadcasts Information Service
FO	Foreign Office (Britain)
FRUS	Foreign Relations of the United States
HA	Hagana Archives
IDF	Israel Defense Forces
IDFA	Israel Defense Forces Archive
ISA	Israel State Archives
IZL	Irgun Zvai Leumi (National Military Organization)
JAE	Jewish Agency Executive
JNF	Jewish National Fund
Lehi	Lohamei Herut Israel (Fighters for the Freedom of Israel, "Stern Gang")
Mapai	Mifleget Poalei Eretz Israel (Land of Israel Workers Party, Labor Party)
Mapam	Mifleget Hapoalim Hameuhedet (United Workers Party, Israel)
NA	National Archives (Britain)
NC	National Committee
PA	Palestinian Authority
PLO	Palestine Liberation Organization
PRO	Public Record Office
SWB	Summary of World Broadcasts (BBC)
UN	United Nations
UNSCOP	United Nations Special Committee on Palestine
WO	War Office (Britain)

Notes

Introduction

1. Yona Cohen, *Jerusalem under Siege: Pages from a 1948 Diary* (Los Angeles: Ridgefield, 1982), p. 39.
2. This was a higher human toll than that suffered by Britain in World War II and approximately four times the American toll during the same conflict, not to mention the Korean, and Vietnam wars where American fatalities accounted for one-fiftieth and one-thirtieth of 1 percent of the total population, respectively. Translated into British and US World War II terms, the Jewish death toll during the 1948 war equaled some 467,468 British and 1,342,818 American fatalities (the actual figures being 355,276 and 362,561 fatalities, respectively). See, for example, Martin Gilbert, *The Second World War* (London: Fontana, 1990), p. 746; National Register of the United Kingdom and the Isle of Man, *Statistics of Population on 29 September 1939* (London: HMSO, 1939); Maldwyn A. Jones, *The Limits of Liberty: American History 1607–1992* (Oxford: Oxford University Press, 1995).
3. Walid Khalidi, *From Haven to Conquest: Readings in Zionism and the Palestine Problem until 1948* (Washington, D.C.: Institute for Palestine Studies, 1987), p. lxix.
4. Sir J. Troutbeck, "Summary of General Impressions Gathered during Week-End Visit to the Gaza District," June 16, 1949, FO 371/75342/E7816, p. 123.
5. Qustantin Zuraiq, *Ma'na al-Nakba* (Beirut: Dar al-Ilam li-l-Malayin, 1948), p. 6; Musa Alami, "The Lesson of Palestine," *Middle East Journal*, Vol. 3, No. 4 (Oct. 1949), p. 381.
6. Muhammad Amin Husseini, *Haqa'iq an Qadiyat Filastin* (Cairo: Maktab al-Hay'a al-Arabiyya al-Ulya li-Filastin, 2nd ed., 1956), pp. 9, 15–16, 22.
7. In a letter to the Mufti in May 1947, the veteran Palestinian Arab politician Rashid Hajj Ibrahim wrote: "The Jews covet Egypt because this is where Moses was born; they desire Syria and Lebanon – because their Temple was built from Lebanese cedars; they have set their sights on Iraq and the Hijaz – respective birthplaces of Abraham the patriarch and his son Ishmael; and they fancy Transjordan because it is a part of Palestine and was a part of Solomon's kingdom." Hagana Archive (HA), 105/249, pp. 56–59. See also a circular by the AHC National Orientation Section, Jerusalem, Feb. 21, 1948, HA 105/146, p. 167.
8. Muhammad Nimr Khatib, *Min Athar al-Nakba* (Damascus: al-Matba'a al-Amumiya, 1951), pp. 177–78.
9. Walid Khalidi, "Benny Morris and before their Diaspora," *Journal of Palestine Studies*, Vol. 22, No. 3 (spring 1993), p. 108; Edward Said, *The Question of Palestine* (New York: Vintage, 1980), pp. 12–13.
10. Rashid Khalidi, "The Palestinians and 1948: The Underlying Causes of Failure," in Eugene L. Rogan and Avi Shlaim (eds.), *The War for Palestine: Rewriting the History of 1948* (Cambridge: Cambridge University Press, 2001), pp. 16–17.
11. Benny Morris, *Righteous Victims: A History of the Zionist-Arab Conflict 1881–2001* (New York: Vintage Books, 2001), p. 676.
12. Thus, for example, Benny Morris (of Ben-Gurion University in Beersheba) admitted that in writing *The Birth of the Palestinian Refugee Problem* (1987), he had "no access to" – elsewhere

he said he "was not aware of" – the voluminous documents in the archives of the specific
Israeli institutions whose actions in 1948 formed the burden of his indictment: the Hagana
underground organization and the Israel Defense Forces (IDF). See Morris, "Revisiting the
Palestinian Exodus of 1948," in Rogan and Shlaim, *The War for Palestine*, p. 37.
13. Troutbeck, "Summary."

Chapter 1: Jews and Arabs in the Holy Land

1. According to the ninth-century Muslim historian Baladhuri, at the time of the Muslim
   conquest of Palestine the Jews of Caesaria alone numbered some 200,000 people.
   Although this figure is probably an exaggeration, it gives an indication of the size of the
   country's Jewish community, which nearly 200 years later was still large enough to
   launch a local revolt. Moshe Gil, *A History of Palestine, 634–1099* (Cambridge:
   Cambridge University Press, 1992), pp. 59, 282–83.
2. Arthur Ruppin, *Shloshim Shnot Binyan Beeretz Israel* (Jerusalem: Shocken, 1937), p. 59.
3. Memorandum by Brigadier General Gilbert Clayton, June 16, 1918, Public Record
   Office/National Archives, FO 371/3395/130342, p. 3 (179); "Report on the Existing
   Political Condition in Palestine and Contiguous Areas by the Political Officer in Charge
   of the Zionist Commission, Aug. 27, 1918," FO 371/3395/147225, p. 5 (231).
4. For pre-World War I Arab-Jewish relations, see: Neville Mandel, *The Arabs and Zionism
   before World War I* (Berkeley: University of California Press, 1976); Michael Asaf,
   Hayahasim bein Arvim Veyehudim Beeretz Israel 1860–1948 (Tel Aviv: Tarbut Vehinuh,
   1970), pp. 9–120; Eliezer Be'eri, *Reshit Hasikhsukh Israel-Arav, 1882–1911* (Tel Aviv:
   Sifriyat Poalim, 1985).
5. For early protests over the Balfour Declaration, see: *Wathaiq al-Muqawama al-Filastiniyya
   al-Arabiyya did al-Ihtilal al-Baritani wa-l-Sihyuniyya* (Beirut: Center for Palestine Studies,
   1968), pp. 1–13; Bayan Nuwaihid al-Hut, *Watha'iq al-Haraka al-Wataniyya al-Filastiniyya
   1918–1939: Min Awraq Akram Zu'aytir* (Beirut: Palestinian Research Center, 1984;
   2nd ed.), pp. 4–34; Emile Ghouri, *Filastin Abra Sittin Aman* (Beirut: Dar al-Nahar,
   1972), pp. 36–40.
6. Walter Laqueur (ed.), *The Israel-Arab Reader* (Harmondsworth: Penguin, 1970), pp. 37–39.
7. J. H. Kann, *Some Observations on the Policy of the Mandatory Government of Palestine with
   Regard to the Arab Attacks on the Jewish Population in August 1929 and the Jewish and the
   Arab Sections of the Population* (Hague: Martinus Nijhoff, 1930), p. 10.
8. See, for example, David Ben-Gurion's Diary (Sde Boker), Nov. 24, 1929 (hereinafter
   BGD); Z. Abramowitz and Y. Guelfat, *Hameshek Haarvi Beeretz Israel Uveartzot Hamizrah
   Hatichon* (Tel Aviv: Hakibbutz Hameuhad, 1944), pp. 5–7.
   The decline in Arab emigration from Palestine was particularly marked in comparison
   with the neighboring Arab states. While over 103,000 people left Syria and Lebanon
   from 1920 to 1931, only 9,272 non-Jews left Palestine during the same period: less than
   half the Syrian/Lebanese rate given that their population was five times as large. Aharon
   Cohen, *Israel and the Arab World* (London: W. H. Allen, 1970), p. 225.
9. Palestine Royal Commission, *Report. Presented to the Secretary of State for the Colonies in
   Parliament by Command of his Majesty, July 1937* (London: HMSO; repr. 1946; hereinafter
   Peel Commission Report), p. 93 (vii).
10. *Ibid.*, pp. 94, 157–58; Abramowitz and Guelfat, *Hameshek Haarvi*, pp. 48–50.
11. *A Survey of Palestine. Prepared in December 1945 and January 1946 for the Information of
    the Anglo-American Committee of Enquiry* (repr. 1991 in full with permission from Her
    Majesty's Stationery Office by the Institute for Palestine Studies, Washington, D.C.),
    Vol. 2, pp. 708–15.
12. *Ibid.*, pp. 570–80; *Peel Commission Report*, p. 94; Cohen, *Israel*, p. 228.
13. *A Survey of Palestine*, pp. 699–700, 710–14, 719–20; *Peel Commission Report*, pp. 93
    (vi), 231.
14. See, for example, Colonial Office, *Palestine: Report on Palestine Administration, 1923*
    (London: HMSO, 1924), p. 26; Colonial Office, *Palestine: Report on Palestine*

Administration, 1924 (London: HMSO, 1925), pp. 28, 32, 50; Colonial Office, *Palestine: Report on Palestine Administration, 1926* (London: HMSO, 1927), p. 33; Chaim Weizmann, "Progress and Problems," confidential report to Colonial Office, Feb. 15, 1922, *The Letters and Papers of Chaim Weizmann. Vol. I, Series B, August 1898–July 1931* (New Brunswick & Jerusalem: Transaction Books & Israel Universities Press, 1983), p. 366.

15. Frederick H. Kisch, *Palestine Diary* (London: Victor Gollancz, 1938), pp. 48–49, 54, 73. See also Cohen, *Israel*, pp. 249–50.

16. Colonial Office, *Palestine: Report of the High Commissioner on the Administration of Palestine 1920–1925* (London: HMSO, 1925), pp. 40–41.

17. Extrapolation of currency fluctuations throughout the book are based on Dominic Webb "Inflation: The Value of the Pound 1750–2005" (House of Commons Library Research Paper 06/09, Feb. 3, 2006).

18. David Ben-Gurion, *My Talks with Arab Leaders* (Jerusalem: Keter, 1972), pp. 15–16; Kenneth W. Stein, *The Land Question in Palestine, 1917–1939* (Chapel Hill: University of North Carolina Press, 1984), pp. 182, 228–39.

19. *Peel Commission Report*, pp. 63, 271.

20. This is according to two of the Mufti's biographers; others note different dates ranging from 1893 to 1897. See: Philip Mattar, *The Mufti of Jerusalem: Al-Hajj Amin al-Husayni and the Palestinian National Movement* (New York: Columbia University Press, 1988), pp. 6, 128; Zvi Elpeleg, *The Grand Mufti* (London: Cass, 1993), p. 1; Khairiyya Qasmiyya, *al-Qiyyadat wa-l-Mu'asasat al-Siyasiya fi Filastin 1917–1948* (Beirut: Palestine Research Center, 1986), p. 201; Maurice Pearlman, *Mufti of Jerusalem: The Story of Hajj Amin El Husseini* (London: Gollancz, 1946), p. 10.

21. Ronald Storrs, *Orientations* (London: Riders Union, 1939), p. 343.

22. Years after Amin's appointment, a prominent Indian Muslim scholar, taken aback by his religious ignorance, lamented "how such a person could become a Mufti in Islam's holy city" (Eliahu Epstein's report, London, May 12, 1937, HA 080/153P/0011). See also: "Tahir Husseini's Meeting with [Yitzhak] Ben-Zvi and A. Laniado," Apr. 1, 1930, Central Zionist Archives (CZA), S25/3051; *Haaretz*, Apr. 15, 1927; *Peel Commission Report*, pp. 129–30.

23. Uri M. Kupperschmidt, *The Supreme Muslim Council: Islam under the British Mandate for Palestine* (Leiden: Brill, 1987), pp. 69–71; Yehoshua Porath, *The Emergence of the Palestinian-Arab National Movement 1918–1929* (London: Cass, 1974), p. 49; "Conversation with Awni Abdel Hadi," June 3, 1920, HA 80/145/11.

24. Yehuda Taggar, *The Mufti of Jerusalem and Palestine Arab Politics, 1930–1937* (New York & London: Garland, 1986), p. 187; "Notes from an Interview Accorded to Members of the Arab Higher Committee by His Excellency the High Commissioner on the 7th November, 1936," CZA, S25/22704, pp. 15–16.

25. Bernard Lewis, *The Jews of Islam* (Princeton: Princeton University Press, 1984), pp. 165–66.

26. Gad Frumkin, *Derekh Shofet Beyerushalaim* (Tel Aviv: Dvir, 1956), pp. 216, 280–90; Eliahu Elath, *Shivat Zion Vearav*, (Tel Aviv: Dvir, 1974), p. 245; Taggar, *The Mufti*, p. 83. In January 1935, the Mufti told a Jerusalem conference of *ulama* (Islamic legal scholars) that "he used only Arab manufactured goods."

27. Dov Joseph, *The Faithful City: The Siege of Jerusalem 1948* (New York: Simon and Schuster, 1960), p. 194.

28. The Mufti's Diary, HA 80/972/1F. In public, the Mufti was more temperate, if hardly less xenophobic. "The Jews have changed the life of Palestine in such a way that it must inevitably lead to the destruction of our race," he lamented to a Western journalist. "They have also spread here their customs and usages which are opposed to our religion and to our whole way of life. Above all, our youth is being morally shattered. The Jewish girls who run around in shorts demoralize our youths by their mere presence." Told that "running around in shorts" was in full accordance with the climate of Palestine, let alone commonplace in all European countries, the Mufti retorted: "It is not a matter of climatic conditions, but of tradition. This is foreign to our tradition. And it is dangerous,

so radical, almost revolutionary to bring 'the other world' before the eyes of the youth."
Ladislas Farago, *Palestine on the Eve* (London: Putnam, 1936), pp. 62–63.

29. See, for example, Muhammad Amin Husseini, *Haqa'iq an Qadiyat Filastin* (Cairo: Maktab al-Hay'a al-Arabiyya al-Ulya li-Filastin, 2nd ed., 1956), pp. 27–45.

30. Kisch, *Palestine Diary*, p. 268.

31. High Commissioner for Palestine to Secretary of State for the Colonies, Dec. 17, 1931, FO 141/728/10. See also *al-Jami'a al-Arabiyya*, Dec. 12, 1931; *Times*, Nov. 6, Dec. 4, 5, 6, 7, 9, 12, 16, 1931; Haim Arlosoroff, *Yoman Yerushalaim* (Tel Aviv: Labor Party Printing House, 2nd ed., 1949), pp. 138–39.

32. *Times*, Sept. 2, 1929. See also *ibid.*, Oct. 29, 30, & Nov. 8, 1929.

33. *Report of the Commission on the Palestine Disturbances of August, 1929. Presented by the Secretary of State for the Colonies to Parliament by Command of His Majesty, March, 1930* (London: HMSO, 1930), especially pp. 58, 73–82, 156–59, 172–83.
    The commission noted the virulent incitement prior to the riots by religious societies, officials, and dignitaries, on the one hand, and by nationalist activists and the Arabic press, on the other. Yet it chose to exonerate the Mufti and the Arab Executive Committee (AEC), the umbrella organization of the Palestinian Arabs, "on the charges of complicity in or incitement to the disturbances," euphemistically regretting that "during the week which preceded those disturbances, the Moslem religious authorities and the Arab political leaders did not make a more determined attempt to control their followers by declaring publicly and emphatically that they were on the side of law and order." This was too much for one of the commissioners, who, in a dissenting opinion, attributed to the Mufti "a greater share in the responsibility for the disturbances than is attributed to him in the report," and stated that "the Mufti must bear the blame for his failure to make any effort to control the character of an agitation conducted in the name of a religion of which in Palestine he was the head." He likewise rejected the report's "acquitting of the Moslem religious authorities of all but the slightest blame" for the incitement campaign. So did the head of the Palestine Section in the Colonial Office. "I think I may say that it is our private opinion in the office that the Mufti, and some of his supporters, were probably very much more responsible for some of the deplorable incidents which have occurred in Palestine than the majority of the Shaw Commission appear to think," he commented on the report, "and such intelligence information as we have had since the outbreak has tended to confirm this impression." Indeed, the prominent Palestinian activist Izzat Darwaza, a close associate of the Mufti who at the time served as the SMC's director of religious endowments, reaffirmed these views years later by revealing that the riots had been orchestrated from behind the scenes. See: Muhammad Izzat Darwaza, *Hawla al-Haraka al-Arabiyya al-Haditha: Ta'rikh wa-Mudhakkirat wa-Ta'liqat* (Sidon & Beirut: al-Matba'a al-Asriyya, 1950), Vol. 3, pp. 61–63; Taggar, *The Mufti*, p. 100.

34. For discussion of this episode, see: Efraim Karsh and Inari Karsh, *Empires of the Sand: The Struggle for Mastery in the Middle East, 1789–1923* (Cambridge: Harvard University Press, 1999), Chapter 20.

35. Theodor Herzl, *Altneuland* (New York: Bloch Publishing & Herzl Press, 1941), Book III, Part 2 (internet ed.: www.wzo.org.il/en/resources/view.asp?id=1602).

36. Ruppin, *Shloshim*, p. 60.

37. David Ben-Gurion, "Toward the Future" (1915), in his *Anahnu Ushkheneinu* (Tel Aviv: Dvir, 1931), pp. 7–9; Ben-Gurion, *Bamaaraha* (Tel Aviv: Mapai Publishing House, 1949), Vol. 4, Part 2, pp. 260–66.

38. Ahad Ha'am, "Truth from the Land of Israel," in *Kol Kitvei Ahad Ha'am* (Tel Aviv: Dvir, 1961), pp. 23–24. See also: Ze'ev Jabotinsky, "On the Issue of Territorialism," in *Ktavim Zioniim Rishonim* (Jerusalem: Eri Jabotinsky, 1949), p. 151; Max Nordau, *Ktavim Zioniim* (Tel Aviv: Mitzpe, 1930), Vol. 2, p. 120.

39. Max Nordau, "The Arabs and Us" (1918), in his *Ktavim Zioniim* (Jerusalem: Zionist Library, 1962), Vol. 4, pp. 49–55; Nordau, "Jews and Arabs in Palestine" (1920), *ibid.*, p. 108.

40. Kisch, *Palestine Diary*, p. 53.

41. "The Yishuv's Security: The Basic Zionist Question," in Ze'ev Jabotinsky, *Neumim, 1905–26* (Jerusalem: Eri Jabotinsky, 1947), pp. 191, 198–99.

42. Originally published in Russian under the title "O Zheleznoi Stene," in *Rassvyet*, Nov. 4, 1923, the "Iron Wall" was reprinted several times, including in the *Jewish Herald* (South Africa), Nov. 26, 1937 (*www.mideastweb.org/ironwall.htm*; emphasis in the original).

43. Jabotinsky's address to the Institute for the Resolution of National Problems (Warsaw), in his *Neumim 1927–1940* (Jerusalem: Eri Jabotinsky, 1948), p. 216; Palestine Royal Commission, *Notes of Evidence Taken in London on Thursday, 11th February, 1937. Sixty-Sixth Meeting (Public)* (London: His Majesty's Stationery Office, 1937), p. 370.

44. Jabotinsky, *Neumim 1927–1940*, p. 278.

45. Vladimir Jabotinsky, *The Jewish War Front* (London: George Allen & Unwin, 1940), p. 212.

46. *Ibid.*, p. 216.

47. Ze'ev Jabotinsky, "What Is to Be Done?" (1905), in *Ktavim Zioniim Rishonim*, pp. 209–10; "The Iron Wall."

48. Jabotinsky, *The Jewish War Front*, pp. 216–20; Palestine Royal Commission, "Notes of Evidence," p. 379.

49. Ben-Gurion, "The Rights of the Jews and the Non-Jews in Palestine" (1918), in his *Anahnu Ushkheneinu*, pp. 31–32; Ben-Gurion, "The Hebrew Worker and the Arab Worker" (1926), *ibid.*, p. 105.

50. "The Congress as a Political Committee," third meeting, Saturday night, Aug. 7, 1937, S25/1543, pp. 109–10.

51. "Memorandum on the Treatment of Minorities," submitted by M. Shertok, Executive of the Jewish Agency, to the Secretary, Palestine Partition Commission, Jerusalem, on 31st July 1938, S25/8929.

52. Haim Arlosoroff, "The May Disturbances" (1921), in Jacob Steinberg (ed.), *Haim Arlosoroff: Ktavim* (Tel Aviv: Shtibel, 1934), Vol. 1, pp. 8–10.

53. *Peel Commission Report*, p. 57; Kisch, *Palestine Diary*, p. 95.

54. Arlosoroff, "Stocktaking" (1929) & "Address to the 17th Zionist Congress" (1931), in Steinberg (ed.), *Haim Arlosoroff*, Vol. 1, pp. 101–14 & Vol. 6, pp. 75–76. See also Arlosoroff, "A Press Conference" (1931), *ibid.*, Vol. 6, pp. 96–97.

55. David Ben-Gurion's address to the Vaad Leumi, June 10, 1919, in Neil Caplan, *Futile Diplomacy. Vol. 1: Early Arab-Zionist Negotiations Attempts 1913–1931* (London: Frank Cass, 1983), p. 7.

56. Ben-Gurion, *Anahnu Ushkheneinu*, pp. 173–75; BGD, Oct. 9, 1929.

57. Ben-Gurion, *My Talks*, pp. 13–14; BGD, Dec. 6, 12, 1933; Shabtai Teveth, *Ben-Gurion: The Burning Ground 1886–1948* (Boston: Houghton Mifflin, 1987), pp. 458, 531.

58. The Jewish Agency was established by the World Zionist Organization at the Sixteenth Zionist Congress (Aug. 1929) in accordance with the stipulation in the League of Nations' Mandate for Palestine that a "Jewish Agency comprised of representatives of world Jewry assist in the establishment of the Jewish National Home . . . in Palestine."

59. BGD, Sept. 4, 1934; "Minutes of a Meeting of Mapai's Political Committee, Aug. 5, 1934," p. 2, *Ben-Gurion Archives* (Sde Boker; hereinafter BGA); Ben-Gurion, *My Talks*, pp. 16, 20–21.

60. These included the Jerusalem notable Hassan Sidqi Dajani and Tahir Husseini, son of the late mufti, Kamil Husseini, as well as the prominent journalist and editor Yusuf Francis. Jewish contacts with non-Palestinian Arabs included meetings with Syrian and Lebanese leaders, notably the Lebanese president, as well as conversations with the Saudi and Iraqi representatives in London, with senior Egyptian journalists in Cairo, and with the prominent Syrian politician Abdel Rahman Shahbandar. See, for example: "Conversation with Hassan Sidqi Dajani on Jan. 11, 1932," S25/3051; Dov Hoz, "Precis of a Conversation with Hassan Sidqi Dajani (King David Hotel, Nov. 1, 1935)," *ibid.*; Elias Sasson, "Conversation with Hassan Sidqi Dajani," Dec. 15, 1935, *ibid.*; "Conversation with Awni Abdel Hadi at Mr. Agronsky's Home on Friday, Feb. 12, 1932," *ibid.*; Elias Sasson's reports on conversations with Yusuf Francis on July 15, Sept. 3, 5, 13, 1935, Mar. 3, 18, 1936,

ibid.; "Minutes of the JAE Meeting on Aug. 28, 1934," BGA; "Minutes of Mapai's Political Committee on Aug. 19, 1934," BGA; "Minutes of JAE Meeting, Apr. 22, 1934," *ibid.*

61. Ben-Gurion, *My Talks*, pp. 32–33; BGD, Sept. 4, 7, 1934; Geoffrey Furlonge, *Palestine Is my Country: The Story of Musa Alami* (London: John Murray, 1969), p. 103. For Abdel Hadi's version of his talks with Ben-Gurion, see Khairiyya Qasmiyya, *Awni Abdel Hadi: Awraq Khassa* (Beirut: PLO Research Center, 1974), pp. 68–73.

62. Kisch, *Palestine Diary*, p. 316.

63. "The Arab Political Parties of Palestine," Jan. 1945, S25/9228; M. Kapeliuk, "The Warfare Methods of the Mufti and his Faction," Nov. 1938, S25/3483, pp. 11–12.

64. Francis R. Nicosia, *The Third Reich and the Palestine Question* (New Brunswick: Transaction, 2000; rev. 2nd ed.), pp. 85–86; Yehoshua Porath, *Mimhumot Limrida: Hatnu'a Haleumit Haarvit Hafalestinit 1929–1939* (Tel Aviv: Am Oved, 1978), pp. 100–01.

65. "Tahir Husseini's Meeting with Ben-Zvi and A. Laniado"; Daniel Auster, "A Precis," June 24, 1935, S25/3051.

66. The AHC comprised the heads of the six parties – Awni Abdel Hadi, Ragheb Nashashibi, Yaqub Ghussein, Jamal Husseini, Hussein Khalidi, and Abdel Latif Salah. The other members were Ahmad Hilmi, head of the Umma Bank (neutral with Istiqlal affinities), the Christian Jaffa notable Alfred Rock (a Husseini supporter), and the Christian Jerusalemite Yaqub Faraj (a Nashashibi sympathizer). See Yaacov Shimoni, *Arviyei Eretz Israel* (Tel Aviv: Am Oved, 1947), pp. 297–98.

67. *Peel Commission Report*, pp. 71–75.

68. *Ibid.*, pp. 271–75.

69. "Evidence of Haj Amin El Husseini before the Royal Commission on Jan. 12, 1937," S25/10211; *Peel Commission Report*, p.102.

70. General Staff H.Q., Jerusalem, "History of the Disturbances in Palestine 1936–1939," Dec. 1939, WO 191/88; Yuval Arnon-Ohana, *Herev Mibait: Hamaavak Hapnimi Batnuah Haleumit Hafalestinit* (Tel Aviv: Yariv-Hadar, 1981), pp. 278–83; Joseph B. Schechtman, *The Mufti and the Fuehrer: The Rise and Fall of Hajj Amin el-Husseini* (New York & London: Thomas Yoseloff, 1965), p. 74; Pearlman, *Mufti*, pp. 21–22; Hillel Cohen, *Army of Shadows: Palestinian Collaboration with Zionism, 1917–1948* (Berkeley: University of California Press, 2008), Chapter 5.

71. *A Survey of Palestine*, Vol. 1, pp. 38, 46, 49; Arnon-Ohana, *Herev*, p. 286; Kenneth Waring, "Arab against Arab: Evidence of Rebel Documents," *Times*, Jan. 18, 1939. For an annotated Hebrew translation of a comprehensive collection of original documents of the Arab gangs, see Ezra Danin (ed.), *Teudot Udmuyot Meginzei Haknufiot Haarviot Bemeoraot 1936–1939* (Jerusalem: Magnes Press, 1981 [1944]).

72. Pearlman, *Mufti*, p. 29 (emphasis in the original); Ben-Zion Dinur (general editor), *Sefer Toldot Hahagana. Vol. 2, Part 2: Mehagana Lemaavak* (written by Yehuda Slotzky) (Jerusalem & Tel Aviv: The Zionist Library & Ministry of Defense Publishing House, 1972), p. 777.

73. Ben-Gurion, *My Talks*, pp. 42–55.

74. "Mapai's Political Committee Meeting," June 21, 1936, p. 21, BGA.

75. Protocol of JAE Meeting, May 2, 1937; Miriam Glickson, "Attempts at an Agreement with Arabs," Mar. 5, 1946, CZA, S25/3311.

Chapter 2: Pan-Arab Ambitions

1. Abu Khaldun Sati al-Husri, *al-Uruba Awalan* (Beirut: Dar al-Ilm li-l-Malain, 1955), pp. 11–13; Hearing before the Anglo-American Committee of Inquiry, Washington, D.C., State Department, Jan. 11, 1946, Central Zionist Archives (CZA), V/9960/g, pp. 10–11.

2. *Arab Bulletin*, June 23, 1916, p. 47 & Feb. 6, 1917, pp. 57–58, FO 882/25. See also McMahon to Grey, Oct. 20, 1915, FO 371/2486/154423; "Intelligence Report," Dec. 28, 1916, FO 686/6, p. 176.

3. Hussein to McMahon (Cairo), July 1915–Mar. 1916, presented to British parliament, Cmd. 5957, London, 1939, p. 3 (hereinafter – "Hussein-McMahon Correspondence").

4. Hussein's letter of Nov. 5, 1915, *ibid.*, p. 8; McMahon's letter of Dec. 14, 1915, *ibid.*, pp. 11–12; "Report of Conversation between Mr. R.C. Lindsay, C.V.O., Representing the Secretary of State for Foreign Affairs, and His Highness the Emir Faisal, Representing the King of the Hedjaz. (Held at the Foreign Office on Thursday, Jan. 20, 1921)" CO 732/3, fol. 366.

5. For the text of Hussein's letter, see *Times*, May 19, 1923. See also Husseini's letter to High Commissioner Samuel, Nov. 3, 1923, CZA, S25/10690.

6. B. H. Liddell Hart, *T. E. Lawrence to his Biographer* (London: Cassell, 1962), p. 142 (recording a conversation with Lawrence, Aug. 1, 1933).

7. Abu Khaldun Sati al-Husri, *Yawm Maisalun: Safha min Tarikh al-Arab al-Hadith* (Beirut: Dar al-Ittihad, 1964, rev. ed.), p. 261. For discussion of Faisal's attempts to win his Syrian empire, see Efraim Karsh and Inari Karsh, *Empires of the Sand: The Struggle for Mastery in the Middle East, 1789–1923* (Cambridge: Harvard University Press, 1999), chapters 17–18.

8. Jamal Husseini, "Report of the State of Palestine during the Four Years of Civil Administration, Submitted to the Mandate's Commission of the League of Nations Through H.E. the High Commissioner for Palestine, by the Executive Committee of the Palestine Arab Congress – Extract," Oct. 6, 1924, p. 1, S25/10690 (CZA); "Minutes of the JAE Meeting on Apr. 19, 1937," BGA (Ben Gurion Archive); "The Arabs Reject Partition," quoted from *Palestine & Transjordan*, Vol. II, No. 57 (July 17, 1937), p. 1, S25/10690.

9. General Nuri Said, *Arab Independence and Unity: A Note on the Arab Cause with Particular Reference to Palestine, and Suggestions for a Permanent Settlement to Which Are Attached Texts of All the Relevant Documents* (Baghdad: Government Press, 1943), p. 11.

10. "First Conversation on Trans-Jordania, Held at Government House, Jerusalem, Mar. 28, 1921," FO 371/6343, fols. 99–101; "Second Conversation on Trans-Jordania" & "Third Conversation on Trans-Jordania," *ibid.*, fols. 101–02.

11. Taha al-Hashemi, *Mudhakkirat Taha al-Hashemi. Vol. 2–1942–1955* (Beirut: Dar al-Tali'a li-l-Taba'a wa-l-Nashr, 1978), p. 90 (diary entry for Sept. 29, 1945).

12. Clayton to Foreign Office, Dec. 12, 1947, FO 371/62226/E11928.

13. *Haprotokolim shel Havaad Hapoel Hazioni 1919–1929. Vol. 3: Sep. 1921–Jun. 1923* (Jerusalem: Zionist Library, 2003), pp. 165–69, 211–17; *The Letters and Papers of Chaim Weizmann. Series A, Vol. 10, Jul. 1920–Dec. 1921* (New Brunswick & Jerusalem: Transaction Books & Israel Universities Press, 1977), p. 338.

14. See, for example, Max Nordau, "Jews and Arabs in Palestine" (1920), in his *Ktavim Zioniim* (Jerusalem: Zionist Library, 1962), Vol. 4, pp. 109–11. See also Berl Katznelson's scathing criticism of Weizmann's contacts with the Hashemites: *Kitvei Berl Katznelson* (Tel Aviv: Mapai Publishing House, 1946), pp. 46–49.

15. Kinahan Cornwallis, "Zionists and Syrians in Egypt," *Arab Bulletin*, No. 87 (Apr. 30, 1918), FO 882/27; Chaim Weizmann to Nahum Sokolow, Apr. 18 & July 17, 1918, *The Letters and Papers of Chaim Weizmann. Series A, Vol. 8, Nov. 1917–Oct. 1918*, pp. 137, 233–34; Jeremy Wilson, *Lawrence of Arabia: The Authorized Biography of T. E. Lawrence* (London: Minerva, 1990), pp. 511–13.

16. "Dr. Weizmann's Interview with Emir Faisal at the Carlton Hotel, Dec. 11, 1918, Colonel Lawrence Acting as Interpreter," Z4/40065; Weizmann to Balfour, Apr. 9 & Sept. 27, 1919, *The Letters and Papers of Chaim Weizmann. Series A, Vol. 9, Oct. 1918–Jul. 1920*, pp. 129–30, 230–31; Jon Kimche, *There Could Have Been Peace* (New York: Dial Press, 1973), p. 70.

17. Weizmann to Balfour, Sept. 27, 1919 & Weizmann to the Zionist Executive (London), Mar. 25, 1920 & Weizmann to Sir Louis Bolls, Mar. 31, 1920, *The Letters and Papers of Chaim Weizmann. Series A, Vol. 9, Oct. 1918–Jul. 1920*, pp. 230, 329, 332–33.

18. Palestine Royal Commission, *Report: Presented to the Secretary of State for the Colonies in Parliament by Command of His Majesty, July 1937* (London: HMSO; repr. 1946; hereinafter *Peel Commission Report*), p. 57. See also A. H. Cohen, "Conversation with

M[uhammad] U[nsi] on Mar. 5, 1934" & "Conversation with M[uhammad] U[nsi] on July 28, 1934," S25/3051.

19. Negib Azury, *Le Réveil de la Nation Arabe dans l'Asie Turque* (Paris: Librairie Plon, 1905), p. 246; Sylvia G. Haim (ed.), *Arab Nationalism: An Anthology* (Berkeley: University of California Press, 1964), pp. 46–47.

20. Thomas Mayer, *Egypt and the Palestine Question, 1936–1945* (Berlin: Klaus Schwartz, 1983), pp. 9–40; Israel Gershoni and James P. Jankowski, *Egypt, Islam, and the Arabs: The Search for Egyptian Nationhood, 1900–1930* (New York: Oxford University Press, 1986), pp. 247–54.

21. M. Shertok, "Note of a Call on His Highness the Emir Abdullah, Nov. 24, 1936," S25/188; A. H. Cohen, "The Political Department and the Emirate's Palace," HA 80/153F/10a.

22. "Minutes of the Meeting with the Arab National Bloc of Syria (Arab Nationalist Party) at Bludan (near Damascus) on August 1st, 1936," S25/22656.

23. Eliahu Epstein, "Conversation with the Syrian Prime Minister Jamil Mardam, Damascus, Feb. 26, 1937," HA 080/153/P/011; Protocol of the JAE Meeting, May 2, 1937, BGA.

24. David Ben-Gurion's Diary (BGD), June 8, 9, 10, 11, 18, 25, 26, 27, 28, 1936; Norman A. Rose (ed.), *Baffy: The Diaries of Blanche Dugdale 1936–1947* (London: Vallentine, Mitchell, 1973), p. 23 (diary entry for June 29, 1936); Chaim Weizmann to Sir Archibald Clark-Kerr, Baghdad, June 29, 1936 & to William G.A. Ormsby-Gore, London, June 28, 1936, *The Letters and Papers of Chaim Weizmann. Series A, Vol. 17, Aug. 1935–Dec. 1936*, pp. 290–92.

25. Elias Sasson, *Baderekh el Hashalom: Igrot Vesihot* (Tel Aviv: Am Oved, 1978), p. 58; Minutes of JAE Meeting, Mar. 3, 1937, BGA; BGD, Feb. 14, 1937.

26. Eliahu Epstein, "Meeting between D. Ben-Gurion and Fuad Bey Hamza," Apr. 13, 1937, HA 80/183/32; Minutes of JAE Meeting, Apr. 19, 1937, BGA.

27. Eliahu Elath, *Shivat Zion Vearav*, (Tel Aviv: Dvir, 1974), p. 325; David Ben-Gurion, *My Talks with Arab Leaders* (Jerusalem: Keter, 1972), pp. 127–40; BGD, May 18, 26, 1937.

28. Anthony Eden to Sir Miles Lampson (Cairo), July 16, 1937, FO 141/676.

29. BGD, June 11, 1937; *Egyptian Gazette*, July 25, 1937. For reports on the Bludan conference and the text of its resolutions, see FO 684/10; S25/22656.

30. Sir A. Clark-Kerr (Baghdad) to Foreign Office, July 17, 18, 1937, FO 141/678.

31. D. V. Kelly (Cairo) to Foreign Office, Sept. 11, 1937, FO 141/678; Mr. A. C. Trott, (Jeddah) to Foreign Office, enclosing a Note Verbale from Ibn Saud, Aug. 27, 1937, 1937, FO 141/678; Reader W. Bullard to Anthony Eden, Dec. 16, 1937, FO 141/678.

32. "Minute of an Interview of Dr. Bernard Joseph with the President of the Lebanese Government on Friday, Aug. 6, 1937," HA 80/153F/10a.

33. E. Sasson to M. Shertok, "Conversation with the Prime Minister of Syria," Damascus, July 25, 1938, S/25/63.

34. David Ben-Gurion, "Note of Interview with His Excellency Hafiz Wahba, Saudi Minister in London, 25th Aug. 1938, at 4 p.m.," S25/22656.

35. BGD, June 9, 1937.

36. Mr. Howard, Colonial Officer, "Palestine: Miscellaneous, July 21, 1938," KV 2/2084.

37. See CO memorandum "Suggestions for Increased Propaganda for Palestine to Deal with German and Italian Propaganda," sent to Rushbrook Williams of the Ministry of Information, Jan. 20, 1939, CO 733/387/20. See also Owen Tweedy's memorandum "Publicity: Propaganda in the Middle East," Nov. 29, 1938, CO 733/387/2. For the full text of the White Paper, see "Cmd. 6019: Palestine, Statement of Policy," May 1939.

38. "Palestine Jews to Protest," *Times*, May 16, 1939; Weizmann to Mr. Justice Louis D. Brandeis, May 8, 1939, *Foreign Relations of the United States* (hereafter FRUS), 1939, *Vol. 4: The Far East, Near East and Africa*, p. 749; Rabbi Stephen S. Wise to the Secretary of State, May 22, 1939, *ibid.*, 761; "Political Report of the London Office of the Executive of the Jewish Agency," submitted to the Twenty-Second Zionist Congress at Basle, Dec. 1946, pp. 9–10.

39. Undated letter by Bedouin sheiks and tribal heads to the high commissioner for Palestine, S25/10690.
40. Bernard Joseph, "Minute of an Interview with M[uhammad] U[nsi] in my Home on Dec. 11, 1938," S25/3485, pp. 2–3.
41. William Manchester, *The Last Lion: Winston Spencer Churchill – Alone 1932–1940* (New York: Dell, 1988), pp. 397–98.

Chapter 3: "The Most Important Arab Quisling"

1. "Putting the Jews into a Ghetto," *Palestine Post*, Aug. 20, 1939; Weizmann to Chamberlain, Aug. 29, 1939, *The Letters and Papers of Chaim Weizmann. Series A, Vol. 19, Jan. 1939–Jun. 1940* (New Brunswick & Jerusalem: Transaction Books & Israel Universities Press, 1977), p. 145.
2. D. Gurewitz to Political Department, "Figures on Jewish-Owned Lands at the Beginning of 1940," Apr. 4, 1944, BGA; Weizmann to Malcolm J. MacDonald, Sept. 15, 1939 & MacDonald's response on Sept. 20, *The Letters and Papers of Chaim Weizmann. Series A, Vol. 19*, pp. 157–58; Jewish Agency for Palestine, *The Jewish Case before the Anglo-American Committee of Inquiry on Palestine* (Jerusalem: Jewish Agency for Palestine, 1947), pp. 294–99; Monty Noam Penkower, *Decision on Palestine Deferred: America, Britain, and Wartime Diplomacy 1939–45* (London: Cass, 2002), p. 35.
3. "Short Note of Talk at Dinner with W.S.C., 19.9.39, 5.30 p.m.," BGA; Bernard Joseph, "Minute of an Interview with the General Officer Commanding Lieut. Gen. M. G. H. Barker, C. B., on 25.9.39," BGA; Ben-Gurion, "Note of Conversation with General Barker, G.O.C., Jerusalem, Nov. 1, 1939" & "Hebrew Translation of the Meeting's Protocol," BGA; Dov Hoz, "Conversation with General Barker, G.O.C., on Nov. 2, 1939," BGA; BGD, Nov. 1, 5, 8, 1939; Martin Kolinsky, "After the Arab Rebellion – Part I: The Defense of Mandatory Palestine in British Strategy for the Eastern Mediterranean/Middle Eastern Region, 1938–40," *Israel Affairs*, Vol. 2, No. 2 (winter 1995), pp. 37–69; *idem*, "After the Arab Rebellion – Part II: The Defense of Palestine in British Strategy, 1941–42," *ibid.*, Vol. 5, No. 1 (autumn 1998), pp. 149–84; BGD, Nov. 1, 15, 1939.
4. BGD, Nov. 28, 1939; Moshe Sharett, *Yoman Medini 1940–42* (Tel Aviv: Am Oved, 1979), p. 205; "The British Plan for Palestine: Reported Acceptance by Mufti," *Times*, Nov. 2, 1939.
5. Reader Bullard, *Two Kings in Arabia: Letters from Jeddah 1923–5 and 1936–9* (Reading: Ithaca Press, 1993), p. 266 (diary entry for May 19, 1939).
6. "Record of the Reception of the Royal Counselor Khalid al-Hud al-Gargani, the Special Envoy of King Abdul Aziz ibn Saud," June 20, 1939, *Documents on German Foreign Policy 1918–1945* (London: HMSO, 1949; hereinafter DGFP), Ser. D, Vol. 6, pp. 743–44. See also Lukasz Hirszowicz, *The Third Reich and the Arab East* (London: Routledge & Kegan Paul, 1966), Chapters 2–3; Francis R. Nicosia, *The Third Reich and the Palestine Question* (New Brunswick: Transaction, 2000; rev. 2nd ed.), pp. 85–102, 180–92; R. Melka, "Nazi Germany and the Palestine Question," *Middle Eastern Studies*, Vol. 5, No. 3 (Oct. 1969), pp. 221–33.
7. Minister in Iran to the Foreign Ministry, Apr. 15, 1941, DGFP, Ser. D, Vol. 12, pp. 558–60; Minutes of JAE Meeting, May 21, 1941, BGA.
8. Elias Sasson, "Why and How the Mufti Moved to Iraq," Nov. 2, 1939, S25/3750; Majid Khadduri, "General Nuri's Flirtations with the Axis Powers," *Middle East Journal*, Vol. 16, No. 3 (summer 1962), pp. 328–29.
9. "The Mufti," Nov. 30, 1939, PRO, KV2/2085; "Palestine. The Mufti's Intention to Keep the Revolt Simmering; Propaganda in Favor of his Return to Palestine, Etc.," Dec. 7, 1939, *ibid.*; "The Mufti's Activities and Interests," Feb. 5, 1940, *ibid.*; "Palestine. Miscellaneous Arab Information," Mar. 15, 1940, *ibid.*; "The Mufti's Propaganda at Nabi Musa," May 10, 1940, *ibid.*; "Palestine. Revival of Pro-Mufti Activities," June 11, 1940, *ibid.*

10. "Activities of the Mufti. Possibility of Intrigue in the Middle Euphrates," Jan. 18, 1940, KV2/2085; "The Mufti's Activities," Feb. 21, 1940, *ibid.*; "The Mufti. Summoning of Followers to Baghdad to Discuss Plans, Etc.," May 15, 1940, *ibid.*

11. The Ambassador in Turkey to the Foreign Ministry (Enclosure), July 6, 1940, DGFP, Ser. D, Vol. 10, pp. 143–44; "Memorandum by an Official of the Foreign Ministry," Aug. 27, 1940, *ibid.*, pp. 556–59; "The State Secretary to the Embassy in Italy," Sept. 9, 1940, DGFP, Ser. D, Vol. 11, pp. 44–46; State Secretary to the Embassy in Italy, Oct. 6, 1940, *ibid.*, pp. 268–69; "Conversation of the State Secretary with the Private Secretary of the Grand Mufti on the Occasion of the Communication of a Statement of German Policy toward the Arabs," Oct. 18, 1940, *ibid.*, pp. 320–22; "The Grand Mufti to Adolf Hitler," Jan. 20, 1941, *ibid.*, pp. 1151–55; Uthman Haddad, *Rashid Ali al-Kailani Sanat 1941* (Sidon: al-Maktaba al-Asriya, 1957), pp. 24–46, 75–97; Abdel Rahman Abdel Ghani, *Almania al-Naziya wa-Filastin 1933–1945* (Beirut: Muasassat al-Dirasat al-Filastiniyya, 1990), pp. 240–52, 260–69.

12. I have discussed the Anglo-Hashemite negotiations at some length in *Empires of the Sand: The Struggle for Mastery in the Middle East, 1789–1923* (Cambridge: Harvard University Press, 1999), especially chapters 13–15 & "Myth in the Desert, or Not the Great Arab Revolt," *Middle Eastern Studies*, Vol. 33, No. 2 (Apr. 1997), pp. 267–312.

13. Memorandum by the Head of Political Division IM, Feb. 5, 1941 & Memorandum on the Arab Question by the Director of the Political Department, Mar. 7, 1941, DGFP, Ser. D, Vol. 12, pp. 30–32, 234–43; Ambassador in Italy to the Foreign Ministry, Sept. 10 & 14, 1940, DGFP, Ser. D, Vol. 11, pp. 48–49, 74–75; Memorandum by the Director of the Political Department, Sept. 28, 1940, *ibid.*, pp. 220–21; State Secretary to Embassy in Italy, Sept. 30, 1940, *ibid.*, p. 228; Ambassador in Turkey to the Foreign Ministry, Jan. 2, 1941, *ibid.*, pp. 1004–05; Minister Rahn, "Report on the German Mission in Syria from May 9 to July 11, 1941," July 30, 1941, DGFP, Ser. D, Vol. 13, p. 250.

14. Chargé d'Affaires in Italy to the Foreign Ministry, May 27, 1941, DGFP, Ser. D, Vol. 12, p. 890; Minister Grobba to the Foreign Ministry, May 30, 1941, *ibid.*, pp. 925–26; State Secretary to the Legation in Iran, June 1, 1941, *ibid.*, pp. 958–59; Minister in Iran to the Foreign Ministry, Aug. 21, 1941, DGFP, Ser. D, Vol. 13, pp. 344–45; Chargé d'Affaires in Italy to the Foreign Ministry, Oct. 13 & 28, 1941, *ibid.*, pp. 641–42, 704–05; Memorandum by Grobba, Nov. 6, 1941, *ibid.*, pp. 746–49; "Record of the Conversation between the Führer and the Grand Mufti of Jerusalem on Nov. 28, 1941, in the Presence of Reich Foreign Minister and Minister Grobba in Berlin," Nov. 30, 1941, *ibid.*, pp. 881–85.

15. Abdel Karim Umar, *Mudhakkirat al-Hajj Muhammad Amin al-Husseini* (Damascus: Ahali, 1999), pp. 107, 124–27.

16. G.3/D. (C. & D.), "Intelligence Report on the Mufti," Dec. 16, 1943, KV 2/2085.

17. *A Survey of Palestine: Prepared in December 1945 and January 1946 for the Information of the Anglo-American Committee of Enquiry* (repr. 1991 in full with permission from Her Majesty's Stationery Office by the Institute for Palestine Studies, Washington, D.C.), Vol. 1, pp. 337–38; "Note on Potential Arab Political Violence in Palestine," Apr. 1946, FO 141/1090; editorial, *Palestine Post*, Nov. 21, 1939; "Citrus Purchase Being Discussed," *ibid.*, Sep. 11, 1940; "Arab and Jewish Farmers Benefit," *ibid.*, Nov. 14, "Bulk of Valencia Orange Crop Sold to the Army," *ibid.*, May 7, 1941; 1940; telegrams in brief, *Times*, Jan. 18, 1940.

18. Director of Land Registration to Statistician, Jewish Agency for Palestine, Apr. 9, 1944, BGA; "MacDonald's 'Cordial Support' of Youth Immigration: Arab applications for Land Sales in Prohibited Zones," *Palestine Post*, Apr. 25, 1940; "Chief Rabbis Lead Pilgrimage," *ibid.*, Apr. 9, 1940; "Tel Aviv Police Win against Arab Side," *ibid.*, Apr. 12, 1940; "Rishon Maccabi Draw with Jaffa Arab S.C.," *ibid.*, Mar. 4, 1941; "Ramat Gan Hapoel Draw with Jaffa S.C.," *ibid.*, Apr. 15, 1941; "Jaffa Arab National Club Extend Tel Aviv Maccabi," *ibid.*, May 20, 1941; "Situation in the Near East," *Times*, July 12, 1940; Memorandum by the Head of Political Division VII, Dec. 9, 1940, DGFP, Ser. D, Vol. 11, p. 827; Hillel Cohen, *Army of Shadows: Palestinian Collaboration with Zionism, 1917–1948* (Berkeley: University of California Press, 2008), pp. 172–77.

19. Yaacov Shimoni, *Arviyei Eretz Israel* (Tel Aviv: Am Oved, 1947), pp. 318–24; Bayan Nuwaihid al-Hut, *al-Qiyadat wa-l-Muasasat al-Siyasiyya fi Filastin 1917–1948* (Beirut: Muasassat al-Dirasat al-Filastiniyya, 1986), pp. 469–74.

20. General Nuri Said, *Arab Independence and Unity: A Note on the Arab Cause with Particular Reference to Palestine, and Suggestions for a Permanent Settlement to Which Are Attached Texts of All the Relevant Documents* (Baghdad: Government Press, 1943), pp. 1–5, 11–12.

21. For Unsi's wartime meetings with Zionist officials, see: E. Sasson to Dr. B. Joseph, "Conversation with M[uhammad] U[nsi]," Nov. 28, 1939, S25/3485; Sasson to Joseph, "Conversation with M.U.," Dec. 22, 1939, S25/3051; Sasson to M. Shertok, "Conversation with M.U.," Apr. 30, 1940, S25/3054; "Conversation with M.U.," Apr. 30, 1940, S25/3051; Sasson to Shertok, "A New Partition Proposal," Sept. 21, 1943, S25/63; Elias Sasson, *Baderekh el Hashalom: Igrot Vesihot* (Tel Aviv: Am Oved, 1978), pp. 177–78, 183–84, 197–98, 200–01, 204–12, 215–18, 253–57, 277–78, 291–94, 327–37. For Shertok and Sasson's Amman visit, see Minutes of JAE Meeting, Nov. 21, 1942.

22. Ben-Gurion told Lawrence that he would rather have the Negev in the Jewish state than the Transjordanian territories offered in compensation. He also rejected the two schemes' envisaged transfer of the Palestinian Arabs from the country. See: Minutes of JAE Meeting, Nov. 26, 1939 & "Protocols of the Meetings of Mapai's Political Committee on Nov. 27, 1939" & BGD, Nov. 8, 17, 1939," BGA.

23. Yehoshua Porath, *In Search of Arab Unity 1930–1945* (London: Cass, 1986), p. 92.

24. "Short Minutes of Meeting Held on Thursday, Nov. 11, 1943, at the Dorchester Hotel, London, W1, at 5.50 P.M.," BGA; "Short Minutes of Meeting Held on Monday, Nov. 15, 1943, at 77 Great Russell Street, London, WC1," *ibid.*; "Short Minutes of Meeting Held on Monday, Nov. 16, 1943, at 77 Great Russell Street, London, WC1," *ibid.*; Harold B. Hoskins, "Results of Mission of Lt. Col. Harold B. Hoskins to Saudi Arabia," Nov. 3, 1943, FO 371/34963A; Jedda to Foreign Office, Feb. 3, 1945, FO 371/45231; Jedda to Foreign Office, Aug. 29, 1943, FO 371/35037; Chaim Weizmann, *Trial and Error* (New York: Shocken Books, 1949), pp. 427–28, 432–33.

25. Jedda to Foreign Office, Feb. 3, 1945, FO 371/45231.

26. During World War II, for example, a steady flow of Iraqi dignitaries arrived in Palestine, where they held working and social meetings with Zionist officials, while Jewish experts were sent to Iraq to help develop the local agriculture. So popular had the Hadassah hospital in Jerusalem become with upper-class Iraqis that the Iraqi consul in the city half-jokingly quipped that a special wing would have to be built to accommodate them. Likewise, the Zionists held a string of wartime meetings with prominent Egyptian politicians and intellectuals (notably minister of education Muhammad Hussein Heikal, the leading pan-Arabist Muhammad Ali Alluba, and the renowned author Taha Hussein), though none of these made real headway toward Arab-Jewish reconciliation. Secret contacts with prime minister Ismail Sidqi in the summer and autumn of 1946 proved equally futile.
See: Minutes of the Meeting of the Committee for the Study of the Arab Problem, Mar. 12, 1942, S25/22205, pp. 18–19; Minutes of JAE Meeting, July 27, 1941 & Jan. 31, Aug. 22, Nov. 7, Dec. 27, 1943 & Jan. 30, Feb. 27, 1944, BGA; Miriam Glickson (Jewish Agency's Political Department), "Attempts to Reach an Agreement with Arabs," Feb. 28, 1946, pp. 1–3 & "Attempts to Reach an Agreement with Arabs," Mar. 5, 1946, p. 6, both in S25/8085; Sasson, *Baderekh*, pp. 209–15, 281–82, 286–87, 289–90, 326–27.

27. Minutes of JAE Meeting, Nov. 7, 1943.

28. Minutes of JAE Meeting, Oct. 4, 1942 & Nov. 7, 1943.

29. Telegram from the prime minister to the deputy prime minister, Apr. 29, 1944, FO 371/40135.

30. See memorandum on "Developments in Palestine during Recent Months," n.d. (1942), FO 371/35034; memorandum "Dr Weizmann's Policies," British Embassy, Washington to Eastern Department, FO, July 9,1942, FO 371/31379; MacMichael to Malcolm MacDonald, Nov. 23, 1938, CO 753/387/5; Colonial Office memorandum, "Control of Jewish Land Transfers in Palestine," Jan. 5, 1939, CO 753/387/15; Washington

Embassy to Foreign Office, Jan. 6, 1943, FO 371/35031; Efraim Karsh and Rory Miller, "Freya Stark in America: Orientalism, Anti-Semitism, and Political Propaganda," *Journal of Contemporary History*, Vol. 39, No. 3 (July 2004), pp. 315–32.

31. Minutes of JAE Meeting, Feb. 13, 1944; Minutes attached to "Information about the Jews for Miss Freya Stark," FO 371/35039. See also: Halifax to Eden, June 9, 1944, FO 371/40131; Washington Embassy to Foreign Office, May 15, 1944, FO 371/40131.

32. "A Policy for Palestine," in the report on "International Postwar Settlement," *Manchester Guardian*, Apr. 24, 1944.

33. In a JAE meeting on May 7, 1944, and a Mapai central committee session the next day, Shertok, fresh from a working trip to London, told of his debates with a few Labour politicians about the prudence of their "transfer" recommendation. Ben-Gurion was similarly antagonistic. "Were they to ask [me]: 'What should our program be?' I would have found it inconceivable to tell them [to introduce] the transfer idea," he told his JAE colleagues. For the minutes of both meetings, see BGA.

34. Alan Bullock, *Ernest Bevin: Foreign Secretary, 1945–1951* (London: Heinemann, 1983), pp. 181–82; Weizmann's address of the Convention of the Zionist Organization of America at Atlantic City, Nov. 19, 1945, FO 371/51128. For the Foreign Office's attitude to the Jewish refugee problem, see H. Henderson, "Memorandum on Jewish Refugees," Oct. 19, 1946, FO 371/52646.

35. CAB 128/1, 38th Conclusions, Oct. 4, 1945; Bevin to Halifax, Oct. 12, 1945, FO 371/45381/E7757; "Future of Palestine," *Times*, Nov. 14, 1945; "Short Minutes of Meeting Held at 77 Great Russell Street, London, WC1, on Friday, Nov. 2, 1945," BGA.

36. Bevin to Halifax, Oct. 12, 1945. See also "Report by Mr. Ben-Gurion on his Visit to the Camps Given at a Meeting at 77 Gt. Russell St., London, WC1, on Tuesday, Nov. 6, 1945," BGA.

37. "Future of Palestine"; Walter Laqueur (ed.), *The Israel-Arab Reader* (Harmondsworth: Penguin, 1970), pp. 54–55.

38. "Short Minutes of Meeting Held at 77 Great Russell Street, London, WC1, on Tuesday, Oct. 23, 1945," BGA; "Jews' Prospects in Europe," *Times*, Nov. 14, 1945.

39. See, for example, Bullock, *Ernest Bevin*, p. 167, 181–82.

40. "Palestine: Future Policy," Secret Memorandum by the Secretary of State for the Colonies, Jan. 16, 1947, Annex I, CAB 129/16, C.P. (47) 31.

41. Richard Crossman, *Palestine Mission: A Personal Record* (New York: Harper, 1947), p. 131. The venomously anti-Zionist and anti-Semitic head of the Cairo Middle East Office, Sir John Troutbeck, described the Arabs condescendingly as "silly, feckless people . . . of medieval outlook," incapable of "the same kind of loyalty to each other that one expects but does not always get from Europeans." Troutbeck to Wright, May 18, 1948, 371/68386/E8738; Troutbeck to Bevin, Jan. 24, 1949, FO 371/75054/E3518; Troutbeck to Wright, Mar. 3, 1949, FO 371/75064.

42. Anthony Parsons, *From Cold War to Hot Peace: UN Interventions 1947–1994* (London: Michael Joseph, 1995), p. 3.

43. CAB 128/6, C.M. (46), 71st Conclusions, July 22, 1946; CAB 128/11 C.M. (47), 6th Conclusions, Minute 3, Jan. 15, 1947; "An Analysis of the Palestine Situation, Apr. 1948," Cunningham Papers, Middle East Centre, St Antony's College, Oxford University.

Chapter 4: The Road to Partition

1. "You are making a serious mistake in thinking that through the committee of inquiry you'll be able to suppress us," Weizmann told Lord Halifax. "We have got 120,000 young men who are prepared to fight and to sacrifice their lives [for Jewish independence], and you can count me among them" (Minutes of JAE Meeting, Dec. 16, 1945).

2. "Reply of the League on Mr. Bevin's Statement on Palestine," Dec. 5, 1945, FO 371/45396; Cairo to Foreign Office, Dec. 4, 1945, *ibid.*; "Arabs' Boycott of Jewish Goods," *Times*, Dec. 4, 1945; "Arabs Declare Boycott of Jewish Goods" & "Arabs Prepared for Counter-Boycott," *Palestine Post*, Dec. 4, 5, 1945; "Arab League Issues Reply

to Bevin" & "Arab League Rejects Bevin Plan" & "Arabs Refuse to Admit Any Jews," *ibid.*, Dec. 7, 12, 1945 & Jan. 10, 1946. For the full text of the Arab League's response, see Jewish Agency's Political Department, Arabic Section, "News," Dec. 12, 1945, BGA.

3. *Report of the Anglo-American Committee of Enquiry Regarding the Problems of European Jewry and Palestine, Lausanne, 20th April, 1946. Presented by the Secretary of State for Foreign Affairs to Parliament by Command of his Majesty* (London: HMSO, 1946; Cmd. 6088), pp. 1–2, 7, 44.

4. "Bayan min Ijtima Muluk al-Arab wa-Ru'asaihim wa-Umaraihim," May 29, 1948 (sent with a summary translation from the Cairo embassy to the foreign office), FO 141/1084; Jamil Arif, *al-Watha'iq al-Sirriya li-Dawr Misr wa-Suriya wa-l-Saudiya: Shahid ala Mawlid Jami'at al-Duwal al-Arabiya* (Cairo: al-Duwaliya li-l-Ilm wa-l-Nashr, 1995), pp. 170–80; Muhammad Izzat Darwaza, *Hawla al-Haraka al-Arabiyya al-Haditha: Ta'rikh wa-Mudhakkirat wa-Ta'liqat* (Sidon & Beirut: al-Matba'a al-Asriyya, 1950), Vol. 5, pp. 52–54; "The Inshas Resolutions," *Meahorei Hapargod* (Hebrew translation of an Iraqi parliamentary report on the 1948 war, published in Sept. 1949) (Tel Aviv: Maarachot, 1954), pp. 38–39; Jewish Agency Political Department, "Arab Political News: The Meeting of the Arab Kings & Attempts at Military Organization," May 29, 1946, pp. 1–4, S25/9229; Cairo to Foreign Office, May 30, 31, 1946, FO 371/52313; "Mr. Attlee's Warning to Illegal Armies" & "Meeting of Arab Rulers End" & "Arabs United over Palestine" & "Arab Rulers in Conclave," *Times*, May 2, 30, 31, 1946; "Arab Leaders Want 'Peace in Middle East,' " *Palestine Post*, May 31, 1946.

5. "The Bludan Resolutions," *Meahorei Hapargod*, pp. 40–42; Darwaza, *Hawla*, Vol. 5, pp. 55–60; Fadel Jamali, *Dhikrayat wa-Ibar: Karithat Filastin wa-Atharuha fi-l-Waqi al-Arabi* (Beirut: Dar al-Kitab al-Jadid, 1965), pp. 53–54; Arif, *al-Watha'iq*, pp. 184–90. See also: "Arab Political News: After Bludan," June 25, 1946, pp. 2–4, S25/9229; Arab States' League Secretariat General, "Memorandum" & "Remarks and Observations on the Recommendations of the Anglo-American Committee" & "Comments on the Recommendations of the Anglo-American Committee" & "Extraordinary Session No. 2," Bludan, June 15, 1946, FO 371/52314; Research Department, Foreign Office, "The Activities of the Arab League from its Formation in March 1945 to 15th May 1948," Sept. 30, 1948, FO 371/68322; Beirut to Foreign Office, June 13, 1946, *ibid.*; Beirut to Foreign Office, June 14, 1946, FO 141/1084; "Arab Fight Against Zionism" & "The Arab League and Palestine" *Times*, June 14, 15, 1946; "Negotiations Precede Bludan Arab Meeting" & "Arab League Wants Talks with Britain" & "Bludan Rejects U.S. Intervention" & "Echoes of Bludan," *Palestine Post*, June 9, 12, 13, 17, 1946.

6. Cairo to Foreign Office, Mar. 23, 1945, FO 954/15; Cairo to Foreign Office, Dec. 5, 1945, FO 371/45396; Jerusalem to Cairo, Jan. 14, 1946, FO 141/1084; Clayton to Smart, May 29, 1946, *ibid.*; Baghdad to Foreign Office, Feb. 11, 1947, FO 371/61523; W. Smart, Cairo, "Memorandum," Mar. 20, 1945 & British Embassy, Cairo, to Foreign Office, July 4, 1945, FO 371/45238.
   For inter-Arab divergences preceding the League's formation, see: "Record of Conversations between Ibn Saud, Sheik Yusuf Yasin and His Majesty's Minister on Arab Unity," Sept. 20–22, 1943, FO 371/34962; "Translation of Letter Dated September 7th, 1943, from Nahhas Pasha to Ibn Saud," *ibid.*; "From Abdul Aziz ibn Abdel Rahman al-Faisal to His Excellency Mustafa al-Nahhas Pasha, Prime Minister of Egypt," Sept. 24, 1943, *ibid.*; R[ichard] L[aw], Foreign Office, "Iraqi Prime Minister's Proposals Relating to Arab Unity," Sept. 10, 1943, *ibid.*; Jedda to Foreign Secretary, Oct. 2, 1943, *ibid.*; Jedda to Foreign Office, Apr. 26, 1943, FO 371/34957; Cairo to Foreign Office, Aug. 31, 1943, FO 371/34961; Cairo to Foreign Office, Sept. 3, 1944, FO 371/39990; Commander-in-Chief Middle East to War Office, Oct. 14, 1943, FO 371/34962; Cairo to Foreign Office, "Summary of the Procès Verbaux of the Discussions between Nahhas and Nuri Pashas at Alexandria Regarding Arab Union," Aug. 29, 1943, FO 371/34961.

7. Arif, *al-Watha'iq*, pp. 190–92; "Memorandum by the [Arab League's] Internal Committee," Bludan, June 10, 1946, CZA S25/10965; Atara, "At the Arab League Summit," Apr. 11, 1946, S25/9020; untitled report by Sasson on Bludan, June 18, 1946,

ibid.; M. S. Comay to B. Joseph, "Bludan – Impressions," June 16, 1948, *ibid.*; M. Comay to B. Gering, Apr. 30 & May 29, 1946; Sasson to E. Epstein, June 18, 1946, in World Zionist Organization, Israel State Archives, and Tel Aviv University, *Political Documents of the Jewish Agency. Volume 1 May 1945–December 1946* (Jerusalem: Publishing House of the World Zionist Organization, 1996), pp. 382–83, 421, 434–38; Clayton to Smart, May 29, 1946, FO 371/52313; Cunningham to Secretary of State for the Colonies, June 4, 1946, FO 371/52314; Jedda to Foreign Office, June 16, 1946, *ibid.*; Baghdad to Foreign Office, June 22, 1946, *ibid.*; "Arabs and Jews Not Opposed," *Palestine Post,* July 9, 1946.

8. Jedda to Foreign Office, May 29, 1945, PRO, KV2/2085; "Arab Political News," Sept. 4, 1945, p. 5 & Sept. 12, 1945, p. 4, S25/9229; Eliahu Epstein, "Conversation with Abdel Rahman Azzam-Pasha, Secretary General of the Arab League," June 20, 1947, BGA; Esptein to Members of the Jewish Agency Executive in Jerusalem, "Conversation with Mr. Cecil Hourani, Director of the Arab Office in Washington, June 16, 1947," in World Zionist Organization, Israel State Archives, and Tel Aviv University, *Political Documents of the Jewish Agency. Volume 2: January–November 1947* (Jerusalem: Publishing House of the World Zionist Organization, 1998), pp. 408–09; Elias Sasson, *Baderekh el Hashalom: Igrot Vesihot* (Tel Aviv: Am Oved, 1978), p. 374; Cairo to Foreign Office, July 6, 1946, FO 141/1117.

9. Beirut to Foreign Office, June 13, 1946, FO 371/52314; Egypt to Foreign Office, June 21, 28, 1948, FO 141/1117; "The Mufti in Cairo" & "The Mufti in Egypt," *Times,* June 20, 21, 1946.

10. Campbell (Alexandria) to Foreign Office, Sept. 16, 1946, *ibid.*

11. Amman to Cairo, Oct. 26, 1946, FO 141/1091; report by the General Headquarters, Middle East Land Forces (Cairo) on the "People's Arab League," Nov. 8, 1946, FO 141/1084; Tene, "In the Arab Camp: News Summary," Nov. 22 & Dec. 31, 1946, IDFA 2004/535/479.

12. Foreign Office, Research Department, "The Activities of the Arab League from its Formation in March 1945 to 15th May 1948," Sept. 30, 1948, FO 371/68322, p. 4; Sasson to Shertok, Dec. 1, 2, 1946, S25/63; "Activities of the Arab Higher Committee since its Establishment (June 12, 1946)," HA 105/69, pp. 26–45; Tene, "In the Arab Camp: News Summary," Nov. 27, 1946, IDFA 2004/535/479.

13. The Arab League's November 1945 reconstitution of the AHC proved stillborn as the Palestinian factions continued their infighting, and in June 1946 the Bludan summit formed a new five-member AHC, with Hajj Amin as president, Jamal Husseini as vice-president, and Hussein Khalidi as secretary. The other two members were Emile Ghouri and Ahmad Hilmi.

	For the November 1945 AHC, see: "Arab Political News: League Delegation Secures Preliminary Agreement on Higher Committee," Nov. 21, 1945, pp. 1–2, S25/9229; Darwaza, *Hawla,* Vol. 5, pp. 39–40; "Arab Talks on Mr. Bevin's Statement," *Times,* Nov. 17, 1945; "Arab Envoys Gather in Jerusalem" & "New Committee in the Making" & "Mardam Reports New Committee" & "Local Delegates to Arab League," *Palestine Post,* Nov. 18, 21, 23, 26, 1945.

	For the June 1946 AHC, see: "Arab Political News: Higher Committee Members Not Yet Reconciled," Jan. 8, 1946, p. 4, S25/9229; "Dissension in the Higher Arab Committee," Feb. 27, 1946, p. 2, *ibid.*; "Arab Political News: The Higher Committee," Mar. 20, 1946, pp. 1–2, *ibid.*; "Arab Political News: Reform of the Higher Committee," Mar. 27, 1946, pp. 1–2, *ibid.*; "Arab Political News: The Arab Higher Committee," Apr. 3, 1946, pp. 1–3, *ibid.*; "Arab Political News: The Cleavage in the Arab Higher Committee," Apr. 10, 1946, pp. 1–2, *ibid.*; "Arab Differences in Palestine" & "The Mufti Leaves France" & "Mufti's Flight to Cairo" & "The Mufti in Cairo" & "The Mufti's Escape" & "The Mufti in Egypt," *Times,* May 29 & June 10, 13, 20, 21, 1946; "Jamal Asks Withdrawal of British Troops" & "Rival Arab Political Organization Formed," *Palestine Post,* May 26 & June 4, 1946; "The Bludan Resolutions," *Meahorei Hapargod,* p. 40.

14. Sasson to Shertok, Dec. 3, 1946, S25/63.

15. Jamal Husseini's interview with *al-Musawwar* (Cairo), Dec. 27, 1946 & *al-Wahda*, Dec. 30, 1946, HA 105/358, p. 122. For the Husseini efforts to gain control over the Palestinian Arabs, see: Tene, "In the Arab Camp: News Summary," Nov. 12, 22, 27, 1946, Dec. 10, 17, 1946, Jan. 15, 30, 1947, Feb. 25, 1947, IDFA 2004/535/479; Armon, "The Najada," Sept. 15, 1946, HA 105/69, pp. 46–52; "Fortnightly Intelligence Newsletter No. 39," issued by HQ British Troops in Palestine (for period Mar. 29–Apr. 11, 1947), WO 275/64; "Fortnightly Intelligence Newsletter No. 41," issued by HQ British Troops in Palestine (for period Apr. 26–May 9, 1947), *ibid.*

16. See, for example, Dr. Nahum Goldman, "Address before the Executive of the Jewish Agency," Paris, Aug. 3, 1946 & "Political Resolutions of JAE Meeting," Aug. 4, 1946 & "Meeting of the Executive of the Jewish Agency," Aug. 5, 1946 & "Dr. Goldman's Mission to Washington," Aug. 5, 1946 & JAE Meeting of Aug. 13, 1946, Morning Session, all in BGA.

17. "The Zionist Case," *Times*, Dec. 27, 1946; Ben-Gurion to Bevin, Feb. 14, 1947, *Political Documents: Volume 2*, pp. 197–98.

18. "Long-Term Policy in Palestine. Memorandum by the Secretary of State for the Colonies," July 8, 1946, CAB 129/11; "Short Minutes of Meeting Held at the Colonial Office on Jan. 29th, 1947, at 2.30 p.m." & "Short Minutes of Meeting at the Colonial Office on Monday, 3rd February, 1947, at 3 p.m." & "Short Minutes of Meeting at the Colonial Office on Thursday, February 6th, 1947, at 5 p.m." & "Short Minutes of Meeting at the Colonial Office on Monday, February 10th, 1947, at 4.30 p.m." & "Meeting between the Right Honourable Ernest Bevin and Mr. Ben-Gurion, Foreign Office, 12th February, 1947, 9.45 a.m." & "Short Minutes of Meeting at the Colonial Office on Thursday, February 13th, 1947, at 3.10 p.m." & "Short Note of Conversation with the Lord Chancellor, House of Lords, Thursday, February 13th, 1947, at 9.15 p.m." & "Short Minutes of Meeting at the Colonial Office on Wednesday, February 19th, 1947, at 4 p.m." & "Short Note of Conversation between Mr. Shertok and Mr. Creech Jones, Thursday, February 20th, 1947, at 1 p.m." & "Short Minute of Meeting with Mr. Creech Jones, Wednesday, 26th February, 1947, at 4 p.m. at the House of Commons" & "Short Minutes of Meeting at the Colonial Office on Thursday, February 27th, 1947, at 6 p.m.," all in BGA. See also Eliahu Elath, *Hamaavak al Hamedina, Washington 1945–1948* (Tel Aviv: Am Oved & The Zionist Library, 1979), Vol. 1, pp. 368, 400.

19. "Palestine," *House of Commons* (Government Policy), Feb. 25, 1947, PREM 8/627, Part 6. See also: "New Approach to Palestine" & "Basis of British Decision on Palestine," *Times*, Feb. 19, 1947.

20. Trygve Lie, *In the Cause of Peace: Seven Years with the United Nations* (New York: Macmillan, 1954), pp. 162–63; David Horowitz, *State in the Making* (New York: Knopf, 1953), p. 143; Cunningham to Creech Jones, Mar. 25, 1948, Cunningham Papers, III/2.

21. "Mufti of Jerusalem Warns of Bloodshed," *New York Times*, Sept. 11, 1947; "Top Secret: Hajj Amin Eff. El Husseini," Sept. 21, 1947, KV 2/2091.

22. Amram, "Oral Report from the Meetings of the Political Committee in Sofar," Oct. 1, 1947, S25/9020; Maimon to Shimoni and Zaslani, Sept. 14, 1947, S25/9013; Foreign Office, Research Department, "The Activities of the Arab League," pp. 4–5; *Meahorei Hapargod*, Annexes 8–10, pp. 49–53; Tene, "Sofar's Secret Resolutions," Sept. 28, 1947, IDFA 2004/535/479; Beirut to Foreign Office, Sept. 16, 17, 19, 20, 25, 1947, FO 371/61529; Baghdad to Foreign Office, Sept. 24, 1947, *ibid.*; Amman to Foreign Office, Sept. 14, 24, 1947, *ibid.*; I.O.C, N.Y., "Palestine: Attitude of the Arab States," Sept. 24, 1947, FO 371/61530; Taha al-Hashemi, *Mudhakkirat Taha al-Hashemi. Vol. 2 – 1942–1955* (Beirut: Dar al-Tali'a li-l-Taba'a wa-l-Nashr, 1978), p. 157 (diary entry for Oct. 14, 1947); Darwaza, *Hawla*, Vol. 5, pp. 98–101; Bayan Nuwaihid al-Hut, *al-Qiyadat wa-l-Muasasat al-Siyasiyya fi Filastin 1917–1948* (Beirut: Muasassat al-Dirasat al-Filastiniyya, 1986), pp. 571–72.

23. United Nations, "Official Record of the Second Session of the General Assembly. Ad Hoc Committee on the Palestinian Question, Summary Records of Meetings, 25 September–25 November 1947" (Lake Success, New York, 1947), pp. 3–4; Jamil

Mardam to Fares Khuri, Oct. 31, 1947, S25/9020; *Meahorei Hapargod,* p. 54; "The Activities of the Arab League," p. 5; Tene, "In the Arab Camp: News Summary," Oct. 19, 1947, IDFA 2004/535/479; Beirut to Foreign Office, Oct. 10, 16, 1947, FO 371/61530; Baghdad to Foreign Office, Oct. 14, 1947, *ibid.*; Beirut to Cairo, Oct. 8, 12, 16, 1947, FO 141/1186; Darwaza, *Hawla,* Vol. 5, pp. 101–07; al-Hut, *al-Qiyadat,* p. 573.

24. Beirut to Foreign Office, Oct. 12, 1947, FO 371/61530; Beirut to Cairo, Oct. 11, 1947, FO 141/1233; "Passage from the Minutes of the Third Meeting of the Arab League's Regular Sixth Session," Mar. 23, 1947, S25/9020.

25. See, for example, "The Riots in Tripolitania," Nov. 11, 1945, BGA.

26. "Official Record of the Second Session of the General Assembly," pp. 185, 200–01.

27. UN General Assembly Special Session on Palestine, "Fifty-Fifth Meeting, Held at Lake Success, New York, on Monday, 12 May 1947, at 3 p.m.," p. 272.

28. *Ibid.,* pp. 10, 30–31, 66–67, 80–81, 101, 200–01.

29. Radio Beirut, Nov. 12, 1947, in Foreign Broadcasts Information Service (FBIS), European Section: Near & Middle East and North African Transmitters, Nov. 13, 1947, II2; Radio Damascus, Nov. 20, 24, 1947, FBIS, Nov. 21, II2 & Nov. 25, 1947, II1; Radio al-Sharq al-Adna (Jaffa), Nov. 3, 1947, FBIS, Nov. 4, 1947, II2. See also: Radio Beirut, Nov. 9, 27, 1947, FBIS, Nov. 10, 1947, II1 & Nov. 28, 1947, II2; Radio Damascus, Oct. 27, 1947, in BBC, *Summary of World Broadcasts: Western Europe, Middle East, Far East and Americas* (hereinafter SWB), Part III, No. 23, Oct. 30, 1947, p. 54; *ibid.,* Oct. 31, 1947, SWB, Part III, No. 24, Nov. 6, 1947, p. 50.

30. Protocol of the JAE Meeting of May 22, 1947.

31. See, for example, Sasson to Sharef, Aug. 9, 1946 & N. Goldman to E. Bevin, Aug. 19, 1946 & "Report on Meetings in Egypt," Aug. 29, 1946 & "Meeting: E. Sasson-Sidqi Pasha," Sept. 3, 1946 & "Memorandum by E. Sasson," Sept. 23, 1946 & "Meeting: E. Sasson-I.N. Clayton (Cairo)," Sept. 8, 1946 & "Meeting: E. Sasson-I. Sidqi Pasha," Sept. 16, 1946 & "Memorandum by E. Sasson," Sept. 23, 1946, in *Political Documents: Volume 1,* pp. 508–21, 538–39, 554–57, 575–77, 584–87, 601–03, 618–21; Sasson, *Baderekh,* pp. 364–66, 373–74; Ismail Sidqi, *Mudhakkarati* (Cairo: n.p., 1950); Cairo to Foreign Office, Sept. 17, 1946, FO 141/1090; Clayton to Smart, Aug. 13, 30, 1946, FO 141/1090; Cairo to Foreign Office, Aug. 29 & Sept. 2, 1946, *ibid.*; Foreign Office to Cairo, Aug. 19, 1948, FO 141/1091.

32. Elath, *Hamaavak,* Vol. 2, p. 204–06; Shertok to Epstein, July 14, 1947 & "Meeting: A. Eban and D. Horowitz – E.F. Sandstrom (Geneva, Aug. 1, 1947)," *Political Documents: Volume 2,* pp. 452, 504–05; Baghdad to Ankara, Apr. 21, 1947, FO 371/61524.

33. Epstein, "Conversation with Abdel Rahman Azzam"; Elath, *Hamaavak,* Vol. 2, p. 128.

34. A. S. Eban to the Executive of the Jewish Agency, "Conversation with Abdul Rahman Azzam, 15th September 1947," Sept. 29, 1947, S25/9020; Horowitz, *State in the Making,* pp. 231–35; Shertok to Meyerson, Sept. 7, 1947 & Sharef to Shertok, Sept. 11, 1947, *Political Documents: Volume 2,* pp. 631, 651.

35. Ezra Danin, "Conversation with Abdullah, 17.11.47," S25/4004; Sasson to Shertok, Nov. 20, 1947, S25/1699; Golda Meyerson's verbal report to the Provisional State Council on May 12, 1948, Israel State Archives, *Provisional State Council: Protocols, 18 April–13 May 1948* (Jerusalem: Israel Government Publishing House, 1978), pp. 40–41.

36. Translation of a letter from Abdullah to the Iraqi regent, Nov. 29, 1947, FO 816/111.

37. Hashemi, *Mudhakkirat,* Vol. 2, p. 156 (diary entry for Oct. 13, 1947); Hazza al-Majali, *Mudhakkirati* (Amman: al-Tab'a al-Ula, 1960), p. 63; *al-Sharq al-Adna,* Oct. 26, 1947, SWB, Part III, No. 23, Oct. 30, 1947, p. 53.

38. See below pp. 195–96.

39. Hashemi, *Mudhakkirat,* Vol. 2, pp. 152–61, 166, 169 (diary entries for Oct. 4, 13, 14, 15, 16 & Nov. 3, 8, 16, 1947).

40. "Fortnightly Intelligence Newsletter No. 55," issued by HQ British Troops in Palestine (for the period Nov. 8–21, 1947), Nov. 22, 1947, WO 275/64; "Tene News – Daily Precis," Nov. 16, 1947, IDFA 1952/900/58.

41. Hashemi, *Mudhakkirat*, Vol. 2, pp. 165–66, 170–73 (diary entries for Nov. 8, 21, 29, 1947); "Biographical Material on Sami Taha," Sept. 25, 1944, S25/9228a; "In the Arab Camp: News Summary," Sept. 14, 28 & Oct. 8, 19, 24 & Nov. 2, 9, 16, 23, 1947, IDFA 2004/535/479; *al-Sharq al-Adna*, Oct. 24, 1947, SWB, Part III, No. 23, Oct. 30, 1947, p. 52; Sixth Airborne Division, "Weekly Intelligence Review," No. 137, issued Nov. 14, 1947, WO 275/120; "Fortnightly Intelligence Newsletter No. 54," issued by HQ British Troops in Palestine, Nov. 8, 1947, WO 275/64; "Fortnightly Intelligence Newsletter No. 55," issued by HQ British Troops in Palestine (for the period Nov. 8–21, 1947), Nov. 22, 1947, *ibid.*

42. For Sasson's meetings with Abdullah, see: Sharif to Linton, Aug. 13, 1946, S25/9035; Correspondence between Sasson and Shertok (then detained in Latrun), Aug. 11–Sept. 10, 1946, S25/3959; Sasson to Shertok, Aug. 12, 19, 1946, S25/9036; Sasson, *Baderekh*, pp. 367–72; *al-Wahda*, Aug. 20, 1946; *Barada* (Damascus), Oct. 9, 1946; WGT to Agronsky, "Confidential," S25/9035.

Chapter 5: Kingdoms are Established over Dead Bodies and Skulls

1. GSO 1 (Ops), "Log of Events" Nov. 30, 1947, Sheets 213–16, Stockwell Collection, Liddell Hart Military Archives, King's College London; Sixth Airborne Division, "Riot at Acre Gaol – 30 Nov 47," WO 275/61; 01203 to Tene, "The Attack on the Buses" & "Attack on Egged Bus on the Petach Tikva-Lydda Road on 30.11.47," Dec. 2, 1947 & Tiroshi, "The Attack on the Buses Near Petach Tivka on 30.11," Dec. 3, 1947, IDFA 1949/481/62; "7 Jews Murdered" & "Prisoners Attacked," *Palestine Post*, Dec. 1, 1947.

2. "List of [Jewish] Fatalities," Feb. 27, 1948, BGA; "Third Jewish State," *Times*, Dec. 1, 1947. See also: Zeev Sharef, *Three Days* (London: W. H. Allen, 1962), p. 37; High Commissioner for Palestine to Secretary of State for the Colonies, "Weekly Intelligence Appreciation," Jan. 3, 1948, Cunningham Papers, Middle East Centre, St Antony's College, Oxford University.

3. Golda Meyerson's report to the JAE meeting of Dec. 7, 1947, CZA, pp. 12718–19; Information Office (Jerusalem) to Hagana Members in Jerusalem, "What Happened in the Jerusalem Commercial Center," Dec. 10, 1947, HA 105/61, pp. 27–28; GSO 1 (Ops), "Log of Events" Dec. 3, 1947, Sheet No. 227; "Arab Mob Loots, Burns and Stabs," *Palestine Post*, Dec. 3, 1947; "Arab Riots in Jerusalem," *Times*, Dec. 3, 1947; Richard Graves, *Experiment in Anarchy* (London: Victor Gollancz, 1949), p. 102; Yona Cohen, *Jerusalem under Siege: Pages from a 1948 Diary* (Los Angeles: Ridgefield, 1982), p. 42; Ben-Zion Dinur (general editor), *Sefer Toldot Hahagana. Vol. 3, Part 2: Memaavak Lemilhama* (written by Yehuda Slotzky) (Jerusalem & Tel Aviv: The Zionist Library & Ministry of Defense Publishing House, 1972), p. 1372.

4. "From Today's News," Dec. 2, 1947, HA 105/61, pp. 7–8; "Protocol of the Histadrut's Executive Committee Meeting of Dec. 10, 1947," pp. 9–10, BGA; Agam/Matkal, "Annex to Circular No. 2: Lessons of Enemy Actions from 1.1.48 to 20.1.48," IDFA 1949/481/23; "Diary of the Trials and Tribulations of Tel-Aviv and its Environs," based on newspaper clippings from Nov. 29 1947–May 13, 1948, IA, K4-8/1; Uri Milstein, *History of Israel's War of Independence. Vol. II: The First Month* (Lanham: University Press of America, 1997), p. 72; Yossef Olitski, *Mimeoraot Lemilhama: Prakim Betoldot Hahagana al Tel Aviv* (Tel Aviv: Hagana Headquarters, 1949), p. 210; Dinur, *Sefer. Vol. 3, Part 2*, pp. 1376–78.

5. David Ben-Gurion, *Yoman Hamilhama Tashah-Tashat* (Tel Aviv: Ministry of Defense Publishing House, 1982), Vol. 1, p. 63 (entry for Dec. 22, 1947).

6. David Ben-Gurion, *Bamaaraha* (Tel-Aviv: Mapai Publishing House, 1949), Vol. 4, Part 2, p. 278.

7. Milstein, *History. Vol. II*, pp. 118–19.

8. "Fortnightly Intelligence Newsletter No. 57," issued by HQ British Troops in Palestine (for the period Dec. 6–2359 hrs- Dec. 18, 1947), Dec. 20, 1947, WO 275/64; Ben-Gurion, *Yoman Hamilhama*, Vol. 1, p. 67 (entry for Dec. 23, 1947); Tene, "Daily

News," Dec. 8, 1947, BGA; Dinur, *Sefer. Vol. 3, Part 2*, p. 1431; "Darkening Scene in Palestine," *Times*, Dec. 10, 1947; "Many Dead in Palestine," *Times*, Dec. 15, 1947.

9. Ben-Gurion, *Yoman Hamilhama*, Vol. 1, p. 77 (entry for Dec. 27, 1947); Tene, "Report on Clashes in Kfar Uriya on Jan. 11, 1948," BGA; Hatzer 1, "Daily Events," Jan. 11 & Feb. 2, 1948, IDFA 1949/8275/127; "Tene News-Daily Summary," Jan. 15, 1948, HA 105/61a, p. 68; Hagana Operational Directorate, "Logbook of the War of Independence, 3.1.48–14.5.48," IDFA, 1954/464/2, pp. 52, 62–63.

10. "Logbook of the War of Independence," pp. 71–72, 77, 78, 79a–83, 94–95; Tene News, "The Etzion Bloc Battles," Jan. 20, 1948, HA 105/61a, p. 96; Hatzer 1, "Daily Events," Jan. 14, 17, 18, 1948, IDFA 1949/8275/127; "The Mood in Hebron," Jan. 21, 1948, IDFA 1948/500/60; Tene, "Events in the Negev," Jan. 26, 1948, IDFA 1975/922/1110; untitled intelligence report, Jan. 21, 1948, IDFA 1949/2504/15; Dinur, *Sefer. Vol. 3, Part 2*, pp. 1431–32; Lt. General G. H. A. MacMillan, "Palestine: Narrative of Events from February 1947 until Withdrawal of All British Troops," Appendices Maps, Stockwell Collection, 6/25/2, pp. 22; "The Massacre of the Hebron Jews Was Avenged in Kfar Etzion," *Haboker*, Feb. 4, 1948.

11. See, for example, "The Arab World. Diary of Events 9.12.1947–21.12.1947," BGA; "Arab Riots in Jerusalem," *Times*, Dec. 3, 1947; "Riots in Aleppo. Synagogues, Houses Burn," *Palestine Post*, Dec. 2, 1947; "Riots in Egypt in Spite of Ban," *Palestine Post*, Dec. 5, 1947; "75 Jews, Arabs Dead in Aden," *ibid.*, Dec. 7, 1947; "Baghdad Protest March," *Times*, Dec. 3, 1947; Norman A. Stillman, *The Jews of Arab Lands in Modern Times* (Philadelphia: Jewish Publications Society, 1991), pp. 147–48. For Azzam's speech (on Dec. 4, 1947), see Ibrahim Shakib, *Harb Filastin 1948: Ru'ya Misriya* (Cairo: al-Zahra li-l-I'lam al-Arabi, 1976), p. 63.

12. H.M. Minister, Amman, to Foreign Office, London, Dec. 21, 1947, FO 816/111. See also "From British Middle East Office, Cairo, to Foreign Office," Dec. 12, 1947, FO 371/62226: "Note on Proceedings of the Meeting of the Arab Premiers in Cairo. Dec 8th to 17th 1947," FO 371/68364; I. Clayton, "Conference of Arab Prime Ministers-December 1947," FO 141/1246.

13. In addition, a national garrison force was to oversee the defense of the cities. See Ismail Safwat, "Forming the Forces and Defining their Operational Zones and Fronts," Jan. 1, 1948, HA 8/230.

14. For the text of the Cairo Summit's decisions, see *Meahorei Hapargod* (Hebrew ed. of an official report by an Iraqi parliamentary committee on the 1948 war, published in Sept. 1949) (Tel Aviv: Maarachot, 1954), pp. 55–56. See also Arif Arif, *al-Nakba: Nakbat Bait al-Maqdis wa-l-Firdaws al-Mafqud* (Beirut: al-Maktaba al-Asriya, 1956), Vol. 1, pp. 33–37; Taha al-Hashemi, *Mudhakkirat Taha al-Hashemi. Vol. 2–1942–1955* (Beirut: Dar al-Tali'a li-l-Taba'a wa-l-Nashr, 1978), pp. 180–84, 200–02 (diary entries for Dec. 21–24, 27, 1947, Feb. 4–5, 1948); Sasson to Shertok, report on the Arab League's summit, Dec. 20, 1947, in Israel State Archives, World Zionist Organization, Central Zionist Archives, *Political and Diplomatic Documents. December 1947–May 1948* (Jerusalem: Government Printer, 1979), pp. 90–91; Ben-Gurion, *Yoman Hamilhama*, Vol. 1, pp. 65–66 (entry for Dec. 22, 1947); "The Arab World. Diary of Events 9.12.1947–21.12.1947," BGA; High Commissioner for Palestine to Secretary of State for the Colonies, "Weekly Intelligence Appreciation," Feb. 14, 1948, Cunningham Papers; "Arab League War Council," *Times*, Dec. 18, 1947; "Arabs Considering British Proposal," *Palestine Post*, Dec. 15, 1947; "Arab League Council Meeting Ends Today," *Palestine Post*, Dec. 16, 1947; "Communiqué Is Moderate," *ibid.*, Dec. 19, 1947.

15. High Commissioner for Palestine to Secretary of State for the Colonies, Dec. 28, 1947, Cunningham Papers, Middle East Centre, St Antony's College, Oxford University.

16. High Commissioner for Palestine to Secretary of State for the Colonies, "Weekly Intelligence Appreciation," Jan. 16 & 24, 1948, Feb. 1, 7, & 21, 1948, Mar. 20, Apr. 17, 1948, Cunningham Papers; High Commissioner for Palestine to UKDEL, Mar. 11, 1948, No. 666, Cunningham Papers, III/2/20–21; MacMillan, "Palestine," pp. 20, 22, 23, 25, 26, 27, 28, 29; Hagana Operational Directorate, "Logbook of the War of

Independence, 3.1.48–14.5.48," pp. 92, 99, 100, 106, 112, 123, 136; Tene to Yadin,
"The Arab Liberation Army," Feb. 13, 1948, IDFA 1975/922/1110; Tene News,
Jan. 24–29, 1948, Feb. 2–3, 8, 1948, HA 105/61a, pp. 121–27, 132, 137, 140, 153,
161, 170; Tene News, Apr. 1, 4, 1948, HA 105/62, pp. 8, 22; Tene News, Feb. 3, 15,
23, 25, 1948, Mar. 1, 10, 14, 25, 1948, Apr. 5, 1948, HA 105/62a, pp. 2, 18, 59, 75,
94, 127, 139, 155, 174; "Invasion of Foreign Fighters of Palestine," Apr. 15, 1948, IDFA
1969/661/36; "The Arab Liberation Army," Feb. 13, 1948, S25/3999; Don Burke,
Dispatch 3 (from Damascus), Mar. 6, 1948, S25/5635.

17. Hagana Operational Directorate, "Logbook of the War of Independence, 3.1.48–14.5.48,"
pp. 96–102, 105–06, 155–60; Hatzer 1, "Events of the Day," Jan. 20, 1948, IDFA
1949/8275/127 & Tene News, Jan. 24–26, 1948, HA 105/61a, p. 124; "Fortnightly
Intelligence Newsletter No. 60," issued by HQ British Troops in Palestine (for the period
2359 hrs, Jan. 14–2359 hrs, Jan. 28, 1948), Jan. 30, 1948, WO 275/64, p. 4; High
Commissioner for Palestine to Secretary of State for the Colonies, "Weekly Intelligence
Appreciation," Jan. 16 & 24, 1948, Cunningham Papers.

18. "Fortnightly Intelligence Newsletter No. 62," issued by HQ British Troops in Palestine
(for the period 2359 hrs, Feb. 11–2359 hrs, Feb. 25, 1948), Feb. 27, 1948, WO 275/64,
pp. 1, 4; Hatzer 1, "Events of the Day, Feb. 16, 17, 1948 & "Weekly Review," Feb. 21,
1948, IDFA 1949/8275/127; MacMillan, "Palestine," pp. 21, 23, 26; Commander of
the 2nd company, Yarmuq Battalion, "Administrative Order No. 7," Feb. 26, 1948,
IDFA, 1975/922/648; Fauzi al-Qawuqji, "Memoirs, 1948. Part I," *Journal of Palestine
Studies*, Vol. 1, No. 4 (summer 1972), pp. 35–36.

19. Ben-Gurion, *Bamaaraha*, Vol. 4, Part 2, pp. 136–37; Ben-Gurion, "Security" (address to
the Zionist Executive Committee, Zurich), Aug. 26, 1947, BGA.

20. David Ben-Gurion, "The Hagana Covenant," June 18, 1947 (and a slightly different
version of the same date, "Our Defense"), BGA; Dinur, *Sefer*. Vol. 3, Part 2, p. 1338.

21. "Jerusalem Dressed in Blue and White" & "Yishuv Celebrates Jewish State Decision,"
Palestine Post, Dec. 1, 1947.

22. *Davar*, Dec. 3, 1947.

23. Michael Asaf, "The Egyptian Demonstrations," *Davar*, Dec. 12, 1947. See also Asaf,
"Summing Up the League's Position," *ibid.*, Dec. 26, 1947.

24. David Ben-Gurion's address to the representative council, Nov. 25, 1947, BGA (a somewhat shorter English version was published in the monthly *Palestine and Middle East*,
Vol. XIX, Nos. 10–11, Nov.–Dec. 1947, BGA).

25. Sasson to Azzam, Dec. 5, 1947, *Political and Diplomatic Documents*, pp. 27–30.

26. See, for example, Protocol of the Situation Committee's meetings on Nov. 24 and
Dec. 22, 1947, BGA; Protocol of the Subordinate Committee C meetings on Dec. 1, 2,
22, 1947, *ibid.*; Secretariat of Subordinate Committee B, "Proposal for the
Establishment of Police in the Hebrew State," Dec. 31, 1947, *ibid.*

27. "Jews and Arabs Will Be Equal Citizens in Jewish State," *Palestine Post*, Dec. 1, 1947. See
also: David Ben-Gurion's address to the Histadrut's Executive Committee on Dec. 3,
1947, BGA (published on the same day by *Haaretz*); Ben-Gurion, "On the Founding of
the State," *Hapoel Hatzair*, Vol. 10, No. 13 (Dec. 16, 1947), pp. 1–15.

28. HA 14/27; "Fortnightly Intelligence Newsletter No. 56," issued by HQ British Troops
in Palestine (for the period Nov. 22–Dec. 5, 1947), Dec. 6, 1947, WO 275/64, p. 1;
Protocol of the Meeting of the Histadrut's Executive Committee, Dec. 10, 1947, p. 8,
BGA; Protocol of the JAE Meeting on Dec. 9, 1947, p. 12740, CZA; Ben-Gurion,
Yoman Hamilhama, Vol. 1, pp. 27–28 (entry for Dec. 9, 1947); "Meeting of the Security
Committee," Tel Aviv, Dec. 18, 1947, BGA.

29. Ben-Gurion, *Yoman Hamilhama*, Vol. 1, pp. 77, 97 (entries for Dec. 27, 1947 & Jan. 1,
1948, fn. 3); "Protocol of the Meeting on Arab Affairs, January 1–2, 1948," Hakibbutz
Hameuhad Archive, Ramat-Efal, Israel, Galili Section, Box 45, File 1–4, pp. 51–52; "For
our Members in the Bases, Bulletin No. 15," Dec. 10, 1947, HA 105/61, p. 24; 01227
to Tene, "For our Members in the Bases, Bulletin No. 17," Dec. 11, 1947, *ibid.*,
pp. 39–41; "A Retaliatory Action in the Qazaza Village," Dec. 22, 1947, IDFA

1949/481/62; "To our Members – Daily Information Bulletin: A Reply to Queries" (regarding the Khasas tragedy), Jan. 2, 1948, HA 105/61, p. 141; "Information Bulletin No. 28," Dec. 28, 1947, HA 57/109 (Beit Sureiq raid).

30. According to a report by the *Palestine Post*'s Haifa correspondent, the Arab workers in the refinery had already set upon their Jewish colleagues before the IZL bombing (Sakran to Tene, Dec. 31, 1947, IDFA 1949/481/62). This claim was amplified by an IZL radio broadcast on Jan. 4, 1948, which pointed out that prior to the bombing Armenian workers at the plant had warned their Jewish friends of an imminent attack, and some Jewish workers took notice and left the place before the massacre. The broadcast also noted the pre-positioning of cold arms throughout the plant and the fact that the massacres ensued in the farthest corner of the refinery, some 3 km (2 miles) from the bombing, where the explosion could not be heard. See David Niv, *Maarachot Hairgun Hatzvai Haleumi* (Tel Aviv: Hadar, 1980), Vol. 6, pp. 19–20.

For contemporary reports on the massacre, see: "Report of the Commission of Inquiry on the Haifa Refinery's Disaster (Dec. 30, 1947), Jan. 25, 1948," HA 80/460/11; "The Refinery Massacre," HA 80/460/11; "Information Bulletin," No. 30, Dec. 30, 1947, HA 105/61, p. 117; "To our Members – Daily Information Bulletin," Dec. 31, 1947, HA 105/61, p. 126.

31. From the Moetza to the Knesset, "Report on the Balad al-Sheik Retaliation," Jan. 6, 1948, HA 100/61.

32. High Commissioner for Palestine to Secretary of State for the Colonies, "Weekly Intelligence Appreciation," Jan. 3, 1948, Cunningham Papers.

33. David Ben-Gurion, *Behilahem Israel* (Tel Aviv: Mapai Publishing House, 1951; 3rd ed.), pp. 23–24.

34. "Protocol of the Meeting on Arab Affairs, January 1–2, 1948," p. 36; "To our Members – Daily Information Bulletin No. 21," Haifa, Jan. 2, 1948, HA 105/61, p. 140.

35. High Commissioner for Palestine to Secretary of State for the Colonies, "Notes of an Interview with Mr. Ben-Gurion, 6th January 1948," Cunningham Papers; Protocol of the JAE Meeting of Jan. 6, 1948, p. 12409, CZA; *Meahorei Hapargod*, p. 101; Arif, *al-Nakba*, Vol. 1, pp. 138–39.

36. Ben-Gurion, *Bamaaraha*, Vol. 4, Part II, pp. 283–84, 286–87, 302–03; Hagana broadcast in Arabic, Mar. 16 & 18, 1948, *BBC Summary of World Broadcasts: Western Europe, Middle East, Far East and Americas* (SWB), No. 43, Mar. 25, 1948, Part III, p. 68.

37. "Summary Report of a Meeting between a Hagana Representative and Fawzi K on April 1, 1948," ISA, Hetz 364/3; "A Meeting with Fawzi Qawuqji in Nir Shams – 1.4.48," Apr. 4, 1948, BGA; Dr. Matzliah, "Meeting of Jews with Qawuqji," Apr. 3, 1948, BGA; Zafrira Din, "Interview with Josh Palmon on June 28, 1989," HA 80/721/3; Ben-Gurion, *Yoman Hamilhama*, Vol. 1, p. 330 (diary entry for Mar. 31, 1948); Larry Collins and Dominique Lapierre, *O Jerusalem* (London: Pan Books, 1973), p. 237.

In his memoirs, Qawuqji gives a fictional account of the meeting, substituting Palmon for a delegation of oriental Jews from a number of localities who allegedly came to his camp "with a view to surrendering, so as to obtain our protection." According to him, the Jews accepted the surrender terms and departed to inform their colleagues, after which they were to return and place themselves under ALA protection. In the end, nothing came out of the episode since "the Jewish Agency in Tel Aviv got wind of the meeting and took disciplinary measures against those who attended it" (Qawuqji, "Memoirs, 1948. Part I," p. 35).

38. Ehud to Carmeli, "Report on an Attack on an Arms Convoy and Arab Commanders on Mar. 17, 1948," Mar. 19, 1948, IDFA 1949/815/1.

39. For a first-hand account of the Nebi Daniel battle passed to Ben-Gurion, see Aharon Gilad, "Notes Made in the Course of Fighting," Mar. 27, 1948, BGA; for Arab accounts, see: "Report on the Kfar Etzion Convoy" & "Annexes A & B: Report on the Kfar Etzion Convoy," Apr. 4, 1948, IDFA 1948/550/55; Arif, *al-Nakba*, Vol. 1, pp. 141–44. See also: Hagana Operational Directorate, "Logbook of the War of Independence," pp. 228–32, 234, 236 & "Events of the Day," Mar. 28, Apr. 1, 1948, IDFA 1949/8275/127 (Gush Etzion, Yehiam, and Hulda & convoys); undated report by commander of the Yarmuq

battalion on the Yehiam attack, IDFA 1975/922/648; "Fortnightly Intelligence Newsletter No. 65," issued by HQ British Troops in Palestine (for the period 2359 hrs, Mar. 23–2359 hrs, Apr. 7, 1948), Apr. 9, 1948, WO 275/64, pp. 2–3.

40. Etzioni to Amitai, Mar. 28, 1948, IDFA 1948/500/48; Yavne to Tene, Mar. 29, 1948, *ibid.*; Golan to Amitai, Mar. 29, 1948, *ibid.*; Haim Solomon to JAE, Mar. 29, 1948, *ibid.* See also High Commissioner for Palestine to Secretary of State for the Colonies, Apr. 3, 1948, Cunningham Papers, III/3.

41. Ben-Gurion, *Bamaaraha*, Vol. 4, Part II, p. 288.

42. "An Analysis of the Palestine Situation, Apr. 1948," Cunningham Papers, IV/5/33.

43. David Shaltiel to Amitai, Dan, Hillel and Yadin, Mar. 28, 1948, BGA. See also Leo Kohn's letter to Ben-Gurion, Mar. 29, 1948, *ibid.*; "Irgun Communal Circular No. 47," IA, K4-12/1/31, Apr. 2, 1948.

44. David McCullough, *Truman* (New York: Simon & Schuster 1992), p. 597.

45. Dinur, *Sefer. Vol. 3, Part 2*, p. 1456.

46. Ben-Gurion, *Yoman Hamilhama*, Vol. 1, pp. 330–31 (diary entry for Mar. 31, 1948).

47. *Ibid.*, p. 349 (diary entry for Apr. 14, 1948); Arif, *al-Nakba*, Vol. 1, pp. 158–60.

48. "Fortnightly Intelligence Newsletter No. 61," issued by HQ British Troops in Palestine (for the period 2359 hrs, Jan. 28–2359 hrs, Feb. 11, 1948), Feb. 13, 1948, WO 275/64, p. 4. See also pp. 178–79 below.

49. "Arab News Items," Apr. 8 & 12, 1948, IDFA 1948/500/55; "Fortnightly Intelligence Newsletter No. 61," issued by HQ British Troops in Palestine (for the period 2359 hrs, Jan. 28–2359 hrs, Feb. 11, 1948), Feb. 13, 1948, WO 275/64, p. 4; "Fortnightly Intelligence Newsletter No. 66," issued by HQ British Troops in Palestine (for the period 2359 hrs, Apr. 7–2359 hrs, Apr. 19, 1948), Apr. 21, 1948, WO 275/64, p. 1.

50. Thus according to "a serious Arab report" a day after the event ("Deir Yasin," Apr. 10, 1948, IDFA 1949/2605/6 & Yavne, "Arab News Items," Apr. 10, 1948, IDFA 1948/500/55). The Palestinian Arab historian Arif Arif puts the number of dead at 110. The public figure mentioned at the time of the event, however, was more than twice as high. See Arif, *al-Nakba*, p. 173.

51. Arif concedes the occurrence of heavy fighting. He claims that the villagers killed more than 100 Jewish fighters (the actual figure was 4 dead and 32 wounded), but alleges that only seven of the 110 Arab fatalities were killed in action and that the rest were peaceful civilians murdered in their homes (*ibid.*, p. 173). By contrast, a Hagana intelligence report issued three days after the event underscores the operational incompetence and disarray of the attacking forces, and lack of discipline, manifested inter alia in acts of plunder, but makes no mention of a massacre. See Yavne to Tene, "The Etzel and Lehi Operation in Deir Yasin," Apr. 12, 1948, IDFA 1948/500/35.

52. Irgun Command, "Statement on the Deir Yasin Affair" & "Statement" & "Condemn the Hypocrisy," April 1948, IA, K4-4/10. For mid-1950s affidavits of battle participants denying any massacre, see IA, K4-1/10, 9/10. An extensive collection of press and scholarly writings can be found in IDFA 2004/26/70. See also: Arif, *al-Nakba*, pp. 169–80; "Deir Yasin Occupied by the Irgun and Lehi" & "The Jewish Agency Condemns the Irgun and Lehi Operation in Deir Yasin" & "The Chief Rabbinate Strongly Condemns the Deir Yasin Incident," *Ha'aretz*, Apr. 11, 12, 1948; "Battle Participant Evidence: 60 Hours in Deir Yasin," *Mivrak*, Apr. 19, 1948, IA K4; High Commissioner for Palestine to Secretary of State for the Colonies, "Deir Yasin," Apr. 13, 1948, Cunningham Papers; High Commissioner for Palestine to Secretary of State for the Colonies, "Weekly Intelligence Appreciation," Apr. 17, 1948, Cunningham Papers; "An Arab from Deir Yasin Reveals on the Deir Yasin Anniversary: The Jews Didn't Plan a Massacre But Conducted a Battle," *Herut*, June 3, 1953; "Prime Minister Menachem Begin in Interview with Lord Bethel: Deir Yasin – A Tragedy in the Irgun's History, But Casualties Were Caused in the Course of Fighting; There Was No Massacre," *Yediot Aharonot*, June 22, 1979.

53. "Conclusions of the Commission of Inquiry about the Sheik Jarah Disaster of Apr. 13, 1948," Apr. 18, 1948 HA 57/95; "Report by Shalom Hurwitz on the Mount Scopus Convoy Disaster in Sheik Jarah on Apr. 13, 1948," June 6, 1948, BGA.

54. See, for example, *Filastin*, Apr. 13, 14, 16, 1948; *al-Difa*, Apr. 11, 12, 13, 14, 15, 16, 1948; Radio Jerusalem in Arabic to the Middle East, Apr. 13, 1948 & Radio Damascus, Apr. 14, 1948, in Foreign Broadcast Information Service (FBIS–NME), *European Section: Near & Middle East–North African Transmitters*, Apr. 15, 1948, p. II4; Radio al-Sharq al-Adna (Jerusalem), Apr. 15, 1948, *ibid.*, Apr. 16, 1948, p. II5. See also Hiram to Carmeli, "News Bulletin, 23.4.48," noting Deir Yasin as a cause of the mass flight (HA 105/149, p. 286).
55. "Tene News: Daily Precis," Apr. 14, 1948, IDFA 1952/900/58.
56. Hiram to Tene, "The Attack on Ramat Yohanan," Apr. 27, 1948, IDFA, 1975/922/648; Zuri to Tene, "The Mishmar Haemek Battle," May 8, 1948, HA 105/127; correspondence of the ALA northern command during the Mishmar Haemek battle, IDFA, 1975/922/648; Commander of the Second Company to Commander of the Hittin Battalion, "Lessons of the Mishmar Haemek Battle," IDFA, 1957/100001/373; Hashemi, *Mudhakkirat*, p. 213 (diary entry for Apr. 14, 1948); Hagana Operational Directorate, "Logbook of the War of Independence, pp. 240, 244–46, 248–51, 253–58; Ben-Gurion, *Yoman Hamilhama*, Vol. 1, p. 356 (diary entry for Apr. 18, 1948); Qawuqji, "Memoirs. Part I," pp. 38–47; "Fortnightly Intelligence Newsletter No. 65," issued by HQ British Troops in Palestine (for the period 2359 hrs, Mar. 23,–2359 hrs, Apr. 7, 1948), Apr. 9, 1948, WO 275/64, p. 3; Qawuqji speech on al-Inqaz (ALA) radio in Arabic, Apr. 11, 1948, FBIS, Apr. 12, 1948, II6.
57. Hashemi, *Mudhakkirat*, pp. 214–16 (diary entries for Apr. 17, 22, 1948); Tzuri to Golani, "News Summary: Tiberias," Apr. 21, 1948, HA 105/143, p. 275; Hagana Operational Directorate, "Logbook of the War of Independence," p. 260; MacMillan, "Palestine: Narrative of Events," Apr. 17/18, 18, 1948, p. 37; Nahum Ab (Abu), *Hamaavak al Tveria* (Tel Aviv: Ministry of Defense Publishing House, 1991), pp. 199–217.

Chapter 6: Fleeing Haifa

1. Yehoshua Ben-Arieh, "The Population of the Large Towns in Palestine during the First Eighty Years of the Nineteenth Century, According to Western Sources," in Moshe Maoz (ed.), *Studies on Palestine during the Ottoman Period* (Jerusalem: Magness Press, 1975), p. 68; Government for Palestine, *Supplement to Survey of Palestine: Notes Compiled for the Information of the United Nations Special Committee of Palestine* (London: HMSO, June 1947; reprinted in full with permission by the Institute for Palestine Studies, Washington, D.C.), p. 12.
2. Sixth Airborne Division, "Weekly Intelligence Summary No. 61, Based on Information Received up to Oct. 23, 1947," WO 275/120, p. 3; "Fortnightly Intelligence Newsletter No. 54," issued by HQ British Troops in Palestine, Nov. 8, 1947, WO 275/64, p. 2.
3. Sixth Airborne Division, Historical Section: GHQ MELF, "Weekly Intelligence Review," issued on Nov. 21, 1947, WO 275/120, No. 138.
4. David Ben-Gurion, *Yoman Hamilhama, Tashah-Tashat* (Tel Aviv: Ministry of Defense Publishing House, 1982), Vol. 1, pp. 114, 171, 177 (entries for Jan. 5, 22, 1948). See also: "Tene News," Jan. 2–4, 1948, HA 105/61, p. 158; "Yishuv Circular No. 18," Feb. 6, 1948, IZL Archive (IA), K4-31/1/12.
5. Mahmoud Yazbaq, *al-Hijra al-Arabiya ila Haifa fi Zaman al-Intidab* (Nazareth: n.p., 1988), pp. 112–17, 149–53; Yazbak, *Haifa in the Late Ottoman Period 1864–1914: A Muslim Town in Transition* (Leiden: Brill, 1998), pp. 127–39, 158–62; Yazbak, "The Arab Migration to Haifa 1933–1948: A Quantitative Analysis on the Basis of Arab Sources," *Katedra*, No. 45 (Sept. 1987), p. 143; May Seikaly, *Haifa: Transformation of a Palestinian Arab Society* (London: I. B. Tauris, 1998), pp. 34–35; Yaacov Shimoni, *Arviyei Eretz Israel* (Tel Aviv: Am Oved, 1947), pp. 119–25, 236; Yossef Waschitz, "Rural Migration to Haifa during the Mandate: An Urbanization Process?" *Katedra*, No. 45 (Sept. 1987), pp. 119–28.
6. "Tene News," Dec. 11, 25, 1947, Jan. 2–5, 1948, HA, 105/61, pp. 43, 84, 155, 158, 164; "For our Members: Daily Information Bulletin No. 16," Dec. 26, 1947, *ibid.*,

p. 91; "Tene News – Daily Summary," Jan. 12, 1948, HA 105/61a, p. 32; Muhammad Nimr Khatib, *Min Athar al-Nakba* (Damascus: al-Matba'a al-Amumiya, 1951), pp. 247, 276; Ben-Gurion, *Yoman Hamilhama*, Vol. 1, p. 114 (entry for Jan. 5, 1948); 317 Airborne Field Security Section, "Report No. 63 for the Week Ending 21 Jan 48," para. 8, WO 275/79.

7. Hanagid, "The Haifa Rally," July 14, 1947, HA 105/358, p. 124; "The Mufti's Letter to the Great Palestine National Gathering," July 6, 1947, as translated from *al-Ikhwan al-Muslimin*, HA 105/358, pp. 127–28; Hanoch, "A Monthly Report on the Arab Sector in March 1947," Apr. 8, 1947, HA 105/143, p. 36; *idem*, "Haifa and its Environs," in "Among the Arabs: Report for April 1947," May 14, 1947, *ibid.*, pp. 42–43; Hanagid, "Miscellaneous," May 20, 1947, *ibid.*, p. 46; Hanoch, "Moods and Opinions [in Haifa]," *ibid.*, p. 58; *idem*, "Haifa and its Environs," in "Report on Arab Affairs for June 1947," *ibid.*, pp. 62–64; Hiram, "Haifa and its Environs," in "A Monthly Report on Arab Affairs, August 1947," *ibid.*, pp. 68–70; Hiram, "A Monthly Report on the Developments among the Haifa Arabs during August 1947," *ibid.*, pp. 83–85.

8. 01011 to Tene, HA 105/215, p. 26.

9. See, for example, "Protocol of the Haifa NC's 9th Meeting, Held at the Residence of Hajj Muhammad Awwa on Dec. 16, 1947, 10.10am," HA 100/60, p. 14; "Protocol of the Haifa NC's 27th Meeting, Held at the Committee's Headquarters on Feb. 10, 1948," *ibid.*, p. 46; "Proposals Accepted and Submitted to the Office for Implementation on Dec. 6, 1947," *ibid.*, p. 9; "Protocol of the Haifa NC's 34th Meeting, Held at the Committee's Headquarters on Tuesday, Mar. 30, 1948," *ibid.*, p. 57.

10. See, for example, payment of £4.4, for miscellaneous expenses to Salah al-Din Abbasi, "Protocol of the Haifa NC's 32nd Meeting, Held at the Committee's Office on Tuesday, Mar. 16, 1948," HA 100/60, p. 55; Khatib, *Min Athar al-Nakba*, p. 140.

11. See, for example, "Protocol of the Haifa NC's 9th Meeting, Held at the Residence of Hajj Muhammad Awwa," p. 15; "Protocol of the Haifa NC's 11th Meeting, Held at the Committee's Office on Sunday, Dec. 21, 1947, 0900," HA 100/60, p. 18; "Protocol of the Haifa NC's 14th Meeting, Held at the Committee's Office on Dec. 26, 1947, 11.00," *ibid.*, p. 22; "Protocol of the Haifa NC's 15th Meeting, Held at the Committee's Office on Dec. 30, 1947," *ibid.*, p. 22; "Protocol of the Haifa NC's 25th Meeting, Held at the Committee's Office on Tuesday, Jan. 27, 1948, 10.00," *ibid.*, p. 42; "Protocol of the Haifa NC's 31st Meeting, Held on Mar. 9, 1948," *ibid.*, p. 51; "Protocol of the Haifa NC's 32nd Meeting, Held at the Committee's Office on Tuesday, Mar. 16, 1948," *ibid.*, p. 55; "Protocol of the NC's 37th Meeting, Held at the Committee's Office on Tues. Apr. 13, 1948," *ibid.*, p. 59.

12. 317 Airborne Field Security Section, "Report No. 63 for the Week Ending 21 Jan 48," para. 8d, WO 275/79. See also Taha Hashemi, *Mudhakkirat Taha al-Hashemi. Vol. 2: 1942–1955* (Beirut: Dar al-Tali'a li-l-Taba'a wa-l-Nashr, 1978), p. 173 (entry for Nov. 29, 1947).

13. "Protocol of the Haifa National Committee's 6th Meeting, Held at the Islamic Committee Center on Friday, Dec. 12, 1947," HA 100/60, p. 10; "Protocol of the Haifa National Committee's 7th Meeting, Held at the Islamic Committee Center on Saturday, Dec. 13, 1947," *ibid.*, p. 11. See also Khatib, *Min Athar al-Nakba*, pp. 150–51; Bayan Nuwaihid Hut, *al-Qiyadat wa-l-Muasasat al-Siyasiyya fi Filastin 1917–1948* (Beirut: Muasassat al-Dirasat al-Filastiniyya, 1986), p. 628.

14. Hiram to Tene, Jan. 18, 1948, HA 105/32a, p. 18; "Report on the Haifa Situation on Friday, Jan. 16, 1948," *ibid.*, p. 23; Hiram, Jan. 19, 1948, *ibid.*, p. 25; "Report on Developments among the Haifa Arabs during January 1948," Feb. 1, 1948, HA 105/69, pp. 272–73; HA 105/61a, p. 112; 317 Airborne Field Security Section, "Report No. 62 for the Week Ending 14 Jan 48," para. 8e & "Report No. 63 for the Week Ending 21 Jan 48," pp. 1, 3–5, both in WO 275/79.

15. "Protocol of the Haifa National Committee's 22nd Meeting," HA 100/60, pp. 36–37; "Tene News – Daily Brief," Jan. 20, 1948, HA 105/61a, pp. 98, 105; "Developments among the Arabs," Jan. 22, 1948, HA 105/54, p. 108; "A Report on Developments in

Haifa on the Jan. 20," HA, 105/72, p. 62; Hadad to Adina, "Details of Notes Taken Yesterday and Today of Various Conversations with Arabs Held in Haifa during the Last Couple of Days," entry for Jan. 19, 1948, pp. 4–5, CZA, S25/7721.

16. "Protocol of the Haifa National Committee's 25th Meeting, Held at the Committee's Headquarters on Tuesday, Jan. 27, 1948," HA 100/60, pp. 40–41; Hiram-Nagid, "The Mufti and Haifa," HA 105/54a, p. 24; "Yishuv Circular No. 18, Feb. 6, 1948," IA, K4-31/1/12; Hadad to Adina, "On the Haifa Situation: the Delegation to Egypt," Jan. 31, 1948, CZA, S25/7721; "Fortnightly Intelligence Newsletter No. 61, issued by HQ British Troops in Palestine, for the Period 2359 hrs 28 Jan–2359 hrs 11 Feb 48," Feb.13, 1948, WO 275/64, p. 3.

17. Hashemi, *Mudhakkirat*, pp. 199–200 (diary entry for Feb. 4, 1948); Khatib, *Min Athar al-Nakba*, pp. 140–42; Arif Arif, *al-Nakba: Nakbat Bait al-Maqdis wa-l-Firdaws al-Mafqud* (Beirut: al-Maktaba al-Asriya, 1956), Vol. 1, pp. 210–12; Hiram, "Report on Developments Among the Haifa Arabs, October 1947," HA 105/143, p. 98; "Protocol of the Haifa NC's 22nd Meeting, Held at the Committee's Headquarters on Sunday, Jan. 18, 1948, 14.30," HA 100/60, pp. 35–36.

18. "Protocol of the Haifa NC's 15th Meeting, Held at the Committee's Office on Dec. 30, 1947," HA 100/60, p. 23; "Protocol of the Haifa NC's 22nd Meeting, Held at the Committee's Office on Sunday, Jan. 18, 1948, 14.30," *ibid.*, pp. 36–37; "Conversation with Justice Ahmad Khalil, Jan. 18, 1948," HA 105/54a, p. 15; Hajj Amin Husseini to the Haifa NC, Jan. 29, 1948, no. 521, IDFA, 1957/1/20.

19. 317 Airborne Field Security Section, "Report No. 65 for the Week Ending 4 Feb 48," para. 8c & "Report No. 66 for the Week Ending 11 Feb 48," para. 8b, both in WO 275/79; "Protocol of the Haifa National Committee's 25th Meeting, pp. 41–42; "Tene News: Daily Summary," Feb. 2, 1948, 105/61a, p. 152; "Report on Developments among the Haifa Arabs during January 1948," Feb. 1, 1948, HA 105/69, pp. 273–74; "Tene News," Feb. 12 & 23, HA 105/98, pp. 15, 25; Hiram to Tene, "Report on the Haifa Situation," Feb. 10 & 13, 1948, HA 105/32a, pp. 65, 71; Hiram to Tene, Feb. 15, 1948, *ibid.*, p. 73; Hiram to Tene, "Various News Items," Feb. 18, 1948, *ibid.*, p. 83; "Tene News," Feb. 18 & 22, 1948, HA 105/98, pp. 21, 24.

20. Hajj Amin Husseini to the Haifa National Committee, Feb. 12, 1948, No. 608, IDFA, 1957/1/20.

21. See, for example, Hiram to Tene, "Summary of Ahitofel-Nitzoz News from Feb. 20, 1948," HA 105/32a, p. 87; Hiram to Tene, "Report on the Haifa Situation on Friday, Feb. 20," *ibid.*, p. 90; Hiram to Tene, "Report on the Haifa Situation on Saturday, Feb. 21," *ibid.*, p. 89; Hiram, Feb. 23, 24, 25, 1948, *ibid.*, pp. 98–99; Hiram to Tene, "Report on the Haifa Situation on Friday, Feb. 27," *ibid.*, p. 102; "Tene News," Feb. 25, 1948, HA 105/98, p. 29; report by Hiram, Mar. 7, 1948, HA 105/257, p. 55.

22. Hajj Amin Husseini to Rashid Hajj Ibrahim, Mar. 3, 1948, IDFA, 1957/1/20; Hiram to Tene, "Evacuation of Women and Children from Haifa," Mar. 8, 1948, HA 105/257 p. 1; Hiram, "Evacuation of Women," Mar. 10, 1948 & Dr. Yatsliah, "Haifa," Mar. 10, 1948, *ibid.*, p. 112; Hiram, report on AHC instructions to evacuate women, children, and the elderly, Mar. 17, 1948 & "Removal of Children to Beirut," Mar. 14, 1948, *ibid.*, p. 108; Hiram, report on the evacuation, *ibid.*; "Tene News," Mar. 21, 1948, HA 105/98, p. 53; "Précis of Hiram News," Mar. 25, 1948, HA, 105/143, p. 121.

23. Khatib, *Min Athar al-Nakba*, pp. 248, 250–51; Zadoq Eshel, *Maarachot Hahagana Behaifa* (Tel Aviv: Ministry of Defense Publishing House, 1978), p. 338. For the detailed Hagana report on the battle, see Ehud to Carmeli, "Report on an Operation against Arms Convoy and Arab Commanders on 17.3.48," Mar. 19, 1948, IDFA 1949/815/1.

24. See, for example, 317 Airborne Field Security Section, "Report No. 71 for the Week Ending 24 Mar 48," pp. 1–3, WO 275/79; Hiram, "Migration from Haifa to Acre," Mar. 25, 1948 & untitled report from Mar. 24, 1948, HA 105/257, p. 106; Hiram, "Departure from the Country," Apr. 2, 1948, HA 105/257; Hiram to Tene, "Flight of Christians to Lebanon," Apr. 4, 1948 & "The Flats of the Christian Families," Apr. 4, 1948, *ibid.*, p. 222; Hiram to Tene, "The Haifa Residents," Apr. 8, 1948, *ibid.*, p. 30.

25. Hiram to Tene, "The Food [Situation] in the City," Apr. 6, 1948, HA 105/257, p. 53; Haifa National Committee, "Protocol of a Meeting at the Arab Bank, Apr. 12, 1948," HA 105/400, p. 45; *Haaretz*, Apr. 14, 1948, p. 4.

26. See, for example, Haifa National Committee, "Protocol of a Meeting at the Arab Bank"; "Protocol of the Haifa NC's 36th Meeting, Held at the Committee's Headquarters on Tuesday, Apr. 6, 1948," 100/60, p. 58; Hiram to Tene, "The Qaraman, Dick & Salti Factory," Mar. 31, 1948, Ha 105/257, p. 34; Hiram to Tene, "Transfer of Part of a Factory to Acre," Apr. 8, 1948, *ibid.*, p. 50; Hiram to Tene, untitled report & "[Removal of] Children to Beirut," Apr. 15, 1948, *ibid.*, p. 89; "Tene News," Mar. 21, 1948, HA 105/98, p. 53; "Tene News," Mar. 29, 1948, HA 105/98, p. 62; "Tene News," Apr. 18, 1948, *ibid.*, p 83; "In the Arab Public Sector," HA 105/100, Mar. 30, 1948, p. 15; "News from the Arab Economy," Bulletin No. 1, Apr. 11, 1948 & "Haifa from Operation Dichduch (Gloom) to the City's Occupation," HA 100/31a, p. 26.

27. "Protocol of the Haifa National Committee's 36th Meeting, Held at the Committee's Headquarters on Tuesday, Apr. 13, 1948," 100/60, p. 59.

28. Hiram to Tene, "Various Messages from Abu Zaidan," Apr. 5, 948, HA 105/257, p. 52.

29. Hiram, Apr. 2, 1948, HA 105/257, p. 23; Hiram-Kafri, untitled report, Apr. 20, 1948, *ibid.*, p. 57; Hiram-Farid, untitled report, Apr. 8, 1948, *ibid.*; "Tene News," Mar. 25 & 26, 1948, HA 105/98, pp. 59–60.

30. "257 and 317 FS Section Weekly Report No. 2 for Week Ending 21 April 1948," pp. 1–2, WO 275/79; Logbook of the Sixth Airborne Division, Apr. 15, 1948, Sheet 65, Serials 283 & 284; Apr. 16, 1948, Sheet 69, Serial 306 (see also serials 307, 314, 316, 323, 350, 352, 366, 380, 385, 386, 387, 399 of Apr. 16–20, 1948), Liddell Hart Centre for Military Archives, King's College London, Stockwell Collection, 6/17; *Davar* & *Haaretz*, Apr. 14, 16, 18, 1948; Carmeli Brigade, "Summary of Events," Apr. 16, 1948, 0900, BGA.

31. First Battalion Coldstream Guards, "Battalion Sitrep, No. 13, Apr. 19, 1948, 1630 hrs," WO 261/297; Logbook of the Sixth Airborne Division, Apr. 20, 1948, Sheet 90, Serial 399. For descriptions of the clashes see also *Filastin*, Apr. 10, 11, 14, 1948; *al-Difa*, Apr. 14, 15, 19, 1948; *Haaretz*, Apr. 11, 12, 15, 18, 19, 1948.

32. Stockwell to HQ, Palestine, "Withdrawal from Palestine," Mar. 1, 1948, annex in Lt. General G. H. A. MacMillan, "Palestine: Narrative of Events from February 1947 until Withdrawal of All British Troops," Stockwell Collection 6/25/2.

33. For the text of Stockwell's message, see "To:- The Arab and Jewish Executives in Haifa," Apr. 21, 1948, Stockwell Collection, 6/13. See also "Appreciation of the Situation by Maj Gen HC Stockwell CB.CBE.DSO. at 0900 hrs 20 April 1948 at Haifa," Stockwell Collection, 6/13, pp. 1–3.

34. Second Brigade (Carmeli), Battalion 22, "War Diary," entries for Apr. 20 & 21, 1948, IDFA 1972/721/389.

35. From Hiram, "Report on Events in Haifa on Wednesday, 24.3.48," Mar. 28, 1948, IDFA 1949/7249/152; ALA, General Headquarters of the Palestine Forces, "Operational Orders: Specifically for the Commander of the Haifa District," Mar. 28, 1948 & "Operational Order No. 1 Regarding the Establishment of an Independent Headquarters in the Haifa District," Mar. 28, 1948, IDFA, 1957/100001/64.

36. Khatib, *Min Athar al-Nakba*, p. 265; "Report by GOC North Sector Major General HC Stockwell CB.CBE.DSO. Leading up to, and after the Arab-Jewish Clashes in Haifa on 21/22 April 1948," Haifa, Apr. 24, 1948, Stockwell Collection, 6/15, p. 4, para. 14 (hereinafter Stockwell Report); Hiram to Tene, "News Bulletin," Apr. 21, 1948, HA 105/143, p. 282; "257 and 317 FS Section Weekly Report No. 3 for Week Ending 28 April 1948," para. 4, WO 275/79.

37. See, for example, Hiram to Tene, "News Bulletin," Apr. 23, 1948, HA 105/149, p. 287; Hiram to Tene, "General Moods," Apr. 25, 1948, HA 105/257, p. 355; Lippincott (American Consulate, Haifa) to the Secretary of State, Airgram A-5, Apr. 23, 1948, p. 3, NA Record Group 84, Haifa Consulate, 800 – Political Affairs.

38. Walid Khalidi, "Why Did the Palestinians Leave? An Examination of the Zionist Version of the Exodus of 1948," Information Paper No. 3 (London, n.d.), p. 22.

39. See, for example, NorthSec to Troopers, Apr. 23, 1948, 0030, Stockwell Collection, 6/13; Lippincott to Secretary of State, Aigram A-5, Apr. 23, 1948, pp. 2–3, NA Record Group 84, Haifa Consulate, 800 – Political Affairs; and his telegram 33 of the same day (1300 hours), *ibid.*

40. Stockwell Report, p. 5, para. 14e; Lippincott, airgram A-5 of Apr. 23, 1948.

41. Stockwell Report, p. 5, para. 14d; "Fortnightly Intelligence Newsletter No. 67, issued by HQ British Troops in Palestine, for the Period 2359 hrs 19 April–2359 hrs 3 May 48," WO 275/64, p. 1; Lippincott's airgram A-5 of Apr. 23, 1948.

42. Logbook of the Sixth Airborne Division, Apr. 22, 1948, Sheet 101, Serials 444 & 446; Sheet 102, Serial 450; "Intelligence Diary: the Occupation of Haifa," entry for Apr. 22, 1948, 0805, IDFA 1949/815/1.

43. Stockwell Report, p. 5, para. 15. See also NorthSec to Troopers, Apr. 23, 1948, Stockwell Collection, 6/13; report by the Superintendent of the District Police, "General Situation – Haifa District," Apr. 23, 1948.

44. Broadmead (Damascus) to Foreign Office, Apr. 22, 1948, FO 371/68544/E5019 & E5028.

45. "Precis of a Meeting Held in the Town Hall Haifa between the Representatives of the Arab and Jewish Communities under the Chairmanship of the GOC North Sector on 22 April," Appendix "A" to HQ North Sector letter 383/G (Ops) dated Mar. 24, 1948, Stockwell Collection, 6/15, p. 1.

46. For the original terms of the truce and the amended version, see: "Terms of the Hagana Command for a Truce in Haifa," Haifa, Apr. 24, 1948, Annexure I: to HQ North Sector letter 383/G (Ops) dated   Apr. 24, 1948, Stockwell Collection, 6/15; "Terms of the Hagana Command for a Truce in and Applicable to Haifa, between Jews and Arabs, Haifa 22 April 48," Annexure II: to HQ North Sector letter 383/G (Ops) dated Apr. 24, 1948, Stockwell Collection, 6/15.

47. Arab Emergency Committee, "Mudhakkira Hawla Hujum al-Yahud ala-l-Arab fi Haifa Masa Yawm al-Arbi'a al-Waqi fi 21.4.1948," p. 8, ISA 69.04/940F/15. The document was given to Yaacov Salomon by his personal friend and member of the Emergency Committee George Muammar. See Yaacov Salomon, *Bedarki Sheli* (Jerusalem: Idanim, 1980), pp. 134–35.

48. Stockwell Report, p. 6, paragraph 24; Harry Beilin, "Operation Haifa," Apr. 25, 1948, S25/10584.

49. Salomon's report to the Political Department, Israel's Foreign Office, Apr. 1, 1949, ISA, FM 2401/11; Beilin, "Operation Haifa," pp. 2–3; recollection of Abraham Kalfon (participant in the truce negotiations), Feb. 24, 1972, HA, File 284 (David Nativ's personal archive), p. 27; Dan Kurzman, *Genesis 1948: The First Arab-Israeli War* (New York: New American Library, 1972), pp. 191–92; Moshe Carmel, *Maarachot Tsafon* (Tel Aviv: Hakibbutz Hameuhad, 1949), p. 107.

50. Cyril Marriott (Haifa) to Secretary of State for Foreign Affairs, "Report on the Events Leading Up to, During, and After the Arab-Jewish Clashes in Haifa on 21st/22nd April," Apr. 26, 1948, FO 371/68505, para. 14 (hereinafter – Marriott Report); al-Inqaz, Arab Liberation Radio, clandestine, in Arabic to the Near East, Apr. 23, 1948, 6:00 am Est, FBIS-NME, Apr. 26, 1948, p. II/4.

51. From Secretary of State for the Colonies to High Commissioner for Palestine, Apr. 24, 1948, Cunningham Collection, III/4/23. Palestinian scholar Bayan Nuwaihid Hut has similarly claimed (*al-Qiyadat*, p. 630) that the Jews refused to make the slightest amendment to the truce terms, thus making them unacceptable to the Arab delegates.

52. Khalidi, "Why Did the Palestinians Leave?" p. 8; Erskine Childers, "The Other Exodus," *Spectator*, May 12, 1961, p. 673; Arthur Koestler, *Promise and Fulfillment: Palestine 1917–1949* (New York: Macmillan, 1949), pp. 187, 207.

53. See "Terms of the Hagana Command for a Truce in Haifa," Haifa, 22 April 48, Annexure I: to HQ North Sector letter 383/G (Ops) dated 24 April 1948," Stockwell Collection, 6/15.

54. Hagana Haifa Command, "Announcement No. 2 to the Haifa Arab Residents," Apr. 22, 1948, 1200, HA 15/14.

55. Hagana Arabic broadcasts, Apr. 23, 24, & 26, 1948, in BBC, *Summary of World Broadcasts: Western Europe, Middle East, Far East and Americas,* Part III, No. 48, Apr. 29, 1948, p. 61; Part III, No. 49, May 6, 1948, p. 70; *Haaretz* & *Palestine Post,* Apr. 27, 1948.

56. ISA, "Protocol of the Joint Committee Meeting," Apr. 23, 1948, 69–4/941/440a.

57. CZA, "Protocol of the Jewish Agency Executive Meeting," May 6, 1948, p. 125867.

58. Lippincott to the Secretary of State, No. 40, Apr. 25, 1948; No. 44, Apr. 26, 1948; Airgram A-6, Apr. 29, 1948; all in NA Record Group 84, Haifa Consulate, 800 – Political Affairs.

59. Superintendent of Police (CID), "Subject:- General Situation – Haifa District," Apr. 26 & 28, 1948, HA 8/15, pp. 158, 161; Logbook of the Sixth Airborne Division, May 1, 1948, Sheet 135, Serial 602; "257 and 317 FS Section Weekly Report No. 4 for Week Ending 5 May 1948," para. 4, WO 275/79.

    Several reports in the same vein were sent by the British authorities in Palestine to their superiors in London. On April 25, for example, High Commissioner Cunningham reported that at the Jewish-Arab committee established following the Arab decision to evacuate Haifa, under the mayor's chairmanship, the "Jews fearing for the economic future of the town, pressed [the] Arabs to reconsider their decision of complete evacuation." A fortnight later, Cyril Marriott, the British consul-designate in Haifa, reported that "they [i.e., the Jews] obviously want the Arab labour to return and are doing their best to instil confidence. Life in [the] town is normal even last night except of course for the absence of Arabs. I see no reason why [the] Palestine Arab residents of Haifa should not return." And a fortnightly intelligence brief by the headquarters of the British forces in Palestine reported that "if it had not been for [the] conference held under the auspices of the British authorities (which included representatives from both communities), together with great efforts made by the Jews themselves and the voluntary return of a very small number of Arabs who had met with a cold reception in their places of asylum, the position in Haifa would have been a great deal worse than it now is." See: Cunningham to Secretary of State, Apr. 25, 1948, Cunningham Collection, III/4/52; Marriott to Foreign Office, May 15, 1948, FO 371/68553/E6322; "Fortnightly Intelligence Newsletter No. 67, Issued by HQ British Troops in Palestine, for the Period 2359 hrs 19 April–2359 hrs 3 May 48," WO 275/64, p. 2.

60. UP Haifa report of Apr. 24, 1948, as quoted by *Haaretz,* Apr. 25, 1948. See also *Davar,* Apr. 25, 1948.

61. Hiram to Tene, "The Returning Arabs to Haifa," Apr. 28, 1948, HA 105/257, p. 365; report by Kafri, "Occurrences in Haifa on Sunday, May 9, 1948," May 11, 1948, IDFA, 1949/7249/152; Hiram, "Tour of the Christian Neighborhoods in Haifa," May 9, 1948, *ibid.*

62. Hiram to Tene, "The Situation of the Arabs in Abbas Street," Apr. 25, 1948, HA 105/257, p. 354; Hiram to Tene, "The Arabs' Evacuation of Haifa," Apr. 29, 1948, *ibid.*, p. 3.

63. Testimony of Ephraim Elroi (who carried out the tapping operation), Dec. 24, 1972, p. 10, HA, File 284 (David Nativ's personal archive); testimony of Aharon Kari (Kramer) (who recorded the conversation), Jan. 17, 1973, *ibid.*, pp. 6–7; testimony of Naftali Lifschitz (participant in the truce negotiations), Sept. 19, 1978, *ibid.*, p. 1; testimony of Yaacov Salomon (participant in the truce negotiations), Mar. 10, 1971, *ibid.*, p. 8; interview with Naftali Lifschitz (Apr. 13, 1994), in Tamir Goren, "Why Did the Arab Residents Leave Haifa? Examination of a Disputed Issue," *Katedra,* No. 80 (1996), p. 189, fn. 92.

64. Marriott to Foreign Office, Apr. 25, 1948, Stockwell Collection, 6/13.

65. Protocol of the JAE Meeting, May 6, 1948, p. 12586.

66. Salomon's report to the political department, Israel's Foreign Office, Apr. 1, 1949, ISA, FM 2401/11.

67. Lippincott (American Consulate, Haifa) to Department, No. 40, Apr. 25, 1948 & No. 44, Apr. 26, 1948, NA Record Group 84, Haifa Consulate, 800 – Political Affairs.

68. Cunningham to Secretary of State, Apr. 25, 1948, Cunningham Collection, III/4/52; Sixth Airborne Division's Logbook of 1805 hrs, May 4, 1948, Sheet 148, Serial 653.

69. "257 and 317 FS Section Weekly Report No. 3 for Week Ending 28 April 1948," paragraph 4, WO 275/79.
70. Cairo Radio, Apr. 26, 1948, 20:00, in BBC, *Summary of World Broadcasts: Western Europe, Middle East, Far East and Americas*, Part III, No. 48, Apr. 29, 1948, p. 57.

Chapter 7: Why Don't You Stay and Fight?

1. S. Tolkowsky, *The Gateway of Palestine: A History of Jaffa* (London: Routledge, 1924), pp. 133, 138; Yehoshua Ben-Arieh, "The Population of the Large Towns in Palestine during the First Eighty Years of the Nineteenth Century according to Western Sources," in Moshe Ma'oz (ed.), *Studies on Palestine during the Ottoman Period* (Jerusalem: Magnes Press, 1975), p. 68.
2. During the Crimean War, for example, rioting Muslim mobs in Jaffa plundered many homes of Christians and Jews. A few years later, in 1860, the Jaffa Christians narrowly escaped slaughter at the hands of their Muslim neighbors, who sought to repeat the massacres of Christians in Lebanon and Syria. As late as the autumn of 1912, a large number of Arab Bedouins entered Jaffa with the explicit aim of massacring Christian Arabs in revenge for an Ottoman setback in the Balkan war; only the prompt intervention of the Ottoman governor prevented bloodshed. See, for example, Vice-Consul McGregor (reporting from Jaffa), Nov. 12, 1912, FO 371/1507/50271.
3. Ruth Kark, *Jaffa: A City in Evolution 1799–1917* (Jerusalem: Yad Yitzhak Ben-Zvi Press, 1990), Chapters 2, 3, 5; Tolkowsky, *The Gateway*, pp. 183–84.
4. Thus, for example, during the Jaffa riots of April 19, 1936, which sparked the 1936–39 "revolt," many Jews were sheltered by Arab acquaintances or local public servants. Likewise, Arab sailors and port workers continued to ship Jewish travelers, including new immigrants, despite the officially declared national boycott of the Jewish community. See: Ben-Zion Dinur (general editor), *Sefer Toldot Hahagana. Vol. II Mehagana Lemaavak* (written by Yehuda Slotzky) (Jerusalem & Tel Aviv: The Zionist Library & Ministry of Defense Publishing House, 1976), p. 634; Michael Asaf, *Hayahasim bein Arvim Veyehudim Beeretz Israel 1860–1948* (Tel Aviv: Tarbut Vehinuh, 1970), p. 101.
5. Government for Palestine, *A Survey of Palestine: Prepared in December 1945 and January 1946 for the Information of the Anglo-American Committee of Inquiry* (London: HMSO, 1946–47; reprinted in full with permission by the Institute for Palestine studies, Washington, D.C.), Vol. 2, pp. 939–44; Government for Palestine, *Supplement to Survey of Palestine. Notes compiled for the Information of the United Nations Special Committee of Palestine* (London: HMSO, June 1947; reprinted in full with permission by the Institute for Palestine Studies, Washington, D.C.), p. 13.
6. So strained were the relations between the city's Christian and Muslim communities that there was scarcely a sports competition that did not end in a riot, driving the Christians to demand that such events be held in Christian neighborhoods. There was also secret incitement for the exclusion of Christian members from the trade board, and it was only after Christian threats to leave the board altogether that a Christian delegate was introduced into its ranks. More importantly, many Christians were arming themselves for self-defense against their Muslim neighbors. See, for example, "Report for May 1947: Jaffa and its Environs," June 2, 1947, HA 105/143, p. 59.
7. "Review [of Arab Affairs] for May 1947: Jaffa and its Environs," June 2, 1947, HA 105/143, pp. 60–61; "Review of Arab Affairs for the Month of June," July 7, 1947, *ibid.*, p. 65; Yogev, "Further Details from the Youth Gathering in Jaffa on July 13, 1947," HA 105/358, p. 710.
8. "Monthly Review of Arab Affairs: Tel-Aviv and its Environs," Aug. 1947, HA 105/143, pp. 70–71; "Monthly Report, Aug. 1947," Sept. 7, 1947, *ibid.*, p. 87; Avram, "A Monthly Report for Oct. 1947: Jaffa and its Environs," Nov. 7, 1947, *ibid.*, pp. 100, 101.
9. Avram, "In Jaffa," Dec. 25, 1947, HA 105/72, p. 15.
10. By the end of February 1948, almost 7,500,000 boxes of citrus had been shipped from Palestine: 3,926,402 from Haifa, 2,600,340 from Jaffa, and 837,465 from Tel Aviv. Arab

exporters had shipped 1,100,000 cases from Haifa, but had subsequently stopped sending citrus from this port and began using Jaffa exclusively. See "Ships Waiting for Citrus," *Palestine Post*, Mar. 2, 1948.

11. Avram, "The Jabaliya Mukhtar," Dec. 23, 1947, HA 105/72, p. 13.

12. Tene, "Daily News," Dec. 1, 3, 4, 1947, HA 105/61, pp. 6–9; Avram, "Riots in the Borderline Areas and their Perpetrators," Dec. 9, 1947, HA 105/22, p. 65; Tene, "News Bulletin No. 15," Dec. 10, 1947, HA 105/61, p. 24; Hillel to Qiryati, Dec. 10, 1947, IDFA 1948/321/88; Tiroshi/Whiskey, Dec. 18, 1947, HA 105/23; "Tene News," Dec. 25, 1947, HA, 105/61, p. 84; "Yishuv Circular No. 7," Jan. 17, 1948, IZL Archive (IA) K4–31/1/12; "Protocol of the Histadrut's Executive Committee Meeting on Dec. 10, 1947," pp. 5–6, BGA; David Ben-Gurion, *Yoman Hamilhama Tashah-Tashat* (Tel Aviv: Ministry of Defense Publishing House, 1982), Vol. 1, pp. 29, 35, 173, 178 (entries for Dec. 9, 10, 1947, Jan. 22, 1948); Yossef Olitski, *Mimeoraot Lemilhama: Prakim Betoldot Hahagana al Tel Aviv* (Tel Aviv: Hagana Headquarters, 1949), pp. 84–89, 131, 148, 201–02; Taha al-Hashemi, *Mudhakkirat Taha al-Hashemi. Vol. 2: 1942–1955* (Beirut: Dar al-Tali'a li-l-Taba'a wa-l-Nashr, 1978), pp. 199–200; "Jaffa-T.A. Truce," *Palestine Post*, Dec. 12, 1947; Abraham Nahum, "Jaffa at War" (IDF History Branch, 1959), IDFA, 1975/922/246, p. 8; Muhammad Nimr Hawari, *Sir al-Nakba* (Nazareth: Matba'at Hakim, 1955), pp. 41–46.

13. "Tene News – Daily Summary," Dec. 9, 1947, HA 105/61, p. 23; Tene to Dan & Hillel, Nov. 30, 1947, *ibid.*, p. 5; Tene to Dan & Hillel, "Regarding the Situation," Dec. 1, 1947, *ibid.*, p. 6; "News from Jaffa," Jan. 5, 1948, HA, 105/215a, p. 47; Avram, Jan. 2, 1948, HA, 105/215, p. 78; Yogev, Jan. 5, 1948, HA 105/215a, p. 48; "Tene News," Jan. 5, 1948, HA 105/61, p. 175; "Yishuv Circular No. 7," Jan. 17, 1948, IA, K4-31/1/12; "On the Jaffa Situation," HA 105/32a, p. 80.

14. "Tene News," Jan. 7, 1948, HA 105/61a, p. 6; Avram, Jan. 11, 1948, HA 105/215, p. 26; "Tene News – Daily Summary," Jan. 11, 1948, HA 105/61a, p. 25; "Transcript of a Phone Conversation between a Journalist (*al-Sha'b* Editorial Office) and a Clerk in Jaffa's Central Post Office," Jan. 6, 1948, 10:50, IA, K4-9/8, p. 7; "Death Toll Rises in Jaffa Bombing" & "Serail Was Arsenal," *Palestine Post*, Jan. 6, 9, 1948; Nahum, "Jaffa at War," pp. 12–13.

15. "Transcript of a Phone Conversation between Mrs. Heikal and Arif Jaburi (Jaffa Municipality)," Jan. 6, 1948, 11:30, IA, K4-9/8, p. 8; "Tene News," Jan. 7, 1948, HA 105/61a, p. 6.

16. Ibrahim Abu Lughod, "After the Matriculation," *Al-Ahram Weekly* (internet ed.), "Special Pages Commemorating *50 Years of Arab Dispossession* since the Creation of the State of Israel." (1998).

17. "Tene News," Dec. 30, 1947, HA 105/61, p. 125; *Filastin* & *al-Difa*, apparently from Jan. 19–21, 1948 and/or Feb. 1 (undated copy in HA 105/215, p. 17); Avner to Tene, "Jaffa: Miscellaneous," Apr. 18, 1948, HA 105/257; "Life Stands Still in Jaffa," *Palestine Post*, Mar. 21, 1948.

18. "Transcript of a Phone Conversation between Rafiq Tamimi and Abdel Rahman Labab," Jan. 6, 1948, IA, K4-9/8, p. 6; "Nejada Leader Flees Country," *Palestine Post*, Dec. 31, 1947; "National Committee Losing Grip in Gaza," *Palestine Post*, Jan. 18, 1948.

19. *Al-Sha'b* as quoted in Richard Mower, "Arab State in Balance," *Palestine Post*, Jan. 27, p. 4.

20. Yerubaal, "Subject: a) Hassan Salame; b) Situation in the Villages and in Jaffa," Dec. 21, 1947, HA 105/22, pp. 112–13; "Tene News," Dec. 30, 1947, HA 105/61, p. 125; *Filastin* & *al-Difa*, apparently from Jan. 19–21, 1948 and/or Feb. 1 (undated copy in HA 105/215, p. 17); Yogev to Tene, Feb. 8, 1948, HA 105/215, p. 16; Nahum, "Jaffa at War," pp. 1–2, 13–15.

21. "Transcript of a Phone Conversation between an Unidentified Journalist and the Editorial Office of *al-Difa*," Jan. 4, 1948, IA, K4-9/8, p. 1.

22. "Transcript of a Phone Conversation between Abdel Rahman Hababi and Rafiq Tamimi," Jan. 4, 1948, IA, K4-9/8, p. 4.

23. "Transcript of a Phone Conversation between Rafiq Tamimi and Ali Dabagh (of the Jaffa NC)," Jan. 4, 1948 & between Tamimi and the Mufti, Jan. 4, 1948, IA K4-8/9, pp. 2–3;

"Transcript of a Phone Conversation between Amin Aqil (Speaking from Tamimi's Home) and Hajj Khalid (Standing in for the Mufti)," Jan. 12, 1948, IA K4-9/8, p. 20; "Transcript of Phone Conversations between Amin Aqil and Rafiq Tamimi," Jan. 14, 15, 1948, IA, K4-9/8, pp. 28, 32.

24. "Transcript of a Phone Conversation between an Identified Caller from *al-Difa* Editorial Office and Flanagan, Police District Superintendent," Jan. 4, 1948, IA, K4-9/8, p. 4.

25. "Transcript of a Phone Conversation between Rafiq Tamimi and Muhammad Khouri," Jan. 6, 1948, IA, K4-9/8, p. 9; "Transcript of a Phone Conversation between Tamimi and Muhammad Kanaana (*Filastin* Editorial Office)," Jan. 12 1948, IA, K4-9/8, p. 20; "Transcript of a Phone Conversation between Tamimi and Sheik Muhammad (Manshiya)," Jan. 15, 1948, IA, K4-9/8, p. 32.

26. "Tene News," Dec. 31, 1947, HA 105/61, p. 121; "Tene News," Jan. 13, 15–16, 28, 29 & Feb. 8, 1948, HA 105/61a, pp. 50, 71, 132, 141, 143, 170; Avram, Feb. 10, 1948, HA 105/215, p. 15; Tene, "The Maintenance of the Iraqi and Syrian Volunteers," Feb. 20, 1948, HA 105/215a, p. 71; "Yishuv Circular No. 3," IA, K4-31/1/12, Jan. 9, 1948; Ben-Gurion, *Yoman Hamilhama*, Vol. 1, p. 169 (entry for Jan. 21, 1948); *Filastin*, Apr. 4, 6, 1948.

27. Haderati to Tene, "Foreigners in Jaffa and Tubas," Feb. 9, 1948, HA 105/215a, p. 23; "News from Jaffa," Feb. 10, 1948, HA 105/215, p. 140; Amir, "From a Conversation with Yogev," Feb. 11, 1948, HA 105/215a, p. 22; Sixth Airborne Division, "Weekly Intelligence Summary No. 154," Mar. 19, 1948, WO 275/120, p. 5.

28. Ben-Gurion to Shertok (New York), Feb. 12, 1948, in State of Israel, *Political and Diplomatic Documents, December 1947–May 1948* (Jerusalem: Israel State Archives, 1979), p. 333.

29. Avram to Tene, "The Impact of the Jewish Attack in the Tel Aviv Area," Feb. 15, 1948, HA 105/32a, p. 72; intelligence report, Feb. 17, 1948, HA 105/215, p. 52; Avner to Tene, Feb. 20, 1948, HA 105/32a, p. 90; Hashemi, *Mudhakkirat*, p. 203; "Resignation of the Jaffa Commander and its Causes," Mar. 3, 1948, HA 105/257. For daily logbooks and weekly reports of Arab military operations between early February and mid-April 1948, see ISA, P-11/ 339 (Arabic).

30. Avner to Tene, "From the Plans of the Iraqi Commander in Jaffa," Feb. 18, 1948, HA 105/215a, p. 77; Avner to Tene, "Change of Iraqi Commanders in Jaffa," Feb. 23, 1948, *ibid.*, p. 125; Qiryati to Dromi, "Change of Iraqi Commanders in Jaffa," Feb. 27, 1948, IDFA 1949/8275/130.

31. Hashmonai to Dromi, Feb. 2, 1948, IDFA 1948/500/60; Avner to Tene, "Clashes in Jaffa between Iraqis, Syrians, and the Jaffa People," Mar. 28, 1948, HA 105/257; Avner to Tene, "Jaffa: Miscellaneous," IDFA, 1975/922/648; Muhammad Nimr Khatib, *Min Athar al-Nakba* (Damascus: al-Matba'a al-Amumiya, 1951), pp. 334–36; "Three Iraqis Killed in Jaffa," *Palestine Post*, Apr. 25, 1948.

32. Zeev Sharef, *Three Days* (London: W. H. Allen, 1962), p. 201.

33. Hashemi, *Mudhakkirat*, p. 211; Seret to Givati & Qiryati, "In the Arab Camp: Jaffa, Villages", Mar. 30, 1948, HA, 105/143, pp. 149–51; *al-Sarih*, Mar. 30, 1948, as summarized by the Hagana intelligence, IDFA, 1949/4944/504; Tiroshi (Allon) to Tene, "The Situation in Salame," Mar. 23, 1948, HA 105/32a, p. 136; Qiryati/Daphne to front commanders, "Jaffa: Miscellaneous," Apr. 2, 1948, IDFA 1949/8275/123; "Bulletin No. 2: Occurrences in the Arab Camp in Jaffa and the Neighboring Villages," Apr. 4, 1948, HA, 105/143, pp. 161–63; Avner to Tene, "Rumors in the Neighboring Villages after the Blowing Up of Hassan Salame's Headquarters," Apr. 13, 1948, HA, 105/31, p. 9; "Bulletin No. 5: Occurrences in the Arab Camp in Jaffa and the Adjoining Villages," Apr. 20, 1948, IDFA 1949/8275/123.

34. "Bulletins Nos. 5 & 6: Occurrences in the Arab Camp in Jaffa and the Adjoining Villages," Apr. 20 & 22, 1948, IDFA 1949/8275/123; Observation Post Shaar Tikva, "Summary of News on Arab Transportation," Apr. 19–20, 1948, IDFA 1949/8275/162; Qiryati-Dafna to Seret, "Occurrences in Jaffa," Apr. 23, 1948, *ibid.*; Seret to Givati & Qiryati, "Occurrences in Jaffa: News Summary," Apr. 21, 1948, IDFA 1949/8275/130;

"Operations Hametz and Dror (Jaffa's Surrender and Capitulation) and the Qiryati Brigade's Role in these Events," Nov. 1, 1948, p. 10, IDFA 1975/922/251.

35. "An Analysis of the Palestine Situation, April 1948," Cunningham Papers, IV/5/33; Hagana Operational Directorate, "Logbook of the War of Independence, 3.1.48–14.5.48," IDFA, 1954/464/2, pp. 268, 273.

36. For ALA correspondence regarding Jaffa's defense, see: IDFA 1975/922/648; Fawzi Qawuqji, "Memoirs, 1948. Part I," *Journal of Palestine Studies*, Vol. 1, No. 4 (summer 1972), pp. 50–58. For the fighting over the city, see: ALA, Hittin Battalion Command, "Order of Movement for the Hittin Battalion," Apr. 27, 1948, IDFA, 1957/100001/373; Hagana Command, Operations Directorate, "Operation Hametz: Draft Plan," Apr. 22, 1948 & "Instructions for Operation Hametz," Apr. 26, 1948 & "Order of Battle and Deployment for Operation Hametz," Apr. 27, 1948 & "Summary of Operation Hametz," May 2, 1948, IDFA 1975/922/255; Operations Directorate, "Logbook of Events, Apr. 27–29, 1948 & "Summary of the Battle for Jaffa from Apr. 16–May 2," IDFA 1975/922/255; Hatzer 1, "Events of the Day," Apr. 28–May 5, 1948, IDFA 1949/8275/127.

37. "Bulletin No. 4: Occurrences in the Arab Camp in Jaffa and the Adjoining Villages," Apr. 19, 1948, IDFA 1949/8275/123; Qiryati-Dafna to the Fronts, "The Situation in Jaffa," May 1, 1948, *ibid.*; *idem*, "Occurrences in Jaffa, [Apr.] 30," May 1, 1948, IDFA, 1949/8275/162; Qiryati-Dafna to the Fronts, "Occurrences in Jaffa and its Environs, 30 [Apr.], 1920–01 [May] 1815," May 1, 1948, IDFA 1949/8275/10; "The Movement from Jaffa, May 1, 1948," IDFA 1949/8275/123; "The Situation in Jaffa," May 3, 1948, *ibid.*; Qiryati-Dafna to the Fronts, "Occurrences in Jaffa, [Apr.] 30, 1350–1505" & May 11, 1948, IDFA 1949/8275/162; "Occurrences in Jaffa," May 4, 1948, *ibid.*; Commander of the Second Company to Commander of the Hittin Battalion, Apr. 26, 1948, IDFA 1957/10001/151; Commander of the Second Company to Commander of the Hittin Battalion, May 3, 1948, IDFA, 1957/100001/373; "Extract from ME Daily Situation Report 144. Information Dispatched at 2100, 2nd May 1948," CO 537/3875.

38. Ben-Gurion, *Yoman Hamilhama*, Vol. 1, p. 389 (entry for May 5, 1948); Kenneth W. Bilby, *New Star in the Near East* (New York: Doubleday, 1950), p. 30.

39. "Extract from Middle East Special Situation Report 29 April 1948," CO 537/3875.

40. High Commissioner for Palestine to Secretary of State, Apr. 28, 1948, Cunningham Papers, III/4/119; High Commissioner for Palestine to Amman, Apr. 29, 1948, Cunningham Papers, III/4/134; High Commissioner for Palestine to Secretary of State, Apr. 30, 1948, Cunningham Papers, III/4; Lt. General G. H. A. MacMillan, "Palestine: Narrative of Events from February 1947 until Withdrawal of All British Troops," Appendices Maps, Stockwell Collection, Liddell Hart Military Archives, King's College London, 6/25/2, pp. 39–41; Haim Lazar (Litai), *Kibbush Yafo* (Tel Aviv: Shelah, 1951), pp. 201–16.

41. Cunningham to Secretary of State, Apr. 26 & May 1, 3, 1948, Cunningham Papers, III/4/71, III/5/25, III/5/43.

42. Cunningham to Secretary of State, May 5, 1948, Cunningham Papers, III/5.

43. Gurney Diary, May 5, 1948, Middle East Centre, St Antony's College, Oxford University.

44. Qiryati, "Daily Summary," May 1–5, IDFA, 1949/8275/154; "The State of Equipment, and the Events in Jaffa following the IZL Attack of Apr. 25, 1948," IDFA 1949/8275/162; "Transportation from and to Jaffa Related to the IZL Operation on Apr. 26, 1948," *ibid.*; "Current Moods (in Relation with Operation Hametz), Apr. 28, 1948," *ibid.*; "Movement of Forces from and to Jaffa (in Relation with Operation Hametz), Apr. 28, 1948," *ibid.*; "Moods," Apr. 29, 1948, *ibid.*; "Transportation from Jaffa," Apr. 29, 1948, *ibid.*; "Movement from Jaffa from 0800am," Apr. 29, 1948, *ibid.*; "Movement from Jaffa," Apr. 30, 1948, *ibid.*; "Movement from Jaffa," May 1, 1948, "Transportation from Jaffa," May 3, 1948, *ibid.*; IDFA 1949/8275/162; "Summary of Arab Transportation, 0700–16.30, May 4, 1948," *ibid.*; "Transportation to Jaffa," May 5, 1948; *ibid.*; "Summary of Arab Transportation, May 7, 1948," *ibid.*; from Hatzer 1, "Internal – Read and Destroy," Apr. 29, 1948, IA, K4-8/26; Nahum, "Jaffa at War," p. 21.

45. Qiryati-Dafna to All Fronts, "Occurrences in Jaffa, [Apr.] 11, 1948–[Apr.] 20, 0740," May 2, 1948, IDFA 1949/8275/162.

46. Palestine (Cunningham) to the Secretary of State for the Colonies, May 1, 1948, FO 371/68547/E5665/4/71.

47. "Transportation from Jaffa, May 1, 1948," IDFA 1949/8275/123; "Movement in the Port," IDFA 1949/8275/162, May 2, 1948; Tene, "Evacuation of Jaffa," May 3, 1948, HA 105/31, p. 38.

48. MacMillan, "Palestine," p. 41; Avner to Tene, "Occurrences in Jaffa and its Environs 041000–041230," IDFA, 1949/8275/162; *idem*, "Occurrences in Jaffa, May 7, 1948 1845–May 8, 1948 1000," *ibid.*; Qiryati/Daphne to Natani, "In Ramle and Jaffa," May 4, 1948, *ibid.*; "The Number of the Residents, May 8, 1948," IDFA 1949/8275/123, p. 41; "Among the Arabs," May 5, 1948, IDFA, 1949/8275/162; Qiryati/Operations, "Daily Summary, 101800–111800," IDFA 1948/321/92. For the somewhat larger figure of 5,000–8,000 remaining residents, see: Qiryati, "Operational Order 'Dror,' " May 12, 1948, 1949/8275/123; "Arab Exodus Brings Chaos," *Palestine Post*, May 6, 1948.

49. "Minutes of a Meeting between the Tel Aviv Hagana Commander and his Deputies and the Jaffa Representatives, Tel Aviv, May 12, 1948," IDFA 1948/321/97; "Second Meeting between the Tel Aviv Hagana Commander and Delegates of the Jaffa Emergency Committee, Tel Aviv, May 13, 1948, 1045am," *ibid.*; Qiryati Headquarters, "Special Order of the Day Following the Fall of Jaffa," May 14, 1948, *ibid.*

50. "The Palestinians," television documentary prepared and presented by Edward Said and Ibrahim Abu Lughod (early 1990s).

Chapter 8: Jerusalem Embattled

1. Ben Halpern, *The Idea of the Jewish State* (Cambridge: Harvard University Press, 1961), pp. 373–75. At the beginning of 1947, according to British figures, Jerusalem's population totaled some 164,440 people: 99,320 Jews, 65,010 Arabs, and 31,330 Christians. Government for Palestine, *Supplement to Survey of Palestine Notes Compiled for the Information of the United Nations Special Committee of Palestine* (London: HMSO, June 1947; reprinted in full with permission by the Institute for Palestine Studies, Washington, D.C.), p.13.

2. "Protocol of a Meeting of the Histadrut's Executive Committee," Dec. 3, 1947, BGA, p. 4.

3. Robert B. Macatee (American Consul-General, Jerusalem) to Secretary of State, Feb. 9, 1948, RG 84/800, National Archives (NA), Washington, D.C., pp. 1–2; Yavne to Tene, "The State of the Arab Neighborhoods in the South of the City," Mar. 26, 1948, HA 105/143, pp. 130–31; "Fortnightly Intelligence Newsletter No. 64," issued by HQ British Troops in Palestine (for the period 2359 hrs, Mar. 23–2359 hrs, Apr. 7, 1948), WO 275/64, p. 2. It should be noted, however, that the availability of food products in Arab Jerusalem did not prevent occasional local shortages owing to mismanagement, corruption, private hoarding, lack of collective solidarity, and central control.

4. Dov Joseph, *The Faithful City: The Siege of Jerusalem, 1948* (New York: Simon and Schuster, 1960), p. 84; Harry Levin, *Jerusalem Embattled: A Diary of the City under Siege, March 25th, 1948 to July 18th, 1948* (London: Victor Gollancz, 1950), p. 35. See also: "Fish, Flowers, Papers Arrive," *Palestine Post*, Dec. 5, 1947; Larry Collins and Dominique Lapierre, *O Jerusalem!* (London: Pan Books, 1972), p. 122.

5. "Report on the Situation in the Old City, Dec. 5–12, 1947," IDFA 1949/481/23; Joseph, *The Faithful City*, p. 27.

6. Macatee to Secretary of State, Dec. 31, 1947, RG 84/800, p. 5; Macatee to Secretary of State, Feb. 9, 1948, RG84/800; High Commissioner for Palestine to Secretary of State, Cunningham Papers, Middle East Centre, St Antony's College, Oxford University.

7. Jerusalem Logbook of Events, Dec. 2, 1947, 1550 hrs, S25/9210; Hashmonai, "British Incite Hebronites to Attack Jews," Dec. 22, 1947, IDFA 1948/500/32; Jonathan to Ben Yehuda, "A British Provocation," Dec. 28, 1947, IDFA, 1948/500/28; Hashmonai to

Ben Yehuda, "Report for 27–28/12/47," IDFA 1948/500/56; Hashmonai to David, "Report for 11–12.2.48," *ibid.*; Abraham Halperin to Members of the JAE and the National Committee, "Preserving the Jewish Community in the Old City," Apr. 5, 1948, IDFA 1950/553/25; Joseph, *The Faithful City*, pp. 36–37; Ben-Zion Dinur (general editor), *Sefer Toldot Hahagana. Vol. 3, Part 2: Memaavak Lemilhama* (written by Yehuda Slotzky) (Jerusalem & Tel Aviv: The Zionist Library & Ministry of Defense Publishing House, 1972), pp. 1397–98.

8. Joseph, *The Faithful City*, pp. 74–75; Levin, *Jerusalem Embattled*, p. 70; protest letters by Leo Kohn to General Macmillan & to Jacques de Reynier, Apr. 16, 1948, S25/5634; Kohn to Macmillan, Apr. 26, *ibid.*; Jerusalem Headquarters, "Hadassah University, Feb. 17–June 22, 1948," IDFA 1948/500/44; "Conclusions of the Commission of Inquiry about the Sheik Jarah Disaster of Apr. 13, 1948," Apr. 18, 1948 HA 57/95; "Report by Shalom Hurwitz on the Mount Scopus Convoy Disaster in Sheik Jarah on Apr. 13, 1948," June 6, 1948, BGA.

9. Tene to Dan & Hillel, Nov. 30, 1947, HA 105/61, p. 5; 00004 to Tene, "Report Summary, Dec. 7, 1947," HA 105/61, p. 9; Yavne to Tene, "For our Members in the Bases," Dec. 9, 1947, *ibid.*, p. 18; "For our Members in the Bases," Bulletin Nos. 15 & 16, Dec. 10 & 11, 1947, *ibid.*, pp. 24, 37; Yavne, "Evacuation of Women and Children from Lifta," Dec. 28, 1947, HA 105/215, p. 23; 00004 to Tene, "Arabs Erecting Military Posts in Lifta," Dec. 14, 1947, IDFA 1949/5253/104; "The Old City," Dec. 26, 1947, *ibid.*; "Families Leaving Lifta," Jan. 1, 1948, *ibid.*

10. Yavne, "Arms Cache in Qatamon," Dec. 12, 1947, HA 105/148, p. 177; Hashmonai to Shadmi, "Qatamon," Dec. 20, 1947, IDFA 19484/500/32; Hashmonai to Shadmi, "Semiramis Hotel," Jan. 2, 1948, IDFA 1948/500/28; Tzadik to Hashmonai, "The Semiramis Hotel Bombing," Jan. 5, 1948, IDFA, 1948/500/32; Hashmonai to Ben Yehuda, "Report for 4–5.1.48," IDFA 1948/500/56.

11. Yavne, "Arab Departure from Romema and Lifta," Jan. 1, 1948 & "Families Leaving Lifta," Jan. 2, 1948 & "Arabs Begin to Vacate Qatamon," Jan. 2, 1948 & "Mass Flight from Qatamon and Sheik Jarrah," Jan. 8, 1948, HA 105/215, pp. 78–79; "Tene News," Jan. 2–4, 1948, HA 105/61, pp. 155–59; "Tene News," Jan. 7, 1948, HA 105/61a, p. 5; Hashmonai, "News Items," Jan. 1, 2, 4, 7, 1948, IDFA 1948/500/60, pp. 37, 44, 48, 49; "The Mood in Qatamon after the Bombing," Jan. 7, 1948, *ibid.*, p. 49; Hashmonai, "Fear and Discipline," Jan. 13, 1948, *ibid.*, p. 36; "Reliable Arab News," Feb. 29, 1948, *ibid.*; Yavne to Syria and Tahkemoni, "Shneler and its Neighborhood," Jan. 9, 1948 & Yavne to Architect, "A Rumor in Musrara," Jan. 11, 1948, HA 105/215, p. 26; Tzadik to Mathan & Hashmonai, "Report for 14–15.1.48," IDFA 1948/500/61; "The Preparations in Qatamon before the Semiramis Bombing," Jan. 12, 1948, IDFA 1949/5254/104; 02204 to Tene, "Rumors in the Old City," Jan. 19, 1948, HA 105/215a, p. 49; "In the Arab Camp: News Summary," Jan. 18, 1948, IDFA 2004/535/479; "Hashmonai, "Demographic Changes in Jerusalem," Jan. 25, 1948, IDFA 1948/500/60; "In the Arab Camp," Jan. 25, 1948, *ibid.*; "Anger in Beit Safafa over the Use of the Village by Armed Gangs for Attacks on Mekor Haim," Jan. 28, 1948, *ibid.*; "Beit Safafa" & "The Evacuation of Beit Safafa," Feb. 15 & 18, 1948, *ibid.*; Yavne to Tene, "Deir Abu Tur," Feb. 21, 1948, HA 105/215, p. 81; Hashmonai, "Annexes to News Bulletin No. 114," Mar. 16, 1948, IDFA 1949/2605/2; 01204 (Hatzil) to Tene, Jan. 21, 1948, HA 105/72, p. 52; Yavne to Tene, "Complaint by the Beit Safafa Mukhtar to the NC," Feb. 16, 1948, *ibid.*, p. 105; David Ben-Gurion, *Yoman Hamilhama Tashah-Tashat* (Tel Aviv: Ministry of Defense Publishing House, 1982), Vol. 1, pp. 118, 120, 121 (entries for Jan. 6, 7, 1948); "Fortnightly Intelligence Newsletter No. 60," issued by HQ British Troops in Palestine (for the period 2359 hrs, Jan. 14–2359 hrs, Jan. 28, 1948), WO 275/64, p. 4.

12. Ben-Gurion, *Yoman Hamilhama*, Vol. 1, p. 165 (entry for Jan. 20, 1948).

13. Tzadik to Mathan & Hashmonai, "Report for 10.2.48," IDFA 1948/500/61; Tiroshi to Tene, "Moods," Feb. 12 & 13, 1948, HA 105/215, pp. 15, 45; Hashmonai to David, "Report for 10–11.2.48," IDFA 1948/500/56; Yavne to Tene, Feb. 24, 1948, *ibid.*, p. 82; Yavne to Tene, "The Evacuation of the Arab Residences in Talbieh," HA 105/32a, p. 76;

"[Arab] Moods," Feb. 12, 1948, IDFA 1948/500/60; 90004 to Aluqa, "Certified News Items," Feb. 11, 1948, *ibid.*; "Certified News Items," Feb. 13, 1948, *ibid.*; Hashmonai, "Evacuation of Arab Homes in Talbieh," Feb. 22, 1948, *ibid.*; "News Items," Feb. 21, 1948, *ibid.*; "Army Prevents New Attack on Yemin Moshe," *Palestine Post*, Feb. 12, 1948; "Two Zones Grow in Jerusalem," *Palestine Post*, Feb. 16, 1948.

14. Ben-Gurion, *Yoman Hamilhama*, Vol. 1, pp. 112–13 (entry for Jan. 4, 1948).

15. *Ibid.*, pp. 134, 141, 156, 169 (entries for Jan. 11, 12, 15, 21, 1948); "Arab News Agency," Dec. 12, 1947, as brought by BBC, "Summary of World Broadcasts" (hereinafter SWB), Part III, No. 30, Dec. 16, 1947, p. 58.

16. "Fortnightly Intelligence Newsletter No. 60," issued by HQ British Troops in Palestine (for the period 2359 hrs, Jan. 14–2359 hrs, Jan. 28, 1948), WO 275/64, p. 3.

17. "In the Arab Camp," No. 5/48 (Feb. 1, 1948), HA 105/142, p. 105; "Tene News: Daily Summary," Feb. 2, 1948, HA 105/61a, p. 152; "Fortnightly Intelligence Newsletter No. 57," issued by HQ British Troops in Palestine (for the period, Dec. 6–2359 hrs-Dec. 18, 1947), WO 275/64, p. 2; Macatee to Secretary of State, Jan. 30, 1948, RG 84/800.

18. "Arab News Agency," Nov. 18, 1947, SWB, Part III, No. 27, Nov. 27, 1947, p. 51; "Fortnightly Intelligence Newsletter No. 56," issued by HQ British Troops in Palestine (for the period Nov. 22 Dec. 5, 1947), WO 275/64, p. 4; "02204 to Tene," Dec. 31, 1947, IDFA 1948/500/60; "Tene News," Jan. 2–4, 5, 1948, HA 105/61, pp. 155, 164; "Tene News – Daily Summary," HA 105/61a, Jan. 11, 12, 1948, pp. 25, 32; "The Mood in Qatamon," Jan. 5, 1948, IDFA 1949/5254/104; "News Items: Thefts in the Arab Cities," Feb. 3/4, 1948, IDFA 1948/500/60; "Abdel Qader Husseini's Trials," Feb. 2, 1948, *ibid.*; "Thieving Gangs in the National Guard," Feb. 4, 1948, *ibid.*; Ben-Gurion, *Yoman Hamilhama*, Vol. 1, pp. 112, 141 (entries for Jan. 4 & 12, 1948).

19. Hashmonai to Ben-Yehuda, "Security Officials and Matters of Guards and Security," Dec. 21, 1947, IDFA 1948/500/29; "Meetings of the Military Committee Elected on 28/12/47," IDFA 1957/100001/927; "02204 to Tene," Dec. 30, 1947, IDFA 1948/500/60; Hashmonai, "A Movement against the Official Arab Leadership," *ibid.*; "Fortnightly Intelligence Newsletter No. 57," issued by HQ British Troops in Palestine (for the period Dec. 6–2359 hrs-Dec. 18, 1947), WO 275/64, p. 3; "The Christians and Muslims in Qatamon and Upper Baq'a," Jan. 21, 1948, IDFA 1949/5254/104.

20. Khalil Sakakini, *Kaze Ani, Rabotai* (Jerusalem: Keter, 1990), pp. 228–32 (diary entries from Jan. 1–8, Mar. 16 & 20, 1948); Hashmonai, "Annexes to News Bulletin No. 114," Mar. 15, 1948, IDFA 1949/2605/2.

21. Hashmonai, "Qatamon," Jan. 1, 1948, IDFA 1948/500/32; "Certified Arab News for Mar. 1, 1948," IDFA 1948/500/55; Sakakini, *Kaze Ani, Rabotai*, pp. 233–34 (diary entry for Mar. 28, 1948); Cunningham to Secretary of State, May 1, 1948, Cunningham Papers; Levin, *Jerusalem Embattled*, p. 110.

22. Hashmonai to Dromi, "Arab Reinforcement to the South of the City," Feb. 20, 1948, IDFA 1948/500/28; "Certified Arab News Items," Feb. 26, 1948, IDFA 1948/500/60; Hashmonai to Dromi, "Arab Reinforcement of the South of the City," Feb. 20, 1948, *ibid.*; "In the Arab Camp: News Summary," Feb. 28, 1948, pp. 2–3, IDFA 2004/535/479; "Certified Arab News for Mar. 3, 1948," IDFA 1948/500/55; "In the Arab Camp: News Summary," Mar. 9, 1948, p. 3, *ibid.*; Hashmonai, "Annex to News Bulletin No. 100," Feb. 26, 1948, IDFA 1949/2605/2; "Annexes to News Bulletin No. 105," Mar. 7, 1948, *ibid.*; "Annexes to News Bulletin No. 108," Mar. 10, 1948, *ibid.*; "Annexes to News Bulletin No. 109," Mar. 11, 1948, *ibid.*; "Annexes to News Bulletin No. 111," Mar. 12, 1948, *ibid.*; "Annexes to News Bulletin No. 114," Mar. 15, 1948, *ibid.*; "Annexes to News Bulletin No. 118," Mar. 21, 1948, *ibid.*; "Annexes to News Bulletin No. 122," Mar. 23, 1948, *ibid*; "Certified Arab News Items," Mar. 17, 1948, IDFA 1948/500/55; "Fortnightly Intelligence Newsletter No. 63," issued by HQ British Troops in Palestine (for the period 2359 hrs, Feb. 25–2359 hrs, Mar. 10, 1948), WO 275/64, p. 3.

23. "Statement by the Committee of the Christian Union of Palestine Addressed to All World Religious and Political Bodies," sent by the US Consulate General in Jerusalem to Washington, Mar. 8, 1948, RG 84/800; "News Items," Feb. 21, 1948, IDFA

1948/500/60; "Moods and General Policy," Feb. 27, 1948, *ibid.*; "In the Arab Camp: News Summary," Feb. 15, 1948, p. 3, IDFA 2004/535/479; "In the Arab Camp: News Summary," Feb. 29, 1948, p. 3, *ibid.*; "Fortnightly Intelligence Newsletter No. 63," issued by HQ British Troops in Palestine (for the period 2359 hrs, Feb. 25–2359 hrs, Mar. 10, 1948), WO 275/64, p. 3.

24. High Commissioner for Palestine to Secretary of State, Mar. 3, 1948, Cunningham Papers; Radio Beirut in Arabic, Mar. 31, 1948, in Foreign Broadcasts Information Service (FBIS), European Section: Near & Middle East and North African Transmitters, Apr. 1, 1948, II2.

25. "Moods and General Policy," Feb. 23, 27 & Mar. 14, 1948, IDFA 1948/500/60; "In the Arab Camp: News Summary," Feb. 29, 1948, p. 4, IDFA 2004/535/479; "News from the Arab Press," Mar. 23, 28, 30, 31 & Apr. 1, 1948, IDFA 1949/4944/504.

26. Yavne to Tene, "Moods and Rumors among the Arabs" & "The Mood among the Arabs" & "Fears of Jewish Retaliation" Apr. 15, 1948, HA 105/31, p. 22; Committee for Economic Defense, "News from the Arab Economy," Bulletin No. 1, Apr. 11, 1948, HA 105/143, pp. 181–82; Committee for Economic Defense, "News from the Arab Economy," Bulletin No. 3, Apr. 13, 1948, *ibid.*, p. 199; Committee for Economic Defense, "News from the Arab Economy," Bulletin No. 5, Apr. 14–16, 1948, *ibid.*, pp. 217–19; Committee for Economic Defense, "News Summary for Apr. 5–20," Bulletin No. 8, Apr. 26, 1948, *ibid.*, p. 306; Committee for Economic Defense, "A Survey of the Jerusalem Economic Situation," Bulletin No. 10, May 5, 1948, *ibid.*, pp. 337–38; Yavne, "Arab News Items," Apr. 18, 19, 1948, *ibid.*, pp. 246, 258; Yavne to Tene, "Arab News Items," Apr. 15, 1948, HA 105/143, p. 222.

27. Committee for Economic Defense, "News from the Arab Economy," Bulletin No. 4, Apr. 10–18, 1948, HA 105/143, p. 178.

28. "In the Arab Camp: News Summary," Mar. 14, 1948, p. 2, IDFA 2004/535/479; "In the Arab Camp: News Summary," Mar. 29, 1948, p. 2, *ibid.*; Yavne to Tene, Feb. 15, 1948, HA 105/215, p. 41.

29. Yeruham, "The Arab Command in the Jerusalem District Jan.–May 1948" (late May 1948), IDFA 1949/7249/283; Yavne to Tene, "Arab News Items," Apr. 17, 23, 24, 26, 27, 29, 30, May 2, 4, 1948, HA 105/143, pp. 238, 290–91, 294, 304, 309–10, 317, 319, 327, 336; "Arab News Items," Apr. 25, 1948, IDFA 1948/500/55; "In the Arab Camp – News Summaries," May 3, 1948, HA 105/142, p. 141; from Albert, Apr. 7, 1948, S25/5634.

30. "Gurney Diary," pp. 85, 86–87 (entries for Apr. 28, 29, 1948), Cunningham Papers; Yeruham, "Arab News Items," May 5, 6, 8, 1948, HA 105/143, pp. 339, 348, 357, 360; "Arab News Items," Mar. 29, 1948, IDFA 1948/500/55; Hashmonai, "Annexes to News Bulletin No. 133," Apr. 3, 1948, IDFA 1949/2605/2; "Annexes to News Bulletin No. 180," Apr. 18, 1948, *ibid.*; "Annexes to News Bulletin No. 198," Apr. 26, 1948, *ibid.*; "Annexes to News Bulletin No. 203," Apr. 28, 1948, *ibid.*; "Certified Arab News for Apr. 27, 1948," IDFA 1948/500/53; Hashmonai, "News Items," Apr. 27, 1948, *ibid.*; Tzadik, "The Situation in Musrara," Apr. 8, 1948, IDFA 1949/840/192; "Arab News Items," Apr. 17, 27, 28, 1948, IDFA 1948/500/55; Eilon to Tzadik, "Talbieh," Apr. 26, 1948, IDFA 1949/71/15.

31. "Gurney Diary," pp. 4, 19, 22 (entries for Mar. 16, 25, 27, 1948); Marie Syrkin, *Golda Meir: Woman with a Cause* (London: Gollancz, 1964), p. 153; Wasson (US Jerusalem Consulate General) to Secretary of State, Apr. 6, 1948, RG 84/800.

32. "Atarot and Neve Yaacov" (logbook of events Feb. 21–May 17, 1948), IDFA 1948/500/42; Cunningham to Secretary of State for the Colonies, Apr. 30, 1948, Cunningham Papers; Ernest to Eldad & Moria, "The Arnona Youth Institute," Apr. 17, 1948, IDFA 1950/553/25; "Observation Post Opposite Nabi Samuel, 27.4.48–6.5.48," IDFA 1949/5545/114.

33. In late March, for example, the Isawiyya residents were ordered to vacate the village so as to allow its use as a base for anti-Jewish attacks. In mid-April, all women and children were removed from Beit Iqsa, which was occupied by some 200 Iraqi fighters.

Shortly afterward, women and children were evacuated from Beit Hanina to Ramallah, leaving in the village some 500 fighters. A similar evacuation was reported in Maliha on April 15.

34. Hashmonai, "Annexes to News Bulletin No. 126," Mar. 30, 1948, IDFA 1949/2605/2; "Annexes to News Bulletin No. 172," Apr. 15, 1948, *ibid.*; "Annexes to News Bulletin No. 180," Apr. 18, 1948, *ibid.*; "Annexes to News Bulletin No. 185," Apr. 20, 1948, *ibid.*; Yavne, "Arab News Item" Apr. 18, 1948, HA 105/143, p. 243, 245; "Ein Karim," Dec. 15, 1947–Apr. 17, 1948, IDFA 1949/2605/6; "Gurney Diary," p. 66 (entry for Apr. 18, 1948); Hashmonai, "News Items," Apr. 27, 1948, IDFA 1948/500/53.

35. Cunningham to UKDEL, New York, Apr. 25, 1948, Cunningham Papers; Wasson to Secretary of State, May 13, 1948, RG 84/800.

36. Levin, *Jerusalem Embattled*, pp. 96–97.

37. Cunningham to Washington (for UKDEL), Apr. 30, 1948, Cunningham Papers.

38. *ibid.*; Cunningham to Secretary of State, May 1, 1948, *ibid.*

39. "Arab News Items," May 3, 1948, IDFA 1948/500/55; Cunningham to UKDEL New York, May 2, 1948, Cunningham Papers; "The Qatamon Affair" (summary of Hagana reports of military events in the suburb between Mar. 12 and May 5, 1948), IDFA 1948/500/47.

40. "Gurney Diary," p. 90 (entry for May 2, 1948).

41. "Discussion on Truce in Jerusalem. Meeting at Jericho at 1500 Hours 7th May 1948," Cunningham Papers; Wasson to Secretary of State, May 7, 1948, RG84/800.

Chapter 9: All Fall Down

1. Hisham Sharabi, *al-Jamr wa-l-Ramad: Dhikrayat Muthaqqaf Arabi* (Beirut: Dar al-Tali'a li-l-Tiba'a wa-l-Nashr, 1978), p. 12.

2. Meron to Amitai, Dan & Hillel, "Hebrew Translation of the Arab-Language Communiqué," Dec. 19, 1947, IDFA 1949/481/62.

3. Hashmonai to Ben Yehuda, "Relations with Neighboring Villages," Dec. 24, 1947, IDFA 1948/500/28. See also: Hashmonai to Shadmi, "The Suba Village," Dec. 22, 1947, IDFA, 1948/500/32; 01104 to Tene, "Relations between Qatanna and Maale Hahamisha," Dec. 23, 1947, *ibid.*; "Fortnightly Intelligence Newsletter No. 58," issued by HQ British Troops in Palestine (for the period 2359 hrs, Dec. 18, 1947–2359 hrs, Jan. 1, 1948), WO 275/64, p. 2.

4. Yavne, "Beit Hanina," Jan. 2, 1947 & "The Qiryat Anavim-Abu Gosh Area," Jan. 7, 1948, HA 105/72, pp. 27–28; Segal to Ben Yehuda, "Peace with Maliha," Jan. 10, 1948, IDFA 1949/2644/402.

5. Ben-Zion Dinur (general editor), *Sefer Toldot Hahagana. Vol. 3, Part 2: Memaavak Lemilhama* (written by Yehuda Slotzky) (Jerusalem & Tel Aviv: The Zionist Library & Ministry of Defense Publishing House, 1972), p. 1375; Zafrira Din, "Interview with Josh Palmon on June 28, 1989," HA 80/721/3; 01123 to Tene, "An Arab Peace Overture," Jan. 14, 1948, HA 105/72, p. 46.

6. Noam, "Aqir's Peace Overture," Dec. 12, 1947, HA 105/72, p. 6; Tzefa, "Peace Offer by Ghuweir Abu Shusha," Dec. 16, 1948, *ibid.*; Tiroshi, "Requests by Neighborhood Arabs for Peace with the Jews," Dec. 18, 1947, *ibid.*, p. 8; "01112 to Tene, "Kafr Qara and Kfar Glikson," Jan. 25, 1948, *ibid.*, p. 68; 01101 to Tene, "Meeting between the Ard Saris Mukhtar and Dr. Bihem, Head of the Kfar Atta Municipality," Jan. 22, 1948, *ibid.*, p. 71; "Tene News – Daily Summary," Dec. 16, 1947, HA 105/61, p. 59; "For Our Members, Daily News Bulletin No. 19," Dec. 31, 1947, *ibid.*, p. 127.

7. "To Members in the Bases, Bulletin No. 16," Dec. 11, 1947, HA 105/61, p. 38; "Tene News," Jan. 2–4, 1948, *ibid.*, pp. 158–59; from Tzova's Head of Security, "An Attempt to Save Jews," Dec. 10, 1947, 105/72, p. 3; Haganan to Hiram, Dec. 26, 1947, *ibid.*, p. 10; British informer to Yavne, "Beit Hanina," Jan. 2, 1947, *ibid.*, p. 27; Noam, "Happenings in Aqir," Jan. 4, 1948, *ibid.*, p. 29; Yavne, "Shots," Dec. 11, 1948, *ibid.*, p. 4; Yavne, "The

Maliha Situation," Dec. 23, 1947, *ibid.*, p. 11; Tiroshi to Tene, "Arab Gang near Abu Kishk," Feb. 29, 1948, *ibid.*, p. 119.

8. Naim, "In the Villages," Dec. 25, 1947, HA 105/22, p. 123; 00004 to Tene, "Qalandiya Opposes Gang Concentrations," Dec. 30, 1947, IDFA 1948/500/28; Yavne, "Occurrences in Romema," Jan. 2, 1948, HA 105/72, p. 27; Yavne, "Silwan-Ramat Rahel," Jan. 1, 1948, *ibid.*, p. 30; Yavne, "Dissatisfaction with Abdel Qader Husseini," *ibid.*, p. 32; Qiryat Anavim residents to Yavne, "Qatanna Residents Expelled an Arab Gang from the Village," Jan. 5, 1948, *ibid.*, p. 32; 02104 to Tene, "Workers from Maliha and Qaluniya Who Refuse to Attack Jews," Jan. 7, 1948, *ibid.*, p. 33; 00004 to Tene, "Meeting of Bani Hassan in Maliha to Discuss Attitude to Armed Gangs," Jan. 14, 1948, *ibid.*, p. 46; 02204 to Tene, "Maliha," Jan. 14, 1948, *ibid.*, p. 47; 02204 to Tene, "Qattana," Jan. 17, 1948, *ibid.*, p. 50; 02104 to Tene, "Anti-Gang Resistance," Jan. 28, 1948, *ibid.*, p. 72; 02104 to Tene, "Refusal to Provide Volunteers," Feb. 1, 1948, *ibid.*, p. 76; 02104 to Tene, "Villages' Fear of Retaliation," Feb. 1, 1948, *ibid.*, p. 80; Yavne, "Battir and Other Villages," Feb. 4, 1948, *ibid.*, p. 84; 02204 to Tene, "Opposition to Abdel Qader's Operation by Qastel," Feb. 6, 1948, *ibid.*, p. 91; Yavne to Tene, "Shu'fat," Feb. 24, 1948, *ibid.*, p. 114; Hiram to Tene, "Shafa Amr," Feb. 26, 1948, *ibid.*, p. 116; "Tene News," Dec. 31, 1947 & Jan. 2–4, 1948, HA 105/61, pp. 121–22, 158–59; "Annex to News Concentration No. 100," Feb. 20 & 24, 1948, IDFA 1949/2605/2; "Maliha," Jan. 1, 1948, IDFA 1949/2504/4; log of events in Suba, Mar. 2–Apr. 13, 1948, IDFA 1949/5545/114, p. 141.

9. Tiroshi, "Arab Jalad," Dec. 16, 1947, HA 105/72, p. 8; Noam, "Incitement in Tel al-Safi," Dec. 22, 1947, *ibid.*, p. 13; Hiram, "A Visit to Hawasa," Dec. 23, 1947, *ibid.*, p. 20; Hiram, Dec. 29, 1947, HA 105/72, p. 21; "Incitement in Bashshit," Jan. 9, 1948 & "Survey of Events in the Sidoni District," Feb. 2, 1948, *ibid.*, p. 36; 02122 to Tene, "Robbers Gang," Jan. 12, 1948, *ibid.*, p. 38; 01011 to Tene, "In Yajur," Jan. 12, 1948, *ibid.*, p. 40; 01207 to Tene, "Meeting with Hajj Muhammad Khalil al-Uzi," Jan. 16, 1948, *ibid.*, p. 49; 02112 to Tene, "A Gang in Ein Ghazal," Jan. 19, 1948, *ibid.*, p. 54; 01101 to Tene, "Gangs Try to Gain Control of Kababir," Jan. 21, 1948 & "Shafa Amr," Jan. 20, 1948, *ibid.*, pp. 62–63; 02112 to Tene, "Mobilization of Arabs," Dec. 25, 1947, *ibid.*, p. 68; 01237 to Tene, "Thoughts among Gaza Bedouins," Feb. 5, 1948, *ibid.*, p. 89; "Tene News," Jan. 2–4, 1948 & "Daily Summary," Jan. 6, 1948, HA 105/61, pp. 158, 168.

10. "For Our Members. Daily Information Circular No. 12," Dec. 21, 1947, HA 105/61, p. 70; "Tene New," Dec. 31, 1947, *ibid.*, p. 125; Avram, "Jammasin: News Items," Jan. 9, 1948, HA 105/23, p. 114; Tiroshi, "Dispatch of Arab Merchandise," Dec. 15, 1947, HA 105/72, p. 7; Naim to Tene, "Position of the Gaza Felaheen," Feb. 15, 1948, *ibid.*, p. 103; Naim to Tene, "Evacuation of the Wahidat Territory," Feb. 22, 1948, *ibid.*, p. 111; 00004 to Tene, "Moods in Sur Bahir," Dec. 22, 1947, IDFA 1948/500/60; Avram, "The Miska Arabs," Jan. 8, 1948, HA 105/54a, p. 19; Hiram to Tene, "Meeting between the Yehiam Mukhtar and Tarshiha's Mayor," Feb. 22, 1948, *ibid.*, p. 31; Tiroshi to Tene, "Appeal for a Ceasefire and Good Neighborly Relations," Apr. 7, 1948, *ibid.*, p. 53; Tiroshi to Tene, "Peace Overtures by Baqa Gharbiya," Apr. 20, 1948, *ibid.*, p. 79; Grar to Tene, "Yasur," Apr. 21, 1948, *ibid.*, p. 84.

11. Naim, "In the Azzi Family," Jan. 9, 1948, HA 105/23, p. 130; Naim, "Abdel Rahman Azzi," Dec. 30, 1947 & Jan. 19, 1948, HA 105/72, pp. 22, 25; "In the Faluja-Beit Jubrin Area," Jan. 20, 1948, *ibid.*, p. 60.

12. 02204 to Tene, "The Reasons for Villagers Joining of Abdel Qader's Forces," Jan. 19, 1948, HA 105/358, p. 42.

13. David Ben-Gurion, *Behilahem Israel* (Tel Aviv: Mapai Publishing House, 1951; 3rd ed.), pp. 43, 54; Ben-Gurion, *Bamaaraha* (Tel-Aviv: Mapai Publishing House, 1949), Vol. 4, Part 2, p. 284 (see also his speech at Mapai party center on Jan. 8, 1948, *Behilahem*, p. 28).

14. David Ben-Gurion's address at a meeting of Mapai security operatives, Jan. 15, 1948, BGA, p. 4.

15. "Tene News," Jan. 27, 1948, HA 105/61a, p. 128; to Segal (for Ytzhar), "Evacuation of Qastel," Mar. 25, 1948, IDFA 1948/500/28; log of events in Suba, Mar. 2–Apr. 13, 1948, IDFA 1949/5545/114, p. 141.

16. "Tene News – Daily Summary," Feb. 3 & 15, 1948, HA 105/62a, pp. 2, 18; 02112 to Tene, "Foreigners in Sabbarin," Feb. 3, 1948, HA 105/72, p. 82; Tzefa to Tene, "Adib Shishakli's Gang," Feb. 9, 1948, *ibid.*, p. 93; 02122 to Tene, "Moods and Occurrences in Villages," Feb. 9, 1948, *ibid.*, p. 94; Tiroshi to Tene, "Training in Qalansuwa" & "Training in Taiyiba" & "Training in Tira," HA 105/148, p. 222; Tiroshi to Tene, "Iraqis in Sabbarin," Mar. 27, 1948, HA 105/257, p. 217; Naim to Tene, "Search in Idnibba," Mar. 14, 1948, *ibid.*, p. 256; Naim to Tene, "Searches and Arrests in Idnibba," Mar. 15, 1948, *ibid.*, p. 257; 02112 to Tene, "Qannir and Kefar Glickson," Jan. 29, 1948, IDFA 1949/6400/66; Alexandroni, "Qannir: A General Survey," Feb. 19, 1948, *ibid.*; Tiroshi to Tene, "Syrians in Qannir," Feb. 19, 1948 & "Abdullah Assad," Feb. 19 & "Foreigners in Qannir," Mar. 2, *ibid.*

17. Yavne, "Training in Ein Karim for Neighborhood Arabs," Dec. 11, 1947 & "Arab Preparations in Ein Karim," Dec. 16, 1947, HA 105/148, pp. 175–76; "Bren Machine Guns in Ein Karim" & "Syrians in the Neighborhood," Feb. 23, 1948, IDFA 1949/2605/4; "Lifta, Beit Iksa," Mar. 8, 1948, *ibid.*; "Ein Karim," Dec. 15, 1947–Apr. 17, 1948, IDFA 1949/5545/114; "Maliha and Ein Karim," Apr. 1, 1948 & "Visits to Maliha," Apr. 10, 1948 & "Maliha, Ein Karim," Apr. 10, 1948, IDFA 1949/2504/4; Yavne to Tene, "Arab News Items," Apr. 20, 1948, HA 105/143, p. 266; Yeruham, "Arab News Items," May 6, 1948, *ibid.*, p. 339.

18. Avram to Tene, "Reinforcement from Syria," HA 105/215a, p. 83; "Arab News Items," Apr. 17, 1948, IDFA 1948/500/55; 02112 to Tene, "Arab al-Fuqara," Feb. 9, 1948, IDFA 1949/6400/66; 02122 to Tene, "From Salim Abdel Rahman," Dec. 12, 1947, *ibid.*; 01122 to Tene, "Assorted News Items," Dec. 2, 1947, *ibid.*

19. "Tene News," Jan. 19, 1948, HA 105/61a, p. 85.

20. 02117 to Tene, "In Wadi Hunein," Jan. 5, 1948, HA 105/148, p. 195; Tiroshi to Tene, "Dannaba," Feb. 17, 1948, *ibid.*, p. 219; 01132 to Tene, "Vacation of Mir," Feb. 8, 1948 & "The Evacuation of Jamala," Feb. 8, 1948, HA 105/215, p. 44; Tiroshi to Tene, "Arab Hawarith," Feb. 18, 1948, *ibid.*, p. 14.

21. "Annexes to News Bulletin No. 114," Mar. 16, 1948, IDFA 1949/2605/2; "Annexes to News Bulletin No. 122," Mar. 23, 1948, *ibid.*; "Annexes to News Bulletin No. 126," Mar. 30, 1948, *ibid.*; "Urgent Arab News Items," Mar. 29, 1948, IDFA 1948/550/55.

22. Tzefa to Tene, "Vacation of Khisas," Mar. 26, 1948, HA 105/257, p. 106; Tzefa to Tene, "Ulmaniya and Waddi Luz," Mar. 5, 1948, *ibid.*, p. 33; Tiroshi to Tene, "Bureika," Mar. 6, 1948, *ibid.*, p. 33; Yavne to Tene, "Isawiya," Mar. 30, 1948, *ibid.*; Tzefa to Tene, "Vacation of Women and Children from Arab Villages in the Upper Galilee," Feb. 25, 1948, HA 105/215, p. 20; Tiroshi to Tene, "Sarkas," Feb. 19, 1948, *ibid.*; p. 14; Tirsohi to Tene, "Arab al-Nufeiat," Mar. 30, 1948 & "Sarkas," Apr. 20 & "Evacuation of Sarkas," Apr. 22, IDFA 1949/6400/66; Alexandroni "Sarkas," Mar. 11, 1948, *ibid.*; Yosef Weitz, *Yomani Veigrotai Labanim* (Tel Aviv: Masada, 1965), Vol. 3, p. 257 (diary entry for Mar. 28, 1948).

23. Yavne to Tene, "Departure of Inhabitants and Entry of Foreigners," Apr. 18, 1948, HA 105/257; Hiram to Tene, "Arab Propaganda Regarding Evacuations," Apr. 30, 1948, *ibid.*; Bulgarim to Matkal, "Daily Report," May 3, 1948, p. 312.

24. These villagers' resentment of their forced eviction was illustrated, inter alia, by the subsequent negotiations with their Jewish neighbors on the possibility of their return. The Jews agreed to ensure their protection provided all weapons in the villages were surrendered. The Arabs promised to consult the ALA, which apparently rejected the proposed arrangement. Tzuri to Golani, "News Summary," May 6, 1948, HA 105/143, p. 346.

25. Tene, "Migration of the Palestinian Arabs in the Period 1.12.47–1.6.48. Annex 1: Vacated Arab Villages," June 30, 1948, IDFA, 1957/100001/781, p. 4; Naim to Tene, "Evacuation of Arabs," Apr. 8, 1948, HA 105/143, pp. 171, 185; Yavne, "Arab News

Items," Apr. 27, 30, 1948, *ibid.*, pp. 309, 319; Tzuri to Tene, "Assorted News," May 6, 1948, *ibid.*, p. 343; Naim to Tene, "Vacation of Sarafand Kharab," Apr. 8, 1948, HA 105/257, p. 290; Tzefa to Tene, "Vacation of Arab Villages," Apr. 6, 1948, *ibid.*, pp. 24, 53; Tiroshi to Tene, "Fajja Vacated of its Residents," Apr. 14, 1948, *ibid.*, p. 8; Tiroshi to Tene, "Partial Vacation of Qannir," Apr. 29, 1948 & "The Qannir Residents Moved to Arara," Apr. 29 & "Qanir," May 3, 1948, IDFA 1949/7249/129; Weitz, *Yomani,* Vol. 3, p. 277 (diary entry for May 4, 1948); Yosef Weitz diary, May 4, 1948, CZA, A246/13, pp. 2373–74; Hiram to Tene, "Vacation of the Arab Zubeidat Tribe," Apr. 16, 1948, HA 105/54a, p. 67; report by an Arab source on the Arab Legion's order to vacate villages, May 12, 1948, IDFA 1949/5545/114, p. 11; Yeruham to Mamaz, "Urgent Arab News Items," May 12, 1948, IDFA 1948/500/55.

26. Yossef Olitski, *Mimeoraot Lemilhama: Prakim Betoldot Hahagana al Tel Aviv* (Tel Aviv: Hagana Headquarters, 1949), pp. 72, 75; Tene to Dan & Hillel, "On the Situation," Dec. 1, 1948, HA 105/61, p. 6; "News of the Day," Dec. 2, 3, 1947, *ibid.*, pp. 7–8; "Tene News," Jan. 2–4, 1948, *ibid.*, p. 159; from Avram, Jan. 8, 1948, HA 105/215, p. 79; Avram, "Jammasin: News Items," Jan. 9, 1948, HA 105/23, p. 114; Tiroshi to Tene, "Evacuation of Arab Abu Kishk" & "Evacuation of Sheik Muwannis and its Neighborhood," Mar. 31, 1948, HA 105/257, pp. 97–98; Tene, "Migration of the Palestinian Arabs," Annex 1, pp. 8, 9; "Yishuv Circular No. 46," Apr. 1, 1948, IA, K4–31/1/12; "Yishuv Circular No. 52," Apr. 7, 1948, *ibid.*; Ezra Danin, *Zioni Bekhol Tnai* (Jerusalem: Kidum, 1987), Vol. 1, p. 218.

27. "Tene News – Daily Summary," Dec. 16, 1947, HA 105/61, p. 59; "For Our Members, Daily News Bulletin No. 19," Dec. 31, 1947, *ibid.*, p. 127; *al-Ayam* (Damascus), Dec. 21, 1947, as brought in "News on Arab Military Preparations," Jan. 1, 1948, CZA S25/3999.

28. "Tene News," Dec. 31, 1947, Jan. 1 & 2–4, 1948 HA 105/61, pp. 124–25, 137, 157; "Village Files," Dec. 22, 1947, HA 105/134, p. 198; Naim, "Refugees," Dec. 22, 1947, HA 105/215a, p. 62; Tiroshi, "Partial Evacuation of Khirbat Azzun," Dec. 21, 1947, *ibid.*; Tene, "Migration from December to the End of February," HA 105/102, p. 14.

29. 01011 to Tene, "Partial Evacuation of the Gawarina," Jan. 8, 1948, HA 105/23, p. 80; 02204 to Tene, "The Lifta People's Position," Feb. 9, 1948, HA 105/32a, p. 61; "Tene News," Jan. 2–4, 6, 1948, HA 105/61, pp. 157, 170; "Yishuv Circular No. 4," Jan. 13, 1948, IA 12/1/31-K4; 01101 to Tene, "Meeting between the Ard Saris Mukhtar and Dr. Bihem, Head of the Kfar Atta Municipality," Jan. 22, 1948, HA 105/72, p. 71; 01227 to Tene, "Seida," Jan. 20, 1948, HA 105/215, p. 25; 01112 to Tene, "Qisariya," Jan. 12 & Feb. 9, 1948, *ibid.*, pp. 16, 27; Tsefa to Tene, "Migration of Arabs from their Villages," Feb. 17, 1948, *ibid.*, p. 13; Avner/Haderati, Feb. 18, 1948, HA 105/215, p. 14 (Yazur); Tene, "Migration from December to the End of February"; Tene, "Migration of the Palestinian Arabs," Annex 1, pp. 2, 7, 8, 9, 14.

30. Lt. General G. H. A. MacMillan, "Palestine: Narrative of Events from February 1947 until Withdrawal of All British Troops," Appendices Maps, Stockwell Collection, Liddell Hart Military Archives, King's College London, 6/25/2, p. 32. For the British figures, see Yavne to Tene, "Abandonment of Arab Villages," Apr. 20, 1948, HA 105/257. In my estimate, between 29,000 and 32,000 Arabs had fled their villages by early April 1948 (see Appendix). See also David Ben-Gurion, *Yoman Hamilhama Tashah-Tashat* (Tel Aviv: Ministry of Defense Publishing House, 1982), Vol. 1, p. 325 (entry for Mar. 29, 1948).

31. Damascus Radio in Arabic, May 5, 1948, in Foreign Broadcasts Information Service (FBIS), European Section: Near & Middle East and North African Transmitters, May 6, 1948, II3; Yavne to Tene, "Fate of Abandoned Villages," Apr. 19, 1948, HA 105/257, p. 329.

32. Tene, "Migration of the Palestinian Arabs," Annex 1, pp. 4, 6, 7, 14, 15; "Hametz Plan," Apr. 27, 1948, IDFA 1975/922/250; Matkal/Agam, "Hametz Orders," Apr. 26, 1948, IDFA 1975/922/255; Matkal/Agam, "Summary of Hametz Activities," May 2, 1948, *ibid.*; Qaman Hametz to Matkal/Agam2, "Summary of Operation Hametz," May 1, 1948, *ibid.*; Tiroshi to Tzuri to Tene, "Assorted News," May 6, 1948, HA 105/143, p. 343; Tene,

"Survey of Arab Events in the District for the Fortnight Ending May 4, 1948," May, 6, 1948, *ibid.*, p. 344; Tene, "Happenings in the Neighborhood on Apr. 26, 1948," HA 105/62, p. 156; Hiram to Tene, "Tira," Apr. 17, 1948, HA 105/257, p. 28; Tiroshi to Tene, "The Arabs of Kafr Ana and Saqiya," Apr. 27, 1948, *ibid.*, p. 29; Tzuri to Tene, "Happenings in Nazareth," Apr. 28, 1948, *ibid.*; "Tene News," Apr. 28 & May 3, 1948, HA 105/98, pp. 94, 97; "Fortnightly Intelligence Newsletter No. 67," issued by HQ British Troops in Palestine (for the period 2359 hrs, Apr. 19–2359 hrs, May 3, 1948), WO 275/64, p. 1; Sixth Airborne Division, 257 and 317 FS Section, "Weekly Report No. 3 for Week Ending 28 Apr. 1948," WO 275/79, p. 3; Lt. General G. H. A. MacMillan, "Palestine: Narrative of Events from February 1947 until Withdrawal of All British Troops," Part III, Stockwell Collection, 6/25/2, p. 12.

33. Damascus to Foreign Office, May 4, 1948 & Damascus to High Commissioner for Palestine, May 4, 1948, Cunningham Papers, Middle East Centre, St Antony's College, Oxford University; US London Embassy to Department of State, May 6, 1948, RG 84/800, National Archives (NA), Washington, D.C.

34. At the end of 1946, according to British figures, the Safad population totaled some 12,610 people: 2,400 Jews and 10,210 Arabs (9,780 Muslims and 430 Christians). Government for Palestine, *Supplement to Survey of Palestine: Notes Compiled for the Information of the United Nations Special Committee of Palestine*, (London: HMSO, June 1947; reprinted in full with permission by the Institute for Palestine Studies, Washington, D.C.), p.12; Gurney Diary, Cunningham Collection, May 7, 1948; Dan Kurzman, *Genesis 1948: The First Arab-Israeli War* (New York: Signet, 1972), pp. 194–96.

35. For nineteenth-century population figures, see Yehoshua Ben-Arieh, "The Population of the Large Towns in Palestine during the First Eighty Years of the Nineteenth Century according to Western Sources," in Moshe Ma'oz (ed.), *Studies on Palestine during the Ottoman Period* (Jerusalem: Magnes Press, 1975), pp. 66–67.

36. Ben-Gurion, *Yoman Hamilhama*, Vol. 1, pp. 16, 70–71, 237 (entries for Dec. 2, 23, 1947, Feb. 12, 1948).

37. To Dan from Magee, Dec. 30, 1847, IDFA 1949/481/23; Lt. Colonel, Commanding, 1st Battalion Irish Guards, "Report on the Events Leading Up to the Evacuation of Safad Town," Apr. 17, 1948, Stockwell Collection, p. 2; Arif al-Arif, *al-Nakba: Nakbat Bait al-Maqdis wa-l-Firdaws al-Mafqud* (Beirut: al-Maktaba al-Asriya, 1956), Vol. 1, pp. 301–02.

38. Nafez Nazzal, *The Palestinian Exodus from the Galilee 1948* (Beirut: Institute for Palestine Studies, 1978), p. 40; Bulgarim to Matkal, "Daily Report," Apr. 16, 28, 1948, IDFA, 1975/922/1044, p. 317.

39. "Fortnightly Intelligence Newsletter No. 67," issued by HQ British Troops in Palestine (for the period 2359 hrs, Apr. 19–2359 hrs, May 3, 1948), WO 275/64, p. 1. See also Bulgarim to Matkal, "Daily Report," May 3, 1948, IDFA 1975/922/1044, p. 312.

40. Nazzal, *The Palestinian Exodus*, p. 41; Arif, *al-Nakba*, pp. Vol. 1, pp. 302–09; Fauzi Qawuqji, "Memoirs, 1948. Part II," *Journal of Palestine Studies*, Vol. 2, No. 1 (fall 1972), p. 6; Hagana Operational Directorate, "Logbook," pp. 280, 287–90; Yiftah Brigade, "Logbook of Daily Reports," May 10/11, 1948, IDFA 1975/922/1226; Tzuri to Tene, "Report on Various Operations in the Upper Galilee from May 1–May 13, 1948," HA 105/143, p. 400; Tzuri to Tene, May 15, 1948, HA 105/31, p. 76; Tzuri, brief reports on the collapse of Arab Safad, May 16, 1948, HA 105/92, p. 58.

41. Jerusalem Radio, May 9, 1948, *BBC Summary of World Broadcasts: Western Europe, Middle East, Far East and Americas* (SWB), No. 50, May 13, 1948, Part III, p. 59; Cairo Radio, May 9, 1948, *ibid.*, p. 62; Damascus Radio in Arabic, May 6, 8, 10, 1948, FBIS, May 7, 1948, II5, May 10, II3, May 11, II2; "Tene News," May 20, 1948, HA 105/98, p. 118.

42. "Tene News," Apr. 18 & May 10, 1948, HA 105/98, pp. 84, 105; "Tene News – Daily Summary," Apr. 20, 23, 25, 1948, HA 105/62, pp. 110, 136, 150; "Tene News – Daily Summary," Feb. 16, HA 105/62a, p. 21; Avner to Tene, "In the Arab Camp," Apr. 18, 1948, HA 105/143, p. 248; Doron to Tene, "The Enemy's Campaigns in the South, Bulletin No. 14," Apr. 25, 1948, *ibid.*, p. 297; Tiroshi, "Summary of News for the Alexandroni Brigade, Apr. 27, 1948," *ibid.*, p. 236; Yovav to Tene," Report on the Situation

in the Negev," May 7, 1948, *ibid.*, p. 350; MacMillan, "Palestine: Narrative of Events. Appendices Maps," p. 43.

Chapter 10: The Scramble for Palestine

1. "Fortnightly Intelligence Newsletter No. 58," issued by HQ British Troops in Palestine for the period 2359 hrs, Dec. 18, 1947–2359 hrs, Jan. 1, 1948, WO 275/64, p. 2.
2. "Fortnightly Intelligence Newsletter No. 57," issued by HQ British Troops in Palestine for the period Dec. 6–18, 1947, WO 275/64, p. 2; Paris Radio, Dec. 23, 1947, in *BBC Summary of World Broadcasts: Western Europe, Middle East, Far East and Americas* (SWB), No. 32, Jan. 8, 1948, Part III, p. 64.
3. Kirkbride to Burrows, Nov. 3, 1947, FO 816/89.
4. Research Department, Foreign Office, "The Activities of the Arab League from its Formation in March 1945 to 15th May 1948," Sept. 30, 1948, FO 371/68322, p. 6; "Translation of a Communiqué Issued by [the] Arab League on 7th February," FO 371/68381; Arab League, Press & Publication Section, "Official Communiqué," Cairo, Feb. 22, 1948, *ibid.*; Cairo to Foreign Office, Feb. 23, 1948, *ibid.*; Secretary of State for the Colonies to a number of embassies, Mar. 3, 1948, *ibid.*; British Middle East Office (BMEO), Cairo, to Foreign Office, Feb. 17 & Mar. 10, 1948, *ibid.*; *Meahorei Hapargod* (Hebrew translation of an Iraqi parliamentary report on the 1948 war, published in Sept. 1949) (Tel Aviv: Maarachot, 1954), pp. 22–24, 57–61; Azzam's statement to Arab News Agency (Cairo) & to Cairo Radio, Feb. 16, 1948, SWB, No. 38, Feb. 19, 1948, Part III, pp. 64–66; Arab News Agency, Dec. 8, 1947, *ibid.*, No. 29, Dec. 11, 1947, Part III, p. 46; al-Sharq al-Adna (Jerusalem), Feb. 24, 1948, *Foreign Broadcasts Information Service* (FBIS), European Section: Near & Middle East and North African Transmitters, Feb. 25, 1948, 115.
5. *Meahorei*, pp. 93–103, 144; Taha al-Hashemi, *Mudhakkirat Taha al-Hashemi. Vol. 2–1942–1955* (Beirut: Dar al-Tali'a li-l-Taba'a wa-l-Nashr, 1978), pp. 206–10 (diary entries for Mar. 14 & 19, 1948); "Fortnightly Intelligence Newsletter No. 64," issued by HQ British Troops in Palestine for the period 2359 hrs, Mar. 10–2359 hrs, Mar. 23, 1948, WO 275/64, pp. 3, 5.
6. "Fortnightly Intelligence Newsletter No. 65," issued by HQ British Troops in Palestine for the period 2359 hrs, Mar. 23–2359 hrs, Apr. 7, 48, WO 275/64, p. 2; Beirut Radio, Mar. 19, 1948, SWB, No. 43, Mar. 25, 1948, Part III, pp. 62–63; Arab News Agency, Mar. 26, 1948, SWB, No. 44, Apr. 1, 1948, Part III, p. 63.
7. *Meahorei*, pp. 83–84.
8. Kirkbride to Bevin, Oct. 29, 1947, FO 371/62226; Kirkbride to Bevin, Dec. 20, 1947, FO 371/61583; "Correspondence between King Abdullah and the Secretary of State," Nov. 4, 1947, *ibid.*; Troutbeck to Bevin, Nov. 15, 1947, FO 141/1182; Busk to Foreign Office, Dec. 17, 1947, FO 816/115.
9. CAB 128/6, C.M. 67 (46), July 11, 1946; Bevin to Kirkbride, Nov. 11, 1947 & Kirkbride to Bevin, Nov. 17, 1947, FO 816/89; Bevin to Abdullah, Nov. 1947 & Kirkbride to Bevin, Dec. 8, 1947 & Clayton to Foreign Office, Dec. 15, 1947, FO 371/62226; TRL, "Main Points from a Conversation with Omar Dajani, Personal Envoy of King Abdullah of Transjordan," Jan. 7, 1948, FO 371/68364.
10. Foreign Office to Amman, Cairo, Baghdad, Beirut, Damascus, Jedda, Jerusalem, Dec. 20, 1947, FO 371/62226; Cunningham to Foreign Office, Dec. 20, 1947, *ibid.*; Amman to Foreign Office, Dec. 23, 1947, FO 371/61583; Baghdad to Foreign Office, Dec. 31, 1947, FO 371/68364; H. Beeley, "Possibilities of Transjordan Plans to Seize Parts of Palestine," Jan. 6, 1948, *ibid.*
11. Bevin to Kirkbride, Jan. 10, 1948, FO 371/62226.
12. Sir John Bagot Glubb, *A Soldier with the Arabs* (London: Hodder & Stoughton, 1957), pp. 63–66; Bevin to Kirkbride, "Conversation with the Transjordan Prime Minister," Feb. 9, 1948, FO 371/68366; Bevin to Kirkbride, Feb. 10, 1948, FO 371/68818; Bevin to Kirkbride, Dec. 11, 1947, FO 816/111.

13. Within this framework the British prevented the United Nations Palestine Commission (UNPC), charged with ensuring Palestine's smooth transition to independence, from entering the country in February 1948 as stipulated by the partition resolution, and rejected the commission's request for a month "overlap" with the mandatory administration to facilitate the transition to statehood, driving the UN to condemn British policy as "bordering on obstruction." No less important, Britain failed to comply with the stipulation by the partition resolution "that the Mandatory Power shall use its best endeavor to ensure that an area situated in the territory of the Jewish State, including a seaport and hinterland adequate to provide facilities for a substantial immigration, shall be evacuated at the earliest possible date and in any event not later than 1 February 1948."

The British also obstructed the Jewish proposal for the deployment of an international force in Palestine to administer the country's peaceful transition to independence; prevented Jewish immigration, the elixir of life of the prospective Jewish state, up to the last stages of the British presence in Palestine; and detained dozens of thousands of Holocaust survivors in concentration camps in Cyprus, including the illegal retention of some 9,000 "able-bodied" men for nine months after the establishment of the state of Israel to prevent their possible participation in the ongoing war.

14. Memorandum by B. A. B. Burrows, Feb. 9, 1948, FO 371/68368.

15. Comments by FO officials on telegram from Kirkbride, dated Feb. 13, 1948, on "Plans for Transjordan Occupation of Arab Parts of Palestine," FO 371/68367; M. T. Walker, "Arab Legion after May 15th," Mar. 3, 1948, FO 371/38366.

16. Abul Huda (London) to the Rais of the Diwan (Amman), Feb. 8, 1948, FO 816/112.

17. Cunningham to the Secretary of State for the Colonies, "Weekly Intelligence Appreciation," Apr. 25, 1948, CO 537/3869.

18. Jerusalem Radio in Arabic, Apr. 20, 1948, FBIS, Apr. 21, 1948, 113; ALA Radio, Apr. 24, 1948, FBIS, Apr. 26, 1948, 114–5; Arif al-Arif, *al-Nakba: Nakbat Bait al-Maqdis wa-l-Firdaws al-Mafqud* (Beirut: al-Maktaba al-Asriya, 1956), Vol. 1, pp. 196–97; David Ben-Gurion, *Yoman Hamilhama Tashah-Tashat* (Tel Aviv: Ministry of Defense Publishing House, 1982), Vol. 1, p. 369 (entry for Apr. 25, 1948); "Arab Mayors Court King," *Palestine Post*, Apr. 27, 1948.

19. Kirkbride to Foreign Office, Apr. 16, 1948, FO 371/68852; Jedda to Foreign Office, Mar. 11, 1948, FO 371/68369; "Tene News: Daily Précis," Apr. 20, 1948, IDFA 1952/900/58; "The Activities of the Arab League," p. 6; "Fortnightly Intelligence Newsletter No. 66," issued by HQ British Troops in Palestine for the period 2359 hrs, Apr. 7–2359 hrs, Apr. 19, 1948, WO 275/64, p. 2; Sasson to Shertok, Apr. 8, 9, 13, 14, 18, 20, 22 1948, S25/5634; interview [by] Clare Hollingowith with Azzam Pasha, Mar. 23, 1948, S25/9020; Radio al-Sharq al-Adna, Apr. 12, 15 & Beirut Radio, Apr. 12, 1948, FBIS, Apr. 13 & 16, 1948, 111–2 & 115–6.

20. Kirkbride to Foreign Office, Apr. 17, 1948, PREM 8, 859, Part III; al-Sharq al-Adna, Apr. 13, 20, 23, 1948, FBIS, Apr. 14, 21, 26, 1948, 111 & 111 & 112.

21. Cunningham to Secretary of State for the Colonies, Apr. 20, 1948, FO 371/68852; Sasson to Shertok, Apr. 22, 1948, S25/5634; "Arab News Bulletin," Apr. 27, 28, 1948, IDFA 1948/500/55; al-Sharq al-Adna, Apr. 26, 1948, FBIS, Apr. 27, 1948, 111–2; Beirut Radio, Apr. 25, 1948, SWB, No. 48, Apr. 29, 1948, Part III, p. 58; Hashemi, *Mudhakkirat*, pp. 215–16 (diary entry for Apr. 25, 1948); "Arab Decisions in Amman," *Times*, Apr. 26, 1948; "Declaration by Transjordan," Apr. 27, 1948, *ibid.*; "Abdullah Exhorts Arabs to Fight," *New York Times*, Apr. 24, 1948; "Syrians Expect Invasion," *ibid.*; "Plans Studied in Amman," *ibid.*, Apr. 25, 1948; "Arab King Warns Palestine Invasion by Saturday Is Set," Apr. 27, 1948, *ibid.*

22. "Record of Conversation Which the Prime Minister and Secretary of State Had with the United States Ambassador on the 28th April 1948," FO 800/487; Douglas to the Secretary of State, Apr. 29, 1948, *Foreign Relations of the United States 1948* (FRUS) (Washington, D.C.: Government Printing Office, 1976), Vol. 5, Part, pp. 876–77.

23. Hashemi, *Mudhakkirat*, pp. 216–18 (diary entries for Apr. 24, 25, 26, 1948); Sasson to Shertok, Apr. 18, 1948, S25/5634; "Abdullah Worries Syrians," *New York Times*, Apr. 28, 1948.

24. "Arab Public Affairs," May 5, 1948, HA 105/100, p. 24; "In the Arab Camp: News Summary," May, 3, 1948, IDFA 479/535/04; Arab News Bulletin," Apr. 30, May 1, 2, 1948, IDFA 1948/500/55; Damascus Radio, Apr. 28, 1948, FBIS, Apr. 29, 1948, 113; al-Sharq al-Adna, Apr. 29, 1948, FBIS, Apr. 30, 1948, 116; Beirut Radio, May 2, 1948, FBIS, May 3, 1948, 111; *Meahorei*, pp. 144–45; Arif, *al-Nakba*, Vol. 1, pp. 282–89; Hashemi, *Mudhakkirat*, p. 218 (diary entry for Apr. 28, 1948); Kirkbride to Foreign Office, May 1, 1948, Cunningham Papers.

25. Cairo to Department of State, "Arab League Decision Regarding Ceasefire Proposal in Palestine," May 5, 1948, RG 84 – Jerusalem Consulate. 800 – Egypt.

26. See, for example, Meyerson to Cunningham, Dec. 17, 1947, in Israel State Archives, World Zionist Organization, Central Zionist Archives, *Political and Diplomatic Documents. December 1947–May 1948* (Jerusalem: Government Printer, 1979), pp. 83–84; "Meeting: Representatives of the Jewish Agency-Secretary of State for the Colonies and Colonial Office Staff (London, Dec. 23, 1947)," *ibid.*, pp. 96–97; Danin to Sasson, Jan. 4, 1948, *ibid.*, p. 127; Minutes of JAE Meetings of Nov. 16 & Dec. 7, 1947 & Jan. 9, 1948; BGD, Dec. 9, 1947 & Jan. 1 (emphasis in the original), Mar. 7, 1948.

27. Shertok to Zaslani, Apr. 25, 1948, *Documents*, p. 674; Jewish Agency to Abdullah, Apr. 12, 1948, *ibid.*, pp. 625–26; Chief of the Royal Court (Amman) to the Jewish Agency, Apr. 12, 1948, S25/5635.

28. For the text of the Deir Yasin exchange, see S25/5634. See also: Kirkbride to Foreign Office, Apr. 23 & 24, 1948, FO 371/28852; al-Sharq al-Adna, May 4, 1948, FBIS, May 5, 1948, 111; "Abdullah Seeks 'Trust,' " *New York Times*, Apr. 27, 1948; Hagana Radio, Apr. 29, 1948, FBIS, Apr. 30, 1948, 115; "Legion Obeys Abdullah's, Not Britain's Commands," *Palestine Post*, May 3, 1948.

29. Golda Meyerson's verbal report to the Provisional State Council on May 12, 1948. Israel State Archives, *Provisional State Council: Protocols, 18 April–13 May 1948* (Jerusalem: Government Printer, 1978), pp. 40–44; Zeev Sharef, *Three Days* (London: W. H. Allen, 1962), pp. 72–76; Ben-Gurion, *Yoman Hamilhama*, Vol. 1, pp. 382, 400–01, 409 (entries for May 1, 8, 11, 1948); Ben-Gurion to Eban, May 11, 1948, *Documents*, p. 778.

30. "Truce Commission Warns Abdullah," *Palestine Post*, May 2, 1948; Beirut Radio, May 2, 6 & 13, 1948, FBIS, May 7 & 14, 111 & 111 & 113.

31. Hashemi, *Mudhakkirat*, pp. 219–21 (diary entries for May 11–14, 1948); *Meahorei*, pp. 144–45; Jerusalem Radio in Arabic, May 6, 1948, FBIS, May 7, 1948, 114; Beirut Radio, May 10, 1948, FBIS, May 11, 1948, 113; "Ibn Saud to Do 'Utmost,' " *New York Times*, May 5, 1948; "Safwat Reported Going Home," May 9, 1948, *ibid.*; "Abdullah Hits Arab Group," *ibid.*, May, 12, 1948; "King Abdullah Dismisses Arab Higher Committee," *Palestine Post*, May 12, 1948; "League Appoints Abdullah C. in C.," *ibid.*, May, 13, 1948.

32. Hagana Radio in Arabic, May 11, 1948, FBIS, May 13, 1948, 111–2.

33. In a conversation with the UN mediator to Palestine, Folke Bernadotte, on May 29, Nuqrashi confirmed that his government had reluctantly decided on war only on May 8, "when it became apparent that no settlement would be worked out." Folke Bernadotte, *To Jerusalem* (London: Hodder and Stoughton, 1951), p. 24.

34. Cairo Radio, May 11, 1948, FBIS, May 12, 1948, 111; al-Sharq al-Adna, May 13, 1948, FBIS, May 14, 1948, 113; AFP (Paris), May 15, 1948, FBIS, May 17, 1948, KK2; Muhammad Hassanein Heikal, *al-Urush wa-l-Juyush: Kadhalik Infajara al-Sira fi Filastin* (Cairo: Dar al-Shuruq, 1998), p. 84; Ibrahjim Shakib, *Harb Filastin 1948: Ru'iya Masriyya* (Cairo: al-zahra li-l-I'lam al-Arabi, 1986), pp. 123–32; "Egypt Allots $16,000,000 for Army Near Palestine," *New York Times*, May 10, 1948; "Egyptian Senate Approves Invasion," *ibid.*, May 12, 1948; "Farouk Gives Stand," *ibid.*; "Activity in Cairo," *Times*, May 10, 1948.

35. Tene to Hillel, "Arab Public Affairs," HA 105/147, p. 2; Beirut Radio, May 15, 1948, SWB, No. 51, May 20, 1948, Part III, p. 56.

36. Hashemi, *Mudhakkirat*, p. 222 (diary entry for May 13, 1948); Rony E. Gabbay, *A Political Study of the Arab-Jewish Conflict: The Arab Refugee Problem (A Case Study)*

(Geneva: Librairie E. Droz, 1959), p. 88; Sir Alec Kirkbride, *From the Wings: Amman Memories 1947–1951* (London: Cass, 1976), p. 24.

Chapter 11: Shattered Dreams

1. The declaration of the establishment of Israel stipulated that "with effect from the moment of the termination of the Mandate being tonight, the eve of Sabbath, the 6th Iyar, 5708 (15th May, 1948), until the establishment of the elected, regular authorities of the State in accordance with the Constitution which shall be adopted by the Elected Constituent Assembly not later than the 1st October 1948, the People's Council shall act as a Provisional Council of State, and its executive organ, the People's Administration, shall be the Provisional Government of the Jewish State, to be called 'Israel'." As it turned out, the first parliamentary elections were held on January 25, 1949, and on February 14 the Knesset, as the new parliament was to be called, held its first session. The provisional government continued to serve until March 10, when it was replaced by Israel's first elected government.

2. Protocol of Israel's Provisional Government Meeting, May 16, 1948, Israel State Archives (ISA), pp. 7–8.

3. Dr. Joseph to Ben-Gurion, June 8, 1948, IDFA 1950/2169/76; Protocol of Israel's Provisional Government Meeting, June 8, 1948, pp. 2–5, 14 & June 14, 1948, pp. 4–5.

4. General Staff Headquarters/Operations/Intelligence, "Situation Report on the Eve of the Truce," June 1948, IDFA 1949/15/34; Tzuri to Tene, "Report on the Attack on Mishmar Hayarden, 10.6.48–11.6.48," June 14, 1948, HA 105/127a, p. 35.

5. Doron to Tene, "The Capture of Mughar," May 18, 1948, HA 105/92a, p. 184; Doron to Tene, "Arms, Ammunition, and Prisoners from the Abu Shusha Village," May 21, 1948, *ibid.*, p. 49; "Tantura Is Captured," *Haaretz*, May 24, 1948; Doron to Tene, "An Attack on Hamama," June 9, 1948, HA 105/92a, p. 193; Tzuri to Tene, "Umm Zinat," May 18, 1948, HA 105/92b, p. 71; "Interrogation of Khalil Hajj Ahmad Muslih," June 21, 1948, *ibid.*, p. 102; Tene, "Migration of the Palestinian Arabs in the Period 1.12.47–1.6.48. Annex 1: Vacated Arab Villages," June 30, 1948, IDFA, 1957/100001/781.

6. "Situation Report on the Eve of the Truce."

7. On May 12, the Red Cross estimated the city's remaining population at 1,500. See: Hiram to Tene, "Acre after its Conquest on May 17," May 21, 1948, HA 105/92b, p. 125; Hiram to Tene, "Red Cross Telegram," June 1, 1948, *ibid.*, p. 129; Hiram to Tene, "The Conquest of Acre and its Present Situation," June 6, 1948, *ibid.*, pp. 78–79.

8. Shertok's report to the Provisional Israeli Government, June 1, 1948, p. 9; James C. McDonald, *My Mission in Israel 1948–1951* (New York: Simon and Schuster, 1951), p. 65.

9. Folke Bernadotte, *To Jerusalem* (London: Hodder & Stoughton, 1951), pp. 33, 131.

10. For example, in a meeting with the US ambassador to London on May 25, 1948, Bevin said, inter alia, that "the inclusion of Gaza and the Negev in the Jewish State had been a terrible mistake as there were no Jews there, and this must be righted." See "Record of Meeting with the U.S. Ambassador to Discuss the Palestine Situation," May 25, 1948, FO 800/487.

11. On September 11, the British chargé d'affaires in Beirut, Trefon Evans, cabled the Foreign Office: "Of course if Syria could also be given a share albeit small in the spoils Abdullah's position would be stronger. But practical difficulties particularly the strength of Jewish position in Houleh area would appear to exclude this possibility." Two days later, the Foreign Office relayed this idea to Sir John Troutbeck, head of the British Middle East Office (BMEO), which acted as Britain's main liaison with Bernadotte: "I have been considering the suggestion that Syrian acquiescence in the aggrandizement of Transjordan would be more easily obtained if there could be some session of territory in Northern Palestine to Syria. The difficulty is that the north-eastern corner of Palestine, including the Huleh concession area, is a district to which the Jews are likely to attach a very great importance." Evans to Foreign Office, Sept. 11, 1948, FO 371/68861/E11891; Foreign Office to Rhodes, Sept. 13, 1948, FO 800/487.

12. See, for example, "Palestine: Memorandum by the Secretary of State for Foreign Affairs," CAB 129/29, C.P. (48) 207, Aug. 24, 1948; CAB 128/13, C.M. (48), 57th Conclusions, Aug. 26, 1948; Foreign Office to BMEO in Cairo, Aug. 28 & Sept. 11, 1948, 800/487; Beirut to Foreign Office, Sept. 11, 1948, FO 371/68861/E11891; Michael Wright, "Palestine," June 15, 1948, FO 371/68650/E8409.

13. Michael Wright, "Palestine," June 15, 1948, FO 371/68650/E8409; Foreign Office to the British Ambassador in Washington, June 18, 1948, FO 371/68650/E8626.

14. UN Security Council, "Text of Suggestions Presented by the United Nations Mediator on Palestine to the Two Parties on 28 June 1948," S/863, June 28, 1948.

15. "Letter Dated 7 July 1948 from the Representative of the Provisional Government of Israel to the Secretary-General Containing Israel's Reply to the United Nations Mediator's Suggestions," July 8, 1948, S/870; UN Security Council, "Telegram from the United Nations Mediator Dated 8 July Addressed to the Secretary-General Concerning the Statement of the Mediator on the Arab and Jewish Replies to the Mediator's Proposal for Prolongation of Truce," July 8, 1948, S/873; "Telegram from the United Nations Mediator Dated 9 July to the Secretary-General Concerning the Arab Reply to the Mediator's Proposal for Prolongation of the Truce," July 9, 1948, S/876; League of Arab States Secretariat-General to Bernadotte, July 3, 1948, FO 141/1247.

16. Bernadotte, To Jerusalem, pp. 144–45, 159, 164–65; Tene, "Arab Public Affairs," June 27, 1948, HA 105/147, p. 71; Pirie-Gordon (Amman) to Burrows (Foreign Office), July 25, 1948, FO 371/6822; Campbell (Cairo) to Foreign Office, July 8, 1948, FO 141/1247.

17. David Ben-Gurion, Yoman Hamilhama Tashah-Tashat (Tel Aviv: Ministry of Defense Publishing House, 1982), Vol. 2, pp. 468, 492 (entries for May 30, June 6, 1948); Hassan Hindi to Madlul Bey (ALA), May 17, 1948, IDFA 1957/100001/2062; Lydda and Ramle mayors reporting on an Israeli attack to the Egyptian headquarters (Gaza & Jerusalem) and news agencies, May 31, 1948, HA 105/92a, p. 53.

18. For Lydda's and Ramle's population figures, see Government for Palestine, Supplement to Survey of Palestine: Notes Compiled for the Information of the United Nations Special Committee of Palestine (London: HMSO, June 1947; reprinted in full with permission by the Institute for Palestine Studies, Washington, D.C.), p. 13

19. Operation Danny HQ to General Staff (Operations), July 12, 1948, 11:30 am, IDFA 1975/922/1233, p. 215; Operation Danny HQ to the Yiftach Brigade, July 10, 1948, 1600 hrs, ibid., p. 209; intercepted Legion communication, July 11, 1948, HA 105/92b, p. 23; Danny HQ to General Staff, July 10, 1948, 1145 hrs, IDFA, 1975/922/1176, p. 23.

20. According to Arif, some 50,000 people were expelled by the Israelis. A contemporary Israeli military report put the figure at 30,000. See: Arif, al-Nakba, Vol. 3, p. 655; Seret to Qiryati, "Details on the City of Lydda," May 28, 1948, HA 105/228.

21. See, for example, Danny Headquarters to Brigade Commanders, "Operation Danny (1st Stage)," July 8, 1948, IDFA 1949/6450/98; Operation Danny HQ, "To the Lydda and Ramle Residents and All Arms Bearers," July 11, 1948, IDFA 1975/922/1237.

22. Dan Kurzman, Genesis 1948: The First Arab-Israeli War (New York: New American Library, 1972), pp. 576–77; Keith Wheeler, "Blitz Tactics Won Lydda," Palestine Post, July 13, 1948; "Thus Fell Lydda, Ramle, and their Environs," Haaretz, July 13, 1948; Moshe Kelman, "The Difference between Deir Yasin and Lydda," Yediot Aharonot, May 2, 1972; Yeroham Cohen, Leor Hayom Uvamahshach (Tel Aviv: Amiqam, 1969), p. 157. See also: intercepted Legion communications, July 10–12, 1948, HA 105/92b, pp. 23, 26, 33, 36, 37, 68, 70–72, 76; Yeruham, "Arab News," July 12, 1948, ibid.; Deputy Governor to Amman & Commander of 4th Division, July 11, 1948, ibid., p. 23.

23. Yiftach to Danny HQ, July 12, 1948, 1315 hrs, IDFA 1975/922/1237; Intelligence Officer, 3rd Battalion, "Report from July 12," ibid.; "Comprehensive Report of the 3rd Battalion's Activities from Friday July 7 to Sunday, July 18," July 19, 1948, IDFA 1975/922/1231. Arif Arif claims 426 fatalities (al-Nakba, vol. 3, p. 605), while Muhammad Nimr Khatib notes the fantastical figure of 1,700 fatalities (Min Athar al-Nakba, Damascus, al-Matba'a al-Amumiya, 1951, p. 350).

24. Mula to Danny HQ, July 12, 1948, 0845 hrs, IDFA 1975/922/1237; Yiftach to Danny, July 12, 1948, "Hanes Hagadol" (General Staff's Operational Logbook), IDFA 1975/922/1176, p. 30.

25. Avi Yiftach (Shmarya Guttmann), "Lydda Goes to Exile," *Mebifnim* (Nov. 1948), repr. in Alon Kadish et al., *Kibbush Lod, July 1948* (Tel Aviv: Ministry of Defense Publishing House, 2000), p. 135.

26. Ben-Gurion, *Yoman Hamilhama*, Vol. 2, pp. 582–83 (entry for July 12, 1948).

27. David K. Shipler, "Israel Bars Rabin from Relating '48 Eviction of Arabs," *New York Times*, Oct. 23, 1979. This excerpt was removed from the published memoirs, in both the Hebrew and English versions, by a censorship board comprising five cabinet members. A copy of the manuscript, however, was passed by the translator to the *New York Times*, which in turn gave it publicity.

28. Operation Danny HQ to Yiftach, July 12, 1948, 1330 hrs, IDFA 1975/922/1237, p. 190; Operation Danny HQ to Yiftach's and Qiryati's Forward HQ, July 13, 1948, 0035 hrs, *ibid.*, p. 206. See also Qiryati HQ to Yitzhak Rapaport, "Ramle," July 13, 1948, IDFA 1949/6450/98.

29. "Surrender Conditions of the City of Ramle," signed in Naan on July 12, 1948, IDFA 1975/922/1025.

30. Cohen, *Leor Hayom*, p. 160; Avi Yiftach, "Lydda," pp. 137–43; Shipler, "Israel Bars Rabin."

31. Central Galilee Front, "List of Arab Villages That Fell to our Hands on July 15–18, 1948," IDFA 1949/7249/119; Golani/Intelligence, "Daily Summary," June 16, the night of June 17/18, June 18, 1948, IDFA 1951/128/84.

32. Golani Brigade, "Weekly Summary," May 1, 1948, IDFA 128/51/70; Yeruham, "Arab News," June 24, 1948, HA 105/147, p. 67; Ben-Gurion to Yadin and Northern Front Command, July 15, 1948 & Commander of the Northern Front, "Day Command," July 16, 1948 & Carmel's telegram to the general staff headquarters & Ben-Gurion's comment, July 17, 1948, IDFA 1975/922/1025; Ben-Gurion, *Yoman Hamilhama*, Vol. 2, p. 599 (entry for July 18, 1948); "Surrender Terms of the City of Nazareth to the IDF," July 16, 1948, IDFA 1975/922/1025; Tzuri to Tene, "Occurrences in the North of the Country," July 29, 1948 & "The Conquest of Nazareth," July 19, 1948, HA 105/92b, pp. 112, 158.

33. Front A, "Operation Hiram Command," Oct. 26, 1948, IDFA 1949/7249/133; Front A, "Hiram Operational Report 1: 281500–290800," & "2: 290800–29200," *ibid.*; "Operation Hiram – Intelligence Report, Oct. 28–31, 1948," IDFA 1992/164/1; Front A, "Hiram Operational Report 3: 292000–300600 & "4: 300800–302000," & "5: 302000–310000," & "6: 310800–312000," *ibid.*

34. "Arab Refugees Increase," *New York Times*, Oct. 31, 1948; Beirut to Foreign Office, Nov. 6, 1948, FO 371/68682. In Carmel's estimate, some 30,000 villagers and refugees had fled as a result of Operation Hiram (Ben-Gurion, *Yoman Hamilhama*, Vol. 3, p. 788; diary entry for Oct. 31, 1948).

35. First Brigade/Intelligence, "Daily Brief, Nov. 7, 1948," IDFA 1951/128/84; Acting British Consul General (Jerusalem) to Foreign Office, Oct. 30, 1948, FO 371/68643 & Nov. 4, 1948, FO 141/1247; Amman to Foreign Office, Oct. 25, 1948, FO 371/68418; Intelligence Officer, Negev District, "Circular by the Egyptian HQ in Gaza to the City's Inhabitants," Nov. 11, 1948, IDFA 1975/922/1025; Damascus to Foreign Office, Nov. 12, 1948, FO 141/1247.

36. Protocol of a Security Meeting on Jan. 9, 1948, BGA, p. 5; "The Four Month Campaign and its Lessons," in Ben-Gurion, *Behilahem*, pp. 87.

37. Ezra Danin, *Zioni Bekhol Tnai* (Jerusalem: Kidum, 1987), Vol. 1, pp. 216–17; Zafrira Din, "Interview with Josh Palmon, June 28, 1989," HA 80/721/3; Shertok to Zaslani, Apr. 25, 1948, Israel State Archives, World Zionist Organization, Central Zionist Archives, *Political and Diplomatic Documents. December 1947–May 1948* (Jerusalem: Government Printer, 1979), p. 674; Protocol of the Provisional Government Meeting, May 23, 1948, pp. 19–20.

38. Protocol of the Provisional Government Meeting, June 16, 1948, pp. 20–22, 29, 35–36, 42, 46–47.

39. "Meetings: M. Shertok-Count Bernadotte and Assistants (Tel Aviv, June 17, 18 & July 26, 1948)," Israel State Archives, *Documents on the Foreign Policy of Israel. Vol. 1: 14 May–30 September 1948* (Jerusalem: Government Printer, 1981), pp. 185, 412–13; "Reply of the Provisional Government of Israel to the Proposal Regarding the Return of Arab Refugees. Letter from the Minister for Foreign Affairs of the Provisional Government to the United Nations Mediator," Aug. 1, 1948, FM 2451/13; Protocol of the Provisional Government Meeting, June 20, 1948, p. 24 & July 28, 1948, pp. 11–13, 20, 26.

40. See, for example, Bernadotte, *To Jerusalem*, pp. 227–30; Z. Zeligson to Y. Shimoni, "Conversation with Emile Eddé on July 3, 1948," FM 3766/6; Sasson (Paris) to Shimoni, Aug. 31, 1948 & T. Arazi (Paris) to Shimoni, Sept. 20, 1948, FM 64/14; Sasson (Paris), "Conversation with Dr. Ahmad Qadi," Sept. 4, 1948, *ibid*.

41. M. Shertok to Count Bernadotte (Tel Aviv), Aug. 6, 1948 & "Meetings: M. Shertok-Count Bernadotte (Jerusalem, Aug. 10, 1948)," *Documents on the Foreign Policy of Israel. Vol. 1*, pp. 492, 503–04; UN General Assembly, "Progress Report of the United Nations Mediator on Palestine Submitted to the Secretary-General for Transmission to the Members of the United Nations in Pursuance of Paragraph 2, Part II, of Resolution 186 (S-2) of the General Assembly of 14 May 1948" (General Assembly Official Records: Third Session Supplement No. 11; A/648, Sept. 16, 1948), p. 18.

42. McDonald, *My Mission*, p. 176; Ben-Gurion, *Yoman Hamilhama*, Vol. 2, pp. 657, 677 (diary entries for Aug. 20 & Sept. 8, 1948).

43. State of Israel, "Provisional State Council," Eleventh Session, July 22, 1948, pp. 19–20 (Tel Aviv: The New Press, 1948).

44. Protocol of the Provisional Government Meeting, Sept. 12, 1948, pp. 9, 11.

45. "Report from the Meeting of the Provisional State Council's Foreign Affairs Committee," Oct. 7, 1948, BGA.

46. "Text of Suggestions Presented by the United Nations Mediator on Palestine to the Two Parties on 28 June 1948," Article 9.

47. Thus according to two of Bernadotte's top aides, John Reedman and Ralph Bunche, who would become acting mediator after the count's assassination. See: M. Comay to the Israeli Mission to the United Nations General Assembly Session in Paris, *Documents on the Foreign Policy of Israel. Vol. 1*, pp. 643–44; Ben-Gurion, *Yoman Hamilhama*, Vol. 3, p. 737 (diary entry for Oct. 7, 1948).

48. "Progress Report of the United Nations Mediator," pp. 24, 31.

49. UN General Assembly, "194(III). Palestine – Progress Report of the United Nations Mediator," A/Res/194(III), Dec. 11, 1948.

50. UN General Assembly, "Hundred and Eighty-Sixth Plenary Meeting. Held at the Palais de Chaillot, Paris, on Saturday 11 December 1948, at 8.30 p.m.," A/PV 186, Dec. 11, 1948.

51. Israel Foreign Office, Middle Eastern Department, "Arab Broadcasts: Daily Summary," No. 36, Sept. 12–13, 1948, HA 105/88, p. 153; summary of Ghouri's article in HA 105/102, pp. 43–44. See also *Davar*, May 23, 1948.

52. UN General Assembly, "Two Hundred and Seventh Meeting. Held at the Palais de Chaillot, Paris, on Monday, 22 Nov. 1948, at 3 p.m.", pp. 697–704.

53. C. Waterlow, "Arab Refugees," Oct. 22, 1948, FO 371/68681.

54. "Arabs Firm on Refugees," *New York Times*, Sept. 9, 1948; Bernadotte, *To Jerusalem*, p. 228; British Middle East Office (Cairo) to Foreign Office, Sept. 11, 1948, FO 371/68341; *Davar*, Aug. 8, 1948; *al-Masri*, Oct. 11, 1948 as quoted in Israel's Foreign Ministry, Research Department, "Refugee Repatriation – A Danger to Israel's Security," Sept. 4, 1951, FM 2564/1.

Chapter 12: A Self-Inflicted Catastrophe

1. Muhammad Izzat Darwaza, *Fi Sabil Qadiyat Filastin wa-l-Wahda al-Arabiya wa-Min Wahy al-Nakba wa-li-Ajli Mu'alajatiha* (Beirut: al-Maktaba al-Asriya, 1972), p. 12.

2. According to a British intelligence report, 967 Arabs and 875 Jews were killed in the four-month period from November 30, 1947 to April 1948. The Arab League's Jerusalem

office set Arab fatalities during this period at 963 (249 fighters and 714 civilians) compared with 1,169 Jews killed (629 fighters and 544 civilians). "Casualties in Palestine since the United Nations Decision, Period 30th November, 1947 to 3rd April, 1948," CO 733/483/5, p. 19; "News from the Arab Press," Apr. 4, 1948, IDFA 1949/4944/504.

3. Beirut Radio, May 7, 1948, in *BBC Summary of World Broadcasts: Western Europe, Middle East, Far East and Americas* (SWB), No. 50, May 13, 1948, Part III, p. 57.

4. *Meahorei Hapargod* (Hebrew edition of an official report by an Iraqi parliamentary committee on the 1948 war, published in Sept. 1949; Tel Aviv: Maarachot, 1954), pp. 9, 98–99; "Fortnightly Intelligence Newsletter No. 64," issued by HQ British Troops in Palestine (for the period 2359 hrs, Mar. 10–2359 hrs, Mar. 23, 1948), WO 275/64, p. 4.

5. Beirut Radio, May 4, 1948, in Foreign Broadcasts Information Service (FBIS), European Section: Near & Middle East and North African Transmitters, May 5, 1948, II2; Tzuri to Tene, "News from Semakh after the Evacuation," May 10, 1948, HA 105/31, p. 46; "Summary of News for the Alexandroni Brigade," Apr. 9, 1948, HA 105/143, p. 174; Philip Ernst (American Consul in Port Said) to Department of State, "Arrival of Palestine Arab Refugees," Apr. 29, 1948 (dispatched May 11), RG 84, 800 – Refugees; Beirut Radio, Apr. 25, 1948, SWB, No. 48, Apr. 29, 1948, p. 60; Cairo to High Commissioner for Palestine, May 1, 1948, Cunningham Papers.

6. Arab Legion, "Situation Report," May 21, 1949, HA 105/114, p. 27; "News Summary," Aug. 4, 1948 HA 105/147, p. 149; summary of Ghouri's article in HA 105/102, pp. 43–43; Sir J. Troutbeck, "Summary of General Impressions Gathered during Week-End Visit to the Gaza District," June 16, 1949, FO 371/75342/E7816, p. 123.

7. David Ben-Gurion's Diary (BGD), June 2, 1949; see also. "The Gaza Strip and Refugees," July 4, 1949, FO 371/75432/E8543; Sir R. Campbell, "Comments on British and United States Representations to the Egyptian Government Regarding its Attitude to the Arab Refugee Problem," July 4–5, 1949, FO 371\75431/E8161.

8. A.S. Eban to the Executive of the Jewish Agency, "Conversation with Abdul Rahman Azzam, 15th September 1947," Sept. 29, 1947, S25/9020; United Nations, "Seventy-Eighth Plenary Meeting. Held in the General Assembly Hall at Flushing Meadow, New York, on Wednesday, May 14, 1947, at 3 p.m.," pp. 135–36.

9. "Fortnightly Intelligence Newsletter No. 57," issued by HQ British Troops in Palestine for the period Dec. 6–18, 1947, WO 275/64, p. 2; Cunningham to Creech Jones, Feb. 24, 1948, Cunningham Papers, VI/1/80; Kirkbride to Bevin, Dec. 23, 1947, FO 371/61583.

10. "Interview [by] Clare Hollingworth with Azzam Pasha, Mar. 23, 1948, S25/9020; Cairo to London, June 4, 1948, FO 371/68527.

11. Protocol of the Provisional Government Meeting, Oct. 21 & Nov. 11, 1948; Sasson to Foreign Office, Sept. 23, 1948, Israel State Archives, *Documents on the Foreign Policy of Israel. Vol. 1: 14 May–30 September 1948* (Jerusalem: Government Printer, 1981), pp. 632–34; David Ben-Gurion, *Yoman Hamilhama Tashah-Tashat* (Tel Aviv: Ministry of Defense Publishing House, 1982), Vol. 3, pp. 739–40, 859–60 (entries for Oct. 8 & Dec. 1, 1948); Cairo to Foreign Office, Sept. 29, 1948, FO 371/68642; Beeley to Burrows, Nov. 11, 1948, FO 371/68643; Amman to Foreign Office, Dec. 10, 1948, FO 371/68603; Cairo to Foreign Office, Dec. 17, 1948, FO 371/68644; BGD, June 2, 1949.

12. Musa Alami, "The Lesson of Palestine," *Middle East Journal*, Vol. 3, No. 4 (Oct. 1949), p. 385.

13. Protocol of the Provisional Government Meeting, June 16, 1948, pp. 23–24. Two months later, in a telegram to the minister of minority affairs, Bechor Shalom Shitrit, Shertok argued that "Without being able to totally remove from the agenda the possible annexation of the Arab part of western Palestine to Transjordan [as a result of Bernadotte's efforts], we must prefer the establishment of an independent Arab state in western Palestine. In any event we should strive to explore this possibility and to underscore its desirability in our eyes over the annexation proposal." Shertok to Shitrit, Aug. 8, 1948, in *Documents on the Foreign Policy of Israel. Volume 1*, p. 498.

14. "Meeting: M. Shertok-Count Bernadotte (Jerusalem, Aug. 10, 1948)," *Documents on the Foreign Policy of Israel*, pp. 502, 504; Folke Bernadotte, *To Jerusalem* (London: Hodder & Stoughton, 1951), p. 211. Shertok repeated the same position at a meeting with US Special Representative (later ambassador) James McDonald. See Protocol of the Provisional Government Meeting, Sept. 8, 1948, p. 3.

15. Ben-Gurion, *Yoman Hamilhama*, Vol. 3, p. 885 (diary entry for Dec. 18, 1948).

16. "Had we been able to afford a purely theoretical approach to this question, I would have preferred a separate government in the Arab part of Palestine to its annexation to Transjordan," Shertok told the Provisional State Council on September 27. "But saying this now will imply supporting the Mufti's rule in Arab Palestine. Suffice it that we do not openly oppose the Gaza government for an outright rejection will have been interpreted as endorsement of the annexation of the Arab part to Transjordan." See State of Israel, "Provisional State Council, Twentieth Session: The Mediator's Report," Sept. 27, 1948 (Tel Aviv: The New Press, 1948), p. 17.

17. David Ben-Gurion, *Bama'araha* (Tel-Aviv: Mapai Publishing House, 1949), Vol. 4, Part 2, p. 260. Ben-Gurion reiterated this pledge on May 4, 1948, ten days before the proclamation of Israel: "We hope to have soon a free parliament in the state of Israel, democratically elected by all its citizens: all the Jewish citizens and all Arab citizens who would like to remain in Israel." David Ben-Gurion, *Behilahem Israel* (Tel Aviv: Mapai Publishing House, 1951; 3rd ed.), p. 102.

18. Hagana Commander-in-Chief to Brigade Commanders, "The Arabs Residing in the Enclaves," Mar. 24, 1948, HA/46/199z.

19. Commander of the Jerusalem District and Brigade, "Appointment of Governors in Conquered Territories," May 15, 1948, IDFA 1949/5254/13. See also: "Plan D – March 1948," Matkal/Agam, Mar. 10, 1948, HA 73/94, pp. 5–8; "Guidelines for Treating Surrendering Villages," Apr. 22, 1948, IDFA 1949/4663/84, p. 12; IDF Chief of Staff, "Discipline," July 6, 1948, *ibid.*, p. 19; "Summary of a Meeting of Arab Affairs Advisors in Natanya," May 9, 1948, *ibid.*, p. 30; "Proposal for the Administration of Surrendering Arab Cities and Villages," Apr. 1948, IDFA 1949/481/14; Matkal, "Abandoned Property," May 3, 1948, HA 105/54, p. 118; Hagana Arabic Broadcasts, Mar. 18, 1948, (SWB), No. 43, Mar. 25, 1948, Part III, p. 68.

20. Voice of Israel in Arabic, May 16, 1948, SWB, No. 51, May 20, 1948, Part III, pp. 55–57.

21. Protocol of Israel's Provisional Government Meeting, May 16, 1948, pp. 11–18, 20; Protocol of the Provisional Government Meeting, Sept. 5, 1948, p. 5.

22. From Palestine (General Sir A. Cunningham) to the Secretary of State for the Colonies, "Weekly Intelligence Appreciation," Dec. 22, 1947, Cunningham Papers, Middle East Centre, St Antony's College, Oxford University; Cunningham to the Secretary of State for the Colonies, "Weekly Intelligence Appreciation," Jan. 24, 1948, CO 537/3869.

23. Thus, for example, after an attack on Ramat Hakovesh (on April 19) by the neighboring village of Miska, the kibbutz *mukhtar* told the villagers to leave or bear the consequences of their aggression, which they did. Likewise, in the midst of a Jewish operation in the eastern Galilee, the secretary of the Genossar kibbutz, together with the *mukhtar* of the Arab village of Majdal, convinced the Majdal inhabitants to vacate the village and surrender their weapons. In Khirbat Beit Lid and Khirbat Azzun, the villagers were advised to leave since the Jewish forces would not be able to ensure their safety. See: Tiroshi, "Summary of News for the Alexandroni Brigade, Apr. 27, 1948," HA 105/143, p. 235; Tiroshi to Tene, "Vacation of Miska," Apr. 27, 1948, HA 105/257, p. 79; Tzuri to Tene, "Arab Majdal," Apr. 23, 1948, *ibid.*, p. 4; Tiroshi to Tene, "Departure of Arabs from the Neighborhood," Apr. 16, 1948, *ibid.*, p. 89; Tiroshi to Tene, "Vacation of Khirbat Azzun," Apr. 20, 1948, *ibid.*, p. 3.

24. High Commissioner for Palestine to Secretary of State, May 5, 1948, Cunningham Papers. See also: Tzuri to Golani, "News Summary: Tiberias," Apr. 21, 1948, HA 105/143, p. 275; Hagana Operational Directorate, "Logbook of the War of Independence," p. 260; MacMillan, "Palestine: Narrative of Events," Apr. 17/18, 18, 1948, p. 37.

25. See, for example, Qiryati-Dafna to All Fronts, "Occurrences in Jaffa, [Apr.] 11, 1948–[Apr.] 20, 0740," May 2, 1948, IDFA 1949/8275/162; Palestine (Cunningham) to

the Secretary of State for the Colonies, May 1, 1948, FO 371/68547/E5665/4/71; Tene to Dan & Hillel, Nov. 30, 1947, HA 105/61, p. 5; 00004 to Tene, "Report Summary, Dec. 7, 1947," HA 105/61, p. 9; Yavne to Tene, "For Our Members in the Bases," Dec. 9, 1947, *ibid.*, p. 18; "For Our Members in the Bases," Bulletin Nos. 15 & 16, Dec. 10 & 11, 1947, *ibid.*, pp. 24, 37; Yavne, "Evacuation of Women and Children from Lifta," Dec. 28, 1947, HA 105/215, p. 23; 00004 to Tene, "Arabs Erecting Military Posts in Lifta," Dec. 14, 1947, IDFA 1949/5253/104; "The Old City," Dec. 26, 1947, *ibid.*; "Families Leaving Lifta," Jan. 1, 1948, *ibid.*; Hashmona'i, "Demographic Changes in Jerusalem," Jan. 25, 1948, IDFA 1948/500/60; "In the Arab Camp," Jan. 25, 1948, *ibid.*; "Anger in Beit Safafa over the Use of the Village by Armed Gangs for Attacks on Mekor Haim," Jan. 28, 1948, *ibid.*; "Beit Safafa" & "The Evacuation of Beit Safafa," Feb. 15 & 18, 1948, *ibid.*; Yavne to Tene, "Deir Abu Tur," Feb. 21, 1948, HA 105/215, p. 81; Hashmona'i, "Annexes to News Concentration No. 114," Mar. 16, 1948, IDFA 1949/2605/2; 01204 (Hatzil) to Tene, Jan. 21, 1948, HA 105/72, p. 52; Yavne to Tene, "Complaint by the Beit Safafa Mukhtar to the NC," Feb. 16, 1948, *ibid.*, p. 105; "In the Arab Camp: News Summary," Mar. 14, 1948, p. 2, IDFA 2004/535/479; "In the Arab Camp: News Summary," Mar. 29, 1948, p. 2, *ibid.*; Yavne to Tene, Feb. 15, 1948, HA 105/215, p. 41.

26. Sasson to Shertok, Apr. 25, 1948, S25/5635.

27. "Fortnightly Intelligence Newsletter No. 60," issued by HQ British Troops in Palestine (for the period 2359 hrs, Jan. 14–2359 hrs, Jan. 28, 1948), WO 275/64, p. 4.

28. Sixth Airborne Division, "Weekly Intelligence Summary No. 61. Based on Information Received up to 23 Oct 47," WO275/60, pp. 3–4; Hiram/Nagid, "The Mufti and Haifa," Feb. 8, 1948, HA 105/54a, p. 24; 02112 to Tene, "Abdel Qader Husseini in Zeita," Jan. 25, 1948, IDFA 1949/6400/66; "Fortnightly Intelligence Newsletter No. 56," issued by HQ British Troops in Palestine (for the period Nov. 22–Dec. 5, 1947), WO 275/64, p. 3; Khatib, *Min Athar al-Nakba*, pp. 197, 266; Arif al-Arif, *al-Nakba: Nakbat Bait al-Maqdis wa-l-Firdaws al-Mafqud* (Beirut: al-Maktaba al-Asriya, 1956), Vol. 1, pp. 206–07; Hajj Amin Husseini to Rashid Hajj Ibrahim, Mar. 13, 1948, IDFA, 20/1/57 (captured Arab documents).

29. Ireland to Department of State, Apr. 28, 1948, RG 84 – Jerusalem Consulate; al-Inqaz in Arabic, Apr. 27, 1948, SWB, No. 49, May 6, 1948, Part III, p. 70; "Tene News," Apr. 28, 1948, HA 105/98, p. 94.

30. See, for example: Ben-Gurion, *Yoman Hamilhama*, Vol. 1, p. 369 (entry for Apr. 25, 1948); Yavne to Tene, "Rumor about the Transfer of Arab Women and Children from Jerusalem," Feb. 15, 1948, HA 105/215, p. 41; Hiram to Tene, "Evacuation of Women and Children from Haifa," Mar. 8, 1948, HA 105/257, p. 1; Hiram, "Transfer of Children to Beirut," Mar. 14 & report on AHC instructions to evacuate women, children, and the elderly, Mar. 17, 1948 *ibid.*, p. 108; Hiram, "Evacuation of Women," Mar. 10, 1948 & Dr. Yatsliah, "Haifa," Mar. 10, 1948, *ibid.*, p. 112; AHC circular, Mar. 8, 1948, *ibid.*, pp. 227–28; Yavne to Tene, "Arabs Going Abroad," Apr. 6, 1948, *ibid.*, p. 52; "Tene News," Mar. 21, 1948, HA 105/98, p. 53; "Précis of Hiram News," Mar. 25, 1948, HA, 105/143, p. 121.

31. Abdel Karim Umar, *Mudhakkirat al-Hajj Muhammad Amin al-Husseini* (Damascus: Ahali, 1999), p. 394; Muhammad Nimr Khatib, *Min Athar al-Nakba* (Damascus: al-Matba'a al-Amumiya, 1951), p. 287.

32. Hashmonai, "News Items: Economy," Feb. 2, 1948, IDFA 1948/500/60; "In the Arab Camp: News Summary," Feb. 29 & Mar. 28, 1948, IDFA 2004/535/479, pp. 3–4; "Yishuv Circular No. 16," Jan. 31, 1948, K4-31/1/12, IA; Committee for Economic Defense, "News from the Arab Economy, Bulletin No. 6," Apr. 17–19, 1948, HA 105/143, p. 240.

33. Hayogev, Jan. 5, 1948, HA 105/215a, p. 48; "Among the Arabs," Feb. 22, 1948, IDFA 1948/500/60; 02204 to Tene, "The Lifta People's Position," Feb. 9, 1948, HA 105/32a, p. 61; Tiroshi to Tene, "Situation of the Refugees," Apr. 12, 1948, HA 105/257; Hiram to Tene, "Acre Inhabitants and Defenders Refuse to Receive More Refugees," Apr. 27,

1948, *ibid.*; Tiroshi, "News Summary for the Alexandroni Brigade," Apr. 16, 1948, HA 105/143, p. 231; Director of Operations/Intelligence Directorate, "News Summary on the Eastern and Northern Fronts," June 3, 1948, IDFA 1975/922/1044; "Arab News Items," Apr. 25, 1948, IDFA 1948/500/55; "Annexes to News Bulletin No. 205," Apr. 29, 1948, IDFA 1949/2605/2.

34. "Annexes to News Bulletin No. 185," Apr. 20, 1948, IDFA 1949/2605/2; "Deir Yasin," Apr. 17, 1948, IDFA 1949/2605/6, p. 7.

35. Macatee to Secretary of State, Dec. 31, 1947, pp. 1–2, RG 84/800.

36. Cunningham to Creech Jones, Apr. 25 & 28, 1948, Cunningham Papers, III/4/52 & III/4/117; Tzuri to Tene, "News Items about the Tiberias Exodus," Apr. 21, 1948, HA 105/257, p. 347; "Tene News-Daily Summary," Apr. 18, 1948, HA 105/62, p. 93; Kenneth W. Bilby, *New Star in the Near East* (New York: Doubleday, 1950), p. 30; *Filastin*, Apr. 13, 14, 16, 1948; *al-Difa*, Apr. 11, 12, 13, 14, 15, 16, 1948; Radio Jerusalem in Arabic to the Middle East, Apr. 13, 1948 & Radio Damascus, Apr. 14, 1948, in FBIS, Apr. 15, 1948, p. II4; Radio al-Sharq al-Adna (Jerusalem), Apr. 15, 1948, *ibid.*, Apr. 16, 1948, p. II5; BBC Television Channel 2, "The Fifty Years War: Israel and the Arabs," Program 1, broadcast on March 15, 1998.

37. Secretary of State for the Colonies to High Commissioner for Palestine (attaching a report by the British ambassador to Cairo), Apr. 23, 1948, Cunningham Papers, III/4/6.

38. For the impact of the scaremongering on the flight, see, for example: Tiroshi to Tene, "A Day of Mourning in Lydda," Apr. 27, 1948, HA 105/31, p. 32; Hiram to Carmeli, "News Bulletin," Apr. 23, 1948, HA 105/149, p. 286; Doron to Tene, "Report on Ben Shemen and its Neighborhood from Apr. 14 to Apr. 23," May 10, 1948, HA 105/143, p. 366; "Occurrences in the Area in the Week Ending on May 9, 1948," *ibid.*, p. 361; "Occurrences in the Area in the Week Ending on May 16, 1948," *ibid.*, p. 406.

39. Sir Henry Gurney's Diary, Apr. 28, 1948, Cunningham Papers. Cunningham described the situation with quintessential English understatement. "You should know that the collapsing Arab morale in Palestine is in some measure due to the increasing tendency of those who should be leading them to leave the country," he reported to London. "For instance in Jaffa the Mayor went on 4 days leave 12 days ago and has not returned, and half the National Committee has left. In Haifa the Arab members of the municipality left some time ago; the two leaders of the Arab Liberation Army left actually during the recent battle. Now the Chief Arab Magistrate has left. In all parts of the country the effendi class has been evacuating in large numbers over a considerable period and the tempo is increasing" (Cunningham to Secretary of State for the Colonies, Apr. 26, 1948, *ibid.*). See also: "Fortnightly Intelligence Newsletter No. 67," issued by HQ British Troops in Palestine (for the period 2359 hrs, Apr. 19–2359 hrs, May 3, 1948), WO 275/64, p. 1; Cunningham to the Secretary of State for the Colonies, "Weekly Intelligence Appreciation," May 1, 1948, CO 537/3869.

40. Giora to Utz, May 18, 1948, HA 105/92b, p. 51; Hiram to Tene, "The city of Acre after its Conquest on May 17," May 21, 1948, HA 105/92b, p. 125; Tzuri to Tene, "Reports from Samakh after its Evacuation," May 10, 1948, *ibid.*, p. 109; Tzuri to Tene, "The Conquest of Nazareth," July 19, 1948, *ibid.*, p. 158.

41. Arif Arif, *al-Nakba*, p. 179.

Epilogue

1. "Meetings: M. Shertok-Count Bernadotte and Assistants (Tel Aviv, 17 and 18 June 1948)," Israel State Archives, *Documents on the Foreign Policy of Israel. Vol. 1: 14 May–30 September 1948* (Jerusalem: Government Printer, 1981), pp. 183–84; Protocol of the Provisional Government Meeting, June 20, 1948, pp. 20–21.

2. Jerusalem Radio (Arabic), May 29, 1948, in *BBC Summary of World Broadcasts: Western Europe, Middle East, Far East and Americas* (SWB), No. 53, June 3, 1948, Part III, p. 65; Muhammad Ibrahim Kamel, *The Camp David Accords: A Testimony* (London: KPI, 1986), p. 321.

3. P. J. Vatikiotis, *Nasser and his Generation* (London: Croom Helm, 1978), p. 245.

4. Ephraim Dowek, *Israeli-Egyptian Relations 1980–2000* (London: Cass, 2001), pp. 120–21.

5. See, for example, Damascus Radio, Dec. 13, 1981.

6. Gamal Abdel Nasser, "Speech to National Assembly Members on May 29, 1967," in Walter Laqueur (ed.), *The Arab-Israeli Reader* (Harmondsworth: Penguin, 1970), p. 228.

7. Baghdad Radio, Aug. 12, 1990.

8. Damascus Radio, Mar. 8, 1974.

9. Palestinian leaders went out of their way to reassure their constituents that this was merely a tactical ploy aimed at enhancing the PLO's international standing and, as a consequence, its ability to achieve the ultimate objective of Israel's destruction. "We vowed to liberate Palestine before 1967," declared Abu Iyad, Arafat's second-in-command. "We will restore Palestine step by step and not in one fell swoop, just as the Jews had done. We are learning from them and there is nothing wrong in this." "The borders of our state noted [by the PLO declaration] represent only a part of our national aspirations," he added. "We will strive to expand them so as to realize our ambition for the entire territory of Palestine." A few days later he reiterated this pledge: "The establishment of a Palestinian state on any part of Palestine is but a step toward the [liberation of the] whole of Palestine" (*Al-Anba*, Kuwait, Dec. 5 & 13, 1988). For other Palestinian statements in the same vein, see, for example, interview by Khaled Hassan, head of the Palestine National Council's (PNC) committee for external and parliamentary relations, with *al-Musawar* (Cairo), Jan. 20, 1989; interview with Salim Zaanun (aka Abu Adib), the PNC's deputy chairman, with *al-Anba* (Kuwait), Nov. 21, 1988; interview by Rafiq al-Natsha (Abu Shakir), a member of the PLO's central committee, with *al-Sharq al-Awsat* (London), Dec. 9, 1988 & with *al-Jazira* (Saudi Arabia), Jan. 1, 1989; interview by Ahmad Sidqi Dajani, a senior PLO member, with *Ukaz* (Saudi Arabia), Nov. 22, 1988.

10. During this interim period the territories would be administered by a Palestinian council, to be freely and democratically elected after the withdrawal of Israeli military forces both from the Gaza Strip and from the populated areas of the West Bank.

11. Arafat's interview with *al-Anwar* (Beirut), Aug. 2, 1968.

12. *Al-Arabi* (Cairo), June 24, 2001.

13. Uzi Mahanaimi, "Arafat: I Know There Is an Agreement between Israel and Damascus," *Haolam Haze*, Sept. 8, 1993, pp. 3–4.

14. "Political Program for the Present Stage Drawn Up by the 12th PNC, Cairo, June 9, 1974," *Journal of Palestine Studies*, summer 1974, pp. 224–25.

15. John Laffin, *The PLO Connections* (London: Corgi Books, 1983), p. 127.

16. State of Israel, Central Bureau of Statistics (CBI), "Statistical Abstract of Israel 2008. 2.1: Population Estimates," pp. 85–86; CBI, "Projections of Israel's Population until 2020," Table 2: "Base Population in 1995 and Projections for 1995 and 2020, by Population Group and the Various Variants."

17. See, for example: al-Jazeera (Doha), Jan. 13, 2002; *al-Hayat al-Jadida* (Gaza) Dec. 8, 25, 1997 & Sept. 26, 2000 & Dec. 24, 2001; *Jerusalem Post*, Mar. 17, 1997; Reuters, Nov. 11, 1999.

18. See, for example: *Al-Musawwar* (Cairo), Aug. 18, 2000, quoting a "high-ranking source in the Palestinian delegation to Camp David." Other Palestinian officials gave similar accounts of the Camp David talks. According to the PLO senior official Nabil Shaath, the Israelis offered the Palestinians the equivalent of 1 percent of the West Bank's territory on the border with Gaza in return for the annexation of 9 percent of the West Bank, only to be rejected by the Palestinian delegation, while Tayyib Abdel Rahim, the Palestine secretary-general, reported that Israel agreed to withdraw from 92 percent of the West Bank during the Camp David summit. See, *al-Quds*, Aug. 30, 2000.

19. Palestinian Authority Television, Oct. 2, 2000. For discussion of the origin of the latest Palestinian-Israeli war, see Efraim Karsh, *Arafat's War: The Man and his Battle for Israel Conquest* (New York: Grove, 2003).

20. Ion Pacepa, *Red Horizons. Inside the Romanian Secret Service – The Memoirs of Ceausescu's Spy Chief* (London: Coronet Books, 1989), p. 28.

21. Khalil Shikaki, "Palestinian Public Opinion about the Peace Process, 1993–1999" (Washington, D.C.: Center for Policy Analysis on Palestine, 1999); "New Beginning," *U.S. News & World Report*, Sept. 13, 1993, p. 27.

22. "Results of Public Opinion Poll, No. 19: The West Bank and the Gaza Strip, Aug./Sept. 1995," Nablus, Center for Palestine Research and Studies (CPRS), p. 10; "Results of Public Opinion Poll, No. 20: The West Bank and the Gaza Strip, Oct. 13–15, 1995," CPRS, p. 5; "Results of Public Opinion Poll, No. 25," Dec. 26–28, 1996, CPRS, p. 14; "Public Opinion Poll No. 31 – Part I on Palestinian Attitudes toward Politics," Jerusalem Media & Communications Center (JMCC), March 1999, p. 3; *Maariv*, Mar. 14, 1995; Peter Hirschberg, "The Dark Side of Arafat's Regime," *Jerusalem Report*, Aug. 21, 1997, p. 25.

23. For the text of the Covenant, see "The Palestine National Charter Adopted by the Fourth Palestine National Assembly, Cairo, July 18, 1968," in Zuhair Diab (ed.), *International Documents on Palestine 1968* (Beirut: Institute for Palestine Studies, 1971), pp. 393–95.

24. "Exclusive Interview with Hamas Leader," Sept. 22, 2005, *The Media Line*, http://www.themedialine.org/news/news_detail.asp?NewsID=11354.

25. Hamas Covenant (*www.yale.edu/lawweb/avalon/mideast/hamas.htm*), articles 11, 13, 15, 27.

26. See, for example, Nabil Shaath as quoted in *Haaretz*, Sept. 9, 1993; Abu Ala's interview with *al-Ittihad* (internet ed.), June 24, 1996; Yasir Abed Rabbo's interview with *Le Monde*, Sept. 26, 2000; Faisal Husseini's interview with *Al-Arabi* (Cairo), June 24, 2001.

27. Mahmoud Abbas, *al-Wajh al-Akhar: al-Alaqat al-Sirriya bayna al-Naziya wa-l-Sihyuniya* (Amman: Dar Ibn Rushd, 1984).

28. *Al-Ra'i* (Ramallah), No. 33, July 15–Aug. 2000, p. 9; *al-Hayat* (London), Nov. 23–24, 2000.

29. *www.palestine-pmc.com/details.asp?cat=1&id=888*; *http://english.wafa.ps/body.asp?field=Enews&id =2658* (both are PA official sites).

30. Jackson Diehl, "Abbas's Waiting Game," *Washington Post*, May 29, 2009; "Chief Palestinian Negotiator Saeb Erekat: Abu Mazen Rejected the Israeli Proposal in Annapolis Like Arafat Rejected the Camp David 2000 Proposal," The Middle East Research Institute (MEMRI), TV clip 2074, Mar. 27, 2007; Palestinian Media Watch Bulletin, Nov. 28, 2007 (pmw.org.il/bulletins_nov2007.htm#b2811070); Aluf Ben, "Olmert Almost Made History," *Haaretz*, June 26, 2009.

31. "Abbas Won't Recognize Israel as a Jewish State," *Ynet.news.com*, Apr. 27, 2009.

32. "Mubarak: Demand to Recognize Israel as Jewish State Hindering Peace," *Ynet*, June 15, 2009; "Palestinians Reject Netanyahu Speech," *Independent Online*, June 14, 2009; MEMRI, "Fatah's Sixth General Conference Resolutions: Pursuing Peace Options without Relinquishing Resistance or Right to Armed Struggle," Aug. 13, 2009.

Appendix

1. Asher Goren (Israel's Foreign Ministry's Middle East Department), "The Palestinian Arab Refugee Problem," Sept. 27, 1948, p. 2, CZA A457/113; "Refugees Strain Arab Towns," *New York Times*, July 26, 1948; "Official Puts Arab Refugees at 300,000," *ibid.*, July 24, 1948; "Disease Threatens Refugees," *ibid.*, Aug. 3, 1948,.

2. David Ben-Gurion, *Yoman Hamilhama Tashah-Tashat* (Tel Aviv: Ministry of Defense Publishing House, 1982), Vol. 2, p. 487 (diary entry for June 5, 1948).

3. Tene, "Migration of the Palestinian Arabs in the Period 1.12.47–1.6.48," June 30, 1948, pp. 1–2, IDFA, 1957/100001/781; Y. Weitz, E. Danin, and Z. Lifshitz, "Memorandum on the Settlement of the Arab Refugees. Submitted to the Prime Minister of the Provisional Government," Oct. 31, 1948, p. 4, HA 80/58/13.

4. UN General Assembly, "Progress Report of the United Nations Mediator on Palestine Submitted to the Secretary-General for Transmission to the Members of the United Nations in Pursuance of Paragraph 2, Part II, of Resolution 186 (S-2) of the General

Assembly of 14 May 1948" (General Assembly Official Records: Third Session Supplement No. 11; A/648, Sept. 16, 1948), p. 78; Beirut to Foreign Office, Oct. 1, 1948, FO 371/68679; "Plight of 472,000 Arab Refugees," *Times*, Oct. 21, 1948.

5. "Refugees Put at 700,000," *New York Times*, Aug. 17, 1948; Rony E. Gabbay, *A Political Study of the Arab-Jewish Conflict: The Arab Refugee Problem (A Case Study)* (Geneva: Librairie E. Droz, 1959), pp. 167–68.

6. Beirut to Foreign Office, Oct. 1, 3, 1948, FO 371/68679; "The Number of Arab Refugees (Revised Version)," Israel State Archives (ISA), FM 347/2 (apparently written in Aug./Sept. 1949); W. de St. Aubin, "Peace and Refugees in the Middle East," *Middle East Journal*, Vol. 3, No. 3 (July 1949), p. 249.

7. Sir J. Troutbeck, "Summary of General Impressions Gathered during Week-End Visit to the Gaza District," June 16, 1949, FO 371/75342/E7816.

8. Partial food rationing was imposed by the British authorities in 1941 after serious shortages arose in some commodities. In cities people had to register with groceries which were to supply them with the rationed commodities. Arab villages and townships were allocated quantities of rationed commodities in accordance with the size of their population, to be distributed by a local authority. This applied mainly to sugar, the entire requirements of which were imported, so that all stocks and supplies were fully controlled by the food controller. Arab village heads provided food control officers, through Arab district officers, with exaggerated population figures in order to get excessive quantities of sugar and other rationed commodities. Thus the Food Controller's ration's allocation figures for most of the Arab rural, and to some extent also urban, population exceeded considerably the actual number of inhabitants. The inclusion of the Food Controller records in the total volume of data from which the Village Statistics figures were worked out resulted in a "leap" of over 10 percent in the rate of annual increase of the Muslim population from 1943 onward.

9. Palestine Office of Statistics, *Village Statistics 1945* (Jerusalem, 1945), "Explanatory Note," p. 2 (A5).

10. Government for Palestine, *Supplement to Survey of Palestine: Notes Compiled for the Information of the United Nations Special Committee of Palestine*, (London: HMSO, June 1947; reprinted in full with permission by the Institute for Palestine Studies, Washington, D.C.), p. 14.

11. *Supplement to Survey on Palestine*, pp. 10–11; Israeli Foreign Ministry, Middle East Department, "The Palestinian Refugee Problem (Report No. 3)," Feb. 2, 1949, ISA FM 347/23; *idem*, "Notes on Arab Refugees, the Boundaries of Israel, and Jerusalem," Aug. 22, 1949, *ibid.*; "The Number of Arab Refugees (Revised Version)"; Military Government HQ, "Tables of the Arab Population Categorized by Settlements and Religions, Feb. 15, 1950," IDFA 1960/28/29, May 9, 1959; Walter Pinner, *How Many Arab Refugees? A Critical Study of UNRWA's Statistics and Reports* (London: MacGibbon & Kee, 1959), Part III.

    In its report, submitted to the General Assembly on Dec. 28, 1949, the United Nations Conciliation Commission for Palestine estimated the number of Arab refugees outside Israel's territory at 726,000, of whom 627,000 were eligible for relief from the United Nations. See "Final Report of the United Nations Economic Survey Mission for the Middle East: An Approach for Economic Development in the Middle East" (Lake Success: United Nations, Dec. 28, 1949), A/AC.25/6, pp. 18, 22–24.

12. Urban population figures are taken from *Supplement to Survey of Palestine*, pp.12–13.

13. Ministry of Minorities Affairs & Central Bureau of Statistics, "List of City Residents," Sept. 26, 1948, FM 2564/22.

14. "Survey of the Arab Situation in Haifa," Sept. 22, 1948, IDFA 1954/219/240.

15. "Protocol of a Meeting to Discuss the Problems in the Cities of Jaffa, Lydda, and Ramle," Aug. 16, 1948, IDFA 1949/1331/54; Ministry of Minorities Affairs & Central Bureau of Statistics, "List of City Residents," Sept. 26, 1948, FM 2564/22.

16. Tene, "Migration of the Palestinian Arabs in the Period 1.12.47–1.6.48. Annex 1: Vacated Arab Villages," June 30, 1948, IDFA, 1957/100001/781, p. 2.

17. "Protocol of a Meeting to Discuss the Problems in the Cities of Jaffa, Lydda, and Ramle."
18. Unless otherwise indicated, rural population figures are based on the *Village Statistics 1945* & Tene, "Migration of the Palestinian Arabs," Annex 1: Vacated Arab Villages. Departure dates are based on the latter study, unless indicated otherwise.
19. Administrative divisions and transliterations of village names are based on the *Village Statistics 1945*.
20. Tzadok Eshel, *Hativat Carmeli Bemilhemet Haqomemiut* (Tel Aviv: Maarachot, 1973), p. 291.
21. Hagana Operational Directorate, "Logbook of the War of Independence, 3.1.48–14.5.48," IDFA, 1954/464/2, p. 291.
22. Intercepted communications from the ALA forces in north Palestine & the residents of Birwa, June 14, 1948, HA 105/92b, p. 91; Hiram to Tene, "The Battle for Birwa according to Acre Residents," July 4, 1948, *ibid.*, p. 159.
23. Seventh Brigade/Intelligence, "News Logbook 8," July 14, 1948 & Seventh Brigade/Operational HQ, "Dekel Operational Order," July 18, 1948, IDFA 1952/273/5.
24. Front A, "Hiram Operational Report, No. 4: 300800–302000," IDFA 1992/164/1.
25. Eshel, *Hativat Carmeli*, p. 290.
26. "Operation Hiram – Intelligence Report, Oct. 28–31, 1948," IDFA 1992/164/1.
27. Agam/Matkal, "Hanes Hagadol" (General Staff's Operational Logbook), May 22, IDFA 1975/922/1175, p. 48.
28. "Hiram Operational Report, No. 4."
29. Eshel, *Hativat Carmeli*, p. 291.
30. *Ibid.*, p. 290.
31. "Hiram Operational Report, No. 4."
32. Eshel, *Hativat Carmeli*, p. 290.
33. *Ibid.*, p. 292.
34. Front A, "Hiram Operational Report, No. 3: 292000–300600," IDFA 1992/164/1.
35. "Logbook of the War of Independence," p. 291.
36. *Ibid.*
37. "Hiram Operational Report, No. 4."
38. Eshel, *Hativat Carmeli*, p. 290.
39. "Logbook of the War of Independence," p. 291.
40. Golani/Intelligence, "List of Arab Villages Captured by the 13th Battalion," June 25, 1948, IDFA, 1951/128/84.
41. Beisan National Committee (mid-March 1948), IDFA 1975/922/648.
42. Tzefa to Tene, "Evacuation of Arab Villages," Apr. 6, 1948, HA 105/257, p. 24.
43. Beisan National Committee; Tene, "Migration."
44. Beisan National Committee.
45. "Carmeli Brigade: News Summary No. 6 for May 25, 1948," IDFA 1949/6127/117.
46. Beisan National Committee.
47. *Ibid.*; Golani/Intellgence, "List of the Arab Villages in our Hands. Captured by the 12th Battalion," June 25, 1948, IDFA 1951/84/128.
48. Beisan National Committee.
49. Golani/Intellgence, "List of the Arab Villages in our Hands. Captured by the 12th Battalion," June 25, 1948, IDFA 1951/84/128.
50. *Ibid.*
51. Tene, "Migration."
52. "Hanes Hagadol," p. 25.
53. Galilee Front, "List of Villages (and Cities) That Fell to our Hands on July 15–18, 1948," IDFA 1949/7249/119.
54. *Ibid.*
55. "First Brigade: Operational Logbook," May 16, 1948, IDFA 1951/665/1; Eshel, *Hativat Carmeli*, p. 291.
56. Weitz, Danin, and Lifshitz, "Memorandum."
57. *Ibid.*;"Logbook of the War of Independence," p. 265.

58. "Operation Hiram – Intelligence Report, Oct. 28–31, 1948."
59. "Logbook of the War of Independence," p. 283.
60. Weitz, Danin, and Lifshitz, "Memorandum."
61. "Hiram Operational Report, No. 4."
62. Front A, "Hiram Operational Report, No. 5: 302000–310000," IDFA 1992/164/1.
63. IDF History Branch, *Toldot Milhemet Haqomemiut* (Tel Aviv: Maarachot, 1975 [1959]), pp. 243–44.
64. "Operation Hiram – Intelligence Report, Oct. 28–31, 1948."
65. Golani-Intelligence, "Daily Summary," Nov. 6, 1948, IDFA 1951/128/84; "Hiram Operational Report, No. 4."
66. Bulgarim to Matkal, "Daily Report," May 2, 1948, 1975/922/1044, p. 313; Tene, "Migration."
67. "Logbook of the War of Independence."
68. "Hiram Operational Report, No. 4."
69. "Logbook of the War of Independence," p. 285.
70. "Tene News," Apr. 24 & 28, 1948, HA 105/98, pp. 89, 93; Tene, "Migration"; Weitz, Danin, and Lifshitz, "Memorandum."
71. Tene, "Migration."
72. "Hiram Operational Report, No. 5."
73. Bulgarim to Matkal, "Daily Report," May 29, 1948, IDFA 1975/922/1214; "Operation Hiram – Intelligence Report, Oct. 28–31, 1948."
74. Bulgarim to Matkal, "Daily Report," May 2, 1948, IDFA, 1975/922/1044, p. 313; Tene, "Migration."
75. "Hiram Operational Report, No. 4."
76. "Operation Hiram – Intelligence Report, Oct. 28–31, 1948."
77. "Hiram Operational Report, No. 4."
78. *Ibid.*
79. Front A, "Hiram Operational Report, No. 3: 292000–300600," IDFA 1992/164/1.
80. "Hiram Operational Report, No. 4."
81. Eshel, *Hativat Carmeli*, p. 291.
82. Tzefa to Tene, "Evacuation of Arab Villages," Apr. 6, 1948, HA 105/257, p. 24; Golani/Intellgence, "List of the Arab Villages in our Hands. Captured by the 12th Battalion," June 25, 1948, IDFA 1951/84/128; "Logbook of the War of Independence," p. 280.
83. Golani/Intelligence, "Daily Summary," July 17, 1948, IDFA 1951/128/84.
84. "Tene News," Apr. 24, 1948, HA 105/98, p. 89; "List of the Arab Villages in our Hands. Captured by the 12th Battalion."
85. Golani/Intelligence, "Daily Summary," July 17, 1948, IDFA 1951/128/84.
86. Tzefa to Tene, "Evacuation of Arab Villages"; "List of the Arab Villages in our Hands"; "Logbook of the War of Independence," p. 280.
87. "List of Arab Villages in our Hands. Captured by the 12th Battalion."
88. *Ibid.*
89. Golani/Intelligence, "Daily Summary," July 18, 1948, IDFA 1951/128/84.
90. "List of the Arab Villages in our Hands."
91. *Ibid.*
92. Tzuri to Tene, "Ubeidiya Arabs Vacated their Village and Moved to Transjordan," Apr. 21, 1948, HA 105/257, p. 3.
93. Tzefa to Tene, "Evacuation of Arab Villages"; "List of the Arab Villages in our Hands"; "Logbook of the War of Independence," p. 291.
94. Galilee Front, "List of Villages (and Cities) That Fell to our Hands on July 15–18, 1948," IDFA 1949/7249/119.
95. Golani/Intelligence, "List of Arab Villages Captured by the 14th Battalion," June 25, 1948, IDFA, 1951/128/84; "Logbook of the War of Independence," p. 251.
96. "List of Arab Villages Captured by the 14th Battalion."
97. Weitz, Danin, and Lifshitz, "Memorandum."

98. Tiroshi to Tene, "Evacuation of Bureika," Apr. 26, 1948, HA 105/257, p. 11; "Tene News," Apr. 24, 1948, HA 105/98, p. 89.

99. "Hanes Hagadol,", p. 9; "Tene News," Apr. 24, 1948, HA 105/98, p. 89; "List of the Arab Villages Captured by the 14th Battalion."

100. "Logbook of the War of Independence," p. 255.

101. Alexandroni Report, July 25, 1948, IDFA 1975/922/1176.

102. Eshel, *Hativat Carmeli*, p. 291.

103. "List of Arab Villages Captured by the 14th Battalion"; "Logbook of the War of Independence," pp. 248, 255, 257.

104. "Logbook of the War of Independence," p. 296.

105. Alexandroni Report, July 25, 1948, IDFA 1975/922/1176.

106. Golani/Intelligence, "List of Arab Villages Captured by the 13th Battalion," June 25, 1948, IDFA, 1951/128/84.

107. "Tene News," May 13, 1948, HA 105/98, p. 107; "Hanes Hagadol," May 17, 1948, p. 26; IDF, *Toldot Milhemet Haqomemiut*, p. 252.

108. "Logbook of the War of Independence," pp. 253–54.

109. Golani to Matkal, May 15, 1948, IDFA 1954/464/1.

110. "List of Arab Villages Captured by the 14th Battalion"; "Logbook of the War of Independence," p. 257.

111. "Hanes Hagadol," May 17, 1948, p. 26.

112. Tiroshi to Tene, "Qannir," Apr. 26, 1948, HA 105/257, p. 16; "Tene News," Apr. 29, 1948, HA 105/98, p. 95.

113. Weitz, Danin, and Lifshitz, "Memorandum."

114. "Logbook of the War of Independence," p. 255.

115. "Tene News," May 13, 1948, HA 105/98, p. 107; Eshel, *Hativat Carmeli*, p. 291.

116. "Hashmonai Bulletin No. 68," July 17, 1948, IDFA 1949/2504/9.

117. Tirsohi to Tene, "Evacuation of Umm Zinat," Apr. 26, 1948, HA 105/257, p. 16; "List of Arab Villages Captured by the 14th Battalion."

118. Tene, "Migration"; "List of Arab Villages Captured by the 14th Battalion"; Bulgarim to Matkal, "Daily Report," Apr. 16, 1948, 1975/922/1044, p. 317.

119. "List of Arab Villages Captured by the 13th Battalion."

120. "Hanes Hagadol," p. 93.

121. 01132 to Tene, "The Evacuation of Jalama," Feb. 8, 1948, HA 105/215, p. 44.

122. "Qaqun in the Triangle and Arab Yibna in the South Captured by our Armies," *Haaretz*, June 6, 1948.

123. Fifth Brigade/Intelligence, "Summary of Operations," Oct. 24, 1948, IDFA 1975/922/900; Fifth Brigade/Intelligence, "Summary of Operations," Oct. 15–Dec. 9, *ibid.*

124. Avraham Ayalon, *Hativat Givati Mul Hapolesh Hamitsri* (Tel Aviv: Maarachot, 1963), p. 254.

125. "Hashmonai Bulletin No. 65," July 13, 1948, IDFA 1949/2504/9; Ayalon, *Hativat Givati*, pp. 557–58; Ben-Gurion, *Yoman Hamilhama*, Vol. 3, p. 779 (diary entry for Oct. 27, 1948).

126. Netanel Lorch, *The Edge of the Sword: Israel's War of Independence 1947–1949* (Jerusalem: Massada, 1961), p. 431.

127. Ayalon, *Hativat Givati*, p. 558.

128. *Ibid.*, p. 550.

129. *Ibid.*, p. 558.

130. Fifth Brigade/Intelligence, "Summary of Operations, Oct. 22/23, 1948," IDFA 1975/922/900; Fifth Brigade/Intelligence, "Summary of Operations, Oct. 15–Dec. 9," *ibid.*

131. Agam to Givati, July 16, 1948, IDFA 1975/922/1226.

132. Ayalon, *Hativat Givati*, p. 558.

133. Fifth Brigade/Intelligence, "Summary of Operations, Oct. 22/23, 1948" & "Summary of Operations, Oct. 15–Dec. 9."

134. Ayalon, *Hativat Givati*, p. 254.
135. Fifth Brigade/Intelligence, "Summary of Operations, Oct. 22/23, 1948."
136. Ayalon, *Hativat Givati*, p. 254; "Hanes Hagadol," p. 48.
137. Weitz, Danin, and Lifshitz, "Memorandum"; Fifth Brigade/Intelligence, "Summary of Operations, Oct. 22/23, 1948," IDFA 1975/922/900; Fifth Brigade/Intelligence, "Summary of Operations, Oct. 15–Dec. 9," *ibid.*
138. Salim Tamari (ed.), *Jerusalem 1948: The Arab Neighborhoods and their Fate in the War* (Jerusalem: Institute of Jerusalem Studies, 1999), p. 86.
139. *Ibid.*
140. "Arab News Bulletin," July 18, 1948, IDFA 1949/5254/75.
141. Tamari, *Jerusalem 1948*, p. 86.
142. "Logbook of the War of Independence," p. 289.
143. "Arab News Bulletin," July 8, 1948, IDFA 1949/5254/75.
144. Elhannan Orren, *Baderekh el Hair: Mivtsa Danny* (Tel Aviv: IDF Publishing House, 1976), p. 133.
145. *Toldot Milhemet Haqomemiut*, p. 260.
146. Ben-Gurion, *Yoman Hamilhama*, Vol. 3, p. 753 (diary entry for Oct. 19, 1948).
147. Yeruham, "Weekly Report of Jerusalem District Departments," July 14–20, 1948, IDFA 1949/2504/7.
148. Ben-Gurion, *Yoman Hamilhama*, Vol. 3, p. 753 (diary entry for Oct. 19, 1948).
149. IDF History Branch, *Toldot Milhemet Haqomemiut*, p. 263.
150. Tamari, *Jerusalem 1948*, p. 86.
151. "Hashmonai Bulletin No. 65," July 13, 1948, IDFA 1949/2504/9; Ben-Gurion, *Yoman Hamilhama*, Vol. 2, p. 589 (entry for July 15, 1948); Yeruham, "Weekly Report of Jerusalem District Departments," July 14–20, 1948, IDFA 1949/2504/7.
152. Harel to General Staff, July 10, 1948, IDFA 1975/922/1237; *Toldot Milhemet Haqomemiut*, p. 263.
153. Harel to General Staff, July 10, 1948, IDFA 1975/922/1237.
154. Tamari, *Jerusalem 1948*, p. 86.
155. "Hashmonai Bulletin No. 76," July 26, 1948, IDFA 1949/5254/49.
156. "Arab News Bulletin," July 14, 1948, IDFA 1949/5254/75.
157. Orren, *Baderekh*, p. 133.
158. Tamari, *Jerusalem 1948*, p. 86.
159. "Hashmonai Bulletin No. 65," July 13, 1948, IDFA 1949/2504/9; Ben-Gurion, *Yoman Hamilhama*, Vol. 2, p. 589 (entry for July 15, 1948); Yeruham, "Weekly Report of Jerusalem District Departments," July 14–20, 1948, IDFA 1949/2504/7.
160. Tamari, *Jerusalem 1948*, p. 86.
161. *Toldot Milhemet Haqomemiut*, p. 311.
162. "Evacuation of Qastel," Mar. 25, 1948, IDFA 1948/500/28; Tene, "Migration."
163. Tamari, *Jerusalem 1948*, p. 86.
164. Harel to General Staff, July 10, 1948, IDFA 1975/922/1237; "Hashmonai Bulletin No. 65," July 13, 1948, IDFA 1949/2504/9.
165. "Logbook of the War of Independence," p. 258; Tene, "Migration."
166. Orren, *Baderekh*, p. 133.
167. Intercepted Arab military communications, July 13, 1948, HA 105/92a, p. 58; "Hashmonai Bulletin No. 63," July 13, 1948, IDFA 1949/5254/75.
168. *Toldot Milhemet Haqomemiut*, p. 311.
169. Lorch, *The Edge*, p. 432.
170. "Tene News," May 9, 1948, HA 105/98, p. 102.
171. Weitz, Danin, and Lifshitz, "Memorandum."
172. *Ibid.*; Tiroshi to Tene, "Vacation of Jalil," Mar. 23, 1948, HA 105/257.
173. Gershon Rivlin and Zvi Sinai (eds.), *Hativat Alexandroni Bemilhemet Haqomemiut* (Tel Aviv: Maarachot, 1964), p. 285.
174. Tiroshi to Tene, "The Rantiya Villagers on the Move," Apr. 28, 1948, HA 105/257, p. 64; "Tene News," May 14, 1948, HA 105/98, p. 110.

175. Weitz, Danin, and Lifshitz, "Memorandum."
176. *Ibid.*; "Arab News Bulletin," July 10, 1948, IDFA 1949/5254/75.
177. "Flight from Aqir," May 5, 1948, HA 105/92a, p. 244.
178. "Hashmonai Bulletin No. 68," July 17, 1948, IDFA 1949/2504/9; Agam report, July 15, 1948, IDFA 1975/922/1226.
179. Yiftach to General Staff, May 1, 1948, IDFA 1975/922/1226; Yiftach HQ, "Daily Report," July 11, 1948, IDFA 1975/922/1237.
180. Tene, May 12, 1948 HA 105/92a, p. 252.
181. "Hashmonai Bulletin No. 68," July 17, 1948, IDFA 1949/2504/9; Danny HQ to General Staff, July 16, 1948, IDFA 1975/922/1176, p. 42.
182. *Ibid.*; Danny HQ to General Staff, July 16, 1948, IDFA 1975/922/1176, p. 42.
183. Yiftach/Intelligence, "Daily Report," July 13, 1948, IDFA 1975/922/1237.
184. Harel to Matkal, May 16, 1948, IDFA 1954/464/1.
185. Naim to Tene, "Operation Nahshon," Apr. 7, 1948, HA 105/92a, p. 181; "Tene News," Apr. 22, 1948, HA 105/98, p. 87.
186. "Arab News," July 11, 1948, HA 105/92b, p. 141.
187. Rivlin and Sinai, *Hativat Alexandroni*, p. 280; Allon to General Staff, July 13, 1948, 1975/922/1176; "More Villages Captured," *Palestine Post*, July 14, 1948.
188. Givati to General Staff, July 16, 1948, 1975/922/1176, p. 43; Ayalon, *Hativat Givati*, p. 254.
189. "Arab News Bulletin," July 10, 1948, IDFA 1949/5254/75; Givati Operational Logbook, July 16, 1948, IDFA 1975/922/1226.
190. Givati Operational Logbook, July 16, 1948.
191. Debriefing of a Jimzu resident, July 13, 1948, HA 105/92b, p. 77.
192. Yiftach/Intelligence, "Daily Report," July 11, 1948, IDFA 1975/922/1237.
193. Givati Operational Logbook, July 16, 1948.
194. Orren, *Baderekh*, p. 147.
195. Naim to Tene, "Operation Nahshon," Apr. 7, 1948, HA 105/92a, p. 181; "Summary of Conquests in the Southern Sector up to June 11, 1948," HA 105/92b, p. 149.
196. "Hanes Hagadol," p. 18.
197. *Toldot Milhemet Haqomemiut*, p. 258.
198. Tene, "Migration from December to the End of February," HA 105/102, p. 14; Village Files, HA 105/134, p. 76; "Summary of Conquests in the Southern Sector up to June 11, 1948," HA 105/92b, p. 149.
199. *Ibid.*; Givati to Matkal, May 15, 1948, IDFA 1954/464/1.
200. Weitz, Danin, and Lifshitz, "Memorandum"; Tene, "Migration from December to the End of February," p. 14.
201. Orren, *Baderekh*, pp. 178–83.
202. Weitz, Danin, and Lifshitz, "Memorandum"; Agam/Hashmonai, "Hashmonai Bulletin No. 17," June 14, 1948, IDFA 1949/2504/6.
203. "Summary of Conquests in the Southern Sector," p. 149.
204. Doron to Tene, "Qazaza Evacuation," HA 105/257, p. 10; Ayalon, *Hativat Givati*, p. 254.
205. Village Files, HA 105/134, p. 208; "The Qubab Village Is Captured," *Haaretz*, June 4, 1948.
206. Doron to Tene, "Report on the Qubeiba Operation," May 30, 1948, HA 105/92a, p. 55; Ayalon, *Hativat Givati*, p. 254.
207. Rivlin and Sinai, *Hativat Alexandroni*, pp. 288, 291–99.
208. Ayalon, *Hativat Givati*, p. 254.
209. "Hashmonai Bulletin No. 68," July 17, 1948, IDFA 1949/2504/9.
210. "Summary of Conquests in the Southern Sector," p. 149.
211. *Ibid.*
212. *Toldot Milhemet Haqomemiut*, p. 262.
213. Ayalon, *Hativat Givati*, p. 263.
214. Rivlin and Sinai, *Hativat Alexandroni*, p. 288.

215. 02117 to Tene, "In Wadi Hunein," Jan. 5, 1948, HA 105/148, p. 195; "Summary of Conquests in the Southern Sector," p. 149.
216. "Qaqun in the 'Triangle' and Arab Yibna in the South Captured by our Armies," *Haaretz*, June 6, 1948.
217. Doron to Tene, "The Zarnuqa Village," May 30, 1948, HA 105/92a, p. 225.
218. Operational Headquarters to General Staff/Operations, "Evacuation of the Coastal Plain," Dec. 2, 1948, IDFA 1975/922/1025.
219. Doron to Tene, "Batani Sharqi," May 13, 1948, HA 105/92a, p. 47; "Tene News," May 12, 1948, HA 105/98, p. 106.
220. "Capture of Villages," June 14, 1948, HA 105/92b, p. 91.
221. "Tene News," May 23, 1948, HA 105/98, p. 121; Arif Arif, *al-Nakba: Nakbat Bait al-Maqdis wa-l-Firdaws al-Mafqud* (Beirut: al-Maktaba al-Asriya, 1956), Vol. 3, p. 720.
222. "Evacuation of the Coastal Plain"; Front D to General Staff, Nov. 5, 1948, IDFA 1975/922/1176, p. 136; Ayalon, *Hativat Givati*, p. 571.
223. "Hanes Hagadol," p. 95.
224. Ayalon, *Hativat Givati*, p. 254.
225. Fifth Brigade/Intelligence, "Summary of Operations," Oct. 18, 1948, IDFA 1975/922/900.
226. Doron to Tene, "An Attack on Hamama," June 9, 1948, HA 105/92a, p. 193; "Evacuation of the Coastal Plain."
227. Ayalon, *Hativat Givati*, p. 324.
228. *Ibid.*, p. 571; "Evacuation of the Coastal Plain."
229. Fifth Brigade/Intelligence, "Summary of Operations, Oct. 15–Dec. 9," IDFA 1975/922/900; Benjamin Magen to General Staff, Oct. 20, 1948, IDFA 1975/922/1176, p. 118.
230. "Tene News," May 23, 1948, HA 105/98, p. 121.
231. Fifth Brigade/Intelligence, "Summary of Operations," Oct. 16–17, 1948, IDFA 1975/922/900.
232. *Ibid.*, Nov. 10, 1948; Arif, *al-Nakba*, Vol. 3, p. 718.
233. "Evacuation of the Coastal Plain."
234. "Tene News," May 23, 1948, HA 105/98, p. 121; Ayalon, *Hativat Givati*, p. 263.
235. Ayalon, *Hativat Givati*, p. 571; "Evacuation of the Coastal Plain."
236. Weitz, Danin, and Lifshitz, "Memorandum"; "Capture of Villages," June 14, 1948, HA 105/92b, p. 91; "Tene News," May 23, 1948, HA 105/98, p. 121.
237. Ayalon, *Hativat Givati*, p. 571.
238. "Interrogation of Khalil Hajj Ahmad Muslih," June 21, 1948, HA 105/92b, p. 102.
239. "Tene News," May 23, 1948, HA 105/98, p. 121.
240. Sergei to General Staff, Aug. 16, 1948, IDFA 1975/922/1176; Yiftach/Intelligence to General Staff, Sept. 24, 1948, IDFA 1975/922/1214.
241. Fifth Brigade/Intelligence, "Summary of Operations, Oct. 15–Dec. 9," IDFA 1975/922/900.
242. "Evacuation of the Coastal Plain."
243. Ayalon, *Hativat Givati*, p. 263.
244. Sergei to Matkal, May 28, 1948, IDFA 1954/464/1.
245. Ayalon, *Hativat Givati*, p. 571; "Evacuation of the Coastal Plain."
246. Ayalon, *Hativat Givati*, p. 262.
247. "Summary of Conquests in the Southern Sector," p. 149; Doron to Tene, "Capture of the Sawafirs," May 19, 1948, HA 105/92a, p. 14.
248. "Capture of the Sawafirs"; Doron to Tene, "The Capture of Beit Daras," May 13, 1948, *ibid.*, p. 46; Village Files, HA 105/143, pp. 39, 46; "Summary of Conquests in the Southern Sector," p. 149.
249. Ayalon, *Hativat Givati*, p. 254.
250. *Ibid.*, p. 263.
251. "Capture of Villages," June 14, 1948, HA 105/92b, p. 91.

252. Bulgarim to Matkal, "Daily Report," June 12, 1948, IDFA, 1975/922/1214.

253. Tene, "Migration."

254. The *Village Statistics* sets the number of the Negev Bedouins at 47,980; 17,470 of these, according to Israeli figures, remained in situ. See Military Administration HQ, "Table of the Arab Population by Settlements and Religions, Feb. 15, 1950," IDFA 1960/28/29.

255. *Ibid.*

Index